1st Annual Meeting of the ELRA/ISCA Special Interest Group on Under-Resourced Languages (SIGUL2022)

Held at LREC 2022

Marseille, France
20 – 25 June 2022

Editors:

Maite Melero
Sakriani Sakti
Claudia Soria

ISBN: 978-1-7138-6138-6

Printed from e-media with permission by:

Curran Associates, Inc.
57 Morehouse Lane
Red Hook, NY 12571

Some format issues inherent in the e-media version may also appear in this print version.

Association for Computational Linguistics
209 N. Eighth Street
Stroudsburg, Pennsylvania 18360

Phone: 1-570-476-8006
Fax: 1-570-476-0860

acl@aclweb.org

Additional copies of this publication are available from:

Curran Associates, Inc.
57 Morehouse Lane
Red Hook, NY 12571 USA
Phone: 845-758-0400
Fax: 845-758-2633
Email: curran@proceedings.com
Web: www.proceedings.com

LREC 2022 Workshop
Language Resources and Evaluation Conference
20-25 June 2022

The 1st Annual Meeting of the ELRA/ISCA Special Interest Group on Under-Resourced Languages (SIGUL2022)

PROCEEDINGS

Editors:
Maite Melero
Sakriani Sakti
Claudia Soria

Sponsored by
Google

Proceedings of the LREC 2022 Workshop of the 1st Annual Meeting of the ELRA/ISCA Special Interest Group on Under-Resourced Languages (SIGUL 2022)

Edited by:
Maite Melero, Sakriani Sakti, Claudia Soria

For more information:
European Language Resources Association (ELRA)
9 rue des Cordelières
75013, Paris
France
http://www.elra.info
Email: lrec@elda.org

Message from the Workshop Chairs

Over the last years, research in text and speech processing for less-resourced languages has taken momentum. Initiatives and events have flourished, as well as hackathons, toolkits, special interest groups, and journals' special issues. The topic of less-resourced languages has ceased to be niche and has gained space in major conferences such as LREC, ACL, and Interspeech.

The multiplication of research interest makes it even more necessary for the community that revolves around less-resourced languages to find opportunities for aggregation and discussion. It is also very important that these occasions leave space for communities and representatives of under-resourced and endangered languages, in order to ensure that the research and development of technological solutions are in line with the needs and demands of those communities, with a view to open and inclusive research with strong social impact.

The 1st Annual Meeting of the ELRA/ISCA Special Interest Group on Under-Resourced Languages (SIGUL 2022) spans the research interest areas of less-resourced, under-resourced, endangered, minority and minoritized languages. SIGUL 2022 carries on the tradition of the CCURL-SLTU (Collaboration and Computing for Under-Resourced Languages – Spoken Language Technologies for Under-resourced languages) Workshop Series, which has been organized since 2008 and, as LREC Workshops, since 2014. As usual, SIGUL provides a forum for the presentation of cutting edge research in text and speech processing for under-resourced languages to both academic and industry researchers. In addition, it offers a venue where researchers in different disciplines and from varied backgrounds can fruitfully explore new areas of intellectual and practical development while honouring their common interest in sustaining less-resourced languages.

In order to promote synergies and to increase cross-fertilization between neighbouring disciplines, this year's workshop holds a joint session together with the 18th Workshop on Multiword Expressions (MWE 2022) and hosts a shared task on unsupervised Machine Translation techniques for the benefit of under-resourced languages, organized by the MT4All project (CEF 2019-EU-IA-0031).

This year, we have the pleasure to welcome 19 oral and 8 poster presentations, addressing a vast array of topics in NLP, Speech, Data and General issues. Accepted papers display a huge variety of languages, covering 76 different languages from Europe, Asia, Africa and the Americas. This workshop, together with at least five other LREC2022 workshops in neighbouring topics and the main conference track on less-resourced and endangered languages, clearly show how the topic of language resources and speech and natural language processing for less-resourced language is now a mature and well-established field.

The SIGUL 2022 workshop is organised and sponsored by the SIGUL organization, which serves as the Special Interest Group in under-resourced languages for both ELRA and ISCA associations. It is also endorsed by SIGEL, the ACL special interest group on endangered languages. In addition, this year's event has received a sponsorship grant from Google Inc.

Organizers

Maite Melero – Barcelona Supercomputing Center, Spain
Sakriani Sakti – JAIST, Japan
Claudia Soria – CNR-ILC, Italy

Program Committee:

Gilles Adda (LIMSI/IMMI CNRS, France)
Tunde Adegbola (African Language Technology Initiative)
Manex Agirrezabal (University of Copenhagen, Denmark)
Shyam S Agrawal (KIIT, India)
Begona Altuna (University of the Basque Country, Spain)
Raghuram Mandyam Annasamy (Google, US)
Antti Arppe (University of Alberta, Canada)
Dorothee Beermann (NTNU, Norway)
Delphine Bernhardt (Lilpa, Université de Strasbourg, France)
Laurent Besacier (Naver Labs Europe, France)
Steven Bird (Charles Darwin University, Australia)
Federico Boschetti (CNR-ILC, Italy)
Klara Ceberio Berger (Elhuyar, Spain)
Matt Coler (University of Groningen, Campus Fryslân, The Netherlands)
Omar Farooq (ZH College of Engineering and Technology, India)
Dafydd Gibbon (Bielefeld University, Germany)
Itziar Gonzalez-Dios (University of the Basque Country, Spain)
Jeff Good (University at Buffalo, USA)
Atticus Harrigan (University of Alberta, Canada)
Lars Hellan (NTNU, Norway)
Dewi Bryn Jones (Bangor University, UK)
John Judge (ADAPT DCU, Ireland)
Alexey Karpov (SPC RAS, Russian Federation)
Heysem Kaya (Utrecht University, The Netherlands)
Laurent Kevers (Università di Corsica Pasquale Paoli, France)
Irina Kipyatkova (SPC RAS, Russian Federation)
Andras Kornai (Hungarian Academy of Sciences, Hungary)
Jordan Lachler (University of Alberta, Canada)
Richard Littauer (University of Saarland, Germany)
Joseph Mariani (LIMSI-CNRS, France)
Satoshi Nakamura (NAIST, Japan)
Win Pa Pa (UCS Yangon, Myanmar)
Delyth Prys (Bangor University, UK)
Carlos Ramisch (Université Marseille, France)
Kevin Scannell (Saint Louis University, Missouri, US)
Nick Thieberger (University of Melbourne / ARC Centre of Excellence for the Dynamics of Language, Australia)
Trond Trosterud (Tromsø University, Norway)
Daan Van Esch (Google)
Charl Van Heerden (Saigen (Pty) Ltd, South Africa)
Marcely Zanon Boito (LIA – Avignon University, France)

Table of Contents

Unsupervised Word Segmentation from Discrete Speech Units in Low-Resource Settings
Marcely Zanon Boito, Bolaji Yusuf, Lucas Ondel, Aline Villavicencio and Laurent Besacier 1

An Open Source Web Reader for Under-Resourced Languages
Judy Fong, Þorsteinn Daði Gunnarsson, Sunneva Þorsteinsdóttir, Gunnar Thor Örnólfsson and Jon Gudnason 10

Text-to-Speech for Under-Resourced Languages: Phoneme Mapping and Source Language Selection in Transfer Learning
Phat Do, Matt Coler, Jelske Dijkstra and Esther Klabbers 16

ReadAlong Studio: Practical Zero-Shot Text-Speech Alignment for Indigenous Language Audiobooks
Patrick Littell, Eric Joanis, Aidan Pine, Marc Tessier, David Huggins Daines and Delasie Torkornoo 23

Corpus Creation for Sentiment Analysis in Code-Mixed Tulu Text
Asha Hegde, Mudoor Devadas Anusha, Sharal Coelho, Hosahalli Lakshmaiah Shashirekha and Bharathi Raja Chakravarthi 33

Crowd-sourcing for Less-resourced Languages: Lingua Libre for Polish
Mathilde Hutin and Marc Allassonnière-Tang 41

Tupían Language Ressources: Data, Tools, Analyses
Lorena Martín Rodríguez, Tatiana Merzhevich, Wellington Silva, Tiago Tresoldi, Carolina Aragon and Fabrício F. Gerardi 48

Quality versus Quantity: Building Catalan-English MT Resources
Ona de Gibert Bonet, Ksenia Kharitonova, Blanca Calvo Figueras, Jordi Armengol-Estapé and Maite Melero 59

A Sentiment Corpus for South African Under-Resourced Languages in a Multilingual Context
Ronny Mabokela and Tim Schlippe 70

CUNI Submission to MT4All Shared Task
Ivana Kvapilíková and Ondrej Bojar 78

Resource: Indicators on the Presence of Languages in Internet
Daniel Pimienta 83

Language Technologies for Low Resource Languages: Sociolinguistic and Multilingual Insights
A. Seza Doğruöz and Sunayana Sitaram 92

Sentiment Analysis for Hausa: Classifying Students' Comments
Ochilbek Rakhmanov and Tim Schlippe 98

Nepali Encoder Transformers: An Analysis of Auto Encoding Transformer Language Models for Nepali Text Classification
Utsav Maskey, Manish Bhatta, Shiva Bhatt, Sanket Dhungel and Bal Krishna Bal 106

CoSwID, a Code Switching Identification Method Suitable for Under-Resourced Languages
Laurent Kevers 112

A Neural Network Approach to Create Minangkabau-Indonesia Bilingual Dictionary
Kartika Resiandi, Yohei Murakami and Arbi Haza Nasution 122

Machine Translation from Standard German to Alemannic Dialects
Louisa Lambrecht, Felix Schneider and Alexander Waibel 129

Question Answering Classification for Amharic Social Media Community Based Questions
Tadesse Destaw, Seid Muhie Yimam, Abinew Ayele and Chris Biemann 137

Automatic Detection of Morphological Processes in the Yorùbá Language
Tunde Adegbola.. 146

Evaluating Unsupervised Approaches to Morphological Segmentation for Wolastoqey
Diego Bear and Paul Cook...155

Baseline English and Maltese-English Classification Models for Subjectivity Detection, Sentiment Analysis, Emotion Analysis, Sarcasm Detection, and Irony Detection
Keith Cortis and Brian Davis 161

Building Open-source Speech Technology for Low-resource Minority Languages with SáMi as an Example – Tools, Methods and Experiments
Katri Hiovain-Asikainen and Sjur Moshagen 169

Investigating the Quality of Static Anchor Embeddings from Transformers for Under-Resourced Languages
Pranaydeep Singh, Orphee De Clercq and Els Lefever.....................................176

Introducing YakuToolkit. Yakut Treebank and Morphological Analyzer.
Tatiana Merzhevich and Fabrício Ferraz Gerardi 185

A Language Model for Spell Checking of Educational Texts in Kurdish (Sorani)
Roshna Abdulrahman and Hossein Hassani 189

SimRelUz: Similarity and Relatedness Scores as a Semantic Evaluation Dataset for Uzbek Language
Ulugbek Salaev, Elmurod Kuriyozov and Carlos Gómez-Rodríguez..........................199

ENRICH4ALL: A First Luxembourgish BERT Model for a Multilingual Chatbot
Dimitra Anastasiou 207

Workshop Program

Friday, June 24, 2022

14:00–14:10 SIGUL 2022 Opening Talk

14:10–15:10 Session 1: Speech

14:10–14:25 *Unsupervised Word Segmentation from Discrete Speech Units in Low-Resource Settings*
Marcely Zanon Boito, Bolaji Yusuf, Lucas Ondel, Aline Villavicencio and Laurent Besacier

14:25–14:40 *An Open Source Web Reader for Under-Resourced Languages*
Judy Fong, Þorsteinn Daði Gunnarsson, Sunneva Þorsteinsdóttir, Gunnar Thor Örnólfsson and Jon Gudnason

14:40–14:55 *Text-to-Speech for Under-Resourced Languages: Phoneme Mapping and Source Language Selection in Transfer Learning*
Phat Do, Matt Coler, Jelske Dijkstra and Esther Klabbers

14:55–15:10 *ReadAlong Studio: Practical Zero-Shot Text-Speech Alignment for Indigenous Language Audiobooks*
Patrick Littell, Eric Joanis, Aidan Pine, Marc Tessier, David Huggins Daines and Delasie Torkornoo

15:10–16:00 Keynote Speech
Sovereignty for Under-resourced Languages
Keoni Mahelona

16:00–16:30 Coffee break

16:30–17:45 Session 2: Data

16:30–16:45 *Corpus Creation for Sentiment Analysis in Code-Mixed Tulu Text*
Asha Hegde, Mudoor Devadas Anusha, Sharal Coelho, Hosahalli Lakshmaiah Shashirekha and Bharathi Raja Chakravarthi

16:45–17:00 *Crowd-sourcing for Less-resourced Languages: Lingua Libre for Polish*
Mathilde Hutin and Marc Allassonnière-Tang

17:00–17:15 *Tupían Language Ressources: Data, Tools, Analyses*
Lorena Martín Rodríguez, Tatiana Merzhevich, Wellington Silva, Tiago Tresoldi, Carolina Aragon and Fabrício F. Gerardi

Friday, June 24, 2022 (continued)

17:15–17:30 *Quality versus Quantity: Building Catalan-English MT Resources*
Ona de Gibert Bonet, Ksenia Kharitonova, Blanca Calvo Figueras, Jordi Armengol-Estapé and Maite Melero

17:30–17:45 *A Sentiment Corpus for South African Under-Resourced Languages in a Multilingual Context*
Ronny Mabokela and Tim Schlippe

Saturday, June 25, 2022

9:00–10:00 Session 3: MT4All

9:00–9:15 *General overview of unsupervised MT for under resourced languages*
Â Jordi Armengol

9:15–9:30 *Technical approach in MT4All*
Iakes Goenaga

9:30–9:45 *MT4All generated resources and Shared Task scope and results*
Ona de Gibert

9:45–10:00 *CUNI Submission to MT4All Shared Task*
Ivana Kvapilíková and Ondrej Bojar

10:00–10:30 Session 4: General Issues

10:00–10:15 *Resource: Indicators on the Presence of Languages in Internet*
Daniel Pimienta

10:15–10:30 *Language Technologies for Low Resource Languages: Sociolinguistic and Multilingual Insights*
A. Seza Doğruöz and Sunayana Sitaram

10:30–11:00 Coffee break

11:00–12:45 Session 5: NLP

11:00–11:15 *Sentiment Analysis for Hausa: Classifying Students' Comments*
Ochilbek Rakhmanov and Tim Schlippe

11:15–11:30 *Nepali Encoder Transformers: An Analysis of Auto Encoding Transformer Language Models for Nepali Text Classification*
Utsav Maskey, Manish Bhatta, Shiva Bhatt, Sanket Dhungel and Bal Krishna Bal

11:30–11:45 *CoSwID, a Code Switching Identification Method Suitable for Under-Resourced Languages*
Laurent Kevers

Saturday, June 25, 2022 (continued)

11:45–12:00 *A Neural Network Approach to Create Minangkabau-Indonesia Bilingual Dictionary*
Kartika Resiandi, Yohei Murakami and Arbi Haza Nasution

12:00–12:15 *Machine Translation from Standard German to Alemannic Dialects*
Louisa Lambrecht, Felix Schneider and Alexander Waibel

12:15–12:30 *Question Answering Classification for Amharic Social Media Community Based Questions*
Tadesse Destaw, Seid Muhie Yimam, Abinew Ayele and Chris Biemann

12:30–12:45 *Automatic Detection of Morphological Processes in the Yorùbá Language*
Tunde Adegbola

12:45–14:00 Lunch break

14:00–15:00 Joint SIGUL2022-MWE Poster session

Evaluating Unsupervised Approaches to Morphological Segmentation for Wolastoqey
Diego Bear and Paul Cook

Baseline English and Maltese-English Classification Models for Subjectivity Detection, Sentiment Analysis, Emotion Analysis, Sarcasm Detection, and Irony Detection
Keith Cortis and Brian Davis

Building Open-source Speech Technology for Low-resource Minority Languages with SáMi as an Example – Tools, Methods and Experiments
Katri Hiovain-Asikainen and Sjur Moshagen

Investigating the Quality of Static Anchor Embeddings from Transformers for Under-Resourced Languages
Pranaydeep Singh, Orphee De Clercq and Els Lefever

Introducing YakuToolkit. Yakut Treebank and Morphological Analyzer.
Tatiana Merzhevich and Fabrício Ferraz Gerardi

A Language Model for Spell Checking of Educational Texts in Kurdish (Sorani)
Roshna Abdulrahman and Hossein Hassani

SimRelUz: Similarity and Relatedness Scores as a Semantic Evaluation Dataset for Uzbek Language
Ulugbek Salaev, Elmurod Kuriyozov and Carlos Gómez-Rodríguez

ENRICH4ALL: A First Luxembourgish BERT Model for a Multilingual Chatbot
Dimitra Anastasiou

Saturday, June 25, 2022 (continued)

15:00–16:00 **Joint SIGUL2022-MWE Keynote Speech**
Multiword Expressions and the Low-Resource Scenario from the Perspective of a Local Oral Culture
Steven Bird

16:00–16:30 **Coffee break**

16:30–17:30 **Panel discussion**

17:30–17:50 **General discussion**

17:50–18:00 **Closing**

Proceedings of SIGUL2022 @LREC2022, pages 1–9
Marseille, 24-25 June 2022

Unsupervised Word Segmentation from Discrete Speech Units in Low-Resource Settings

Marcely Zanon Boito[1,*], Bolaji Yusuf[2,3], Lucas Ondel[4], Aline Villavicencio[5], Laurent Besacier[6]
[1]Avignon University, FR, [2]Bogazici University, TR
[3]Brno University of Technology, CZ
[4]LISN CNRS, FR [5]University of Sheffield, UK
[6]Naver Labs Europe, FR and University Grenoble Alpes, FR
* Research done while at University Grenoble Alpes.
contact: marcely.zanon-boito at univ-avignon dot fr

Abstract

Documenting languages helps to prevent the extinction of endangered dialects – many of which are otherwise expected to disappear by the end of the century. When documenting oral languages, unsupervised word segmentation (UWS) from speech is a useful, yet challenging, task. It consists in producing time-stamps for slicing utterances into smaller segments corresponding to words, being performed from phonetic transcriptions, or in the absence of these, from the output of unsupervised speech discretization models. These discretization models are trained using raw speech only, producing discrete speech units that can be applied for downstream (text-based) tasks. In this paper we compare five of these models: three Bayesian and two neural approaches, with regards to the exploitability of the produced units for UWS. For the UWS task, we experiment with two models, using as our target language the Mboshi (Bantu C25), an unwritten language from Congo-Brazzaville. Additionally, we report results for Finnish, Hungarian, Romanian and Russian in equally low-resource settings, using only 4 hours of speech. Our results suggest that neural models for speech discretization are difficult to exploit in our setting, and that it might be necessary to adapt them to limit sequence length. We obtain our best UWS results by using Bayesian models that produce high quality, yet compressed, discrete representations of the input speech signal.

Keywords: unsupervised word segmentation, speech discretization, acoustic unit discovery, low-resource settings

1. Introduction

Popular models for speech processing still rely on the availability of considerable amounts of speech data and their transcriptions, which reduces model applicability to a limited subset of languages considered *high-resource*. This excludes a considerable number of *low-resource* languages, including many from oral tradition. Besides, learning supervised representations from speech differs from the unsupervised way infants learn language, hinting that it should be possible to develop more data-efficient speech processing models.

Recent efforts for *zero-resource* processing (Glass, 2012; Jansen et al., 2013; Versteegh et al., 2016; Dunbar et al., 2017; Dunbar et al., 2019; Dunbar et al., 2020) focus on building speech systems using limited amounts of data (hence *zero resource*), and without textual or linguistic resources, for increasingly challenging tasks such as acoustic or lexical unit discovery. Such zero resource approaches also stimulated interest for computational language documentation (Besacier et al., 2006; Duong et al., 2016; Godard et al., 2018; Bird, 2021) and computational language acquisition (Dupoux, 2018).

In this paper we address the challenging task of unsupervised word segmentation (UWS) from speech. This task consists of outputting time-stamps delimiting stretches of speech, associated with class labels corresponding to word hypotheses, without access to any supervision. We build on the work presented in Godard et al. (2018): they proposed a cascaded model for UWS that first generates a discrete sequence from the speech signal using the model from Ondel et al. (2016), and then segments the discrete sequence into words using a Bayesian (Goldwater, 2007) or a neural (Boito et al., 2017) approach. Since then, much progress has been made in automatic speech discretization: efficient Bayesian models for acoustic unit discovery (AUD) emerged (Ondel et al., 2019; Yusuf et al., 2021), and self-supervised models based on neural networks – typically made of an auto-encoder structure with a discretization layer – were also introduced (van den Oord et al., 2017; Baevski et al., 2020a; Chorowski et al., 2019).

Therefore, in this work we revise and extend Godard et al. (2018) by empirically investigating the *exploitability* of five recent approaches for speech discretization for the UWS task in a rather low-resource scenario, using approximately 4 hours of speech (roughly 5k sentences). More precisely, we train three Bayesian speech discretization models (*HMM* (Ondel et al., 2016), *SHMM* (Ondel et al., 2019) and *H-SHMM* (Yusuf et al., 2021)), and two neural models (*VQ-VAE* (van den Oord et al., 2017) and *vq-wav2vec* (Baevski et al., 2020a)). We extract discrete speech units from them using only 4 hours of speech, and we perform UWS from the sequences produced. Our pipeline targets the Mboshi language (Bantu C25), an unwritten language from Congo-Brazzaville. Additionally, we perform experiments in equal data settings for Finnish, Hungarian, Romanian and Russian. This allows us to assess the language-related impact in our UWS pipeline.

Our experiments show that neural models for speech discretization are difficult to exploit for UWS, as they output very long sequences. In contrast to that, the Bayesian speech discretization approaches from Ondel et al. (2019) and Yusuf et al. (2021) are robust and generalizable, producing high quality, yet compressed, discrete speech sequences from the input utterances in all languages. We obtain our best results by using these sequences for training the neural UWS model from Boito et al. (2017).

This paper is organized as follows. Section 2 presents related work, and Section 3 details the speech discretization models we experiment with. Section 4 presents our experimental setup, and Section 5 our experiments. Section 6 concludes our work.

2. Related Work

The work presented here revises the UWS model from speech in low-resource settings presented in Godard et al. (2018). Boito et al. (2019) complemented that work by tackling different neural models for bilingual UWS, but they did not address the discretization portion of the pipeline, working directly from manual phonetic transcriptions. In Kamper and van Niekerk (2021), the authors propose constraining the VQ-VAE model in order to generate a more exploitable output representation for direct application to the UWS task in English. Different from that, in this work we focus on providing an empirical comparison of recent discretization approaches, extending Godard et al. (2018) and providing results in low-resource settings, and in five different languages.

This work falls into the category of computational language documentation approaches. Recent works in this field include the use of aligned translation for improving transcription quality (Anastasopoulos and Chiang, 2018), and for obtaining bilingually grounded UWS (Duong et al., 2016; Boito et al., 2017). We find pipelines for obtaining manual (Foley et al., 2018) and automatic (Michaud et al., 2018) transcriptions, and for aligning transcription and audio (Strunk et al., 2014). Other examples are methods for low-resource segmentation (Lignos and Yang, 2010; Goldwater et al., 2009), and for lexical unit discovery without textual resources (Bartels et al., 2016). Finally, direct speech-to-speech (Tjandra et al., 2019) and speech-to-text (Besacier et al., 2006; Bérard et al., 2016) architectures could be an option for the lack of transcription, but it remains to be seen how exploitable these architectures can be in low-resource settings.

Lastly, we highlight that recent models based on self-supervised learning (Schneider et al., 2019; Baevski et al., 2019; Wang et al., 2020; Liu et al., 2020; Baevski et al., 2020b; Hsu et al., 2021) provide an interesting novel option for reducing the amount of labeled data needed in downstream tasks such as automatic speech recognition and speech translation. In this work we experiment with the vq-wav2vec model, a predecessor of the popular wav2vec 2.0 (Baevski et al., 2020b). We however, do not extend our investigation to the latter, or to models such as HuBERT (Hsu et al., 2021). This is because, while these models do produce a certain discretization of the speech (for wav2vec 2.0 via quantization module, for HuBERT via clustering of MFCC features), we judge this discretization to be insufficiently exploitable for downstream text-based approaches due to their excessive length.[1] We do, however, find promising the integration of self-supervised speech features into Bayesian AUD models as in Ondel et al. (2022).

3. Unsupervised Speech Discretization Models

Speech discretization consists in labeling the speech signal into discrete speech units, which can correspond or not to the language phonetic inventory. This problem can be formulated as the learning of a set of U discrete units with embeddings $\mathbf{H} = \{\boldsymbol{\eta}^1, \dots, \boldsymbol{\eta}^U\}$ from a sequence of untranscribed acoustic features $\mathbf{X} = [\mathbf{x}_1, \dots, \mathbf{x}_N]$, as well as the assignment of frame to unit $\mathbf{z} = [z_1, \dots, z_N]$. Depending on the approach, neural (Section 3.1) or Bayesian (Section 3.2), the assumptions and the inference regarding these three quantities will differ.

3.1. Neural (VQ-based) models

VQ-VAE. It comprises an encoder, a decoder, and a set of unit-specific embeddings $\mathbf{H}$. The encoder is a neural network that transforms the data into a continuous latent representation $\mathbf{V} = (\mathbf{v}_1, \dots, \mathbf{v}_N)$. Each frame is then assigned to the closest embedding in the Euclidean sense (Equation 1). The decoder transforms the sequence of quantized vectors into parameters of the conditional log-likelihood of the data $p(\mathbf{x}_n|\mathbf{z})$, and the network is trained to maximize this likelihood. Since the quantization step is not differentiable, the encoder is trained with a straight through estimator (Bengio et al., 2013). In addition, a pair of ℓ_2 losses are used to minimize the quantization error, and the overall objective function that is maximized is presented in Equation 2, where $\text{sg}[\cdot]$ is the stop-gradient operator. We define the likelihood $p(\mathbf{x}_n|z_n) = \mathcal{N}(\mathbf{x}_n; \boldsymbol{\mu}(\boldsymbol{\eta}^{z_n}), \mathbf{I})$. Under this assumption, the log-likelihood reduces to the mean-squared error $||\mathbf{x}_n - \boldsymbol{\mu}(\boldsymbol{\eta}^{z_n})||_2^2$.

$$z_n = \arg\min_u ||\mathbf{v}_n - \boldsymbol{\eta}^u||_2. \quad (1)$$

[1] For instance, wav2vec 2.0 trains on a joint *diversity* loss for inciting the use of its discrete units. Their large codebook of $G = 8; V = 8$ results in an upper-bound of 8^8 units.

$$\mathcal{L} = \frac{1}{N}\sum_{n=1}^{N}\Big(\ln p(\mathbf{x}_n|z_n) - k_1||\operatorname{sg}[\boldsymbol{\eta}^{z_n}] - \mathbf{v}_n||_2^2 - k_2||\boldsymbol{\eta}^{z_n} - \operatorname{sg}[\mathbf{v}_n]||_2^2\Big), \quad (2)$$

vq-wav2vec. This model is composed of an encoder ($f : \mathbf{X} \rightarrow \mathbf{Z}$), a quantizer ($q : \mathbf{Z} \rightarrow \hat{\mathbf{Z}}$) and an aggregator ($g : \hat{\mathbf{Z}} \rightarrow \mathbf{C}$). The encoder is a CNN which maps the raw speech input $\mathbf{X}$ into the dense feature representation $\mathbf{Z}$. From this representation, the quantizer produces discrete labels $\hat{\mathbf{Z}}$ from a fixed-size codebook $\mathbf{e} \in \mathbb{R}^{V \times d}$ with V representations of size d. Since replacing an encoder feature vector $\mathbf{z}_i$ by a single entry in the codebook makes the method prone to model collapse, the authors independently quantize partitions of each feature vector by creating multiple *groups* G, arranging the feature vector into a matrix $\mathbf{z}' \in \mathbb{R}^{G \times (d/G)}$. Considering each row as an integer index, the full feature vector is represented by the indices $\mathbf{i} \in [V]^G$, with V being the possible number of *variables* for a given group, and each element $\mathbf{i}_j$ corresponding to a fixed codebook vector ($j \in |G|$). For each of the G groups, the quantization is performed by using Gumbel-Softmax (Jang et al., 2017) or online k-means clustering. Finally, the aggregator combines multiple quantized feature vector time-steps into a new representation $\mathbf{c}_i$ for each time step i. The model is trained to distinguish a sample k steps in the future $\hat{\mathbf{z}}_{i+k}$ from *distractor* samples $\tilde{\mathbf{z}}$ drawn from a distribution p_n. This is done by minimizing the contrastive loss for steps $k = \{1, \ldots, K\}$ as in Equation 3, where T is the sequence length, $\sigma(x) = 1/(1 + exp(-x))$, $\sigma(\hat{\mathbf{z}}_{i+k}^{\intercal} h_k(\mathbf{c_i}))$ is the probability of $\hat{\mathbf{z}}_{i+k}$ being the true sample, and $h_k(\mathbf{c}_i)$ is the step-specific affine transformation $h_k(\mathbf{c}_i) = W_k\mathbf{c}_i + b_k$. Finally, this loss is accumulated over all k steps $\mathcal{L} = \sum_{k=1}^{K} \mathcal{L}_k$.

$$\mathcal{L}_k = \sum_{i=1}^{T-k}\Big(\log \sigma(\hat{\mathbf{z}}_{i+k}^{\intercal} h_k(\mathbf{c_i})) + \lambda \mathbb{E}_{\tilde{\mathbf{z}} \sim p_n}[\log \sigma(-\tilde{\mathbf{z}}^{\intercal} h_k(\mathbf{c}_i))]\Big) \quad (3)$$

Training. For **VQ-VAE**, the encoder has 4 Bi-LSTM layers each with output dimension 128 followed by a 16-dimensional feed-forward decoder with one hidden layer. The number of discovered units (quantization centroids) is set to 50. This setting is unusually low but it helps to reduce the length of the output sequence. We set $k_1 = 2$ and $k_2 = 4$ (Equation 2), and train[2] with Adam (Kingma and Ba, 2015) with an initial learning rate of 2×10^{-3} which is halved whenever the loss stagnates for two training epochs.

For **vq-wav2vec**, we use the small model from (Baevski et al., 2020a),[3] but with only 64 channels, residual scale of 0.2, and warm-up of 10k. For vocabulary we set $G = 2$ and experimented with having both $V = 4$, resulting in 16 units (*VQ-W2V-V16*), and $V = 6$, resulting in 36 units (*VQ-W2V-V36*). Larger vocabularies resulted in excessively long sequences which could not be used for UWS.[4] We also experimented reducing the representation by using byte pair encoding (BPE) (Sennrich et al., 2016), hypothesizing that phones were being modeled by a combination of different units. In this setting, BPE serves as a method for identifying and clustering these patterns. Surprisingly, we found that using BPE resulted in a decrease in UWS performance. This hints that this model might not be very consistent during its labeling process.

3.2. Bayesian Generative Models

For generative models, each acoustic unit embedding $\boldsymbol{\eta}_i$ represents the parameters of a probability distribution $p(\mathbf{x}_n|\boldsymbol{\eta}_{z_n}, z_n)$ with latent variables $\mathbf{z}$. Discovering the units amounts to estimating the posterior distribution over the embeddings $\mathbf{H}$ and the assignment variables $\mathbf{z}$ given by:

$$p(\mathbf{z}, \mathbf{H}|\mathbf{X}) \propto p(\mathbf{X}|\mathbf{z}, \mathbf{H})p(\mathbf{z}|\mathbf{H}) \prod_{u=1}^{U} p(\boldsymbol{\eta}^u). \quad (4)$$

From this, we describe three different approaches.

HMM. In this model each unit is a 3-state left-to-right HMM with parameters $\boldsymbol{\eta}^i$. Altogether, the set of units forms a large HMM analog to a "phone-loop" recognition model. This model, described in Ondel et al. (2016), serves as the backbone for the two subsequent models.

SHMM. The prior $p(\boldsymbol{\eta})$ in Equation 4 is the probability that a sound, represented by an HMM with parameters $\boldsymbol{\eta}$, is an acoustic unit. For the former model, it is defined as a combination of exponential family distributions forming a prior conjugate to the likelihood. While mathematically convenient, this prior does not incorporate any knowledge about phones, i.e. it considers all possible sounds as potential acoustic units. In Ondel et al. (2019), they propose to remedy this shortcoming by defining the parameters of each unit u as in Equation 5, where $\mathbf{e}^u$ is a low-dimensional unit embedding, $\mathbf{W}$ and $\mathbf{b}$ are the parameters of the *phonetic subspace*, and the function $f(\cdot)$ ensures that the resulting vector $\boldsymbol{\eta}^u$ dwells in the HMM parameter space. The subspace, defined by $\mathbf{W}$ and $\mathbf{b}$, is estimated from several labeled source languages. The prior $p(\boldsymbol{\eta})$ is defined over the low-dimensional embeddings $p(\mathbf{e})$ rather than $\boldsymbol{\eta}$ directly, therefore constraining the search of units in the relevant region of the parameter space. This model is denoted as the Subspace HMM (SHMM).

$$\boldsymbol{\eta}^u = f(\mathbf{W} \cdot \mathbf{e}^u + \mathbf{b}) \quad (5)$$

[2]Implementation available at: `https://github.com/BUTSpeechFIT/vq-aud`

[3]Implementation available at: `https://github.com/pytorch/fairseq/tree/master/examples/wav2vec`

[4]For instance, the `dpseg` original implementation only processes sequences shorter than 350 tokens.

H-SHMM. While the SHMM significantly improves results over the HMM, it also suffers from an unrealistic assumption: it assumes that the phonetic subspace is the same for all languages. Yusuf et al. (2021) relax this assumption by proposing to adapt the subspace for each target language while learning the acoustic units. Formally, for a given language λ, the subspace and the acoustic units' parameters are constructed as in Equation 6-8, where the matrices $\mathbf{M}_0, \dots, \mathbf{M}_K$ and vectors $\mathbf{m}_0, \dots, \mathbf{m}_K$ represent some "template" phonetic subspace linearly combined by a language embedding $\boldsymbol{\alpha}^\lambda = [\alpha_1^\lambda, \alpha_2^\lambda, \dots, \alpha_K^\lambda]^\top$. The matrices $\mathbf{M}_i$ and the vectors $\mathbf{m}_i$ are estimated from labeled languages – from multilingual transcribed speech dataset for instance. The acoustic units' low-dimensional embeddings $\{\mathbf{e}_i\}$ and the language embedding $\boldsymbol{\alpha}$ are learned on the target (unlabeled) speech data. We refer to this model as the Hierarchical SHMM (H-SHMM).

$$\mathbf{W}^\lambda = \mathbf{M}_0 + \sum_{k=1}^{K} \alpha_k^\lambda \mathbf{M}_\mathbf{k} \tag{6}$$

$$\mathbf{b}^\lambda = \mathbf{m}_0 + \sum_{k=1}^{K} \alpha_k^\lambda \mathbf{m}_\mathbf{k} \tag{7}$$

$$\boldsymbol{\eta}^{\lambda,u} = f(\mathbf{W}^\lambda \cdot \mathbf{e}^{\lambda,u} + \mathbf{b}^\lambda) \tag{8}$$

Inference. For the three generative models, the posterior distribution is intractable and cannot be estimated. Instead, one seeks an approximate posterior $q(\{\boldsymbol{\eta}_i\}, \mathbf{z}) = q(\{\boldsymbol{\eta}_i\})q(\mathbf{z})$ that maximizes the variational lower-bound $\mathcal{L}[q]$. Concerning the estimation of $q(\mathbf{z})$, the *expectation* step is identical for all models and is achieved with a modified *forward-backward* algorithm described in Ondel et al. (2016). Estimation of $q(\boldsymbol{\eta})$, the *maximization* step, is model-specific and is described in Ondel et al. (2016) for the HMM, in Ondel et al. (2019) for SHMM models, and in Yusuf et al. (2021) for the H-SHMM model. Finally, the output of each system is obtained from a modified Viterbi algorithm that uses the expectation of the log-likelihoods with respect to $q(\{\boldsymbol{\eta}_i\})$, instead of point estimates.

Training. The models are trained with 4 Gaussians per HMM state and using 100 for the Dirichlet process' truncation parameter. SHMM and H-SHMM use an embedding size of 100, and H-SHMM models have a 6-dimensional language embedding. For the methods that use subspaces estimation (SHMM and H-SHMM), this estimation uses the following languages: French, German, Spanish, Polish from the Globalphone corpus (Schultz et al., 2013), as well as Amharic (Abate et al., 2005), Swahili (Gelas et al., 2012) and Wolof (Gauthier et al., 2016) from the ALFFA project (Besacier et al., 2015). We use 2-3 hours subsets of each, for a total of roughly 19 hours.

4. Experimental Setup

From the discrete speech units produced by the presented speech discretization models, we produce segmentation in the symbolic domain by using two UWS models. A final speech segmentation is then inferred using the units' time-stamps and evaluated by using the *Zero-Resource Challenge* 2017 evaluation suite, track 2 (Dunbar et al., 2017)[5]. We now detail the UWS models used in this work, which are trained with the same parameters from Godard et al. (2018). We also detail the datasets and the post-processing for the discrete speech discrete units.

		#Types	#Tokens	Avg Token Length	Avg #Tokens per Sentence
MB-FR	MB*	6,633	30,556	4.2	6.0
	FR	5,162	42,715	4.4	8.3
MaSS	FI*	12,088	70,226	6.0	13.2
	HU*	12,993	69,755	5.9	13.1
	RO*	6,795	84,613	4.5	15.9
	RU*	10,624	67,176	6.2	12.6
	FR	7,226	94,527	4.1	17.8

Table 1: Statistics for the datasets, computed over the text (FR), or over the phonetic representation (*).

		HMM	SHMM	H-SHMM
RAW	# Units	77 (+9)	76 (+8)	49 (-19)
	Avg #Units per sequence	27.5 (+8.7)	24.0 (+5.2)	21.7 (+2.9)
	Max Length	68 (+17)	69 (+18)	63 (+12)
+SIL	# Units	75 (+7)	75 (+7)	47 (-21)
	Avg #units per sequence	20.9 (+2.1)	19.9 (+1.1)	19.4 (+0.6)
	Max Length	69 (+18)	62 (+11)	60 (+9)
		VQ-VAE	**VQ-W2V-16**	**VQ-W2V-36**
RAW	# Units	50 (-18)	16 (-52)	36 (-32)
	Avg #units per sequence	65.2 (+46.4)	81.7 (+62.9)	111.0 (+92.2)
	Max Length	217 (+166)	289 (+238)	361 (+310)
+SIL	# Units	50 (-18)	16 (-52)	36 (-32)
	Avg #units per sequence	43.4 (+24.6)	52.6 (+33.8)	76.2 (+57.4)
	Max Length	143 (+92)	229 (+178)	271 (+220)

Table 2: Statistics for the discrete speech units produced for the Mboshi, with the difference between the produced and reference representation between parentheses. RAW is the original output from speech discretization models, +SIL is the result after silence post-processing. Other languages follow the same trend.

Bayesian UWS approach (monolingual). Non-parametric Bayesian models (Goldwater, 2007; Johnson and Goldwater, 2009) are statistical approaches for UWS and morphological analysis, known to be robust in low-resource settings (Godard et al., 2016). In these models, words are generated by a unigram or bigram model over an infinite inventory, through the use of a Dirichlet process. In this work, we use the unigram model from *dpseg* (Goldwater et al., 2009)[6], which was shown to be superior to the bigram model in low-resource settings (Godard, 2019).

Neural UWS approach (bilingual). We follow the bilingual pipeline from Godard et al. (2018). The discrete speech units and their sentence-level translations are fed to an attention-based neural machine transla-

[5]Resources are available at `http://zerospeech.com/2017`

[6]Implementation available at `http://homepages.inf.ed.ac.uk/sgwater/resources.html`

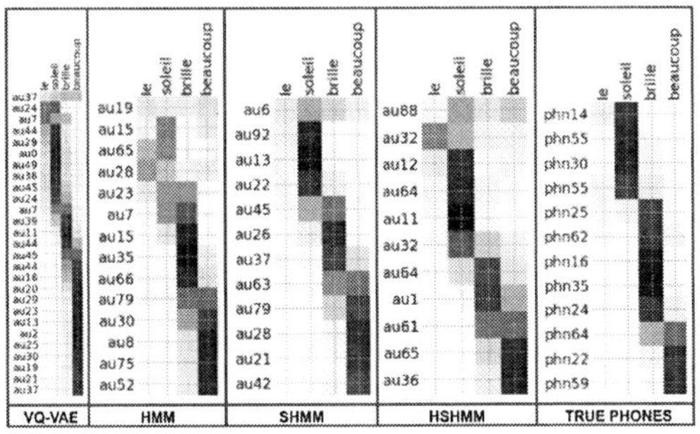

Figure 1: Heatmaps for the soft-alignment probability matrices generated by the neural UWS models (bilingual) trained on different discrete speech units, for the same French-Mboshi sentence. The darker the square, the higher the pair probability. The rows present the automatically generated units from the different discretization models, informed in the bottom.

tion system that produces soft-alignment probability matrices between source and target sequences. For each sentence pair, its matrix is used for clustering together (segmenting) neighboring phones whose alignment distribution peaks at the same source word. Examples of these matrices are provided in Figure 1. We refer to this model as *neural*.

Datasets. We use the Mboshi-French parallel corpus (MB-FR) (Godard et al., 2018), which is a 5,130 sentence corpus from the language documentation process of Mboshi (Bantu C25), an oral language spoken in Congo-Brazzaville. We also report results using an extract from the MaSS corpus (Boito et al., 2020), a multilingual speech-to-speech and speech-to-text dataset. We use the down-sampling from Boito et al. (2020), which results in 5,324 aligned sentences. We exclude French and Spanish, as these languages are present in the subspace prior from SHMM and H-SHMM models, and we exclude English as it was used as to tune the hyperparameters of the subspace models and the VQ-VAE. We also exclude Basque, as the sequences produced were too long for UWS training. The final set of languages is: Finnish (FI), Hungarian (HU), Romanian (RO) and Russian (RU). In all cases, the French (FR) translations are used as supervision for the neural UWS approach. Statistics are presented in Table 1.

Discrete Speech Units Post-processing. We experiment with reducing the representation by removing units predicted in silence windows. For this, we use the gold references' silence annotations. Removing these allow us to focus the investigation on the quality of the units generated in *relevant* portions of the speech. We see in Table 2 that removing windows that we *know* correspond to silence considerably reduces the number of units generated by all models. Before UWS evaluation, the silence windows are reintroduced to ensure that their segmentation boundaries are taken into account. This approach is justified because a silence detector is an inexpensive resource to obtain. For instance, popular software such as Praat (Boersma, 2006) are able to handle this task in any language. Figure 2 exemplifies the discrete speech units discovered by the models before applying this post-processing.

		dpseg		*neural*	
		RAW	**+SIL**	**RAW**	**+SIL**
1	**HMM**	32.4	59.9	35.1	61.2
2	**SHMM**	43.7	**61.4**	41.4	**64.7**
3	**H-SHMM**	**45.3**	**61.4**	**44.8**	63.9
4	**VQ-VAE**	39.0	52.7	32.1	60.1
5	**VQ-W2V-V16**	37.4	52.2	32.0	50.6
6	**VQ-W2V-V36**	-	48.0	-	49.8
7	**True Phones**	-	**77.1**	-	74.5

Table 3: UWS Boundary F-scores for the MB-FR dataset.

5. Experiments

We first present our results for the MB-FR dataset, the language which corresponds to the true low-resource scenario that we are interested in. Table 3 presents UWS Boundary F-scores for UWS models (dpseg and neural) trained using different discrete speech units for the MB-FR dataset. We include results for both the direct output (RAW) and the post-processed version (+SIL). The RAW VQ-W2V-V36 is not included as its output sequences were excessively large for training our UWS models (Table 2).

We observe that in all cases, post-processing the discrete speech units with the silence information (+SIL) creates *easier* representations for the UWS task. We believe this is due to the considerable reduction in average length of the sequences (Table 2). For Bayesian models, we also observe a reduction in the number of units, meaning that some units were modelling silence windows, even though these models already produce an independent token for silence, which we remove before UWS training.

Looking at the results for UWS models trained using the output of VQ-based models (rows 4-6), we see that the best segmentation result is achieved using the one with the smallest average sequence length (VQ-VAE). In general, we believe that all VQ-based models underperform due to the excessively long sequences produced, which are challenging for UWS. Figure 2 illustrates this difference in representation length, by presenting the discrete speech units produced by Bayesian and neural models for a given utterance: the latter produce considerably more units.

Overall, we find that UWS models trained using the discrete speech units from Bayesian models produce better segmentation, with models trained with SHMM and H SHMM presenting the best results. In Yusuf et al. (2021) both systems showed competitive results for the AUD task. A noticeable difference between these two models is the compression level: H-SHMM

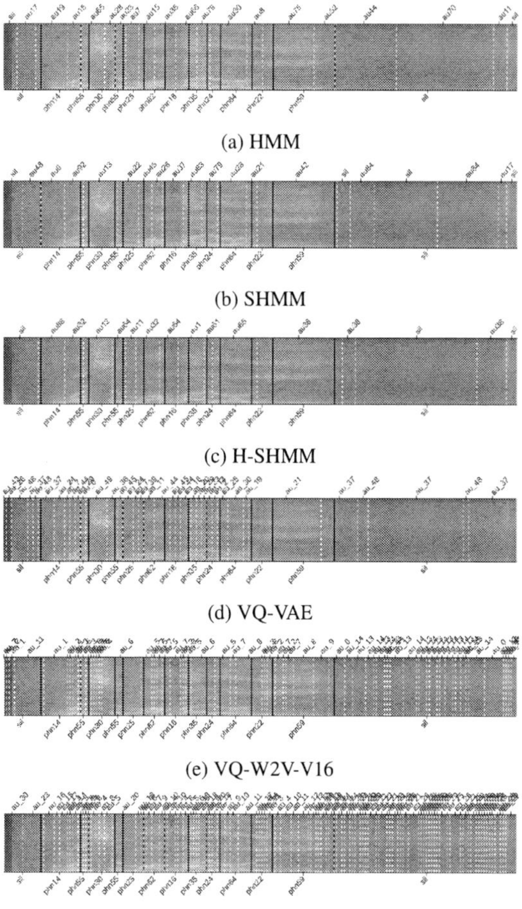

(a) HMM

(b) SHMM

(c) H-SHMM

(d) VQ-VAE

(e) VQ-W2V-V16

(f) VQ-W2V-V36

Figure 2: Speech discrete units produced by the five models for the same Mboshi sentence. Black lines denote the true boundaries, while dashed white lines denote the discovered units boundaries. For each example, discrete speech units (top) and reference (bottom).

	dpseg				*neural*			
	FI	**HU**	**RO**	**RU**	**FI**	**HU**	**RO**	**RU**
HMM	45.6	49.9	53.5	47.1	53.4	51.2	56.6	54.9
SHMM	49.0	52.3	53.5	50.5	56.0	**53.9**	57.7	**57.7**
H-SHMM	50.5	52.9	58.0	52.9	**56.1**	53.3	**59.6**	56.0
True Phones	87.1	83.3	88.0	85.9	68.4	63.4	75.7	68.4

Table 4: UWS Boundary F-scores for the MaSS dataset using Bayesian models (+SIL only). Best UWS results from speech discrete units (**bold**) and from true phones (underlined) are highlighted.

uses 27 fewer units than SHMM. Regarding type retrieval, the models scored 12.1% (SHMM), 10.7% (H-SHMM), and 31% (topline). We also find that SHMM models produced more types and fewer tokens, reaching a higher Type-Token Ratio (0.63) compared to H-SHMM (0.55).

Focusing on the generalization of the presented speech discretization models, we trained our models using four languages from the MaSS dataset. We observed that due to the considerably larger average length of the sentences (Table 1), the VQ-based models produced sequences which we were unable to directly apply to UWS training. This again highlights that these models need some constraining, or post-processing, in order to be directly exploitable for UWS. Focusing on the Bayesian models, which performed the best for generating exploitable discrete speech units for UWS in low-resource settings, Table 4 present UWS results. We omit results for RAW, as we observe the same trend from Table 3. Looking at the results for the four languages, we again observe competitive results for SHMM and H-SHMM models, illustrating that these approaches generalize well to different languages.

Comparing the UWS results present in Table 3 (Mboshi) and Table 4 (languages from MaSS), we notice overall lower results for the languages from the MaSS dataset (best result: 59.6) compared to Mboshi (best result: 64.7). We believe this is due to the MaSS data coming from read text, in which the utterances correspond to verses that are consistently longer than sentences (Table 1). This results in a more challenging setting for UWS and explains the lower results. Lastly, our results over five languages show that the neural UWS model produces better segmentation results from discrete speech units than dpseg, which in turn performs the best with the true phones (topline). This confirms the trend observed by (Godard et al., 2018). The neural UWS models have the advantage of their word-level aligned translations for grounding the segmentation process, which might be attenuating the difficulty of the task in this noisier scenario, with longer sequences and more units. Moreover, a benefit of these models is the potentially exploitable bilingual alignment discovered during training. Boito et al. (2019) used these alignments for filtering the generated vocabulary, increasing type retrieval.

6. Conclusion

In this paper we compared five methods for speech discretization, two neural models (VQ-VAE, VQ-WAV2VEC), and three Bayesian approaches (HMM, SHMM, H-SHMM), with respect to their performance serving as direct input to the task of unsupervised word segmentation (UWS) in low-resource settings. Our motivation for such a study lies in the need of processing oral and low-resource languages, for which obtaining transcriptions is a known bottleneck (Brinckmann, 2009).

In our UWS setting, and using five different languages (Finnish, Hungarian, Mboshi, Romanian and Russian), we find that VQ-based methods are not a good fit for our pipeline, as they output very long and inconsistent sequences, which are difficult to treat. This was also recently observed in Kamper and van Niekerk (2021). In contrast to that, the Bayesian SHMM and H-SHMM models perform the best, as they produced concise yet highly exploitable representations from just few hours of speech. We believe this difference in performance is due to HMM-based models explicitly performing acoustic unit discovery. This means the discretization produced by them aims not only to summarize the speech signal, but to closely match the language's phonology. Moreover, the subspace estimation performed by both SHMM and H-SHMM, might also play a significant role. This is because these models are able to learn from an additional 19 hours of data in different languages. The other models (HMM and VQ-based models) do not have access to any form of pretraining or prior.

Finally, comparing the neural and Bayesian UWS approaches, we notice that the neural model is competitive in the *noisier* setting, reaching better UWS boundary scores working with the output of speech discretization models. The Bayesian model is however better at segmenting true phones (topline scenario). Concluding, this work updates Godard et al. (2018) by using more recent speech discretization models, and presenting better UWS results for Mboshi.

7. Bibliographical References

Anastasopoulos, A. and Chiang, D. (2018). Leveraging translations for speech transcription in low-resource settings. In *Proc. Interspeech 2018*, pages 1279–1283.

Baevski, A., Auli, M., and Mohamed, A. (2019). Effectiveness of self-supervised pre-training for speech recognition. *arXiv preprint arXiv:1911.03912*.

Baevski, A., Schneider, S., and Auli, M. (2020a). vq-wav2vec: Self-supervised learning of discrete speech representations. In *International Conference on Learning Representations (ICLR)*.

Baevski, A., Zhou, Y., Mohamed, A., and Auli, M. (2020b). wav2vec 2.0: A framework for self-supervised learning of speech representations. *Advances in Neural Information Processing Systems*, 33:12449–12460.

Bartels, C., Wang, W., Mitra, V., Richey, C., Kathol, A., Vergyri, D., Bratt, H., and Hung, C. (2016). Toward human-assisted lexical unit discovery without text resources. In *Spoken Language Technology Workshop (SLT), 2016 IEEE*, pages 64–70. IEEE.

Bengio, Y., Léonard, N., and Courville, A. (2013). Estimating or propagating gradients through stochastic neurons for conditional computation. *arXiv:1308.3432*.

Bérard, A., Pietquin, O., Servan, C., and Besacier, L. (2016). Listen and translate: A proof of concept for end-to-end speech-to-text translation. In *NIPS Workshop on End-to-End Learning for Speech and Audio Processing*.

Besacier, L., Zhou, B., and Gao, Y. (2006). Towards speech translation of non written languages. In *Spoken Language Technology Workshop, 2006. IEEE*, pages 222–225. IEEE.

Besacier, L., Gauthier, E., Mangeot, M., Bretier, P., Bagshaw, P., Rosec, O., Moudenc, T., Pellegrino, F., Voisin, S., Marsico, E., et al. (2015). Speech technologies for african languages: example of a multilingual calculator for education. In *Sixteenth Annual Conference of the International Speech Communication Association*.

Bird, S. (2021). Sparse transcription. *Computational Linguistics*.

Boersma, P. (2006). Praat: doing phonetics by computer. *http://www. praat. org/*.

Boito, M. Z., Bérard, A., Villavicencio, A., and Besacier, L. (2017). Unwritten languages demand attention too! word discovery with encoder-decoder models. In *2017 IEEE Automatic Speech Recognition and Understanding Workshop (ASRU)*, pages 458–465. IEEE.

Boito, M. Z., Villavicencio, A., and Besacier, L. (2019). Empirical evaluation of sequence-to-sequence models for word discovery in low-resource settings. In *Proc. Interspeech 2019*, pages 2688–2692.

Boito, M. Z., Villavicencio, A., and Besacier, L. (2020). Investigating language impact in bilingual approaches for computational language documentation. In *Proceedings of the 1st Joint SLTU and CCURL Workshop (SLTU-CCURL 2020)*.

Brinckmann, C. (2009). Transcription bottleneck of speech corpus exploitation. In *Proceedings of the Second Colloquium on Lesser Used Languages and Computer Linguistics (LULCL II). Combining efforts to foster computational support of minority languages*.

Chorowski, J., Weiss, R. J., Bengio, S., and van den Oord, A. (2019). Unsupervised speech representation learning using wavenet autoencoders. *IEEE/ACM transactions on audio, speech, and language processing*, 27(12):2041–2053.

Dunbar, E., Cao, X. N., Benjumea, J., Karadayi, J., Bernard, M., Besacier, L., Anguera, X., and Dupoux, E. (2017). The zero resource speech challenge 2017. In *2017 IEEE Automatic Speech Recognition and Understanding Workshop (ASRU)*, pages 323–330. IEEE.

Dunbar, E., Algayres, R., Karadayi, J., Bernard, M., Benjumea, J., Cao, X.-N., Miskic, L., Dugrain, C., Ondel, L., Black, A. W., Besacier, L., Sakti, S., and Dupoux, E. (2019). The Zero Resource Speech Challenge 2019: TTS Without T. In *Proc. Interspeech 2019*, pages 1088–1092.

Dunbar, E., Karadayi, J., Bernard, M., Cao, X.-N., Algayres, R., Ondel, L., Besacier, L., Sakti, S., and Dupoux, E. (2020). The Zero Resource Speech Challenge 2020: Discovering Discrete Subword and Word Units. In *Proc. Interspeech 2020*, pages 4831–4835.

Duong, L., Anastasopoulos, A., Chiang, D., Bird, S., and Cohn, T. (2016). An attentional model for speech translation without transcription. In *Proceedings of the 2016 Conference of the North American Chapter of the Association for Computational Linguistics: Human Language Technologies*, pages 949–959.

Dupoux, E. (2018). Cognitive science in the era of artificial intelligence: A roadmap for reverse-engineering the infant language-learner. *Cognition*.

Foley, B., Arnold, J., Coto-Solano, R., Durantin, G., Mark, E., van Esch, D., Heath, S., Kratochvil, F., Maxwell-Smith, Z., Nash, D., et al. (2018). Building speech recognition systems for language documentation: the coedl endangered language pipeline and inference system (elpis).

Glass, J. (2012). Towards unsupervised speech processing. In *Information Science, Signal Processing and their Applications (ISSPA)*. IEEE.

Godard, P., Adda, G., Adda-Decker, M., Allauzen, A., Besacier, L., Bonneau-Maynard, H., Kouarata, G.-N., Löser, K., Rialland, A., and Yvon, F. (2016). Preliminary experiments on unsupervised word discovery in mboshi. In *Proc. Interspeech*.

Godard, P., Boito, M. Z., Ondel, L., Bérard, A., Yvon, F., Villavicencio, A., and Besacier, L. (2018). Unsupervised word segmentation from speech with attention. In *Proc. Interspeech 2018*, pages 2678–2682.

Godard, P. (2019). *Unsupervised word discovery for computational language documentation*. Ph.D. thesis, Paris Saclay.

Goldwater, S., Griffiths, T. L., and Johnson, M. (2009). A bayesian framework for word segmentation: Exploring the effects of context. *Cognition*, 112(1):21–54.

Goldwater, S. J. (2007). *Nonparametric Bayesian models of lexical acquisition*. Ph.D. thesis, Citeseer.

Hsu, W.-N., Bolte, B., Tsai, Y.-H. H., Lakhotia, K., Salakhutdinov, R., and Mohamed, A. (2021). Hubert: Self-supervised speech representation learning by masked prediction of hidden units. *IEEE/ACM Transactions on Audio, Speech, and Language Processing*, 29:3451–3460.

Jang, E., Gu, S., and Poole, B. (2017). Categorical reparameterization with gumbel-softmax. In *ICLR*.

Jansen, A., Dupoux, E., Goldwater, S., Johnson, M., Khudanpur, S., Church, K., Feldman, N., Hermansky, H., Metze, F., Rose, R., et al. (2013). A summary of the 2012 jhu clsp workshop on zero resource speech technologies and models of early language acquisition. In *2013 IEEE International Conference on Acoustics, Speech and Signal Processing*, pages 8111–8115. IEEE.

Johnson, M. and Goldwater, S. (2009). Improving nonparameteric bayesian inference: experiments on unsupervised word segmentation with adaptor grammars. In *Proc. NAACL-HLT*, pages 317–325. Association for Computational Linguistics.

Kamper, H. and van Niekerk, B. (2021). Towards Unsupervised Phone and Word Segmentation Using Self-Supervised Vector-Quantized Neural Networks. In *Proc. Interspeech 2021*, pages 1539–1543.

Kingma, D. P. and Ba, J. (2015). Adam: A method for stochastic optimization. In Yoshua Bengio et al., editors, *ICLR 2015, Conference Track Proceedings*.

Lignos, C. and Yang, C. (2010). Recession segmentation: simpler online word segmentation using limited resources. In *Proceedings of the fourteenth conference on computational natural language learning*, pages 88–97.

Liu, A. T., Yang, S.-w., Chi, P.-H., Hsu, P.-c., and Lee, H.-y. (2020). Mockingjay: Unsupervised speech representation learning with deep bidirectional transformer encoders. In *ICASSP 2020-2020 IEEE International Conference on Acoustics, Speech and Signal Processing (ICASSP)*, pages 6419–6423. IEEE.

Michaud, A., Adams, O., Cohn, T. A., Neubig, G., and Guillaume, S. (2018). Integrating automatic transcription into the language documentation workflow: Experiments with na data and the persephone toolkit.

Ondel, L., Burget, L., and Černockỳ, J. (2016). Variational inference for acoustic unit discovery. *Procedia Computer Science*, 81:80–86.

Ondel, L., Vydana, H. K., Burget, L., and Černocký, J. (2019). Bayesian Subspace Hidden Markov Model for Acoustic Unit Discovery. In *Interspeech*, pages 261–265.

Ondel, L., Yusuf, B., Burget, L., and Saraclar, M. (2022). Non-parametric bayesian subspace models for acoustic unit discovery. *IEEE/ACM Transactions on Audio, Speech, and Language Processing*.

Schneider, S., Baevski, A., Collobert, R., and Auli, M. (2019). wav2vec: Unsupervised Pre-Training for Speech Recognition. In *Proc. Interspeech 2019*, pages 3465–3469.

Sennrich, R., Haddow, B., and Birch, A. (2016). Neural machine translation of rare words with subword units. In *Proceedings of the 54th Annual Meeting of the Association for Computational Linguistics (Volume 1: Long Papers)*, pages 1715–1725, Berlin, Germany, August. Association for Computational Linguistics.

Strunk, J., Schiel, F., Seifart, F., et al. (2014). Untrained forced alignment of transcriptions and audio for language documentation corpora using webmaus. In *LREC*, pages 3940–3947.

Tjandra, A., Sakti, S., and Nakamura, S. (2019). Speech-to-speech translation between untranscribed unknown languages. *arXiv:1910.00795*.

van den Oord, A., Vinyals, O., and kavukcuoglu, k. (2017). Neural discrete representation learning. In I. Guyon, et al., editors, *Advances in Neural Information Processing Systems*, volume 30, pages 6306–6315. Curran Associates, Inc.

Versteegh, M., Anguera, X., Jansen, A., and Dupoux, E. (2016). The zero resource speech challenge 2015: Proposed approaches and results. *Procedia Computer Science*, 81:67–72.

Wang, W., Tang, Q., and Livescu, K. (2020). Unsupervised pre-training of bidirectional speech encoders via masked reconstruction. In *ICASSP 2020-2020 IEEE International Conference on Acoustics, Speech and Signal Processing (ICASSP)*, pages 6889–6893. IEEE.

Yusuf, B., Ondel, L., Burget, L., Černocký, J., and Saraclar, M. (2021). A hierarchical subspace model for language-attuned acoustic unit discovery. In *ICASSP 2021-2021 IEEE International Conference on Acoustics, Speech and Signal Processing (ICASSP)*, pages 3710–3714. IEEE.

8. Language Resource References

Abate, S. T., Menzel, W., and Tafila, B. (2005). An amharic speech corpus for large vocabulary continuous speech recognition. In *Ninth European Conference on Speech Communication and Technology*.

Boito, M. Z., Havard, W. N., Garnerin, M., Ferrand, É. L., and Besacier, L. (2020). Mass: A large and clean multilingual corpus of sentence-aligned spoken utterances extracted from the bible. *Language Resources and Evaluation Conference (LREC)*.

Gauthier, E., Besacier, L., Voisin, S., Melese, M., and Elingui, U. P. (2016). Collecting Resources in Sub-Saharan African Languages for Automatic Speech Recognition: a Case Study of Wolof. *LREC*.

Gelas, H., Besacier, L., and Pellegrino, F. (2012). Developments of Swahili resources for an automatic speech recognition system. In *SLTU - Workshop on Spoken Language Technologies for Under-Resourced Languages*, Afrique Du Sud.

Godard, P., Adda, G., Adda-Decker, M., Benjumea, J., Besacier, L., Cooper-Leavitt, J., Kouarata, G.-N., Lamel, L., Maynard, H., Mueller, M., Rialland, A., Stueker, S., Yvon, F., and Boito, M. Z. (2018). A very low resource language speech corpus for computational language documentation experiments. In *Proceedings of the Eleventh International Conference on Language Resources and Evaluation (LREC 2018)*, Miyazaki, Japan, May. European Language Resources Association (ELRA).

Schultz, T., Vu, N. T., and Schlippe, T. (2013). Globalphone: A multilingual text & speech database in 20 languages. In *International Conference on Acoustics, Speech and Signal Processing*. IEEE.

Proceedings of SIGUL2022 @LREC2022, pages 10–15
Marseille, 24-25 June 2022

An Open Source Web Reader for Under-Resourced Languages

**Judy Y. Fong, Þorsteinn Daði Gunnarsson, Sunneva Þorsteinsdóttir,
Gunnar Thor Örnólfsson, Jon Gudnason**
Reykjavík University
Menntavegur 1 - Reykjavík Iceland
judy@judyyfong.xyz, thorsteinng@ru.is, sunnevatorstein@gmail.com
gunnaro@ru.is, jg@ru.is

Abstract

We have developed an open source web reader in Iceland for under-resourced languages. The web reader was developed due to the need for a free and good quality web reader for languages which fall outside the scope of commercially available web readers. It relies on a text-to-speech (TTS) pipeline accessed via a cloud service. The web reader was developed using the Icelandic TTS voices Alfur and Dilja, but could be connected to any language which has a TTS pipeline. The design of our web reader focuses on functionality, adaptability and user friendliness. Therefore, the web reader's feature set heavily overlaps with the minimal features necessary to provide a good web reading experience while still being extensible enough to be adapted to work for other languages, high-resourced and under-resourced. The web reader works well on all the major web browsers and has a Web Content Accessibility Guidelines 2.0 Level AA: Acceptable compliance, meaning that it works well for the largest user groups, people in under-resourced languages with visual impairments and difficulty reading. The code for our web reader is available and published with an Apache 2.0 license at https://github.com/cadia-lvl/WebRICE, which includes a simple demo of the project.

Keywords: text-to-speech, web reader, accessibility, human-computer interaction

1. Introduction

The proposed open source web reader for under-resourced languages is a language technology tool for everyday users. Web readers are added to websites to let visitors listen to the content of the webpage instead of reading it. They are analogous to audiobooks made from ebooks. However, audiobooks are generally manually recorded and edited, and are labour-intensive to produce. Manually rendering text on websites into speech at scale is generally not viable. Thus, web readers use automatic text-to-speech (TTS) voices produced for the target language. In this way, web readers are a scalable way to make a website more accessible.

1.1. Language Technology Tools

Language technology (LT) tools such as web readers are scalable, which benefits under-resourced languages. It means with less effort and few resources, a wide audience can still be reached, like how web readers can allow a single TTS voice to be used on any given number of websites. One of the main goals of language technology development is to facilitate the use of natural language in today's digital age. A web reader achieves this by allowing users to listen to a given website in addition to reading it. More importantly, people visit websites in their under-resourced language every day. These smaller language communities, like Icelandic, often lack resources. In some cases, national governments can counteract this by implementing national language technology initiatives. These initiatives are often crucial to bring an under-resourced language into the digital age. For example, the Estonian language is now viable in the digital age through a government initiative described by (Meister and Vilo, 2008). With this inspiration and knowledge, the Icelandic government has implemented the five year language technology programme for Icelandic as described by (Nikulásdóttir et al., 2020), to bring the Icelandic language and the digital age together. Nikulásdóttir et al. (2021) enumerates the language technology tools and datasets created by this initiative and hosted at CLARIN-IS. One of the core areas of this initiative is text-to-speech.

1.1.1. TTS technologies

The research and development for each part of a typical TTS pipeline is considered in the Icelandic programme mentioned by Nikulásdóttir et al. (2020). For example, collecting data as in (Sigurgeirsson et al., 2020) and creating the free and open Talrómur and Talrómur 2 TTS datasets as mentioned by (Sigurgeirsson et al., 2021) and (Gunnarsson, Þ. et. al., 2021). Model training recipes have been developed for the datasets, both for unit selection[1] and neural network-based TTS methods[2][3]. TTS models from (Gunnarsson Þ. et. al., 2022) have been trained and published. Important TTS pre-processing steps like text normalization in (Sigurðardóttir et al., 2021) and grapheme to phoneme conversions as in (Nikulásdóttir, A. et. al., 2022) are also considered. A TTS web service has been developed[4], which allows anyone to host their own TTS voices.

[1]https://github.com/cadia-lvl/unit-selection-festival/
[2]https://github.com/cadia-lvl/FastSpeech2
[3]https://github.com/cadia-lvl/espnet
[4]https://github.com/tiro-is/tiro-tts

These serve as a template for providing a TTS web service in any under-resourced language. An instance of that service has been made accessible[5] as a result of the project. This allows the development of TTS applications such as the main subject of this paper: the web reader.

1.2. Other Web Readers

Under-resourced languages usually attract less commercial interest than better resourced ones. One of the reasons can be the smaller size of the language community. For example, the Icelandic language has only a few hundred thousand speakers which make up the whole market for Icelandic LT solutions. That is a tiny fraction of the millions or billions of speakers and users, which heavily resourced languages like French and English have.

This smaller commercial interest was noticeable when researching existing web readers used in the world and in Iceland. Our research delved into NaturalReader, Read Aloud, and ReadSpeaker. NaturalReader[6] seems to only offer English as it does not mention multilingual support, only a variety of voices. Also, it is a proprietary software solution. Read Aloud is offered only as a web browser extension. It is not offered as a web reader embedded into websites. It is a free in-browser web reader which connects to various proprietary TTS cloud service providers. While the extension itself is free, listening to Icelandic neural voices is only possible through paid services. Finally, ReadSpeaker[7] does support Icelandic directly but it is also a proprietary option. In addition to web readers, we also looked into screen readers such as Ivona, ClaroRead, and JAWS[8]. Screen readers are installed directly onto one's operating system and can read most text on a computer or mobile device. However, screen readers are operating system dependent and are out of scope for developing an open source web reader despite the overlap. The research results are twofold: first and foremost many web readers are commercial and second that they offer limited or no support for Icelandic, nor other under-resourced languages. The most widely adopted web reader on Icelandic websites is ReadSpeaker, built with heavy involvement from the Icelandic community a decade ago. To provide users of under-resourced languages a nearly seamless experience when using our web reader on websites, compared to proprietary readers, it would be best for our web reader to offer the same core features.

1.3. An Open Source Web Reader

As mentioned previously, under-resourced languages attract less commercial interest. In order to get international companies to implement tools for these languages, TTS language resources and tools must be open, standardized, and accessible. Only then will the needs of the under-resourced language community and commercial interests be aligned. The same is true for smaller under-resourced language companies, public entities, and individuals who usually have limited resources. So they cannot include commercial web readers. Having these language resources open and freely available also means that language technology research is more likely to be done. The result should be more websites with web readers. It is an important accessibility feature for websites to have a web reader, especially popular and required websites such as for the government, schools, and the media. Without a web reader, many under-served communities struggle to get equal access to information and events. Therefore, an open source web reader is crucial for under-resourced languages because it gets text-to-speech technology into the hands of language users immediately.

1.4. Language support

To improve an under-resourced language's chance of being included in the commercial offerings of international companies' technologies, it would appear that the most feasible option would be to make the language resources and other tools open and accessible enough for them to be incorporated easily. One way is to use the same standards of data and tools as used in these companies. This is what we have done to make sure our web reader and TTS web service support Icelandic. Our aim in making the web reader was to reach the largest possible internet audience in Iceland, meaning be good for both users (listeners) from the under-served communities and the general Icelandic population. Our open source web reader's development goal is to work with any natural language, under-resourced and highly-resourced alike, and with any TTS cloud services available. In the Icelandic case, the most popular commercial TTS cloud service offering Icelandic during initial development was Amazon Polly[9], due to it being the only TTS web service available directly for producing spoken Icelandic. But now Icelandic is also offered on two other platforms, Google[10] and Microsoft Azure[11]. Having a selection of voices is important for users and companies to choose the voice that best reflects themselves. This is why the web reader is capable of connecting to TTS cloud services from different companies.

Now that the web reader infrastructure is provided, it can be connected to TTS web services in any language. Due to the default design of our web reader, it works with Icelandic currently. But it can easily be changed to use a TTS web service from any other under-resourced language. Thus, machine learning engineers can focus

[5]https://tts.tiro.is/

[6]https://www.naturalreaders.com/index.html

[7]https://www.readspeaker.com/

[8]https://www.freedomscientific.com/products/software/jaws/

[9]https://aws.amazon.com/polly/

[10]https://cloud.google.com/text-to-speech/

[11]https://azure.microsoft.com/en-us/services/cognitive-services/text-to-speech/

solely on providing great TTS voices behind a standard HTTP POST request.

1.5. Overview

The following is a summary of our software design, implementation, and tests. It consists of requirements and features for both the web reader and integration requirements with TTS web services and websites. The software development was categorized into required and optional. In this paper, we will mainly be talking about our required features.

2. Web reader

When developing software, the first steps are to identify the core features, to understand how a web reader is used and to understand what differentiates a good web reader from a poor web reader. People rarely use bad web readers. Our web reader was developed in consultation with the target user groups, which should translate to a good user experience. More information about the target user groups is discussed later.
The web reader's visual design focus is on a high quality suite of buttons as seen in Figure 1. The web reader must be able to play, pause, resume, speed up, slow down, stop and restart audio for the given text. The buttons must also be large and visible. There are several constraints. Functionality must be intuitive; for example, the settings module must close if a user clicks away from the settings module. The web reader must work on even the longest texts. It needs to be mobile friendly, as most users browse the web on mobile devices. As the basic user interface needs to meet the "WCAG 2.0 Level AA: Acceptable compliance" accessibility standards, the keyboard interface is implemented in two ways. First is the standard keyboard interface where users or screen readers can tab through the buttons on the web reader, like on any accessible website. Second are shortcut keys on each button directly. These shortcut keys are pretty similar to the ones offered by the most popular Icelandic web reader. If a user wants to use the shortcut keys, they can read the instructions on the web reader's help menu. The web reader is also customisable, like setting reading speed. Good documentation is essential. The final requirement is it must connect to a TTS web service. To meet the need for an open source web reader, we have built a web reader whose primary focus is synthesizing text and playing audio for any language. Our web reader meets all the aforementioned requirements.
In short, our web reader consists of multiple modules. There are the button modules: play/pause, stop, speed, and settings. Other modules are highlighting, speech manager, and client store manager. Highlighting handles all the highlighting features. Text can be highlighted while users listen to the generated speech, as shown in Figure 2. Text highlighting is possible using time alignments (speech marks) to the generated speech. The speech manager module interacts with the TTS web services, and the client store manager handles all the user settings and preferences across multiple sessions.

Figure 1: The play (including the ear), stop, speed, and settings buttons with some text below. The pause button replaces the play button during playback.

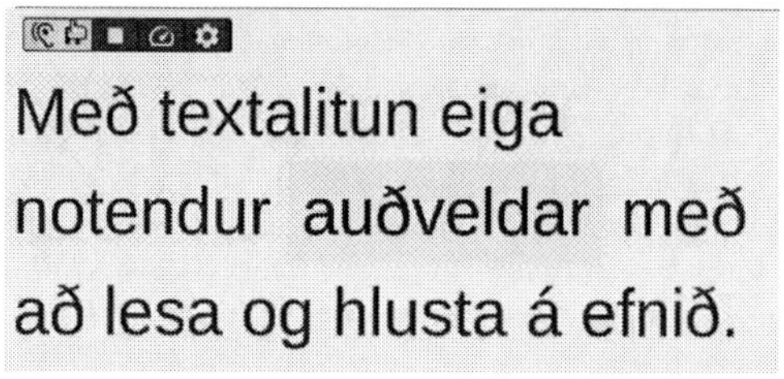

Figure 2: A word being highlighted as the audio is played. The English translation of the text is as follows: With text highlighting users have an easier (highlighted word) time reading and listening to content.

Then, we have several workflows. In the preliminary workflow, the user first loads a website containing our web reader. Then, the buttons are created within the HTML tag with the web reader's ID. Next, any saved settings from a previous session are loaded from client storage. Finally, the text is extracted from the website. The main workflow starts when a user presses or selects play. The web reader fetches the generated speech and speech marks from the TTS web service. Then, we check if the user has text highlighting enabled. If so, then that is applied to the text displayed to the user.

3. Integration

Our web reader has been developed with integration heavily in mind. It has been turned into a webpack library, which can be embedded to websites with a single pre-compiled JavaScript link. Customizing the look of the web reader can be done outside of the web reader's code base, meaning developers can customize the color palette of the web player easier. A business can customize our web reader to seamlessly integrate the web reader into its own brand experience. This experience is not readily offered by any other web readers we have found on the internet.

3.1. TTS web services

Our design depends on having a separate TTS web service. The reasoning is two-fold. First, to allow our web reader to connect to multiple TTS web services. Generally, users will not use web readers with long loading times and poor quality voices. This allows users a greater choice in TTS voices, providers, and natural languages. As TTS web services are provided as standard HTTP POST requests, it would be easy to switch out the current TTS web service with TTS web services in other languages or from other providers. For example, people from under-resourced languages can connect it to their TTS cloud services and deploy the web reader for their language. Second, this separates the TTS development from the web reader development, allowing us to use both the best voices and the best user interface. But in order to connect to a variety of TTS web services, there must be a common minimum feature set that our web reader has to support: good quality voices, low latency, and speech synthesis markup language (SSML) support. Also, it should offer speech marks, which are time alignments between text and generated speech used for highlighting text.

3.1.1. TTS models

Our web reader for under-resourced languages' default integration is with a TTS web service built from Tiro's open source code repository[12]. The underlying TTS web service provides four voices in total: Karl, Dóra, Álfur and Diljá.

The data for the Álfur and Diljá voices come from Sigurgeirsson et al. (2021)'s Talrómur corpus. Two iterations of these voices have been developed. The first iteration was created from the FastSpeech 2 implementation[13] (Chien et al., 2021) as specified in (Ren et al., 2021) and has been released to the public by (Gunnarsson Þ. et. al., 2022). These models are the first publicly available open-source TTS models for Icelandic. An accompanying MelGAN[14](Kumar et al., 2019) vocoder trained on both all the voices from (Sigurgeirsson et al., 2021) for Álfur and only on Diljá for Diljá is used to synthesize the voices. Text normalization was very naive and consisted only of removing all punctuation marks and skipping all numbers. A Sequitur[15] (Bisani and Ney, 2008) grapheme-to-phoneme converter, developed by (Nikulásdóttir et al., 2018), was used for phonetic transcription[16].

We observed significant issues with these initial models, both originating in the acoustic models and the vocoder models as well as the lack of text preprocessing. Phones would often be mispronounced and noise inserted where silence would be expected. Furthermore, significant vocoder artefacts are present, especially in the Diljá voice. Thus, a second iteration of the Álfur and Diljá voices was created using the ESPNet toolkit's[17] implementation of FastSpeech 2 (Hayashi et al., 2020) and trained on the same voice data as before. Additionally, both a Parallel WaveGAN (Yamamoto et al., 2020) and a multi-band MelGAN (Yang et al., 2021) model were trained[18] on the entire Talrómur corpus (Sigurgeirsson et al., 2021). Whereas the Parallel WaveGAN model provides slightly better synthesis quality, the multi-band MelGAN model can generate samples much faster. The TTS web service which provides access to these models currently supports limited text normalization to improve the TTS output, e.g. by expanding abbreviations which should be read letter by letter rather than read as a word. The knowledge and experience gained from (Nikulásdóttir and Guðnason, 2019) shaped the text normalization created by (Sigurðardóttir et al., 2021) and which is used in the web service. Grapheme-to-phoneme conversion for out-of-vocabulary words is done using a LSTM encoder-decoder sequence-to-sequence model[19]. The web service is still in active development so expect the text normalization and other speech features to continue to improve.

3.2. Website Testing

To make sure our web reader works on various websites, we performed integration tests. During the initial development, the web reader was tested on three websites: our web reader's webpage, a local company's webpage and on our university's webpage. The web reader's color palette was also customized to match the websites' own colors. Now, in the later development stages, the web reader is being integrated into websites which did not have a web reader. These websites touch on many parts of society: including financial, government, and innovation organizations. Since the web reader is available as open source software, the organizations are able to perform this later stage of testing themselves.

4. User Tests

For web readers, some of the biggest end-users are under-served communities. Within Iceland, a large proportion of the dyslexic and visually impaired inhabitants often need to rely on spoken word for two reasons: to fully understand everything and to operate independently. However, web readers are not the best option for everyone. People who are blind or significantly visually impaired need a screen reader paired with Símarómur[20], an Android TTS engine which offers the same voices as our web reader: Álfur and Diljá. With language technology, these overlapping groups can in-

[12]https://github.com/tiro-is/tiro-tts

[13]https://github.com/cadia-lvl/FastSpeech2

[14]https://github.com/seungwonpark/melgan

[15]https://github.com/sequitur-g2p/sequitur-g2p

[16]https://github.com/atliSig/g2p

[17]https://github.com/espnet/espnet

[18]https://github.com/kan-bayashi/ParallelWaveGAN/

[19]https://github.com/grammatek/ice-g2p

[20]https://play.google.com/store/apps/details?id=com.grammatek.simaromur

dependently navigate the internet using screen or web readers, whichever best fits their situation.

In addition to the integration tests, we conducted user tests with The Iceland Dyslexia Association and the Icelandic Association of the Visually Impaired. The results revealed that these users primarily use smartphones with computers as a close second. Over 50% of respondents use web readers at least monthly. So they are recurring monthly users. Their strictest requirement is low latency voices; they have a lower tolerance than the general population for slow TTS due to TTS being a primary means of communication. Meanwhile, their most desired optional feature is selecting text and listening to it while following along with the highlighted text. However, the users did clarify that this is optional and not strictly necessary for an enjoyable web reading experience. From the results of our user tests, we are confident that users will like and use our web reader when it becomes available on websites with under-resourced languages like Icelandic.

We later extended the survey to people not in these groups and the percentage of users who use web readers monthly is significantly different in the two groups: over 50% of users in the original user tests versus under 25% of the general population. The general populace also favors browsing the internet on computers over mobile devices. So, the survey results show that web readers are disproportionately used by those with visual impairments in some way.

The results of the user tests mostly confirmed our initial research before development. However there were a few surprises. For example, that users would be satisfied by a simple interface. Users are also remarkably opposed to a nearly but not quite good TTS voice. But they are more forgiving when they know these voices will continue to improve.

5. Conclusion

The proposed open source web reader for under-resourced languages is now published and available with good documentation that describes the integration process for web developers. Connected to the web reader are two state-of-the-art Icelandic TTS voices, Álfur and Diljá. The codebase and demo for our web reader is licensed under Apache 2.0 on GitHub[21].

Now that the open source web reader is published, the aim is to integrate it to popular Icelandic websites and to make web readers more accessible to the public. This involves browser and content management system (CMS) extensions. Browser extensions allow anyone, tech savvy or not, to easily download, install and use them right away on any website. The stores for browser extensions are also an easy way for developers to easily distribute updates and bug fixes automatically for their users.

[21]https://github.com/cadia-lvl/WebRICE

6. Acknowledgements

The authors thank Luke O'brien, Tiro ehf[22], Félag lesblindra á Íslandi (The Iceland Dyslexia Association)[23], and Blindrafélagið (Icelandic Association of the Visually Impaired)[24]. This project was funded by the Language Technology programme for Icelandic 2019-2023. The programme, which is managed and coordinated by Almannarómur[25], is funded by the Icelandic Ministry of Education, Science and Culture.

7. Bibliographical References

Bisani, M. and Ney, H. (2008). Joint-sequence models for grapheme-to-phoneme conversion. *Speech Communication*, 50(5):434–451.

Chien, C.-M., Lin, J.-H., Huang, C.-y., Hsu, P.-c., and Lee, H.-y. (2021). Investigating on incorporating pretrained and learnable speaker representations for multi-speaker multi-style text-to-speech. In *ICASSP 2021 - 2021 IEEE International Conference on Acoustics, Speech and Signal Processing (ICASSP)*, pages 8588–8592.

Hayashi, T., Yamamoto, R., Inoue, K., Yoshimura, T., Watanabe, S., Toda, T., Takeda, K., Zhang, Y., and Tan, X. (2020). Espnet-tts: Unified, reproducible, and integratable open source end-to-end text-to-speech toolkit. In *ICASSP 2020 - 2020 IEEE International Conference on Acoustics, Speech and Signal Processing (ICASSP)*, pages 7654–7658.

Kumar, K., Kumar, R., de Boissiere, T., Gestin, L., Teoh, W. Z., Sotelo, J., de Brébisson, A., Bengio, Y., and Courville, A. C. (2019). Melgan: Generative adversarial networks for conditional waveform synthesis. *Advances in neural information processing systems*, 32.

Meister, E. and Vilo, J. (2008). Strengthening the Estonian language technology. In *Proceedings of the Sixth International Conference on Language Resources and Evaluation (LREC'08)*, Marrakech, Morocco, May. European Language Resources Association (ELRA).

Nikulásdóttir, A. B. and Guðnason, J. (2019). Bootstrapping a text normalization system for an inflected language. numbers as a test case. In *INTERSPEECH*, pages 4455–4459.

Nikulásdóttir, A. B., Guðnason, J., and Rögnvaldsson, E. (2018). An icelandic pronunciation dictionary for tts. In *2018 IEEE Spoken Language Technology Workshop (SLT)*, pages 339–345. IEEE.

Nikulásdóttir, A., Guðnason, J., Ingason, A. K., Loftsson, H., Rögnvaldsson, E., Sigurðsson, E. F., and Steingrímsson, S. (2020). Language technology programme for Icelandic 2019-2023. In *Proceedings of the 12th Language Resources and Evaluation*

[22]https://tiro.is

[23]https://www.lesblindir.is/english/

[24]https://www.blind.is/en

[25]https://almannaromur.is

Conference, pages 3414–3422, Marseille, France, May. European Language Resources Association.

Nikulásdóttir, A. B., Arnardóttir, Þ., Guðnason, J., Daði, Þ., Gunnarsson, A. K. I., Jónsson, H. P., Loftsson, H., Óladóttir, H., Sigurðsson, E. F., Sigurgeirsson, A. Þ., et al. (2021). Help yourself from the buffet: National language technology infrastructure initiative on clarin-is. In *CLARIN Annual Conference 2021*, page 124.

Ren, Y., Hu, C., Tan, X., Qin, T., Zhao, S., Zhao, Z., and Liu, T. (2021). FastSpeech 2: Fast and High-Quality End-to-End Text to Speech. In *Proceedings ICLR 2021 – 9th International Conference on Learning Representations*, Online, may.

Sigurðardóttir, H. S., Nikulásdóttir, A. B., and Guðnason, J. (2021). Creating data in Icelandic for text normalization. In *Proceedings of the 23rd Nordic Conference on Computational Linguistics (NoDaLiDa)*, pages 404–412, Reykjavik, Iceland (Online), May 31–2 June. Linköping University Electronic Press, Sweden.

Sigurgeirsson, A., Örnólfsson, G., and Guðnason, J. (2020). Manual speech synthesis data acquisition - from script design to recording speech. In *Proceedings of the 1st Joint Workshop on Spoken Language Technologies for Under-resourced languages (SLTU) and Collaboration and Computing for Under-Resourced Languages (CCURL)*, pages 316–320, Marseille, France, May. European Language Resources association.

Sigurgeirsson, A., Gunnarsson, Þ., Örnólfsson, G., Magnúsdóttir, E., Þórhallsdóttir, R., Jónsson, S., and Guðnason, J. (2021). Talrómur: A large Icelandic TTS corpus. In *Proceedings of the 23rd Nordic Conference on Computational Linguistics (NoDaLiDa)*, pages 440–444, Reykjavik, Iceland (Online), May 31–2 June. Linköping University Electronic Press, Sweden.

Yamamoto, R., Song, E., and Kim, J.-M. (2020). Parallel wavegan: A fast waveform generation model based on generative adversarial networks with multi-resolution spectrogram. In *ICASSP 2020-2020 IEEE International Conference on Acoustics, Speech and Signal Processing (ICASSP)*, pages 6199–6203. IEEE.

Yang, G., Yang, S., Liu, K., Fang, P., Chen, W., and Xie, L. (2021). Multi-band melgan: Faster waveform generation for high-quality text-to-speech. In *2021 IEEE Spoken Language Technology Workshop (SLT)*, pages 492–498. IEEE.

8. Language Resource References

Gunnarsson, Þ. et. al. (2021). *Talrómur 2 (21 12)*. CLARIN-IS.

Gunnarsson Þ. et. al. (2022). *Talrómur Utils*. CLARIN-IS.

Nikulásdóttir, A. et. al. (2022). *Icelandic Pronunciation Dictionary for Language Technology 22.01*. CLARIN-IS.

Proceedings of SIGUL2022 @LREC2022, pages 16–22
Marseille, 24-25 June 2022

Text-to-Speech for Under-Resourced Languages: Phoneme Mapping and Source Language Selection in Transfer Learning

Phat Do[1], Matt Coler[1], Jelske Dijkstra[2], Esther Klabbers[3]
[1]University of Groningen, Campus Fryslân, Leeuwarden, the Netherlands
[2]Fryske Akademy/Mercator Research Centre, Leeuwarden, the Netherlands
[3]ReadSpeaker, Driebergen-Rijsenburg, the Netherlands
{t.p.do, m.coler}@rug.nl, jdijkstra@fryske-akademy.nl, esther.judd@readspeaker.com

Abstract

We propose a new approach for phoneme mapping in cross-lingual transfer learning for text-to-speech (TTS) in under-resourced languages (URLs), using phonological features from the PHOIBLE database and a language-independent mapping rule. This approach was validated through our experiment, in which we pre-trained acoustic models in Dutch, Finnish, French, Japanese, and Spanish, and fine-tuned them with 30 minutes of Frisian training data. The experiment showed an improvement in both naturalness and pronunciation accuracy in the synthesized Frisian speech when our mapping approach was used. Since this improvement also depended on the source language, we then experimented on finding a good criterion for selecting source languages. As an alternative to the traditionally used language family criterion, we tested a novel idea of using Angular Similarity of Phoneme Frequencies (ASPF), which measures the similarity between the phoneme systems of two languages. ASPF was empirically confirmed to be more effective than language family as a criterion for source language selection, and also to affect the phoneme mapping's effectiveness. Thus, a combination of our phoneme mapping approach and the ASPF measure can be beneficially adopted by other studies involving multilingual or cross-lingual TTS for URLs.

Keywords: neural text-to-speech synthesis, under-resourced languages, cross-lingual transfer learning, phoneme mapping, language family

1. Introduction

Research in text-to-speech synthesis (TTS) has seen rapid advancement recently. Since the 2010s, there has been a paradigm shift to neural network-based speech synthesis (neural TTS), which produces much higher output quality in both naturalness and intelligibility compared to previous paradigms such as concatenative synthesis and statistical parametric speech synthesis (Tan et al., 2021).

However, neural TTS requires a large amount of training data. In TTS, training data refers to recordings of human speakers, preferably recorded with high quality (e.g., no or little background noise, good recording equipment, consistent speaking style and pronunciation), have reliable annotations (e.g., split into text-audio pairs with minimal or no discrepancies), and, in regards to quantity: the more the better. For an example, LJSpeech (Ito and Johnson, 2017), a public domain data set recorded by an American English female speaker that is widely used in neural TTS studies, has a duration of nearly 24 hours. Such an amount, though generally not hard to obtain for relatively highly-resourced languages, would likely be problematic for under-resourced languages (URLs).

One solution to address this challenge for URLs is to use cross-lingual transfer learning. This involves pre-training the acoustic model in a different language (called the "source language") that has sufficient training data, before fine-tuning that acoustic model with the limited training data of the URL ("target language"). This helps with the mapping between the input (text or phoneme sequence) and the output (speech features) in the URL, owing to the underlying similarities (e.g., patterns in pronunciation, semantic structures) among the language pair (Tan et al., 2021).

Cross-lingual transfer learning, however, comes with its own challenges. Firstly, there is often a mismatch between the input embeddings of the source and target languages, due to differences in their sets of phonemes or orthographic characters. To overcome this, Chen et al. (2019) proposed a Phonetic Transformation Network, fitted with a preceding automatic speech recognition component, to automatically map input symbols across languages based on their sounds. More recently, Wells and Richmond (2021) experimented between using phonemes and phonological features as input and made use of linguistic expertise (in the source and target languages) to map the embeddings. Notwithstanding these valuable findings, there is yet to be a solution that: a) is simpler but still sufficiently effective, b) can be easily replicated for other languages, and c) does not require specific linguistic expertise in the languages involved. We posit that such qualities are greatly helpful in cross-lingual transfer learning for URLs.

Secondly, numerous previous studies have shown that, for the same target language, transfer learning from different source languages leads to different effects in output quality. This leads to another consideration: by what criterion should the source language be chosen? Traditionally, language family classification has been widely used, with the implication that languages in the same family have more similarities that help in trans-

fer learning (or more generally, in sharing knowledge in a multilingual setting). However, an extensive study by Gutkin and Sproat (2017) found no conclusive evidence for this. In addition, in a meta-analysis of studies involving multilingual and cross-lingual TTS for URLs, Do et al. (2021) also concluded that language family classification was not an effective criterion for selecting source languages.
Accordingly, we aim to make the following contributions in this study:

1) We experiment on using a set of universal phonological features as a guide to map phoneme embeddings across source and target languages. (2.1)

2) We investigate a new criterion for selecting source languages: a measure of cross-lingual phoneme distribution similarity, and compare it with the conventional language family criterion. (2.3)

2. Databases and Proposed Metric

2.1. Phonological Inventory Data

PHOIBLE (Moran and McCloy, 2019) is a database of phonological inventories of 2,186 distinct languages. PHOIBLE uses a fixed set of 37 phonological features to describe all the phonemes in its database and ensures that each phoneme, represented by a unique IPA symbol, has a distinct set of binary attributes from these features. In other words, each IPA symbol representing a phoneme has a unique set of 37 binary attributes (corresponding to the phonological features) associated with that phoneme's pronunciation. This facilitates our proposed method for cross-lingual phoneme mapping, which is described in more detail in 4.2.2.

2.2. Language Classification Data

For language family classification, Ethnologue (Eberhard et al., 2021) is likely the most comprehensive and commonly used reference. It has been used by, e.g., Tan et al. (2019) as the reference for language clustering in their multilingual experiments, and by Do et al. (2021) as a potential factor in the effectiveness of multilingual or cross-lingual TTS models. To enable comparisons, we also use Ethnologue in this study.

2.3. Angular Similarity of Phoneme Frequencies (ASPF)

Cosine similarity (S_C or $\cos(\theta)$) is traditionally used in the field of natural language processing (NLP) to measure similarities between text documents, e.g., by Huang et al. (2011). Recently, a study by Cer et al. (2018) stated that the angular distance (D_θ, calculated from $\cos(\theta)$) performed better. Motivated by this, we experimented with using angular similarity ($S_\theta := 1 - D_\theta$) between the vectors of phoneme frequencies of two languages to measure the similarity between their phoneme systems. For language A with phoneme set P_A, we defined a vector of phoneme frequencies PF_A containing frequencies of all phonemes in P_A, calculated from A's data set. To compare languages A and B, we calculated $\cos_\theta$ and then S_θ between PF_A and PF_B (with padding where necessary to avoid size mismatch):[1]

$$S_C(PF_A, PF_B) := \cos_\theta = \frac{PF_A \cdot PF_B}{\|PF_A\| \|PF_B\|}$$

$$S_\theta := 1 - \frac{2 \cdot \arccos(\cos_\theta)}{\pi}$$

Hereafter we use the name Angular Similarity of Phoneme Frequencies (ASPF) for these S_θ values, which represent the degrees of similarities between the phoneme systems of the two languages from which they are calculated ($0 \leq ASPF \leq 1$).

3. Data Sets and Preparation

3.1. Target Language Data Set

3.1.1. Frisian

Frisian ("Frysk") is the local language of the province of Friesland ("Fryslân"), which is located in the north of the Netherlands. The language has roughly 350,000 native speakers (Gorter, 2003), and has been recognized as the second official language of the Netherlands since 2013. Frisian is formally referred to as West Frisian (to distinguish from North Frisian and East Frisian), but in this study we simply call it Frisian.

3.1.2. Frisian Data Set

Although there are Frisian audio corpora, they were designed for other purposes than TTS. The FAME project (Yilmaz et al., 2016) corpus was designed to study code-switching and the Boarnsterhim Corpus (Sloos et al., 2018) was part of a longitudinal study. As such, they are not ideal for TTS research. Therefore, we created a small single-speaker corpus by using recordings and corresponding texts from a Frisian audiobook. We split the recordings by silence periods and also trimmed the preceding and trailing silences. Following LJSpeech, we further split long excerpts (while still respecting clause boundaries) so that the longest duration was 10 seconds. The corresponding texts had their sentences tokenized, abbreviations and numbers checked and expanded, and were thoroughly inspected to ensure good correspondence between text-audio pairs. From this corpus, we used 30 minutes of recordings (316 utterances) for this study and show their duration histogram in Figure 1.

3.2. Source Language Data Sets

CSS10 (Park and Mulc, 2019) is a publicly available single-speaker data set of 10 languages, consisting of short audio clips cut from audiobooks in the LibriVox project[2]. We chose it for this study since its wide range of languages enables the testing of the language family

[1] This is the formula for when the vectors do not contain negative values, which matches our case.

[2] `https://librivox.org`

factor, and its audio format and structure are similar to what we had for Frisian. From its 10 languages, considering a balance between language family variation and available audio duration, we chose to experiment with the following languages (in alphabetical order): Dutch, Finnish, French, Japanese, and Spanish.

We manually inspected these languages' subsets by listening to the audio files, skimming the paired texts, and remedying (or removing) the mismatches. The most common discrepancies included numbers that were not spelled out in the texts, book and chapter names that were read but not included in the texts, and differences in the audio/text splitting boundaries. To conform to the Frisian data set, we also excluded utterances longer than 10 seconds. Ultimately, each target language had approximately 9 hours of total duration, with similar duration distributions. Figure 1 shows the duration histogram of the Spanish data set as an example.

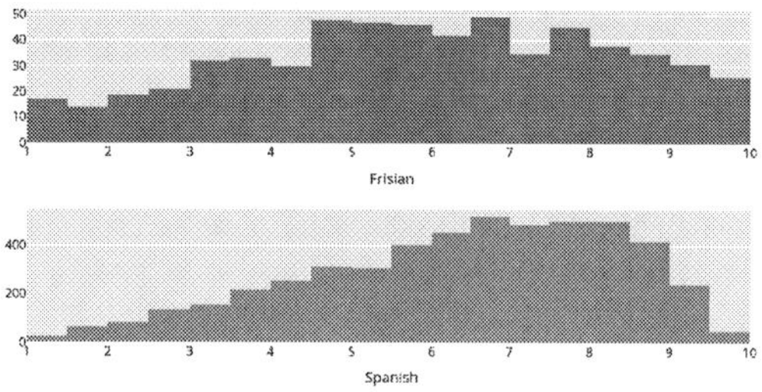

Figure 1: Duration (s) histograms of data sets

3.3. Data Sets Phonemization

We converted all data sets in this study using lexicons (pronunciation dictionaries). The Carnegie Mellon University Pronouncing Dictionary (CMU, 2014) (CMUdict) is a public domain dictionary for American English that is widely used in TTS research. We followed its conventions for phoneme annotations, with the following exceptions: a) we used IPA symbols from the PHOIBLE database instead of the modified ARPABET system in CMUdict, and b) we only included primary stress marks (i.e., secondary stress was treated as unstressed). The latter was in order to accommodate all the source languages involved, since not all of them can be said to have secondary stresses.

We used PHOIBLE to define the phoneme sets of all the languages. For languages that have more than one listed phoneme inventories (i.e., from several "doculects"), we used a union set from all of these, and then removed all the phonemes that were not used (i.e., not present) in the corresponding lexicon.

Frisian: We used the lexicon included as part of the FAME project, modifying it slightly to match the annotation method described above and supplementing it with the corresponding stress information provided by the Fryske Akademy.

Dutch: We used the e-Lex lexicon from the Instituut voor de Nederlandse Taal (INT, 2014), which uses phoneme representations from the Corpus Gesproken Nederlands (CGN) (Oostdijk, 2000) and was thus converted into IPA symbols following its manual. e-Lex includes stress information, and the majority of the entries are already manually checked by the authors.

All the other source languages used lexicons from the *ipa-dict* project (Doherty, 2019), which already uses IPA symbols and thus no conversion was needed.

Finnish: The lexicon readily contains stress information, so we only needed to exclude the secondary stresses.

French: As French does not have lexical stress, the lexicon does not contain stress information. Therefore, we determined the stressed phonemes using the rules from Kelton et al. (2019)[3], with the phrase boundaries predicted from punctuation marks and/or short breaks in the audio. We acknowledge that this is a rudimentary and oversimplifying approach, e.g., compared to that in de Dominicis et al. (2000). Nevertheless, we posited that this would suffice for the current study's purposes.

Japanese: One major challenge was that Japanese texts contain many homographs, which complicates the selection of the right pronunciation from the lexicon. CSS10 dealt with this by including *romaji* annotations (romanized transcriptions) that were post-edited by a native speaker. Although these still contain occasional mistakes, we used them as reference to determine the stressed phonemes. It should be noted that Japanese is not a stress-oriented language (de Dominicis et al., 2000) and instead has pitch (high-low) patterns. However, for the purposes in this study, we treated the vowels in high-pitched morae as stressed. Specifically, we used MeCab (Kudo, 2006) to parse the Japanese orthographic texts, compared them with CSS10's *romaji* annotations for the homographs, and obtained the stress information from a dictionary by javdejong (2022).

Spanish: The lexicon already contains stress marks for accented words. For the others, we followed the guide by Collins (2022) to determine the stress position.

For out-of-vocabulary (OOV) words in all languages, we used OpenNMT (Klein et al., 2017) to train a grapheme-to-phoneme (G2P) model for each language to predict the pronunciations and, to the extent possible, manually inspected and corrected the obvious errors.

4. Training and Evaluation

4.1. Source Language Pre-Training

We chose the FastSpeech 2 architecture (Ren et al., 2020), implemented by Chien et al. (2021) for the acoustic model. Pitch and energy prediction was done at the phoneme-level, following the authors' recommendation. For the vocoder, we used the universal generator of HiFi-GAN V1 (Kong et al., 2020) for all

[3]Available at https://www.laits.utexas.edu/fi/html/pho/03.html

source and target language models without fine-tuning, since the duration of the data sets (especially Frisian) was not sufficient for effective fine-tuning.
We trained a separate acoustic model for each source language. As done in the original FastSpeech 2 paper, we used the Montreal Forced Aligner (McAuliffe et al., 2017) to obtain phoneme-level alignments between the annotations and the audio recordings. We then trained each acoustic model for 100K parameter updates, with a batch size of 16 and the Adam optimizer (Kingma and Ba, 2017) with $\beta_1 = 0.9$, $\beta_2 = 0.98$, and $\epsilon = 10^{-9}$. To make sure they were trained successfully, for each model, we synthesized the corresponding set of 20 test sentences used in the CSS10 paper (Park and Mulc, 2019). The results had subjectively good quality and can be found online[4].

4.2. Target Language Fine-Tuning

To verify this study's proposed approach to phoneme mapping, we tested two scenarios for each source language: without and with phoneme mapping. We call the corresponding models *separate* and *mapped*, respectively, and describe them below.

4.2.1. Without Phoneme Mapping (*separate*)

In this scenario, we directly fine-tuned the source language model (described in 4.1) on the 30-minute Frisian data set. In other words, for the phonemes that are present in Frisian but not in the source language, the model would have their parameters initialized from scratch and "learn" from the Frisian data.

4.2.2. Phoneme Mapping (*mapped*)

In this scenario, for each phoneme not present in the source language, instead of initializing from scratch, we mapped it to the model parameters of its closest phoneme, which was predicted with a simple rule. The rule is expected to be universal (i.e., independent of the language pairs) and is as follows: for each target language phoneme that needed mapping, we looked for source language phoneme candidates with the most similar sets of PHOIBLE phonological features (represented as a vector of length 37). In case of ties, we compared the cosine similarities (2.3) of the phoneme distributions in the immediately preceding and succeeding positions of the phoneme in question, i.e., the candidate with the most similar adjacent phoneme distributions would be selected. For certain diphthongs and long vowels, no single target phoneme could be found. In that case, the source phonemes were decomposed into unitary vowels, which were subsequently mapped as if they were individual phonemes. All the resulting mapping decisions are reported in Appendix 8.

4.2.3. Model Fine-Tuning

Following the above descriptions, each of the 5 source languages had two separate fine-tuning scenarios: *separate* and *mapped*, both starting from the same pre-trained model. This resulted in a total of 10 fine-tuned models. Each model was trained on the 30-minute Frisian data set for another 100K parameter updates with a batch size of 4 (to better accommodate the small data size), with the other hyperparameters unchanged.

4.3. Evaluation

4.3.1. Test Sentences

We selected a total of 20 unseen test sentences, divided into 5 small sets of 4 sentences each, so that each set: a) contains all phonemes (regardless of frequency) from the Frisian data set[5], b) has a set-wide phoneme distribution as close as possible to that of the Frisian data set, and c) has an average duration of 5 seconds.

4.3.2. Listening Experiment

We used PsyToolkit (Stoet, 2010; Stoet, 2017) for an online listening experiment to obtain subjective evaluation, following the MUSHRA framework (Series, 2014). Each participant was randomly assigned a set of 4 sentences, each with a reference audio sample resynthesized from that sentence's ground-truth mel-spectrogram. The participant was then asked to listen to 10 synthesized samples (from the 10 models described in 4.2.3), together with a hidden resynthesized anchor, before being asked to rate each sample on its naturalness and pronunciation accuracy on a 0-100 scale. We collected answers from 50 participants that fully completed their panels, but had to exclude participants with lower self-rated Frisian proficiency. In the end, we used answers from 46 participants for data analysis ($n = 2024$). The audio samples are available online[4].

5. Results and Discussion

5.1. Phoneme Mapping

The MUSHRA scores are reported in Figure 2. To verify the effect of phoneme mapping, we conducted paired Wilcoxon tests between the scores of the models with and without phoneme mapping (*map* and *sep*). Table 1 reports the effects of phoneme mapping (differences in median scores between *map* and *sep*) and the p-values of the corresponding paired Wilcoxon tests, with statistically significant effects in bold.
Despite significantly increasing both naturalness and pronunciation accuracy ratings in the Dutch and Finnish models, phoneme mapping only increased accuracy ratings in the French model, and did not have a significant effect in the Spanish and Japanese models. To investigate this in more detail, we used a linear mixed effect model (Bates et al., 2014), with mapping as the fixed effect, and participants and sentences as random effects (to account for the by-participant and by-sentence variation). For both naturalness and pronunciation accuracy, phoneme mapping did affect the

[4] https://phat-do.github.io/sigul22

[5] This is usually not enforced by other studies, but we believe this would test the phoneme mapping more effectively, despite likely affecting the models' subjective evaluation negatively.

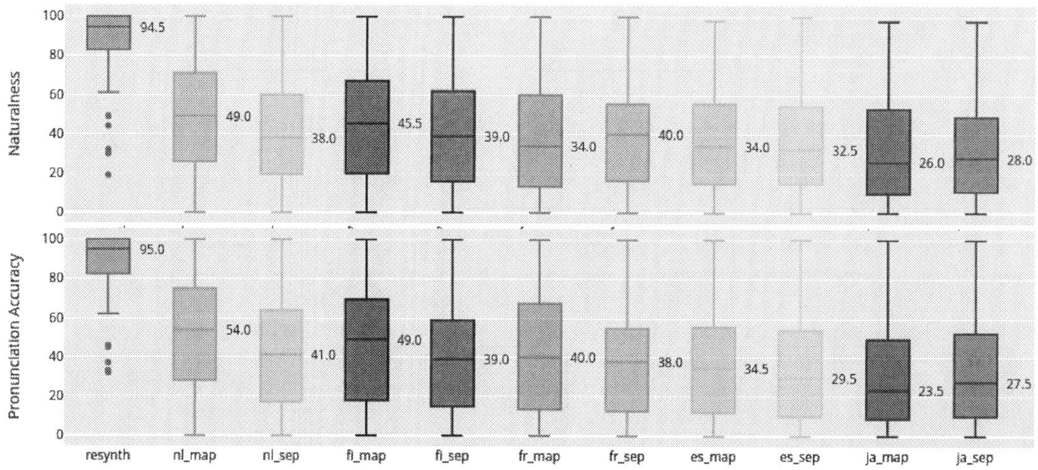

Figure 2: MUSHRA scores in Naturalness and Pronunciation Accuracy (central bars: median scores)

Source language	Naturalness ($M_{map} - M_{sep}$)	Accuracy ($M_{map} - M_{sep}$)
nl (Dutch)	**11 (*p* <.001)**	**13 (*p* <.001)**
fi (Finnish)	**6.5 (*p* = .003)**	**10 (p <.001)**
fr (French)	-6 (*p* = .82)	**2 (*p* = .02)**
es (Spanish)	1.5 (*p* = .17)	5 (*p* = .21)
ja (Japanese)	-2 (*p* = .56)	-4 (*p* = .11)

Table 1: Effect of phoneme mapping

MUSHRA score ($p = .004$ and $p < .001$, respectively), increasing it by 2.42 ($\pm$ 0.85) and 3.79 ($\pm$ 0.88), respectively. This means phoneme mapping did have an overall positive effect, but this effect also depended on the source language. This observation further motivated the analysis in the next stage.

5.2. Source Language Selection Criterion

5.2.1. Language Family

Acknowledging the complexity of measuring in detail the concept of language family distance, similar to Tan et al. (2019), we counted only the first level in the phylogenetic language classification tree (following the terms in Gutkin and Sproat (2017)). Accordingly, Frisian, Dutch, French, and Spanish were considered to be in the same language family (Indo-European), while Finnish (Uralic) and Japanese (Japonic) were not.

5.2.2. ASPF

Following 2.3, we calculated two versions of ASPF: a data set-level ASPF that compares two languages' whole data sets, and a sentence-level ASPF that involves the frequencies of only the phonemes present in each sentence. We posited that the latter was more accurate as a variable, and it also helped alleviate the issue of modeling a continuous variable with very few observed values, as the data set-level ASPF had only 5 values. It was still useful, however, in reaching a recommendation for source language selection criterion.

5.2.3. Results

Linear mixed effect models were used to test the effects of language family and sentence-level ASPF. When tested as the only fixed effect, they both had statistically significant effects on the MUSHRA score. However, since they are collinear by nature (languages in the same family are likely to have similar phoneme characteristics), we wanted to find the true effect that could explain the variation. Therefore, we used likelihood tests between these models and another model with both of them as fixed effects. This showed that language family indeed did not have a significant effect on either naturalness ($p = .56$) or accuracy ($p = .50$), while sentence-level ASPF significantly affected both ($p < .001$), increasing them by 2.93 ($\pm$ 0.36) and 3.66 ($\pm$ 0.37), respectively, for every increase of 10 percentage point in ASPF.

Sentence-level ASPF, however, is not very useful for generalization to other scenarios with other languages. Thus, we also tested for the correlation between data set-level ASPF (reported in Table 2) and the median MUSHRA scores, using the "Spearman" method. This showed that they were significantly correlated, with a coefficient of 1 and $p = .01$, confirming the usefulness of using data set-level ASPF as a criterion for choosing source languages (the higher, the better).

Source language	nl	fi	fr	es	ja
ASPF	0.73	0.47	0.38	0.35	0.33

Table 2: Data set-level ASPF (compared to Frisian)

6. Conclusion

We propose a novel approach for phoneme mapping in cross-lingual transfer learning, using phonological features of the PHOIBLE database and a language-independent mapping rule. We experimented with Dutch, Finnish, French, Japanese, and Spanish as source languages and Frisian as the target language. Listening scores showed that our approach improved both naturalness and pronunciation accuracy compared to without mapping. This effect also depended on the source language, motivating the investigation into a criterion to select source languages.

We then tested the idea of using Angular Similarity of Phoneme Frequencies (ASPF) as a criterion for selecting source languages, and proved through our experiment that it was more effective than the traditional criterion of language family classification.

Future research is intended to expand into experimenting in the setting of a directly multilingual model, with a wider range of languages, and in the scenario of having no available lexicons for the target language.

7. Acknowledgements

We thank the Center for Information Technology of the University of Groningen for their support and for providing access to the Peregrine high performance computing cluster. We are thankful for the permission to use, for research purposes, the original recordings by Geartsje de Vries of books written by Kookos Tiemersma and published by the publisher Audiofrysk. We would also like to thank the Fryske Akademy (Leeuwarden, the Netherlands) for their support with the Frisian lexicon and the dissemination of the listening experiment.

8. Bibliographical References

Bates, D., Mächler, M., Bolker, B., and Walker, S. (2014). Fitting linear mixed-effects models using lme4. *arXiv preprint arXiv:1406.5823*.

Cer, D., Yang, Y., Kong, S.-y., Hua, N., Limtiaco, N., John, R. S., Constant, N., Guajardo-Cespedes, M., Yuan, S., Tar, C., Sung, Y.-H., Strope, B., and Kurzweil, R. (2018). Universal Sentence Encoder.

Chen, Y.-J., Tu, T., chieh Yeh, C., and Lee, H.-Y. (2019). End-to-End Text-to-Speech for Low-Resource Languages by Cross-Lingual Transfer Learning. In *Proc. Interspeech 2019*, pages 2075–2079.

Chien, C.-M., Lin, J.-H., Huang, C.-y., Hsu, P.-c., and Lee, H.-y. (2021). Investigating on incorporating pretrained and learnable speaker representations for multi-speaker multi-style text-to-speech. In *ICASSP 2021-2021 IEEE International Conference on Acoustics, Speech and Signal Processing (ICASSP)*, pages 8588–8592. IEEE.

CMU. (2014). cmusphinx/cmudict.

Collins. (2022). Which syllable to stress | Learning Spanish Grammar | Collins Education.

de Dominicis, A., Hirst, D., and Cristo, A. D. (2000). Intonation Systems: A Survey of Twenty Languages. *Language*, 76(2):460.

Do, P., Coler, M., Dijkstra, J., and Klabbers, E. (2021). A Systematic Review and Analysis of Multilingual Data Strategies in Text-to-Speech for Low-Resource Languages. In *Proc. Interspeech 2021*, pages 16–20.

Doherty, L. (2019). ipa-dict - Monolingual wordlists with pronunciation information in IPA.

Eberhard, D. M., Simons, G. F., and Fennig, C. D. (2021). *Ethnologue: Languages of the World. Twenty-fourth edition.* SIL International.

Gorter, D. (2003). Nederlands en Fries op gespannen voet. *Waar gaat het Nederlands naar toe*.

Gutkin, A. and Sproat, R. (2017). Areal and Phylogenetic Features for Multilingual Speech Synthesis. In *Proc. Interspeech 2017*, pages 2078–2082.

Huang, C.-H., Yin, J., and Hou, F. (2011). A text similarity measurement combining word semantic information with tf-idf method. *Jisuanji Xuebao (Chinese Journal of Computers)*, 34(5):856–864.

INT. (2014). e-Lex.

Ito, K. and Johnson, L. (2017). The lj speech dataset. `https://keithito.com/LJ-Speech-Dataset/`.

javdejong. (2022). javdejong/nhk-pronunciation.

Kelton, K., Guilloteau, N., and Blyth, C. (2019). *Français interactif.* Lulu. com.

Kingma, D. P. and Ba, J. (2017). Adam: A Method for Stochastic Optimization. *arXiv:1412.6980 [cs]*.

Klein, G., Kim, Y., Deng, Y., Senellart, J., and Rush, A. (2017). OpenNMT: Open-source toolkit for neural machine translation. In *Proceedings of ACL 2017, System Demonstrations*, pages 67–72, Vancouver, Canada, July. Association for Computational Linguistics.

Kong, J., Kim, J., and Bae, J. (2020). HiFi-GAN: Generative Adversarial Networks for Efficient and High Fidelity Speech Synthesis. *arXiv:2010.05646 [cs, eess]*.

Kudo, T. (2006). MeCab: Yet Another Part-of-Speech and Morphological Analyzer.

McAuliffe, M., Socolof, M., Mihuc, S., Wagner, M., and Sonderegger, M. (2017). Montreal Forced Aligner: Trainable Text-Speech Alignment Using Kaldi. In *Proc. Interspeech 2017*, pages 498–502.

Steven Moran et al., editors. (2019). *PHOIBLE 2.0*. Max Planck Institute for the Science of Human History, Jena.

Oostdijk, N. (2000). Het corpus gesproken nederlands.

Park, K. and Mulc, T. (2019). CSS10: A Collection of Single Speaker Speech Datasets for 10 Languages. In *Proc. Interspeech 2019*, pages 1566–1570.

Ren, Y., Hu, C., Tan, X., Qin, T., Zhao, S., Zhao, Z., and Liu, T.-Y. (2020). Fastspeech 2: Fast and high-quality end-to-end text to speech. *arXiv preprint arXiv:2006.04558*.

Series, B. (2014). Method for the subjective assessment of intermediate quality level of audio systems. *International Telecommunication Union Radiocommunication Assembly*.

Sloos, M., Drenth, E., and Heeringa, W. (2018). The Boarnsterhim Corpus: A Bilingual Frisian-Dutch Panel and Trend Study. In *Proceedings of the Eleventh International Conference on Language Resources and Evaluation (LREC 2018)*.

Stoet, G. (2010). PsyToolkit: A software package for programming psychological experiments using Linux. *Behavior Research Methods*, 42(4):1096–1104.

Stoet, G. (2017). PsyToolkit: A Novel Web-Based Method for Running Online Questionnaires and Reaction-Time Experiments. *Teaching of Psychology*, 44(1):24–31.

Tan, X., Chen, J., He, D., Xia, Y., Qin, T., and Liu, T.-Y. (2019). Multilingual Neural Machine Translation with Language Clustering. *arXiv:1908.09324 [cs]*. arXiv: 1908.09324.

Tan, X., Qin, T., Soong, F., and Liu, T.-Y. (2021). A Survey on Neural Speech Synthesis. *arXiv:2106.15561 [cs, eess]*.

Wells, D. and Richmond, K. (2021). Cross-lingual Transfer of Phonological Features for Low-resource Speech Synthesis. In *11th ISCA Speech Synthesis Workshop (SSW 11)*, pages 160–165. ISCA.

Yilmaz, E., Andringa, M., Kingma, S., Dijkstra, J., Kuip, F., Velde, H., Kampstra, F., Algra, J., Heuvel, H., and van Leeuwen, D. A. (2016). A longitudinal bilingual Frisian-Dutch radio broadcast database designed for code-switching research.

Appendix

Table 3 reports all the mappings resulted from the rule in 4.2.2, with vowels at the top and consonants at the bottom. Frisian phonemes are on the left column (*fy*). An empty cell means no mapping was needed, and a cell with two vowels mean they were converted from either a long vowel or a diphthong.

fy	nl	fi	fr	es	ja
a		ɑ			
aː	ɑː	ɑː	a a	a a	
ai	aɪ	ɑ i	a i		a i
eː			e e	e e	
ə		e		e	e
ɛ		e		e	e
ɛː	eː	eː	ɛ ɛ	e e	eː
ɛi	ɛ i	ɛ i	ɛ i	ei	e i
i					
iː	eː		i i	i i	
iə	i ə	i e	i ə	i e	i e
ɪ		i		i	i
ɪə	ɪ ə	i e	ɪ ə	i e	i e
o	ɔ				
ø				o	o
oː			o o	o o	
øː	yː		ø ø	o o	o o
œ	ʏ	ø		o	o
oə	ɔ ə	o e	o ə	o e	o e
ou	ɔ u	o u	o u	o u	o o
ɔ		o		o	o
ɔː		oː	ɔ ɔ	o o	oː
ɔu	ʌu	o u	ɔ u	o u	o o
u					o
uː	oː		u u	u u	oː
uə	u ə	u e	uə	u e	o e
ui	u i	u i	u i	oi	o i
y				u	o
yː			y y	u u	o o
yə	y ə	y e	y ə	u e	o e
b					
d					
f					ɸ
g					
h			f	f	
j					
k					
l					ɾ
m					
n					
ɲ		ŋ			ç
ŋ					ɴ
p					
r			l		ɾ
s					
t					
v				β	
x					k
z					

Table 3: Phoneme mapping results

Proceedings of SIGUL2022 @LREC2022, pages 23–32
Marseille, 24-25 June 2022

ReadAlong Studio: Practical Zero-Shot Text-Speech Alignment for Indigenous Language Audiobooks

Patrick Littell[1], Eric Joanis[1], Aidan Pine[1], Marc Tessier[1],
David Huggins-Daines[2], Delasie Torkornoo[3]
[1] National Research Council Canada
1200 Montreal Road, Ottawa, ON K1A 0R6
{Patrick.Littell, Eric.Joanis, Aidan.Pine, Marc.Tessier}@nrc-cnrc.gc.ca

[2] dhdaines@gmail.com

[3] Carleton University
1125 Colonel By Dr, Ottawa, ON K1S 5B6
delasie.torkornoo@carleton.ca

Abstract

While the alignment of audio recordings and text (often termed "forced alignment") is sometimes treated as a solved problem, in practice the process of adapting an alignment system to a new, under-resourced language comes with significant challenges, requiring experience and expertise that many outside of the speech community lack. This puts otherwise "solvable" problems, like the alignment of Indigenous language audiobooks, out of reach for many real-world Indigenous language organizations. In this paper, we describe ReadAlong Studio, a suite of tools for creating and visualizing aligned audiobooks, including educational features like time-aligned highlighting, playing single words in isolation, and variable-speed playback. It is intended to be accessible to creators without an extensive background in speech or NLP, by automating or making optional many of the specialist steps in an alignment pipeline. It is well documented at a beginner-technologist level, has already been adapted to 30 languages, and can work out-of-the-box on many more languages without adaptation.

Keywords: forced alignment, text-speech alignment, Indigenous languages

1. Introduction

Despite recent advances in speech and natural language processing, many practical technologies remain out of reach for languages with few digitized resources, such as the vast majority of the roughly seventy Indigenous languages spoken in Canada (Littell et al., 2018).

Text-speech alignment, the alignment of timestamps in a speech recording with sentences, words, or subword elements in its transcription (Robert-Ribes and Mukhtar, 1997; Moreno et al., 1998; Schiel, 1999; Yuan and Liberman, 2008; Gorman et al., 2011; McAuliffe et al., 2017), is a potential exception to this; such systems can be bootstrapped with little-to-no pre-existing data required. For example, a typical cross-linguistic alignment workflow in the Festival family of speech tools (Black et al., 1998) is to transliterate the input document into another language's phoneme inventory (often English), and then use an off-the-shelf aligner for that language to align the transliterated document to the recording. This allows the approximate alignment of documents in a new language, even without any pre-existing training data in that language.

However, in practice, non-specialists often have trouble adapting forced-alignment workflows to new languages and speech varieties (MacKenzie and Turton, 2020). Even accomplishing the zero-data workflow described above typically requires: having access to (and installation permissions on) a UNIX workstation, understanding Unicode and handling potentially noisy user-generated inputs, coping with out-of-vocabulary tokens and code mixing, mapping phonetic near-neighbours between languages, knowing speech-specific protocols like ARPABET, setting reasonable values for beam search, etc. While these may seem minor individually, there are many potential snags to navigate, and together these skills add up to a relatively rare expertise. So while the *data* requirements of alignment are potentially quite low, the corresponding bar for *expertise* is still set rather high.

The *ReadAlongs* collaboration seeks to lower this bar to entry, so that more organizations can adapt text-speech alignment technology to their languages. ReadAlong Studio[1] is a suite of software tools for UNIX, MacOS, and Windows that automates or makes optional some specialist steps that stymie non-expert users. To give just one example here, the system uses `PanPhon` (Mortensen et al., 2016) to automate cross-linguistic approximate phone matching that, otherwise, would have required specialist intervention.

Some technological background is still recommended

[1]`https://github.com/ReadAlongs/Studio`

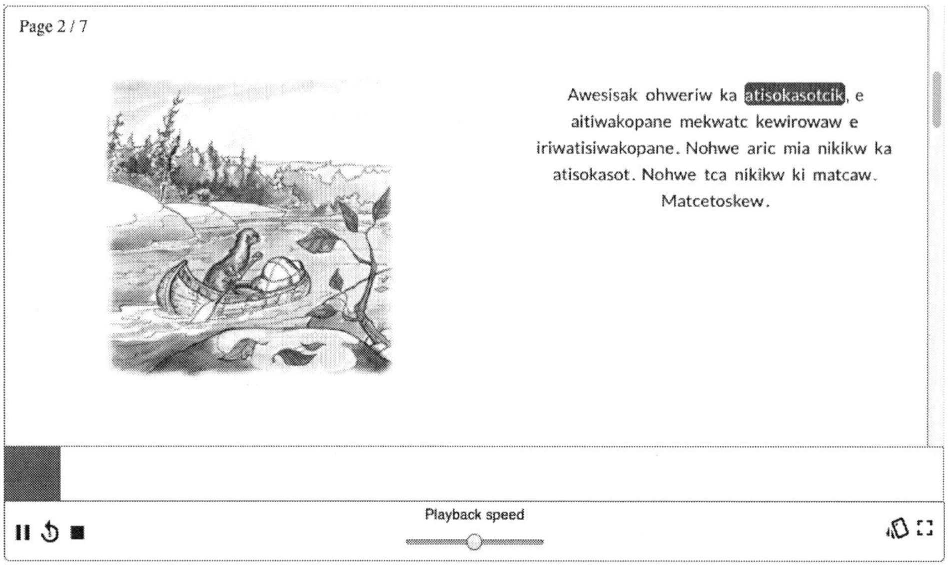

Figure 1: A screenshot of a web component ReadAlong published for Atikamekw. Other ReadAlongs published for Atikamekw can be found at `https://atikamekw.atlas-ling.ca/lecture-audio/`. Highlighting guides the reader to the word currently being spoken in the recording, and the reader can play single words by clicking on them.

(complete, fluent use of the tools requires some familiarity with the command line and XML), but a speech/NLP background is not.

It should be emphasized that this system, and this paper, do not present a novel *model* of forced alignment (we use a lightweight, off-the-shelf English acoustic model); we do not feel that inadequate modeling is where the main barrier lies. Rather, our approach is about automating aspects of the larger *workflow*, and this larger approach could mix and match with other approaches to the modeling problem proper.

1.1. Motivation

The world's languages have vastly different amounts of digitized resources available. Among Indigenous languages spoken in Canada, for example, there are a few "medium-resourced" languages like Inuktitut, one of the official languages of the Nunavut territory, with a 1.3 million-line parallel corpus with English (Joanis et al., 2020). However, many have very limited digital resources: word lists of a few thousand words, a few hours of transcribed recordings, etc.

In light of these constraints, Littell et al. (2018) surveyed different language technologies in terms of the feasibility of developing and deploying them for *any* Indigenous languages spoken in Canada. Among these technologies, text-speech alignment stood out as a low-hanging fruit, since it can feasibly be done with no training data in the target language.

Meanwhile, the ability to align text and audio dovetailed with a real educational need. Many Indigenous language organizations (schools, publishers, etc.) already have books and other literacy materials that have been recorded by fluent speakers: often, as a printed book with an accompanying CD. However, we have heard from teachers and librarians that modern students are not necessarily using them: what kid uses a CD player these days?

Teachers need these resources to be converted into online content, which requires some level of time alignment to coordinate the different sections of the text and audio. This can be (and usually is) done manually at the page, paragraph, or sentence level, but alignment to a finer granularity can provide richer added value, like word-level highlighting and the ability to play single words by clicking them (Figure 1), or syllable-level highlighting for a sing-along karaoke video (Figure 2).

Figure 2: A screenshot of a bouncing-ball sing-along video in Kitigan Zibi Anishinàbemowin, made with ReadAlong Studio by aligning syllables rather than words.

In particular, we were inspired by online read-along/sing-along activities for East Cree[2] (Luchian and Junker, 2004). However, fine-grained manual alignment of text is very time-consuming, and requires a skilled annotator. Realizing that this process could be automated was the genesis of the ReadAlongs collaboration.

Upon seeing initial prototypes, the response from Indigenous language teachers and organizations has been highly enthusiastic. Teachers have mentioned to us on several occasions that their languages are traditionally oral, and that they are trying to train *speakers* and not just readers/writers, so they are always looking for ways to incorporate real speech into the curriculum. Another teacher noted that many language technologies are geared more towards advanced learners in a university-like setting, as opposed to younger students; read-along/sing-along activities are a rare language technology that even toddlers can use.

1.2. Special Considerations

Most speech/NLP libraries assume workflows where the input is being extracted and transformed, and only the transformed representations are of interest. Existing forced alignment libraries are typically conceptualized as a step in this kind of workflow, especially for the preparation of training data for speech processing or synthesis systems, or the isolation of speech segments for phonetic analysis.

It is worth highlighting some of the unspoken assumptions inherent in conventional speech pipelines:

- Documents are plain text to begin with, or structured documents have had the relevant textual material extracted.
- Formatting, capitalization, and non-phonetic material like punctuation can often be discarded as irrelevant to the downstream task.
- If a document fails to align, we can ignore it, discard the results, and move on to the next document: we do not, after all, want to train our systems or make measurements using text/audio pairs where the contents might not actually correspond.

On the other hand, for a read-along audiobook or other digital publishing product, the document in question is generally the whole point, and must be fully preserved:

- Documents have structure (pages or chapters, paragraphs, sometimes lines), formatting, capitalization, and punctuation that must be retained in the end product.
- A document that fails to align cannot be ignored or discarded; whatever is wrong with it has to be detected and fixed, whether by human or automated means.

There are also special considerations that arise due to the specific nature of our users' documents:

- English or French words (loanwords, personal and place names, etc.) occur fairly frequently. We cannot assume the document is monolingual; the software should be able to respect language annotations at any structural level (document, sentence, word), and have reasonable fallback behaviors when language tags are not used.
- Many documents for second-language learners are bilingual (e.g., where each line is accompanied by a translation), but with one of the languages not spoken in the recording.
- Conversely, the recording often has intro/outro speech that is untranscribed. In both this and the previous case, there must be some "do not align" annotation that the aligner respects, while still retaining the content in the final document.

This is not to say that existing libraries cannot be used in this context; our early versions used the Montreal Forced Aligner (McAuliffe et al., 2017) internally, although we later happened to swap it out for a more lightweight acoustic library (detailed in §2.4.6) for speed of alignment and ease of installation. However, these libraries cannot easily be used *alone* for this task, since their plain-text focus means that the original document must somehow be re-associated with the outputs or re-constructed.

Not all considerations related to the target languages introduce *greater* challenge. Most Indigenous languages, having had a shorter tradition of writing, have orthographies that are relatively transparent and organized on a phonemic basis. Grapheme-to-phoneme (G2P) transduction in these languages is often straightforward, and even rough ad-hoc G2P can suffice for many languages.

2. ReadAlong Studio

2.1. Internal Formats

In light of the above considerations, ReadAlong Studio (RAS) takes a philosophy of "non-destructive NLP": only *adding* information to a document, never transforming the document in a way where information is lost or the transformation cannot be undone.

To achieve this, RAS assumes XML-structured text internally; each step proceeds by adding elements or attributes, but leaves the text and previously-added information alone. If a more technically-advanced user has already added (say) tokenization or G2P, the system will respect it rather than overwriting it. The pipeline can be stopped at any step for advanced users to add markup by hand or by script, and restarted taking into account this markup.

RAS is usually intended for use with the ReadAlong Web Component display interface, which has a particular XML format it expects, but the aligner itself does not require this format; it could be used with a variety of XML document formats.

[2] `https://eastcree.org`

2.2. Text Standards: TEI

The intermediate XML formats, as well as the final output intended for visualization by the ReadAlong Web Component (§3.1), conform to the TEI P5 conventions for the digital humanities (TEI Consortium, 2021).

However, while the aligner should at least be able to align most TEI documents, the TEI standard is not so much a format as a collection of practices for defining a new format, specific to the sort of document one is dealing with. (That is, it is intended to allow a certain amount of interoperability and predictability whether one is working on Shakespeare folios or children's books, without requiring the scholar to coerce one sort of document into a format intended for the other.) It is *not* the case that an arbitrary TEI document will be able to be viewed in ReadAlong Web Component. We use a subset of the TEI conventions appropriate for the kinds of books our collaborators have needed to align: often children's books, but sometimes longer-form narratives for adults as well.

2.3. Alignment Standards: EPUB3/SMIL

For alignment outputs, we follow the EPUB3 e-book accessibility guidelines (Garrish et al., 2022), formerly part of the DAISY Consortium guidelines for audiobooks for the visually impaired. Rather than maintaining separate standards for plain-text books and audio-aligned accessible books, the EPUB3 standards keep the text document intact and treat aligned audio as a "media overlay" that publishers, manufacturers, and software developers can choose to support.

In the EPUB3 media overlay standards, a SMIL file (Bulterman et al., 2008) is used to express time-aligned parallelism between document elements in different kinds of media. In this case, it associates IDs within an XML document with start and end timestamps in one or more audio files. This association allows visualization software to (in one direction) drive the highlighting of text in time with accompanying media or (in the other) play snippets of media in response to the reader clicking/tapping text elements.

While the RAS library does not currently automate the creation of EPUB e-books with accessibility overlays, our compatibility with this standard means that it is fairly straightforward to convert/compile our outputs into an accessible EPUB and view it in software that supports them (e.g. Apple iBooks).

2.4. The Alignment Pipeline

2.4.1. Initial Document Generation

Although RAS uses TEI XML internally, it does not require the user to input the document in this format, and most users do not. The user can simply provide a plain-text document, and a minimal TEI document will be created from it with an appropriate structure for further processing. Additional metadata can be provided to, for example, associate images with particular pages in a picture book or mark some audio span as "do-not-align" to exclude it from the alignment process.

An advanced user can skip this step and write the XML by hand, or output it from another program, but most users let the system generate the initial XML, and (if they need more advanced features like word-level language tags or custom tokenization) modify the generated document before proceeding to subsequent steps.

2.4.2. Tokenization

If the input is not already tokenized, the system will attempt to tokenize the document at the word level.

For the purposes of RAS, "word" refers to the unit that the user wishes to align: the unit that will be highlighted in the ReadAlong Web Component, that readers can click on to hear in isolation, etc. If users have special needs with respect to this unit, they can provide these units themselves; RAS considers any material between `<w>` tags to be "words". For example, the sing-along karaoke video in Figure 2 was made by wrapping `<w>` tags around syllables rather than words.

In the absence of these tags in the input, RAS will assume that word-level alignment is desired and attempt to find these units. This can be difficult given that some languages use punctuation characters phonetically (e.g., comma represents a glottal stop in SENĆOŦEN, and colon represents vowel length in Kanyen'kéha). When the character inventory of the language is known by virtue of being included in our G_i2P_i library (Pine et al., 2022), this will be taken into account, and words will not be split when the punctuation inside them can be parsed as a part of a known character.

This step will also ignore any elements tagged with an XML attribute `do-not-align`, and any elements under that element. As mentioned in §1.2, books for second-language learners often have line-by-line translations, but these are rarely spoken in the audio version; `do-not-align` attributes allow their presence in the text without the system attempting to align them.

2.4.3. ID Assignment

RAS then adds a unique XML ID attribute to each word unit. IDs are necessary because, when the document has finally been aligned, the visualizer does not just need to know that the word "the" was spoken between timestamps 32.41s and 32.65s; it needs to know *which* instance of "the" was said at that time, so it can highlight the appropriate one. In further steps (like constructing the pronunciation dictionary and finite state grammar in §2.4.6), the "words" will actually be these IDs rather than their orthographic forms.

2.4.4. Cross-Linguistic G2P

The system then performs a cross-linguistic G2P step between the target language's orthography and the phone vocabulary of the acoustic model, using the G_i2P_i library (Pine et al., 2022). In our case, the acoustic model is trained on English and thus has an English phone vocabulary, but other languages, or a multilingual model, could be used instead.

The transduction between orthographic form and model vocabulary is achieved by the composition of three transductions. First, the system performs an initial G2P from the orthographic form to the International Phonetic Alphabet (IPA). If the language is already supported in G_i2P_i, this G2P is used. At the time of writing, 30 language-specific mappings have been written: Anishinàbemowin (alq), Atikamekw (atj), Michif (crg), Southern & Northern East Cree (crj), Plains Cree (crk), Moose Cree (crm), Swampy Cree (csw), Western Highland Chatino (ctp), Danish (dan), French (fra), Gitksan (git), Scottish Gaelic (gla), Gwich'in (gwi), Hän (haa), Inuinnaqtun (ikt), Inuktitut (iku), Kaska (kkz), Kwak'wala (kwk), Raga (lml), Mi'kmaq (mic), Kanyen'kéha (moh), Anishinaabemowin (oji), Seneca (see), Tsuut'ina (srs), SENĆOŦEN (str), Upper Tanana (tau), Southern Tutchone (tce), Northern Tutchone (ttm), Tagish (tgx), and Tlingit (tli). English is also supported via the CMU Pronouncing Dictionary (Weide, 1998).

As mentioned in §1.2, there is no requirement that a document be monolingual; the G2P subsystem respects `xml:lang` attributes at any structural level. Also, if G2P fails on a word—for example, if a sentence was marked as being in the target language but it contained an unmarked English loanword with characters not in the target language—the system can fall back to a list of alternative languages provided as an XML attribute or a command-line parameter.

If no language attributes are present, the specified language is ISO 639-3 `und` (undetermined), or G2P happens to fail for the specified language and all fallback languages, the system performs a very rough automatic G2P, which we label `und`. First, the system runs the word through the `text-unidecode` library[3], which assigns each character an ASCII representation that (in most cases) roughly corresponds to its name in the Unicode table. (For example, U+12A8 ETHIOPIC SYLLABLE KA receives the ASCII representation "`ka`".) These ASCII characters are then converted to rough IPA equivalents representing cross-linguistically common usages of these characters.

While the "transcription" resulting from this would probably be inadequate for, say, text-to-speech, and would be entirely inappropriate for difficult cases like Japanese, for many of our target languages this level of rough G2P is adequate for alignment purposes. The kinds of errors that this tends to introduce are often featural (e.g., incorrect voice, glottalization, or velar vs. uvular), and would not necessarily result in different alignment outputs anyway, after the more radical transformation in the following step.

Next, the resulting IPA characters are mapped to their closest equivalents in English (or whatever language(s) the acoustic model has been trained on). This is performed automatically by `PanPhon` (Mortensen et al., 2016), a phonological knowledge base containing feature-level information about any possible human speech sound, and distance metrics between any two speech sounds. During evaluation (§4), we compare two of `PanPhon`'s distance metrics, a weighted feature edit distance and Hamming distance. It is also possible to specify a handwritten mapping, or to hand-edit the automatically generated mapping; from the point of view of the G_i2P_i library this is just another mapping to be composed with others. Finally, the resulting English IPA phones are mapped to the ARPABET vocabulary that the acoustic model expects.

2.4.5. Audio Preparation

Prior to alignment, we convert the audio file into 16-bit signed PCM (if it is not already). Also, if any timespans are marked as `do-not-align` in the user-provided metadata file, these are replaced by silences. These silences are only used for the following step; they do not affect the audio in the final read-along audiobook.

2.4.6. Alignment

For alignment, RAS uses the `SoundSwallower`[4] library, a refactored version of PocketSphinx (Huggins-Daines et al., 2006) with minimal requirements for easy installation across platforms.

It has been previously found that forced alignment at the *sentence* level does not require phonetically precise models, and in fact can be made more robust by the use of universal models estimated over broad categories of phonemes (Hoffmann and Pfister, 2013). Likewise, the context-dependent phone models typically used in large-vocabulary continuous speech recognition are equally counterproductive for alignment even at the phone level (Huggins-Daines and Rudnicky, 2006). We thus hypothesize that to produce a word-level alignment sufficient for the ReadAlongs application, the cross-linguistic G2P should be more than sufficient, and even the automatic `und` fallback should produce acceptable results in many cases.

In theory, forced alignment is quadratic in the length of the input, since every HMM state must be evaluated against every input frame in order to allow any possible alignment. This can, of course, be accelerated using beam search, at the risk of failure to align when the forced phone sequence is too divergent from the acoustic observations. However, there is another option, when state- or phone-level alignments are not needed, which is to treat alignment as a *speech recognition* task with a highly constrained grammar, accepting only the sequence of words in the input text. This allows us to perform alignment many times faster than real-time even on modest hardware, and dramatically faster than full-fledged phone-level alignment such as

[3]`https://github.com/kmike/text-unidecode/`

[4]`https://github.com/ReadAlongs/SoundSwallower`

done by the Montreal Forced Aligner. It is also possible to run the alignment code on the client side by cross-compiling it to JavaScript.

SoundSwallower requires (other than the input audio), two documents: a dictionary file with ARPABET pronunciations of each word (as created in §2.4.4) and a finite-state grammar representing the grammar to be recognized (in this case a trivial grammar, in which each word in the document transitions only to the following word, with 1.0 probability). Both of these (as noted in §2.4.3) use XML ID attributes as the word identifiers, so that outputs can unambiguously be re-associated with particular elements in the document.

3. Output Formats and Visualization

While the primary intended use case for RAS is the development of interactive read-along audiobooks that can be embedded in any website (§3.1), RAS's output files follow existing standards in publishing and the digital humanities that can be visualized in other ways (§3.2). It can also export to other text-audio alignment formats for a variety of use cases (§3.3).

3.1. Web Component

The primary intended downstream application for RAS is a web component[5], written in Stencil[6], that highlights words as they are spoken. Web components can be embedded in any web application for use in any browser, allowing for maximum interoperability and easy embedding in any project.

The structured XML output from RAS is interpreted by the web component such that each page element in the XML has a horizontal scrolling visual metaphor in the web component; paragraph and sentence elements have a vertical scrolling visual metaphor. Each word element becomes clickable and plays the audio for that word, allowing the reader to listen back to specific words in the document.

Deploying a ReadAlong web component involves taking the exported XML text, SMIL and audio, importing the library either with npm or by including the package in the HTML file in which the ReadAlong exists.

While such deployment will work for users who already have a website that they can access and edit, it requires an HTTP server to serve the assets and a developer comfortable with web hosting; it also requires that users have a stable internet connection to view the ReadAlong. To circumvent both of these problems, we also allow RAS to export to a single-file format we label "HTML", which Base64 encodes all of the fonts and assets required by the ReadAlong, and embeds them in a single HTML file that can then be used to view and share the activity offline. This allows readers without an internet connection to view it (provided they have some other means of transferring the HTML file to their computer), and removes the need for a web server, since this file is viewable in any browser without the use of an HTTP server.

3.2. Other Visualizations

Although the ReadAlong Web Component is the default visualizer assumed in our documentation, we target standard output formats (wav, XML, SMIL) that could be visualized and used in other ways. For example, as mentioned in §2.3, the formats are close enough to the EPUB3 accessibility specification that compilation into an accessible e-book is fairly straightforward. For another collaboration, we took output files aligned at the syllable level, rendered them frame-by-frame into PNG images, and then rendered those into MP4 format to make karaoke videos (Figure 2). However, video rendering is a fairly complex process, the details of which are outside of the scope of this paper.

3.3. Formats for Other Downstream Uses

A common request from academic collaborators has been support for ELAN (Brugman and Russel, 2004) and Praat TextGrid (Boersma and van Heuven, 2001) formats. RAS can produce output in these formats, so that the aligner can be used within labs' existing transcription and annotation workflows.

We also can export alignments directly to WebVTT and SRT subtitle formats to provide automatic subtitling for video content in a format compatible with YouTube.

4. Evaluation

While this is not primarily intended as a modeling paper, we performed a small evaluation to show that RAS does indeed produce reasonable outputs, and to illustrate the circumstances in which a handwritten G2P might be necessary.

4.1. Data

We manually annotated three recordings in Kanyen'kéha (Mohawk), SENĆOŦEN, and South Qikiqtaaluk Inuktut in Praat, annotating boundaries at the start and end of each word. The Kanyen'kéha recording is 5m 7s long and has 249 words, the SENĆOŦEN recording is 5m 46s long and has 419 words, and the Inuktut recording is 5m 35s long and has 282 words. Given the small size of this evaluation set, care should be taken in interpreting the results, and small differences are probably insignificant.

While both Kanyen'kéha and SENĆOŦEN use orthographies based on the Roman alphabet, they use the glyphs in very different ways, making an illustrative contrast. The Kanyen'kéha orthography is similar to a phonemic transcription of the language, using letters in much the same way as the IPA does, whereas the SENĆOŦEN orthography is entirely unique. For example, underlined W̱ represents IPA [x^w], and strikethrough Ŧ represents IPA [θ]. A pronunciation "guesser" like our und (see §2.4.4) would

[5]https://github.com/ReadAlongs/Web-Component

[6]https://stenciljs.com/

Language	Mapping type	Distance metric	Accuracy within tolerance (ms)				Span overlap		
			<10	<25	<50	<100	P	R	F1
SENĆOŦEN	Handmade	Weighted	0.23	0.47	0.67	0.87	0.90	0.84	0.87
		Hamming	**0.24**	**0.49**	**0.69**	**0.88**	**0.91**	**0.86**	**0.88**
	Und	Weighted	0.15	0.34	0.49	0.62	0.57	0.66	0.61
		Hamming	0.17	0.37	0.53	0.68	0.61	0.69	0.65
Kanyen'kéha	Handmade	Weighted	0.19	0.37	0.63	0.81	0.94	0.90	0.92
		Hamming	0.19	0.38	0.64	0.81	0.96	0.90	0.93
	Und	Weighted	**0.20**	**0.42**	**0.67**	**0.85**	**0.97**	**0.93**	**0.95**
		Hamming	0.19	0.39	0.64	0.82	0.97	0.91	0.94
Inuktut (Syllabics)	Handmade	Weighted	0.21	0.54	0.74	0.92	0.98	0.94	0.96
		Hamming	0.19	0.46	0.69	0.88	0.98	0.92	0.95
	Und	Weighted	0.22	0.53	0.73	0.91	0.98	0.94	0.96
		Hamming	0.20	0.48	0.71	0.89	0.98	0.94	0.96
Inuktut (Romanized)	Handmade	Weighted	0.22	0.54	0.75	0.92	0.98	0.94	0.96
		Hamming	0.19	0.49	0.70	0.89	0.98	0.92	0.95
	Und	Weighted	0.23	0.54	0.76	0.93	0.98	0.95	0.97
		Hamming	0.20	0.48	0.71	0.90	0.98	0.94	0.96

Table 1: Evaluation of SENĆOŦEN, Kanyen'kéha, and Inuktut forced alignments showing alignment accuracy of word boundaries with varying amounts of tolerance, and an F1 measurement of span overlap. Results are shown for alignments created from handmade G_i2P_i mappings, and mappings from text-unidecode ('Und'), measured against hand-labelled alignments. The results of the best SENĆOŦEN and Kanyen'kéha systems are in bold (statistical significance is not implied), while the Inuktut results are too close to meaningfully label a best system.

not be able to guess this usage from the typical cross-linguistic usage of W and T, so SENĆOŦEN is a case where we expect a human-written G2P mapping to outperform a guessed one.

Meanwhile, the Inuktut dataset evaluates how well RAS handles a non-Roman orthography; the *qaniujaaqpait* orthography uses the Canadian Aboriginal Syllabics abugida. This same text is also available in the *qaliujaaqpait* (Romanized) orthography, letting us observe the relative performance of G2P and `und` in two different orthographies on the same recording.

4.2. Evaluation Procedure

We test two conditions for the G2P mapping from orthographic forms to language-specific IPA phones:

- **Handmade**, a hand-written mapping provided in the G_i2P_i library.
- **Und**, the `und` fallback mapping based on the `text-unidecode` library, described in §2.4.4.

We also test two possibilities for the `PanPhon` edit distance metric, which determines which English phonemes are considered nearest neighbours to the target-language phonemes.

- **Hamming**, in which all articulatory features of each phone are weighted equally.
- **Weighted**, in which some features are weighted more highly than others, according to a phonologist's judgment of their perceptual importance.

We follow the evaluation procedure in McAuliffe et al. (2017), in which system outputs are compared for accuracy at a variety of tolerance thresholds. For example, an accuracy of 0.24 with a threshold of <10ms means that 24% of word boundaries detected were within 10ms of the human-annotated boundaries.[7]

By itself, accuracy within a fixed threshold is not clearly illustrative of whether RAS outputs are appropriate for their intended downstream task: guiding a reader through a text. This can be especially misleading when comparing languages with different word durations, or when comparing different speech styles. SENĆOŦEN typically has shorter words than Kanyen'kéha or Inuktut (in these recordings, 370ms on average compared to 769ms and 834ms, respectively); a 100ms error in SENĆOŦEN is more likely to highlight the wrong word entirely.

Therefore, we also report an F1 metric intended to capture what proportion of the time the highlighting is correctly guiding the reader, as opposed to misleading them.[8] In this metric, recall (R) represents the proportion of timespans in the reference that correctly overlap with their corresponding timespans in the system output. For example, if we were evaluating a one-word document, with a word "hello" spoken from 2.6s to 3.0s, and the system output said that word occurred from 2.8s to 3.1s, the recall would be 0.2s/0.4s = 0.50. In the other direction, precision (P) represents the pro-

[7]It should be noted that human annotations of segment boundaries vary; Schiel et al. (2004) suggest that inter-annotator agreement for phoneme-level segmentation is typically around 85–95% given a tolerance of 20ms.

[8]Many thanks to an anonymous reviewer for inspiring this line of inquiry.

portion of timespans in the system output that overlap with their corresponding timespans in the reference. Because having the highlight linger on a word during periods of silence is not misleading (indeed, it is helpful to keep the highlight on the screen even during silence), we do not penalize system timespans that extend into silences; instead, silences adjacent to the word being evaluated are ignored when calculating the precision of its alignment.

4.3. Results

Results are given in Table 1.[9] We can see that, as expected, the handwritten G2P mapping for SENĆOŦEN substantially outperformed the automatic one. On the other hand, a handwritten mapping did not outperform the automatic mapping for Kanyen'kéha; here, the automatic mapping was slightly better for all tolerances. Small differences on a small dataset should not be over-interpreted, but these results do illustrate that it is probably not necessary, in languages with cross-linguistically typical orthographies like Kanyen'kéha, to write a language-specific G2P mapping just for the purpose of approximate forced alignment.

For Inuktut, G2P and `und` performed very similarly for both orthographies, confirming that the `und` fallback can work even for non-Roman characters.

Comparison between weighted and Hamming distances did not reveal a clear winner. For SENĆOŦEN, Hamming distance performed somewhat better (especially in the poorly-performing `und` condition), but in Kanyen'kéha and Inuktut, the best systems used the weighted distance. Again, however, we should not over-interpret small differences on a small dataset.

For comparison, the Montreal Forced Aligner achieved a top score of 0.97 in the 100ms tolerance condition, in English, but this is after having been trained on approximately 1000 hours of English training data (McAuliffe et al., 2017). Our aligner has not seen *any* target-language data prior to evaluation.[10]

5. Issues and Future Work

Our early users largely agree on a central problem with the RAS workflow. When everything goes correctly and the document aligns adequately, the system seems "magical", replacing hours of human labour with a process taking seconds. However, when the document does *not* align properly, or at all, it is difficult for a novice user to know where the problem occurred (e.g., is there untranscribed text in the audio, or unspoken speech in the text?), and to fix this problem.

In early user tests, we noticed that users took a "divide-and-conquer" approach when alignment failed: dividing both the audio and text into smaller files based on obvious landmarks (like page/chapter breaks and obvious loanwords), aligning those segments separately, and then reassembling the original document. This is effective but tedious, especially when the landmark is deep within an XML structure and splitting the document means introducing matching element tags; while it may have been less labour than manual alignment, it is very frustrating labour, especially when the result of that labour still does not align!

We therefore introduced the idea of "anchors". The user can drop a custom `<anchor/>` element anywhere in the XML document, with a timestamp indicating where in the audio that anchor must be aligned, and the software will perform the division, alignment, and reassembly automatically. Anchors have made error recovery much easier; when an alignment fails or is of poor quality, the user can progressively search for landmarks and drop anchors until the alignment succeeds to their satisfaction.

This still, however, requires a basic knowledge of audio software like Audacity or Praat (to find the timestamp) and XML and text editing (to insert the anchor tag). Our next major milestone in development is a simple graphical user interface for this operation, where a user can "drag" alignments between the waveform and the text, attempt to align again, make further adjustments, etc. This sort of *human-in-the-loop* forced-alignment system, where a human and automated system negotiate the alignment of complex documents until the human is satisfied, will be a focus of future development for ReadAlong Studio.

6. Conclusion

Given the vastly different scales of available resources between languages, we are particularly interested in the "language zero-shot" frontier: what tasks can be achieved at a reasonable accuracy when a system has seen *no* data from the target language before inference?

Text-speech alignment, at least for the relatively-forgiving purpose of helping beginner readers follow along in audiobooks, is among these tasks. However, given the complexity of the pipelines and the special needs of Indigenous language audiobook alignment, it is difficult for more novice users to adapt existing forced alignment workflows to this end.

In this paper, we describe a robust text-speech alignment library that should work out-of-the-box on a variety of languages, and can be adapted via handwritten mappings for languages with more atypical orthographies. This library is open-source, comes with extensive documentation and will, we hope, help more language organizations benefit from automatic text-speech alignment.

[9] Due to fixing some bugs and addressing an issue in the reference data, our SENĆOŦEN and Kanyen'kéha results here are slightly different from those reported in Pine et al. (2022), but not in a way that affects system rankings.

[10] For an additional comparison, we performed forward-backward alignment using the Montreal Forced Aligner on these documents alone, but the systems failed to converge or produce useful alignments on such a small amount of data, so we did not report these.

7. Acknowledgements

This work would not have been possible without the many collaborators who shared their expertise and recordings, including but not limited to the Yukon Native Language Centre, the Kitigan Zibi Cultural Centre, W̱SÁNEĆ School Board, the Pirurvik Centre, Conseil de la Nation Atikamekw, Onwkawenna Kentyohkwa, Owennatekha Brian Maracle, Timothy Montler, Marie-Odile Junker, Hilaria Cruz, Nathan Thanyehténhas Brinklow, Francis Tyers, Fineen Davis, Eddie Antonio Santos, Mica Arseneau, Vasilisa Andriyanets, Christopher Cox, Bradley Ellert, Robbie Jimmerson, Shankhalika Srikanth, Sabrina Yu, Caroline Running Wolf, Michael Running Wolf, Fangyuan (Toby) Huang, Zachery Hindley, Darrel Schreiner, Luyi Xiao, Siqi Chen, Kwok Keung Chung, Koon Kit Kong, He Yang, Yuzhe Shen, Rui Wang, Zirui Wang, Xuehan Yi, and Zhenjie Zhou.

8. Bibliographical References

Black, A. W., Taylor, P., and Caley, R. (1998). The Festival speech synthesis system. http://www.festvox.org/festival.

Boersma, P. and van Heuven, V. (2001). Speak and unSpeak with PRAAT. *Glot International*, 5(9/10):341–347, December.

Brugman, H. and Russel, A. (2004). Annotating multi-media/multi-modal resources with ELAN. In *Proceedings of the Fourth International Conference on Language Resources and Evaluation (LREC'04)*, Lisbon, Portugal, May. European Language Resources Association (ELRA).

Bulterman, D., Jansen, J., Cesar, P., Mullender, S., Hyche, E., DeMeglio, M., Quint, J., Kawamura, H., Weck, D., García Pañeda, X., Melendi, D., Cruz-Lara, S., Hanclik, M., Zucker, D. F., and Michel, T. (2008). *Synchronized Multimedia Integration Language (SMIL 3.0)*. W3C Recommendation.

Garrish, M., Kerscher, G., LaPierre, C., Pellegrino, G., and Singh, A. (2022). *EPUB Accessibility 1.1 Conformance and Discoverability Requirements for EPUB Publications*. W3C Working Draft.

Gorman, K., Howell, J., and Wagner, M. (2011). Prosodylab-aligner: A tool for forced alignment of laboratory speech. *Canadian Acoustics*, 39(3):192–193.

Hoffmann, S. and Pfister, B. (2013). Text-to-speech alignment of long recordings using universal phone models. In Frédéric Bimbot, et al., editors, *INTERSPEECH 2013, 14th Annual Conference of the International Speech Communication Association, Lyon, France, August 25-29, 2013*, pages 1520–1524. ISCA.

Huggins-Daines, D. and Rudnicky, A. I. (2006). A constrained Baum-Welch algorithm for improved phoneme segmentation and efficient training. In *INTERSPEECH 2006 - ICSLP, Ninth International Conference on Spoken Language Processing, Pittsburgh, PA, USA, September 17-21, 2006*. ISCA.

Huggins-Daines, D., Kumar, M., Chan, A., Black, A. W., Ravishankar, M., and Rudnicky, A. I. (2006). PocketSphinx: A free, real-time continuous speech recognition system for hand-held devices. In *2006 IEEE International Conference on Acoustics Speech and Signal Processing Proceedings*, volume 1, pages I–I. IEEE.

Joanis, E., Knowles, R., Kuhn, R., Larkin, S., Littell, P., Lo, C.-k., Stewart, D., and Micher, J. (2020). The Nunavut Hansard Inuktitut–English parallel corpus 3.0 with preliminary machine translation results. In *Proceedings of the 12th Language Resources and Evaluation Conference*, pages 2562–2572, Marseille, France, May. European Language Resources Association.

Littell, P., Kazantseva, A., Kuhn, R., Pine, A., Arppe, A., Cox, C., and Junker, M.-O. (2018). Indigenous language technologies in Canada: Assessment, challenges, and successes. In *Proceedings of the 27th International Conference on Computational Linguistics*, pages 2620–2632, Santa Fe, New Mexico, USA, August. Association for Computational Linguistics.

Luchian, R. and Junker, M.-O. (2004). Developing an on-line Cree read-along with syllabics. *Carleton University Cognitive Science Technical Report*, 2006-01.

MacKenzie, L. and Turton, D. (2020). Assessing the accuracy of existing forced alignment software on varieties of British English. *Linguistics Vanguard*, 6(s1):20180061.

McAuliffe, M., Socolof, M., Mihuc, S., Wagner, M., and Sonderegger, M. (2017). Montreal Forced Aligner: Trainable text-speech alignment using Kaldi. In *Interspeech 2017*, pages 498–502. ISCA, August.

Moreno, P. J., Joerg, C., Thong, J.-M. V., and Glickman, O. (1998). A recursive algorithm for the forced alignment of very long audio segments. In *International Conference on Spoken Language Processing, vol. 8*.

Mortensen, D. R., Littell, P., Bharadwaj, A., Goyal, K., Dyer, C., and Levin, L. S. (2016). PanPhon: A resource for mapping IPA segments to articulatory feature vectors. In *Proceedings of COLING 2016, the 26th International Conference on Computational Linguistics: Technical Papers*, pages 3475–3484. ACL.

Pine, A., Littell, P., Joanis, E., Huggins-Daines, D., Cox, C., Davis, F., Santos, E. A., Srikanth, S., Torkornoo, D., and Yu, S. (2022). G_i2P_i: Rule-based, index-preserving grapheme-to-phoneme transformations. In *Proceedings of The 5th Workshop on The Use of Computational Methods in the Study of Endangered Languages*.

Robert-Ribes, J. and Mukhtar, R. (1997). Automatic

generation of hyperlinks between audio and transcript. In *Eurospeech*.

Schiel, F., Draxler, C., Baumann, A., Elbogen, T., and Steen, A. (2004). The production of speech corpora. https://www.bas.uni-muenchen.de/Forschung/BITS/TP1/Cookbook/.

Schiel, F. (1999). Automatic phonetic transcription of nonprompted speech. In *Proc. of the ICPhS*, pages 607–610.

TEI Consortium. (2021). *TEI P5: Guidelines for Electronic Text Encoding and Interchange*. TEI Consortium.

Weide, R. (1998). The Carnegie Mellon pronouncing dictionary. www.speech.cs.cmu.edu/cgi-bin/cmudict.

Yuan, J. and Liberman, M. (2008). Speaker identification on the SCOTUS corpus. *Proceedings of Acoustics 2008*, pages 5687–5690.

Proceedings of SIGUL2022 @LREC2022, pages 33–40
Marseille, 24-25 June 2022

Corpus Creation for Sentiment Analysis in Code-Mixed Tulu Text

Asha Hegde[1 a]
Mudoor Devadas Anusha[1 b]
Sharal Coelho[1 c]
Hosahalli Lakshmaiah Shashirekha[1 d]
Bharathi Raja Chakravarthi[2 e]
[1]Department of Computer Science, Mangalore University, Mangalore, India
[2]National University of Ireland Galway, Ireland
[e]bharathi.raja@insight-centre.org
{[a]hegdekasha, [b]anugowda251, [c]sharalmucs, ,[d]hlsrekha}@gmail.com

Abstract

Sentiment Analysis (SA) employing code-mixed data from social media helps in getting insights to the data and decision making for various applications. One such application is to analyze users' emotions from comments of videos on YouTube. Social media comments do not adhere to the grammatical norms of any language and they often comprise a mix of languages and scripts. The lack of annotated code-mixed data for SA in a low-resource language like Tulu makes the SA a challenging task. To address the lack of annotated code-mixed Tulu data for SA, a gold standard trlingual code-mixed Tulu annotated corpus of 7,171 YouTube comments is created. Further, Machine Learning (ML) algorithms are employed as baseline models to evaluate the developed dataset and the performance of the ML algorithms are found to be encouraging.

Keywords: Tulu, Code-mixed, Trilingual, Corpus creation, Sentiment Analysis

1. Introduction

Internet-enabled users express their thoughts on any topic through reviews, posts or comments on social media like YouTube, Facebook, Twitter, etc. Users knowing more than one language usually post their impressions about a topic in more than one language as there are no restrictions on the use of the languages or the grammar of any language (Scotton, 1982; Suryawanshi et al., 2020). Mixing multiple languages at different levels such as sentence, word, sub-word in the same text is referred to as code-mixing (Chakravarthi et al., 2019). Despite the fact that many languages have their own scripts, social media users in some parts of the world like India usually use non-native script to pen their comments (Bali et al., 2014). Due to the ease of entering the text in Latin and the usage of common English words, users usually enter the comments combining Latin and native scripts or only in Latin script.

The welcoming nature of online platforms encourages users from various social strata to express their thoughts/feelings on any topic. These thoughts/feelings can be extracted and used for many applications like SA. SA has recently gained popularity as a business strategy that can benefit from the insights gained from user opinions about a product or subject of interest. However, there hasn't been much effort put into analysing the sentiments of code-mixed content in many low-resourced Indian languages (Priyadharshini et al., 2021). These languages face more challenges for SA tasks due to the lack of text processing tools and annotated corpora in those languages. Some Indian languages such as Tulu, Konkani and Kashmiri are rarely explored for SA tasks.

Tulu belongs to the Dravidian language family, with over three million speakers known as Tuluvas in Karnataka, India. The majority of Tuluvas are found in Dakshina Kannada and Udupi, in the state of Karnataka and some in Mumbai, Maharashtra and in Gulf countries. Tulu is also spoken by some people in Kasargod, in the state of Kerala and it has its own script called Tigalari. The earliest written evidence of Tulu dates back to the 17th century AD, although now it exists only as a spoken language and has lost its script over time (Shetty, 2004). Despite the loss of script, Tulu is still a widely spoken language in the Southern part of Karnataka and Kannada script is prominently used to write Tulu. As Tulu is the regional language and Kannada is the official language of Karnataka, Tuluvas usually know both Tulu and Kannada languages fluently. In addition to this, many Kannada words are used in Tulu language. Further, English is predominantly known by many Tulu speaking people, especially those who are active on social media platforms. Tulu songs, videos, movies, comedy programs, skits are popular on social media. The comments posted by Tulu users for Tulu programs on social media will usually be a code-mix of Tulu, Kannada, and English. This has generated a lot of trilingual code-mixed data which is rarely explored for research purposes. In view of the availability of large volume of YouTube comments/posts in code-mixed Tulu, this study gathered comments from various YouTube Tulu songs, movies, comedy programs, skits, and serials to create a code-mixed Tulu dataset for SA. Sample comments from the proposed code-mixed

Sl. No	Type of code-mixing	Example Sentence	English Translation	Description
Eg:1	Inter-sentential	Masth edde ithend. Keep it up Bro.	It was very good. Keep it up brother	Code-mixing occurs when one sentence belongs to a different language from the other sentence in the same comment. The sentence "Keep it up Bro." belongs to English and the sentence "Masth edde ithend", belongs to Tulu exhibiting inter-sentential code mixing.
Eg:2	Intra-sentential	nanala comedy bodu super comedy nikelena	We need more comedy your comedy is super	Code-mixing happens in the same sentence ie., multiple languages are used in the same sentence. The English words comedy and super are used with the Tulu words nanala, bodu, and nikelena in the same sentence.
Eg:3	Word level	Super comedy bokka lastgu Good msg koriar.	super comedy, you gave a good message at the end.	Code-mixing occurs when stem belongs to a language and suffix is added from different language in the same sentence. In the word "lastgu", "last" belongs to English and "gu" belongs to Tulu where this word resides in the same sentence.
Eg:4	Tag-switching	super comedy aanda comedy nanlla bodithnd	may be, i'am coming early.	Code-mixing occurs when there is a switching in the tag in the same comment/sentence. The part of a sentnce "super comedy" indicates the Positive tag and the other part "aanda comedy nanlla bodithnd" indicates the tag Mixed_Feelings.
Eg:5	Multiple script	ಅಜ್ಜ mathergla ರಕ್ಷಣೆ ಕೊರ್ಲೆ	Grandfather save everyone	Code-mixing occurs when multiple scripts are used in the same sentence. In the sentence, "ಅಜ್ಜ", "ರಕ್ಷಣೆ", "ಕೊರ್ಲೆ" belongs to Kannada and "mathergla" beongs to Latin script.

Table 1: Sample code-mixed Tulu comments in the corpus

Tulu dataset along with the type of code-mixing are shown in Table 1.

In view of the lack of annotated code-mixed Tulu dataset for SA, this paper contributes by releasing the gold-standard trilingual code-mixed Tulu dataset to perform SA and presents the comprehensive results of using traditional ML classification methods to set the benchmark for the dataset. In most of the cases usually code-mixing includes two languages. However, the proposed dataset has code-mixing of Tulu, Kannada and English which makes it unique.

The rest of the paper is organized as follows: Section 2 throws light on SA in other Dravidian languages and Section 3 describes the procedure of corpus creation and annotation followed by the description of ML algorithms used to create baseline models in Section 4. Experiments and results are presented in Section 5 followed by the conclusion in Section 6.

2. Related Work

Due to the growth of social media, SA has become significantly important. Extensive research is being carried out on SA of monolingual corpora belonging to high-resource languages such as English, French, and Russian. However, only one work has been reported on SA in Tulu language and very less number of SA works are found for other Dravidian languages too. Some of the recent works on Dravidian languages using code-mixed text are described below:

Chakravarthi et al. (Chakravarthi et al., 2020b) have created a Tamil-English code-mixed annotated corpus for SA of YouTube comments. The corpus contains 15,744 code-mixed comments and each comment in the dataset is annotated by a minimum of three annotators. They implemented traditional ML algorithms, namely: Support Vector Machine (SVM), Decision Trees (DT), Multinomial Naive Bayes (MNB), Logistic Regression (LR), k-Nearest Neighbor (kNN), and Random Forest (RF) using Term-Frequency-Inverse-Document-Frequency (TF-IDF) of word n-grams in the range n = (1, 3) as features. Further, they have implemented Deep Learning (DL) models, namely: 1D Convolutional Long Short Term Memory (1DConvLSTM) and LSTM using the Keras embedding[1] and Dynamic Meta Embedding (DME) respectively. Further, the authors also implemented a transformer based classifier with multilingual Bidirectional Encoder Representations from Transformers (mBERT) for SA of code-mixed Tamil-English language. Among all the models RF model obtained the highest macro F1-score of 0.65.

KanCMD, a Kannada code-mixed dataset was developed by Hande et al. (Hande et al., 2020) by scraping YouTube comments[2]. The comments were segmented into sentences and each sentence was annotated by 5 annotators at three levels. KanCMD consists of 7,671 comments released for multitask learning of Offensive Language Detection (OLD) and SA. Both the tasks were adressed using traditional ML algorithms (SVM, MNB, DT, LR, kNN and RF) and DL based models (1DConvLSTM and LSTM). TF-IDF values, Keras embedding and DME of words were used as features to train ML models, 1DconvLSTM model and LSTM model respectively. Further, they also implemented a transformer based classifier with mBERT to perform SA of KanCMD dataset. The LR model outperformed other models with macro F1-scores of 0.57 and 0.66 for SA and OLD respectively.

Reddy et al. (Appidi et al., 2020b) presented a

[1]https://keras.io/api/layers/core_layers/embedding/

[2]https://github.com/philbot9/youtube-comment-scraper-cli

code-mixed Kannada-English corpus which is a collection of tweets extracted from Twitter on topics like sports, trending, hashtags, politics, movies and events for Parts-Of-Speech (POS) tagging. Conditional Random Fields (CRF), Bidirectional LSTM (BiLSTM), and BiLSTM+CRF are implemented to tag POS for code-mixed Kannada-English corpus. TF-IDF of character n-grams and word n-grams in the range n = (1, 3) followed by the count of common symbols, capitalization of words and numbers are used as features to train their models. Among the three models, BiLSTM+CRF model achieved the best results with macro F1-score of 0.81. Reddy et al. (Appidi et al., 2020a) have adressed the problem of emotion prediction using Kannada-English code-mixed tweets annotated with emotions. The authors trained the SVM classifier using TF-IDF of character n-grams, word tri-grams, and count of English negative words[3], punctuation, capitalization, and repetitive characters as features. They used the Keras embedding to train LSTM model and the LSTM model outperformed the SVM model with an accuracy of 32%.

Kusampudi et al. (Kusampudi et al., 2021) presented Twitter and Blog datasets for code-mixed Telugu-English text to perform SA. The authors implemented traditional ML models (SVM, MNB, DT, LR, KNN and RF), DL models (Convolutional Neural Network, BiLSTM) and hybrid models (BiLSTM+CRF and BiLSTM+LSTM) to predict sentiments in code-mixed Telugu-English text. TF-IDF of character n-grams and word n-grams in the range n=(1,3) followed by hand picked features, namely, count of special characters, capital letters, and digits are used by the authors to train ML models. BiLSTM+LSTM model exhibited a better accuracy of 0.98 on Blog dataset and BiLSTM+CRF model achieved an accuracy of 0.99 on Twitter dataset. Malayalam-English code-mixed annotated dataset for SA is created by Chakravarthi et al. (Chakravarthi et al., 2020a) by scraping the YouTube comments using YouTube comment-scraper[4] to extract the comments. These comments were annotated at three levels by 11 annotators. Further, the authors used Krippendorff's inter-annotator agreement to ensure the agreement between annotators. The annotated English-Malayalam dataset is used to implement traditional ML (LR, SVM, DT, RF, MNB, and kNN) and DL-based models (1DConvLSTM and LSTM) to perform SA. Authors have used TF-IDF of word tri-grams, Keras embeddings and DME as features to train ML, 1DConvLSTM, and LSTM models respectively. Further, they also implemented a transformer based classifier with mBERT and among all the models, mBERT outperformed with a F1-score of 0.75.

Kannadaguli (Kannadaguli, 2021) has created a Tulu-English code-mixed dataset of 5,536 comments for SA by scraping YouTube posts. During dataset construction, the author extracted only Tulu and Tulu-English code-mixed comments written in Latin script. Krippendorff's inter-annotator agreement was calculated to ensure the agreement between annotators. The annotated Tulu-English dataset was used to implement ML models (NB,LR, DT, k-NN, RF, SVM, and Principal Component Analysis), DL models (BiLSTM and Contextualized Dynamic Meta Embeddings), and transformer based classifier with BERT models. TF-IDF values and Keras embeddings are used as features for ML and DL models respectively. Among all the models, BiLSTM model outperformed with considerable F1-scores for all the classes.

From the literature, it is clear that the under-resourced Dravidian languages, namely, Tamil, Kannada, Malayalam, and Telugu have been rarely explored for SA. Further, to the best of our knowledge, there is only one work on SA of code-mixed Tulu text (Kannadaguli, 2021).

Information of Annotators		# of Annotators
Gender	Male	2
	Female	13
Highest Education	Graduate	0
	Postgraduate	12
	Research student	3
Medium of Schooling	English	6
	Native	9
Total		15

Table 2: Details of annotators

3. Corpus Creation and Annotation

The purpose of this work is to construct a code-mixed Tulu dataset for SA. YouTube contains a lot of videos on Tulu movies, movie trailers, skits, songs, and so on, and also the comments posted by users for these videos. These comments are used as corpus for the SA task. The corpus construction work begins by scraping the YouTube comments for the videos in Tulu using the YouTube-comment-scraper tool[5] and the comments collected are anonymized for the privacy of users. The raw data obtained from the scraper is split into sentences consisting of a single comment amounting to 48,000 comments. The comments are written entirely in English, Kannada, Tulu or in a combination of English, Tulu, and Kannada languages in Kannada/Latin script or in a combination of Kannada and Latin scripts. Hence, comments which are entirely in English language written in Latin or Kannada script are filtered out retaining the rest. It may be noted that, after filtering, the comments consist of only code-mixed Tulu content written in either Kannada and/or Latin script. This data filtering is carried out manually as there are

[3] `http://sentiment.christopherpotts.net/lingstruc.html`

[4] `https://github.com/philbot9/`

[5] `https://github.com/g1mishra/Youtube_Comment_Scraper/`

no tools/libraries to identify text in Tulu language. The comments consisting less than 3 words and longer than 15 words were removed as it is difficult to comprehend the sentiments. Further, all the emojis were removed as the majority of the comments contain only emojis without any text. Additionally, duplicate sentences are removed. This process resulted in 7,171 code-mixed comments which are subjected to annotation for SA.

3.1. Annotation Setup

Annotation scheme proposed by Mohammad et al. (Mohammad, 2016) is adopted to annotate the code-mixed Tulu data. Each comment is annotated by a minimum of 3 annotators according to the following guidelines provided to each annotator:

- **Positive :** The text provides an explicit or implicit hint that the speaker is in a positive mood.
  Ex: Masth edde ithend. Keep it up Bro.
  English translation: It was very good. Keep it up brother.

- **Negative :** The comment contains explicit or implicit clues that suggest the speaker is in a negative mood.
  Ex: Ponnu edde ijjal.
  English translation: The girl is not good.

- **Mixed-Feelings :**The text indicates both positive and negative feelings experienced by the speaker.
  Ex: Paniyere aavandina naataka
  English translation: A drama that could not be explained.

- **Neutral :** There is no indication of the speaker's emotional state. For eg: asking for likes or subscriptions, questions about the release date and conveying information etc. This state is considered as neutral state.
  Ex: Yel ganteg sari battnd.
  English translation: It became correct at 7 o'clock.

- **Not_Tulu :** These are the comments that do not contain Tulu content written in Kannada or Latin script. The entire comment may consist of English words written in Kannada script or Kannada words written in Latin and/or Kannada script.
  Ex: tulu artha agaala
  English translation: Do not understand Tulu.

The annotation process involved 15 native Tulu speakers with diversity in gender, medium of education in their schooling, and educational level, as volunteers. Table 2 shows the information about annotators involved in this work. A demonstration was given to the volunteers regarding the annotations and sample sheets with 200 comments were sent to them. If the quality of the sample annotation was good only then that annotator was selected for the annotation of the code-mixed Tulu corpus. Each volunteer was allowed to annotate

Languages	Tulu
Number of Tokens	82,763
Vocabulary Size	24,006
Number of comments	7,171
Average number of Tokens per comment	11

Table 3: Statistics of code-mixed Tulu corpus

Classes	# of Comments
Positive	3,164
Mixed-Feelings	1,212
Neutral	1,201
Negative	670
Not_Tulu	924

Table 4: Class-wise distribution of code-mixed Tulu annotated corpus

as many comments from the corpus as they wish. Annotators were notified that the annotations they were going to do will be recorded and they could opt-out at any time during the annotation process. The annotation setup has two phases: (i) blind annotation where each comment is annotated by two annotators and the annotators were not allowed to discuss regarding the annotations, and (ii) verification of comments and their annotations by an annotator who did not participate in the first phase. If both the annotators in the first phase have tagged the same label for the comment then that label is considered as the final label for that comment. If there is any conflict in the labels assigned by the first two annotators, the third annotator will annotate that comment and that label will be considered as the label of that comment.

3.2. Inter-annotator Agreement

During annotation, the annotator has to select only one of the categories to which the comment belongs adhering to the guidelines supplied. Since multiple annotators were given the task of annotating the same piece of data, a metric is required to compare the annotation qualities. This motivates the use of inter-annotator agreement which measures how well the annotations were carried out by many annotators on the same dataset. It also indicates the degree of agreement about a category among the annotators, but not whether the annotations are accurate. In other words, high inter-annotator agreement implies that guidelines are clear and interpretations are accurate.
Krippendorff's alpha (α) - a popular inter-annotator agreement algorithm is employed to measure the degree of agreement between annotators, despite its computational complexity (Krippendorff, 2011). This agreement is more relevant as it is not affected by miss-

Classes	Train set	Test set
Positive	2,501	663
Mixed-Feelings	953	248
Neutral	984	228
Negative	548	122
Not_Tulu	750	174

Table 5: Details of Train and Test set

ing data, varying sample sizes, categories, or number of annotators and can be applied to any type of measurements, including nominal, ordinal, interval, and ratio. Since the annotation work was carried out by more than two persons and the same person did not annotate all of the comments, Krippendorff's alpha (α) fits better (Artstein, 2017). The range of α must be 0 to 1 and α=1 implies a perfect agreement between annotators. The annotation for code-mixed Tulu corpus produced a nominal metric agreement of 0.6832.

3.3. Difficult Examples

During annotation, it was found that as some of the comments were ambiguous, it was difficult to find out the right feelings of the users who posted those comments. Annotation of such comments seemed difficult and some of such comments are described below:

1. Yes maaatha kadetla inchina jana ippuveru, hilarious show
   -Yes from all the places like this people are there, hilarious show
   Because of using the word 'hilarious show' the comment becomes ambiguous whether the speaker has 'Positive' sentiment or sarcastically giving the comment.

2. Valtaranna erege daye bodu Ladaye?
   - Valter brother why you want fighting?
   The comment conveys in a positive way that fighting is not good. However, the annotator cannot decide whether the comment has 'Positive' sentiment or 'Mixed-Feelings' as there are no explicit clues to identify 'Positive' sentiment.

3. Yappa devare ivaru yalli avaru marre
   -My God from where he is?
   In the comment, the words 'Yappa devare' and 'marre' belong to both Kannada and Tulu. Hence, difficult to decide whether it belongs to 'Not_Tulu' or 'Mixed-Feelings' class.

4. Comedy jaasti uppad. Family emotion drama maata maltar da flop aapundu.
   -Need more comedy. If you add more family sentiments and drama then it will flop.
   From the comment, it is difficult to decide whether the speaker liked the comedy or disliked it.

According to the instructions given to the annotators, the comment which has explicit clues are utilized for annotations. However, some examples have subtle sentiments which are different than the sentiments that can be decided from the explicit clues. Hence, some comments have shown disagreement between the annotators.

3.4. Dataset

Corpus statistics are given in Table 3 and class-wise distribution of the annotated corpus is shown in Table 4. The comments are categorized into five groups: Positive, Negative, Neutral, Mixed-Feelings, and Not_Tulu. Among 7,171 comments, 3,164 comments have a Positive polarity which is the most common category. Since there are only a few YouTube channels in Tulu language compared to other languages, the majority of the viewers encourage such channels with positive comments. The second common categories in this corpus are Mixed-Feelings and Neutral with 1,212 and 1,201 comments respectively. Because, most of the comments collected from YouTube are from Tulu songs, movies, movie trailers and skits, the users show either the ambiguity in their emotion or they just convey some information. Further, Not_Tulu and Negative categories have fewer comments compared to the other categories with 924 and 670 comments respectively. This is because, Tulu channels attract specially Tuluvas and there is least possibility that they post negative comments on the video/work of someone who belongs to their region or community. The dataset will be made available to the research community for exploring different models for SA.

4. Baseline Classifiers

Traditional ML algorithms are implemented using TF-IDF of word bigrams and trigrams as features to predict emotions in code-mixed Tulu data in order to provide baseline. The brief description of ML algorithms along with the hyper-parameters used are given below:

4.1. Multinomial Naive Bayes

Naive-Bayes classifier is a probabilistic model developed from the Bayes theorem that determines the probability of hypothesis activity based on the evidence (Xu et al., 2017). alpha - smoothing parameter value is set to 1 for MNB.

4.2. Logistic Regression

LR algorithm predicts the probability of a target variable using L2 regularization which is the default value for the penalty (Genkin et al., 2007) and the same is used in the baseline LR classifier.

4.3. Support Vector Machine

SVM is an algorithm that determines the best decision boundary between the vectors that belong to a given group (or category) and those which do not belong to

Classes	Classifiers					
	MNB			RF		
	Precision	Recall	F1 score	Precision	Recall	F1 score
Mixed-Feelings	0.39	0.04	0.07	0.53	0.19	0.28
Negative	0.83	0.04	0.08	0.46	0.17	0.25
Neutral	0.71	0.18	0.29	0.35	0.70	0.46
Not_Tulu	1.00	0.17	0.29	0.83	0.28	0.42
Positive	0.50	1.00	0.67	0.72	0.84	0.77
Macro Average	0.69	0.28	0.28	0.58	0.44	0.44
Weighted Average	0.60	0.52	0.41	0.62	0.58	0.55
	LR			SVM		
	Precision	Recall	F1 score	Precision	Recall	F1 score
Mixed-Feelings	0.47	0.25	0.33	0.41	0.29	0.34
Negative	0.49	0.17	0.25	0.45	0.33	0.38
Neutral	0.54	0.40	0.46	0.49	0.43	0.46
Not_Tulu	0.90	0.44	0.59	0.82	0.57	0.68
Positive	0.63	0.96	0.76	0.69	0.89	0.78
Macro Average	0.61	0.44	0.48	0.57	0.50	0.53
Weighted Average	0.61	0.62	0.57	0.61	0.63	**0.60**
	DT			KNN		
	Precision	Recall	F1 score	Precision	Recall	F1 score
Mixed-Feelings	0.35	0.23	0.28	0.28	0.33	0.30
Negative	0.31	0.22	0.26	0.35	0.29	0.32
Neutral	0.32	0.54	0.40	0.40	0.34	0.37
Not_Tulu	0.57	0.32	0.41	0.78	0.42	0.54
Positive	0.72	0.75	0.73	0.71	0.81	0.76
Macro Average	0.45	0.41	0.42	0.50	0.44	0.46
Weighted Average	0.54	0.53	0.52	0.56	0.56	0.55
	MLP			Cross validation		
	Precision	Recall	F1 score	Precision	Recall	F1 score
Mixed-Feelings	0.41	0.36	0.38	0.36	0.47	0.41
Negative	0.43	0.29	0.34	0.50	0.28	0.36
Neutral	0.43	0.46	0.45	0.43	0.56	0.49
Not_Tulu	0.77	0.56	0.65	0.83	0.54	0.66
Positive	0.72	0.83	0.77	0.80	0.77	0.78
Macro Average	0.55	0.50	0.52	0.58	0.52	0.54
Weighted Average	0.60	0.61	**0.60**	0.64	0.61	**0.62**

Table 6: Performance measures of the benchmark systems

that (Tong and Koller, 2001) and is implemented with L2 regularization.

4.4. k Nearest Neighbor

kNN algorithm classifies data by finding the 'k' nearest neighbors in the training data and then predicting the label of the test set based on the labels of these neighbours using the majority voting (Cunningham and Delany, 2021) and the value of 'k' is set to 3.

4.5. Decision Tree

DT algorithm is a tree-structured classifier with internal nodes representing the features of a dataset, branches representing the decision rules, and leaf nodes representing the outcome. In this classifier, classification process begins with a root node and ends with a decision made by leaves based on features (Pranckevičius and Marcinkevičius, 2017). The baseline DT classifier is implemented with max_depth = None, min_samples_split = 2, and criterion = 'gini'.

4.6. Random Forest

RF model consists of a collection of decision trees, each of which is trained using a random subset of features, and the prediction is the result of the majority vote of trees. High-dimensional noisy data can be handled well by this classifier (Shah et al., 2020). RF is implemented with the same hyper-parameter values as in DT.

4.7. Multi-Layer Perceptron

MLP classifiers are widely used in ML models due to their simplicity. It is based on neural network that consists of three types of layers: the input layer, the output layer, and one or more hidden layers. Input layer holds the input features and weighted sums of the input features are calculated by the input function. An activation function is subsequently applied to the result of this computation in order to obtain the output (Bounabi et al., 2018). The MLP model is implemented with random_state = 1 and max_iter = 300.

5. Experiments and Results

Several experiments were conducted using traditional ML algorithms, namely: MNB, LR, SVM, kNN, DT, RF, and MLP. Details of the Train and Test set are shown in Table 5 and Table 6 shows the experimental results using different ML models for SA. Precision, Recall, F1-score, macro average, and weighted average metrics are considered for evaluating the models. A Macro-average computes Precision, Recall, and F1-score independently for each class and then takes the average. Thus, it treats all the classes equally. Weighted average takes metrics from each class similar to the macro average, but the contribution from each class to the average is weighted based on the number of examples available for it.

The results illustrate that all the classification algorithms performed moderately on code-mixed Tulu data. This may be due to the characteristics of the dataset. The scores for different sentiment classes appear to be consistent with the distribution of sentiments in the dataset. Across all the sentiment classes, MLP and SVM classifiers performed comparatively better with the same weighted average F1-score of 0.60. Further, the 5-fold cross validation for SVM classifier resulted in a weighted average F1-score of 0.62.

The dataset does not have a balanced distribution. Table 4 shows that out of 7,171 comments, 44% comments belong to the 'Positive' class while the other sentiment classes share 17%, 17%, 13% and 9% for 'Neutral', 'Mixed-Feelings', 'Not_Tulu' and 'Negative' classes respectively. The Precision, Recall, and F1-score for 'Positive' class are higher than those for other classes. Further, 'Not_Tulu' and 'Negative' are the classes with lowest comments which leads to the poor results. In addition to their low distribution in the dataset, some comments are difficult to annotate even by human annotators, as mentioned in Section 3.3. Comparatively, the 'Negative' and 'Not_Tulu' classes are easy to annotate by human annotators. However, the lack of examples belonging to these classes moderates the performance of the models. Surprisingly in SVM, LR, and MLP models, the 'Negative' and 'Not_Tulu' classes obtained higher F1-scores than the 'Neutral' and 'Mixed-Feelings' classes which have more support data. This is due to more explicit clues for 'Negative' and 'Not_Tulu' words. However, the proposed code-mixed Tulu dataset is imbalanced with more support data for 'Positive' class. This resource could serve as a starting point for further research in SA of code-mixed Tulu data. There is considerable room for exploring code-mixed research with this dataset. Further, the proposed Tulu dataset has three languages and rarely explored for SA ensuring the scope for trilingual code-mixing in SA tasks.

6. Conclusion

In this paper, we have presented code-mixed Tulu dataset construction using YouTube comments for SA. Kripendorff's inter-annotator agreement is used to analyze the agreement between the annotators. Traditional ML algorithms are evaluated using TF-IDF of bi-grams and tri-grams on this code-mixed Tulu annotated corpus to provide baseline results. As the proposed work intends researchers to develop models for SA using this dataset, the dataset will be made available to the research community.

7. Acknowledgements

We thank our Masters students for helping us in creating code-mixed Tulu corpus.

8. References

Appidi, A. R., Srirangam, V. K., Suhas, D., and Shrivastava, M. (2020a). Creation of Corpus and Analysis in Code-Mixed Kannada-English Social Media Data for POS Tagging. In *Proceedings of the 17th International Conference on Natural Language Processing (ICON)*, pages 101–107.

Appidi, A. R., Srirangam, V. K., Suhas, D., and Shrivastava, M. (2020b). Creation of Corpus and Analysis in Code-Mixed Kannada-English Twitter Data for Emotion Prediction. In *Proceedings of the 28th international conference on computational linguistics*, pages 6703–6709.

Artstein, R. (2017). Inter-annotator Agreement. In *Handbook of linguistic annotation*, pages 297–313.

Bali, K., Sharma, J., Choudhury, M., and Vyas, Y. (2014). I am Borrowing ya Mixing? an Analysis of English-Hindi Code Mixing in Facebook. In *Proceedings of the First Workshop on Computational Approaches to Code Switching*, pages 116–126.

Bounabi, M., Moutaouakil, K. E., and Satori, K. (2018). A Probabilistic Vector Representation and Neural Network for Text Classification. In *International Conference on Big Data, Cloud and Applications*, pages 343–355.

Chakravarthi, B. R., Arcan, M., and McCrae, J. P. (2019). Comparison of Different Orthographies for Machine Translation of Under-resourced Dravidian Languages. In *Second Conference on Language, Data and Knowledge (LDK 2019)*, pages 6:1–6:14.

Chakravarthi, B. R., Jose, N., Suryawanshi, S., Sherly, E., and McCrae, J. P. (2020a). A Sentiment Analysis Dataset for Code-Mixed Malayalam-English. In *Proceedings of the 1st Joint Workshop on Spoken Language Technologies for Under-resourced languages (SLTU) and Collaboration and Computing for Under-Resourced Languages (CCURL)*, pages 177–184.

Chakravarthi, B. R., Muralidaran, V., Priyadharshini, R., and McCrae, J. P. (2020b). Corpus Creation for Sentiment Analysis in Code-Mixed Tamil-English Text. In *Proceedings of the 1st Joint Workshop on Spoken Language Technologies for Under-resourced languages (SLTU) and Collaboration and Computing for Under-Resourced Languages (CCURL)*, pages 202–210.

Cunningham, P. and Delany, S. J. (2021). k-Nearest Neighbour Classifiers-A Tutorial. pages 1–25.

Genkin, A., Lewis, D. D., and Madigan, D. (2007). Large-scale Bayesian Logistic Regression for Text Categorization. pages 291–304.

Hande, A., Priyadharshini, R., and Chakravarthi, B. R. (2020). KanCMD: Kannada CodeMixed Dataset for Sentiment Analysis and Offensive Language Detection. In *Proceedings of the Third Workshop on Computational Modeling of People's Opinions, Personality, and Emotion's in Social Media*, pages 54–63.

Kannadaguli, P. (2021). A Code-Diverse Tulu-English Dataset For NLP Based Sentiment Analysis Applications. In *2021 Advanced Communication Technologies and Signal Processing (ACTS)*, pages 1–6.

Krippendorff, K. (2011). Computing Krippendorff's alpha-reliability.

Kusampudi, S. S. V., Chaluvadi, A., and Mamidi, R. (2021). Corpus Creation and Language Identification in Low-Resource Code-Mixed Telugu-English Text. In *Proceedings of the International Conference on Recent Advances in Natural Language Processing (RANLP 2021)*, pages 744–752.

Mohammad, S. (2016). A Practical Guide to Sentiment Annotation: Challenges and Solutions. In *Proceedings of the 7th workshop on computational approaches to subjectivity, sentiment and social media analysis*, pages 174–179.

Pranckevičius, T. and Marcinkevičius, V. (2017). Comparison of Naive Bayes, Random Forest, Decision Tree, Support Vector Machines, and Logistic Regression Classifiers for Text Reviews Classification. pages 209–221.

Priyadharshini, R., Chakravarthi, B. R., Thavareesan, S., Chinnappa, D., Thenmozhi, D., and Ponnusamy, R. (2021). Overview of the DravidianCodeMix 2021 Shared Task on Sentiment Detection in Tamil, Malayalam, and Kannada. In *Forum for Information Retrieval Evaluation*, pages 4–6.

Scotton, C. M. (1982). The Possibility of Code-Switching: Motivation for Maintaining Multilingualism. pages 432–444.

Shah, K., Patel, H., Sanghvi, D., and Shah, M. (2020). A Comparative Analysis of Logistic Regression, Random Forest and KNN Models for the Text Classification. *Augmented Human Research*, pages 1–16.

Shetty, M. (2004). Language Contact and the Maintenance of the Tulu Language in South India.

Suryawanshi, S., Chakravarthi, B. R., Verma, P., Arcan, M., McCrae, J. P., and Buitelaar, P. (2020). A Dataset for Troll Classification of TamilMemes. In *Proceedings of the WILDRE5–5th workshop on indian language data: resources and evaluation*, pages 7–13.

Tong, S. and Koller, D. (2001). Support Vector Machine Active Learning with Applications to Text Classification. pages 45–66.

Xu, S., Li, Y., and Wang, Z. (2017). Bayesian Multinomial Naïve Bayes Classifier to Text Classification. In *Advanced multimedia and ubiquitous engineering*, pages 347–352.

Proceedings of SIGUL2022 @LREC2022, pages 41–47
Marseille, 24-25 June 2022

Crowd-sourcing for Less-resourced Languages: Lingua Libre for Polish

Mathilde Hutin, Marc Allassonnière-Tang
Université Paris-Saclay / LISN-CNRS (UMR 9015),
Muséum national d'Histoire naturelle / EA (UMR 7206)
Rue du Belvedère bât 507, 91405 Orsay, France; 17, place du Trocadéro, 75016 Paris, France
mathilde.hutin@lisn.upsaclay.fr, marc.allassonniere-tang@mnhn.fr

Abstract

Oral corpora for linguistic inquiry are frequently built based on the content of news, radio, and/or TV shows, sometimes also of laboratory recordings. Most of these existing corpora are restricted to languages with a large amount of data available. Furthermore, such corpora are not always accessible under a free open-access license. We propose a crowd-sourced alternative to this gap. Lingua Libre is the participatory linguistic media library hosted by Wikimedia France. It includes recordings from more than 140 languages. These recordings have been provided by more than 750 speakers worldwide, who voluntarily recorded word entries of their native language and made them available under a Creative Commons license. In the present study, we take Polish, a less-resourced language in terms of phonetic data, as an example, and compare our phonetic observations built on the data from Lingua Libre with the phonetic observations found by previous linguistic studies. We observe that the data from Lingua Libre partially matches the phonetic inventory of Polish as described in previous studies, but that the acoustic values are less precise, thus showing both the potential and the limitations of Lingua Libre to be used for phonetic research.

Keywords: Crowd-sourcing, open-access, language description, Polish

1. The "Resource Problem"

Languages are said to be "less-resourced" when the amount of data available and language-specific technologies are less developed for them than for other well-resourced languages such as English, Spanish, French or Chinese. At the root of the problem lies the question of the quantity of data available: This data is necessary in massive amounts to train and then test language technologies. Phoneticians and phonologists, i.e., researchers interested in speech, have to overcome an additional challenge: They cannot use written data as a proxy for language production and need audio recordings when working on vocal languages or video recordings when working on sign languages.

To overcome this challenge, researchers developed two strategies. The first one consists in collecting their own large corpora, either field-recorded, such as the PFC project for French (Durand et al., 2002), or recorded in laboratories such as the TIMIT database for English (Garofolo et al., 1993) or NCCFr for French (Torreira et al., 2010). The second strategy consists in gathering audio recordings from other sources such as TV or radio shows, as was done for instance in the framework of the international project OSEO Quaero (`www.quaero.org`), or from audio books, as exemplified by the LibriSpeech corpus for English (Panayotov et al., 2015, `www.openslr.org/12`). Both options have the disadvantage of being overly costly, both in money and human resources, and sometimes not freely accessible to the community. A third path has been recently explored: crowd-sourced data, recorded by volunteers and therefore much less costly in time and money and generally open-source. The project Common Voice (Ardila et al., 2020, `http://commonvoice.mozilla.org`) for instance was launched in 2017 by Mozilla for the intended purpose of creating a free database for the development of speech recognition software. In March 2022, it contains ~18,000h of speech, 14,000 of which have been validated by other speakers, in 87 languages.

In the present paper, we explore a similar project: Lingua Libre, a participatory linguistic media library developed by Wikimedia France (`www.lingualibre.org`). It was launched in 2015, and, in March 2022, it counts ~700,000 recordings in 148 languages across 777 speakers. This database is interesting to explore because it differs from Common Voice in the fact that its aim is not primarily the development of new technologies, or even linguistic inquiry in general, but patrimonial conservation of languages. Lingua Libre was used only once for academic purposes, i.e., to estimate the transparency of graphic systems in 17 languages with an artificial neural network (Marjou, 2021). With this study, we aim to show that such data is also easily processable and useful for language description. In this proof of concept, we use Lingua Libre to describe the phonetics-phonology interface in Polish, a language we claim can be considered as less-resourced.

In the following, we present an overview of Polish corpora available today to show how Polish can be considered a less-resourced language (Section 2) and describe the Polish phonology and why describing associated phonetic characteristics is essential to both computer scientists and linguists (Section 3). In Section 4, we present our corpus and methodology. In Section 5, we provide counts of the consonants and vowels in our Polish data (5.1) as well as acoustic values of vowels (5.2. Finally, in Section 6, we conclude and discuss the results.

2. Oral Corpora for Polish

In this Section, we provide an overview of oral resources available for Polish and advocate for the need to explore new, open-source, less expensive alternatives. Even today, oral corpora for Polish are indeed problematic: Their scarcity, technical characteristics or expensiveness allow us to define Polish as a less-resourced language.

First, most oral corpora for Polish were designed to train language models, and are thus often expensive to produce and to use. One of the oldest databases for this language, the BABEL Polish Database (ELRA-S0307) [1] is a speech database produced under the COPERNICUS program whose objective was to create a database of languages of Central and Eastern Europe. The Polish part consists in ~16h of read speech (30 males, 30 females) from the 1990s and its license is expensive. Polish is also part of the GlobalPhone corpus (Schultz, 2002), also designed to provide read speech data for the development and evaluation of large continuous speech recognition systems in 22 languages. The Polish part of GlobalPhone was collected from 48 female and 54 male native speakers in Poland aged 18 to 65. Each speaker read ~100 utterances from newspaper articles, resulting in 10130 utterances of journalistic speech (and their transcriptions). The Polish Speecon database (ELRA-S0179) [2] comprises both adult (286 males, 264 females) and child (25 boys, 25 girls) speech, providing 248h of speech recorded in various environments, but is again extremely costly. Most recently, in 2019, the Polish Speech Database (Szwelnik et al., 2019) was developed by VoiceLab. It consists of ~280h of speech (and corresponding transcripts), i.e., 263,424 utterances of Polish speech data from 200 speakers (103 male and 97 female ranging 15 to 60), recorded in Poland. Speakers were asked to record themselves reading a text on a website for at least 60 minutes from their home computer using a headset. The text comprised sentences covering most speech sounds in Polish. The corpus is thus rather representative of read Polish, but its usage is free only to LDC members.

Some of these expensive corpora are not even representative of the actual Polish-speaking community, with only one or few speakers. For instance, the Bonn Open Synthesis System (BOSS) synthesizer (Demenko et al., 2009) has a unit selection corpus for Polish of only 115 minutes of speech read by one professional radio speaker. Similarly, Polish entered the Collins Multilingual database (ELRA-S0383) [3] , covering Real Life Daily vocabulary in a variety of topics in 32 languages (the WordBank, see ELRA-T0376) and a multilingual set of sentences in 28 languages (the PhraseBank, see ELRA-T0377). The audio was recorded by only one native speaker of each language, resulting in 2,000 audio files for each language, and the corpus' license is also very expensive and limited to non-commercial use.

Less representative also are corpora dedicated to specific language domains, such as the ONOMASTICA project (ELRA-S0043)[4], a European project aiming to produce a multi-language pronunciation lexicon of proper names in 11 languages, or the JURISDIC project (Demenko et al., 2008), which aims to create a database to help develop technologies for the dictation of legal texts and includes ~1200h of both semi-spontaneous and read domain-specific speech from ~1000 judges, lawyers, police officers or university staff.

Other corpora can be problematic from a technical point of view. For instance, Polish is represented in the CSLU corpus of telephone speech (Lander, 2005), which contains ~84h of fixed vocabulary and fluent continuous telephone speech (and orthographic transcriptions for a subset of the utterances). Polish is also part of the Multi-Language Conversational Telephone Speech 2011 - Slavic Group (Jones et al., 2016), comprising ~60h of telephone speech in Polish, Russian and Ukrainian. Portions of these telephone calls were also used in the NIST 2011 Language Recognition Evaluation (LRE) (Greenberg et al., 2018), containing 204h of conversational telephone speech and broadcast audio in 24 languages. Yet telephone speech can be challenging to process, since it is usually recorded on reduced bandwidth (4 kHz), which is enough for some usages but may induce an inadequacy with models trained on larger bandwidth (8 kHz).

Finally, the most easily usable oral corpus for Polish is the National Corpus of Polish (NKJP) (Przepiórkowski et al., 2012, `www.nkjp.pl/`). It is mainly a corpus of written Polish, comprising over 1.5 billion words from classical literature, daily newspapers, specialist periodicals and journals, a variety of Internet texts, and transcripts of conversations by both male and female speakers, in various age groups, coming from various regions of Poland. However, the NKJP also comprises a sample of spoken, conversational Polish of ~2 million tokens.

As can be seen from this overview of Polish oral corpora, most were created with the intended purpose

[1] `http://catalog.elra.info/en-us/repository/browse/ELRA-S0307/`

[2] `http://catalog.elra.info/en-us/repository/browse/ELRA-S0179/`

[3] `http://catalog.elra.info/en-us/repository/browse/ELRA-S0383/`

[4] `http://catalog.elra.info/en-us/repository/browse/ELRA-S0043/`

of developing tools or training language technologies, sometimes for specific sociolects. Several are not representative of a large portion of the population or suffer from technical defects, and most of them are expensive to use. In the present paper, we are interested in how everyday vocabulary gathered for free for other purposes than software development can be used to investigate linguistic questions.

3. Polish Phonology

Polish (ISO 639-3) is a Slavic language currently spoken by 36.5 million speakers, mainly in Poland, Europe (`www.ethnologue.com`). In terms of number of speakers, Polish is the largest language in the West Slavic group and the second largest of all Slavic languages after Russian (Lewis et al., 2013). It is a highly inflected language, with a much richer inflection of nouns, adjectives, verbs, pronouns, and numerals than most Germanic languages.

Describing the phonetic characteristics of Polish is important, from a linguistic point of view, for the understanding of its sound system, its variability and its possible evolution. From an applicable perspective, understanding these linguistic characteristics is helpful for Automatic Speech Recognition (ASR) systems, especially for such an inflected language (Demenko et al., 2012).

In terms of phonetic inventory, grammars describe Polish as displaying 31 consonants and 6 vowels (Jassem, 2003).

Consonants are displayed in Table 1. They are divided across 6 modes of articulation: stops, fricatives, and affricates, that have a two-fold distinction between voiceless and voiced, as well as nasals, one lateral, one flap and two approximants, and across 5 places of articulation: labial(-dental), dental, alveolar, (alveo-)palatal, and velar.

	Lab	**L-d**	**(P-)d**	**Al**	**Al-p**	**P**	**V**
Plos	p b		t d			c ɟ	k g
Nas	m		n		ɲ		ŋ
Fri		f v	s z	ʃ ʒ	ɕ ʑ		x
Aff			ts dz	ʧʤ	tɕ dʑ		
Lat			l				
F/t				r			
App						j	w

Table 1: The consonants of Polish. The abbreviations are read as follows. Lab = Labial, L-d = Labiodental, (P-)d = (Post-)dental, Al = Alveolar, Al-p = Alveo-palatal, P = Palatal, V = Velar, Plos = Plosive, Nas = Nasal, Fri = Fricative, Aff = Affricates, Lat = Lateral, F/t = Flap/trill, App = Approximant.

Vowels on the other hand, are displayed in Table 2. They are distributed across three aperture levels, i.e., high, mid and low vowels, and across three anteroposteriority positions (front, central and back vowels). The vowels /i/ and /ɨ/ are debatably positionally-conditioned allophones, at least in non-initial position (Jassem, 1958). Therefore, in the current paper, we only consider the [i] sounds and we do not include /ɨ/.

	Front	Central	Back
High	i	ɨ	u
Mid	e		o
Low		a	

Table 2: The vowels of Polish.

4. Materials and Method

In this paper, we use the data from Wikimedia's participatory linguistic library: Lingua Libre. As a crowdsourcing tool, any speaker can log in, fill in a profile with basic metadata for themselves or for other speakers, and record themselves or their guests reading lists of words in their native language. The device detects pauses, which allows for the recording to end when the word has been read and the next recording to start automatically after, therefore effortlessly generating relatively short audio files for each word. Each audio file is supposed to be titled on the same template of 'Language - Speaker name - Item name'. For example, for the recording 'pol.-KaMan-dokumentalny.wav', the language of the recording is Polish ('pol'), the speaker ID is 'KaMan', and the recorded item is 'dokumentalny', which means 'documentary'. The speaker then checks the validity of their aufio files and uploads them in Creative Commons, meaning that all files are open-source.

We chose to investigate Polish because it is the second most represented language in Lingua Libre, with 81,071 recordings across 15 speakers. The most represented language in Lingua Libre is French, with thrice as much recordings (241,825) across 283 speakers, but since this language can be considered as well-resourced and well-documented, it was less interesting to test our methodology.

The workflow for data extraction is as follows. First, the recordings are scrapped from the Lingua Libre database. In the present study, we extract all the +80,000 recordings available in Lingua Libre. Second, the recordings are segmented and aligned using WebMAUS (Kisler et al., 2017), the online open-access version of the MAUS software (Schiel, 2004), which is used to automatically time-align a recording based on its orthographic transcription. MAUS creates a pronunciation hypothesis graph based on the orthographic transcript of the recording (extracted from the name of the audio file) using a grapheme-to-phoneme converter. During this process, the orthographic transcription is converted to the Speech Assessment Methods Phonetic Alphabet (SAMPA). The signal is then aligned with the hypothesis graph and the alignment with the highest probability is chosen. As an overview of its accuracy, experiments have shown that the MAUS alignments match human alignments 95% of the time (Kipp et al., 1997). At this point, the extracted data allow us to have a frequency count of each phoneme that is found within the data. Third, the recordings of the selected vowels are extracted and analyzed in terms of formants. For each recording of each vowel, the mean F1 and F2 of the entire sound are extracted. The mean formants are considered to attenuate the influence of context-induced noise in the recordings. During this process of data extraction and analysis, the following R packages are used: `emuR` (Winkelmann et al., 2021), `PraatR` (Albin, 2014), and `tidyverse` (Wickham, 2017).

5. Results

Investigating the frequency of phonemes, and of sequences of two or three phonemes (especially across word boundaries compared to word-internally), has been proposed in past research mainly to improve speech recognition system with statistical language modelling (Jassem, 1973; Basztura, 1992; Ziółko et al., 2009; Ziółko and Gałka, 2010; Kłosowski, 2017). However, such explorations are also useful to theorists investigating language variation in synchrony and language evolution through the lens of frequency-based exemplar models (Bybee, 2002).

For this preliminary proof-of-concept, we propose to first investigate the frequency of single phonemes. We will compare the ratio of each phoneme found in the data from Lingua Libre with the ratio of phonemes found in previous studies using controlled linguistic materials. Second, we will focus on Polish vowels and compare the formant values found in previous studies with the formant values of the vowels found in Lingua Libre. We focus on F1 and F2 since it has been shown that the most important acoustic property of vowels are positions and shapes of the first two formants (Izydorczy and Kłosowski, 1999).

5.1. Phoneme Frequency

With regard to the frequency of phonemes, Table 3 displays the results from 5 previous studies, all using written text (converted grapheme-to-phoneme) as data [5], as well as the ratio found from the Lingua Libre data.

We can see in Table 3 that the ratio found in Lingua Libre generally matches the ratio found in previous studies. Taking vowels as an example, /a/, /e/, and /o/ are nearly twice more frequent than the vowels /i/ and /u/. In terms of consonants, we also see that the consonants that have a low ratio in previous studies

	1973	**1992**	**2009**	**2010**	**2017**	LiLi
e	10.2	10.6	9.1	7.8	9.5	8.0
a	9.3	9.7	9.5	8.1	9.5	11.1
o	9.1	8.0	8.9	7.6	9.2	8.7
t	4.4	4.8	4.4	3.7	4.6	3.9
n	4.0	4.0	4.4	3.6	4.3	4.7
ɨ	4.1	3.8	3.6	3.1	4.1	3.1
j	4.5	4.4	3.7	3.2	4.0	3.3
i	3.9	3.4	4.3	3.6	4.0	4.3
r	3.6	3.2	4.6	3.7	3.7	2.5
s	3.0	2.8	3.6	2.9	3.7	3.4
v	3.5	2.9	3.7	3.1	3.4	4.0
p	3.1	3.0	3.2	2.7	3.4	2.8
u	3.4	2.8	3.3	2.7	3.3	2.7
m	3.5	3.2	2.9	2.6	3.1	2.6
k	2.7	2.5	2.9	2.4	2.9	4.8
ŋ	2.6	2.4	2.0	1.8	2.5	3.3
d	2.2	2.1	2.8	2.3	2.2	2.0
l	2.1	1.9	2.6	2.1	2.2	3.1
w	2.2	1.8	1.6	1.6	1.9	1.6
ʃ	2.0	1.9	1.2	1.1	1.7	1.6
f	1.5	1.3	1.6	1.3	1.6	1.4
z	1.8	1.5	1.9	1.6	1.6	1.7
ts	1.5	1.2	1.6	1.3	1.4	1.4
b	1.5	1.5	1.4	1.3	1.4	1.7
g	1.5	1.3	1.5	1.3	1.3	1.2
ɕ	1.5	1.6	0.9	0.9	1.3	1.3
tɕ	1.3	1.2	0.6	0.6	1.1	2.4
x	1.1	1.0	1.4	1.1	1.1	0.9
ʧ	1.2	1.2	0.9	0.8	1.1	1.4
ʒ	1.2	1.3	0.9	0.8	1.1	1.0
ɛ̃	0.7	0.6	0.6	0.5	0.7	0.1
c	n.a.	0.7	0.6	0.5	0.6	n.a.
dʑ	0.8	0.7	0.5	0.5	0.5	0.1
dz	0.2	0.2	0.2	0.2	0.2	0.1
ʑ	0.2	0.2	0.1	0.1	0.1	n.a.
ɟ	n.a.	0.1	0.2	0.1	0.1	n.a.
ʤ	0.0	0.1	0.1	0.1	0.1	0.1

Table 3: Rates (%) of each phoneme in 5 past corpora (Jassem, 1973; Basztura, 1992; Ziółko et al., 2009; Ziółko and Gałka, 2010; Kłosowski, 2017) and in Lingua Libre (abbreviated as LiLi). The frequencies from Lingua Libre are extracted based on all the recorded words available in Lingua Libre. The cells with 'n.a.' indicate that a phoneme was not found in the sample.

(e.g., dʑ, dz, ʑ, and ʤ) are also rare in the Lingua Libre data. As another example, the voiceless stops /p, k/ are regularly more frequent than their nasal counterparts /m, ŋ/, and both voiceless stops and nasals /t, n/, /p, m/ and /k, ŋ/ are more frequent than their voiced oral counterparts /d/, /b/ and /g/. Finally, alveolar obstruants are generally more frequent than labials and labials than velars, and voiceless obstruants than their voiced counterparts.

[5]Other studies, such as (Ziółko et al., 2014), have explored the frequency of diphones and triphones in oral corpora, but not that of single phonemes.

In Lingua Libre, however, compared to the lowest rate in the past five research papers, there are less /r/ (δ=0.7%) and, to a lesser extent, less /ɛ̃/ (δ= 0.4%), /dʑ/ (δ=0.4%), /d/ (δ=0.1%), /g/ (δ=0.1%) and /dz/ (δ=0.1%). On the other hand, compared to the highest rate from the past five analyses, there are much more /a/ (δ=1.4%) and /k/ (δ=1.9%), more /v/ (δ=0.3%), /ŋ/ (δ=0.7%) and /l/ (δ=0.5%), and, to a lesser extent, more /tʃ/ (δ=0.2%). This may be due to the fact that we investigate isolated words, i.e., mostly lexical words, whereas previous studies analyzed (written) connected speech, i.e., mixing lexical and functional words. It may also be due to the fact that contemporary vocabulary has evolved to some extent.

5.2. Vowel Qualities

In this subsection, we analyze the first and second formants of vowels. As a reference point, consider the values from 10 speakers analyzed with a Sona-Gram (Jassem, 1968) reproduced in Table 4, and the values from 10 other speakers analyzed spectrographically (Krzyśko et al., 1999) in Table 5.

	F1 (S-G)	F2 (S-G)	F1 (LiLi)	F2 (LiLi)
a	630-900	1100-1600	500-990	1300-2500
e	520-630	1600-2200	320-830	1670-2520
i	190-270	2100-2200	210-410	2220-2670
o	490-680	790-1100	420-810	1050-2650
u	240-340	560-780	300-650	950-2670

Table 4: Ranges of F1 and F2 values (in Hertz) for the 5 cardinal vowels of Polish according to the Sona-Gram analysis (S-G) of 8 male and 2 female speakers (Jassem, 1968) on the left and to our own analysis of Lingua Libre (LiLi) on the right.

As one can see from Table 4 , the values for F1 and F2 in Lingua Libre are much less precise, expanding on a larger range than in Jassem (1968)'s data. This effect is especially obvious for the F2 values of /a/, /o/ and /u/, which display, between their lowest and their highest values, a 1200 Hz delta for /a/, a 1600 Hz delta for /o/ and a 1720 Hz delta for /u/ in Lingua Libre, *vs* a 500 Hz delta for /a/, a 310 Hz delta for /o/ and a 220 Hz delta for /u/. The values for /e/ are more precise, as they span across 110 Hz for F1 and 600 Hz for F2 according to Jassem (1968) and across 510 Hz for F1 and 850 Hz for F2 according to our Lingua Libre data. The acoustic analysis is the most precise for /i/, which spans across 80 Hz for F1 and 100 Hz for F2 according to Jassem (1968), and across 200 Hz for F1 and 450 Hz for F2 according to the data from Lingua Libre. This may be due to the fact that our data come from 15 speakers with various sociolinguistic markers (e.g., 5 male, 3 female and 7 unknown), which is a known source of phonetic variation (Adda-Decker and Lamel, 2005). Another factor that could add noise in the data is the segmentation process, which might have included co-articulatory effects for the vowels, which could result in a larger variation of formants as well.

	F1 (spec)	F2 (spec)	F1 (LiLi)	F2 (LiLi)
a	724	1473	769	1891
e	538	1941	566	2126
i	322	2424	331	2446
o	556	1110	618	1850
u	386	940	470	1960

Table 5: Mean F1 and F2 values (in Hertz) for the 5 cardinal vowels of Polish according to the spectrographic analysis of 5 male and 5 female speakers (Krzyśko et al., 1999) on the left and to our own analysis of Lingua Libre (LiLi) on the right.

The means are also different in Lingua Libre and in Krzyśko et al. (1999)'s data, as can be seen in Table 5, with F1 and F2 being generally higher, especially for F2 with /u/ (δ=1020 Hz), /o/ (δ=764 Hz), /a/ (δ=418 Hz) and, to a lesser extent, /e/ (δ=185 Hz). This could be due, however, to the distribution of pre-palatal consonants in each dataset (Cavar et al., 2017), which advocates for more in depth analyses, in particular regarding immediate left and right contexts. An exception is /i/, for which our results match previous results, with only a 9 Hz difference between Krzyśko et al. (1999)'s and Lingua Libre's F1 and a 22 Hz difference between Krzyśko et al. (1999) and Lingua Libre's F2. These results are encouraging for future research.

6. Conclusion and Discussion

The main goal of this paper was to compare the phoneme inventory and the vowel formants extracted from Lingua Libre with similar data from previous studies on Polish phonetics, and show that such crowd-sourced data can be useful for linguistic investigations.

For the phoneme inventory, the distribution generally matches the existing knowledge. However, for formants, we observe a partial divergence with the formants' ranges and mean values identified in previous research. This divergence in formant values is, in a way, expected, since the recording environment of Lingua Libre is much less controlled than published phonetic experiments.

This divergence could be interpreted in two ways. On the one hand, it shows the limitation of the Lingua Libre data. On the other, it also shows that there is a considerable variation between crowd-made recordings and controlled recordings, while both data sources reflect a different facet of natural production of Polish. This divergence in absolute values thus does not negate the potential of Lingua Libre data, as the recordings could still be used to investigate the relative variation of formants across vowels of the same language. As an example, the data of Lingua Libre could still be used to measure the intra-speaker variation of Polish vowels.

The use of MAUS is also to be further analyzed, as the model could have induced noise in the data by including the surrounding context of different vowels during the segmentation process.

Finally, the issue of metadata is problematic in Lingua Libre. While each contributor can provide profile information such as gender or geographical location, not all contributors do so (as shown within the Polish contributors). Therefore, it is hard to control for such variables during our analysis based on data from Lingua Libre, although they would affect phonetic realization.

As a summary, while the Lingua Libre data is not as controlled as are materials in phonetic studies, we show that it still partially matches the output of existing studies. The variation of formants also hints toward the possibility that formants observed in daily recorded speech differ from those observed in controlled environments. Both environments are relevant not only for technological purposes such as speech recognition, but also for scientific aims such as typological comparisons. Therefore, they should both be considered in future studies. In the short-term, we hope to use our methodology to investigate diphones and triphones as well as more precise acoustic measures on vowels (i.e., F3, F4 and F5) and on consonants, especially /r/ and the fricatives, while controlling for gender and regional variation as much as possible.

7. Acknowledgements

This research was partially supported by Institut DATAIA and the MSH Paris-Saclay in the framework of the Excellency Award for the project OTELO - OnTologies pour l'Enrichissement de l'analyse Linguistique de l'Oral (PI Ioana Vasilescu and Fabian Suchanek), and by the French National Research Agency in the framework of the grant EVOGRAM: The role of linguistic and non-linguistic factors in the evolution of nominal classification systems, ANR-20-CE27-0021 (PI Marc Allassonnière-Tang). The authors would also like to thank the Wikimedia community for their interest in the project, and in particular Lucas Lévêque for his help on the Lingua Libre tool.

8. Bibliographical References

Adda-Decker, M. and Lamel, L. (2005). Do speech recognizers prefer female speakers? In *INTERSPEECH*.

Albin, A. (2014). Praatr: An architecture for controlling the phonetics software "praat" with the r programming language. *Journal of the Acoustical Society of America*, 135(4):2198.

Basztura, C. (1992). *Rozmawiac z komputerem*. Wydaw.

Bybee, J. (2002). Word frequency and context of use in the lexical diffusion of phonetically conditioned sound change. *Language Variation and Change*, 14(3):261–290.

Cavar, M. E., Lulich, S. M., and Nelson, M. (2017). Allophonic variation of polish vowels in the context of prepalatal consonants. *The Journal of the Acoustical Society of America*, 141(5):3820–3820.

Demenko, G., Möbius, B., and Klessa, K. (2009). The design of polish speech corpus for unit selection speech synthesis. In *Language Technology*.

Izydorczy, J. and Kłosowski, P. (1999). Acoustic properties of polish vowels. *Bulletin of the Polish Academy of Sciences. Technical Sciences*, Vol. 47, nr 1:29–37.

Jassem, W. (1958). A phonologic and acoustic classification of polish vowels. *STUF - Language Typology and Universals*, 11(1-4):299–319.

Jassem, W. (1968). Vowel formant frequencies as cues to speaker discrimination. *Speech Analysis and Synthesis*, 1:9–41.

Jassem, W. (1973). *Podstawy fonetyki akustycznej*. Panstwowe Wydaw Naukowen.

Jassem, W. (2003). Polish. *Journal of the international Phonetic Association*, 33(1):103–107.

Kipp, A., WesenickM, M.-B., and Schiel, F. (1997). 2004): Maus goes iterative. In *Proceedings of the Fifth European Conference on Speech Communication and Technology EUROSPEECH 1997*.

Kisler, T., Reichel, U., and Schiel, F. (2017). Multilingual processing of speech via web services. *Computer Speech & Language*, 45:326–347, September.

Kłosowski, P. (2017). Statistical analysis of orthographic and phonemic language corpus for word-based and phoneme-based polish language modelling. *EURASIP Journal on Audio, Speech, and Music Processing*, 1.

Krzyśko, M., Jassem, W., and Czajka, S. (1999). The formants of polish vowels:a multivariate analysis of variance with two factors. *Speech and Language Technology*, 3(3):173–189.

Lewis, M. P., Simons, G., and Fennig, C. D. (2013). Ethnologue: Languages of the world. *SIL International*.

Marjou, X. (2021). Oteann: Estimating the transparency of orthographies with an artificial neural network. In *Proceedings of the Third Workshop on Computational Typology and Multilingual NLP*, pages 1–9. Association for Computational Linguistics.

Schiel, F. (2004). 2004): Maus goes iterative. In *Proceedings of the LREC 2004*, pages 1015–1018.

Wickham, H. (2017). tidyverse: Easily install and load the Tidyverse. *R package version*, 1.2.1.

Winkelmann, R., Jaensch, K., Cassidy, S., and Harrington, J., (2021). *emuR: Main Package of the EMU Speech Database Management System*. R package version 2.3.0.

Ziółko, B. and Gałka, J. (2010). Polish phones statistics. In *Proceedings of the International Multiconfer-*

ence on *Computer Science and Information Technology*, pages 561–565. IEEE.

Ziółko, B., Gałka, J., Manandhar, S., Wilson, R. C., and Ziółko, M. (2009). Triphone statistics for polish language. In Zygmunt Vetulani et al., editors, *Human Language Technology. Challenges of the Information Society*, pages 63–73, Berlin, Heidelberg. Springer Berlin Heidelberg.

Ziółko, B., Żelasko, P., and Skurzok, D. (2014). Statistics of diphones and triphones presence on the word boundaries in the polish language. applications to asr. In *XXII Annual Pacific Voice Conference (PVC)*, pages 1–6.

9. Language Resource References

Ardila, R., Branson, M., Davis, K., Henretty, M., Kohler, M., Meyer, J., Morais, R., Saunders, L., Tyers, F. M., and Weber, G. (2020). Common voice: A massively-multilingual speech corpus. In *LREC*.

Demenko, G., Grocholewski, S., Klessa, K., Ogórkiewicz, J., Wagner, A., Lange, M., Śledziński, D., and Cylwik, N. (2008). Jurisdic: Polish speech database for taking dictation of legal texts. In Nicoletta Calzolari (Conference Chair), et al., editors, *Proceedings of the Sixth International Conference on Language Resources and Evaluation (LREC'08)*, Marrakech, Morocco, may. European Language Resources Association (ELRA). http://www.lrec-conf.org/proceedings/lrec2008/.

Demenko, G., Szymański, M., Cecko, R., Kuśmierek, E., Lange, M., Wegner, K., Klessa, K., and Owsianny, M. (2012). Development of large vocabulary continuous speech recognition for polish. *Acta Physica Polonica A*, 121(1A1A):A–086–A–091.

Durand, J., Laks, B., and Lyche, C. (2002). La phonologie du français contemporain: usages, variétés et structure. *Romanistische Korpuslinguistik-Korpora und gesprochene Sprache/Romance Corpus Linguistics – Corpora and Spoken Language*, 1.2.1:93–106.

Garofolo, J. S., Lamel, L. F., Fisher, W. M., Fiscus, J. G., Pallett, D. S., Dahlgren, N. L., and Zue, V. (1993). Timit acoustic-phonetic continuous speech corpus. *Linguistic Data Consortium*.

Greenberg, C., Martin, A., Graff, D., Walker, K., Jones, K., and Strassel, S. (2018). 2011 nist language recognition evaluation test set. *Linguistic Data Consortium*.

Jones, K., Graff, D., Walker, K., and Strassel, S. (2016). Multi-language conversational telephone speech 2011 – slavic group. *Linguistic Data Consortium*.

Lander, T. (2005). Cslu: 22 languages corpus. *Linguistic Data Consortium*.

Panayotov, V., Chen, G., Povey, D., and Khudanpur, S. (2015). Librispeech: An asr corpus based on public domain audio books. In *2015 IEEE International Conference on Acoustics, Speech and Signal Processing (ICASSP)*, pages 5206–5210.

Przepiórkowski, A., Bańko, M., Górski, R. L., and Lewandowska-Tomaszczyk, B. (2012). Narodowy korpus języka polskiego. *Wydawnictwo Naukowe PWN*.

Schultz, T. (2002). Globalphone: A multilingual speech and text database developed at karlsruhe university. In *Proceedings of the ICSLP*, pages 345–348.

Szwelnik, T., Kawalec, J., and Gutowska, D. (2019). Polish speech database. *Linguistic Data Consortium*.

Torreira, F., Adda-Decker, M., and Ernestus, M. (2010). The nijmegen corpus of casual french. *Speech Communication*, 52:201–212.

Proceedings of SIGUL2022 @LREC2022, pages 48–58
Marseille, 24-25 June 2022

Tupian Language Resources

Data, Tools, Analyses

Lorena Martín Rodríguez[*]
Tatiana Merzhevich[*]
Wellington Silva[O]
Tiago Tresoldi[‡]
Carolina Aragon[†]
Fabrício Ferraz Gerardi[*]
[*]Universität Tübingen
lorena.martin-rodriguez, tatiana.merzhevich, fabricio.gerardi@uni-tuebingen.de

[O]Fundação Getúlio Vargas-RJ
wellington.71319@gmail.com

[‡]Uppsala Universitet
tiago.tresoldi@lingfil.uu.se

[†]Universidade Federal da Paraíba
carolinac.aragon@gmail.com

Abstract

TuLaR (Tupian Language Resources) is a project for collecting, documenting, analyzing, and developing computational and pedagogical material for low-resource Brazilian indigenous languages. It provides valuable data for language research regarding typological, syntactic, morphological, and phonological aspects. Here we present TuLaR's databases, with special consideration to TuDeT (Tupian Dependency Treebanks), an annotated corpus under development for nine languages of the Tupian family, built upon the Universal Dependencies framework. The annotation within such a framework serves a twofold goal: enriching the linguistic documentation of the Tupian languages due to the rapid and consistent annotation, and providing computational resources for those languages, thanks to the suitability of our framework for developing NLP tools. We likewise present a related lexical database, some tools developed by the project, and examine future goals for our initiative.

Keywords: Tupian Languages, NLP, Amazonian Languages, Historical Linguistics, Treebanks, Morphology, Finite-State

1. Introduction

The Tupian Language Resources (TuLaR) project follows the precept of promoting linguistic resource development for minority or under-studied languages (Hinton, 2003; Pine and Turin, 2017), especially considering how limited availability interferes with the subsequent production of scientific knowledge and commercial support (Mager et al., 2018; Hedderich et al., 2021). In many scenarios, the lack of such resources leads scientific and commercial initiatives for computational linguistics to only engage with majority or dominant languages, even when there are multi- and cross-linguistic concerns. Such an effect builds up hidden biases against low-resourced languages, even from their own speakers, and, as such, our effort is in line with the objectives of the conference's call: by providing the computational foundations and facilitating the production of teaching material, we aim at fostering the direct participation of minority language communities in the development of computational resources and theoretical knowledge.

The goal of TuLaR is to contribute to the production of computational resources and linguistic knowledge for research and for cooperative work with indigenous communities, especially for those whose languages are categorized as threatened or vulnerable (Eberhard et al., 2021; Languages Project, 2020). It aims to improve the understanding of its morphology and syntax interrelations, thus facilitating their use in natural language processing tasks. For this, we are building different databases (lexical, syntactic, morphological, and fauna-flora) that also aim to consider the historical relations among Tupian languages, as well as its contemporary use, in order to support multilingual tasks that can contribute in increasing the linguistic and cultural knowledge of South American indigenous languages.

TuLaR comprises four databases: TuLeD (Tupian

Lexical Database) (Gerardi et al., 2021b; Gerardi et al., 2021a) with 90 languages (upcoming release), TuMoD (Tupian Morphological Database) (Gerardi, 2022a) with 51 languages, TuPAn (Tupian Plants and Animals) (Gerardi, 2022b) with 25 languages, and TuDeT (Tupian Dependency Treebanks) (Gerardi et al., 2022) with 9 languages. All databases are work-in-progress in different stages of completion.

Among this project databases, this work focuses on the specifications of TuDeT in view of its applicability and results (current and future outcomes). On the scientific side we are concentrating on measuring syntactic complexity of the languages, but we extend our tools used so that we can apply them for all treebanks in Universal Dependencies (UD) (De Marneffe et al., 2021).

On the practical side, we also intend to use the collection of sentences in TuDeT to create educational materials for the communities. One of the main goals of TuDeT is to raise literacy by promoting new teaching materials in indigenous context, to help the communities in stand against language domination.[1]

It would not be out of place at this point to discuss available tools or corpora for Tupian languages, but none exists. TuDeT is the first collection of sentences open-access, despite its inceptive state, as are the tools being built within, such as the Guajajara morphological analyzer (see Section 4.3.). One almost obvious exception is Paraguayan Guarani, a language that enjoys official status and spoken by about six million people. We are aware of a morphological analyzer (Kuznetsova and Tyers, 2021), but not of annotated or tokenized corpora. A parallel corpus Guarani-Spanish is being developed (Chiruzzo et al., 2020). Additional documentation data exists for Aweti (Drude and Reiter, 2005) and Ache (Thompson et al., 2012), but their access is restricted.

Here we introduce our project and discuss its purpose (this section), before describing its main components: the dependency treebanks in terms of their basis and process and annotation (Section 2.) and the lexical database (Section 3.). We address the incipient development of related NLP tools (Section 4.) before concluding remarks that discuss the relevance and potential outcomes of the project's output (Section 5.).

2. The Tupian Dependency Treebanks (TuDeT)

All languages in TuDeT belong to the Tupian family, one of the largest language families in South-America (Rodrigues and Cabral, 2002; Rodrigues and Cabral, 2012; Galucio et al., 2015). The vitality level of these languages varies significantly. A sociolinguistic fact about them is the non-correlation between the amount of speakers and the status of the languages. Some languages with only a few hundred speakers each (such as Ka'apor and Karo) are less threatened than others with thousands of speakers (such as Guajajara and Munduruku) which, however, are in an alarmingly rapid process of shifting to Portuguese and abandoning native languages. The nine languages in TuDeT are shown with their respective number of speakers and status from (Eberhard et al., 2021) in Table 1. The presence of two extinct languages, Tupinamba and Old Guarani, plays an important role in understanding diachronic aspects of this language family. The geographic distribution of the languages in TuDeT is shown in Figure 1.

Annotated sentences in TuDeT stem from various sources. For the extinct languages, Tupinamba and Old Guarani, all texts known for these languages are being annotated: grammatical descriptions, e.g. (de Anchieta, 19331595; de Montoya, 1876a), religious texts, e.g. (Araújo, 19521618; de Montoya, 1876b), poetry and theater plays. For the modern languages, we took sentences from grammatical descriptions e.g. (Gabas Jr, 1999; Braga, 2005; Rose, 2011; Aragon, 2014), fieldwork data collection, articles describing aspects of the languages and stories told by native speakers, e.g. (Castro and Guajajara, 2020; Campos Castro and Gervason Defilippo, 2021). The current state of TuDeT treebanks is given in Table 2.

Language	Glottocode	Speakers	Status
Akuntsu	akun1241	3	Nearly extinct
Guajajara	guaj1255	12000	Vigorous
Ka'apor	urb1250	600	Developing
Karo	karo1305	200	Vigorous
Makurap	maku1278	40	Moribund
Munduruku	mund1330	5000	Threatened
Old Guarani	oldp1258	0	Extinct
Teko	emer1243	400	Vigorous
Tupinamba	tupi1273	0	Extinct

Table 1: Languages in TuDeT.

A relevant feature of TuDeT is its unified terminology for the morphological annotations. Having consulted various language descriptions, we have arrived at a general terminology so that the morphological features and their values are the same, as far as possible, for all languages (in TuDeT). Since different descriptions often treat the same constructions in different ways and using different terminology, we have adapted these observations to the framework of Universal Dependencies considering diachronic and synchronic aspects of the

[1]The project is about to publish a book for the alphabetization of Makurap children (Tupi, Tupari) (Aragon and Makurap, 2022).

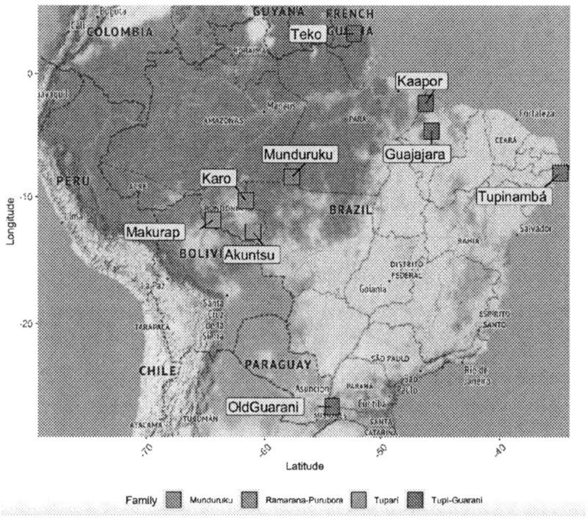

Figure 1: Languages in TuDeT.

languages.

2.1. The Universal Dependencies Framework

Universal Dependencies (De Marneffe et al., 2021) is a multilingual formalism for treebanking, including annotation guidelines[2] for dependency relations, morphological analysis, part-of-speech tagging, and other linguistic features. Besides the languages in TuDeT, one more Tupian language is present in UD, Mbya Guarani, so that ten languages represent the Tupian family in UD. Although we acknowledge some drawbacks of UD, e.g., (Osborne and Gerdes, 2019), it is still the best open-access possibility available. The annotations use the standard UD style POS tag inventory, morphological features and universal dependency relations from Universal Dependencies v2 (Nivre et al., 2020), and are encoded using the CoNLL-U format[3]. They are enriched with additional dependency subtypes and language-specific morphological features to reflect specific traits of Tupian languages.

This combination of standard annotations with specification through subtypes makes UD a satisfactory annotation framework for the analysis of individual languages and for the study of linguistic typology. Each of the treebanks is accompanied by a documentation for all features, syntactic, morphological and POS.

The adaptability of the UD framework to language-specific features is relevant to treat characteristic features of Tupian languages and facilitating NLP tasks. One example of specific values that characterize these languages are ideophones, which show unique syntactic patterns as they can co-occur with certain lexical items in the sentence (restricted collocations) and they are usually exposed to different reduplication processes (Voeltz and Kilian-Hatz, 2001). In UD, ideophones are not part of the POS tag-set, therefore their description in our treebanks requires special treatment. Another case concerns the so called relational prefixes (Rodrigues, 2009), a feature described uniquely for some Brazilian indigenous languages, which mark syntactic contiguity or non-contiguity of heads and their dependents.

Another advantage of the UD framework is that its extended documentation and highly standardized annotations make it suitable for rapid, consistent annotation as well as easily comprehended by non-linguist audiences. This contributes to our goal of increasing the linguistic documentation and understanding of the Tupian languages.

Moreover, the competitive scores reached in the ConLL 2017 and 2018 Shared Tasks, illustrate the suitability of the framework in developing high-accuracy computer parsers and other downstream NLP tasks (Zeman et al., 2018). Thanks to this, we can develop NLP tools employing the annotated data (see Section 4.), such as the morphological analyzers that are being built for Guajajara and Munduruku, which rely almost exclusively on the respective treebanks.

Alternatives such as SUD (Gerdes et al., 2018) are worth consideration and a future conversion to a surface-syntactic annotation schema and parallel maintenance is planned.

2.2. The Annotation Process

Initially, all annotations were/are being carried out manually by linguists and computational linguists with a strong background knowledge of Tupian languages. Each treebank has one main annotator and all annotations are revised by the two Tupian specialists in the team.

2.2.1. Data standardization

Most of the languages present in TuDeT either lack a standardized orthography or have only recently acquired one. Therefore, we employ rule-based approaches to unify the orthographic differences found in the texts to be annotated. This is done with a two-fold approach:

Phonetic representation: the different sources annotated employ different symbols for certain sounds. We unify the texts in a single orthographic representation of the phonemes. For example, the glottal stop /ʔ/ is generally represented by an apostrophe ('), but we represent it using its IPA symbol (ʔ).

Word boundaries: the sources do not agree whether or not certain morphemes are bound. This affects mainly affixes, clitics, and certain particles.

[2]https://universaldependencies.org/guidelines.html
[3]https://universaldependencies.org/format.html

We decide the status of these morphemes based on diachronic, typological, and syntactic criteria.

2.2.2. Manual annotation

We combine manual approaches with supervised computational methods for the annotation of the linguistic corpora. We start by manually annotating a subset of the linguistic data according to the UD framework described above. The morphosyntactic features of the sentences are encoded using three main linguistic aspects: POS tags, morphological features, and dependency relations.

POS tags: Parts-of-speeches in UD are a predefined tag-set, but it allows for a language-specific tag-set as well. Tupian languages are challenging for theories of word-classes as also are native American languages or languages of Southeast-Asia (Mithun, 2001; Van Valin Jr, 2008; Enfield, 2021). In establishing word-classes for the languages in TuDeT, we adopt an approach suggested by the literature (Croft, 1991; Croft, 2001; Croft, 2022a; Haspelmath, 2021) which avoids the splitting and lumping of word-classes (Croft, 2022b; Croft, 2022a) and accounts for the fact that all lexical roots in many Tupian languages are (existential) predicates, which require additional morphology for functioning as arguments, even roots that are semantically "things or objects". Some treebanks lack the adjective label (ADJ) as a POS, since this label is not relevant – a feature already noticed in the early Jesuitic descriptions of (Old) Guarani and Tupinamba (Alexander-Bakkerus et al., 2020).

Features: The morphological information of each token also stems from a predefined tag-set expanded with language-specific features and values. All features and values are explained in the standardized UD documentation style.

Based on the experience of some team members with Tupian languages, as linguists and field workers, we have adopted some unified terminology for morphological features which often contradicts descriptions of these languages. One example is the controversial status of the so called relational morpheme (R_2), which marks the non-contiguity of head and its dependent (Meira and Drude, 2013; Cabral, 2000). Many authors (Rose, 2011; Harrison and Harrison, 2013) treat it as a third person marker, but in the TuDeT treebanks, similar constructions are marked with the same features and values.

(1) a. Mari **i**-purag
Mari **r₂**-beauty
"Mari is beautiful"

b. Kujã **i**-poraŋ
Woman **r₂**-beauty
"The woman is beautiful"

c. Wãĩwĩ **i**-puruʔa
woman **r₂**-pregnant
"The woman is pregnant"

Dependency relations: We use the dependency relations from the UD guidelines along with certain language-specific subtypes, e.g. the relations *obl:subj* and *obl:obj* are employed in strictly head-marking languages such as Tupinamba, where the core arguments are bound to the predicate as a single phonological word, so that NPs related to these arguments cannot be the argument themselves and thus must be in a different dependency relation. This can be seen in Figures 2 and 3, where the strictly head-marking character is considered by the subtypes of the oblique relation, since the root contains the predicate and two core-arguments.

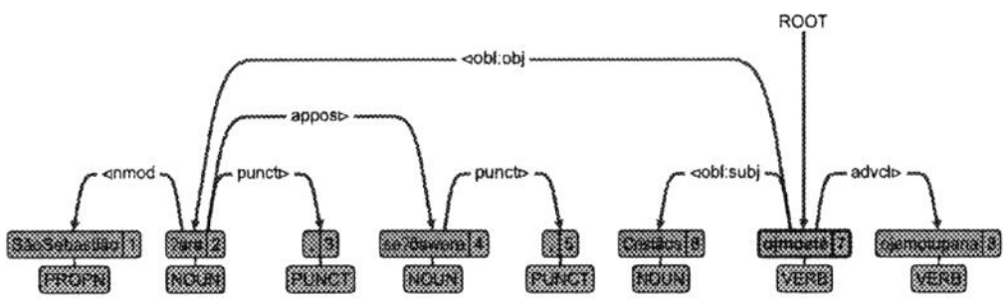

Figure 2: Example of dependency annotation from the Tupinamba UD-treebank.

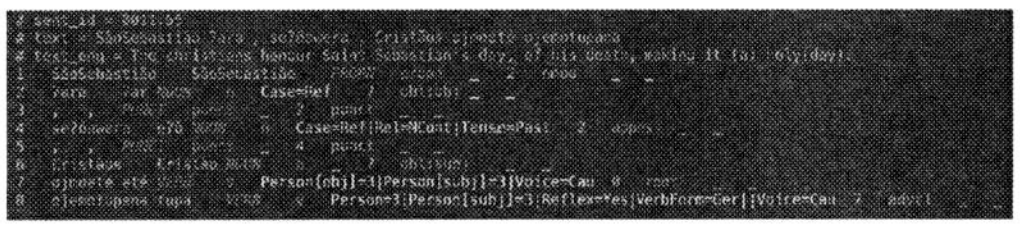

Figure 3: Example of annotation in CoNLL-U format from the Tupinamba UD-treebank.

2.2.3. Supervised annotation

For the supervised annotation, we employ UDPipe 2 (Straka, 2018), a multi-task system for automatic annotation within the UD framework which performs with high accuracy for several languages. We train the model using the manually annotated corpora of sentences available. The resulting annotations are then revised and corrected before their insertion into the treebanks. As expected, the output of the model improves proportionally to the number of annotated sentences. Guajajara is a good example for this approach: the first release of the Guajajara UD-treebank contained 276 sentences. After 500 sentences were reached, this manually annotated dataset served as a training model for automatic dependency parsing. The accuracy of a predictive model has been proven positive, with an accuracy of 99.96%. Currently, the treebank has been enlarged up to 1126 sentences, which should allow for more precision and consequently better quality of the automatically annotated sentences. Transfer approaches have been implemented for Paraguayan Guarani (Mager et al., 2021), but the performance showed lower automatic scores. Therefore, we initially excluded the possibility of using transfer approaches. However, there has been recent promising work regarding zero-shot methods (Blum, 2022), so transfer approaches could be considered to improve the annotation process.

Table 2 contains the number of sentences and tokens that are part of each TuDeT treebank. It is relevant to mention that not all the treebanks have been created at the same time, which is reflected in the quantity of annotated texts.

Language	Sentences	Tokens
Akuntsu	243	1056
Guajajara	1126	8702
Ka'apor	83	366
Karo	674	2319
Makurap	31	146
Munduruku	158	1016
Old Guarani	59	212
Teko	100	232
Tupinamba	546	4089

Table 2: Amount of sentences and tokens in each TuDeT treebank.

3. TuLeD

The Tupian Lexical Database (TuLeD) is the largest online database dedicated to languages of a South-American family. It is an open-source database[4], which provides an extensive list of lexical items with cognate assignment, phonetic alignment (shown in Figure 4), cultural or linguistic notes, and borrowing information. The data is presented in a standardized format according to the CLDF (cross-linguistic data format) standards (Forkel et al., 2018), and corresponds to the main principles of FAIRness (Findability, Accessibility, Interoperability, and Reusability) (Wilkinson et al., 2016), which enables ease of access, straightforward sharing and manipulation. Such word lists can be applied in typological language comparison and other linguistic tasks. This database comprises 78 languages, 404 concepts[5]. The concepts are connected to CONCEPTICON glosses (List et al., 2016), which allow for a network of semantic relationships cross-linguistically. The geographic distribution of the languages and language families presented in TuLeD is shown in Figure 5.

[4]https://tular.clld.org/contributions/tuled

[5]The next release of TuLeD will comprise 91 languages and 650 concepts.

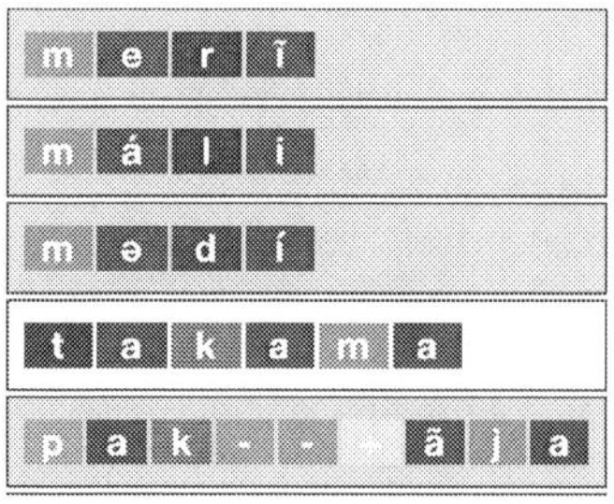

Figure 4: Example of phonetic alignment from TuLeD for three different cognate classes.

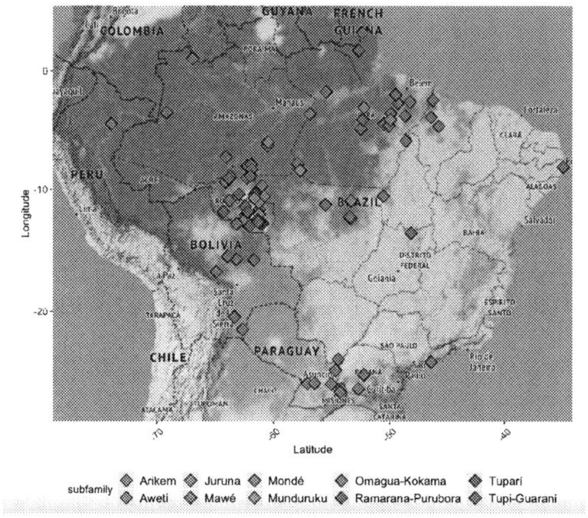

Figure 5: Map of languages in TuLeD colored according to sub-group.

Although TuLeD cannot yet be considered as a dictionary (it does not supply information about, for example, grammar, usage, and synonym discrimination), it plays an important role in laying out ways to help the process of vocabulary learning besides accommodating the phonetic-phonological profile of the languages. TuLeD, besides containing the traditional items of the Swadesh List (Swadesh, 1955), which are said to be the most borrowing-resistant items of languages, also contains culturally relevant items for the Tupian populations (Ferraz Gerardi et al., 2021).

Two additional databases are part of TuLaR: TuMoD (Tupian morphological database) and TuPAn (Tupian plants and animals). As they are under intensive development and have not been publicly released yet, they are not discussed here.

4. TuDeT Tools

The development of NLP tools is an important part of the project and is still in its initial phase. As of now, two tools are almost ready for release, and are presented below.

4.1. TuDeTstats

In order to track relevant statistics from the treebanks and measure syntactic complexity, which are informative of synchronic and diachronic aspects of the languages, we have built a web application which uses two different approaches. On one side, complexity measures are computed (e.g. MDD: mean dependency distance in a sentence (Gibson, 1998), LEFT: proportion of left dependents (Chen and Gerdes, 2017), NDD: normalized dependency distance (Lei and Jockers, 2020)) along with part-of-speech tags and syntactic dependencies (using code from (van Cranenburgh, 2019))[6]. On the other side, we have added unigrams, and selected bi- and trigrams of POS tags along with a raw count of left dependents [7].

The combination of these complexity measures with n-grams, as we show, performs better than the complexity measures alone. With Linear Discriminant Analysis (LDA), for example, the inclusion of n-grams can account for family membership. The family-cluster is less clear when only complexity measures are used. This is shown in Figure 6 where only complexity measures were used to cluster according to family membership languages of five different families in UD[8]. Figure 7 shows the clusters combining complexity measures and selected n-grams alongside with HeadLeft. Measures such as these are important because they can tell us how structurally different text types are for the family's internal analyzes.

4.2. Visualization

TuDeTstats is built in the R programming language (R Core Team, 2021) with the Shiny package (RStudio, Inc, 2014) for reactive web applications. Together, they provide access to modern analytics and visualization algorithms for linguistic research. Figure 8 shows the TuDeTStats application with selected measures displayed for the Tupian treebanks in UD.

4.3. Morphological analyzers

Based on the collected texts and the morphology presented in the treebank, a finite-state transducer for Munduruku is being built using HFST (Lindén et al., 2009) and Xerox functions. The analyzer contains a lexicon of root words, morphological and phonological rules, and composition operators. Another morphological analyzer for Guajajara is in the early stages of development, also using HFST, and we have plans to experiment with FOMA (Hulden, 2009) and OpenFST (Allauzen et al., 2007). The training set for the lexicon was extracted from the Guajajara UD-treebank, which contains 700 unique lemmas. Unfortunately, it is difficult to evaluate the analyzer at an early stage. However, a test-set for accuracy evaluation is being developed as the amount of rules increase.

A significant advantage of these morphological analyzers is that they can be adapted to other languages of the Tupian family. For example, we have already started to build a analyzer of Tupinamba based on the templates available for Guajajara. Rule-based systems of a morphological analyzer can be used for future NLP applications, such as morphological inflection and derivation tasks, automatic annotation of morphological features and machine translation. An example of an output from the Munduruku morphological analyzer is shown in Figure 9[9].

5. Conclusion

TuLaR contributes to expanding the linguistic description, documentation, and computational linguistic resources available for under-researched and low-resource languages of the Tupian family through nine languages following the Universal Dependencies framework and allows developing NLP tools, providing analyzes at different levels (phonology, morphology, and syntax). Future directions may focus on the development of NLP tools such as tokenizers, lemmatizers, morphological analyzers or automatic translation of written texts, as well as web-based systems with new language resources. All these are valuable initiatives to increase linguistic policies regarding endangered languages, rekindling ways to revitalize not only the language and culture, but also the indigenous community identity (Hinton, 2003; Pine and Turin, 2017).

Thus, the creation of linguistic resources presented for the Tupian family in this paper is an example of how computational linguistics products correlate with linguistic research and indigenous communities' necessities in a way to implement efforts to ensure the triad **documentation-conservation-revitalization**, contributing towards a more inclusive computational linguistics.

An important aspect of the work here presented lies is that all tools and the data are available in open access. We are glad to engage in academic cooperation, as well as with the communities. We

[6]We are aware of the controversial topic of complexity in language and measures of syntactic complexity, nonetheless it is appropriate to employ the term for the measures implemented in our application– see (Jiménez, 2018).

[7]The web application can be accessed in its pre-release version from `https://ffgerardi.shinyapps.io/TuDeT-Stats/`.

[8]We have included larger figures in Appendix A.

[9]The Munduruku finite-state morphological analyzer can be accessed from `https://github.com/LanguageStructure/Munduruku_FST`.

look forward to participating in similar projects, but we also welcome collaborators in our projects.

6. Acknowledgements

The research presented in this paper is supported by the by European Research Council (ERC) under the European Union's Horizon 2020 research and innovation programme (Grant agreement No. 834050).

7. Bibliographical References

Alexander-Bakkerus, A., Rebeca, R. F., Zack, L., Zwartjes, O., and Case, J., (2020). *Were there ever any adjectives? The recognition of the absence of an autonomous adjective class in Tupi-Guarani as demonstrated in the earliest missionary grammars.*, page 139–155. Brill.

Allauzen, C., Riley, M., Schalkwyk, J., Skut, W., and Mohri, M. (2007). Openfst: A general and efficient weighted finite-state transducer library. In *International Conference on Implementation and Application of Automata*, pages 11–23. Springer.

Aragon, C. C. and Makurap, A. O. (2022). *Ensinando a língua Makurap*, volume 1. Oikos: São Leopoldo.

Aragon, C. C. (2014). *A grammar of Akuntsú, a Tupían language.* Ph.D. thesis, University of Hawai 'i„ at Mānoa. unpublished PhD thesis.

Araújo, A. d. (1952[1618]). *Catecismo na língua brasílica.* Pontifícia Universidade Católica do Rio de Janeiro.

Blum, F. (2022). Evaluating zero-shot transfers and multilingual models for dependency parsing and POS tagging within the low-resource language family tupían. In *Proceedings of the 60th Annual Meeting of the Association for Computational Linguistics: Student Research Workshop*, pages 1–9, Dublin, Ireland, may. Association for Computational Linguistics.

Braga, A. d. O. (2005). *Aspects morphosyntaxiques de la langue Makurap/Tupi.* Ph.D. thesis, Toulouse 2. unpublished PhD thesis.

Cabral, A. (2000). Flexão relacional na família tupí-guaraní. *ABRALIN, Boletim da Associação Brasieira de Lingüística*, 25:233–262.

Campos Castro, R. and Gervason Defilippo, J. (2021). Histórias originárias em tenetehára (tupí-guaraní) como estratégia de revitalização linguística. In Patrícia Goulart Tondineli, editor, *(Re)vitalizar línguas minorizadas e/ou ameaçadas: teorias, metodologias, pesquisas e experiências*, pages 109–138. Coleção Pós-Graduação da UNIR - EDUFRO.

Castro, R. C. and Guajajara, P. C. (2020). Izipi mehe: Cibercaminhos linguísticos e literários para a preservação da cultura tenetehára. *Revista Brasileira de Linguística Antropológica*, 12:251–282.

Chen, X. and Gerdes, K. (2017). Classifying languages by dependency structure. typologies of delexicalized universal dependency treebanks. In *Proceedings of the fourth international conference on dependency linguistics (Depling 2017)*, pages 54–63.

Chiruzzo, L., Amarilla, P., Ríos, A., and Giménez Lugo, G. (2020). Development of a Guarani - Spanish parallel corpus. In *Proceedings of the 12th Language Resources and Evaluation Conference*, pages 2629–2633, Marseille, France, May. European Language Resources Association.

Croft, W. (1991). *Syntactic categories and grammatical relations: The cognitive organization of information.* University of Chicago Press.

Croft, W. (2001). *Radical construction grammar: Syntactic theory in typological perspective.* Oxford University Press on Demand.

Croft, W. (2022a). *Morphosyntax: Constructions of the World's Languages.* Cambridge University Press. Draft version of 2021.

Croft, W. (2022b). Word classes in radical construction grammar. In Eva van Lier, editor, *Oxford handbook of word classes.* Oxford University Press.

de Anchieta, J. ((1933)[1595]). *Arte de gramática da língua mais usada na costa do Brasil.* Imprensa Nacional.

De Marneffe, M.-C., Manning, C. D., Nivre, J., and Zeman, D. (2021). Universal dependencies. *Computational linguistics*, 47(2):255–308.

de Montoya, A. R. (1876a). *Arte de la lengua guarani o mas bien tupi.* Faesy & Frick.

de Montoya, A. R. (1876b). *Catecismo de la lengua guaraní*, volume 4. BG Teubner.

Drude, S. and Reiter, S. (2005). Collection "awetí".

Eberhard, D. M., Simons, G. F., and Fennig, C. D. (2021). *Ethnologue: Languages of the World. Twenty-fourth edition*, volume 16. SIL international, Dallas, TX.

Enfield, N. J. (2021). *The Languages of Mainland Southeast Asia.* Cambridge Language Surveys. Cambridge University Press.

Ferraz Gerardi, F., Aragon, C. C., and Reichert, S. (2021). When the macaw teaches you to eat the brazil nut: Introducing a concept list of tupían languages. Computer-Assisted Language Comparison in Practice, 01/12/2021, https://calc.hypotheses.org/2988, 12.

Forkel, R., List, J.-M., Greenhill, S., Rzymski, C., Bank, S., Cysouw, M., Hammarström, H., Haspelmath, M., Kaiping, G., and Gray, R. (2018). Cross-linguistic data formats, advancing data sharing and re-use in comparative linguistics. *Scientific Data*, 5:180205, 10.

Gabas Jr, N. (1999). *A Grammar of Karo*. Ph.D. thesis, University of California, Santa Barbara. unpublished PhD thesis.

Galucio, A. V., Meira, S., Birchall, J., Moore, D., Gabas Júnior, N., Drude, S., Storto, L., Picanço, G., and Rodrigues, C. R. (2015). Genealogical relations and lexical distances within the tupian linguistic family. *Boletim do Museu Paraense Emílio Goeldi. Ciências Humanas*, 10(2):229–274.

Gerardi, F. F., Reichert, S., and Aragon, C. C. (2021a). Tuled (tupían lexical database): introducing a database of a south american language family. *Language Resources and Evaluation*, 55(4):997–1015.

Gerardi, F. F., Reichert, S., Aragon, C., List, J.-M., and Wientzek, T. (2021b). Tuled: Tupían lexical database, 03.

Gerardi, F. F., Reichert, S., Aragon, C., Martín-Rodríguez, L., Godoy, G., and Merzhevich, T. (2022). Tudet: Tupían dependency treebank, 05.

Gerardi, F. F. (2022a). Tumod: Tupían morphological database. Forthcoming.

Gerardi, F. F. (2022b). Tupan: Tupían plants and animals. Forthcoming.

Gerdes, K., Guillaume, B., Kahane, S., and Perrier, G. (2018). SUD or surface-syntactic Universal Dependencies: An annotation scheme near-isomorphic to UD. In *Proceedings of the Second Workshop on Universal Dependencies (UDW 2018)*, pages 66–74, Brussels, Belgium, November. Association for Computational Linguistics.

Gibson, E. (1998). Linguistic complexity: Locality of syntactic dependencies. *Cognition*, 68(1):1–76.

Harrison, C. and Harrison, C. (2013). *Dicionário guajajara-português*. Anápolis: International Linguistic Association (SIL).

Haspelmath, M. (2021). Word class universals and language-particular analysis. In Fulano, editor, *Oxford handbook of word classes*. Oxford University Press.

Hedderich, M. A., Lange, L., Adel, H., Strötgen, J., and Klakow, D. (2021). A survey on recent approaches for natural language processing in low-resource scenarios. In *Proceedings of the 2021 Conference of the North American Chapter of the Association for Computational Linguistics: Human Language Technologies*.

Hinton, L. (2003). Language revitalization. *Annual Review of Applied Linguistics*, 23:44–57.

Hulden, M. (2009). Foma: a finite-state compiler and library. In *Proceedings of the Demonstrations Session at EACL 2009*, pages 29–32.

Jiménez, C. C. (2018). *Complejidad lingüística: orígenes y revisión crítica del concepto de lengua compleja*. Peter Lang.

Kuznetsova, A. and Tyers, F. M. (2021). A finite-state morphological analyser for paraguayan guaraní. In *Proceedings of the First Workshop on Natural Language Processing for Indigenous Languages of the Americas*, pages 81–89.

Languages Project, E. (2020). Catalogue of endangered languages.

Lei, L. and Jockers, M. L. (2020). Normalized dependency distance: Proposing a new measure. *Journal of Quantitative Linguistics*, 27(1):62–79.

Lindén, K., Silfverberg, M., and Pirinen, T. (2009). Hfst tools for morphology – an efficient open-source package for construction of morphological analyzers. In Cerstin Mahlow et al., editors, *State of the Art in Computational Morphology*, volume 41, pages 28–47, 08.

List, J.-M., Cysouw, M., and Forkel, R. (2016). Concepticon: A resource for the linking of concept lists. In *Proceedings of the Tenth International Conference on Language Resources and Evaluation (LREC'16)*, pages 2393–2400, Portorož, Slovenia, May. European Language Resources Association (ELRA).

Mager, M., Gutierrez-Vasques, X., Sieera, G., and Meza, I. (2018). Challenges of language technologies for the indigenous languages of the americas. In *Proceedings of the 27th International Con- ference on Computational Linguistics*, pages 55–69.

Mager, M., Oncevay, A., Ebrahimi, A., Ortega, J., Rios, A., Fan, A., Gutierrez-Vasques, X., Chiruzzo, L., Giménez-Lugo, G., Ramos, R., Meza Ruiz, I. V., Coto-Solano, R., Palmer, A., Mager-Hois, E., Chaudhary, V., Neubig, G., Vu, N. T., and Kann, K. (2021). Findings of the AmericasNLP 2021 shared task on open machine translation for indigenous languages of the Americas. In *Proceedings of the First Workshop on Natural Language Processing for Indigenous Languages of the Americas*, pages 202–217, Online, June. Association for Computational Linguistics.

Meira, S. and Drude, S. (2013). Sobre a origem histórica dos "prefixos relacionais" das línguas tupí-guaraní. *Cadernos de Etnolingüística*, 5(1):1–30.

Mithun, M. (2001). *The languages of native North America*. Cambridge University Press.

Nivre, J., de Marneffe, M.-C., Ginter, F., Hajič, J., Manning, C. D., Pyysalo, S., Schuster, S., Tyers, F., and Zeman, D. (2020). Universal Dependencies v2: An Evergrowing Multilingual Treebank Collection.

Osborne, T. and Gerdes, K. (2019). The status of function words in dependency grammar: A critique of universal dependencies (ud). *Glossa: a journal of general linguistics*, 4(1):1–28.

Pine, A. and Turin, M. (2017). *Language revitalization*. Oxford University Press.

R Core Team, (2021). *R: A Language and Environment for Statistical Computing*. R Foundation for Statistical Computing, Vienna, Austria.

Rodrigues, A. D. and Cabral, A. (2002). Revendo a classificação interna da família Tupí-Guaraní. *Línguas Indígenas Brasileiras. Fonologia, Gramática e História, Atas do I Encontro Internacional do GTLI da ANPOLL*, 1.

Rodrigues, A. D. and Cabral, A. S. (2012). Tupían. In Lyle Campbell et al., editors, *The Indigenous Languages of South America*, volume 2, pages 495–574. de Gruyter, Berlin.

Rodrigues, A. D. (2009). A case of affinity among tupí, karíb, and macro-jê. *Revista Brasileira de Linguística Antropológica*, 1(1):137–162.

Rose, F. (2011). *Grammaire del L'Émérillon Teko, une langue Tupi-Guarani de Guyane Française*. Peeters.

RStudio, Inc, (2014). *shiny: Easy web applications in R*. URL: `http://shiny.rstudio.com`.

Straka, M. (2018). UDPipe 2.0 prototype at CoNLL 2018 UD shared task. In *Proceedings of the CoNLL 2018 Shared Task: Multilingual Parsing from Raw Text to Universal Dependencies*, pages 197–207, Brussels, Belgium, October. Association for Computational Linguistics.

Swadesh, M. (1955). Towards greater accuracy in lexicostatistic dating. *International journal of American linguistics*, 21(2):121–137.

Thompson, W. M., Roessler, E.-M., Hauck, J. D., Susnik, B., and Sousa, L. T. (2012). Collection "aché".

van Cranenburgh, A. (2019). udstyle. `https://github.com/andreasvc/udstyle`. unpublished code.

Van Valin Jr, R. D. (2008). Rps and the nature of lexical and syntactic categories in role and reference grammar. In Robert D Van Valin Jr, editor, *Investigations of the syntax-semantics-pragmatics interface*, pages 161–78. John Benjamins, Amsterdam.

Voeltz, F. E. and Kilian-Hatz, C. (2001). *Ideophones*. John Benjamins Publishing.

Wilkinson, M. D., Dumontier, M., Aalbersberg, I. J., Appleton, G., Axton, M., Baak, A., Blomberg, N., Boiten, J.-W., da Silva Santos, L. B., Bourne, P. E., et al. (2016). The fair guiding principles for scientific data management and stewardship. *Scientific data*, 3(1):1–9.

Zeman, D., Hajič, J., Popel, M., Potthast, M., Straka, M., Ginter, F., Nivre, J., and Petrov, S. (2018). CoNLL 2018 shared task: Multilingual parsing from raw text to universal dependencies. In *Proceedings of the CoNLL 2018 Shared Task: Multilingual Parsing from Raw Text to Universal Dependencies*, pages 1–21, Brussels, Belgium, October. Association for Computational Linguistics.

A Appendix

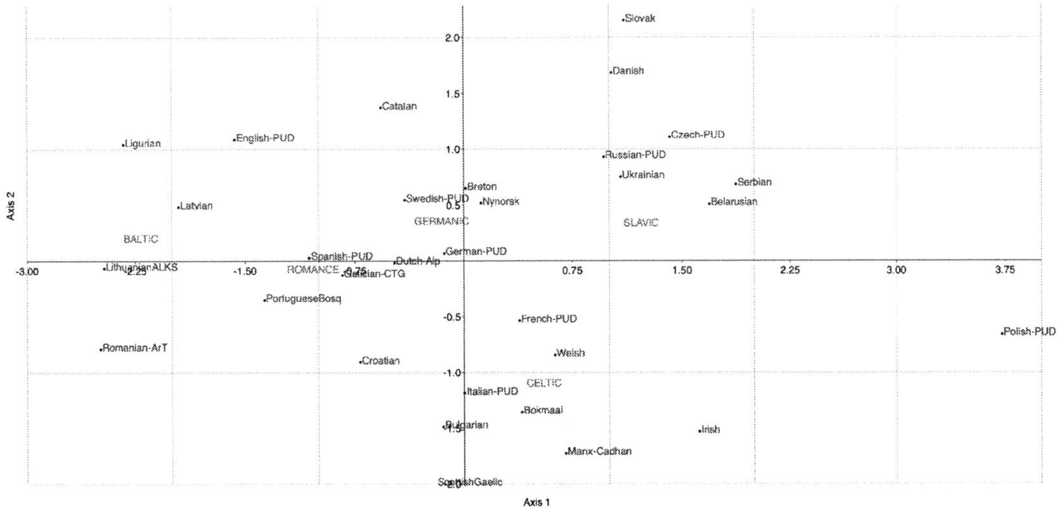

Figure 6: LDA using complexity measures.

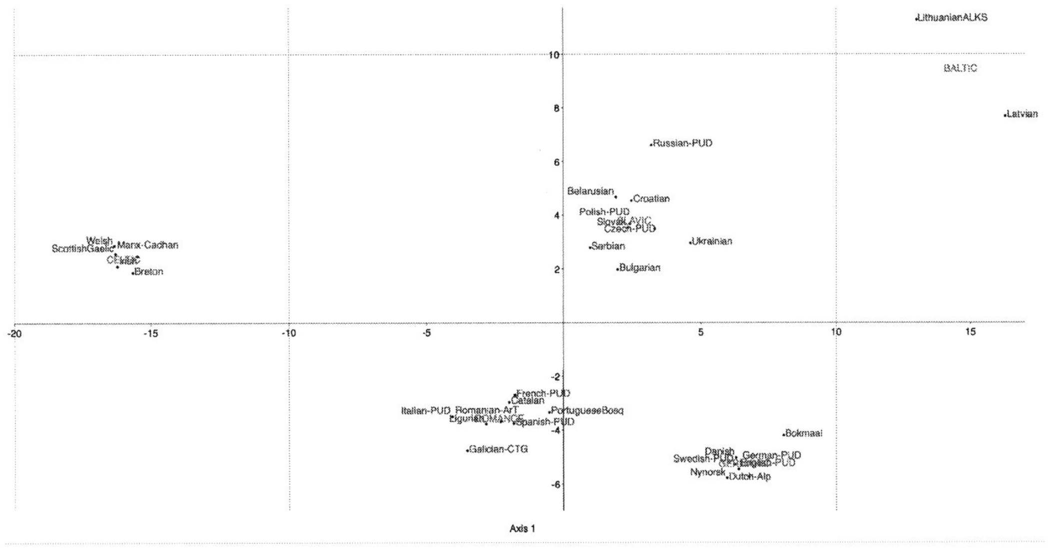

Figure 7: LDA combining complexity measures with n-grams.

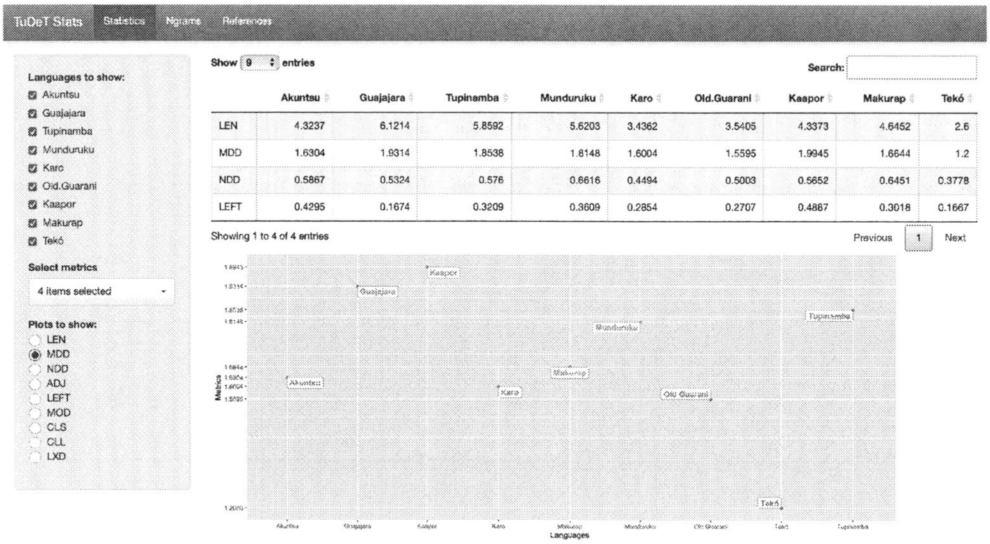

Figure 8: Example of Mean Dependency Distance for languages in TuDeT.

```
apply up ooroĝ
NUMBER=SING|PERSON=1+Perfective+(hunt)

apply up oxi
1SG+R1+mother

apply down 1SG+R1+arrow
odop

apply up tao
R2+leg
```

Figure 9: Output examples of the Munduruku finite-state morphological analyzer.

Proceedings of SIGUL2022 @LREC2022, pages 59–69
Marseille, 24-25 June 2022

Quality versus Quantity: Building Catalan-English MT Resources

Ona de Gibert, Ksenia Kharitonova, Blanca Calvo Figueras, Jordi Armengol-Estapé, Maite Melero
Barcelona Supercomputing Center
Plaça Eusebi Güell 1-3, Barcelona 08034, Spain
{ona.degibert, ksenia.kharitonova, blanca.calvo, jordi.armengol, maite.melero}@bsc.es

Abstract

In this work, we make the case of quality over quantity when training a MT system for a medium-to-low-resource language pair, namely Catalan-English. We compile our training corpus out of existing resources of varying quality and a new high-quality corpus. We also provide new evaluation translation datasets in three different domains. In the process of building Catalan-English parallel resources, we evaluate the impact of drastically filtering alignments in the resulting MT engines. Our results show that even when resources are limited, as in this case, it is worth filtering for quality. We further explore the cross-lingual transfer learning capabilities of the proposed model for parallel corpus filtering by applying it to other languages. All resources generated in this work are released under open license to encourage the development of language technology in Catalan.

Keywords: Machine Translation, Catalan, Under-Resourced Languages, Parallel Corpus, Data Cleaning

1. Introduction

In recent years, the arrival of the transformers (Vaswani et al., 2017) has opened up new lines of research with a clear focus on under-resourced languages (Zoph et al., 2016). The transfer-learning capabilities of pre-trained language models, such as BERT (Devlin et al., 2019), have successfully been used to solve downstream tasks employing much less task-specific annotated data. This has encouraged the development of multilingual and language-specific pre-trained language models (Martin et al., 2020). For instance, Liu et al. (2020) demonstrated that using a multilingual BART-like model (Lewis et al., 2019) for Machine Translation (MT) showed performance gains in low-resource language settings.

In the past, building MT resources has been ruled by quantity over quality, especially in low-resource scenarios, where there is little data available. In the quest for as much data as possible, large multilingual corpora such as CCAligned (El-Kishky et al., 2020), WikiMatrix (Schwenk et al., 2019) or Paracrawl (Bañón et al., 2020) are collected in mass from the web, without actively assessing their quality. The task of parallel corpus filtering aims at filtering noisy data originating from unreliable sources or misalignments to improve the quality of a bilingual dataset.

In this work, we focus on the collection and filtering of Catalan-English corpora. Despite the status of English as *lingua franca*, there are not many publicly available parallel resources for this language pair. We present new resources, both for training and evaluation, diverse in sizes and domains. Our contributions sum up to:

- A high-quality dataset for Catalan-English MT
- A quality filter for Catalan-English Parallel Corpora
- Three new evaluation datasets

Our code is openly available on Github[1] for the sake of reproducibility. We also release the resources created.

The rest of the paper is organised as follows. Section 2 provides an overview of the previous work done in the field. Section 3 describes in detail the resources presented. Section 4 outlines the human assessment of the datasets' quality. Section 5 describes our approach to the task of parallel corpus filtering. Finally, section 6 concludes our work and opens future lines of research.

2. Related Work

Typical resources to train MT models are composed of parallel corpora, i.e. bilingual aligned sentences. When trying to gather parallel training corpora for low-resource languages, a starting point is collecting large multilingual datasets, such as the ones found in OPUS (Tiedemann, 2012). OPUS includes many such datasets in a variety of languages, sizes, and domains (e.g. software handbooks, religious texts, Wikipedia articles...). Catalan is included in many of the large web-crawled corpora, however, as Kreutzer et al. (2021) point out, most data coming from online sources is of poor quality. For this reason, there is a growing interest in evaluating the quality of the released datasets. While several works focus on the quality assessment of monolingual corpora (Caswell et al., 2020), Kreutzer et al. (2021) are the first to evaluate the quality of MT datasets. They perform a large-scale human evaluation of publicly available datasets and find severe quality issues, especially for low-resource languages.

Once the quality has been assessed, a second necessary step is to improve the quality of a given dataset. Parallel corpus filtering, also known as sentence alignment filtering, is the task of automatically filtering out bad aligned sentences or sentences that are not good enough

[1] `https://github.com/TeMU-BSC/seq-to-seq-catalan/tree/main/machine_translation`

for MT training. The relevance of this task is gaining importance in recent years, as proven by the organisation of a Shared Task on Parallel Corpus Filtering and Alignment in WMT (Koehn et al., 2020).
This task has been approached using different methods that can be summarized as follows (Koehn et al., 2020):

- Filtering based on heuristic rules such as sentence length, length ratio, alpha-numerical tokens ratio, token overlap, mismatched Named Entities.
- Filtering based on automatic scores obtained by sentence embeddings or pre-trained language models.
- Filtering as a binary classification task that takes some positive and negative examples as input.

After building your model, evaluation resources are needed to test your MT system. These are much shorter in size, humanly produced, and are used as gold standards for validation. Catalan is part of the multilingual benchmark Flores-101 (Goyal et al., 2021). Other datasets for Catalan-English MT evaluation are: the Catalan United Nations test set (Costa-jussà, 2020), which is the Catalan translation of the United Nations Parallel Corpus test set (Ziemski et al., 2016), and the Catalan translation of WMT20 Biomedical Shared Task test set (Bawden et al., 2020).

3. Language Resources

In order to build a large parallel corpus for Catalan-English MT, we have compiled a total of 19 available open-source bilingual Catalan-English datasets, and we have created a brand new dataset, GEnCaTa. In total, we obtain a moderately large Catalan-English corpus of over 11.55 million aligned sentences.

3.1. Parallel Corpora Compilation

The collected datasets originate from different sources and belong to different domains. The characteristics of the corpora can be found in Table 1.
Most datasets belong to the general domain. Nonetheless, we also gather sources originating from software translations, known to contain many boilerplate sentences; Wikipedia articles, from which we expect well-constructed sentences; and specific domains, such as Health or Legislation.
We are aware that the quality of each corpus varies greatly and is difficult to measure. Furthermore, the datasets have been constructed using different methods, either produced by human translations and manual revision, or by using automatic alignment algorithms. Regarding the collected datasets, 9 out of the 20 are produced by humans.
If we look at the statistics, we can see that CCaligned contains almost as many sentences as all the other datasets together. However, it should be noted that CCaligned has been recently shown to have poor quality translations, as well as Wikimatrix (Kreutzer et al., 2021), which also has a big representation within the collected corpora for this work. Memories Lliures is the largest manually produced dataset, although its average sentences are shorter in size since it consists of a compilation of freely available translation memories, mostly coming from software. The corpora with the smallest average sentence length are Open Subtitles, movie dialogues; Tatoeba, voluntary translations; and Ubuntu, software handbooks. Not surprisingly, the longest sentences originate from Wikipedia sources, namely, Wikimedia and Wikimatrix.
To further understand the scale of the datasets, we provide a treemap visualization in the Appendix in Figure 3.

3.2. GEnCaTa: a High Quality Parallel Corpus

GEnCaTa is a high-quality Catalan-English parallel corpus composed of 38,595 segments. It has been compiled by leveraging parallel data from crawling the `gencat.cat` domain and subdomains, belonging to the Catalan Government and containing bilingual sites, both in English and Catalan.

Crawling and preprocessing We use the cleaning pipeline described in Armengol-Estapé et al. (2021) to process the WARC files obtained from the crawlings and retrieve monolingual data. Using the pipeline allows us to maintain the metadata and retrieve the original URL per each visited page.

Document alignment We extract the content of the fetched URLs from the metadata that has non-empty crawled data in both languages. We obtain 4,429 comparable sites with an average of 27.64 sentences and 382.91 and 401.65 tokens for Catalan and English, respectively. We consider each of these sites as our documents.

Sentence alignment and deduplication To align the sentences at document-level, we use the alignment algorithm Vecalign (Thompson and Koehn, 2019) based on sentence embeddings. We use multilingual sentence embeddings provided by LASER[2] for the alignment. After the automatic alignment, we obtain 126,674 aligned segments. We then perform sentence deduplication and find that almost 60% of the sentences are duplicates, leaving 51,908 parallel segments.

Manual revision A first inspection of the resulting segments has shown that the alignment was of considerable quality, which prompted us to perform a manual revision of the full dataset. Several native Catalan annotators have revised the aligned segments and labeled each pair as valid or not valid for MT training. This involves labeling as negative misaligned sentences, truncated sentences, and non-linguistic sentences.
After the manual revision of the alignment, only 38,595 segments remain (i.e. 24.98% of the aligned segments are removed).

[2] `https://github.com/facebookresearch/LASER`

	Dataset	Sentences	Tokens	Tokens/Sent	Source	Domain
1	CCaligned	5,787,682	89,606,874	15.48	(El-Kishky et al., 2020)	General
2	COVID-19 Wikipedia	1,531	34,836	22.75	(Tiedemann, 2012)	Health
3	CoVost ca-en*	263,891	809,660	10.17	(Wang et al., 2020)	General
4	CoVost en-ca*	79,633	2,953,096	11.19	(Wang et al., 2020)	General
5	Eubookshop	3,746	82,067	21.91	(Tiedemann, 2012)	Legislation
6	Europarl	1,965,734	50,417,289	25.65	(Koehn, 2005)	Legislation
7	GEnCaTa*	38,595	858,385	22.24	New	General
8	Global Voices	21,342	438,032	20.52	(Tiedemann, 2012)	General
9	Gnome*	2,183	30,228	13.85	(Tiedemann, 2012)	Software
10	JW300	97,081	1,809,252	18.64	(Agić and Vulić, 2019)	General
11	KDE4*	144,153	1,450,631	10.06	(Tiedemann, 2012)	Software
12	Memories Lliures*	1,173,055	9,452,382	8.06	Softcatalà	Software
13	Open Subtitles	427,913	2,796,350	6.53	(Lison and Tiedemann, 2016)	General
14	Opus Books	4,580	73,416	16.03	(Tiedemann, 2012)	Narrative
15	QED*	69,823	1,058,003	15.15	(Abdelali et al., 2014)	Education
16	Tatoeba*	5,500	34,872	6.34	(Tiedemann, 2012)	General
17	Tedtalks	50,979	770,774	15.12	Softcatalà	General
18	Ubuntu	6,781	33,321	4.91	(Tiedemann, 2012)	Software
19	Wikimatrix	1,205,908	28,111,517	23.31	(Schwenk et al., 2019)	Wikipedia
20	Wikimedia*	208,073	5,761,409	27.69	(Tiedemann, 2012)	Wikipedia
	Total	11,558,183	196,582,394	15.78		

Table 1: Collected parallel corpora for Catalan-English MT. *Tokens* refers to Catalan tokens. The symbol * refers to manually produced or revised datasets.

Alignment Scores We perform a further analysis of the obtained results and notice that only 19.8% of the 5,000 highest scored segments ranked by Vecalign are also selected after the manual revision. This posits the question of how much we can rely on alignment algorithms for building parallel corpora by only looking at the given score.
We release the GEnCaTa dataset with an open license, together with relevant metadata such as the source URLs and the alignment scores given by Vecalign.

4. Human Audit

As mentioned, the quality of the compiled parallel corpora differs greatly depending on domain, origin, and creation method. For that reason, as a way to uncover the unknown quality of each dataset, we follow Kreutzer et al. (2021) and perform a human evaluation of the quality of each dataset. They perform a large-scale human audit of five major multilingual datasets, including CCaligned, WikiMatrix, and Paracrawl, based on the following error taxonomy:

- **CC**: Correct translation, natural sentence
- **CS**: Correct translation, but single word or short phrase
- **CB**: Correct translation, but boilerplate
- **X**: Incorrect translation
- **WL**: Wrong language
- **NL**: Not language

They also annotate whether the segments contain offensive or porn content.
To perform our human evaluation, we randomly sample 100 aligned segments for each of the 20 datasets. Then, two native speakers conduct a blind error analysis on the 2,000 sentences, without knowing their source, and annotate each pair following the taxonomy described above.

4.1. Human Audit Results

The annotator agreement of the task obtains a score of 0.55 Cohen's Kappa, which shows moderate agreement. To compensate for the differences in human perception of the subcategories, we also report a 0.60 Kappa score considering only the binary classification correct labels (CC, CS, CB) and incorrect ones (X, WL, NL).
Results are shown in Figure 1 and in Table 7 in the Appendix. Since only 100 sentences per dataset have been evaluated, the numbers given are only rough estimates. We combine the correct codes (CC, CB, CS) into C for simplicity. The ratio of correct samples (C) ranges from 67% to 98%. The datasets with the bigger amount of correct sentences are CoVost, sentences coming from Common Voice; Tatoeba, originating from user-generated voluntary translations; Europarl, from the European Parliament; and our brand new created GEnCaTa corpus, which is a proof of high quality. Wang et al. (2020) developed the CoVost dataset and performed data quality sanity checks based on language model perplexity, LASER scores, and a length ratio heuristic. The results of their work are in line with our findings.
On the other hand, the datasets with more mistranslations are CCAligned and Eubookshop, both originating from automatic alignments, and Ubuntu, coming from software translations.
Among the correct sentences, the corpora that contain the most boilerplate sentences are KDE4, Memories Lliures, and Ubuntu, all belonging to computer applications and handbooks. These last two also contain the

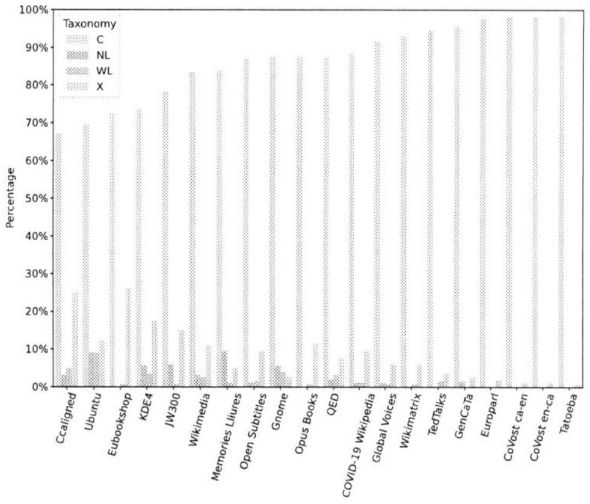

Figure 1: Results of the human audit on 20 different datasets for MT quality

biggest number of non-linguistic sentences.
The datasets containing more short sentences are Open Subtitles and Gnome, composed of dialogue and software texts, respectively.
Translations are almost always in the correct language, but it is worth to note the number of sentences in the wrong language present in Ubuntu, which refer to specific terms of computer programs.
Finally, there is no presence of offensive or porn content in most datasets, except for marginal single cases in CCAligned, CoVost, and QED.
Predictably, our analysis concludes that human revised datasets have higher quality (CoVost, GEnCaTa, Tatoeba). In the next section, we question if the effort that is needed to curate these datasets pays off.

5. Parallel Corpus filtering

Once we have compiled the parallel corpora and analysed their quality, we use the GEnCaTa dataset to build a classifier for parallel corpus filtering, by leveraging the human annotations described in Section 3.2.

5.1. Fine-tuning

Similarly to Açarçiçek et al. (2020), we fine-tune an encoder with a labeled dataset of parallel segments annotated as valid or not valid for MT. In their work, they use two small datasets of 2,000 and 10,000 samples with synthetically generated negative examples. They obtain one of the highest-performance systems in the WMT20 Shared Task on Parallel Corpus Filtering and Alignment.
We make use of the GenCaTa dataset, which consists of 51,908 samples distributed in 38,876 positive and 13,032 negative pairs. These annotations may include misaligned sentences, too short sentences, etc. We also release the labeled dataset to promote further investigations in the field. To our knowledge, this is the largest dataset available of its kind.

Label	Train	Valid	Test
Positive	23,897	7,490	7,489
Negative	8,011	2,510	2,511
Total	31,908	10,000	10,000

Table 2: Train, valid and test splits of the GEnCaTa dataset for parallel corpus filtering

Model	F1	Precision	Recall
mBERT-uncased	0.968	0.966	0.971
mBERT-cased	0.970	0.966	0.974

Table 3: Fine-tuning of mBERT results on the GEnCaTa dataset for parallel corpus filtering

We approach the task as a text classification problem and build a binary classifier that takes as input the pair of Catalan-English aligned sentences and outputs if they are valid for MT or not. Our classifier is based on mBERT (Devlin et al., 2019), a multilingual pre-trained encoder, fine-tuned with our dataset.
As shown in Table 2, we split the GEnCaTa dataset into train, valid, and test splits and then fine-tune both mBERT-cased and mBERT-uncased with the same hyperparameters. We report our results in Table 3 with almost no variability in performance but with excellent scores. We use the classifier with mBERT-cased for the subsequent experiments.

5.2. Filtering

Once we have built our classifier, we use it to filter the compiled resources described in section 3.1.
The number of total filtered sentences per dataset can be seen in Figure 2. On average, 86.87% of the original sentences are valid for MT training.
As could be expected from the human audit results, the corpora with more filtered out sentences are EUBookshop, Ubuntu, and CCaligned. Furthermore, despite the number of correct translations in Opus Books reported in the human audit, this dataset has been filtered heavily as well, since it contains quite a few misalignments and short sentences.
On the other end of the spectrum, the corpora that have been less filtered are CoVost, Tatoeba, GEnCaTa, and Europarl, the same four datasets that had the highest amount of correct sentences.
The Pearson correlation between the human audit results and the percentage of valid sentences is 0.89, a strong correlation. This proves the validity of our model, which could be used as an automatic quality estimator in the future.

5.3. Evaluation on MT Systems

We further investigate the issue of quality by assessing the impact that filtering sentence alignments may have on the quality of MT models.
For that, we build two MT systems. First, we build an MT system using the raw compiled resources (RAW).

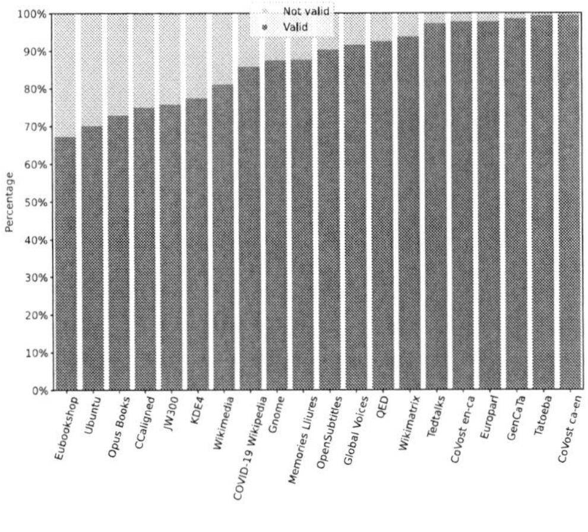

Figure 2: Percentage of filtered sentences by the parallel corpus classifier

Then, we build a new MT system to measure the impact of our parallel filtered corpus (FIL).
Both MT systems are based on mBART (Liu et al., 2020). We first pre-train a default large mBART model with concatenated monolingual data in Catalan and English and later fine-tune it with parallel data in the two languages. As monolingual data, we concatenate CaText (Armengol-Estapé et al., 2021) (in Catalan) and a clean subset of 45k random documents of Oscar (in English) (Ortiz Suárez et al., 2019).
We use default hyperparameters from Liu et al. (2020) both for monolingual pre-training and parallel data fine-tuning. However, the amount of training steps for fine-tuning is considerably lower, notably 8K (appr. 4 epochs) with an update frequency of 512. We use 4 Tesla V100-SXM2-16GB GPUs for training.
We preprocess the parallel sentences by removing duplicates, checking overlap between train and test, and removing those sentences that exceed our length limitations before feeding them to our models.

5.3.1. Evaluation Resources

We use three new in-domain test sets to validate the performance of our systems, as well as the general-domain Flores-101 as a reference. We release them under open licenses. The test sets statistics are included in Table 4.

CyberMT is a brand new test set in Catalan, Spanish, and English that belongs to the cybersecurity domain. It is composed of cybersecurity alerts extracted from the INCIBE Spanish-English corpus[3], which have been manually translated to Catalan.

TaCon is a multilingual dataset from the legal domain that includes translations of the Spanish Constitution to Basque, Catalan, Galician, Spanish, and English. To obtain it, we download the Spanish Constitution from the website of the Agencia Estatal del Boletín Oficial del Estado[4] in the corresponding languages in PDF format. We convert it to plain text, fix the broken sentences, and finally align the sentences manually.

WMT2013-ca consists of the Catalan translation of the WMT 2013 translation shared task test set (Bojar et al., 2013), belonging to the newswire domain. We commissioned the translation from Spanish to Catalan to a professional native translator.

Dataset	Languages	Domain	Sent.	Tokens
CyberMT	ca, es, en	cybersecurity	1,715	33,050
TaCon	ca, es, en eu, ga	legislation	1,110	18,275
WMT13	ca, es, en, de, ru, fr, cs	newswire	3,000	59,340

Table 4: Language resources for MT evaluation. *Tokens* refers to Catalan tokens.

5.3.2. Results

We use BLEU scores (Papineni et al., 2002) to report our results in Table 5, computed with SacreBLEU (sBLEU) (Post, 2018).

Direction	Test set	RAW	FIL
EN → CA	Cyber	40.2	**43.1**
	Flores-101	35.7	**38.0**
	TaCon	28.9	**30.2**
	WMT13	31.2	**32.9**
CA → EN	Cyber	47.4	**49.5**
	Flores-101	34.7	**37.6**
	TaCon	32.4	**35.0**
	WMT13	34.1	**36.0**

Table 5: sBLEU scores for MT evaluation

Results show that MT achieves overall good results for the Catalan-English language pair. Higher scores are obtained for the CA→EN direction, due to English being less morphologically complex.
Regarding in-domain test sets, TaCon is the test set that yields the lowest scores, probably because of the specificity of its language. Surprisingly, the Cyber test set seems to be the easiest to translate, despite being domain-specific. This may be attributed to the numerous non-verbal segments that are kept untranslated, boosting the results up to 49.5 BLEU for the CA→EN direction. Nonetheless, the most remarkable results are obtained by the comparison between the two systems. Even with the modest amount of fine-tuning steps for the two models, FIL outperforms the RAW system in all test sets. The sBLEU scores increase between 1.3 and 2.9 points. General-domain Flores-101 is the test set that shows more clearly the advantage of the quality filtering since the classifier is built on general-domain labeled data.

[3] https://www.elrc-share.eu/repository/browse/descripciones-de-vulnerabilidades-de-la-bbdd-nvd

[4] www.boe.es

	Target						
Source	CA	CS	DE	EN	ES	FR	RU
CA	-	0.952	0.979	-	0.985	0.982	0.954
CS	0.947	-	0.976	0.987	0.948	0.940	0.972
DE	0.879	0.934	-	0.987	0.937	0.949	0.958
EN	-	0.894	0.961	-	0.938	0.957	0.925
ES	0.977	0.947	0.980	0.988	-	0.982	0.971
FR	0.960	0.916	0.979	0.988	0.967	-	0.964
RU	0.936	0.972	0.979	0.981	0.975	0.969	-

Table 6: Zero-shot multilingual parallel corpus filtering

Our results show that automatically filtering sentence alignments significantly boosts MT performance and should be encouraged.

5.4. Zero-Shot Cross-lingual Transfer Learning

To further investigate the capabilities of the proposed filtering method, we explore the possibility of cross-lingual transfer learning by applying our model in zero-shot scenarios. We follow the intuition proposed by (Pires et al., 2019) that mBERT encodes multilingual representations. We use the classifier fine-tuned on CA-EN and apply it to other language pairs.

We make use of the 3,000 sentences of the WMT13 Shared Task test set for evaluation. The reason to have chosen this test set is that we have presented the Catalan version in this work, it includes six additional languages (es, en, de, ru, fr, cs) and contains document boundaries. For the synthetic test set of each language pair, we consider the 3,000 manually translated sentences as valid for MT. Then, we sample 3,000 negative examples by corrupting the alignment. To create a harder test set, we pair each sentence with the sentence of the same document that has the highest fuzzy match score to the correct translation. The final test set contains 6,000 segments.

Accuracy results are shown in Table 6. We tested all language pairs' combinations in both directions. Scores range from 0.879 to 0.988. The first insight we gain from the obtained scores is that mBERT indeed learns multilingual representations, as the results are incredibly positive. The highest scores overall are obtained by the Romance languages (CA, ES, FR); to be expected, since Spanish and French are from the same language family as Catalan. We can observe that the language typology also matters in the language direction. Since we fine-tuned the model with the direction CA→EN, the results are higher for CA and ES as a source, and for DE and EN as a target, being both Germanic languages.

Nonetheless, results are very promising for all tested combinations. While we are aware that we may introduce bias by creating a synthetic test set, we are hopeful for this new line of research that makes use of curated datasets, which may not always be available for all languages, and can later be used with new language pairs.

6. Conclusions & Future Work

In this work, we have presented the process of building high-quality MT resources for the Catalan-English language pair, which until now could be considered low-resource, and have made the case for an automatic quality filter. We have described in detail the compiled resources and the newly created ones, including a high-quality parallel corpus and three in-domain evaluation datasets. Furthermore, we have performed a human evaluation of the datasets' quality and we have devised a parallel corpus filterer, that may be used as a future quality estimator. Finally, we have applied the proposed model to zero-shot scenarios and proved the transfer-learning capabilities of mBERT.

As future lines of research, we plan to further investigate the task of quality estimation of parallel corpora and its impact on the obtained MT engines. We would also like to conduct a more qualitative analysis of the output of the MT systems to gain linguistic insights from the results.

We hope that our work encourages this line of research in the field.

7. Acknowledgements

This work was funded by the MT4All CEF project.[5]

8. Bibliographical References

Açarçiçek, H., Çolakoğlu, T., Hatipoğlu, P. E. A., Huang, C. H., and Peng, W. (2020). Filtering noisy parallel corpus using transformers with proxy task learning. In *Proceedings of the Fifth Conference on Machine Translation*, pages 940–946.

Armengol-Estapé, J., Carrino, C. P., Rodriguez-Penagos, C., de Gibert Bonet, O., Armentano-Oller, C., Gonzalez-Agirre, A., Melero, M., and Villegas, M. (2021). Are multilingual models the best choice for moderately under-resourced languages? A comprehensive assessment for Catalan. In *Findings of the Association for Computational Linguistics: ACL-IJCNLP 2021*, pages 4933–4946, Online, August. Association for Computational Linguistics.

Bawden, R., Di Nunzio, G., Grozea, C., Unanue, I., Yepes, A., Mah, N., Martinez, D., Névéol, A., Neves, M., Oronoz, M., et al. (2020). Findings of the wmt 2020 biomedical translation shared task: Basque, italian and russian as new additional languages. In *5th Conference on Machine Translation*.

Bojar, O., Buck, C., Callison-Burch, C., Federmann, C., Haddow, B., Koehn, P., Monz, C., Post, M., Soricut, R., and Specia, L. (2013). Findings of the 2013 Workshop on Statistical Machine Translation. In *Proceedings of the Eighth Workshop on Statistical Machine Translation*, pages 1–44, Sofia, Bulgaria, August. Association for Computational Linguistics.

Caswell, I., Breiner, T., van Esch, D., and Bapna, A. (2020). Language id in the wild: Unexpected challenges on the path to a thousand-language web text corpus.

[5] `https://ec.europa.eu/inea/en/connecting-europe-facility/cef-telecom/2019-eu-ia-0031`

Devlin, J., Chang, M.-W., Lee, K., and Toutanova, K. (2019). BERT: Pre-training of Deep Bidirectional Transformers for Language Understanding. *arXiv:1810.04805 [cs]*, May. arXiv: 1810.04805.

Koehn, P., Chaudhary, V., El-Kishky, A., Goyal, N., Chen, P.-J., and Guzmán, F. (2020). Findings of the wmt 2020 shared task on parallel corpus filtering and alignment. In *Proceedings of the Fifth Conference on Machine Translation*, pages 726–742.

Kreutzer, J., Caswell, I., Wang, L., Wahab, A., van Esch, D., Ulzii-Orshikh, N., Tapo, A., Subramani, N., Sokolov, A., Sikasote, C., Setyawan, M., Sarin, S., Samb, S., Sagot, B., Rivera, C., Rios, A., Papadimitriou, I., Osei, S., Suárez, P. O., Orife, I., Ogueji, K., Rubungo, A. N., Nguyen, T. Q., Müller, M., Müller, A., Muhammad, S. H., Muhammad, N., Mnyakeni, A., Mirzakhalov, J., Matangira, T., Leong, C., Lawson, N., Kudugunta, S., Jernite, Y., Jenny, M., Firat, O., Dossou, B. F. P., Dlamini, S., de Silva, N., Çabuk Ballı, S., Biderman, S., Battisti, A., Baruwa, A., Bapna, A., Baljekar, P., Azime, I. A., Awokoya, A., Ataman, D., Ahia, O., Ahia, O., Agrawal, S., and Adeyemi, M. (2021). Quality at a glance: An audit of web-crawled multilingual datasets.

Lewis, M., Liu, Y., Goyal, N., Ghazvininejad, M., Mohamed, A., Levy, O., Stoyanov, V., and Zettlemoyer, L. (2019). Bart: Denoising sequence-to-sequence pre-training for natural language generation, translation, and comprehension. *arXiv preprint arXiv:1910.13461*.

Liu, Y., Gu, J., Goyal, N., Li, X., Edunov, S., Ghazvininejad, M., Lewis, M., and Zettlemoyer, L. (2020). Multilingual denoising pre-training for neural machine translation. *Transactions of the Association for Computational Linguistics*, 8:726–742.

Martin, L., Muller, B., Suárez, P. J. O., Dupont, Y., Romary, L., de la Clergerie, É. V., Seddah, D., and Sagot, B. (2020). Camembert: a tasty french language model. In *ACL 2020-58th Annual Meeting of the Association for Computational Linguistics*.

Papineni, K., Roukos, S., Ward, T., and Zhu, W.-J. (2002). Bleu: a method for automatic evaluation of machine translation. In *Proceedings of the 40th annual meeting of the Association for Computational Linguistics*, pages 311–318.

Pires, T., Schlinger, E., and Garrette, D. (2019). How multilingual is multilingual bert? *arXiv preprint arXiv:1906.01502*.

Post, M. (2018). A call for clarity in reporting BLEU scores. In *Proceedings of the Third Conference on Machine Translation: Research Papers*, pages 186–191, Brussels, Belgium, October. Association for Computational Linguistics.

Thompson, B. and Koehn, P. (2019). Vecalign: Improved sentence alignment in linear time and space. In *Proceedings of the 2019 Conference on Empirical Methods in Natural Language Processing and the 9th International Joint Conference on Natural Language Processing (EMNLP-IJCNLP)*, pages 1342–1348.

Vaswani, A., Shazeer, N., Parmar, N., Uszkoreit, J., Jones, L., Gomez, A. N., Kaiser, L., and Polosukhin, I. (2017). Attention is all you need. *CoRR*, abs/1706.03762.

Zoph, B., Yuret, D., May, J., and Knight, K. (2016). Transfer learning for low-resource neural machine translation. In *Proceedings of the 2016 Conference on Empirical Methods in Natural Language Processing*, pages 1568–1575, Austin, Texas, November. Association for Computational Linguistics.

9. Language Resource References

Abdelali, A., Guzman, F., Sajjad, H., and Vogel, S. (2014). The AMARA corpus: Building parallel language resources for the educational domain. In *Proceedings of the Ninth International Conference on Language Resources and Evaluation (LREC'14)*, pages 1856–1862, Reykjavik, Iceland, May. European Language Resources Association (ELRA).

Agić, Ž. and Vulić, I. (2019). JW300: A wide-coverage parallel corpus for low-resource languages. In *Proceedings of the 57th Annual Meeting of the Association for Computational Linguistics*, pages 3204–3210, Florence, Italy, July. Association for Computational Linguistics.

Bañón, M., Chen, P., Haddow, B., Heafield, K., Hoang, H., Esplà-Gomis, M., Forcada, M. L., Kamran, A., Kirefu, F., Koehn, P., et al. (2020). Paracrawl: Web-scale acquisition of parallel corpora. In *Proceedings of the 58th Annual Meeting of the Association for Computational Linguistics*, pages 4555–4567.

Costa-jussà, M. R. (2020). Catalan united nations v1.0 test set, June. This work is supported by the Spanish Ministerio de Economía y Competitividad and European Regional Development Fund, through the postdoctoral senior grant Ramón y Cajal.

El-Kishky, A., Chaudhary, V., Guzmán, F., and Koehn, P. (2020). CCAligned: A massive collection of cross-lingual web-document pairs. In *Proceedings of the 2020 Conference on Empirical Methods in Natural Language Processing (EMNLP 2020)*, November.

Goyal, N., Gao, C., Chaudhary, V., Chen, P.-J., Wenzek, G., Ju, D., Krishnan, S., Ranzato, M., Guzman, F., and Fan, A. (2021). The flores-101 evaluation benchmark for low-resource and multilingual machine translation. *arXiv preprint arXiv:2106.03193*.

Koehn, P. (2005). Europarl: A parallel corpus for statistical machine translation. In *Proceedings of machine translation summit x: papers*, pages 79–86.

Lison, P. and Tiedemann, J. (2016). OpenSubtitles2016: Extracting large parallel corpora from movie and TV subtitles. In *Proceedings of the Tenth International Conference on Language Resources and Evaluation (LREC'16)*, pages 923–929, Portorož, Slovenia, May. European Language Resources Association (ELRA).

Ortiz Suárez, P. J., Sagot, B., and Romary, L. (2019). Asynchronous pipelines for processing huge corpora on medium to low resource infrastructures. Proceedings of the Workshop on Challenges in the Management of Large Corpora (CMLC-7) 2019. Cardiff, 22nd July 2019, pages 9 – 16, Mannheim. Leibniz-Institut für Deutsche Sprache.

Schwenk, H., Chaudhary, V., Sun, S., Gong, H., and Guzmán, F. (2019). Wikimatrix: Mining 135m parallel sentences in 1620 language pairs from wikipedia. *CoRR*, abs/1907.05791.

Tiedemann, J. (2012). Parallel data, tools and interfaces in opus. In *Lrec*, volume 2012, pages 2214–2218. Citeseer.

Wang, C., Wu, A., and Pino, J. (2020). Covost 2: A massively multilingual speech-to-text translation corpus.

Ziemski, M., Junczys-Dowmunt, M., and Pouliquen, B. (2016). The United Nations parallel corpus v1.0. In *Proceedings of the Tenth International Conference on Language Resources and Evaluation (LREC'16)*, pages 3530–3534, Portorož, Slovenia, May. European Language Resources Association (ELRA).

A. Published Resources

- The GEnCaTa Parallel Corpus
- Catalan WMT2013 MT Shared Task Test Set
- Cyber MT Test Set
- TaCon: Spanish Constitution MT Test Set
- The GEnCaTa Dataset for Parallel Corpus Filtering
- Model for English-Catalan Parallel Corpus Filtering

B. Collection of Parallel Corpora

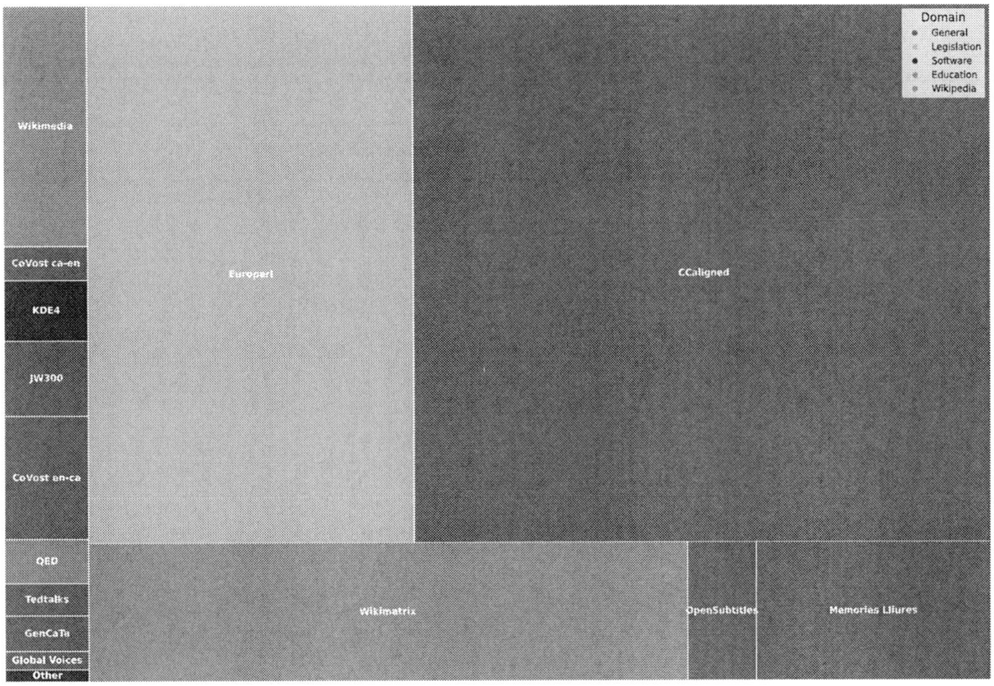

Figure 3: Treemap of the collected English-Catalan parallel corpora by number of sentences

C. Human Audit Results

Dataset	CC	CB	CS	C	X	WL	NL	offensive	porn	% audited
CCAligned	34.50%	21.00%	11.50%	67.00%	25.00%	5.00%	3.00%	0.00%	1.00%	0.0018
COVID-19 Wikipedia	82.00%	6.00%	0.50%	88.50%	9.50%	1.00%	1.00%	0.00%	0.00%	6.5317
CoVost ca-en	92.50%	2.00%	4.50%	99.00%	1.00%	0.00%	0.00%	0.00%	0.00%	0.1256
CoVost en-ca	96.00%	0.50%	2.50%	99.00%	1.00%	0.00%	0.00%	1.00%	0.00%	0.0379
GEnCaTa	79.00%	14.00%	3.00%	96.00%	2.50%	0.00%	1.50%	0.00%	0.00%	0.2592
Eubookshop	63.00%	7.50%	3.00%	73.50%	26.00%	0.50%	0.00%	0.00%	0.00%	2.6696
Europarl	96.00%	1.50%	0.50%	98.00%	2.00%	0.00%	0.00%	0.00%	0.00%	0.0051
Global Voices	77.50%	13.00%	2.00%	92.50%	6.00%	0.50%	1.00%	0.00%	0.00%	0.4686
Gnome	45.00%	25.00%	17.50%	87.50%	2.50%	4.00%	6.00%	0.00%	0.00%	4.5809
JW300	73.50%	3.50%	1.50%	78.50%	15.00%	0.50%	6.00%	0.00%	0.00%	0.1031
KDE4	19.50%	42.50%	11.50%	73.50%	17.50%	3.50%	5.50%	0.00%	0.00%	0.0694
Memories Lliures	16.00%	55.00%	13.50%	84.50%	5.00%	1.00%	9.50%	0.00%	0.00%	0.0086
Open Subtitles	66.00%	2.50%	19.50%	88.00%	9.50%	1.50%	1.00%	0.00%	0.00%	0.0234
Opus Books	74.50%	6.50%	7.00%	88.00%	11.50%	0.50%	0.00%	0.00%	0.00%	2.1835
QED	78.50%	3.00%	6.00%	87.50%	7.50%	3.00%	2.00%	1.00%	0.00%	0.1433
Tatoeba	84.00%	2.50%	13.00%	99.50%	0.50%	0.00%	0.00%	0.00%	0.00%	1.8182
Tedtalks	83.50%	3.50%	8.00%	95.00%	3.50%	1.50%	0.00%	0.00%	0.00%	0.1962
Ubuntu	13.50%	44.00%	12.00%	69.50%	12.00%	9.00%	9.50%	0.00%	0.00%	1.4748
WIkimatrix	91.50%	2.00%	0.00%	93.50%	6.00%	0.50%	0.00%	0.00%	0.00%	0.0103
Wikimedia	72.50%	7.00%	4.00%	83.50%	11.00%	2.50%	3.00%	0.00%	0.00%	0.0481

Table 7: Results of the human audit on 20 different datasets for MT quality

D. Fine-tuning Hyperparameters

D.1. Parallel Corpus Filtering

Hyper-parameter	Value
Learning Rate	0.8e-5
Learning Rate Decay	Linear
Warmup	0.06
Batch Size	64
Batch size per GPU	8
Update freq.	1
GPUs	8
Weight Decay	0.01
Max. Training Epochs	10

Table 8: Hyper-parameters used for fine-tuning the model for parallel corpus filtering. The rest of the parameters are the same as in Devlin et al. (2019)

D.2. MT training

Hyper-parameter	Value
LR scheduler	Polynomial Decay
Peak LR	1e-4
Warmup	0.2K
Total updates for LR scheduler	100K
Batch size	2048
Batch size per GPU	1
Update freq.	512
GPUs	4
Weight Decay	0.01
Max. Training Epochs	5
Dropout	0.1
Attention Dropout	0.1

Table 9: Hyper-parameters used for fine-tuning the MT models. The hyper-parameters for bilingual CA-EN denoising pre-training are the same as in Liu et al. (2020)

Proceedings of SIGUL2022 @LREC2022, pages 70–77
Marseille, 24-25 June 2022

A Sentiment Corpus for South African Under-Resourced Languages in a Multilingual Context

Koena Ronny Mabokela, Tim Schlippe
University of Johannesburg, South Africa
IU International University of Applied Sciences, Germany
krmabokela@gmail.com, tim.schlippe@iu.org

Abstract

Multilingual sentiment analysis is a process of detecting and classifying sentiment based on textual information written in multiple languages. There has been tremendous research advancement on high-resourced languages such as English. However, progress on under-resourced languages remains underrepresented with limited opportunities for further development of natural language processing (NLP) technologies. Sentiment analysis (SA) for under-resourced language still is a skewed research area. Although, there are some considerable efforts in emerging African countries to develop such resources for under-resourced languages, languages such as indigenous South African languages still suffer from a lack of datasets. To the best of our knowledge, there is currently no dataset dedicated to SA research for South African languages in a multilingual context, i.e. comments are in different languages and may contain code-switching. In this paper, we present the first subset of the multilingual sentiment corpus *SAfriSenti* for the three most widely spoken languages in South Africa—*English*, *Sepedi (i.e. Northern Sotho)*, and *Setswana*. This subset consists of over 40,000 annotated tweets in all the three languages including even 36.6% of code-switched texts. We present data collection, cleaning and annotation strategies that were followed to curate the dataset for these languages. Furthermore, we describe how we developed language-specific sentiment lexicons, morpheme-based sentiment taggers, conduct linguistic analyses and present possible solutions for the challenges of this sentiment dataset. We will release the dataset and sentiment lexicons to the research communities to advance the NLP research of under-resourced languages.

Keywords: Multilingual, Sentiment analysis, Under-resourced languages, Code-switching, Sepedi, Setswana, South African languages

1. Introduction

Detecting sentiments or emotions from language has been a significant area of research in natural language processing (NLP) for the past decades (Medhat et al., 2014; Wankhade et al., 2022). Sentiment analysis (SA) is concerned with detecting and categorising emotions from textual information (Pang et al., 2002). SA has garnered a lot of research attention which may be attributed to its numerous essential NLP applications. Recently, SA has given birth to multilingual SA due to the rapid use of mixture of languages on various social media platforms (Balahur and Turchi, 2014). Multilingual SA aims to detect and recognise the sentiment of textual information written in more than one language. It is an emerging NLP research area with promising progress on high-resourced languages, i.e., English and Chinese (Ruder, 2020). However, the same cannot be said for languages with limited resource data which continue to remain highly underrepresented. In addition, the lack of resources poses a significant challenge for language-specific services in developing countries (Dashtipour et al., 2016; Lo et al., 2017).

In context, under-resourced languages are in desperate need of data, digital tools, and resources to overcome the resource barrier and enable NLP to deliver more widespread benefits (Ruder, 2020). Developing such language technologies and curated datasets for these under-resourced languages opens a considerable amount of economic perspectives and it is crucial for data availability and training of NLP applications (Marivate et al., 2020). Past research has yielded relatively limited insights into the relationship between socio-cultural factors, multicultural factors and NLP for under-resourced languages (Lo et al., 2017). However, recent research suggests that socio-cultural factors and multicultural diversity impede NLP for under-resourced languages, possibly leading to economic disparities in many multilingual communities (Weidinger et al., 2021)

With at least 7,000 spoken languages world-wide (Ruder, 2020), not many are represented on the internet, including over 2,000 native languages in Africa[1]. South Africa is with over 60 million people, 11 official spoken languages and over 40 dialects not only the sixth African country with the largest population (Statista, 2022). It is also the most multilingual and multicultural society where most native speakers are fluent in at least two languages. A report shows that in 2020 approximately 40% of South Africa's population were active on social media platforms and approximately 9.3 million of those are on Twitter (Lama, 2020). However, there has been no SA research at all for the indigenous South African languages, especially

[1]https://www.ethnologue.com

not for Twitter. Therefore, a tremendous effort to create digital resources for such under-resourced languages is necessary for future digital language technologies.

In this paper, we present a subset of *SAfriSenti*—our large-scale multilingual Twitter sentiment corpus for the South African languages English, Sepedi, and Setswana. It is to date the largest annotated sentiment dataset combining Sepedi and Setswana as under-resourced languages and English. We further present strategies to perform data collection using a multi-distant supervision approach, data preprocessing and data annotation which can be extended to other languages with limited data. Particularly, we describe our solutions for the missing support of Sepedi and Setswana in the Twitter API. In more detail in this paper, we offer the following contributions:

- We present a subset of our large-scale multilingual sentiment dataset for South African languages *SAfriSenti*. This subset contains Sepedi, Setswana, and English in a multilingual setting.
- We present our sentiment annotation tool *Senti-App* which allows the combination of automatic sentiment labelling and human annotation.
- We leverage the commonly used English sentiment lexicons AFFIN, NRC and VADER (Hutto and Gilbert, 2015; Nielsen, 2011) to built dedicated sentiment lexicons for Sepedi and Setswana.
- We present statistical analyses of *SAfriSenti*'s subset as well as linguistic challenges. Additionally, we describe how we plan to resolve the discovered challenges.

This paper is organised as follows: Section 2 will describe related work. In section 3, we will discuss our data collection, quality assurance and data annotation methods. In Section 4, we will present statistics of the final high-quality subset. Finally, we provide a conclusion of our research work in section 5 and offer suggestion for future work.

2. Related Studies

The research interest to solve the challenges of under-resourced languages has increased (Aguero-Torales et al., 2021; Wankhade et al., 2022). SA for monolingual, code-switched and multilingual comments on under-resourced languages has been studied only for a few African languages, e.g. several Nigerian languages (Hassan Muhammad et al., 2022), Swahili (Martin et al., 2021) and Bambara (Konate and Du, 2018). SA studies on under-resourced languages used datasets which consist of movie reviews, Amazon reviews, YouTube comments, tweets and Facebook comments (Balahur and Turchi, 2012b; Pan et al., 2011; Pak and Paroubek, 2010). As these datasets contain comments in multiple languages, they are interesting for the multilingual SA research (Vilares et al., 2016; Araujo et al., 2016; Can et al., 2018).

Several researchers investigated cross-lingual methods to solve the challenges of under-resourced languages by utilising language knowledge from high-resourced languages like English (Araújo et al., 2020; Balahur and Turchi, 2014; Can et al., 2018; Vilares et al., 2017). Notably, they frequently translate the comments from the original under-resourced language to English. This enables SA to conduct its classification task with high-performing models that have been trained with a large number of English resources. However, even this approach was successful for the high-resourced languages Russian, German and Spanish (Shalunts et al., 2016), (Ghafoor et al., 2021) report that translation from English to German, Urdu, and Hindi had a bad impact on SA performance. Additionally, (Becker et al., 2017) state that SA is dependent on MT quality in cross-lingual SA. According to (Ghafoor et al., 2021), there was a 2-3% SA performance decrease from English to under-resourced languages with help of MT compared to human translation.

Due to the mentioned MT performance issues, there are monolingual SA approaches for under-resourced languages. For these approaches, data in the target language such as sentiment lexica or labelled comments are required. Usually those data are created in a semi-automatic way, i.e. first machine-translated then manually corrected. (Mihalcea et al., 2012) constructed a Romanian sentiment lexicon (also denoted as subjectivity lexicon) with the help of an English sentiment lexicon and an English-Romanian dictionary. Additionally, (Balahur and Turchi, 2012a) generate SA datasets in the target language with the help of MT. They even claim that SA may be done on these translated data without any significant loss of accuracy. However, (Deriu et al., 2017) demonstrated that for German, English, and Italian there is an SA performance degradation after translating the resources into the target language. Previous studies investigated data collection strategies for under-resourced languages on Twitter (Pak and Paroubek, 2010; Vosoughi et al., 2016). The methods focus on labelling only two sentiment classes —positive and negative. Meanwhile other research work has explored strategies to label three sentiment classes in Twitter—positive, neutral, and negative —using human annotators (Vilares et al., 2016; Pak and Paroubek, 2010; Pang et al., 2002; Nakov et al., 2019). Despite the attempt to automate the data labelling process (Kranjc et al., 2015), the hand-crafted annotation is to date the most preferred method of data labelling in many NLP tasks (Muhammad et al., 2022). However, manual annotation presents challenges and it is deemed an expensive process. Notably, the work presented in (Jamatia et al., 2020; Gupta et al., 2021) employed manually annotated tweets, while other studies focus on automated data labelling solutions (Kranjc et al., 2015). (Vosoughi et al., 2016) investigated var-

Language	Tweets	English Translation	Sentiment
Sepedi	le re boledisa kudu baloi	you want us to talk too much witches	negative
English	Those family videos just motivated me to do more for Mpho tomorrow	Those family videos just motivated me to do more for Mpho tomorrow	positive
Setswana	boloi jwa mo ditirong bo bontsi gore	there is is too much witchcraft at work	negative
Mix	how do you guys know so much, **le tshaba maphodisa**	how do you guys know so much, you are running away from the police	negative

Table 1: Example of tweets, their corresponding English translation as well as their associated sentiment labels

ious pipelines to collect data on Twitter using distant supervised learning. In this approach, they use positive and negative emoticons as indicators to annotate tweets. (Go et al., 2009) explore distant supervision methods to label millions of tweets using positive and negative search terms (i.e. term queries) in the Twitter API and emoticons to pre-classify the tweets. (Vilares et al., 2016) also investigate *SentiStrength* scores to label an English-Spanish code-switching Twitter corpus. *SentiStrength* is an online SA system available for a few languages (Thelwall et al., 2011).
Compared to (Cliche, 2017; Jamatia et al., 2020; Vilares et al., 2016), we also investigate distant supervised annotation methods with the help of emoticons, search terms and sentiment lexicons. In addition to these methods, to make sure that we only collect tweets in our target languages, we leverage from Twitter's geolocation functionality and language identification based on word frequencies. Finally, the dataset is double-checked by human annotators. Despite Afrikaans (Kotzé and Senekal, 2018) and English, no other South African language has been investigated for SA to the best of our knowledge. We are the first to develop SA resources and systems for Sepedi and Setswana in a multilingual environment. In the next section, we will discuss our data collection strategies for Sepedi, Setswana and English.

3. Data Collection and Preprocessing

In this section, we will first describe the data collection strategies with the help of the Twitter API. Then we will present our methods for text preprocessing and normalization. Table 1 shows an extract from the dataset with examples of tweets in Sepedi, Setswana and English. It further contains English (marked in blue) and Sepedi (marked in blue) code-switched tweets.

3.1. Twitter Data Collection

Twitter provides easy access to a large amount of public user-generated text. It is used by different people to express their opinion about different topics (Pak and Paroubek, 2010). The Twitter API has evolved over time by introducing a new degree of access to enable developers and academic researchers to investigate the public comments for various NLP tasks[2]. We requested the permission to access the Twitter API by explaining our use-cases, agreeing on theirs terms of usage and policies. Our goal was to collect:

1. tweets only from the target languages.
2. trending tweets.
3. tweets with emotions.

We collected the tweets using the Twitter API for Academic Research[3]. For some languages, this API provides a functionality to only collect tweets in one specific language. However, this is not supported for Sepedi and Setswana. Consequently, we implemented word frequency based language identifications to only collect tweets in our target languages. To collect the trending tweets, we requested several native speakers to provide the trending search keywords and hashtags on a website. With the help of the Twitter API we only collected tweets which contain emoticons to ensure that those tweets contain emotions.

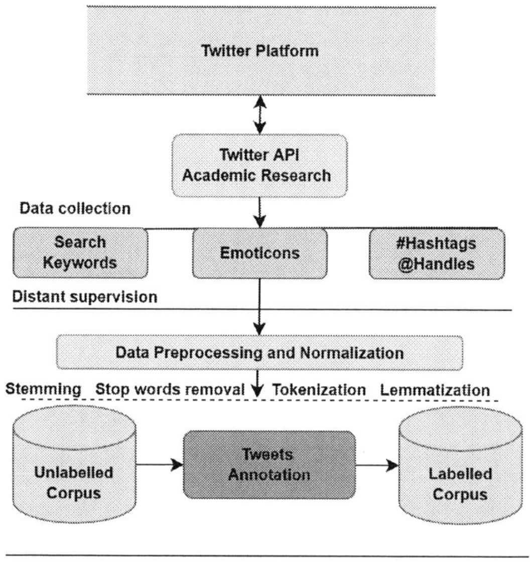

Figure 1: Data collection, cleaning and annotation

Figure 1 summarises these methods for data collection, plus our methods for cleaning and annotation, which we will describe in the upcoming subsection.

[2]https://developer.twitter.com/en/docs/twitter-api

[3]https://developer.twitter.com/en/products/twitter-api/academic-research

3.2. Text Preprocessing and Normalisation

We performed preprocessing, normalisation, lammentazation and tokenization on each tweet as used in (Pang et al., 2002; Pak and Paroubek, 2010). Each tweet was preprocessed in the following steps:

1. We remove very short tweets and duplicated tweets.
2. With the help of the @ symbol, we substitute people's and company's names for the purposes of data protection.
3. We remove punctuations, URLs and the # symbol.
4. We remove characters that appear more than twice (e.g., `Loooool or Whaaaaaat` and `ngwanaaaaaka` is replaced with `Lol` or `What` and `ngwanaka`).
5. We substitute abbreviations by their long form.
6. We set all words to lowercase, remove unnecessary white spaces and tokenize the tweets using the NLTK tokenizer (Bird and Loper, 2004).

In the next subsections, we will describe the preprocessing steps 1 and 3 in more detail.

3.3. Removal of short and duplicated tweets

We remove duplicated tweets in step 1 because they do not contain any additional information. We handle retweets and quote tweets with an `@RT` tag in the following way: We remove tweets which only contain a retweet. In those tweets which contain a quote of another tweet, we only keep the text which is new since we think it contains valuable information. To make sure that we get useful information in the tweets, we remove tweets with less than 5 word tokens.

4. The SAfriSenti Corpus

After we have described the text preprocessing steps, we will depict how we labelled the remaining English, Sepedi and Setswana tweets.

4.1. Pre-annotations

As mentioned in section 2 and recommended by (Go et al., 2009; Vosoughi et al., 2016), we used emoticons as distantly supervised method to pre-classify tweets as *positive*, *neutral* or *negative*. For this, we derived our initial sentiment classes from emoticons representing happy, smile, love, angry and sad as in (Pak and Paroubek, 2010; Nakov et al., 2019). In some tweets, users express their opinions using multiple unrelated emoticons which makes the pre-classification difficult. Consequently, we additionally checked the tweets for words in a sentiment lexicon which will be described in section 5.1. Then human experts verified the pre-classified tweets.

4.2. Annotation Guidelines

We defined strict annotation guidelines which all annotators have to follow in the decision to classify the tweets into *positive* (POS), *neutral* (NEU) and *negative* (NEG) as in (Turney, 2002; Öhman, 2020). We adopted our guidelines from (Mohammad, 2016) and consulted 3 language experts for each language to double-check our guidelines. The annotation guidelines for labelling our sentiment classes are summarised as follows:

- **Positive Sentiment (POS)** - This happens when a tweet expresses a favorable viewpoint, expression of support, appreciation, positive attitude, forgiveness, encouragement, success, cherish or pleasant emotional state.
- **Negative Sentiment (NEG)** - This happens when a tweet contains negative words, such as criticism, judgment, negative attitude, doubting validity/competence, failure or negative emotion.
- **Neutral Sentiment (NEU)** - This happens when a tweet does not directly or indirectly imply any positive or negative words. Typically, these are factual tweets such as reports or general statements.
- **Positive and Negative Sentiment** - This happens when a tweet expresses a positive language in part and negative language in part. For all three languages, these tweets are classified as positive or negative based on a score computed from individual scores in the corresponding sentiment lexicon. For Sepedi and Setswana we additionally apply language-specific morphological rules which will be explained in section 5.2.

Our annotation guidelines further contain the labelling of tweets with code-switches as well as tweets with no sentiments as the following classes:

- **Mixed Language (MIX)** - This happens when a tweet contains text from several languages (i.e. code-switched text).
- **None Sentiment (NOS)** - This happens when a tweet has no indication of the sentiment due to lack of context, e.g. in proverbs, idioms, or sarcasm.

4.3. Annotator's background and training

We recruited 3 native speakers with technical and linguistic background for each language as annotators. To facilitate the labelling process, we developed *SentiApp*, an online platform for organising and annotating the tweets. In a training session, we informed our annotators about our annotation guidelines and demonstrated the use of *SentiApp*. Then they were first asked to annotate 150 tweets. After their annotation process, they received our feedback to improve quality for upcoming tweets as recommended by (Öhman, 2020).

4.4. Annotation Process

After our training session, for organisational reasons, every time our annotators labelled batches with 1,000 tweets in our *SentiApp*. All three representatives of a language always worked on the same batch to be able to compare the resulting labels. In case of disagreement, the final label is determined by a majority voting. We also validated instances where annotators provided the labels `NOS` and `MIX`. As in (Muhammad et al., 2022), tweets with `NOS` are excluded from the dataset since they do not contain any sentiment. In total, the annotators labelled 25,947 monolingual tweets and 14,692 tweets which contain code-switches.

To determine the final label, we used a majority voting approach together with the proposed strategies of (Davani et al., 2021) which deals with the following 4 cases:

- **Three-way disagreement**—This happens when all 3 annotators disagree on a label. For example, if a tweet is labelled as `NEG`, `NEU` and `POS`. In this case, the annotators double-check these tweets or in case of remaining disagreement we discard this tweet.
- **Three-way agreement**—This happens when all 3 annotators agree on a label. For example, if a tweet is labelled as `NEG` by all 3 annotators, then it is `NEG`.
- **Two-way partial disagreement**—This happens when 2 annotators agree on a label but the third annotator chooses the label `NEU`. For example, if a tweet is labelled by 2 annotators as `POS` and by the other annotator as `NEU`, the final label is `POS`.
- **Two-way disagreement**—This happens when 2 annotators agree on a label but the third annotator chooses another label which is not `NEU`. For example, if a tweet is labelled by 2 annotators as `POS` and by the other annotator as `NEG`, the final label is `POS`.

4.5. Data Statistics

In total, we collected over 250,000 tweets for our 3 languages. However, in this paper, we report only the annotated subset of over 40,000 tweets. Tables 2 to 6 show an overview of the monolingual and code-switched tweets in this annotated subset. The monolingual tweets cover 63.4% (25,947 tweets). As demonstrated in Tables 5 and 6, our subset consists of a large number of code-switched tweets (14,692 tweets). 28.9% of those tweets contain code-switches of Sepedi and English (11,830 tweets). 6.9% of those tweets contain code-switches of Setswana and English (2,862 tweets). Sepedi and Setswana share some common words since the languages are closely-related.

Class	Number	%
POS	5,153	47.8
NEG	3,270	30.3
NEU	2,355	21,9
Total	10,778	

Table 2: Distribution of Sepedi tweets

Class	Number	%
POS	3,932	51.3
NEG	2,150	28.0
NEU	1,590	20.7
Total	7,672	

Table 3: Distribution of Setswana tweets

Class	Number	%
POS	2,052	27.4
NEG	3,557	48.4
NEU	1,888	25.2
Total	7,497	

Table 4: Distribution of English tweets

Class	Number	%
POS	3,808	32.2
NEG	4,245	35.9
NEU	3,777	31.9
Total	11,830	

Table 5: Distribution of English-Sepedi code-switched tweets

Class	Number	%
POS	1,498	52.3
NEG	852	29.8
NEU	780	27.3
Total	2,862	

Table 6: Distribution of English-Setswana code-switched tweets

4.6. Linguistic Challenges

Sepedi has diacritics, while Setswana does not have any diacritics. In some Sepedi tweets the diacritics are expressed with Roman characters, e.g. `Š` is replaced by `sh`, `ch` or `x` due to the use of English keyboards. These replacements of Sepedi diacritics sometimes leads to character strings which are very similar to Setswana words. Linguistic challenges, particularly evident in Sepedi, are that some tweets contain spelling errors, local jargon, ambiguities, homographs, and tonal words. Tones in Sepedi give meaning to words, particularly those words which have the same orthographic representation. For example, the word *noka*—depending on the context and tone, means "river" or "waist": The sentence "*ke tlo boya gae ge noka ke sena meetse*" meaning "*I will come back when the river has no water*" has a positive sentiment but the sentence "*o dula o bolaya ke noka buti wa tšwafa*" meaning "*My brother, you are always complaining about your waist, you are lazy*" has a negative meaning. In addition to the linguistic challenges, we encountered that knowledge of socio-cultural background is necessary to correctly label some tweets. We assume that this required additional socio-cultural knowledge could be a challenge for automatic SA systems. Furthermore, some tweets in *SAfriSenti* contain emoticons. On the one hand, these emoticons can be an indicator for the correct sentiment class. On the other hand, for tweets which contain multiple emoticons that expresses contradictory emotions, finding the correct sentiment class can be a challenging task.

5. Additional Resources

In addition to the *SAfriSenti* Corpus, we created sentiment lexicons and morpheme-based sentiment taggers.

5.1. Sentiment Lexicons

Figure 2 depicts the framework for building our sentiment lexicons:

1. Our annotators mark the sentiment-bearing words in each tweet which are only contained in positive and negative tweets.

2. We built a wordlist with the sentiment-bearing words and delete duplicates.

3. To each word we add the sentiment labels of the corresponding tweet and receive a sentiment lexicon.

4. As in (Nielsen, 2011), we let our annotators score the sentiment strength of positive words in a range between $+1$ (very weak) and $+5$ (very strong) and the strength of negative words in a range between -1 (very weak) and -5 (very strong).

5. We translate the words in the sentiment lexicon.

6. We merge our sentiment lexicon with translated versions of the well-known English sentiment lexicons AFFIN and VADER (Hutto and Gilbert, 2015; Nielsen, 2011).

To translate between Sepedi and English, we first used the Google Translate API and between Setswana and English, we used the Autshumato MT Web Service[4]. Autshumato is an open-source translation system, which was developed by *Centre for Text Technology* (CTexT) at the North-West University. Then our annotaters double-checked and corrected the translations.

[4]https://mt.nwu.ac.za

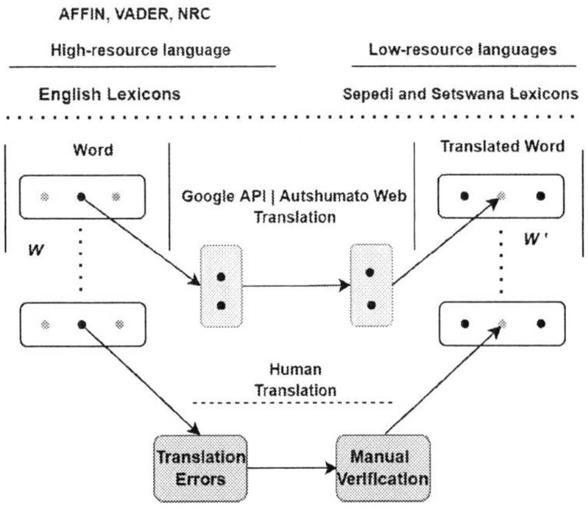

Figure 2: Developing sentiment lexicons.

5.2. Sentiment Taggers

As an additional information source, we looked into the morpheme level of Sepedi and Setwana since those language often contain morphemes that indicate the mood. Consequently, we also developed sentiment taggers for Sepedi and Setswana that first split individual words into morphemes and then label those words based on specific morphemes that indicate positive or negative moods. Examples for Sepedi morphemes which indicate a negative mood are: `/ke be ke sa/ and /ba be ba sa/`. Examples for Sepedi morphemes which indicate a positive mood are: `/ke be ke/ or /ba be ba/`. In the future we plan to investigate the application of our sentiment taggers as additional source for the sentiment classification.

6. Conclusion and Future Work

This paper presented a subset of *SAfriSenti*—a large-scale Twitter-based multilingual sentiment corpus for South African languages in a multilingual setting. We are the first who collected the under-resourced languages Sepedi and Setswana in this corpus. 36.6% of code-switched tweets demonstrate that *SAfriSenti* is highly multilingual. We described our methods for tweets annotation which contain tweets collection via the Twitter API, text processing and normalisation, removal of short and duplicated tweets, pre-annotation based on emoticons, and annotation based on strict guidelines. In addition, we discussed the challenges and mitigation of our data collection process. Additionally, we created sentiment lexicons for Sepedi and Setswana as well as implemented sentiment taggers which use morphemes to indicate the sentiment class.
In the future, we plan to optimize our data annotation process with the help of machine learning to reduce the manual annotation effort iteratively, similar to (Schlippe et al., 2012). Further our goal is to expand *SAfriSenti* with more African under-resourced languages to release a large-scale Twitter based mul-

tilingual sentiment corpus for SA to the NLP research community. Moreover, we will use *SAfriSenti* to investigate and compare different approaches for SA. Since we encountered that knowledge of cultural background is necessary to correctly label some tweets, we will analyze methods to leverage socio-cultural information into SA systems.

7. Acknowledgments

We acknowledge the National Research Foundation (NRF) for sponsorship. We also want to express our gratitude to our annotators and facilitators. Finally, we thank the reviewers for their valuable feedback.

8. References

Aguero-Torales, M. M., Abreu Salas, J. I., and Lopez-Herrera, A. G. (2021). Deep learning and multilingual sentiment analysis on social media data: An overview. *Applied Soft Computing*, 107:107373.

Araujo, M., Reis, J., Pereira, A., and Benevenuto, F. (2016). An evaluation of machine translation for multilingual sentence-level sentiment analysis. In *Proceedings of the 31st Annual ACM Symposium on Applied Computing*, pages 1140–1145.

Araújo, M., Pereira, A., and Benevenuto, F. (2020). A comparative study of machine translation for multilingual sentence-level sentiment analysis. *Information Sciences*, 512:1078–1102.

Balahur, A. and Turchi, M. (2012a). Comparative experiments for multilingual sentiment analysis using machine translation. In *SDAD@ ECML/PKDD*, pages 75–86.

Balahur, A. and Turchi, M. (2012b). Multilingual sentiment analysis using machine translation? In *Proceedings of the 3rd workshop in computational approaches to subjectivity and sentiment analysis*, pages 52–60. Association for Computational Linguistics.

Balahur, A. and Turchi, M. (2014). Comparative experiments using supervised learning and machine translation for multilingual sentiment analysis. *Computer Speech & Language*, 28(1):56–75.

Becker, W., Wehrmann, J., Cagnini, H. E., and Barros, R. C. (2017). An efficient deep neural architecture for multilingual sentiment analysis in Twitter. In *The Thirtieth International Flairs Conference*, pages 246–251.

Bird, S. and Loper, E. (2004). NLTK: The Natural Language Toolkit. In *Proceedings of the ACL Interactive Poster and Demonstration Sessions*, pages 214–217, Barcelona, Spain, July. Association for Computational Linguistics.

Can, E. F., Ezen-Can, A., and Can, F. (2018). Multilingual sentiment analysis: An RNN-based framework for limited data. *arXiv preprint arXiv:1806.04511*.

Cliche, M. (2017). BB_twtr at SemEval-2017 Task 4: Twitter Sentiment Analysis with CNNs and LSTMs. *arXiv preprint arXiv:1704.06125*.

Dashtipour, K., Poria, S., Hussain, A., Cambria, E., Hawalah, A. Y., Gelbukh, A., and Zhou, Q. (2016). Multilingual sentiment analysis: State of the art and independent comparison of techniques. *Cognitive computation*, 8(4):757–771.

Davani, A. M., Díaz, M., and Prabhakaran, V. (2021). Dealing with disagreements: Looking beyond the majority vote in subjective annotations. *CoRR*, abs/2110.05719.

Deriu, J., Lucchi, A., Luca, V. D., Severyn, A., Müller, S., Cieliebak, M., Hofmann, T., and Jaggi, M. (2017). Leveraging large amounts of weakly supervised data for multi-language sentiment classification. *Proceedings of the 26th International Conference on World Wide Web*, pages 1045–1052.

Ghafoor, A., Imran, A., Daudpota, S., Kastrati, Z., Abdullah, Batra, R., and Wani, M. (2021). The impact of translating resource-rich datasets to low-resource languages through multi-lingual text processing. *IEEE Access*, 9:124478 – 124490. Cited by: 0; All Open Access, Gold Open Access, Green Open Access.

Go, A., Bhayani, R., and Huang, L. (2009). Twitter sentiment classification using distant supervision. *Processing*, 150, 01.

Gupta, A., Menghani, S., Rallabandi, S. K., and Black, A. W. (2021). Unconscious self-training for sentiment analysis of code-linked data. *ArXiv*, abs / 2103.14797.

Hassan Muhammad, S., Ifeoluwa Adelani, D., Ruder, S., Said Ahmad, I., Abdulmumin, I., Shehu Bello, B., Choudhury, M., Chinenye Emezue, C., Salahudeen Abdullahi, S., Aremu, A., Jeorge, A., and Brazdil, P. (2022). NaijaSenti: A Nigerian Twitter Sentiment Corpus for Multilingual Sentiment Analysis. *arXiv e-prints*, page arXiv:2201.08277, January.

Hutto, C. and Gilbert, E. (2015). Vader: A parsimonious rule-based model for sentiment analysis of social media text. In *Proceedings of the 8th International Conference on Weblogs and Social Media, ICWSM 2014*, pages 218–225, 01.

Jamatia, A., Swamy, S. D., Gamback, B., Das, A., and Debbarma, S. (2020). Deep Learning Based Sentiment Analysis in a Code-Mixed English-Hindi and English-Bengali Social Media Corpus. *International Journal on Artificial Intelligence Tools*, 29.

Konate, A. and Du, R. (2018). Sentiment Analysis of Code-Mixed Bambara-French Social Media Text Using Deep Learning Techniques. *Wuhan University Journal of Natural Sciences*, 23:237–243, 06.

Kotzé, E. and Senekal, B. (2018). Employing sentiment analysis for gauging perceptions of minorities in multicultural societies: An analysis of Twitter feeds on the Afrikaner community of Orania in South Africa. *TD: The Journal for Transdisciplinary Research in Southern Africa*, 14(1):1–11.

Kranjc, J., Smailovic, J., Podpecan, V., Grcar, M.,

Znidari, M., and Lavrac, N. (2015). Active learning for sentiment analysis on data streams: Methodology and workflow implementation in the clowdflows platform. *Inf. Process. Manag.*, 51:187–203.

Lama. (2020). Talkwalker: Social Media Statistics and Usage in South Africa.

Lo, S. L., Cambria, E., Chiong, R., and Cornforth, D. (2017). Multilingual sentiment analysis: from formal to informal and scarce resource languages. *Artificial Intelligence Review*, 48(4):499–527.

Marivate, V., Sefara, T., Chabalala, V., Makhaya, K., Mokgonyane, T. B., Mokoena, R., and Modupe, A. (2020). Low resource language dataset creation, curation and classification: Setswana and Sepedi - Extended Abstract. *CoRR*, abs/2004.13842.

Martin, G. L., Mswahili, M. E., and Jeong, Y.-S. (2021). Sentiment Classification in Swahili Language Using Multilingual BERT. *African NLP Workshop, EACL 2021*, abs/2104.09006.

Medhat, W., Hassan, A., and Korashy, H. (2014). Sentiment Analysis Algorithms and Applications: A Survey. *Ain Shams Engineering Journal*, 5(4):1093–1113.

Mihalcea, R., Banea, C., and Wiebe, J. (2012). Multilingual subjectivity and sentiment analysis. In *Proceedings of the 50th Annual Meeting of the Association for Computational Linguistics: Tutorial Abstracts*, page 4, Jeju Island, Korea, July. Association for Computational Linguistics.

Mohammad, S. (2016). A practical guide to sentiment annotation: Challenges and solutions. In *Proceedings of the 7th Workshop on Computational Approaches to Subjectivity, Sentiment and Social Media Analysis*, pages 174–179, San Diego, California, June. Association for Computational Linguistics.

Muhammad, S. H., Adelani, D. I., Ruder, S., Ahmad, I. S., Abdulmumin, I., Bello, B. S., Choudhury, M., Emezue, C. C., Abdullahi, S. S., Aremu, A., Jeorge, A., and Brazdil, P. (2022). NaijaSenti: A Nigerian Sentiment Corpus for Multilingual Sentiment Analysis.

Nakov, P., Ritter, A., Rosenthal, S., Sebastiani, F., and Stoyanov, V. (2019). SemEval-2016 task 4: Sentiment analysis in Twitter. *arXiv preprint arXiv:1912.01973*.

Nielsen, F. Å. (2011). A new ANEW: evaluation of a word list for sentiment analysis in microblogs. *CoRR*, abs/1103.2903.

Öhman, E. (2020). Challenges in annotation: Annotator experiences from a crowdsourced emotion annotation task. In *Proceedings of the Digital Humanities in the Nordic Countries 5th Conference*, number 2612 in CEUR workshop proceedings, pages 293–301, International. CEUR Workshop Proceedings.

Pak, A. and Paroubek, P. (2010). Twitter as a corpus for sentiment analysis and opinion mining. In *LREc*, pages 1320–1326.

Pan, J., Xue, G.-R., Yu, Y., and Wang, Y. (2011). Cross-lingual sentiment classification via bi-view non-negative matrix tri-factorization. In *Pacific-Asia Conference on Knowledge Discovery and Data Mining*, pages 289–300. Springer.

Pang, B., Lee, L., and Vaithyanathan, S. (2002). Thumbs up? Sentiment classification using machine learning techniques. In *Proceedings of the ACL-02 conference on Empirical methods in natural language processing-Volume 10*, pages 79–86. Association for Computational Linguistics.

Ruder, S. (2020). Why you should do NLP beyond English. `http://ruder.io/nlp-beyond-english`.

Schlippe, T., Ochs, S., and Schultz, T. (2012). Grapheme-to-phoneme model generation for Indo-European languages. In *The 37th International Conference on Acoustics, Speech, and Signal Processing (ICASSP 2012)*, Kyoto, Japan, 25-30 March.

Shalunts, G., Backfried, G., and Commeignes, N. (2016). The impact of machine translation on sentiment analysis. In *The Fifth International Conference on Data Analytics*.

Statista. (2022). African countries with the largest population as of 2020.

Thelwall, M. A., Buckley, K., and Paltoglou, G. (2011). Sentiment in Twitter events. *J. Assoc. Inf. Sci. Technol.*, 62:406–418.

Turney, P. D. (2002). Thumbs up or thumbs down? Semantic orientation applied to unsupervised classification of reviews. In *Proceedings of the 40th annual meeting on association for computational linguistics*, pages 417–424. Association for Computational Linguistics.

Vilares, D., Alonso, M. A., and Gómez-Rodríguez, C. (2016). EN-ES-CS: An English-Spanish code-switching Twitter corpus for multilingual sentiment analysis. In *Proceedings of the Tenth International Conference on Language Resources and Evaluation (LREC'16)*, pages 4149–4153.

Vilares, D., Alonso, M. A., and Gómez-Rodríguez, C. (2017). Supervised sentiment analysis in multilingual environments. *Information Processing & Management*, 53(3):595–607.

Vosoughi, S., Zhou, H., and Roy, D. (2016). Enhanced Twitter sentiment classification using contextual information. *CoRR*, abs/1605.05195.

Wankhade, M., Rao, A., and Kulkarni, C. (2022). A Survey on Sentiment Analysis Methods, Applications, and Challenges. *Artificial Intelligence Review*, pages 1–50, 02.

Weidinger, L., Mellor, J., Rauh, M., Griffin, C., Uesato, J., Huang, P., Cheng, M., Glaese, M., Balle, B., Kasirzadeh, A., Kenton, Z., Brown, S., Hawkins, W., Stepleton, T., Biles, C., Birhane, A., Haas, J., Rimell, L., Hendricks, L. A., Isaac, W. S., Legassick, S., Irving, G., and Gabriel, I. (2021). Ethical and social risks of harm from language models. *CoRR*, abs/2112.04359.

Proceedings of SIGUL2022 @LREC2022, pages 78–82
Marseille, 24-25 June 2022

CUNI Submission to MT4All Shared Task

Ivana Kvapilíková and Ondřej Bojar
Institute of Formal and Applied Linguistics,
Faculty of Mathematics and Physics, Charles University,
Prague, Czech Republic,
kvapilikova@ufal.mff.cuni.cz, bojar@ufal.mff.cuni.cz

Abstract

This paper describes our submission to the MT4All Shared Task in unsupervised machine translation from English to Ukrainian, Kazakh and Georgian in the legal domain. In addition to the standard pipeline for unsupervised training (pretraining followed by denoising and back-translation), we used supervised training on a pseudo-parallel corpus retrieved from the provided monolingual corpora. Our system scored significantly higher than the baseline hybrid unsupervised MT system.

1. Introduction

Modern machine translation (MT) systems are trained on large parallel corpora, i.e. collections of sentence-aligned text documents translated by humans. While there are public sources of parallel data for several widely-spoken languages, most language pairs have a very limited access to such data. The same problem is faced by translation in high-resource languages but specific domains, since most training data come from newspaper articles and mixed tests crawled from the web. The MT4All project focuses on such low-resource situations and this shared task encourages participants to create unsupervised MT systems for translation from English to nine languages in three different domains: legal, financial and customer support.

In contrast to the standard MT, unsupervised MT models are trained without any parallel documents, but rather use large monolingual corpora to learn the structure of each language separately. Since monolingual texts are significantly easier to obtain (e.g. by web crawling) than parallel texts, unsupervised techniques have substantial amounts of non-translated text at their disposal, which can be leveraged to build a completely unsupervised translation system. Alternatively, parallel corpus (bitext) mining can be used to expand existing data resources by finding parallel sentences in comparable corpora (e.g. Wikipedia) and train an MT system in a supervised fashion even for low-resource languages.

The shared task organizers asked participants to either add value to existing unsupervised systems by adding monolingual training data or to train an unsupervised MT system from scratch. We chose the latter and trained a new MT system, but we also used an existing pretrained model to mine additional training data for our new model. We only participated in Task 1 which entailed unsupervised machine translation from English into Ukrainian, Kazakh and Georgian in the legal domain.

Section 2 of this paper summarizes related research in unsupervised MT. Section 3 describes the data sources and preprocessing, Section 4 gives more details on the parallel corpus we created. In Section 5 we describe the methodology used to build our system for the shared task and in Section 6 we discuss the results. Section 7 concludes.

2. Related Work

Unsupervised machine translation was pioneered by Artetxe et al. (2018b; Artetxe et al. (2018a) and Lample et al. (2018). They proposed unsupervised training techniques for both the phrase-based statistical machine translation (SMT) model and the neural machine translation (NMT) model to extract all necessary translation information from monolingual data. For the SMT model (Lample et al., 2018; Artetxe et al., 2018a), the phrase table is initialized with an unsupervised n-gram embedding mapping. For the NMT model (Lample et al., 2018; Artetxe et al., 2018b), the system is designed with a shared encoder and it is trained on batches of synthetic sentence pairs generated on-the-fly by denoising auto-encoding (Lample et al., 2018) and by back-translation (Sennrich et al., 2016). Artetxe et al. (2019a) push the translation quality higher by combining the two approaches and hybridizing their phrase based system. They train an NMT system with synthetic parallel data produced by the SMT system and jointly refine both systems by back-translation.

Conneau and Lample (2019) obtain similar results when pretraining the encoder and the decoder with a masked language model objective (Devlin et al., 2018) and fine-tuning for unsupervised MT. Song et al. (2019) pretrain the whole encoder-decoder structure on the task of reconstructing a sentence fragment given the remaining part of the sentence. The state of the art performance was reached in the work of Liu et al. (2020) who also pretrain an encoder-decoder model (mBART) and fine-tune using online back-translation. Tran et al. (2020) iteratively fine-tune mBART on the task of multilingual sentence retrieval as well as unsupervised translation and reach an improvement over vanilla mBART.

	en-ka	en-kk	en-uk
monolingual	22.4M x 6.3M	22.4M x 7.6M	22.4M x 9.7M
mined (all)	8.8M	4.7M	21.0M
mined (selected)	400K	300K	600K
mined (cleaned)	230K	169K	496K

Table 1: Final sizes (# of sentences) of cleaned mined parallel corpora in relation to the sizes of monolingual corpora we mined from.

	train (legal)	train (general)	dev	devtest
en	142K	22.4M	997	1,012
ka	264K	6.3M	997	1,012
kk	121K	7.6M	997	1,012
uk	7,601K	9.7M	997	1,012

Table 2: Number of sentences by splits in cleaned monolingual corpora.

3. Data

All provided data sources were monolingual. In addition to domain-specific data sets, the participants were allowed to use any part of the Oscar data set which was primarily intended for pretraining. The Oscar data set is large and we only used a part of it. The details of the data used are summarized in Table 2.

We used the sentence tokenizer from the `nltk` library to split the segments into sentences and we used the `fasttext` language detection model to get rid of sentences which do not appear to be in the desired language. The number of discarded sentences was around 6% of the entire corpus. The resulting size of the clean training corpora is reported Table 2.

Our NMT model processes text segmented into subword units. We used the sentencepiece (Kudo and Richardson, 2018) model trained for mBART50 (Liu et al., 2020) [1] to split the text into subwords and created a shared vocabulary from the most frequent 55k tokens covering 99.90% of the English monolingual training data and 99.97% of the Ukraininan, Kazakh and Georgian monolingual training data. The same vocabulary was used for all our models. The vocabulary size was determined to reasonably cover all training corpora while keeping the final size of the translation model limited.

It was also allowed to use any unsupervised pretrained model available in the Hugging Face Hub. We took the pretrained XLM-100 model and used it to mine parallel sentences from the monolingual corpora as proposed in (Kvapilíková et al., 2020). The details of the mining procedure are given below.

The validation data were taken from the Flores data set which belongs to the general domain. The blind test set was provided by the organizers and came from the legal domain.

4. Parallel Corpus Mining

Pretrained language models produce contextual representations capturing the semantic and syntactic properties of words in their context (Devlin et al., 2018). These representations may be aggregated to represent full sentences and used to assess sentence similarity. Multilingual language models can embed sentences in different languages and these embeddings can be used for parallel corpus mining.

We derive contextualized embeddings from the encoder outputs of the fifth-to-last internal layer of the XLM-100[2] model. It was shown by Kvapilíková et al. (2020) that the representations in the mid layers of the model carry the most multilingual information and are best aligned for the purpose of parallel sentence search.

We use the margin-based approach of (Artetxe and Schwenk, 2019a) to score all candidate sentence pairs rather than simple cosine similarity which cannot deal with the hubness phenomenon of embedding spaces (Artetxe and Schwenk, 2019b). The margin-based score is defined in relative terms to the average cosine similarity between the two sentences and their nearest neighbors, thus reducing the excessive score value of so called *hubs*.

Depending on the total number of retrieved candidates, we selected the top 600,000 sentence pairs for en-uk, 300,000 for en-ka and 400,000 for en-kk. A more careful selection or tuning of the quantities is left to future research. We then used the `clean-corpus-n.perl` script from Moses (Koehn et al., 2007) to get rid of sentences with less than 2 and more than 100 words and sentence pairs with a length ratio higher than 2. The resulting corpus sizes are summarized in Table 1.

An excerpt from the en-uk mined corpus is illustrated in Table 3. Most matched sentences include numerals, special symbols or named entities which probably serve as anchors for the models as they try to represent words in a language-neutral way. However, named entities are also often matched incorrectly. Some sentence pairs have no character overlap indicating that it is not only the identical tokens that drive the parallel sentence search but rather that at least some representations of tokens are properly aligned in the multilingual space. Even though the resulting data set is very noisy with a great number of errors, it seems to be enough to kick

[1] We originally intended to use the pretrained mBART50 model for training.)

[2] `https://huggingface.co/xlm-mlm-100-1280`

	uk	en
1	Encyclopædia Britannica, англ.	Encyclopædia Britannica, Inc.
2	№ 538.	Number 538.
3	Це 100%.	This 100%.
4	Все життя.	Nice life.
5	Їй було 35.	He was 31.
6	Свій!	Sure!
7	І він відмінно працює!	It works perfectly!
8	Це надзвичайно цікава історія.	It's an extraordinarily beautiful work.
9	Ці компанії раніше вже були включені [...]	Search features have been added into [...]
10	Одним з таких є приватна медична практика.	One of those is analytic continuation.
11	6 місяців назад вона народила дитину.	And two years ago she had another healthy baby boy.
12	Сьогодні стає зрозуміло, що боротьба з COVID-19 триватиме не один рік.	Today it is clear that the fight against COVID-19 will last more than one year.
13	Людське тіло містить від 55% до 78% води.	Human beings are made up of 50 – 86% .

Table 3: A sample from the en-uk mined parallel corpus. The translations are of differing quality, e.g. #12 is accurate, #11 and #14 have mistranslated numerals, #10 matches only in the first four words, #4 matches only in the second word.

off the training of an otherwise unsupervised MT system.

5. Training Methodology

We used the unsupervised training pipeline proposed by (Conneau and Lample, 2019). We first pretrained a cross-lingual masked language model (XLM) jointly on all data in English, Ukrainian, Kazakh and Georgian from scratch. The languages with a lower corpus size were upsampled to match the larger corpora. We used the pretrained model to initialize both the encoder and the decoder of an NMT model and fine-tuned with

1. standard MT objective using the mined parallel corpus,
2. online back-translation from monolingual data,
3. denoising from monolingual data.

After reaching convergence, we continued training using only denoising and online back-translation as we suspected that the translation quality of the trained MT system already surpassed the quality of the noisy corpus. After reaching convergence again, we further fine-tuned the model using online back-translation only on the texts from the legal domain.
All models were trained using the XLM toolkit.[3] on 4 GPUs with 16GB of RAM and delayed update of 2 to simulate training on 8 GPUs. The inference was performed with a beam size of 6. Selected training parameters are listed below

```
--tokens_per_batch 3450
--batch_size 30  #for back-translation
--accumulate_gradients 2
--amp 1
--fr16 True
--optimizer adam_inverse_sqrt,beta1=0.9,
beta2=0.98,lr=$LR,
```

[3] https://github.com/facebookresearch/XLM

		en-ka	en-kk	en-uk
1	MT-BT-DN	1.9	1.7	6.7
2	XLM + BT-DN	1.6	1.4	4.5
3	XLM + MT-BT-DN	3.4	2.7	9.0
4	(3) + BT	4.1	3.7	10.6
5	(4) + legal BT	4.1	3.8	8.8

Table 4: Validation results of our models on the Flores dev set. XLM - crosslingual masked LM pretraining; MT - supervised NMT fine-tuning on mined corpus; BT - online back-translation; DN - denoising.

		en-ka	en-kk	en-uk
1	MT-BT-DN	-	-	-
2	XLM + MT-BT-DN	-	-	
3	(2) + BT	**13.8**	7.7	27
4	(3) + legal BT	**13.8**	**9.4**	**28.1**
	Baseline	12	6.4	20.8

Table 5: Results of the submitted models. on the blind test set XLM - crosslingual masked LM pretraining; MT - supervised NMT fine-tuning; BT - online back-translation; DN - denoising.

6. Results

All results are measured on the detokenized data using `sacrebleu` (Post, 2018). In Table 4 we compare different techniques for NMT pretraining and its influence on the final translation quality.
To assess the impact of pretraining on the noisy parallel training data, we measured the performance of an unsupervised MT system trained according to the methodology of Conneau and Lample (2019) and we see an improvement of between 1.3 (en-kk) and 4.5 (en-uk) BLEU points caused by adding the mined parallel corpus. We also measured the effect of XLM pretraining

and we can conclude that for the language pairs in question, XLM pretraining significantly helps while also offering the flexibility of pretraining one multilingual model and using it to initialize all bilingual translation models.

When measured on the general Flores dev set, the effect of domain-specific fine-tuning is negative and leads to a decrease of up to 1.8 BLEU. However, when measured on the domain-specific test set, the fine-tuning adds up to 7.3 BLEU points (en-uk).

We were the only participants to this shared task so we cannot compare ourselves to other candidates but our models scored significantly higher than the baseline provided by the organizers. The baseline is a hybrid model trained from the bilingual word embeddings using the methodology of Artetxe et al. (2019b).

7. Conclusion

The performance of unsupervised models has significantly increased since the first attempts of Artetxe et al. (2018b) and Lample et al. (2018). We were able to train MT systems of reasonable quality for languages and domains where finding genuine parallel data is extremely difficult. We showed that adding a noisy parallel corpus mined from monolingual corpora to the training pipeline helps the final translation quality.

We submitted two unsupervised MT systems to the MT4All shared task, one of which was specifically fine-tuned for translation in the legal domain. Both systems scored significantly higher that the baseline (up to 7.3 BLEU points on the test set) but a comparison with the state-of-the-art mBART model remains for future work.

8. Acknowledgements

This work has received funding from the grant 19-26934X (NEUREM3) of the Czech Science Foundation, and support from the project "Grant Schemes at CU" (reg. no. CZ.02.2.69/0.0/0.0/19_073/0016935). This research was partially supported by SVV project number 260 575.

9. Bibliographical References

Artetxe, M. and Schwenk, H. (2019a). Margin-based parallel corpus mining with multilingual sentence embeddings. In *Proceedings of the 57th Annual Meeting of the ACL*, Florence, Italy. Association for Computational Linguistics.

Artetxe, M. and Schwenk, H. (2019b). Massively multilingual sentence embeddings for zero-shot cross-lingual transfer and beyond. *Transactions of the Association for Computational Linguistics*, 7:597–610, Mar.

Artetxe, M., Labaka, G., and Agirre, E. (2018a). Unsupervised statistical machine translation. In *Proceedings of the 2018 Conference on EMNLP*, Brussels, November. Association for Computational Linguistics.

Artetxe, M., Labaka, G., Agirre, E., and Cho, K. (2018b). Unsupervised neural machine translation. In *Proceedings of the Sixth International Conference on Learning Representations*, April.

Artetxe, M., Labaka, G., and Agirre, E. (2019a). An effective approach to unsupervised machine translation. In *Proceedings of the 57th Annual Meeting of the ACL*, pages 194–203, Florence, July. Association for Computational Linguistics.

Artetxe, M., Labaka, G., and Agirre, E. (2019b). An effective approach to unsupervised machine translation. In *Proceedings of the 57th Annual Meeting of the Association for Computational Linguistics*, pages 194–203, Florence, Italy, July. Association for Computational Linguistics.

Conneau, A. and Lample, G. (2019). Cross-lingual language model pretraining. In H. Wallach, et al., editors, *Advances in Neural Information Processing Systems 32*, pages 7059–7069. Curran Associates, Inc.

Devlin, J., Chang, M., Lee, K., and Toutanova, K. (2018). BERT: pre-training of deep bidirectional transformers for language understanding. *arXiv [e-Print archive]*, abs/1810.04805.

Koehn, P., Hoang, H., Birch, A., Callison-Burch, C., Federico, M., Bertoldi, N., Cowan, B., Shen, W., Moran, C., Zens, R., Dyer, C., Bojar, O., Constantin, A., and Herbst, E. (2007). Moses: Open source toolkit for statistical machine translation. In *Proceedings of the 45th Annual Meeting of the ACL*, pages 177–180, Prague, June. Association for Computational Linguistics.

Kudo, T. and Richardson, J. (2018). SentencePiece: A simple and language independent subword tokenizer and detokenizer for neural text processing. In *Proceedings of the 2018 Conference on Empirical Methods in Natural Language Processing: System Demonstrations*, pages 66–71, Brussels, Belgium, November. Association for Computational Linguistics.

Kvapilíková, I., Artetxe, M., Labaka, G., Agirre, E., and Bojar, O. (2020). Unsupervised multilingual sentence embeddings for parallel corpus mining. In *Proceedings of the 58th Annual Meeting of the Association for Computational Linguistics: Student Research Workshop*, pages 255–262, Online, July. Association for Computational Linguistics.

Lample, G., Ott, M., Conneau, A., Denoyer, L., and Ranzato, M. (2018). Phrase-based & neural unsupervised machine translation. In *Proceedings of the 2018 Conference on EMNLP*, pages 5039–5049.

Liu, Y., Gu, J., Goyal, N., Li, X., Edunov, S., Ghazvininejad, M., Lewis, M., and Zettlemoyer, L. (2020). Multilingual denoising pre-training for neural machine translation. *Transactions of the Association for Computational Linguistics*, 8:726–742.

Post, M. (2018). A call for clarity in reporting BLEU scores. In *Proceedings of the Third Conference on*

Machine Translation: Research Papers, pages 186–191, Brussels, Belgium, October. Association for Computational Linguistics.

Sennrich, R., Haddow, B., and Birch, A. (2016). Neural machine translation of rare words with subword units. In *Proceedings of the 54th Annual Meeting of the ACL*, pages 1715–1725, Berlin, August. Association for Computational Linguistics.

Song, K., Tan, X., Qin, T., Lu, J., and Liu, T.-Y. (2019). MASS: Masked sequence to sequence pre-training for language generation. In Kamalika Chaudhuri et al., editors, *Proceedings of the 36th International Conference on Machine Learning*, volume 97 of *Proceedings of Machine Learning Research*, pages 5926–5936. PMLR, 09–15 Jun.

Tran, C., Tang, Y., Li, X., and Gu, J. (2020). Cross-lingual retrieval for iterative self-supervised training. In H. Larochelle, et al., editors, *Advances in Neural Information Processing Systems*, volume 33, pages 2207–2219. Curran Associates, Inc.

Proceedings of SIGUL2022 @LREC2022, pages 83–91
Marseille, 24-25 June 2022

Resource: Indicators on the Presence of Languages in Internet

Daniel Pimienta
pimienta@funredes.org
Observatory of Linguistic and Cultural Diversity in the Internet
http://funredes.org/lc
Resource link: http://funredes.org/lc2022

Abstract

Reliable and maintained indicators of the space of languages on the Internet are required to support appropriate public policies and well-informed linguistic studies. Current sources are scarce and often strongly biased. The model to produce indicators on the presence of languages in the Internet, launched by the Observatory in 2017, has reached a sensible level of maturity and its data products are shared in CC-BY-SA 4.0 license. It reaches now 329 languages (L1 speakers > one million) and all the biases associated with the model have been controlled to an acceptable threshold, giving trust to the data, within an estimated confidence interval of +-20%. Some of the indicators (mainly the percentage of L1+L2 speakers connected to the Internet per language and derivates) rely on 2021 Ethnologue Global Dataset #24 for demo-linguistic data and ITU, completed by World Bank, for the percentage of persons connected to the Internet by country. The rest of indicators relies on the previous sources plus a large combination of hundreds of different sources for data related to Web contents per language. This research poster focuses the description of the new linguistic resources created. Methodological considerations are only exposed briefly and will be developed in another paper.

Keywords: Linguistic Resource, Languages, Internet, Indicators, Multilingualism

1. Introduction

The Observatory of Linguistic and Cultural Diversity in the Internet[1] has been working with alternative methods for measuring indicators of the presence of languages in the Internet since 1996. The standard method for computing the percentage of Web contents per language is logically to apply a language recognition algorithm to all the existing webpages and count. The huge extension of the Web makes this approach unpractical, except for targeting smaller subsets, as it was done efficiently by the Language Observatory Project, before the project faded out (Mikami et al., 2005). Attempts to use that approach by applying it to a target with a limited number of Webpages supposed to represent faithfully the whole Web, are prone to huge biases, as shown for the method defined by Alis Technologies in 1997[2] and reused) by OCLC (Lavoie and O'Neil, 1999) and (O'Neil et al., 2003. Eight thousand websites were randomly selected by IP numbers and conclusions were derived from a one-shot measurement, instead of a repetitive series treated statistically as a random variable.

Since 2011, W3Techs[3], indeed an excellent and reliable provider of statistics for Web technologies, has been practically the unique source available for Web contents per language, providing daily updated results thru the application of a language recognition algorithm to the home pages of the 10 million of websites classified as the most visited by Alexa.com[4]. The method is analogous to the one used for the other 25 Web technologies that are surveyed by this company, providing extremely interesting results. However, languages are a kind of Web technology quite different from Java Script Libraries or Web servers and processing web content's languages the same way may lead to huge errors. The issue starts by focusing on the home pages of the selection of websites: if you plan counting web contents you need to focus on webpages in order to avoid giving the same weight to a website of ten webpages compared to a website of ten thousand webpages. Furthermore, non-English websites quite often include English words inside their home page (either to introduce the site in English, either because few English words such as *copyright, abstract* or navigation buttons in English are present); this may cause errors to the algorithm. However, the bulk of the error is caused by the lack of consideration to **multilingualism** which makes the algorithm counts as English many websites which offer tenth of language's option in their interfaces. Quite often the website sets the language option automatically, according to user's preference, a practice more and more common, especially for the top sites in the global market (Facebook.com is just one example) and theW3Techs' algorithm is counting only one language per home page, English in those cases. No wonder then why, since 2011, the percentage of English in the Web is kept stable and even growing by

[1] http://funredes.org/lc

[2] https://web.archive.org/web/20010730164601/http://alis.isoc.org/palmares.en.html

[3] http://W3Techs.com

[4] A Web traffic collection and analytics sites belonging to Amazon corporation, about to be retired from the market.

W3Techs, in spite of evidences telling the Internet have changed drastically in the last decade, with Chinese becoming the first language in terms of users, and most Asian languages and Arabic booming. The Web is today probably **more multilingual than the humanity**. According to Ethnologue 2021 data, the ratio of L1+L2 speakers over L1 speakers is 10 361 716 756 / 7 231 699 136 = 1.43. No one shall be surprised then that more than 50% of websites exhibit pages in more than a unique language. Not paying due attention to multilingualism is therefore becoming an inacceptable bias for such studies. W3Techs could, without changing its current selection of websites and core program, fix its biases, with some reworks such as :

- Analyze the language options offered on the homepage and count each language option as well as the English version.
- Find a method to obtain an approximate estimate of the number of pages and multiply each linguistic version by that number in order to count webpages instead of websites.
- When the algorithm reports more than one language on the homepage, as a precaution, do not count the website as English, but rather the second language.

The new results will then be drastically different…

The worrying problem is that, because of the uniqueness of the source, the proven quality of the rest of its surveys, its long-term history and efficient marketing, a large percentage of the linguistic research community (and public policy makers) is taking W3Techs data as reliable inputs. Unfortunately, good theories fed by wrong numbers can hardly provide correct outcomes.

The most symptomatic example of the situation is given by the statistic's aggregator Statista[5] which titles its 2022 announcement about languages in the Internet[6] with a statement which reads as a hard fact: *English Is the Internet's Universal Language*, supported by W3techs data, where English web contents represent 63.7% of the total while Chinese only 1.3%.

At the same time, the Observatory of Linguistic and Cultural Diversity in the Internet computes English and Chinese at the same percentage together, around 20%, while Hindi, with its 224 millions of Internet users, reaches 3.8% (38 times more than the 0.1% measured by W3Techs) and concludes its last announcement with that sentence: *The transition of the Internet between the domination of European languages, English in the lead, towards Asian languages and Arabic, Chinese in the lead, is well advanced and* ***the winner is multilingualism****, but African languages are slow to take their place*.

One, at least, of the two sources shall be extremely wrong and researchers should exercise caution and check the biases of a method before drawing conclusions from its produced data…

2. Alternative Methods

Back in 1998-2007, the alternative method of the Observatory, which provided coherent series for a decade, was limited to English, German and the 5 Latin Languages (French, Italian, Spanish, Portuguese and Romanian). It used Search Engines to count *a comparable vocabulary*[7] for each language (Pimienta, et al. 2009). After 2007, the "marketing evolution" of Search Engines made the method obsolete as their reports of number of occurrences of a searched word become unreliable.

In 2017, the first version of a new Observatory's approach computes 138 languages, those with L1 speakers over 5 million, a limitation adopted to avoid too strong biases as consequence of the working hypothesis of the approach: *all language's speakers in the same country are computed with the same percentage of persons connected to the Internet, the national figure provided by ITU/World Bank.* This hypothesis forbids to compare languages within a country and is hardly applicable to language with low number of speakers. Additionally, it tends to bias positively immigration languages in developing countries (which may be less connected than the average) and to bias negatively European languages in developing countries (which tend to be better connected than the average). Today, the limitation has been extended to L1 > 1M, allowing 329 languages[8] to be processed.

This approach, which has reached maturity in its last version, is an **indirect approximation** to contents, based on the experimental observation that the ratio between world percentage of contents to world percentage of connected speakers has always remained between 0.5 and 1.5 for languages with full digital existence.

There is some kind of *natural economic law* suggested, which would link, for each language, the **offer** (web

[5] http://statista.com Along the line, I will not miss the opportunity to question the ethics of two emerging phenomena which could be correlated. 1) Too many lazy researchers cite Statista as a source of data instead of the very source. 2) Statista offers some data in free access but the identification of the source of that data is only accessible by paid customers.

[6] https://www.statista.com/chart/26884/languages-on-the-internet/

[7] An "equivalent" set of words is selected for each language, with a lot of linguistic precautions (both syntactic and semantic), whose occurrences is counted by Search Engines allowing statistical processing.

[8] Including indigenous languages responding this criterion (for example for languages of the Americas: Aymara, Guarani, Q'eqchi', Kiche and Quechua).

contents and applications) to the **demand** (speakers connected to the Internet). When the number of connected persons increases, the number of webpages logically increases together, in more or less the same proportion. This happens because governments, businesses, educative institutions, etc., and some individuals create contents to respond that demand.

Furthermore, surveys and studies have been consistently reporting that the average Internet users prefer to use their mother tongue and also take opportunity to use, as second option, their second language(s)[9].

Thus, depending of each language, there is some kind of modulation of the mentioned ratio, to make it above or below one. This would mean that some languages have more content production than others, depending on a set of factors related to languages in their country context, such as :

- Obviously, the relative amount of **L2 speakers**, as some people produce, for instance for economic reasons, contents in language different from their mother tongue.

But also:

- The proportion of Internet **traffic** depending of country's tariff, cultural or educational context.
- The number of **subscriptions** to social networks and other Internet applications.
- The digital technological support of the language and its presence in application's **interfaces** and translation programs which would make easier or not the content production.
- The level of submersion of the country where the speaker lives in terms of **Information Society facilities** (e-commerce, government applications to pay taxes and so on).

Then, if it was possible to collect various indicators about each of the mentioned characteristics, one would approximate the fluctuation of the modulation of web contents around one and deduce somehow the contents proportion. This is the core of the method and it is synthetized in the following diagram which shows all the indicators which are processed for each language and the corresponding quantity of sources the model is using. The first and second version of the methodology are fully documented, including the analysis of all identifies biases, see for a lead (Pimienta, 2019). The version 3 detailed methodological description is on the way.

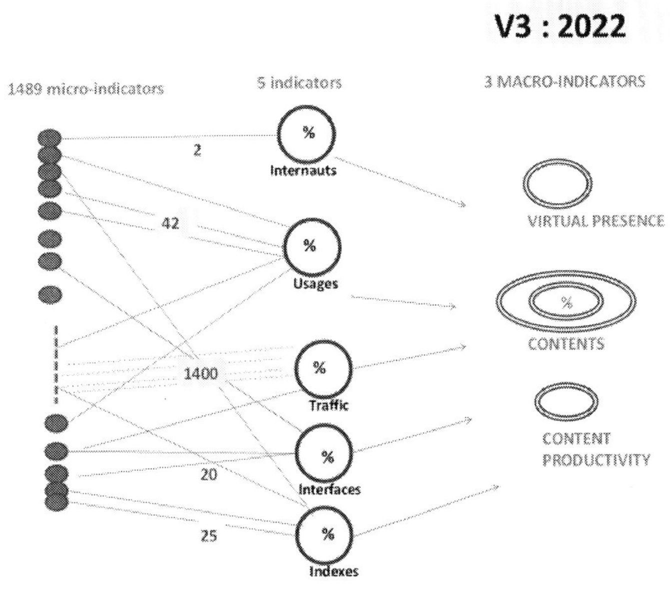

Figure

1: Diagram for indicators creation

This diagram has evolved, from version 1 to version 3, in terms of number of sources and also in terms of indicators, along the hard task of chasing the biases. The computation of the quite complex established

[9] See for instance Union European survey report in https://ec.europa.eu/commission/presscorner/detail/en/IP_1 1_556 or, for the challenging case of India, this report: https://assets.kpmg/content/dam/kpmg/in/pdf/2017/04/Indian-languages-Defining-Indias-Internet.pdf.

model relies extensively in a variety of **weighting operations** to perform the task, with, most of the time, the *vector of percentages of connected persons per country*, which is *the mathematical core* of the process. The source of indicators per language available are scarce; the majority of indicators are obtained per country and most of them only cover a subset of countries. The data source is therefore extrapolated to all countries, weighting with the core data, and the transforming of per country data into per language data is obtained by weighting with the demo-linguistic data (quantity of speakers of each language in each country).

3. Produced Indicators

For each of the 329 languages processed, the model is producing the following indicators per language (note that all world percentages are based on L1+L2 figures and represents the share corresponding for each language).

Intermediary indicators (all are world L1+L2 percentages):
Internauts: speakers connected to the Internet
Usages: relation between users and applications
Traffic: traffic reported to the applications
Interfaces and translation programs: proportion of applications and translation program supported
Indexes: rating of countries in Information Society parameters weighted into language ratings

Model outputs (also called macro-indicators):
Connected speakers : percentage from the total world L1+L2 speakers of those connected to the Internet
Contents : percentage of Web contents (computed as the average of the 5 intermediary indicators)
Content productivity: ratio Contents/Internauts
Virtual presence: ratio Contents/ Speakers

More advanced indicators:
Cyber-geography of languages: repartition of model outputs summed up by language families (European, Asian, Arabic, American, African)
Cyber-Globalization Indicator
CGI (L) = (L1 +L2)/L1(L) x S(L) x C(L)
Where:

L1+L2/L1(L) is the ratio of multilingualism of language L
S(L) is the percentage of world countries which holds speakers of language L
C(L) is the % of speakers of language L connected to the Internet.

This is an indicator of the strategic advantages of a language in cyberspace.

Additionally, for some languages, it has been displayed the list of countries which hold the major percentages of connected speakers.

The Excel files with the final results can be downloaded from http://funredes.org/lc2022.

A data base access to the results, with the possibility to query by language name or iso code, is in project. The plan is to update yearly the model.

4. Examples

Hereafter some examples of produced data are presented, limited, for the majority of the case, to the top results. The same data is available for any of the 329 processed language. The figure 2 inverted pyramid shall be read as an expression of the confidence interval: Chinese (or English) percentage of Web contents is between 16% and 24%, all the remaining languages together represent between 18% and 26% of the total.

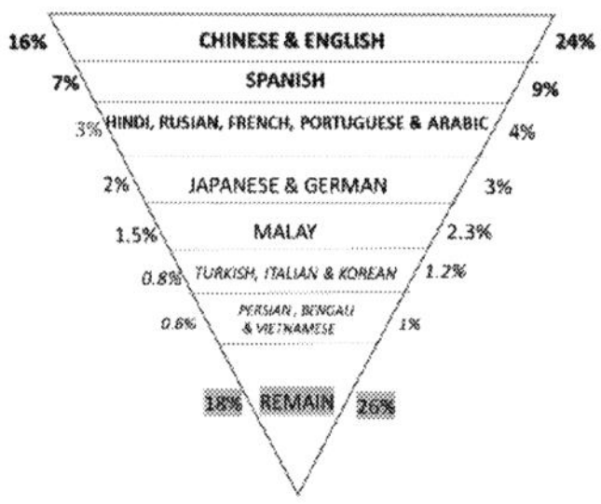

Figure 2: Percentage of contents windows for top languages

. Rank Contents L1+L2	ISO	LANGUAGES	INTERNAUTS L1+L2	World Population L1+L2	Connected Speakers L1+L2	Contents L1+L2	Virtual Presence L1+L2	Content Productivity L1+L2
1	zho	*Chinese*	18.46%	14.72%	71.38%	21.60%	1.47	1.17
2	eng	English	14.83%	13.01%	64.86%	19.60%	1.51	1.32
3	spa	Spanish	6.79%	5.24%	73.72%	7.85%	1.50	1.16
4	hin	Hindi	4.19%	5.80%	41.16%	3.76%	0.65	0.90
5	rus	Russian	3.51%	2.49%	80.32%	3.76%	1.51	1.07
6	fra	French	2.98%	2.58%	65.80%	3.33%	1.29	1.12
7	por	Portuguese	2.99%	2.49%	68.43%	3.13%	1.26	1.05
8	ara	*Arabic*	3.97%	3.53%	63.99%	3.09%	0.87	0.78
9	jpn	Japanese	1.99%	1.22%	92.63%	2.66%	2.18	1.34
10	deu	German	2.04%	1.30%	89.17%	2.37%	1.82	1.16
11	msa	*Malay*	2.36%	2.36%	56.93%	1.96%	0.83	0.83
12	tur	Turkish	1.17%	0.85%	78.05%	1.14%	1.35	0.98
13	ita	Italian	0.87%	0.66%	75.83%	1.00%	1.53	1.14
14	kor	Korean	0.90%	0.79%	65.16%	0.98%	1.24	1.09
15	fas	*Persian*	1.08%	0.81%	75.91%	0.88%	1.09	0.82
16	ben	Bengali	1.11%	2.58%	24.55%	0.88%	0.34	0.79
17	vie	Vietnamese	0.92%	0.74%	70.96%	0.85%	1.15	0.92
18	urd	Urdu	0.95%	2.22%	24.38%	0.66%	0.30	0.70
19	tha	Thai	0.80%	0.59%	77.95%	0.65%	1.12	0.82
20	pol	Polish	0.60%	0.39%	87.09%	0.63%	1.59	1.04
21	mar	Marathi	0.69%	0.96%	41.06%	0.58%	0.60	0.83
22	tel	Telugu	0.68%	0.92%	41.69%	0.56%	0.60	0.82
23	tam	Tamil	0.61%	0.82%	42.15%	0.51%	0.62	0.83
24	jav	Javanese	0.62%	0.66%	53.76%	0.44%	0.66	0.70
25	nld	Dutch	0.38%	0.24%	91.14%	0.41%	1.73	1.08
26	guj	Gujarati	0.44%	0.60%	41.47%	0.36%	0.61	0.83
27	ukr	Ukrainian	0.40%	0.32%	71.02%	0.35%	1.09	0.88
28	kan	Kannada	0.41%	0.57%	41.11%	0.33%	0.59	0.82
29	ron	Romanian	0.32%	0.23%	79.57%	0.30%	1.29	0.93
30	aze	*Azerbaijani*	0.33%	0.23%	81.54%	0.28%	1.21	0.85
		REMAIN	**22.60%**	**30.10%**		**15.13%**		
		TOTAL	**100%**	**100%**		**100%**		

Table 1: Main indicators for 30 top languages in content's percentage

Table 1 shall be read that way: English represents 14.8% of the Internet connected population and 13% of the L1+L2 world population; 64.9% of English L1+L2 speakers are connected to the Internet; 19.6% of the Web contents is in English; the virtual presence coefficient of English is 1.5, meaning that English contents are over-represented in a factor higher than 50%; the content productivity of English is 1.32, the higher after Japanese.

Note that the *macro languages* are mentioned in italics.

The following tables 2, 3, and 4 expose the top languages for each of the output indicators of the model, respectively:

- Percentage of connected speakers.
- Virtual presence (a value normalized to 1).
- Contents productivity (a value normalized to 1).

Table 5 exposes the Cyber-Geography of languages.
Table 6 exposes the Cyber Globalization Indicator.
Tables 7 and 8 expose respectively the first countries in terms of connected speakers for Chinese and Hindi. When appropriate explanations are provided below the tables.

LANGUAGE	CONNECTED SPEAKERS
Norwegian	96.89%
Danish	96.42%
Swedish	93.94%
Catalan	92.88%
Japanese	92.63%
Finnish	92.07%
German, Swiss	91.55%
Limburgish	91.42%
West Flemish	91.30%
Dutch	91.14%
Galician	91.07%
Saxon, Upper	89.81%
Estonian	89.26%
German. Standard	89.17%
Latvian	89.04%
Bavarian	88.24%

Table 2: Top languages in connected speakers

LANGUAGE	VIRTUAL PRESENCE
Japanese	2.18
Norwegian	1.88
German, Standard	1.82
Swedish	1.82
Danish	1.78
Dutch	1.73
Finnish	1.69
Catalan	1.68
German, Swiss	1.63
Polish	1.59
Italian	1.53
Estonian	1.51
Russian	1.51
English	1.51
Hebrew	1.50
Greek	1.50
Spanish	1.50
Chinese	1.47
Latvian	1.46

Table 3: Top languages in virtual presence

LANGUAGE	CONTENTS PROD.
Japanese	1.34
English	1.32
Chinese	1.17
German, Standard	1.16
Spanish	1.16
Italian	1.14
French	1.12
Norwegian	1.10
Swedish	1.10
Korean	1.09
Dutch	1.08
Russian	1.07
Greek	1.07
Kabuverdianu	1.05
Danish	1.05
Portuguese	1.05
Finnish	1.04
Polish	1.04
Catalan	1.03
German, Swiss	1.02
Hebrew	1.00

Table 4: Top languages in contents productivity

LANG. FROM (*)	AFRICA	AMERICAS	ARAB WORLD	ASIA	EUROPE	PACIFIC (**)
Internauts %	29.8%	56.7%	64.0%	49.3%	82.6%	
Contents %	2.89%	0.22%	3.09%	44.77%	45.39%	
POP.L1+L2 %	9.15%	0.31%	3.53%	48.21%	30.91%	
POP. CONN. %	5.18%	0.32%	3.89%	44.60%	39.51%	
Virtual. Pres.	0.28	0.68	0.87	0.65	1.39	
Cont. Prod.	0.51	0.68	0.78	0.72	0.95	
NUMBER OF LANGUAGES	138	8	1	135	47	0

Table 5: Cyber-geography of languages

(*) It has to be understood as native languages.
**) No languages from Pacific are included as none have more than 1 million L1 speakers.

The reading is done that way : African language's L1+L2 speakers have an average connectivity rate of 30% and represent together 3% of Web contents while representing together 9% of world L1+L2 speakers' population and 5% of L1+L2 connected speakers. They have an average virtual presence of 0.3 and a content productivity of 0.5, both indicators quite below the other categories. Note that 138 African languages are processed in the model, a figure slightly higher than the number of Asian languages.

LANGUAGE	CGI	CGI%
English	1.61	14.24%
French	1.09	9.66%
German	0.42	3.75%
Russian	0.31	2.76%
Spanish	0.27	2.40%
Arabic	0.18	1.56%
Malay	0.17	1.51%
Italian	0.17	1.50%
Chinese	0.16	1.46%
Portuguese	0.15	1.37%
Thai	0.15	1.37%
Romani	0.15	1.35%
Turkish	0.15	1.34%
Greek	0.15	1.31%
Ukrainian	0.15	1.31%
Polish	0.13	1.15%
Persian	0.12	1.10%
Rumanian	0.12	1.06%
Hindi	0.12	1.04%

Table 6: Cyber Globalization Indicator

The second column is computed by dividing the CGI value by the total of CGIs for all processed languages. It is mentioned as a way to measure the relative weight[10].

[10] Note that the relative weight of the two first positions, English and French, is close to 25% of the total, showing their strategical advantage. This is coherent with the huge demographic prospects for

CHINESE	L1+L2	%CONN.	CONNECTED	% FROM CONN.
TOTAL	1 525 335 340	71.38%	1 088 735 519	100%
China	1 448 870 000	70.64%	1 023 512 815	94.01%
China–Taiwan	37 320 000	88.82%	33 148 541	3.04%
China–Hong Kong	10 942 800	92.41%	10 112 585	0.93%
Malaysia	7 838 700	89.56%	7 019 949	0.64%
Singapore	4 026 000	75.88%	3 054 766	0.28%
United States	2 894 390	88.50%	2 561 503	0.24%
Viet Nam	2 500 000	70.64%	1 766 054	0.16%
Indonesia	2 054 000	53.73%	1 103 542	0.10%
Thailand	1 729 000	77.84%	1 345 918	0.12%
Canada	1 212 600	97.00%	1 176 222	0.11%
Philippines	1 010 280	43.03%	434 689	0.04%
REST	4 937 570	71.04%	3 507 738	0.32%

Table 7: Repartition of connected Chinese speakers per main countries

HINDI	L1+L2	%CONN.	CONNECTED	% FROM CONN.
TOTAL	600 800 970	41.15%	247 258 401	100%
India	596 000 000	41.00%	244 360 000	98.87%
Kuwait	700 000	98.60%	690 200	0.28%
United States	643 000	88.50%	569 048	0.23%
Nepal	1 307 600	25.00%	326 900	0.13%
South Africa	463 000	68.00%	314 840	0.13%
Saudi Arabia	171 000	97.86%	167 345	0.07%
Australia	160 000	86.54%	138 472	0.06%
Canada	111 000	97.00%	107 670	0.04%
Yemen	316 000	30.00%	94 800	0.04%
REST	929 370	52.63%	489 127	0.20%

Table 8: Repartition of connected Hindi speakers per main countries

5. Bibliographical References

Ethnologue Global Dataset (2022). https://www.ethnologue.com/product/ethnologue-global-dataset-0

Lavoie B.F., O'Neill E. T. (1999). How "World Wide" is the Web? *Annual review of OCLC Research,* https://web.archive.org/web/20031006155123/http://digitalarchive.oclc.org/da/ViewObject.jsp?objid=0000003496

Mikami Y., et al. (2005). The Language Observatory Project (LOP), In *Poster Proceedings of the Fourteenth International World Wide Web Conference*, pp. 990-991, May 2005, Japan

O'Neill E.T., Lavoie B.F., Bennett R. (2003). Trend in the Evolution of the Public Web: 1998 – 2002. *D-Lib Magazine*, 9.4 http://www.dlib.org/dlib/april03/lavoie/04lavoie.html

OIF (2022). Le français dans le monde, Gallimard,

Africa towards 2050: will the African digital divide be overcome those two European languages with higher presence in Africa, will benefit from this phenomenon which will place the African languages which are localized in good situation.

ISBN : 9782072976865. Synthèse en ligne: https://francophonie.org/sites/default/files/2022-03/Synthèse_La_langue_française_dans_le_monde_2022.pdf

Pimienta, D., Prado D., Blanco A. (2009). Twelve years of measuring linguistic diversity in the Internet: balance and perspectives, in *UNESCO Publications for the World Summit on the Information Society*, CI.2009/WS/1 http://unesdoc.unesco.org/images/0018/001870/187016e.pdf

Pimienta D. (2019). Indicators of Languages in the Internet, in Proceedings of International Conference Language Technologies for All (LT4All), 4-6 December 2019, UNESCO, Paris; PP 315-319 https://lt4all.elra.info/proceedings/lt4all2019/pdf/2019.lt4all-1.79.pdf

6. Acknowledgements

The version 3 studies were funded by Organisation Internationale de la Francophonie and the results fed the Internet Chapter of (OIF, 2022).

The idea to use various sources of data by country and transform them into data by language was first conceived by Daniel Prado in 2012.

Proceedings of SIGUL2022 @LREC2022, pages 92–97
Marseille, 24-25 June 2022

Language Technologies for Low Resource Languages: Sociolinguistic and Multilingual Insights

A. Seza Doğruöz, Sunayana Sitaram
Universiteit Gent, Microsoft Research India
Belgium, India
as.dogruoz@ugent.be, sunayana.sitaram@microsoft.com

Abstract

There is a growing interest in building language technologies (LTs) for low resource languages (LRLs). However, there are flaws in the planning, data collection and development phases mostly due to the assumption that LRLs are similar to High Resource Languages (HRLs) but only smaller in size. In our paper, we first provide examples of failed LTs for LRLs and provide the reasons for these failures. Second, we discuss the problematic issues with the data for LRLs. Finally, we provide recommendations for building better LTs for LRLs through insights from sociolinguistics and multilingualism. Our goal is not to solve all problems around LTs for LRLs but to raise awareness about the existing issues, provide recommendations toward possible solutions and encourage collaboration across academic disciplines for developing LTs that actually serve the needs and preferences of the LRL communities.

Keywords: Low Resource Languages, Multilingualism, Sociolinguistics, Language Technologies

1. Introduction

Low resource languages (LRL) refer to the languages spoken in the world with less linguistic resources for language technologies (LTs) (Cieri et al., 2016). Endangered and/or minority languages also overlap with the LRLs in terms of lacking resources for LTs. Different than endangered languages, not all LRLs and minority languages suffer from low numbers of speakers (cf. Pandharipande (2002)) for the situation of minority languages in India).

Joshi et al. (2020) categorize the languages of the world into six categories based on the resources available in terms of labeled and unlabeled data. More than 88% of the world's languages belong to the lowest resource class, with only 25 languages belonging to the two high resource classes. In other words, a majority of the world's languages count as LRLs even when they have large numbers of speakers (e.g. Gondi (Mehta et al., 2020) and Odia (Parida et al., 2020) spoken in India).

Data collection, annotation and analyses remain as challenges for LTs involving LRLs due to limited resources. Even when the data challenges are resolved, the resulting LTs may still not be favored and adopted by the LRL communities.

Recent advances in massive contextual language models (particularly multilingual versions) (Devlin et al., 2018; Conneau et al., 2020) give the impression that LTs for LRLs are solved based on their performance on some benchmarks (mainly covering high resource languages and a few NLP tasks) (Ruder et al., 2021; Liang et al., 2020). However, the majority of (approx. 100) languages covered by these models remain untested by these benchmarks, and the models are not trained on the majority of the world's languages.

Our goal is to highlight the dangers of viewing LRLs the same as high resource languages (HRLs) but only with less data and limited budget. To do this, we provide examples of well-intended but failed LTs for LRLs and explain the reasons through insights from sociolinguistics and multilingualism. Next, we describe the challenges with data (e.g. dangers of focusing on "purity" in LRLs). Lastly, we provide guidelines for different parts of the pipeline (i.e. data collection, annotation and evaluation) to develop better and more informed LTs for LRLs and their speakers.

2. Issues about Sociolinguistic Variation

We start this section with an example of a failed LT for an LRL community in India and explain the reasons with links to sociolinguistics. Voice-based systems are potentially useful LTs for LRL communities with low literacy rates. Spoken Dialogue Systems or Interactive Voice Response (IVR) systems rely on carefully designed prompts and a vocabulary list that needs to be recognized by a speech recognizer. For example, VideoKheti (Cuendet et al., 2013) is a speech and graphics based application targeting speakers of Malvi language in India (a sub-dialect of the Rajashtani dialect of Hindi (Bali et al., 2013)). The application was created to help (illiterate) farmers in rural India to access agricultural online videos by spoken search. During the data collection, a local non-governmental organization (NGO) assisted the project to develop a vocabulary list for the speech recognition system. However, the list contained many technical words which were borrowed from Hindi (and in a formal register) and did not exist in the linguistic repertoires of Malvi speakers in daily and informal communication. Example (1) illustrates one of the problematic technical terms which could (roughly) be translated as "chemical pesticide" (Bali, 2020).

1. **Rasaayanik tarike se kharpatwaar niyantran**
   Chemical technique for weed control

Instead of example (1), Malvi speakers would normally use example (2) in the same context.

2. **keede maarne ki dawaai**
   pest killing medicine

As illustrated with examples above, the terminology used for the linguistic prompts in the app did not match with the daily language use in the Malvi community. This mismatch led to errors in both the recognition and understanding of the prompts produced by the system. Another mismatch in language use was observed in terms of gender differences. More specifically, female Malvi speakers had more difficulty than male speakers using this app. There could be a few reasons behind this observation. Although the new terminology in the app (see example (1)) was unfamiliar to both male and female speakers of the same community, (some) male speakers eventually got familiar with the new terminology through attending the meetings organized by the NGO. For female members, on the other hand, it is not always socially acceptable to attend such public meetings. Second, female members may not always feel comfortable to voice their opinions freely in presence of males or elderly relatives (e.g. parents-in-law) even if they attend such meetings.
Despite the well-intended efforts, the particular app ended up relying mostly on the graphic interface and the speech part was underused by the LRL community members. In other words, it did not serve its development purpose not to mention the unfortunate use of resources and (possible) disappointment among developers and LRL community members who spent time and energy on it. Both of the challenges explained above could have been avoided by a thorough analysis of sociolinguistic variation in the respective LRL community. More concretely, specific farming terminology for the app should not have been developed in a top-down fashion but in a bottom-up way through observing and collecting informal and conversational data from the community members across different backgrounds (e.g. genders, ages, educational background) and in different contexts (e.g. from males and females on different occasions). In this way, the app would have reflected the language used by the LRL community members and it would have served its development purpose.

3. Issues about Multilingualism

Considering that multilingualism is the norm in majority of the world (Dorian, 2014), it is also reasonable to assume (at least some) LRL speakers and communities to be multilingual. In that case, there is a need to analyze their attitudes toward LRLs as well as the power and prestige hierarchies in those contexts before developing any LTs for these communities. For example, speakers of endangered and/or minority languages who had disadvantages in social life (e.g. finding a job) due to lack of language abilities in the dominant language may prefer not to speak LRLs with their children (Dorian, 2014). Pandharipande (2002) gives an example of a housemaid who is a native speaker of Tulu (a LRL) and works in Mumbai (India). She declined to teach and speak Tulu with her children since English and Marathi are the languages that they should be learning for upward mobility (e.g. better education and jobs) according to her.
Similarly, it is quite normal for multilingual LRL community members to switch across languages/dialects in their daily communication. Although there is plenty of research about multilingual language use and code-switching across languages in the world (e.g. an extensive survey by Doğruöz et al. (2021)), multilingualism is not always taken into account while developing LTs for these communities.
For example, in Automatic Speech Recognition (ASR) systems, Srivastava et al. (2018) and Shah et al. (2020) observe that it is not possible to remove all the utterances with foreign words (e.g. code-switching into English) in Hindi since some of these words are already borrowed and got integrated into the language over time. Besides, Hindi has already quite a few borrowings from Persian and Arabic due to centuries-long contact (Jain and Cardona, 2007). Since the distinction between code-switching and borrowing is often blurry (Doğruöz et al., 2021), filtering either of these from the system arbitrarily will lead to system failures. As a result, LRL communities will not approve and adopt the system for which valuable time, energy and resources were invested. Therefore, aiming to create monolingual data sets even for comparisons or benchmarking purposes is not a meaningful effort for LRLs which inherently contain many borrowed words in highly multilingual areas (e.g. India, Africa, Polynesian islands).

4. Issues about Data

Data-driven studies in NLP and speech processing rely on large datasets of text and speech to build models or gain insights automatically. These datasets are curated from naturally occurring data (e.g. social media and/or recorded conversations among humans), or they are created specifically targeting the intended use case scenario.
In general (for most HRLs), there is a tendency to collect only monolingual data, in its standard dialect and with a formal register so that a "pure" target language (e.g. ignoring the inherent sociolinguistic variation in the community) would benefit the accuracy of the system. As a result, the data set becomes very small and artificial in the sense that it does not represent the language spoken in the community anymore (cf. Nguyen et al. (2016)). Although these flaws could be improved for HRLs with enough resources over time, there is (usually) not a second chance for LRLs with limited

manpower, budget and resources. As a result, the LRL communities are left with LTs that do not reflect their language use and do not serve their needs and preferences.

5. Recommendations for Building LTs for LRLs

In the previous sections, we explained how lack of insights in sociolinguistics and multilingualism leads to flaws in developing LTs for LRLs. In this section, we provide guidelines and solutions about how to avoid these pitfalls for the LT pipelines targeting LRLs.

Preparation: Before building any type of LTs and collecting data, making sufficient sociolinguistic inquiries about the dynamics and language use practices among a LRL community is crucial. For example, literacy status of the users, availability of written scripts in a LRL, multilingual and mixed language practices in the community should be researched extensively. In addition, existing data sets (albeit small or not of high quality) for endangered and minority languages (e.g. Pangloss collection by Michailovsky et al. (2014) for endangered Asian, Oceanic, Caucasian, European languages, ELAR (Endangered Languages Archive) collection described by Nathan (2013)) could serve as starting points for LTs in LRLs. They usually come with a description of the meta-data (e.g.participants/community, context) which could give some preliminary insights about the community dynamics. Before collecting any type of data in the LRL community, it is recommended to connect with the Linguistics Department of a local university for their help on available literature, on-going or completed projects on the local LRLs as well as training and employing their students for field work. Instead of allocating resources in a top-down fashion, it is more feasible, less expensive and less time-consuming to start bottom-up with the existing resources and collaborate with fellow researchers in linguistics/sociolinguistics who may already have insights about the LRLs and their communities in depth.

Data Collection: Given that NLP models are becoming larger and require more data than ever before, data collection remains the backbone on which LTs are built upon today. Ideally, the data for LRLs should be collected from the speakers that LTs will benefit. However, this is not always practiced. Instead, it often results in approximating the target LRL by using existing HRL data which is often not representative of the LRLs spoken in the community.

LRL communities should not be expected to adapt to language of the LT developed through random and approximate data sets. Instead, it is crucially important to send multi-disciplinary (e.g. computational (socio)linguists,engineers, multilingualism experts, social workers) teams to spend extended periods of time with the target LRL community with the goal of understanding their (multilingual) needs and preferences as well as the the sociolinguistic variation operating in the particular LRL context. If this is considered a challenge (which should not be), it is at least desirable to collect better approximate data (instead of random ones) which would reflect LRLs in real-life like conversational situations (e.g. movies and soap operas reported by (Biswas et al., 2022)).

Data Cleaning: Language technologies are usually built with monolingual assumptions about character sets, vocabulary and lexicons. The limited amount of data available for LRLs is further reduced if it is also cleaned or filtered to make it (often unnaturally) monolingual. In addition to ignoring the dynamic and multilingual aspects of the data, there is also the danger of not being able to make the best use of naturally occurring data with all its deficiencies and variation (aka "bad language" (Eisenstein, 2013)), or collecting data that does not reflect the real use in the given community.

Prior work on dealing with linguistic variation in the data focused on normalization and domain adaptation. Both of these approaches are problematic. Normalization processes assume that there is a default norm in every language and this norm is often associated with the monolingual, standard dialect and formal register. This assumption results in ignoring communities and speakers who may not use the standard dialect and formal register in their daily communication. Similarly, domain adaptation is not ideal for shifts in medium of expression, like social media. Languages are dynamic and they constantly change even in (supposedly) monolingual contexts. Therefore, LTs should also change and handle linguistic variation simultaneously instead of ignoring and cleaning the data through extensive normalization processes (cf. Nguyen et al. (2016)).

In multilingual contexts and communication, this translates as avoiding to clean the data from foreign influences (e.g. code-switching) to make it "pure" or monolingual, avoiding to create artificial datasets by collecting data in the wrong register (e.g. "formal" instead of "informal"), and avoiding to ignore the foreign language influences (e.g. code-switching and borrowing) during the processing phase.

Annotation: Labeling sociolinguistic variation (e.g. multilingualism, variation in styles, registers, variation across contexts and social variables of users) in the data is challenging due to the lack of standardization. In fact, tailor made solutions are probably more feasible than standard solutions that are assumed to apply across all LRLs. In addition to code-switching, it is also common to switch across scripts in India. For example, annotators use multiple scripts (Devanagari and Latin) to transcribe Hindi-English code-switched speech (Srivastava and Sitaram, 2018) and they may end up transcribing the same word in both scripts in different instances in the corpus. Although it may seem that this problem can be avoided by training the annotators or providing instructions to them, it remains an extremely challenging problem because the distinction between switching and borrowing is blurry (Doğruöz et al., 2021). A related issue is the lack of standardized spellings for borrowed words. Inconsistencies in transcription lead to less training data per word during the model building. As a result, a vicious cycle is created with difficulties in using automated tools to bootstrap labeling due to inconsistently labeled data.

Model building: Models built with monolingual assumptions may produce errors while processing inherently multilingual LRLs and this leads to lower performance of the model. Systems may either ignore content that is not in the expected language, or perform poorly on multilingual utterances. Massive multilingual models such as multilingual BERT (Devlin et al., 2018) and XLMR (Conneau et al., 2020) can process around 100 languages in a single model, however they tend to perform worse on LRLs compared to HRLs (Wu and Dredze, 2020). There is also evidence to show that these models perform poorly on mixed languages (Khanuja et al., 2020). Using these models through few-shot or zero-shot techniques on LRLs may not lead to desired outcomes, since the data they are pre-trained on (e.g. Wikipedia texts or randomly crawled data from the web) does not represent the language use within the LRL community. Adaptation techniques can be explored if the standard variety of the language is used to build the model. However, the adaptation data needs to be collected considering the sociolinguistic variation in the LRL. During the system design phase, there is a need to carefully examine which models are best suited for the intended purpose, instead of assuming that the largest, latest and most accurate models on HRL will also perform best on LRLs. If multiple languages are being served by the same model, there is a need to consider whether the model is fair to all languages (Choudhury and Deshpande, 2021) and that some languages do not benefit at the cost of others. Models that are explainable and easy to debug will also benefit from the feedback provided by the users of LRL communities.

Evaluation: Evaluation benchmarks do not exist for most LRLs (Bhatt et al., 2021). The few and available test datasets may not reflect the way language is used in LRL communities and decrease the usefulness of the benchmarks. Many of these benchmarks (very expensive to create), turn out to be brittle to spurious patterns learned by NLP models (Glockner et al., 2018). Due to over optimization on a small set of benchmarks, it is likely that the performance of NLP models (even on HRLs) is an overestimate. This situation is even more stark in case of LRLs (Wu and Dredze, 2020), where benchmarks do not exist for most languages and tasks.

Code-switching and borrowing make it harder to evaluate systems due to cross-script transcription, multiple ways of conveying the same meaning and the issues (mentioned earlier) with data collection and annotation. Although some NLP benchmarks (e.g. XTREME-R by (Ruder et al., 2021)) cover 50 languages and a set of diverse tasks, each language is still assumed to be strictly monolingual. Currently, there are only two benchmarks that deal with mixed languages (i.e. code-switching, GLUECoS (Khanuja et al., 2020) and LinCE (Aguilar et al., 2020)). However, even these benchmarks cover very few LRLs and a small set of tasks.

Metrics to evaluate LTs are flawed, since they are usually created for HRLs and they do not always reflect the nuances of how the LTs will actually be used in other languages. There is an urgent need to create better metrics and benchmarks, preferably by collecting evaluation data directly from the speakers of the target LRL communities. Accurate and meaningful evaluation of LTs for LRL users can only happen through their participation.

6. Discussion

To conclude, building LTs for LRLs is not a solved problem and there are no simple and quick recipes. LTs built without enough understanding of the LRL communities may not serve their purposes. Therefore, all the aspects mentioned above regarding the data collection, cleaning, annotation, model building and evaluation should be considered by multi-disciplinary teams before building any LTs for LRLs.

Experimenting with LRLs in computational linguistic domains can be a commendable scientific endeavour to test the limits of NLP models (e.g. massive multilingual models), explore new modeling techniques and may also lead to significant improvements in performance for these languages. However, improvements in performance should not be conflated with usefulness of the LTs for the target LRL community without making sure that the factors mentioned above are taken into account, and appropriate evaluation (when possible, including the LRL community members) is carried out.

If the goal is to develop LTs that are actually useful for the LRL community members, there is a need to slow down and understand the social and linguistic dynamics operating in a LRL community through a careful examination. After involving all the stakeholders, appropriate data that reflects real-life language use in the LRL community should be collected without being exposed to a cleaning/normalization phase to increase the accuracy of the models. Fair and explainable models which could also integrate feedback should be favored and evaluated by using the appropriate benchmarks or by testing with the LRL community members.

Ignoring the above-mentioned challenges and pitfalls will only lead to LTs which will remain as experimental trials without any prospects for successful adoptions by the LRL communities. Any serious attempts on building LTs for LRLs can be only be realized through inter-disciplinary collaboration across fields and after following above-mentioned steps closely. We hope that the guidelines in our paper could serve as footprints for the researchers and developers to build better LTs for LRLs and their communities.

7. Bibliographical References

Aguilar, G., Kar, S., and Solorio, T. (2020). Lince: A centralized benchmark for linguistic code-switching evaluation. In *Proceedings of the 12th Language Resources and Evaluation Conference*, pages 1803–1813.

Bali, K., Sitaram, S., Cuendet, S., and Medhi, I. (2013). A hindi speech recognizer for an agricultural video search application. In *Proceedings of the 3rd ACM Symposium on Computing for Development*, pages 1–8.

Bali, K. (2020). The giant leaps in technology - and who is left behind. TEDxMICA.

Bhatt, S., Goyal, P., Dandapat, S., Choudhury, M., and Sitaram, S. (2021). On the universality of deep contextual language models. *arXiv preprint arXiv:2109.07140.*

Biswas, A., Yılmaz, E., van der Westhuizen, E., de Wet, F., and Niesler, T. (2022). Code-switched automatic speech recognition in five south african languages. *Computer Speech & Language*, 71:101262.

Choudhury, M. and Deshpande, A. (2021). How linguistically fair are multilingual pre-trained language models? In *Proceedings of the AAAI Conference on Artificial Intelligence*, volume 35, pages 12710–12718.

Cieri, C., Maxwell, M., Strassel, S., and Tracey, J. (2016). Selection criteria for low resource language programs. In *Proceedings of the Tenth International Conference on Language Resources and Evaluation (LREC'16)*, pages 4543–4549, Portorož, Slovenia, May. European Language Resources Association (ELRA).

Conneau, A., Khandelwal, K., Goyal, N., Chaudhary, V., Wenzek, G., Guzmán, F., Grave, É., Ott, M., Zettlemoyer, L., and Stoyanov, V. (2020). Unsupervised cross-lingual representation learning at scale. In *Proceedings of the 58th Annual Meeting of the Association for Computational Linguistics*, pages 8440–8451.

Cuendet, S., Medhi, I., Bali, K., and Cutrell, E. (2013). Videokheti: Making video content accessible to low-literate and novice users. In *Proceedings of the SIGCHI conference on human factors in computing systems*, pages 2833–2842.

Devlin, J., Chang, M.-W., Lee, K., and Toutanova, K. (2018). Multilingual bert readme document. *Library Catalog: github. com.*

Doğruöz, A. S., Sitaram, S., Bullock, B. E., and Toribio, A. J. (2021). A survey of code-switching: Linguistic and social perspectives for language technologies. In *The Joint Conference of the 59th Annual Meeting of the Association for Computational Linguistics and the 11th International Joint Conference on Natural Language Processing (ACL-IJCNLP 2021)*. Association for Computational Linguistics.

Dorian, N. (2014). *Small-language fates and prospects: Lessons of persistence and change from endangered languages: Collected essays*. Brill.

Eisenstein, J. (2013). What to do about bad language on the internet. In *Proceedings of the 2013 conference of the North American Chapter of the association for computational linguistics: Human language technologies*, pages 359–369.

Glockner, M., Shwartz, V., and Goldberg, Y. (2018). Breaking nli systems with sentences that require simple lexical inferences. In *Proceedings of the 56th Annual Meeting of the Association for Computational Linguistics (Volume 2: Short Papers)*, pages 650–655.

Jain, D. and Cardona, G. (2007). *The Indo-Aryan Languages*. Routledge.

Joshi, P., Santy, S., Budhiraja, A., Bali, K., and Choudhury, M. (2020). The state and fate of linguistic diversity and inclusion in the nlp world. In *Proceedings of the 58th Annual Meeting of the Association for Computational Linguistics*, pages 6282–6293.

Khanuja, S., Dandapat, S., Srinivasan, A., Sitaram, S., and Choudhury, M. (2020). Gluecos: An evaluation benchmark for code-switched nlp. In *Proceedings of the 58th Annual Meeting of the Association for Computational Linguistics*, pages 3575–3585.

Liang, Y., Duan, N., Gong, Y., Wu, N., Guo, F., Qi, W., Gong, M., Shou, L., Jiang, D., Cao, G., et al. (2020). Xglue: A new benchmark datasetfor cross-lingual pre-training, understanding and generation. In *Proceedings of the 2020 Conference on Empirical Methods in Natural Language Processing (EMNLP)*, pages 6008–6018.

Mehta, D., Santy, S., Mothilal, R. K., Srivastava, B. M. L., Sharma, A., Shukla, A., Prasad, V., Venkanna, U., Sharma, A., and Bali, K. (2020). Learnings from technological interventions in a low resource language: A case-study on gondi. In *Proceedings of the 12th Language Resources and Evaluation Conference*, pages 2832–2838.

Michailovsky, B., Mazaudon, M., Michaud, A., Guillaume, S., François, A., and Adamou, E. (2014). Documenting and researching endangered languages: the pangloss collection. *Language Documentation & Conservation*, 8:119–135.

Nathan, D. (2013). Access and accessibility at elar, a social networking archive for endangered languages documentation. *Oral literature in the digital age: archiving orality and connecting with communities*, pages 21–40.

Nguyen, D., Doğruöz, A. S., Rosé, C. P., and De Jong, F. (2016). Computational sociolinguistics: A survey. *Computational linguistics*, 42(3):537–593.

Pandharipande, R. V. (2002). Minority matters: Issues in minority languages in india. *International Journal of Multicultural Societies*, 4:213–235.

Parida, S., Dash, S. R., Bojar, O., Motlicek, P., Pattnaik, P., and Mallick, D. K. (2020). OdiEnCorp

2.0: Odia-English parallel corpus for machine translation. In *Proceedings of the WILDRE5– 5th Workshop on Indian Language Data: Resources and Evaluation*, pages 14–19, Marseille, France, May. European Language Resources Association (ELRA).

Ruder, S., Constant, N., Botha, J., Siddhant, A., Firat, O., Fu, J., Liu, P., Hu, J., Garrette, D., Neubig, G., et al. (2021). Xtreme-r: Towards more challenging and nuanced multilingual evaluation. *arXiv preprint arXiv:2104.07412*.

Shah, S., Sitaram, S., and Mehta, R. (2020). First workshop on speech processing for code-switching in multilingual communities: Shared task on code-switched spoken language identification. *WSTC-SMC 2020*, page 24.

Srivastava, B. M. L. and Sitaram, S. (2018). Homophone identification and merging for code-switched speech recognition. In *Interspeech*, pages 1943–1947.

Srivastava, B. M. L., Sitaram, S., Mehta, R. K., Mohan, K. D., Matani, P., Satpal, S., Bali, K., Srikanth, R., and Nayak, N. (2018). Interspeech 2018 low resource automatic speech recognition challenge for indian languages. In *SLTU*, pages 11–14.

Wu, S. and Dredze, M. (2020). Are all languages created equal in multilingual bert? In *Proceedings of the 5th Workshop on Representation Learning for NLP*, pages 120–130.

Proceedings of SIGUL2022 @LREC2022, pages 98–105
Marseille, 24-25 June 2022

Sentiment Analysis for Hausa: Classifying Students' Comments

Ochilbek Rakhmanov, Tim Schlippe
IU International University of Applied Sciences
ochilbek@rakhmanov.net, tim.schlippe@iu.org

Abstract

We describe our work on sentiment analysis for Hausa, where we investigated monolingual and cross-lingual approaches to classify student comments in course evaluations. Furthermore, we propose a novel stemming algorithm to improve accuracy. For studies in this area, we collected a corpus of more than 40,000 comments—the *Hausa-English Sentiment Analysis Corpus For Educational Environments* (HESAC). Our results demonstrate that the monolingual approaches for Hausa sentiment analysis slightly outperform the cross-lingual systems. Using our stemming algorithm in the pre-processing even improved the best model resulting in 97.4% accuracy on HESAC.

Keywords: sentiment analysis, Hausa, low-resource language, corpus, AI in education

1. Introduction

Sentiment analysis (SA) helps analyze and extract information about polarity from textual feedback and opinions. SA draws attention not only in business environments (Rokade and D, 2019) but also in other areas, like medicine (Zucco et al., 2018). Furthermore, SA is one of the hot research topics in the field of education (Lalata et al., 2019)—a domain that is becoming more and more interesting, also with regards to goal 4 of United Nations' Sustainable Development Goals (UN, 2022). Many educational institutions receive feedback from students—either verbally or in written form—in order to improve the quality of the course contents. But due to the large number of lectures and students, it is often impossible to analyze each of the comments manually. Thus, many research papers focus on how to automate this process in order to extract meaningful information from students' feedback (e.g., (Rani and Kumar, 2017; Kandhro et al., 2019; Sindhu et al., 2019; Rakhmanov, 2020a)).

SA in education generally analyzes such sentiments with machine learning techniques and lexicon-based approaches. Some promising results (up to 95% accuracy) were achieved with random forests and deep neural networks for English students' comments (Rakhmanov, 2020b). Lexicon-based approaches were also used in many studies and good results were obtained, although not as much as in machine learning approaches (Aung and Myo, 2017; Nasim et al., 2017).

The fact that there are many text resources for English has made classification tasks like SA generally successful (Heitmann et al., 2020). But when it comes to low-resource languages, it seems difficult to achieve the same success (Djatmiko et al., 2019). To solve the problem of low-resource languages in SA, cross-lingual approaches with machine translation (MT) are proposed (Balahur and Turchi, 2014; Lin et al., 2014; Can et al., 2018). However, performance of existing MT systems is not always good in low-resource settings having a bad impact on the final SA classification accuracy (Vilares et al., 2017; Inuwa-Dutse, 2021).

Our research was carried out to find solutions to the above-mentioned shortcomings. We investigated different SA methods for Hausa, a low-resource language, which is spoken by approximately 50–100 million people in West Africa (Abubakar et al., 2019). The Hausa people are concentrated mainly in Northwestern Nigeria and in Southern Niger (Burquest, 1992; Koslow, 1995; Schlippe et al., 2012). The cities of this region—Kano, Sokoto, Zari, and Katsina, to name only a few—are among the largest commercial centers of sub-Saharan Africa. Hausa people also live in other countries of West Africa like Cameroon, Togo, Chad, Benin, Burkina Faso, and Ghana. Our goals were:

- To develop a unique English-Hausa data set of more than 40,000 students' comments.
- To conduct a comparative study on monolingual and cross-lingual SA approaches using the Hausa-English data set.
- To test the performance of SA on the Hausa data set with the help of BERT (Devlin et al., 2019), RoBERTa (Liu et al., 2019) and other natural language processing (NLP) models and techniques.
- To investigate if stemming and removal of stop words and duplicates help improve SA accuracy in Hausa.

2. Related Work

While SA resulted in many successful applications in different fields like business (Rokade and D, 2019) and medicine (Zucco et al., 2018), it has also been the subject of research in education (Lalata et al., 2019). Different machine learning algorithms like support vector machines (SVM), decision trees (DT), random forests (RF), multilayer perceptron (MLP) and long short-term memories (LSTM) were analyzed for this task (Balahur and Turchi, 2014; Nguyen et al., 2018; Kumar and Sharan, 2020; Rakhmanov, 2020a). Lexicon-based approaches were also investigated, but machine learning algorithms usually outperform the lexicon-based approaches (Kolchyna et al., 2015; Kotelnikova et al., 2021).

Some researchers propose cross-lingual NLP approaches to solve the problems of low-resource languages by benefiting from rich-resource languages like English (Balahur and Turchi, 2014; Lin et al., 2014; Vilares et al., 2017; Can et al., 2018). For SA, they usually translate the comments from the original low-resource language to English. This allows to do the classification task of SA with well-performing models trained with a lot of English resources. Yet, some NLP models derived from BERT, such as multilingual BERT (m-BERT) (Pires et al., 2019) or RoBERTa (Liu et al., 2019) were trained with a lot of languages and are able to classify comments straightforward from those languages. Unfortunatelly, m-BERT was not trained with Hausa data (Pires et al., 2019). In contrast, RoBERTa was trained with Hausa but its SA performance has not yet been evaluated.

Apart from handling the low-resource languages with multilingual models in cross-lingual SA approaches, monolingual approaches were also tested and appeared to be successful in some cases (Nguyen et al., 2018; Tsakalidis et al., 2018; Fauzi, 2019; Yildirim, 2020). The biggest challenge in the development of monolingual models is that every language has its own characteristics, e.g., different suffix-prefix rules, different tenses, different word formation on genders and many other characteristics. This makes it hard to process the morphology with language-independent algorithms. Thus, it often makes sense to induce language-specific algorithms (Peng et al., 2017; Atif, 2018). Since Hausa's morphology is characterized by complex alternations of phonetic and tonal sequences, where certain consonants in the words are even changed under certain circumstances (Wolff, 2013), language-specific algorithms may also help to process morphology.

Since machine learning algorithms mostly operate on numerical vector representations, different types of word-to-vector methodologies (vectorization, word embeddings) are used as input format. For example, (Balahur and Turchi, 2014) apply TF-IDF (term frequency–inverse document frequency) successfully for vectorization together with classical machine learning algorithms like SVM and RF. More sophisticated vectorization techniques like Word2Vec (Mikolov et al., 2013; Fauzi, 2019) or fastText (Bojanowski et al., 2017; Pathak et al., 2020) are employed for deep learning experiments. Moreover, pre-trained NLP models like BERT (Devlin et al., 2019) or RoBERTa (Liu et al., 2019) provide their own vectorization. Some Hausa-specific methods for word embedding, tagging of word parts, and word stemming have already been investigated (Bashir et al., 2015; Abdulmumin and Galadanci, 2019; Tukur et al., 2019). If this research is further disseminated, a good language processing methodology for Hausa could emerge. Consequently, in this study, we investigated the SA performance of monolingual and cross-lingual systems on Hausa and propose a new stemming algorithm.

A few Hausa text corpora already exist (Atif et al., 2019; Abubakar et al., 2019; Inuwa-Dutse, 2021). Mostly they are based on books and resources like Tanzil (translation of Quran to Hausa with 127k sentences) (Abdulmumin and Galadanci, 2019) or collected texts from websites and social media (Schlippe et al., 2012; Inuwa-Dutse, 2021). Later, such data sets were used for training the multilingual NLP model XLM[1]-RoBERTa (Conneau et al., 2020) which we also analyzed in our experiments. For our studies and to provide a corpus for the research community, we collected a corpus of more than 40,000 comments—the *Hausa-English Sentiment Analysis Corpus For Educational Environments* (HESAC), which will be described in more detail in the next section.

3. The Hausa-English Sentiment Analysis Corpus For Educational Environments (HESAC)

In this section our *Hausa-English Sentiment Analysis Corpus for Educational Environments* (HESAC) is presented. To contribute to the improvement of low-resource languages, we share the corpus with the research community[2]. HESAC is based on an English data set created by (Rakhmanov, 2020a). After we did several corrections and eliminated comments with gibberish, it contains approximately 40,000 English comments. The data set was collected from the 2018/2019 course evaluation database of the Nile University of Nigeria. In this process, 524 courses taught by 203 instructors were evaluated by nearly 4,000 students. Then the data set was labeled with 3 sentiment classes (*negative*, *neutral*, *positive*). Like in other data collections with annotations (e.g., (Mabokela and Schlippe, 2022), the labels were cross-checked. To produce the comments in Hausa, each comment was first machine-translated and then corrected by three PhD students from Nile University of Nigeria with excellent Hausa and English skills. The corrections were cross-checked by all translators and a majority vote was conducted in case of disagreements. The manual correction of the MT output was definitely necessary, since the comparison between the Google's Neural Machine Translation System (Wu et al., 2016) output and the Hausa text created by our diligent correction process showed an MT accuracy of only 46%. If 1-word sentences are not counted, the MT accuracy rises up, but still remains at an unsatisfactory level with 73%.

Tables 1, 2 and 3 demonstrate the distribution of comment lengths and sentiment classes in HESAC. We see

[1]Cross-lingual Language Model

[2]https://github.com/MrLachin/HESAC

Comment length	Frequency
1 word	24,250
2–5 words	10,722
> 5 words	5,150

Table 1: EN-HESAC: Comment length distribution.

Comment length	Frequency
1 word	12,377
2–5 words	23,646
> 5 words	4,094

Table 2: HA-HESAC: Comment length distribution.

that many comments contain only one word. Many of these 1-word comments are repeated in our corpus. If we eliminate the duplicates, 15,856 comments remain in the whole corpus. To investigate the impact of the repetitions that often lead to overfitting in the training of NLP systems, in Section 5 we will compare SA systems trained with all sentences in the HESAC training (*training*) to SA systems where we removed the duplicates in the training data ($training_{uniq}$).

When we asked 60 students in a survey why they prefer to write short comments with less than five words in course evaluations, 80% reported that they give only short feedback since they believe that their comments are not read by the teacher or the school management. This shows the need for automatic SA in the field of education. With the help of AI, educational institutions can communicate to their students that each and every comment will be addressed.

Sentiment class	Frequency
positive	32,084
neutral	4,680
negative	3,360

Table 3: HESAC: Sentiment class distribution.

4. Sentiment Analysis for Hausa

In this section we will describe our SA systems and our new stemming algorithm.

4.1. System Overview

Figure 1 shows the main steps of our systems' pipelines. First, the Hausa students' comments are pre-processed, then vectorized and finally a classification algorithm is applied which outputs a class label for each input text. As shown in the figure, we experimented with different pre-processing components and different SA models and evaluated them not only for Hausa (HESAC (HA), $\text{HESAC}_{\text{uniq}}$ (HA)) but also for English (HESAC (EN), $\text{HESAC}_{\text{uniq}}$ (EN)) as a reference.

4.2. Pre-processing

Since no detailed information on optimal pre-processing for Hausa is described in the literature, we experimented with different pre-processing approaches.

4.2.1. Tokenization, Stop Word Removal, Lemmatization and Stemming

During the pre-processing steps, we applied commonly used textual data cleaning methods (Fauzi, 2019; Yildirim, 2020) such as removal of punctuation marks, removal of stop words, lower-casing, stemming, and lemmatization. Pre-processing steps are usually applied separately before the classical NLP algorithms, but in modern NLP architectures such as BERT (Devlin et al., 2019) and RoBERTa (Liu et al., 2019), the pre-processing steps are included.

For English and Hausa, we therefore used for our traditional classification algorithms (described in Section 4.3.1) first the widely used Porter stemming algorithm[3] (Porter, 1980) provided in NLTK (Bird and Loper, 2004), and for the transformers BERT and RoBERTa (described in Section 4.3.2) the stemming that is included by default in these NLP architectures. Then, to evaluate our stemming algorithms for Hausa, we replaced the default stemming with our algorithm (described in Section 4.2.2).

4.2.2. Our Stemming Algorithm for Hausa

Some libraries like in NLTK (Bird and Loper, 2004) provide methods to conduct pre-processing steps for English. But for low-resource languages, like Hausa, currently no such open-source library exists. A stemming algorithm for Hausa was developed by (Bashir et al., 2015) which achieves an accuracy of 73% of correctly stemmed words. However, they report that the algorithm suffers from over-stemming. The reason for this is the presence of numerous morphological rules in Hausa, all of which have been attempted to be applied—prefix rules, suffix rules, infix rules, correction of gender markers, elimination of stop words and finally elimination of short words. (Bimba et al., 2015) also propose a stemming algorithm, but again due to over-stemming and under-stemming, their results reached only an accuracy of 67%.

Our experiments with HA-HESAC also showed that over-stemming and even removing stop words decrease classification accuracy. Consequently, to avoid these shortcomings, we propose a novel stemming algorithms which consists of 3 parts: The first part applies gender marker removals, the second part prefix and suffix rules, and the third part applies infix rules. The details of this algorithm are demonstrated in Figure 2. Our algorithm is based on two research papers and a book on the Hausa language (Bashir et al., 2015; Crysmann, 2011; Bimba et al., 2015), was checked for validity and tested by two PhD students whose mother tongue is Hausa. We applied this algorithm on HA-HESAC in the pre-processing of our monolingual Hausa SA systems.

[3] https://tartarus.org/martin/PorterStemmer

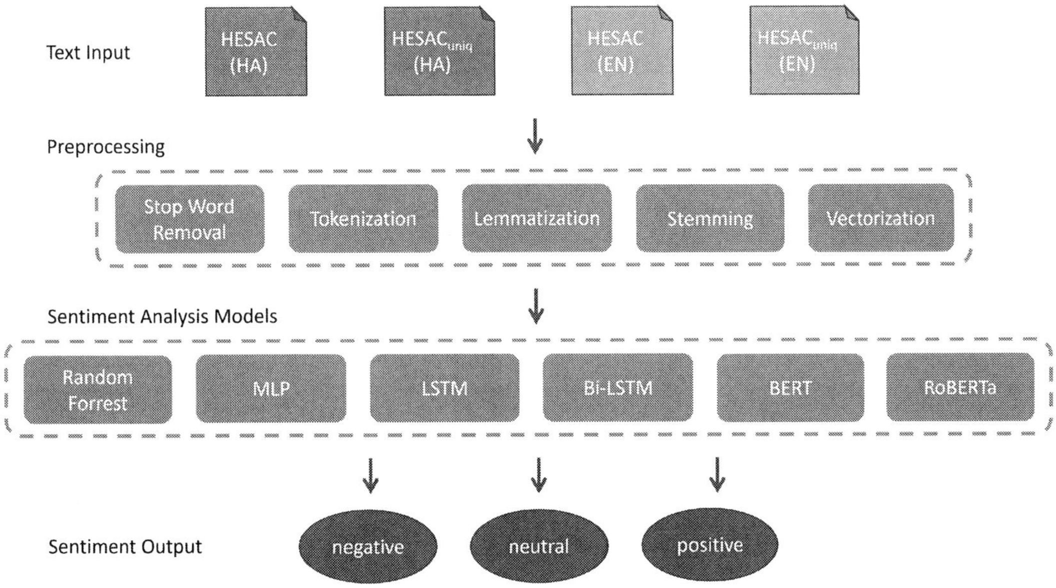

Figure 1: Sentiment Analysis Systems.

4.3. Techniques and NLP Models

We implemented different classification techniques and NLP models for SA and tested them on the HESAC test set.

4.3.1. Traditional Classification Methods

Classification algorithms like random forest (RF), support vector machines (SVM), multilayer perceptrons (MLP), long-short term memory (LSTM) and finally bidirectional LSTM (bi-LSTM) produced promising results in several SA experiments (Kumar and Sharan, 2020; Nasim et al., 2017; Vilares et al., 2017). Our goal was to compare these algorithms and their performances with state-of-art Transformer models like BERT and RoBERTa. For the implementation of RF, we used the Python module scikit-learn[4] and for the implementation of MLP, LSTM, and bi-LSTM the Keras library[5].

4.3.2. Transformers

BERT (Bidirectional Encoder Representations from Transformers) is an open-source framework provided by Google (Devlin et al., 2019). The major technical innovation of BERT is the bi-directional training, which leads to a deeper sense of language understanding. The Transformer encoder reads the entire sequence of words at once, which allows the mechanism to recognize a word's context and make connections to the previous and next words. For the implementation of BERT, we used the Transformers library[6].

Researchers tried to extend the abilities of BERT beyond English. RoBERTa (Robustly optimized BERT pre-training approach) is a leading framework which extends BERT with more languages (Conneau et al., 2020; Liu et al., 2019). For the implementation of RoBERTa, we used the Fairseq(-py) sequence modeling toolkit[7]. Our RoBERTa model XML-R was trained on 100 different languages and provides support for Hausa as well. But the training data set of Hausa was relatively small (0.3 Gigabyte) compared to other popular languages like Russian (278 Gigabyte) or Spanish (53 Gigabyte). BERT and RoBERTa can be used without fine-tuning to some downstream task (Heitmann et al., 2020). We trained our BERT models with 4 epochs and a batch size of 16 using the AdamW optimizer (Loshchilov and Hutter, 2019) with an initial learning rate of 0.00005. The RoBERTa models were trained with 4 epochs and a batch size of 8 using the Adam optimizer (Kingma and Ba, 2015) with an initial learning rate of 0.00001.

5. Experiments and Results

5.1. Experimental Setup

Table 4 demonstrates how we split the HESAC corpus into training and test set. 75% of the students' comments were used to train our SA systems (*training*). On the remaining 25% (*testing*), we evaluated the accuracy of the systems.

To investigate the impact of the repetitions in *training* which often leads to overfitting in the training of NLP systems, we also experimented with $training_{uniq}$ which we received by eliminating the duplicates in *training*. For comparison, all systems were evaluated on the same test set (*testing*).

[4]https://github.com/scikit-learn/scikit-learn

[5]https://github.com/keras-team/keras

[6]https://github.com/huggingface/transformers

[7]https://github.com/pytorch/fairseq

```
Gender marker removal:
for each word in text do
    if word_length>3 then
        if last_letter='r' then
            if pre_last≠'u' or pre_last≠'i' then
                remove last letter from word
            else keep word
        else if last_letter='n'
            remove last letter from word
        else keep word
    else keep word

Suffix-prefix removal:
for each word in text do
    if word_length>3 then
        if word_begins_with='ba' or ='ma'
                                or 'mai' or ='yan' then
            if last_two_letters='wa' then
                remove first and last two letters from word
            else if last_three_letters='iya' or ='uwa' or ='kku'
                remove first two and last three letters from word
            else if last_four_letters='anya'
                remove first two and last four letters from word
            else keep word
        else keep word
    else keep word

Infix removal:
for each word in text do
    if word_length>3 then
        if fourth_from_last_letter=second_from last_letter
            and third_from_last_letter='o'
            and last_letter='i' then
            remove last four letter from word
            add letter 'a' to end
        else keep word
    else keep word
```

Figure 2: Our stemming algorithm for Hausa.

Of the 10,138 students' comments in the test set, 1,450 are completely different to the comments in the training data. A large part is similar or the same, but this is normal in feedback from students on courses when they do not go into detail on certain topics or course content.

Data set	**Sentiment class**		
	negative	**neutral**	**positive**
training	2,533	3,452	24,004
$\text{training}_{\text{uniq}}$	2,172	1,095	12,592
testing	827	1,230	8,081

Table 4: HESAC: Distribution of training and testing.

5.2. Sentiment Analysis on EN-HESAC

To investigate how well our Hausa SA performs compared to English, we first built and evaluated systems with EN-HESAC. Table 5 summarizes the English systems' accuracies.

Method	**training**	$\textbf{training}_{\textbf{uniq}}$
RF	96.3	95.1
MLP	96.3	94.6
LSTM	97.6	94.4
Bi-LSTM	97.5	94.4
BERT	**98.7**	95.9
RoBERTa	98.5	95.3

Table 5: Accuracy (%) on EN-HESAC.

We see that the removal of duplicates in the training data (*$training_{uniq}$*) has a negative impact on performance. All numbers are close to each other ranging between 94.4% and 98.7% accuracy. BERT performs best on EN-HESAC with 98.7%, followed by RoBERTa with 98.5%. Our t-test demonstrates a slight significant difference in the scores between BERT (M=98.7, SD=0.6) and RoBERTa (M=98.5, SD=0.6), where $t(30)=2.9$ and $p<0.01$.
The systems' accuracies of over 94.4% indicate that the models build up an understanding of language and do not just reproduce the sentiment labels from the training data. For comparison, if the sentiments of the completely different comments between training and test data were not recognized and the training data would just be reproduced, the accuracy would be only about 85%.

5.3. Cross-lingual Sentiment Analysis on HA-HESAC

Next, we wanted to find out how close we could get to the English performance with cross-lingual systems for Hausa SA. In the cross-lingual systems, the comments were machine-translated from Hausa to English and then classified with English SA systems.

Method	**training**	$\textbf{training}_{\textbf{uniq}}$
RF	94.7	92.0
MLP	95.7	91.3
LSTM	96.0	92.4
Bi-LSTM	96.0	92.2
BERT	**96.9**	94,9
RoBERTa	96.4	94.5

Table 6: Accuracy (%) on HA-HESAC (*cross-lingual*).

Table 6 shows that the Hausa SA performances with the translation of the Hausa comments and English models (*cross-lingual*) are steadily approximately 2–3% absolute worse than the English SA performances from Table 5. The accuracies range from 91.3% to 96.9%. We find the high Hausa SA accuracies remarkable, since with an Hausa-English MT accuracy of less than 50% we were far from achieving good English translations that were input to the English SA systems. Again BERT performs best, this time with 96.9%, followed by RoBERTa with 96.4%. Our t-test demonstrates a significant difference in the scores between BERT (M=96.9, SD=0.6) and RoBERTa (M=96.4, SD=0.7), where t(30)=14.1 and p<0.0001.

5.4. Sentiment Analysis on HA-HESAC

Finally, we were interested in finding out how well monolingual SA systems perform for Hausa. Additionally, we wanted to analyze whether our stemming algorithm, proposed in Section 4.2.2, has a positive impact on the results.

Method	training	$\text{training}_{\text{uniq}}$
RF	97.1	92.7
$\text{RF}_{\text{stemming}}$	97.3	92,8
MLP	97.0	90.8
$\text{MLP}_{\text{stemming}}$	97.1	91.1
LSTM	96.2	90.9
$\text{LSTM}_{\text{stemming}}$	**97.4**	91.4
Bi-LSTM	96.7	91.0
$\text{Bi-LSTM}_{\text{stemming}}$	97.0	91.4
RoBERTa	96.3	92.0
$\text{RoBERTa}_{\text{stemming}}$	96.3	92.0

Table 7: Accuracy (%) on HA-HESAC (*monolingual*).

Table 7 shows that we also achieve performances above 90% with the monolingual Hausa SA systems. Using our stemming algorithm, we are consistently better than without the language-specific algorithm in pre-processing. For example, a t-test between LSTM (M=96.2, SD=0.4) and $\text{LSTM}_{\text{stemming}}$ (M=97.4, SD=0.4) demonstrated that $\text{LSTM}_{\text{stemming}}$ performs significantly better, where t(30)=29 and p<0.0001. $\text{LSTM}_{\text{stemming}}$ is the best system with 97.4% accuracy, closely followed by $\text{RF}_{\text{stemming}}$ (97.3%). However, our t-test demonstrates no significant difference between both systems.

Concerning the Transformer models: As shown in Table 7, RoBERTa does not perform as strongly as in the experiments with EN-HESAC and HA-HESAC (*cross-lingual*). This could be related to the relatively small amount of Hausa data that was used for RoBERTa (0.3 Gigabyte) as mentioned in Section 4.3.2. Moreover, we could not use BERT for these experiments since a multilingual or monolingual version of BERT that supports Hausa did not exist at the time of our experiments.

5.5. Error Analysis

Overall, all models performed extremely good, achieving a performance of above 90%. Unambiguous comments like "Ina son yadda yake koyarwa.", which means "I love the way he teaches.", were well classified. The majority of misclassified sentiments can be grouped as follows: (1) Comments with more than 10 words which contain misspelled words. (2) Comments with more than 10 words which contain positive and negative aspects but are clear positive or negative statements from the human perspective.

Misclassified comment
Kasancewa malamin lissafi yana da sauki kamar kasancewa wasu darussan darussan da ke da wahalar fahimta game da ilimin lissafi wanda yake buatar bayani koyaushe da kuma hauri. Amma ni ni ba abin da zan ce sai dai shi babban malami ne.
Being a maths lecturer it's as easy as being other courses lecturer. Most students have a hard time understanding mathematics which requires constantly explaining over and over again and not all lecturers have that patience. But as for me, I have nothing much to say but he's a very good lecturer.

Table 8: Misclassified comment (Hausa and English).

Table 8 shows such a long misclassified comment. This comment is manually classified as *positive*. In addition to the positive aspect "he's a very good lecturer", the comment contains word sequences which also present negative parts like "have a hard time", and "explaining ... again", and "not ... have that patience".

6. Conclusion and Future Work

In this paper, we have addressed three issues: First, we collected a corpus of more than 40,000 comments—the *Hausa-English Sentiment Analysis Corpus For Educational Environments* (HESAC). Second, we investigated monolingual and cross-lingual approaches for Hausa to classify student comments in course evaluations. Third, we proposed a novel stemming algorithm for Hausa to improve accuracy. We also experimented with removing duplicates from the training set, but this resulted in deterioration of the systems. Our results demonstrate that the monolingual approaches for Hausa SA slightly outperform the cross-lingual systems. Using our novel stemming algorithm in the preprocessing even improved the best model resulting in an accuracy of 94.6% on HESAC.

We experienced performance losses with long sentences that contain both positive and negative aspects but can be clearly classified by humans. Our systems' performance can still be improved by addressing this challenge. Additionally, we demonstrated that the performances of our cross-lingual and monolingual Hausa SA system are very close. Therefore, in future work it is interesting to consider a system combination which has the potential to even further increase accuracy.

Furthermore, in the context of this work, we were not able to directly compare our stemming algorithm with the other two Hausa stemming algorithms (Bashir et al., 2015; Bimba et al., 2015) or to combine the algorithms. Such further analyses and combinations could be part of future work and may lead to further improvements.

In addition, with the help of topic identification techniques, even more valuable information can be extracted from the students' feedback that can then be used, for example, to supplement and improve curricula and course content (Bothmer and Schlippe, 2022a; Bothmer and Schlippe, 2022b).

7. References

Abdulmumin, I. and Galadanci, B. S. (2019). hauWE: Hausa Words Embedding for Natural Language Processing. *The 2nd Intern. Conference of the IEEE Nigeria Computer Chapter (NigeriaComputConf)*.

Abubakar, A. I., Roko, A., Muhammad, A., and Saidu, I. (2019). Hausa WordNet: An Electronic Lexical Resource. *Saudi Journal of Engineering and Technology*, 4(8):279–285.

Atif, M. M., Aliyu, M. M., and Zimit, S. I. (2019). Towards the Development of Hausa Language Corpus. *International Journal of Scientific Engineering Research*, 10(10):1598–1604.

Atif, M. M. (2018). An Enhanced Framework for Sentiment Analysis of Students' Surveys: Arab Open University Business Program Courses Case Study. *Business and Economics Journal*, 9:1–3.

Aung, K. Z. and Myo, N. N. (2017). Sentiment Analysis of Students' Comment Using Lexicon based Approach. *2017 IEEE/ACIS 16th International Conference on Computer and Information Science (ICIS)*.

Balahur, A. and Turchi, M. (2014). Comparative Experiments using Supervised Learning and Machine Translation for Multilingual Sentiment Analysis. *Comput. Speech Lang.*, 28:56–75.

Bashir, M., Rozaimee, A. B., and Isa, W. M. B. W. (2015). A Word Stemming Algorithm for Hausa Language. *IOSR Journal of Computer Engineering (IOSR-JCE)*, 17(3):25–31.

Bimba, A., Idris, N., Khamis, N., and Noor, N. F. (2015). Stemming Hausa Text: Using Affix-Stripping Rules and Reference Look-Up. *Lang. Resour. Eval.*, 50(3):687–703, September.

Bird, S. and Loper, E. (2004). NLTK: The Natural Language Toolkit. In *The ACL Interactive Poster and Demonstration Sessions*, pages 214–217, Barcelona, Spain. ACL.

Bojanowski, P., Grave, E., Joulin, A., and Mikolov, T. (2017). Enriching Word Vectors with Subword Information. *Transactions of the Association for Computational Linguistics*, 5:135–146.

Bothmer, K. and Schlippe, T. (2022a). Investigating Natural Language Processing Techniques for a Recommendation System to Support Employers, Job Seekers and Educational Institutions. In *The 23rd International Conference on Artificial Intelligence in Education (AIED 2022)*, Durham, UK.

Bothmer, K. and Schlippe, T. (2022b). Skill Scanner: Connecting and Supporting Employers, Job Seekers and Educational Institutions with an AI-based Recommendation System. In *The Learning Ideas Conference 2022 (15th annual conference)*, New York, NY, USA.

Burquest, D. A. (1992). An Introduction to the Use of Aspect in Hausa Narrative. *SIL International Publications in Linguistics*, pages 393–417.

Can, E. F., Ezen-Can, A., and Can, F. (2018). Multilingual Sentiment Analysis: An RNN-Based Framework for Limited Data. In *ACM SIGIR 2018 Workshop on Learning from Limited or Noisy Data*.

Conneau, A., Khandelwal, K., Goyal, N., Chaudhary, V., Wenzek, G., Guzmán, F., Grave, E., Ott, M., Zettlemoyer, L., and Stoyanov, V. (2020). Unsupervised Cross-lingual Representation Learning at Scale. In *The 58th Annual Meeting of the Association for Computational Linguistics*, pages 8440–8451, Online. ACL.

Crysmann, B. (2011). HaG - a Computational Grammar of Hausa. page 321–337, University of Maryland, 2012. Cascadilla Press.

Devlin, J., Chang, M.-W., Lee, K., and Toutanova, K. (2019). BERT: Pre-training of Deep Bidirectional Transformers for Language Understanding. In *NAACL*.

Djatmiko, F., Ferdiana, R., and Faris, M. (2019). A Review of Sentiment Analysis for Non-English Language. In *International Conference of Artificial Intelligence and Information Technology (ICAIIT)*.

Fauzi, M. A. (2019). Word2Vec Model for Sentiment Analysis of Product Reviews in Indonesian Language. *International Journal of Electrical and Computer Engineering (IJECE)*.

Heitmann, M., Siebert, C., Hartmann, J., and Schamp, C. (2020). More than a Feeling: Benchmarks for Sentiment Analysis Accuracy. *Communication & Computational Methods eJournal*.

Inuwa-Dutse, I. (2021). The First Large Scale Collection of Diverse Hausa Language Datasets.

Kandhro, I. A., Wasi, S., Kumar, K., Rind, M. M., and Ameen, M. W. (2019). Sentiment Analysis of Students' Comment by using Long-Short Term Model. *Indian Journal of Science and Technology*, 12(8).

Kingma, D. P. and Ba, J. (2015). Adam: A Method for Stochastic Optimization. In Yoshua Bengio et al., editors, *3rd International Conference on Learning Representations, ICLR 2015, San Diego, CA, USA*.

Kolchyna, O., Souza, T. T. P., Treleaven, P. C., and Aste, T. (2015). Twitter Sentiment Analysis: Lexicon Method, Machine Learning Method and Their Combination. *arXiv: Computation and Language*.

Koslow, P. (1995). *Hausaland: The Fortress Kingdoms (The Kingdoms of Africa)*. Chelsea House Publishers, London.

Kotelnikova, A., Paschenko, D., Bochenina, K., and Kotelnikov, E. (2021). Lexicon-based methods vs. bert for text sentiment analysis. pages 73–81, 11.

Kumar, A. and Sharan, A., (2020). *Deep Learning-Based Frameworks for Aspect-Based Sentiment Analysis*, pages 139–158. Springer Singapore.

Lalata, J., Gerardo, B., and Medina, R. (2019). A Sentiment Analysis Model for Faculty Comment Evaluation Using Ensemble Machine Learning Algorithms. In *The 2019 International Conference on Big Data Engineering*, BDE 2019, page 68–73, New York, NY, USA. ACM.

Lin, Z., Jin, X., Xu, X., Wang, Y., Tan, S., and Cheng, X. (2014). Make It Possible: Multilingual Sentiment Analysis without Much Prior Knowledge. In *2014 IEEE/WIC/ACM International Joint Conferences on Web Intelligence (WI) and Intelligent Agent Technologies (IAT)*, volume 2, pages 79–86.

Liu, Y., Ott, M., Goyal, N., Du, J., Joshi, M., Chen, D., Levy, O., Lewis, M., Zettlemoyer, L., and Stoyanov, V. (2019). RoBERTa: A Robustly Optimized BERT Pretraining Approach.

Loshchilov, I. and Hutter, F. (2019). Decoupled Weight Decay Regularization. In *7th International Conference on Learning Representations, ICLR 2019, New Orleans, LA, USA, May 6-9, 2019*.

Mabokela, R. and Schlippe, T. (2022). A Sentiment Corpus for South African Under-Resourced Languages in a Multilingual Context. In *The 1st Annual Meeting of the ELRA/ISCA Special Interest Group on Under-Resourced Languages (SIGUL 2022)*.

Mikolov, T., Chen, K., Corrado, G., and Dean, J. (2013). Efficient Estimation of Word Representations in Vector Space. In Yoshua Bengio et al., editors, *1st International Conference on Learning Representations, ICLR 2013, Scottsdale, Arizona, USA, May 2-4, 2013, Workshop Track Proceedings*.

Nasim, Z., Rajput, Q., and Haider, S. (2017). Sentiment Analysis of Student Feedback Using Machine Learning and Lexicon based Approaches. *2017 International Conference on Research and Innovation in Information Systems (ICRIIS)*, pages 1–6.

Nguyen, P. X. V., Hong, T. V. T., Nguyen, K. V., and Nguyen, N. L.-T. (2018). Deep Learning versus Traditional Classifiers on Vietnamese Students' Feedback Corpus. *2018 5th NAFOSTED Conference on Information and Computer Science (NICS)*.

Pathak, A. R., Agarwal, B., Pandey, M., and Rautaray, S., (2020). *Application of Deep Learning Approaches for Sentiment Analysis*, pages 1–31. Springer Singapore, Singapore.

Peng, H., Cambria, E., and Hussain, A. (2017). A Review of Sentiment Analysis Research in Chinese Language. *Cognitive Computation*, 9(4):423–435.

Pires, T., Schlinger, E., and Garrette, D. (2019). How Multilingual is Multilingual BERT? In *ACL*.

Porter, M. F. (1980). An Algorithm for Suffix Stripping. *Program*, 14(3):130–137.

Rakhmanov, O. (2020a). A Comparative Study on Vectorization and Classification Techniques in Sentiment Analysis to Classify Student-Lecturer Comments. *Procedia Computer Science*, 178:194–204.

Rakhmanov, O. (2020b). On Validity of Sentiment Analysis Scores and Development of Classification Model for Student-Lecturer Comments Using Weight-Based Approach and Deep Learning. In *The 21st Annual Conference on Information Technology Education*, SIGITE '20, pages 174–179, New York, NY, USA. ACM.

Rani, S. and Kumar, P. (2017). A Sentiment Analysis System to Improve Teaching and Learning. *Computer*, 50(5):36–43.

Rokade, P. P. and D, A. K. (2019). Business Intelligence Analytics using Sentiment Analysis—A Survey. *International Journal of Electrical and Computer Engineering (IJECE)*.

Schlippe, T., Guevara Komgang Djomgang, E., Vu, N. T., Ochs, S., and Schultz, T. (2012). Hausa Large Vocabulary Continuous Speech Recognition. In *The 3rd Workshop on Spoken Language Technologies for Under-resourced Languages (SLTU 2012)*, Cape Town, South Africa.

Sindhu, I., Muhammad Daudpota, S., Badar, K., Bakhtyar, M., Baber, J., and Nurunnabi, M. (2019). Aspect-Based Opinion Mining on Student's Feedback for Faculty Teaching Performance Evaluation. *IEEE Access*, 7:108729–108741.

Tsakalidis, A., Papadopoulos, S., Voskaki, R., Ioannidou, K., Boididou, C., Cristea, A. I., Liakata, M., and Kompatsiaris, Y. (2018). Building and evaluating resources for sentiment analysis in the greek language. *Language Resources and Evaluation*, 52(4):1021–1044.

Tukur, A., Umar, K., and Muhammad, A. (2019). Tagging Part of Speech in Hausa Sentences. *2019 15th International Conference on Electronics, Computer and Computation (ICECCO)*.

UN. (2022). United Nations: Sustainable Development Goals: 17 Goals to Transform our World. https://www.un.org/sustainabledevelopment/sustainabledevelopment-goals. Accessed: 2022-01-16.

Vilares, D., Alonso Pardo, M., and Gómez-Rodríguez, C. (2017). Supervised Sentiment Analysis in Multilingual Environments. *Information Processing Management*, 53, 05.

Wolff, H. E. (2013). Hausa Language. https://www.britannica.com/topic/Hausa-language. Accessed: 2022-01-16.

Wu, Y., Schuster, M., Chen, Z., Le, Q. V., Norouzi, M., Macherey, W., Krikun, M., Cao, Y., Gao, Q., Macherey, K., Klingner, J., Shah, A., Johnson, M., Liu, X., Łukasz Kaiser, Gouws, S., Kato, Y., Kudo, T., Kazawa, H., Stevens, K., Kurian, G., Patil, N., Wang, W., Young, C., Smith, J., Riesa, J., Rudnick, A., Vinyals, O., Corrado, G., Hughes, M., and Dean, J. (2016). Google's Neural Machine Translation System: Bridging the Gap between Human and Machine Translation.

Yildirim, S., (2020). *Comparing Deep Neural Networks to Traditional Models for Sentiment Analysis in Turkish Language*, pages 311–319. Springer Singapore.

Zucco, C., Liang, H., Fatta, G. D., and Cannataro, M. (2018). Explainable Sentiment Analysis with Applications in Medicine. In *2018 IEEE International Conference on Bioinformatics and Biomedicine (BIBM)*, pages 1740–1747.

Proceedings of SIGUL2022 @LREC2022, pages 106–111
Marseille, 24-25 June 2022

Nepali Encoder Transformers: An Analysis of Auto Encoding Transformer Language Models for Nepali Text Classification

Utsav Maskey, Manish Bhatta, Shiva Raj Bhatta, Sanket Dhungel, Bal Krishna Bal
Information and Language Processing Research Lab
Department of Computer Science & Engineering
Kathmandu University,
Dhulikhel, Nepal
bal@ku.edu.np
{um02409118, mb02407218, sb02407118, sd02407618}@student.ku.edu.np

Abstract

Language model pre-training has significantly impacted NLP and resulted in performance gains on many NLP-related tasks, but comparative study of different approaches on many low-resource languages seems to be missing. This paper attempts to investigate appropriate methods for pretraining a Transformer-based model for the Nepali language. We focus on the language-specific aspects that need to be considered for modeling. Although some language models have been trained for Nepali, the study is far from sufficient. We train three distinct Transformer-based masked language models for Nepali text sequences: distilbert-base (Sanh et al., 2019) for its efficiency and minuteness, deberta-base (P. He et al., 2020) for its capability of modeling the dependency of nearby token pairs and XLM-ROBERTa (Conneau et al., 2020) for its capabilities to handle multilingual downstream tasks. We evaluate and compare these models with other Transformer-based models on a downstream classification task with an aim to suggest an effective strategy for training low-resource language models and their fine-tuning.

Keywords: Natural Language Processing, Nepali Language, Language Modeling, Transformers, Auto Encoders

1. Introduction

The Transformer has become the go-to method for neural language modeling. It is highly parallelizable and abides by the scaling laws (i.e. performance gets better in accordance to the number of parameters, dataset size and the amount of compute) (Kaplan et al., 2020). In addition, ULMFiT (Howard & Ruder, 2018) introduced techniques that allowed neural networks to train a base language model which could then be fine-tuned on downstream tasks such as classification, text generation, etc. with much lesser data. Following these techniques, many encoder-based transformer models have achieved state-of-the-art results in text classification including BERT (Devlin et al., 2019), RoBERTa (Liu et al., 2019), XLM (Lample & Conneau, 2019), XLM-RoBERTa (Conneau et al., 2020), ALBERT (Z. He et al., 2018), ALBERT (Lan et al., 2019), ELECTRA (Clark et al., 2020) and DeBERTa (P. He et al., 2020).

However, these models are essentially trained on high-resource languages such as English, French, etc. and sufficient efforts and attention have not been given to low-resourced languages. This is primarily because the transformer model requires huge datasets and hence it is not straightforward and easy task for low-resource languages (Ruder, 2020).

The Nepali language belongs to the Indo-Aryan family which is written in the Devanagari script. It is the official language and lingua franca of Nepal and one of the 22 scheduled languages in India. Furthermore, it is spoken by about a quarter of the population of Bhutan and in Burma and different parts of North East India. According to the 2011 census, there are 16 million native speakers with over 9 million L2 speakers ("Nepali language - Wikipedia", 2022).

Nepali is a free word order language without upper or lower case of the characters. It is written from left to right and follows the Subject Object Verb (SOV) pattern as the sentential grammar structure. There are 33 consonant letters, 11 independent vowel letters and 10 dependent vowel signs or matras in Nepali. The consonant letters may exist independently or in conjunction with dependent symbols (matras, halanta, etc.) to form a compound letter. The halanta symbol (represented by U+094D (्) Devanagari sign Virama in Unicode) is a dependent symbol which is used to suppress the inherent vowel sign in any consonant letter and is mostly used to produce half characters in Nepali. Similarly, there are other dependent symbols including, Chandrabindu (ँ) and Shirbindu (ं) which indicates nasalization of a vowel and consonants respectively. The bisarga (ः) dependent symbol appears in some Nepali words, but they are not usually pronounced. Purna biram (।) marks the end of a sentence, similar to a full stop. The set of digits (०, १, २, ३, ४, ५, ६, ७, ८, ९) are used as numbers in Nepali. ("Nepali alphabet", 2015).

In the context of low-resource language modeling with transformers, Indic-Transformers (Jain et al., 2020) train and benchmark three languages, namely, Hindi, Bengali and Telugu on tasks including classification, POS tagging and Question Answering. Similarly, in line to this, we focus on investigating various approaches to modeling the Nepali language using contemporary transformer models.

As for the Nepali language, attempts have been made to understand the grammatical structure of the Nepali Language in the work of (Bal, 2004a; 2004b). Some notable works related to Nepali language NLP includes, summarization (Mishra et al., 2020), Named entity recognition (Maharjan G., Bal B.K., 2019), etc.

However, not much effort has been made on working with contemporary transformer models. Some encoder-based transformer models including nepaliBERT (Pudasaini, 2022) and NepaliBERT (Rajan, 2021) have been trained for Nepali, whose performance is yet to be analyzed.

In this work, we focus on training three encoder-based transformer models, DistilBERT (Sanh et al., 2019), DeBERTa (P. He et al., 2020) and XLM-R (Conneau et al., 2020) for Nepali. The objective is to find a suitable procedure for training low-resource languages like Nepali.

The contributions of our paper are as follows:

- We train an SPM, Sentence Piece Model (Kudo & Richardson, 2018) for sub-word tokenization of texts. Devanagari characters are different compared to the languages on which most transformer-trained models are trained and therefore, the development of a suitable tokenizer model should be considered. The XLM-R paper (Conneau et al., 2020) shows that they observed negligible loss in performance using SPM as compared to models trained with language-specific pre-processing. This SPM tokenizer will be used for training the language models.
- We train various encoder-based models to compare which transformer architectures are feasible for Nepali Language training.
- We present a comparison of these models by evaluating them on a downstream text-classification task. And since fine-tuning multilingual models is a popular method for modeling a low-resource language, we also reflect the performance of a multilingual model, XLM-R through a comparative study.

2. Background & Related Work

Representation learning aims to learn representations of raw data as useful information for further classification or prediction. Early attempts in this direction account to pre-trained word embeddings on a large and diverse corpus (Mikolov et al., 2013). An inductive transfer is then performed by fine-tuning on top of the learned embeddings that allowed neural networks to train on various NLP tasks. Recurrent neural networks (RNNs) along with usage of techniques including long short-term memory (LSTM) (Hochreiter & Schmidhuber, 1997) and gated recurrent units (GRU) (Chung et al., 2014) on top of learned representations achieved state-of-the-art on many NLP tasks.

The paper, Universal Language Model Fine-tuning (ULMFiT) (Howard & Ruder, 2018) introduced how Causal Language Modeling (CLM) can be pre-trained on neural networks as opposed to word embeddings which used only a single neural network layer for pre-training the diverse corpus. Recent methodologies, however, use Masked Language Modeling (MLM) for pre-training encoder-based transformers.

2.1 Masked Language Modeling (MLM)

As opposed to CLM, where the model attempts to predict the next sequences in a sentence, MLM attempts to predict the middle words in the sentence (Devlin et al., 2019). This ensures that the model learns contextual word representations and the learning is bi-directional. Specifically, given a sequence of text $X = \{x_i\}$, X is corrupted into $\tilde{X}$ by masking some percentile of its tokens at random and then a language model is trained to re-construct X by predicting the masked tokens $\tilde{x}$. The percentile of tokens masked on the original BERT is 15%, however in the work by (Wettig et al., 2022), they suggest that 20% masking performs better for small-sized transformer models whereas huge models favor MLM probability as high as 40%.

2.2 Auto Encoding Transformers

Transformer models are based on attention mechanisms (Vaswani et al., 2017) which consists of Encoder and/or Decoder sub-architectures. The Encoder gets good at understanding the input text and extracting its feature representations, whereas the Decoder gets good at predicting the targeted output sequences. The Encoder part of transformer architecture can independently be used as a many-to-one sequential model, where the sequence length of input tokens may vary provided that the model's output size remains constant. Such auto-encoding transformers pre-trained with language modeling objectives are the state-of-the-art models on the GLUE benchmark (Wang et al., 2018) which measures Natural Language Understanding (NLU) across several tasks of varying difficulty. Auto encoding models that use BERT-like architecture (Devlin et al., 2019) still dominate research and industry when fine-tuned on NLU tasks such as text classification, named entity recognition, and question answering.

3. Experimental Workflow

Our experiments are performed on Auto-encoding Transformers. As for training the language models, we set up a pipelined procedure consisting of data collection, tokenization, language model training and its comparative evaluation on a downstream classification task.

3.1 Nepali Text Data

With the objective of training language models from scratch, we use monolingual unlabeled Nepali texts. We gathered 13 million text sequences (phrases and paragraphs) by combining and de-duplicating three publicly available datasets: OSCAR (Suárez et al., 2020), cc100 dataset (Conneau et al., 2020) and the iNLTK dataset (Arora, 2020).

3.2 Tokenization

Tokenizing Devanagari texts differs from that of English texts due to different ways of combining consonants, vowels and vowel modifiers. For example, the compound letter, 'लु' (ल + ु) is formed by combining the free form character, 'ल' and the vowel-sign, 'ु'. However, the tokenizer used by BERT and the original Multilingual BERT removes some vowel symbols and other dependent symbols, and only the free form character remains. For example, the letter ‘लु’ is tokenized as:

‘लु’ (ल + ु) → ‘ल’ (‘ु’ is removed)

The use of Unicode normalizations causes this behavior in languages with non-Latin alphabets. When tokenizing a decomposed character sequence into multiple pieces, we may break the original meaning of the character. This creates ambiguities in the Nepali Language.

For example, the word, ‘फ्लु’ can be tokenized as:

	Before Tokenization	Tokenized
Decomposition:	फ्लु (फ + ् + ल + ु)	फल (फ+ ल)
Meaning:	Flu	Fruit

Table 1: Decomposition of the word, ‘‘फ्लु’’

The removal of the vowel, ‘ु’ and the halanta, ‘्’ changes the original meaning of the word and causes ambiguity resulting in two different words having the same meaning.

We opted for a Sentence Piece Model (Kudo & Richardson, 2018) for training the tokenizer on the dataset that we collected. This approach is also used by the XLM-R for training multilingual models.

As for testing the tokenizers, we consider two sub-word tokenization approaches:

3.2.1 WordPiece Tokenizer

WordPiece tokenizer is used by nepaliBERT (Pudasaini, 2022) and NepaliBERT (Rajan, 2021). WorldPiece tokenization distinguishes workpieces at the start of a word from pieces starting in the middle (Song et al., 2020). The latter start with a special symbol ‘##’ in BERT, which is called the suffix indicator. For example, the word चन्द्रागिरिमा may be tokenized as [‘चन्द्रागिरि’, ‘##मा’].

3.2.2 Sentencepiece Tokenizer (SPM)

SentencePiece tokenizer treats the input texts just as a sequence of Unicode characters. Even the whitespace is handled as a normal symbol. SentencePiece first escapes the whitespaces with a meta symbol, ‘_’ (U+2581) and tokenizes the input into an arbitrary sub-word sequence.

Input Text : “फ्लुको कारणले हुने पहिलोनेपाली भवकृष्ण भट्टराई”	
Tokenizer	Tokenized output
Shushant/ nepaliBERT	[‘फल’, ‘##को’, ‘कारण’, ‘##ल’, ‘ह’, ##न’,‘पहिलो’, ‘##न’, ‘##पाली’, ‘भव’, ‘##क’, ‘##षण’, ‘भट’, ‘##टर’, ‘##ाई’]
R4J4N/ NepaliBERT	[‘फ्लु’, ‘##को’, ‘कारणले’, ‘हुने’, ‘पहिलो’, ‘##नेपाली’, ‘भव’, ‘##कृष्ण’, ‘भट्टराई’]
Sentence Piece Model [Ours]	[‘_फ्लु’, ‘को’, ‘_कारणले’, ‘_हुने’, ‘_पहिलो’, ‘नेपाली’, ‘_’, ‘भव’, ‘कृष्ण’, ‘_भट्टराई’]

Table 2: Comparison of tokenizer outputs

We observe that the approach used by nepaliBERT frequently misses the dependent symbols. The NepaliBERT tokenizer performs quite well, but we choose to use the SPM tokenizer for its flexibility in generating text sequences on auto-regressive transformers. The tokenizer model is trained with a vocabulary size of 24,576 tokens. We use this tokenizer for all the language models that are trained.

3.3 MLM Training Feasibility Test

With the dataset and tokenizer developed, we train some of the popular language models and analyze the performance based on training data size, training time and computational resource constraints. We set a baseline cut-off perplexity of 54.598 (i.e. training loss of 4.0) and perform a constrained training in order to determine suitable models for training the language model.

Following models are considered for the constrained training:

- De-berta-base (P. He et al., 2020)
- Distilbert-base (Sanh et al., 2019)
- XLM-roberta (XLM-R) (Conneau et al., 2020)

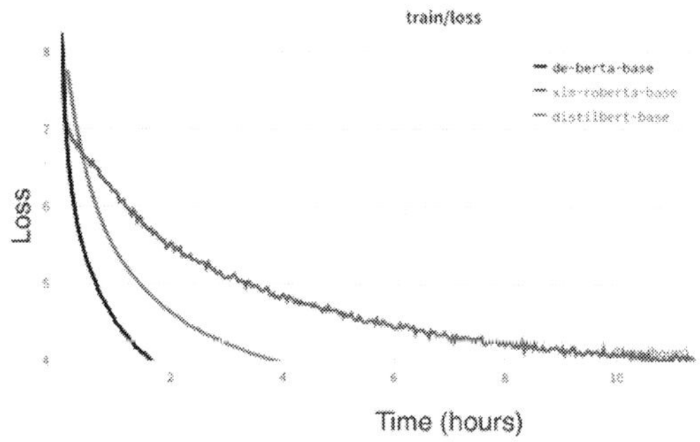

Figure 1: Training loss vs. Time

Model	Batch Size	MLM Probability	Time taken (hh:mm)	No. of training samples
distilbert	28	15%	3:59	406,000
de-berta	6	20%	**1:39**	546,000
xlm-r	1	15%	9:16	**154,000**

Table 3: Summary of the feasibility test. Comparison between the models for reaching the baseline perplexity

The DeBERTa model, despite being trained on a difficult task of MLM probability of 20%, reaches the targeted perplexity the fastest and also by a large margin. The xlm-roberta model, which is trained stochastically (with most training steps), reaches the baseline when trained with the least amount of data; but the training is noisy and the computational training requirement is massive. Therefore, we discarded xlm-roberta-base for its huge architecture and constrained computational training.

We hence decide on training two models: DeBERTa model that focuses on attaining the best performance, and the DistilBERT model which focuses on being lightweight with capabilities of on-device computations.

3.4 Language Model Pre-Training

We proceed with the training of distilbert and de-berta models for 5 epochs on the dataset that we gathered and obtain the following results:

Model	Train/loss	Batch size	Perplexity (eval)
Distilbert-base	2.6412	28	12.3802
De-berta-base	**1.9375**	6	**6.4237**

Table 4: Summary of LM training for 5 Epochs with MLM probability of 20%

In terms of perplexity, we obtain better results using the deberta model. The distilbert model, despite training much faster, produces a respectable performance. We further evaluate the performance of language models by comparing them on a downstream classification task in the next section.

4. Results and Analysis

4.1 Text Classification

The classification task performance evaluation is performed on the "16 Nepali News" dataset (Chaudhary & Sabin, 2017). The dataset consists of approximately 14,364 Nepali language news documents, partitioned (unevenly) across 16 different newsgroups: Auto, Bank, Blog, Business Interview, Economy, Employment, Entertainment, Interview, Literature, National News, Opinion, Sports, Technology, Tourism, and World.

We evaluate Nepali Language Models and compare them in terms of accuracy. The evaluation is performed with varying hyperparameters and for a number of epochs before the models tend to overfit. The following models are considered for the evaluation:

- De-berta-base [Ours]
- Distilbert-base [Ours]
- Shusant/nepaliBERT (Pudasaini, 2022)
- Rajan/NepaliBERT (Rajan, 2021)
- XLM-roberta-base (Conneau et al., 2020)

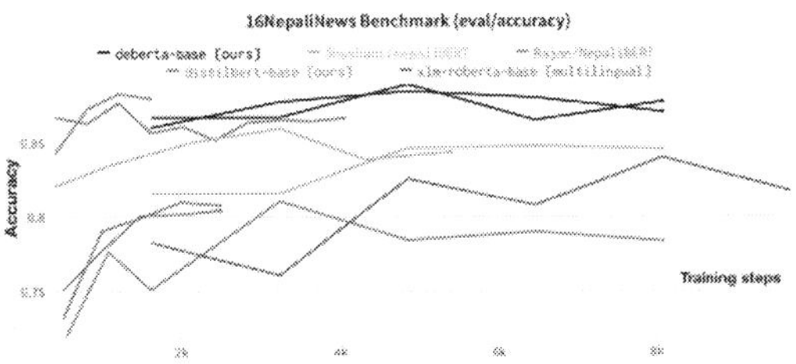

Figure 2: Evaluating language models on "16 Nepali News" Dataset. Training are performed with varying hyperparameters. Each progression in the x-axis represents an Epoch.

Model	Epoch	Train steps	Highest Accuracy
deberta-base [ours]	3	4845	**88.93%**
distilbert-base [ours]	3	**1212**	88.31%
nepaliBERT	4	3231	85.96%
NepaliBERT	6	3230	81.05%
XLM-Roberta	5	8075	84.02%

Table 5: Highest accuracy attained by the models

All the models cross the baseline accuracy of 80%. The de-berta model attains an accuracy of 88.93% which highlights the significance of training domain-adapted language models. Distilbert attains a respectable accuracy of 88.31% with the least number of training steps, which implies that the model trains the fastest for downstream tasks. The performance difference compared to the de-berta model is marginal, and being the smallest and the lightest model, it best suits a production environment with computational constraints.

We note that all models except XLM-roberta-base are domain-adapted to the Nepali language. We can see a general trend of domain-adapted models reaching their peak accuracy on the second or third epoch, whereas multilingual models prefer more training epochs. As a result, domain-adapted language models accelerate downstream task training.

5. Language Model Training and Fine-tuning Approach

We approached language model training and its finetuning with the following considerations:

5.1 Tokenizer:

Language-specific pre-processing of text benefits the training of language models. Modeling a Sentence Piece Model (SPM) tokenization performs comparably with the language-specific approach and can be used for a variety of languages. Using this approach, lesser focus may be given to the language-specific aspects and one may train language models on a language whose structure may not be familiar to them.

5.2 MLM with Less Data Resources

Considering limited data availability constraints, models are trained for multiple epochs by increasing the number of masked tokens on every preceding epoch. This progressive masking approach adds noise to the data and gradually increases the training difficulty in the later epochs. Also, de-duplicating the dataset improves the model performance.

5.3 Fine-tuning on a Downstream Task

As for fine-tuning the language model on a downstream task, our models performed optimally when trained with a learning rate of 2e-5 or 3e-5 with a linear learning rate scheduler.

6. Conclusion

In this work, we have analyzed the need and effectiveness of pre-training Transformer language models for Nepali. We focused on the language-specific aspects that are needed to be considered while modeling a low-resourced language and undertook approaches to tackle data availability constraints. We trained two auto-encoding transformer models, the DeBERTa model that focuses on attaining the best performance, and the DistilBERT model which focuses on being lightweight with capabilities for on-device computations. Our approaches are compared with other transformer models by evaluating them in terms of downstream classification accuracy and the result highlights the need of domain-adapted Language Model training on low-resourced languages.

7. Acknowledgements

This research was supported in part through computational resources provided by the Supercomputer Center Kathmandu University, which was established with equipment donated by CERN.

8. References

Arora, G. (2020). i{NLTK}: Natural Language Toolkit for Indic Languages. *Proceedings of Second Workshop for NLP Open Source Software (NLP-OSS)*, 66–71. https://doi.org/10.18653/v1/2020.nlposs-1.10

Bal, B. K. (2004a). Structure of Nepali Grammar. *PAN Localization, Working Papers 2004-2007*, 332–396.

Bal, B. K. (2004b). A Morphological Analyzer and Stemmer for Nepali. *PAN Localization, Working Papers 2004-2007*, 324–331.

Biewald, L. (2020). Experiment Tracking with Weights and Biases. *Software available from wandb.com*. https://www.wandb.com/.

Chaudhary, A., & Sabin. (2017). 16NepaliNews Corpus. https://github.com/sndsabin/Nepali-News-Classifier

Chung, J., Gulcehre, C., Cho, K., & Bengio, Y. (2014). Empirical evaluation of gated recurrent neural networks on sequence modeling. In *NIPS 2014 Workshop on Deep Learning, December 2014*.

Clark, K., Luong, M. T., Le, Q. V., & Manning, C. D. (2020). Electra: Pre-training text encoders as discriminators rather than generators. *8th International Conference on Learning Representations*.

Conneau, A., Khandelwal, K., Goyal, N., Chaudhary, V., Wenzek, G., Guzmán, F., Grave, E., Ott, M., Zettlemoyer, L., & Stoyanov, V. (2020). Unsupervised Cross-lingual Representation Learning at Scale. *Proceedings of the 58th Annual Meeting of the Association for Computational Linguistics*, 8440–8451. https://doi.org/10.18653/v1/2020.acl-main.747

Devlin, J., Chang, M. W., Lee, K., & Toutanova, K. (2019). BERT: Pre-training of deep bidirectional transformers for language understanding. *NAACL HLT 2019 - 2019 Conference of the North American Chapter of the Association for Computational Linguistics: Human Language Technologies - Proceedings of the Conference*.

He, P., Liu, X., Gao, J., & Chen, W. (2020). Deberta: Decoding-enhanced bert with disentangled attention. *arXiv preprint arXiv:2006.03654*.

He, Z., Bao, S., & Chung, A.C. (2018). 3D Deep Affine-Invariant Shape Learning for Brain MR Image Segmentation. *DLMIA/ML-CDS@MICCAI*.

Hochreiter, S., & Schmidhuber, J. (1997). Long Short-Term Memory. *Neural Computation*, *9*(8), 1735–1780. https://doi.org/10.1162/neco.1997.9.8.1735

Howard, J., & Ruder, S. (2018). Universal language model fine-tuning for text classification. *ACL 2018 - 56th Annual Meeting of the Association for Computational Linguistics, Proceedings of the Conference (Long Papers)*. https://doi.org/10.18653/v1/p18-1031

Jain, K., Deshpande, A., Shridhar, K., Laumann, F., & Dash, A. (2020). Indic-transformers: An analysis of transformer language models for Indian languages. *arXiv preprint arXiv:2011.02323*.

Kaplan, J., McCandlish, S., Henighan, T., Brown, T. B., Chess, B., Child, R., ... & Amodei, D. (2020). Scaling laws for neural language models. *arXiv preprint arXiv:2001.08361*.

Kudo, T., & Richardson, J. (2018). SentencePiece: A simple and language independent subword tokenizer and detokenizer for Neural Text Processing. *EMNLP*.

Lample, G., & Conneau, A. (2019). Cross-lingual Language Model Pretraining. *NeurIPS*.

Lan, Z., Chen, M., Goodman, S., Gimpel, K., Sharma, P., & Soricut, R. (2020). ALBERT: A Lite BERT for Self-supervised Learning of Language Representations. *ArXiv, abs/1909.11942*.

Liu, Y., Ott, M., Goyal, N., Du, J., Joshi, M., Chen, D., Levy, O., Lewis, M., Zettlemoyer, L., & Stoyanov, V. (2019). RoBERTa: A Robustly Optimized BERT Pretraining Approach. *ArXiv, abs/1907.11692*.

Maharjan G., Bal B.K., R. S. (2019). Named Entity Recognition (NER) for Nepali. *Communications in Computer and Information Science*, *1084*(Creativity in Intelligent Technologies and Data Science).

Mikolov, T., Chen, K., Corrado, G., & Dean, J. (2013). Efficient estimation of word representations in vector space. *1st International Conference on Learning Representations, ICLR 2013 - Workshop Track Proceedings*.

Mishra, K., Rathi, J., & Banjara, J. (2020). Encoder Decoder based Nepali News Headline Generation. *International Journal of Computer Applications*, *175*, 975–8887. https://doi.org/10.5120/ijca2020920735

Nepali language - Wikipedia. En.wikipedia.org. (2022). Retrieved 22 May 2022, from https://en.wikipedia.org/wiki/Nepali_language

Nepali alphabet. nepalilanguage.org. (2015). Retrieved 22 May 2022, from https://nepalilanguage.org/alphabet

Pudasaini, S. (2022). Pretraining Nepali Masked Language Model using BERT Architecture. *3rd International Conference on Natural Language Processing, Information Retrieval, and AI*

Rajan. (2021). *NepaliBERT*. https://huggingface.co/Rajan/NepaliBERT

Ruder, S. (2020). *Why You Should Do NLP Beyond English*. https://ruder.io/nlp-beyond-english/

Sanh, V., Debut, L., Chaumond, J., & Wolf, T. (2019). DistilBERT, a distilled version of BERT: smaller, faster, cheaper and lighter. *5th Workshop on Energy Efficient Machine Learning and Cognitive Computing*.

Song, X., Salcianu, A., Song, Y., Dopson, D., & Zhou, D. (2021). Fast WordPiece Tokenization. *EMNLP*.

Ortiz Suarez, P., Romary, L., & Sagot, B. (2020). A Monolingual Approach to Contextualized Word Embeddings for Mid-Resource Languages. *ACL*.

Vaswani, A., Shazeer, N.M., Parmar, N., Uszkoreit, J., Jones, L., Gomez, A.N., Kaiser, L., & Polosukhin, I. (2017). Attention is All you Need. *ArXiv, abs/1706.03762*.

Wang, A., Singh, A., Michael, J., Hill, F., Levy, O., & Bowman, S. R. (2019). {GLUE}: A Multi-Task Benchmark and Analysis Platform for Natural Language Understanding. *International Conference on Learning Representations*.

Wettig, A., Gao, T., Zhong, Z., & Chen, D. (2022). Should You Mask 15% in Masked Language Modeling? *ArXiv, abs/2202.08005*.

9. Appendix

A. Training of Language Models

In this section we show some of the plots of pre-training the language models. Weights and Biases (Biewald, 2020) platform was used to track the training process.

A1. DeBERTa Model

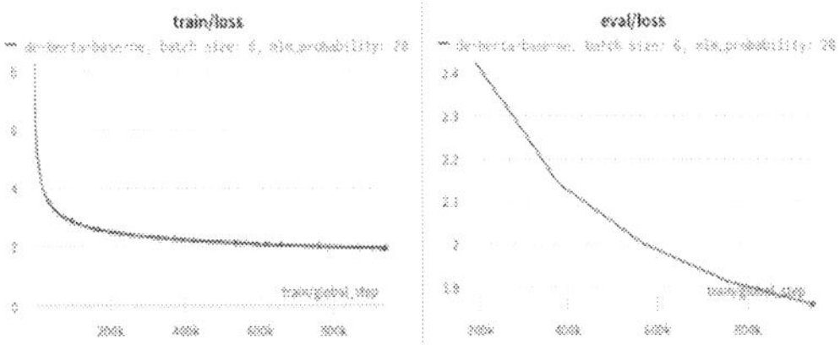

A2. DistilBERT Model

Distilbert Model trained with progressive masking.

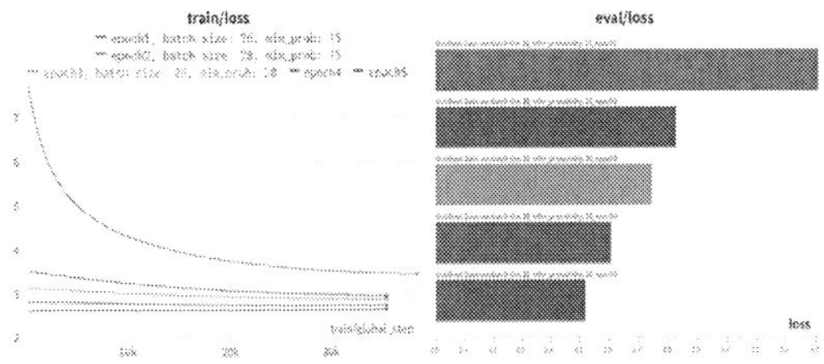

Proceedings of SIGUL2022 @LREC2022, pages 112–121
Marseille, 24-25 June 2022

CoSwID, a Code Switching Identification Method Suitable for Under-Resourced Languages

Laurent Kevers
UMR CNRS 6240 LISA, Università di Corsica - Pasquale Paoli
Avenue Jean Nicoli, 20250 Corte, France
kevers_l@univ-corse.fr

Abstract

We propose a method for identifying monolingual textual segments in multilingual documents. It requires only a minimal number of linguistic resources – word lists and monolingual corpora – and can therefore be adapted to many under-resourced languages. Taking these languages into account when processing multilingual documents in NLP tools is important as it can contribute to the creation of essential textual resources. This language identification task – code switching detection being its most complex form – can also provide added value to various existing data or tools. Our research demonstrates that a language identification module performing well on short texts can be used to efficiently analyse a document through a sliding window. The results obtained for code switching identification – between 87.29% and 97.97% accuracy – are state-of-the-art, which is confirmed by the benchmarks performed on the few available systems that have been used on our test data.

Keywords: language identification, code switching, under-resourced languages, Corsican

1. Introduction

Identifying the language of a document is a task that generally gives very good results. However, there are still various situations where performance tends to lower. Hughes et al. (2006) and Jauhiainen et al. (2018) note, more than ten years apart, that the processing of multilingual documents and the support of under-resourced languages are among the aspects that are not yet fully mastered[1]. In this paper, we focus on these two specific issues by studying the possibility of segmenting a multilingual document – potentially including under-resourced languages – into monolingual sequences whose languages would be identified.

The presence of several languages in a document may have multiple reasons and take different forms. It may be intentional, as in the case of a document which provides the same content in different languages, or even organises language alternation throughout the text[2]. It can also be unintentional – unpremeditated – as in the case of texts transcribing oral interviews where code-switching situations occur.

The localisation of monolingual segments and the identification of languages within a multilingual document is important in many ways, especially for under-resourced languages. Building corpora for these languages is a major challenge that can benefit from fine-grained language identification in order to produce the cleanest possible linguistic resources. This objective can be achieved either by excluding multilingual documents from the corpus or by splitting or annotating sections according to their language. Further linguistic processing of these documents can then take advantage from the language information linked to each word. For example, morphosyntactic annotation – whether done (semi-)manually to create reference data, or automatically using a tagger – can be facilitated and enhanced by this information. At a higher applicative level, search engine indexes or machine translation can also be improved if monolingual segments are correctly located and identified in the documents.

By definition, under-resourced languages often lack the resources and tools to identify them, especially in a multilingual context. We believe that this difficulty must be addressed. Most languages are, as a matter of fact, under-resourced (Joshi et al., 2020), even though they represent a significant number of speakers and constitute a cultural richness whose survival should be encouraged by the development and implementation of appropriate resources and tools.

This paper will first describe the context and objectives of our work (section 2), followed by an overview of the state of the art (section 3). In light of these elements, a solution is then presented (section 4) and evaluated (section 5). Finally, we will discuss the results and outline a method for code switching identification in the context of under-resourced languages (section 6).

2. Context, scope and objectives

In this work on the identification of monolingual sequences within multilingual documents, we are interested both in documents where language diversity is structured and in documents where code switching occurs. In the first case, we can expect fairly homogeneous and well-defined areas, for example a text available in two languages and structured in two columns,

[1] Other issues such as open language detection, the effects of preprocessing, the support of a large number of languages, the distinction between close languages and dialects, as well as language identification for short texts are also identified as problematic.

[2] For example, a switch of language every paragraph if several official or used languages coexist.

or a text where language changes at each paragraph. In the second case, the language switches and the size of the linguistically homogeneous segments may vary greatly and be much more irregular. This is of course the most challenging and interesting problem and will be our main objective.

While many texts will involve only a limited number of languages – for example two or three, possibly known in advance – we also consider, more generally, the situation where it may be higher.

Our approach aims at making the identification of monolingual segments accessible to under-resourced languages. We therefore consider that there is not necessarily an annotated corpus available to describe the phenomenon and to carry out specific and massive machine learning. However, we assume a minimum of resources are available, i.e. an assumed monolingual raw corpus and a word list for each language to include.

Among the under-resourced languages, we are particularly interested in Corsican, for which we have started to develop resources and tools in recent years (Kevers and Retali-Medori, 2020). We have been able to obtain interesting results for the identification of this language at the scale of a whole document (Kevers, 2021), but the treatment of multilingual documents remains unsatisfactory. The presence of words or parts in a language other than the one globally detected is not currently handled, which can be a drawback in some cases. Our concerns for Corsican include the manual or semi-automatic constitution of raw or annotated corpora – in particular morphosyntactically – which can greatly benefit from a language-aware processing. Moreover, we are working on the *Banque de Données Langue Corse* project (BDLC), which is developing a database featuring ethnotexts in Corsican[3]. These texts include segments in French and code switching identification would therefore bring a real added value.

3. State of the art

Language identification has been the focus of much research. While the problem can to some extent be considered solved, there are various situations where this is not the case. In his survey, Jauhiainen et al. (2018) provide an overview of the field and identify open questions. Based on their work – enriched with a few additional references – we take it up again from the angle of the analysis of multilingual documents, as this remained relatively marginal in his original work. Our presentation is necessarily more synthetic, we therefore refer to the original paper for further details.

Some research, such as Prager (2000) or Lui et al. (2014), have addressed the analysis of multilingual documents with the aim of identifying – or even quantifying – the languages they contain, but without locating them precisely. This approach, although it may be useful, is not sufficient for our purposes.

Regarding the identification and characterisation of monolingual segments within a document, some systems introduce a limitation on the number of languages involved. For example, Mandl et al. (2006) or Singh and Gorla (2007) postulate the presence of two or three languages maximum among those recognised by the system. The limitation can also concern one or more specific language pairs, such as English-Spanish (Lignos and Mitch, 2013), Turkish-Dutch (Nguyen and Doğruöz, 2013), English-Spanish and English-Dutch (Chang and Lin, 2014), Hindi-English (Jhamtani et al., 2014), Irish-English, Welsh-English and Breton-English (Minocha and Tyers, 2014), English-Spanish and MSA[4]-Egyptian (Samih et al., 2016), or English-Dutch (Dongen, 2017).

The granularity of the identified units is also variable. While the sentence level is sometimes chosen (Stensby et al., 2010; Lavergne et al., 2014), most methods operate on words or tokens. Some approaches, however, extend the analysis to the character level (Pethő and Mózes, 2014; Kocmi and Bojar, 2017).

Although many approaches could meet our needs (Hammarström, 2007; Rehurek and Kolkus, 2009; Ullman, 2014; Giwa and Davel, 2014; Lavergne et al., 2014; King et al., 2015), we have to note that the availability of tools, in the form of source code or reusable modules, is very limited. Some functional solutions, discussed below, have nevertheless been identified and present the advantage of being comparable and benchmarkable against common data.

With *SegLang*, Yamaguchi and Tanaka-Ishii (2012) propose the division of multilingual documents into monolingual segments for 222 languages, including Corsican. The system, which uses either training data from the *Universal Declaration of Human Rights* or from *Wikipedia*, can also be re-trained with new data. There is no pre-built model as the loading and processing of reference data is done at initialization. The volume of the training set and the data to be processed might be limited according to the available memory[5]. The principle of the analysis is to optimise the segmentation of the text by minimising the *Description Length*. The source code[6] is not ready to use as is, but the authors provide us with a working demo version[7].

[3]The Corsican Language Database project, `https://bdlc.univ-corse.fr`, collects linguistic data on know-how and cultural traditions throughout Corsica by means of oral interviews with native speakers. The lexical surveys are sometimes extended by semi-directed interviews which allow the collection of authentic accounts in Corsican, which once transcribed are integrated into the database as *ethnotexts*.

[4]Modern Standard Arabic.

[5]We did not perform extensive tests to define this limitation, but we were not able to use our full learning data set, even by allocating up to 6 GB of memory to Java. We ended up using about 500 KB of data per language.

[6]`https://github.com/hiroshi-cl/seglang-core`, under BSD license.

[7]We would like to thank them for their help!

King and Abney (2013) present *LangId*, a word-level language identification system designed for the processing of bilingual documents[8]. There are 30 languages initially proposed, Corsican is not among them. It is however possible to generate a model from new data. Again, the size of the data to be processed – for training and to be analysed – depends on the memory that can be allocated. Several classification methods are available, CRF being the one offering the best reported results. The Java code is made available and can be used without any particular dependency[9].

The third available tool is *Codeswitchador* (Lignos and Mitch, 2013), which allows code switching detection by identifying the language at word level. With this system, it is not possible to consider more than two languages, those initially defined being Spanish and English. However, it is possible to generate language models, based on word appearance probabilities. This procedure allows adaptation to other languages. Context-sensitive heuristics are also implemented. The Python code is available[10] and needs *numpy*.

A last system, *LanideNN*[11] (Kocmi and Bojar, 2017), based on neural networks and supporting 131 languages – including Corsican – could have completed this trio. Unfortunately, the installation of the required dependencies[12] could not be achieved. A migration to a more recent framework seems to be envisaged, which could make *LanideNN* usable in the future.

Given these previous works, we highlight the small number of open and reusable tools, as well as some of their limitations. We therefore propose a solution for the identification of monolingual segments within multilingual documents, easily adaptable to different use cases, in particular the simultaneous presence of many languages, possibly under-resourced, as well as code switching situations.

4. A solution to code switching identification : CoSwID

The approach explored is in line with our previous work on **language identification** (Kevers and Retali-Medori, 2020; Kevers, 2021). The experiments carried out have been encouraging and have allowed us to highlight a tool – *ldig*[13] (Nakatani, 2012) – which, in addition to good results at the document level, has shown its ability to efficiently process small texts. We assume that this type of tool can be used to analyse a document through small sequences using a sliding window, and thus determine locally the language of each token.

Unlike most other approaches that extract n-grams of different lengths – for example, ranging from two to four – the analysis performed by *ldig* is based on the concepts of *infinity gram* and *maximal substring* (Okanohara and Tsujii, 2009). The principle consists of extracting a set of character substrings with a priori undefined and variable length. Given their potentially large number, these are aggregated and represented by maximal substrings[14].

The decision to use *ldig* does not imply any exclusive dependency between this component and our developments. Any other language identification module, with similar characteristics, could be used instead.

For this work, we chose to train the language identification module for Corsican as well as for eight other European languages[15]. The limitation to only nine languages was motivated by the need to gather minimal resources (monolingual corpora, dictionaries), as well as by the assumption that very highly multilingual documents are relatively rare. With Corsican in mind, we took care to select, French and Italian, which are languages that are close historically, linguistically and in real-life situations. The other languages have been added in order to be able to handle a slightly larger number of them. Even if the integration of many languages is not a priority, it remains interesting in the perspective of having a more generic approach.

In addition to the language identification module, a set of **monolingual dictionaries**[16] have been collected. Their utility in the analysis process is not fundamental, but they constitute an interesting tool when there is an indecisive decision on some words.

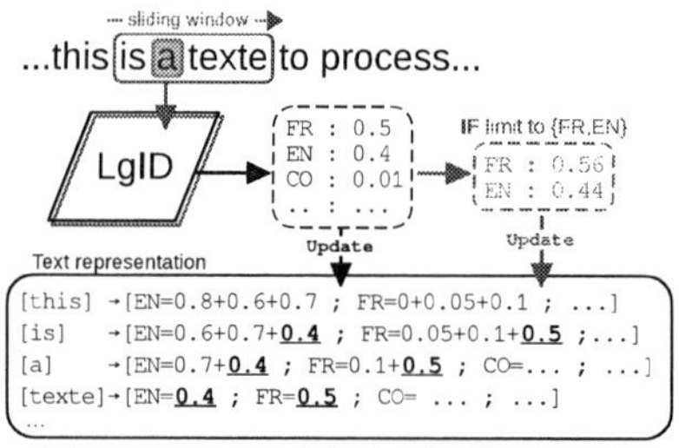

Figure 1: Three tokens wide sliding window parsing

The **parsing** general principle is to split the text into tokens and to analyse them progressively by means of a sliding window which is moved forward from token to token until the end of the text (Figure 1). Besides

[8]The extension to documents containing a larger number of languages is however possible.

[9]`http://www-personal.umich.edu/~benking/resources/langid_release.tar.gz`. Java version 8 is required. There is no user license specified.

[10]`https://github.com/ConstantineLignos/Codeswitchador`, under BSD license.

[11]`https://github.com/kocmitom/LanideNN`

[12]A Python 3.4 version, which is no longer available in recent Linux distributions, and a rather old version of TensorFlow (0.8).

[13]`https://github.com/shuyo/ldig`

[14]For example 'abracadabra' gives the maximal substrings 'a', 'abra' and 'abracadabra' (Nakatani, 2012).

[15]English, French, German, Italian, Dutch, Portuguese, Romanian and Spanish.

[16]These are more precisely word lists, grammatical or inflectional information not being used.

the current token, the window contains a number of additional units taken from the left and right context, and has therefore always an odd size, with a minimum length of one. The resulting snippet is sent to the language identification module, which returns the set of probabilities for all languages known by the system. If we wish to limit the analysis to a subset of languages, irrelevant ones are eliminated from the result – regardless of their importance in this one – and the remaining probabilities are readjusted to keep the sum to 100%. The results obtained for the different languages on a snippet are recorded for each token by adding the probabilities to any scores already produced by a previous segment[17]. Once this has been done for the whole text, each token has a score for each language of the system. In principle, the language with the highest probability is assigned to the token. However, this analysis can be questioned if the difference between the first and subsequent languages does not seem to be sufficient. This is judged according to a configurable margin[18] (*indecision gap*). In this case, a threshold is applied using the same margin[19]. Once this initial selection has been made, various approaches are possible to choose between the candidate languages: consultation of monolingual dictionaries, use of the language identification module on the token alone, or a combination of these two methods. In all cases, if these additional investigations are not successful, the initial scores are maintained and the language that ranks first is selected.
The CoSwID Python code is available[20], as well as an updated version of *ldig*[21].

5. Tests and evaluation

5.1. Data

First of all, regarding the training data needed to create a language identification model with *ldig*, we mainly used, for the eight European languages, sentence corpora from the *Tatoeba* collaborative platform[22]. For Corsican, which is only marginally represented in this source, we used three corpora made available by the BDLC[23]: *Wikipedia*, the *Bible* and *A Piazzetta*, a local news blog in Corsican. Table 1 (*Base* column) gives an overview of the available data.

Language		*Base*	*Filter*	*Filter2*
eng	en	67 948 293	64 653 131	58 824 526
ita	it	32 022 121	22 815 185	20 813 785
deu	de	29 987 665	29 106 064	28 126 760
fra	fr	22 482 372	19 062 318	17 833 313
por	pt	17 399 633	13 688 730	13 054 128
spa	es	15 437 547	12 294 945	11 069 048
cos	co	11 868 620	10 483 557	10 402 975
nld	nl	5 968 644	5 455 944	5 034 300
ron	ro	1 045 723	862 135	782 957

Table 1: Number of characters in the training data (base corpus or after one or two filtering processes)

All these training documents were slightly preprocessed: normalisation to lower case, punctuation removal and space normalisation. As Corsican documents from the *Wikipedia* and *A Piazzetta* corpora may sometimes contain substantial passages in other languages, they were filtered out by means of keywords language detection[24]. Finally, the training data was presented in lines of maximum about 200 characters[25].
The monolingual dictionaries are mainly derived from the lexical resources made available by *Unitex*[26], with the exception of those for Dutch (*OpenTaal*[27]), Romanian (*ELRC*[28]) and Corsican (*BDLC*). The number of items in each dictionary is shown in Table 2.

Language			*Items*
English	eng	en	398 417
Italian	ita	it	95 038
German	deu	de	8 277
French	fra	fr	794 286
Portuguese	por	pt	890 193
Spanish	spa	es	477 976
Corsican	cos	co	43 051
Dutch	nld	nl	401 575
Romanian	ron	ro	19 946

Table 2: Dictionaries data

Finally, we have created several evaluation corpora. The first is a set of synthetic multilingual documents based on the *Universal Declaration of Human Rights* (UDHR)[29] and involving all nine languages. Sev-

[17]If the window size is three, each token will receive three scores which will be summed language by language before being normalised.

[18]With a margin of 10% and the probabilities [Lg1=0.25, Lg2=0.22, Lg3=0.18, Lg4=0.10, Lg5=0.10, Lg6=0.10, Lg7=0.05], the differences between Lg1 and Lg2 (3%) and Lg1 and Lg3 (7%), are not sufficient to choose Lg1 directly.

[19]In the previous example, all languages with a probability greater than or equal to 15% are kept (Lg1, Lg2 and Lg3), the others are eliminated.

[20]https://github.com/lkevers/coswid

[21]https://github.com/lkevers/ldig-python3

[22]https://tatoeba.org, under CC BY 2.0 FR license.

[23]https://bdlc.univ-corse.fr/tal/index.php?page=res

[24]Based on a document-wide count of language-specific keyword occurrences. Keyword lists are from Lucene (https://github.com/apache/lucene), except for the Corsican one. The number of keywords per language varies between 78 and 393. Documents not detected as being mostly in Corsican were discarded (128 documents for *A Piazzetta* and 141 documents for *Wikipedia*).

[25]For performance reasons, it is recommended not to provide *ldig* with too long learning documents.

[26]https://unitexgramlab.org/language-resources, under LGPLLR license.

[27]https://github.com/OpenTaal/opentaal-wordlist, under revised BSD or CC BY 3.0 licenses.

[28]The "Romanian–English parallel wordlists" available at https://elrc-share.eu, under CC-BY 4.0 license.

[29]We used the "udhr2" corpus available in NLTK:

eral versions were produced, depending on the frequency and granularity of the composition between languages. The *UDHR-parag* corpus alternates at paragraph breaks, whereas for *UDHR-sent*, this occurs at the end of each sentence. Finally, the *UDHR-word* corpus provides switching within the sentence itself. The construction of the latter is carried out by replacing, after every three to seven tokens, within a sentence in a "main" language chosen randomly, segments of one to four tokens in another language, chosen randomly again. Even if the mixing has been performed as accurately as possible, a word-for-word replacement respecting the syntactic structure of the sentences is not possible[30]. For these three corpora, all the data are used, so the same text is found nine times in different languages. Finally, it should be noted that the original order of the sentences has not been kept.
The second evaluation corpus (*BDLC-ethno*) is made of authentic ethnotexts containing transcripts of oral interviews conducted in Corsican, in which passages in French may occur.
Beyond their artificial or authentic character, the particularities of these different corpora allow us to take into account different criteria: the frequency of alternation, the length of the segments, as well as the number of languages involved.
The evaluation data, as well as the data used to generate the language identification model, is available[31].

5.2. Experiments

The metric we are trying to maximise is the accuracy of language identification for each token (*overall accuracy*, noted Acc_o). The accuracy obtained specifically on the alternation zones (*targeted accuracy*, noted Acc_t) is also a secondary point of interest.
The experiments were grouped into three tests with different characteristics regarding the frequency of switching, the length of the segments and the number of languages involved.
TEST-1 concerns the *UDHR-parag* and *UDHR-sent* corpora. They consist of relatively long monolingual sequences, and switching is therefore infrequent[32], but involve all nine languages. This test was performed on synthetic data. The language alternation was created artificially from parallel documents, without altering the sentences.
TEST-2 uses the *UDHR-word* corpus, which is marked by short monolingual sequences, frequent switching[33], and again all nine languages. It is a synthetic data set, whose creation process may have led to an alteration of the sentence structure.
Finally, **TEST-3** focuses on the *BDLC-ethno* corpus, composed of authentic data. It is characterised by long sequences in Corsican with insertions of variable size, but rather short, in French[34]. The frequency of switches is slightly higher than in TEST-1, but much lower than in TEST-2.
In order to identify the best configuration for each test, we experimented with several values for the different parameters. First, the **training of the language identification model** was performed either on all data (*Base*) or on a subset (see Table 1). For *Filter*, we applied the keyword filtering method already used for Corsican (see section 5.1 and footnote 24) to all corpora whose documents were transformed into fragments of 200 characters. A second selection (*Filter2*), carried out in accordance with the same approach, but using the language detector CLD3[35], was produced from *Filter*. The **size of the sliding window** used for the analysis was set to 1, 3, 5 or 7 tokens. The **indecision gap** was set to values of 0, 0.05, 0.1 and 0.2. Finally, there are three **verification methods**[36] in case of a questionable language identification: using the dictionary (*dico*), language identification on the single token concerned only (*lgID*), and the combination of these two methods[37] (*full*). Finally, for the *BDLC-ethno* corpus, a **limitation to the two languages** actually present in the corpus can be requested. All the combinations of these parameters – 120 in total[38] – were tested and measured in order to identify the best performing ones.
Finally, our results were compared to those obtained by the three systems that we were able to test: *SegLang*, *LangId* and *Codeswitchador* (see section 3). *SegLang* has built-in data from *Wikipedia* or the *Universal Declaration of Human Rights*. Since TEST-1 and -2 also involved UDHR data, we only used *SegLang* with *Wikipedia* data (SLW) or by using a subset of our own data[39] (SLC). *LangId* (LID) and *Codeswitchador* (CS) also benefited from the same data and were used for TEST-3 in bilingual mode.

https://www.nltk.org/nltk_data/ (public domain).

[30]It could be a drawback if the code switching detection method plans to use this information, which is not our case.

[31]https://github.com/lkevers/coswid

[32]*UDHR-parag* contains 16,095 tokens spread over 531 paragraphs, a switch of language occurring at each paragraph break. *UDHR-sent* contains 16,097 tokens divided into 621 sentences, the language being changed for each new sentence.

[33]*UDHR-word* contains 18,417 tokens and 2,598 language switching sequences (tokens in language X inserted in a sentence globally in language Y).

[34]Out of 79,421 tokens, 74,569 (93.89%) are in Corsican, 4,042 (5.09%) in French – spread over 959 segments – and 810 (1.02%) without an attributed language (abbreviations, proper nouns or speech turn markers when identified).

[35]https://github.com/google/cld3, (Apache-2.0).

[36]When the indecision gap is set to 0, the language with the highest probability is systematically selected and the verification method parameter is not used.

[37]When the two methods have different results, they are compared to the language detected globally for the whole document. If no options emerge, the initial result is retained.

[38](3 filtering modes of learning data * 4 window sizes * 3 indecision gaps (different of 0) * 3 verification methods)=108 + (3 filtering modes of learning data * 4 window sizes * 1 indecision gap (equals to 0 : no verification requiered))=12.

[39]For memory usage reasons, the training corpus was limited to 500KB per language.

5.3. Results

For **TEST-1**, the ten best configurations are detailed for the paragraph (Table 3) or sentence (Table 4) switching level. With a few exceptions, the results tend to converge. The settings that emerge involve exclusively the datasets filtered twice or, to a lesser extent, once. The size of the window is rather large: in general seven tokens, five in a few cases. The values to adopt for these two parameters seem therefore quite clear, which is less the case for the indecision gap. However, the trend points towards values of 10% to 20%. The verification methods based on dictionaries – *dico* and, in a less important way, *full* – emerge as the most effective. The best performing configuration – which is identical in both cases – offers 98.15% of overall accuracy for the paragraph level switching corpus and 98.00% for the one containing sentence level switchings. The accuracy targeted at the language changing points was measured at 88.75% and 89.37% respectively.

SegLang obtained a lower performance than this optimal configuration with the embedded *Wikipedia* data, but outperforms it by 1.39% (paragraph) to 1.61% (sentence) with our filtered training data (*Filter2*).

#	*Configuration*				Acc_o	Acc_t
1	**Filter2**	**7**	**0.2**	**dico**	**0.9815**	**0.8875**
2	Filter	7	0.2	dico	0.9796	0.8865
3	Filter2	7	0.1	dico	0.9785	0.8625
4	Filter2	5	0.2	dico	0.9766	0.8941
5	Filter2	7	0.05	full	0.9762	0.8503
6	Filter2	7	0.05	dico	0.9762	0.8451
7	Filter	7	0.1	dico	0.9751	0.8536
8	Filter2	7	0.1	full	0.9747	0.8658
9	Filter2	5	0.1	dico	0.9740	0.8734
10	Filter2	7	0.05	lgID	0.9739	0.8362
SLW	Built-in Wikipedia data				0.9211	0.7768
SLC	**Custom data 500KB/language**				**0.9954**	**0.9774**

Table 3: Top 10 for TEST-1 (paragraph)

#	*Configuration*				Acc_o	Acc_t
1	**Filter2**	**7**	**0.2**	**dico**	**0.9800**	**0.8937**
2	Filter2	7	0.1	dico	0.9758	0.8663
3	Filter	7	0.2	dico	0.9749	0.8728
4	Filter2	5	0.2	dico	0.9737	0.8933
5	Filter2	7	0.05	dico	0.9715	0.8378
6	Filter2	7	0.1	full	0.9714	0.8619
7	Filter2	7	0.05	full	0.9712	0.8414
8	Filter	7	0.1	dico	0.9708	0.8462
9	Filter2	5	0.1	dico	0.9704	0.8704
10	Filter	5	0.2	dico	0.9695	0.8732
SLW	Built-in Wikipedia data				0.9053	0.7576
SLC	**Custom data 500KB/language**				**0.9961**	**0.9815**

Table 4: Top 10 for TEST-1 (sentence)

The performance[40] observed when varying the parameters one by one with respect to the optimal configuration is shown in Table 5. The use of filtered language identification training data has a positive impact on the overall accuracy (+ 1.35% between *Base* and *Filter2*) as well as on the the targeted accuracy (+1.85%). The size of the window is a decisive criterion, as the results become weaker as the window narrows. The results obtained for windows of seven and five tokens remain fairly close to each other. The setting using only one token has a much lower performance. The use of an indecision gap improves the accuracy, especially for the switching zones. The *dico* verification method is clearly more efficient in terms of overall accuracy (+1.55% with regard to *full* and +2.35% compared with *lgID*) and targeted accuracy (respectively +1.93% and +4.59%).

#	*Configuration*				Acc_o	Acc_t
1	**Filter2**	**7**	**0.2**	**dico**	**0.9800**	**0.8937**
3	**Filter**	7	0.2	dico	0.9749	0.8728
16	**Base**	7	0.2	dico	0.9665	0.8752
4	Filter2	**5**	0.2	dico	0.9737	0.8933
47	Filter2	**3**	0.2	dico	0.9425	0.8776
91	Filter2	**1**	0.2	dico	0.5937	0.6582
2	Filter2	7	**0.1**	dico	0.9758	0.8663
5	Filter2	7	**0.05**	dico	0.9715	0.8378
19	Filter2	7	**0**	n-a	0.9655	0.8019
20	Filter2	7	0.2	**full**	0.9645	0.8744
36	Filter2	7	0.2	**lgID**	0.9565	0.8478

Table 5: Variation of parameters with respect to the optimal solution (TEST-1 sentence)

For **TEST-2** (Table 6), the best performing configurations use again the language identification model trained on the filtered data (*Filter2* and *Filter*), but this time with smaller sliding window sizes (three to five tokens). The trend for the other parameters remains unchanged from TEST-1: a 10% to 20% indecision gap between candidate languages and the dictionary-based verification method. TEST-2, which features more language changes and shorter segments, can be considered as the most complex case we have to analyse. It is therefore not surprising that we find a decrease in both overall (87.29%) and targeted accuracy (82.54%).

SegLang is positioned in the same way as for TEST-1: lower with the *Wikipedia* data, and 0.78% higher with our filtered training data.

The results obtained after varying the parameters with respect to the optimal solution are shown in Table 7. The improvements brought by the filtering operations on the training data are significant for the global and targeted accuracies. They are mainly observable between *Base* and *Filter* (about +4%), while the move to *Filter2* brings an improvement that remains below 1%. The global accuracy obtained with a window of five tokens is very close to the optimal solution (three tokens), but offers a lower accuracy in the switching zones. A window reduced to a single token gives very poor performance. The results observed when the indecision gap varies confirm the orientation towards values be-

[40] These results are related to the sentence level, the paragraph level being comparable.

#	*Configuration*				Acc_o	Acc_t
1	**Filter2**	**3**	**0.2**	**dico**	**0.8729**	**0.8254**
2	Filter2	5	0.2	dico	0.8701	0.8106
3	Filter	3	0.2	dico	0.8672	0.8224
4	Filter	5	0.2	dico	0.8633	0.8017
5	Filter2	3	0.1	dico	0.8611	0.8071
6	Filter2	5	0.1	dico	0.8568	0.7894
7	Filter	3	0.1	dico	0.8563	0.8048
8	Filter2	3	0.05	dico	0.8527	0.7953
9	Filter	5	0.1	dico	0.8501	0.7810
10	Filter2	5	0.1	full	0.8464	0.7817
SLW	Built-in Wikipedia data				0.7061	0.6306
SLC	**Custom data 500KB/language**				**0.8807**	**0.8167**

Table 6: Top 10 for TEST-2

tween 10% and 20%. Finally, it is again the use of dictionaries that emerges as the most appropriate solution to verify the attribution of a language when the probabilities are not strong enough (about +6% compared to *full* and +9% with regard to *lgID*).

#	*Configuration*				Acc_o	Acc_t
1	**Filter2**	**3**	**0.2**	**dico**	**0.8729**	**0.8254**
3	**Filter**	3	0.2	dico	0.8672	0.8224
35	**Base**	3	0.2	dico	0.8282	0.7820
11	Filter2	**7**	0.2	dico	0.8462	0.7701
2	Filter2	**5**	0.2	dico	0.8701	0.8106
91	Filter2	**1**	0.2	dico	0.5892	0.5869
5	Filter2	3	**0.1**	dico	0.8611	0.8071
8	Filter2	3	**0.05**	dico	0.8527	0.7953
19	Filter2	3	**0**	n-a	0.8393	0.7774
56	Filter2	3	0.2	**full**	0.8096	0.7615
75	Filter2	3	0.2	**lgID**	0.7820	0.7300

Table 7: Variation of parameters with respect to the optimal solution (TEST-2)

For **TEST-3** (Table 8), using Corsican ethnotexts, the best configuration involves this time the language identification model trained on *Base*, wich is represented seven times in the Top 10. Filtered models also appear marginally with sligthly lower overall accuracy values. This could be explained by the fact that *Base* had benefited from a first filtering on Corsican, which is the majority language in the *BDLC-ethno* corpus. Interestingly, filtered models consistently achieve higher targeted accuracy results. The optimal sliding window size is unanimously found to be seven tokens, as in TEST-1, while the indecision gap values are scattered between 20% – as for the best setting – and 0%. The verification method is again rather dictionary-based, even if different solutions are represented. In short, only the size of the window seems to have a really clear and decisive influence. The optimal parameters allow to reach the overall accuracy of 96.31%, and a targeted accuracy of 67.27%.

SegLang is again a step behind with the embedded *Wikipedia* data, but slightly better (+1.23%) using our filtered data.

#	*Configuration*				Acc_o	Acc_t
1	**Base**	**7**	**0.2**	**dico**	**0.9631**	**0.6727**
2	Base	7	0.1	dico	0.9620	0.6554
3	Base	7	0.05	dico	0.9612	0.6469
4	Base	7	0.05	full	0.9605	0.6368
5	Base	7	0	n-a	0.9600	0.6370
6	Filter	7	0.2	dico	0.9597	0.7383
7	Base	7	0.1	full	0.9597	0.6340
8	Base	7	0.05	lgID	0.9596	0.6344
9	Filter2	7	0.2	dico	0.9590	0.7602
10	Filter	7	0.1	dico	0.9583	0.7237
SLW	Built-in Wikipedia data				0.9460	0.5648
SLC	**Custom data 500KB/language**				**0.9754**	**0.7120**

Table 8: Top 10 for TEST-3 (9 languages)

For this third test, investigation of changes in the detected optimal parameters (Table 9) highlights again the slightly lower overall accuracy, but higher targeted accuracy, for the language identification models based on filtered data. Similarly to the previous tests, the size of the window has an important impact on the results, which become weaker as the number of tokens decreases. However, the difference between a window of five or seven tokens is relatively small. In spite of the decrease in overall accuracy, a slightly higher targeted accuracy (just over 1%) can be achieved for configurations using smaller windows of five or three tokens. The solution using one token at a time is again lower. As far as the indecision gap is concerned, the results grow relatively slowly but steadily as its size increases. As already pointed out, the modification of the verification method shows that the approach using dictionaries is the most appropriate.

#	*Configuration*				Acc_o	Acc_t
1	**Base**	**7**	**0.2**	**dico**	**0.9631**	**0.6727**
9	**Filter2**	7	0.2	dico	0.9590	0.7602
6	**Filter**	7	0.2	dico	0.9597	0.7383
17	Base	**5**	0.2	dico	0.9554	0.7039
57	Base	**3**	0.2	dico	0.9244	0.7137
91	Base	**1**	0.2	dico	0.6833	0.4212
2	Base	7	**0.1**	dico	0.9620	0.6554
3	Base	7	**0.05**	dico	0.9612	0.6469
5	Base	7	**0**	n-a	0.9600	0.6370
20	Base	7	0.2	**full**	0.9548	0.6253
29	Base	7	0.2	**lgID**	0.9511	0.6179

Table 9: Variation of parameters with respect to the optimal solution (TEST-3, 9 languages)

As the *BDLC-ethno* corpus contains only Corsican and French, we observed the effect of choosing only between these two languages (**TEST-3bis**, Table 10). The global accuracy values obtained for the different configurations are very close to each other, the first ten varying from less than 0.2%, with an optimal configuration at 97.97%. The targeted accuracy results are slightly more variable, with the optimal configuration offering 78.39%. Note that this time there are only so-

lutions based on filtered data (*Filter2* or *Filter*). The window size remains high, between five and seven tokens, while the indecision gap holds around 20%, and the verification methods based on the use of dictionaries (*dico* or *full*) still seem to be the best.
For this last test, no third-party system scored better than ours. *Seglang*, used with our filtered data is the closest with a fairly small difference of 0.28%.

#	*Configuration*				Acc_o	Acc_t
1	**Filter**	**5**	**0.2**	**dico**	**0.9797**	**0.7839**
2	Filter2	7	0.2	dico	0.9788	0.7727
3	Filter	5	0.2	full	0.9786	0.7704
4	Filter	5	0.1	dico	0.9785	0.7706
5	Filter	7	0.2	dico	0.9783	0.7465
6	Filter	5	0.1	full	0.9781	0.7653
7	Filter	5	0.05	dico	0.9779	0.7637
8	Filter	7	0.2	full	0.9778	0.7393
9	Filter2	7	0.2	full	0.9778	0.7668
10	Filter	5	0.05	full	0.9777	0.7618
SLC	Custom data 500KB/language				0.9770	0.7151
LID	Custom data 500KB/language				0.9738	0.6664
CS	Custom data 500KB/language				0.9670	0.7576

Table 10: Top 10 for TEST-3bis, limited to two languages (cos-fra)

For the study of parameter variation (Table 11), we observe mainly small differences. However, we can highlight the usual effect of window size, lengths of seven and five being very close to each other.

#	*Configuration*				Acc_o	Acc_t
1	**Filter**	**5**	**0.2**	**dico**	**0.9797**	**0.7839**
11	**Filter2**	5	0.2	dico	0.9776	0.8066
21	**Base**	5	0.2	dico	0.9768	0.7092
5	Filter	**7**	0.2	dico	0.9783	0.7465
41	Filter	**3**	0.2	dico	0.9742	0.8262
94	Filter	**1**	0.2	dico	0.9021	0.7980
4	Filter	5	**0.1**	dico	0.9785	0.7706
7	Filter	5	**0.05**	dico	0.9779	0.7637
17	Filter	5	**0**	n-a	0.9770	0.7551
3	Filter	5	0.2	**full**	0.9786	0.7704
18	Filter	5	0.2	**lgID**	0.9770	0.7635

Table 11: Variation of parameters with respect to the optimal solution (TEST-3bis, 2 languages: cos-fra)

6. Discussion and conclusion

In the light of our results, no single setting can be identified. However, some trends can be observed and several parameters, such as the size of the sliding window and the magnitude of the indecision gap, can vary depending on the context of use.
The use of fragments of five to seven tokens has generally brought good results. In the case of very frequent and rather short alternations, a shortened window – between three and five tokens – has nevertheless proved to be more effective. In general, it is reasonable to assume that a shorter window is suitable for the analysis of texts in which language alternations occur quite dynamically and/or for short segments. A longer window will maximise accuracy for texts containing mainly long monolingual segments.

Beyond a constant value for optimal configurations (20%), it is not obvious to propose recommendations concerning the choice of the indecision gap. Since it is strongly linked to the verification method, the analysis is tricky and improvements – for example on the content of the dictionaries – could modify the configuration hierarchy. If a benefit is clearly obtained by this verification mechanism when several languages are involved, it is however much more marginal in the case of an alternation of only two languages.

About other parameters, it is worth noting that filtering the training data used for the language identification module is generally beneficial. More data does not always mean better results. Its suitability also matters. Finally, the most effective method for choosing between languages with close probabilities was the dictionary-based method.

We observe that the targeted accuracy sometimes improves by adopting slightly lower values for the window size, but this comes at the cost of a lower overall accuracy. It seems possible to consider a processing in multiple steps using different settings: a first approximation of the segments, followed by a closer review around the detected alternation points, and even a last check of the language attribution at the scale of a potentially homogeneous fragment, once it is defined.

Further work could include the improvement of the learning sets, as well as a closer investigation of language identification results or a wider and finer estimate of the parameters. The extension of the language number could also allow the testing of the reliability of the method, while providing a more universal module. Finally, the automatically performed annotations could be reviewed in some way, so that they can be used as training data for supervised approaches.

Let us conclude by highlighting that the achieved results – an overall accuracy between 87.29% and 97.97% – are in line with the state of the art. CoSwID is between 0.78% and 1.61% less accurate than *SegLang* when using our data, but it is slightly better for the third test featuring the two-language restriction. This leads us to confirm that a highly accurate and powerful language identification module can be used to detect language alternations such as code switching. We therfore consider that the use of CoSwID for language identification in the context of, among other things, morphosyntactic pre-annotation of Corsican corpora is possible. Generally speaking, the proposed approach allows to include without difficulty under-resourced languages with a minimum of resources. The release of the code and data will also contribute to address the small number of open and reusable systems for language identification in multilingual documents, and for the detection of code switching in particular.

7. Acknowledgements

This work was carried out thanks to CPER funding: *Un outil linguistique au service de la Corse et des Corses: la Banque de Données Langue Corse (BDLC).*

8. Bibliographical References

Chang, J. C. and Lin, C.-C. (2014). Recurrent-Neural-Network for Language Detection on Twitter Code-Switching Corpus. *arXiv:1412.4314 [cs]*, December. arXiv: 1412.4314.

Dongen, N. (2017). Analysis and Prediction of Dutch-English Code-switching in Dutch Social Media Messages. Master's thesis, Universiteit van Amsterdam, Amsterdam, Netherlands.

Giwa, O. and Davel, M. (2014). Language identification of individual words with Joint Sequence Models. September.

Hammarström, H. (2007). A Fine-Grained Model for Language Identification. In *Proceedings of Improving Non English Web Searching (iNEWS-07) Workshop at SIGIR 2007*, pages 14–20, Amsterdam, Netherlands.

Hughes, B., Baldwin, T., Bird, S., Nicholson, J., and Mackinlay, A. (2006). Reconsidering language identification for written language resources. In *Proceedings of the fifth international conference on Language Resources and Evaluation (LREC2006)*, pages 485–488. ELRA.

Jauhiainen, T., Lui, M., Zampieri, M., Baldwin, T., and Lindén, K. (2018). Automatic Language Identification in Texts: A Survey. *arXiv:1804.08186 [cs]*, April. arXiv: 1804.08186.

Jhamtani, H., Bhogi, S. K., and Raychoudhury, V. (2014). Word-level Language Identification in Bi-lingual Code-switched Texts. In *Proceedings of the 28th Pacific Asia Conference on Language, Information and Computing*, pages 348–357, Phuket,Thailand, December. Department of Linguistics, Chulalongkorn University.

Joshi, P., Santy, S., Budhiraja, A., Bali, K., and Choudhury, M. (2020). The State and Fate of Linguistic Diversity and Inclusion in the NLP World. In *Proceedings of the 58th Annual Meeting of the Association for Computational Linguistics*, pages 6282–6293, Online, July. ACL.

Kevers, L. and Retali-Medori, S. (2020). Towards a Corsican Basic Language Resource Kit. In *Proceedings of the 12th Language Resources and Evaluation Conference*, pages 2726–2735, Marseille, France, May. European Language Resources Association.

Kevers, L. (2021). L'identification de langue, un outil au service du corse et de l'évaluation des ressources linguistiques. *Traitement Automatique des Langues*, 62(3).

King, B. and Abney, S. (2013). Labeling the Languages of Words in Mixed-Language Documents using Weakly Supervised Methods. In *Proceedings of the 2013 Conference of the North American Chapter of the Association for Computational Linguistics: Human Language Technologies*, pages 1110–1119, Atlanta, Georgia, June. Association for Computational Linguistics.

King, L., Kübler, S., and Hooper, W. (2015). Word-level language identification in The Chymistry of Isaac Newton. *Digital Scholarship in the Humanities*, 30(4):532–540, December.

Kocmi, T. and Bojar, O. (2017). LanideNN: Multilingual Language Identification on Character Window. In *Proceedings of the 15th Conference of the European Chapter of the Association for Computational Linguistics: Volume 1, Long Papers*, pages 927–936, Valencia, Spain, April. Association for Computational Linguistics.

Lavergne, T., Adda, G., Adda-Decker, M., and Lamel, L. (2014). Automatic Language Identity Tagging on Word and Sentence-Level in Multilingual Text Sources: a Case-Study on Luxembourgish. In Khalid Choukri, et al., editors, *Ninth International Conference on Language Resources and Evaluation (LREC'14)*, pages 3300–3304, Reykjavik, Iceland, May. European Language Resources Association (ELRA).

Lignos, C. and Mitch, M. (2013). Toward web-scale analysis of codeswitching. In *87th Annual Meeting of the Linguistic Society of America*.

Lui, M., Lau, J. H., and Baldwin, T. (2014). Automatic Detection and Language Identification of Multilingual Documents. *Transactions of the Association for Computational Linguistics*, 2:27–40.

Mandl, T., Shramko, M., Tartakovski, O., and Womser-Hacker, C. (2006). Language Identification in Multi-lingual Web-Documents. pages 153–163, May.

Minocha, A. and Tyers, F. (2014). Subsegmental language detection in Celtic language text. In *Proceedings of the First Celtic Language Technology Workshop*, pages 76–80, Dublin, Ireland, August. Association for Computational Linguistics and Dublin City University.

Nakatani, S. (2012). Short Text Language Detection with Infinity-Gram, May. https://www.slideshare.net/shuyo/short-text-language-detection-with-infinitygram-1294944.

Nguyen, D. and Doğruöz, A. S. (2013). Word Level Language Identification in Online Multilingual Communication. In *Proceedings of the 2013 Conference on Empirical Methods in Natural Language Processing*, pages 857–862, Seattle, Washington, USA, October. Association for Computational Linguistics.

Okanohara, D. and Tsujii, J. (2009). Text Categorization with All Substring Features. In *Proceedings of SDM 2009*, pages 838–846, April.

Pethő, G. and Mózes, E. (2014). An n-gram-based language identification algorithm for variable-length and variable-language texts. *Argumentum*, 10:56–82.

Prager, J. (2000). Linguini: Language Identification for Multilingual Documents. *J. of Management Information Systems*, 16:71–102, January.

Rehurek, R. and Kolkus, M. (2009). Language Identification on the Web: Extending the Dictionary Method. In *CICLing '09: Proceedings of the 10th International Conference on Computational Linguistics and Intelligent Text Processing*, pages 357–368, March.

Samih, Y., Maharjan, S., Attia, M., Kallmeyer, L., and Solorio, T. (2016). Multilingual Code-switching Identification via LSTM Recurrent Neural Networks. In *Proceedings of the Second Workshop on Computational Approaches to Code Switching*, pages 50–59, Austin, Texas, November. Association for Computational Linguistics.

Singh, A. K. and Gorla, J. (2007). Identification of Languages and Encodings in a Multilingual Document. In Fairon, Cédrick, et al., editors, *Building and Exploring Web Corpora (WAC3 - 2007). Proceedings of the 3rd web as corpus workshop, incorporating cleaneval.*

Stensby, A., Oommen, B., and Granmo, O.-C. (2010). Language Detection and Tracking in Multilingual Documents Using Weak Estimators. volume 6218, pages 600–609, August.

Ullman, E. (2014). Shibboleth - A Multilingual Language Identifier. Master's thesis, Uppsala University,, Uppsala.

Yamaguchi, H. and Tanaka-Ishii, K. (2012). Text Segmentation by Language Using Minimum Description Length. In *Proceedings of the 50th Annual Meeting of the Association for Computational Linguistics (Volume 1: Long Papers)*, pages 969–978, Jeju Island, Korea, July. Association for Computational Linguistics.

Proceedings of SIGUL2022 @LREC2022, pages 122–128
Marseille, 24-25 June 2022

A Neural Network Approach to Create Minangkabau-Indonesia Bilingual Dictionary

Kartika Resiandi, Yohei Murakami, Arbi Haza Nasution
Ritsumeikan University, Ritsumeikan University, Universitas Islam Riau
1-1-1 Noji-higashi, Kusatsu, Shiga, Japan, 1-1-1 Noji-higashi, Kusatsu, Shiga, Japan,
Jl. Kaharuddin Nst 113 Pekanbaru, Riau, Indonesia
gr0502ee@ed.ritsumei.ac.jp, yohei@fc.ritsumei.ac.jp, arbi@eng.uir.ac.id

Abstract

Indonesia has many varieties of ethnic languages, and most come from the same language family, namely Austronesian languages. Coming from that same language family, the words in Indonesian ethnic languages are very similar. However, there is research stating that Indonesian ethnic languages are endangered. Thus, to prevent that, we proposed to create a bilingual dictionary between ethnic languages using a neural network approach to extract transformation rules using character level embedding and the Bi-LSTM method in a sequence-to-sequence model. The model has an encoder and decoder. The encoder functions read the input sequence, character by character, generate context, then extract a summary of the input. The decoder will produce an output sequence where every character in each time-step and the next character that comes out are affected by the previous character. The current case for experiment translation focuses on Minangkabau and Indonesian languages with 13,761-word pairs. For evaluating the model's performance, 5-Fold Cross-Validation is used. The character level seq2seq method (Bi-LSTM as encoder and LSTM as decoder) with an average precision of 83.55% outperforms the sentence piece byte pair encoding (vocab size of 32) with an average precision of 79.93%.

Keywords: Indonesian ethnic language, character level, Bi-LSTM, sequence to sequence model

1. Introduction

Indonesia's riches extend beyond natural resources such as minerals, vegetation, and fauna. Furthermore, the archipelago's culture is highly diversified, and so does a variety of ethnic languages in Indonesia.

The Austronesian language family includes Indonesian, derived from the Malay language. Since prehistoric times, Indonesian ethnic languages have developed, resulting in a different language for each ethnic group in Indonesia (Paauw, 2009). Belong to the same language family and based on the similarity matrix by utilizing the ASJP database (Nasution et al., 2019), most of Indonesian ethnic languages are closely related and similar.

Currently, the phenomenon of ethnic language extinction in Indonesia has become a problem that grabs the attention of scholars, especially linguists. The Summer Institute of Linguistic states that the local languages are endangered and may cease to be spoken in Indonesia. Therefore, we started the Indonesia Language Sphere project that aims at comprehensively creating bilingual dictionaries between the ethnic languages using a neural network approach and crowdsourcing approach, in order to conserve local languages on the verge of extinction (Murakami, 2019). As an expected result, the vocabulary of the ethnic language will expand, more people will learn it, and if there are no more speakers in the future, the language will become extinct.

The current translation experiment case focuses on Minangkabau and Indonesian languages since most of the nationalist writers who contributed to the early development of Indonesian were of Minangkabau ethnicity. Minangkabau language (closely linked to Malay) significantly influenced Indonesian in its formative years (Nasution et al., 2019). Between two languages, we presume they have several phonetic transformation rules. For example, there appears to be a rule in Indonesian and Minangkabau that the last phoneme "a" in Indonesian tends to turn "o" in Minangkabau. Although this rule isn't always valid, it can help predict a rough translation as a preliminary translation.

This study predicts the translation using character level embedding and the Bi-LSTM approach, compared to the sentence piece method using the sequence-to-sequence model.

2. Bilingual Dictionary Induction

Creating a bilingual dictionary is the first crucial step in enriching low-resource languages. Especially for the closely related ones, it has been shown that the constraint-based approach helps induce bilingual lexicons from two bilingual dictionaries via the pivot language (Nasution et al., 2016; Nasution et al., 2017a). However, implementing the constraint-based approach on a large scale to create multiple bilingual dictionaries is still challenging in determining the constraint-based approach's execution order to reduce the total cost. Plan optimization using the Markov decision process is crucial in composing the order of creation of bilingual dictionaries considering the methods and their costs (Nasution et al., 2017b; Nasution et al., 2021).

Heyman et al. (2018) have proposed a method to make bilingual lexical induction as a binary classification task in the biomedical domain for English to Dutch. They create a classifier that predicts whether a pair of words is a translation using character and word level, LSTM method. This study reveals that character-level representations successfully induce bilingual lexicons in the biomedical domain.

Zhang et al. (2016) presented a character-level sequence-to-sequence learning approach proposed in this study. RNN is the encoder-decoder technique used to generate character-level sequence representation for the task of English-to-Chinese.

3. A Neural Network Approach

We would like to extract transformation rules or patterns from the Minangkabau to Indonesia language. The first approach is using character level one hot embedding where words will be separated as characters, and each vector has the same length size adjusted by total characters. Then, sequence to sequence (seq2seq) model, which has two RNN encoders and decoders is utilized. Bi-LSTM as encoder and LSTM as decoder processes are being used in this research. The Bi-LSTM encoder processes the word in the source language (Minangkabau) character by character and produces a representation of the input words. The LSTM decoder takes the output of the encoder as an input and produces a character by character in the target language (Indonesia). Similarly to the first method, the second method employs a sequence to sequence model. The distinction is in the input words, which are tokenized using SentencePiece with byte pair encoding for input to the encoder and decoder in a sequence to sequence model. The tokenization is splitting the words into chunck of characters.

The secondary data is obtained from Nasution et al. (2019) and Koto and Koto (2020) with a total of 13,761-word translation pairs. Pre-processing is completed by deleting duplicate word pairs and constructing an array of word pairs in the form of a data type dictionary given by Python. Because in this case, there are various word pairings of Minangkabau to Indonesian that have several meanings. A dictionary is made up of a set of key-value pairs. Each key-value pair corresponds to a certain value. The model's performance is evaluated using a 5-Fold Cross-Validation.

3.1. Long Short-Term Memory (LSTM)

The Long Short-Term Memory (LSTM) is an upgraded Recurrent Neural Network (RNN) that is used to overcome the problem of vanishing and exploding gradients (Hochreiter and Schmidhuber, 1997). LSTM addresses the problem of long-term RNN reliance, in which RNNs are unable to predict input data stored in long-term memory but can make more accurate predictions based on current information. The LSTM architecture can store large amounts of data for lengthy periods of time. They are applied to time-series data processing, forecasting, and categorization. Memory cells and gate units are the key components of the LSTM architecture. Forget gate, input gate, and output gate are the three types of gates in an LSTM. Figure 1 illustrates the structure of the LSTM model.

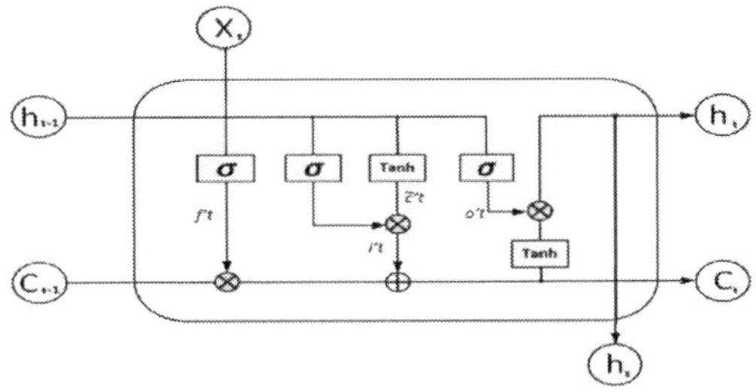

Figure 1: Unit structure of the LSTM

Cell memory tracks the dependencies between components in the input sequence. New values that enter the cell state are handled by the input gate. The LSTM unit utilizes a forget gate to select the value that remains in the cell state. The value in the cell state that remains will be sent to the output gate, where the LSTM activation function, also known as the logistic sigmoid function, will be used to start the calculation. The tanh and sigma symbols represent the types of activation functions employed in the neural network's training layers. Allowing information to flow through it unmodified, a sigmoid gate, which restricts how much information may pass through, is another essential feature of LSTM. The outputs of the sigmoid layer, which vary from zero to one, specify how much of each component should be permitted to pass. The equation that controls the LSTM flow is as follows:

$$f_t = \sigma(w_f \cdot [h_{t-1}, x_t] + b_f$$

$$i_t = \sigma(w_i \cdot [h_{t-1}, x_t] + b_i$$

$$C_t = \tanh(w_c \cdot [h_{t-1}, x_t] + b_c$$

$$C_t = f_t \times C_{t-1} + i_t \star C_t$$

$$o_t = \sigma(w_o \cdot [h_{t-1}, x_t] + b_o$$

$$h_t = o_t \times \tanh C_t$$

where

o_t	: at time t, output gate
i_t	: at time t, input gate
h_t	: output at time t
f_t	: forget gate, at time t
x_t	: input at time t
σ	: sigmoid function
C_t	: the state of the cell at time t
w_o, w_f, w_i, w_c	: weights that have been trained
b_c, b_i, b_f	: trained biases

3.2. Bidirectional Long Short-Term Memory (Bi-LSTM)

RNN has an advantage in the reliance between coding inputs. However, LSTM has an advantage in resolving RNN's long-term issues. Improvements are made with Bi- RNN because only one direction of previous contextual information can be used by LSTM and RNN (Schuster and Paliwal, 1997). As a result of the advantages of each technique, the LSTM form is kept in the cell memory, and Bi-RNN can process information from the previous and next contexts, resulting in Bi-LSTM (Schuster and Paliwal, 1997). Bi-LSTM can leverage contextual information and generate two separate sequences from the LSTM output vector. Each time step's output is a mixture of the two output vectors from both directions, as shown below, where ht is the forward or backward state (Yulita et al., 2017). Figure 2 depicts the combination of LSTM and Bi-RNN.

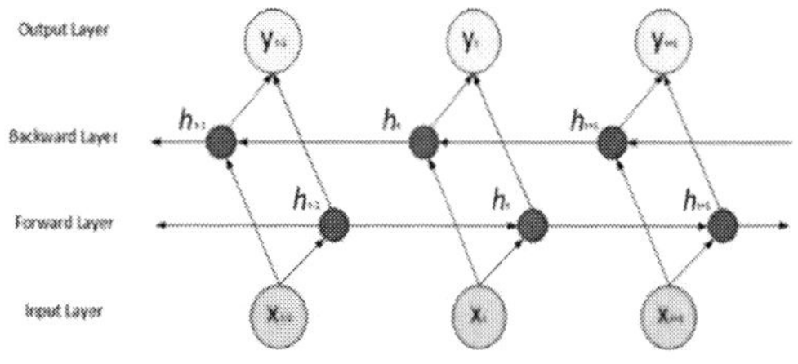

Figure 2: Bi-LSTM Architecture

3.3. Character Level Sequence to Sequence)

Figure 3 shows the Seq2Seq model considered in this study with a two-layered Bi-LSTM encoder and LSTM decoder. The encoder's functions are to character by character read the input sequence, build context, and extract a summary of the input. The decoder will provide an output sequence in which the previous character affects every character in each time step as well as the next character that emerges. The marker <eos> denotes the end of a sentence, and it will determine when we stop predicting the following character in a series (Sutskever et al., 2014).

Following the construction of the encoder and decoder network architectures in this typical end-to-end framework, a training approach may be utilized to obtain an optimal word pair translation model and to keep the character order C_t is referred to as a cell state or memory cell since the horizontal line going across the bottom of the diagram is in the source and target words, the input (Minangkabau) and output (Indonesia) sequence must be treated in time order.

3.4. SentencePiece Sequence to Sequence with Byte Pair Encoding (BPE)

The second method we presented is SentencePiece as subword tokenization. According to Kudo (2018), subword tokenization implements SentencePiece, subword-nmt, and wordpiece model features. Subword vocabulary is built by using the BPE segmentation method to train a SentencePiece tokenization model, which divides words into chunks of characters based on vocabulary size to make pattern detection easier.

BPE was added to our research methodology because Indonesian ethnic languages now utilize an alphabet script established by the Dutch despite having original scripts in the past. Dutch people appeared to assign a chunk of alphabets to phonemes of Indonesian ethnic languages when teaching the alphabets to them (Paauw, 2009). As a result, all Indonesian ethnic languages can use the same tokens.

Furthermore, with each phonetic development, languages belonging to the same language family descended from the same proto-language. As a result, we assume a phonetic-based strategy is preferable to a character-based method. The number of words to be processed into tokenization is known as vocabulary size, which in this case refers to the number of most often occurring characters, including the symbol like < /unk>, and whitespace. We employ a wide range of vocabulary sizes. The following step is the same as the first method.

Figure 4 shows that the encoder and decoder input results as a result of character splitting from BPE in this illustration of the seq2seq model. This approach differs from Figure 3 in that the encoder (Minangkabau word) and decoder (Indonesian word) inputs are different. In the BPE method, we first set the vocabulary size for each language.

BPE builds a base vocabulary consisting of all symbols found in the set of unique words, then learns merge rules to combine two symbols from the base vocabulary to create a new symbol. It continues to do until the vocabulary has grown to the required size. BPE algorithm replaces the data byte pairs that occur most frequently with a new byte until the data can no longer be compressed since no byte pair occurs most frequently. The steps in the training procedure are as follows (Sennrich et al., 2016):

1) Gather a huge amount of training data.
2) Determine the vocabulary's size.
3) At identify the end of a word, add an identifier (< /w>) to the end of each word, and then calculate the word frequency in the text.
4) Calculate the character frequency after dividing the word into characters.
5) Count the frequency of consecutive byte pairs from the character tokens for a predetermined number of rounds and combine the most frequently occurring byte pairing.
6) Repeat step 5 until performed the necessary number of merging operations or reached the specified vocabulary size.

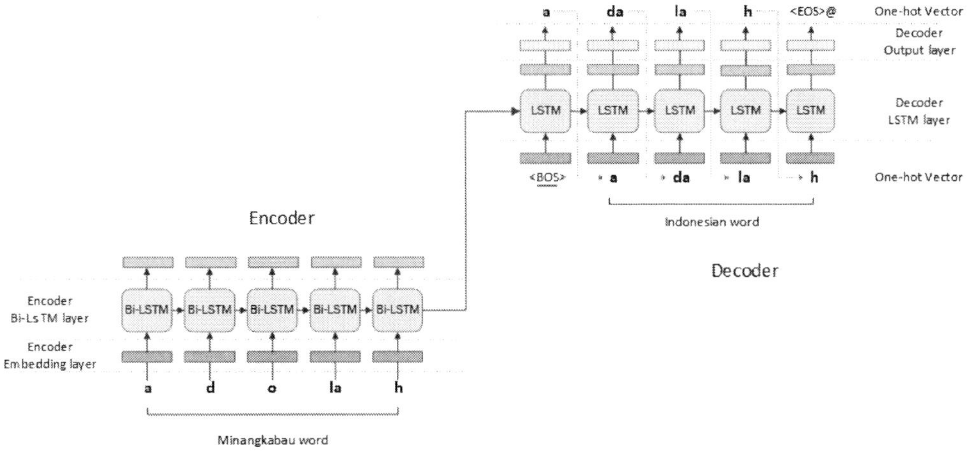

Figure 3: Character Level Sequence to sequence model

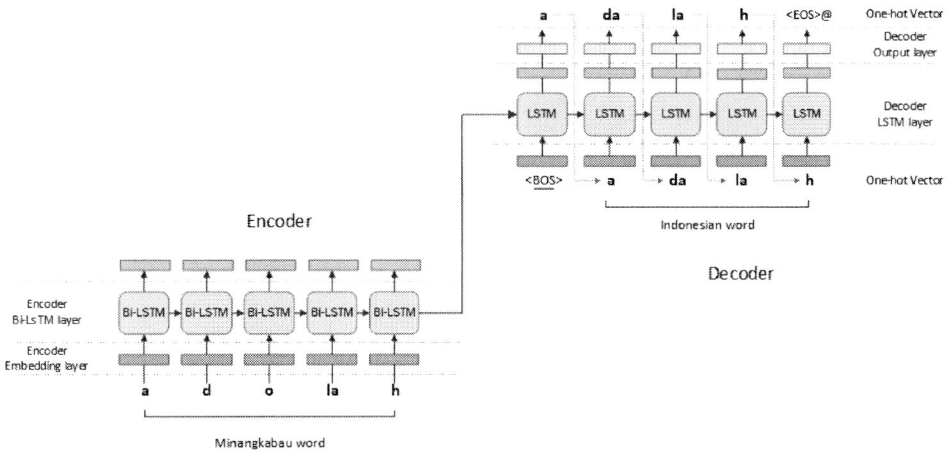

Figure 4: SentencePiece Sequence to sequence model

The input text is treated as a sequence of unicode characters by SentencePiece. Whitespace is also treated like any other symbol. SentencePiece expressly handles whitespace as a fundamental token by first escaping it with the meta symbol "___" (U+2581) (Kudo, 2018). Meanwhile the symbol of '\n' is the end of string. The results of the chunk of characters from the BPE will vary when utilizing a higher vocab size.

Except for alphabets, the vocabularies obtained from BPE 40 and 100 are summarized in the Table 1. For the Minangkabau language, there were 16 and 69 vocabularies obtained, respectively. Indonesian contains 9 and 69 vocabularies, respectively. According to the Table 1, character pieces are more obtained if use larger vocabulary sizes. The alphabet following the "_" symbol is a piece of characters at the beginning of the term in vocabulary that begins with the "_" symbol.

Example in the Minangkabau language, the difference between the character pieces sa and _ sa is that sa indicates that the character is not at the beginning of the word. Tokenization results refer to the Table 2 that shows the words in Minangkabau and Indonesia turned into a piece of characters from BPE.

The tokenization with vocab size=40 is done almost one by one like character-based tokenization except for "an", "ng", "pa" and "la" because vocab size=40 is nearly the same as the number of alphabets.

4. Experiment Design

In the first method, two models to find translation word pairs will be examined by Bidirectional Long Short-Term Memory, and also Long Short-Term Memory to improve and compare performance with previous research (Heyman et al., 2018). We utilize the parameters selected for both models in Table 3. Minangkabau and Indonesian are the language pairs, with a total dataset

Language	Vocab Size=40	Vocab Size=100
Minangkabau	an, _ma, ang, ng, _pa, _di, _ba, si, an, ng, kan, ta, si, ra, _men, nya	an, ng, ra, la, si, ta, _di, _ba, _pa, _ma, _ka, da, kan, nyo, li, ba, ang, ik, ri, ti, tu, ga, ka, bu, ja, ak **_sa**, ma, **sa**, ku, ku, ek, in, _man _ta, ah, di, su, to lu, ca, wa, du, pu, ro, mu, pa, bi, ran, en, lo, _pan, ju, tan, _pe ya, te, de, angan han, _me, gu, er _ke, do, po, gi, le, mi, _se
Indonesia	an, ng, kan, _di ta, si, ra, _men, nya	an, ng, kan, ta, ra, la, _di, da, nya, si, ke, _ber er, ti, ga, ba, li, in, ka, _se, ri, at, bu, tu, ja, ma, sa, en, _men, na di, _per, _a, ya, ku, pa, wa, is, lu _meng, _me, ca, _pen, _p, or, du, _ter, su, ru, ar, un, de, _ba, _mem, on, _ma, _ka, pu, ju, bi, _pe, al, _ko, ran, as, gu, tan, _sa, se

Table 1: Vocabularies obtained from BPE

Vocab Size= 40		Vocab Size= 100	
Minangkabau	Indonesia	Minangkabau	Indonesia
[_,n,an]	[_,y,a,ng,\'n']	[_,n,an]	[_,ya,ng,\'n']
[_pa,d,o]	[_,p,a,d,a,\'n']	[_pa,do]	[_,pa,da,\'n']
[_a,d,o,la,h]	[_a,d,a,l,a,h,\'n']	[_a,do,la,h]	[_a,da,la,h,\'n']
[_,s,a,g,i,r,o]	[_,s,e,g,e,ra,\'n']	[_,sa,gi,ro]	[_,se,ge,ra,\'n']
[_,d,a,s,an,y,o]	[_,d,a,s,a,r,nya,\'n']	[_,da,sa,nyo]	[_,da,sa,r,nya,,\'n']

Table 2: Example of tokenization BPE with different vocabulary size

of 13,761 language pairs split into 5 folds. Drop duplicated data is converted into 13,207 word translation pairs. Then, the total of training data is 10,565 and testing data is 2,642 language pairs.

5. Result and Discussion

This study uses two scenarios to find the optimal seq2seq model with the best performance. When comparing the character level and sentence piece approaches with the seq2seq model, the character level seq2seq method generates a more accurate translation of word pairs.

Character Level and SentencePiece with BPE		
Parameter	**Bi-LSTM**	**LSTM**
Embedding Size	512	512
Epoch	80	80
Batch Size	64	64

Table 3: Model's Parameter

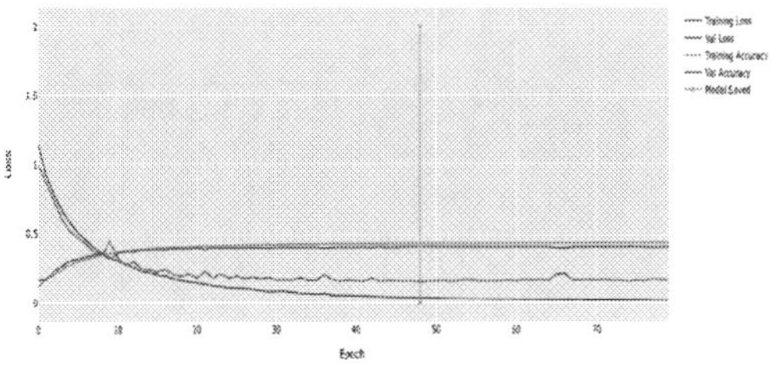

Figure 5: Epoch loss from train and validation on character level seq2seq model

Figure 5 shows the optimal process model that is saved and constructed to generate translation pairs based on the evaluation model using k-fold cross-validation. The model that will be utilized will be better if the loss value is smaller. The loss values for both train and validation remain high in the first epoch and gradually improve. The optimal validation loss value is identified in the 46th epoch using tensorflow's ModelCheckpoint feature, which only saves good models and does not save models in the following epoch if the validation loss value worsens.

Vocab Size	K-Fold Cross-Validation					
	K=1	K=2	K=3	K=4	K=5	Average
32	74.03	77.92	81.55	79.88	**86.27**	79.93
35	71.45	78.03	77.37	79.62	**85.87**	78.46
40	75,34	77,08	80,13	81,51	**83,36**	78,515
50	67.61	73.63	73.23	75.12	**79.99**	73.91
80	65.43	66.41	65.64	64.01	**72.22**	66.74
100	66.6	70.44	**70.91**	65.5	70.62	68.81
300	57.84	62.67	64.34	**67.9**	66.33	63.81

Table 4: Evaluation of SentencePiece with BPE model

The vocabulary size has a minimum and maximum value. The minimum number necessary for this experiment data is 32. The experiment was conducted seven times with various vocabulary sizes, with the largest of number vocab size is 300. As shown in Table 4, using vocabulary size=32, the highest generation of translation pairs accuracy is obtained at 86,27%. Perhaps, because the vector length is shortened, the data is likely to be less informative, making it more difficult for the

Method	K-Fold Cross-Validation					
	K=1	K=2	K=3	K=4	K=5	average
Bi-LSTM (encoder), LSTM (decoder)	78.85	82.23	82.67	86.48	**87.5**	83.55
LSTM (encoder decoder)	64.92	75.19	74.72	**77.01**	75.63	73

Table 5: Evaluation of character-level model

model to recognize. In general, the larger the vocabulary size, the higher the results. It is also probably because the data is word-to-word pairs translation instead of sentence to sentence.

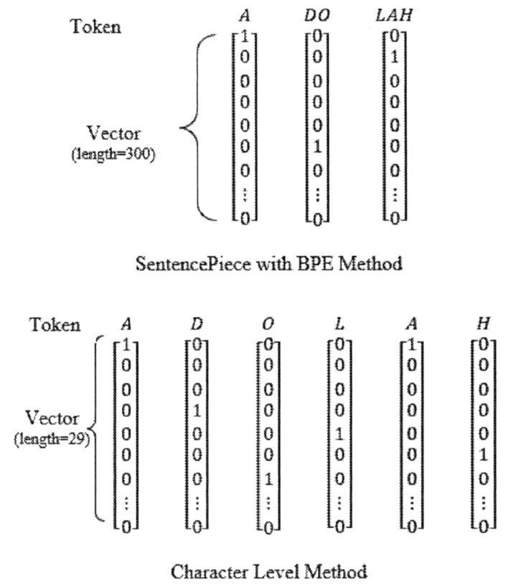

Figure 6: Comparison between SentencePiece with BPE and character level method

However, when we use a small vocab size, it's almost the same as the basic character level. As shown in Table 5, because the Bi-LSTM executes the input in two ways, backward to forward and vice versa, the outcome is better than when LSTM is used as both encoder and decoder at an average precision of 83.55%.

6. Conclusion

According to the comparison of the two approaches used, the character level seq2seq method (Bi-LSTM as encoder and LSTM as decoder) with an average precision of 83.55% outperforms the sentence piece byte pair encoding (vocab size of 32) with an average precision of 79.93%. The model can recognize patterns in both Minangkabau and Indonesian languages, indicating that the two languages are related. In the future, we will adapt the approach utilized in this research to other ethnic languages depending on the translation data pairs, add more experiments and analysis, and find the patterns from generated translation model.

7. Acknowledgements

This research was partially supported by a Grant-in-Aid for Scientific Research (B) (21H03561,2021-2024) and a Grant-in-Aid Young Scientists(A)(17H04706,2017-2020) from the Japan Society for the Promotion of Science(JSPS). This research was also partially supported by the Ministry of Education and Culture of Indonesia, Ministry of Research and Technology of Indonesia.

8. Bibliographical References

Heyman, G., Vulić, I., and Moens, M.-F. (2018). A deep learning approach to bilingual lexicon induction in the biomedical domain. *BMC Bioinformatics*, 19(1), jul.

Hochreiter, S. and Schmidhuber, J. (1997). Long short-term memory. *Neural Computation*, 9(8):1735–1780, nov.

Koto, F. and Koto, I. (2020). Towards computational linguistics in minangkabau language: Studies on sentiment analysis and machine translation. In *Proceedings of the 34th Pacific Asia Conference on Language, Information and Computation*, pages 138–148.

Kudo, T. (2018). Subword regularization: Improving neural network translation models with multiple subword candidates. In *Proceedings of the 56th Annual Meeting of the Association for Computational Linguistics (Volume 1: Long Papers)*. Association for Computational Linguistics.

Murakami, Y. (2019). Indonesia language sphere: an ecosystem for dictionary development for low-resource languages. *Journal of Physics: Conference Series*, 1192:012001, mar.

Nasution, A. H., Murakami, Y., and Ishida, T. (2016). Constraint-based bilingual lexicon induction for closely related languages. In *Proceedings of the Tenth International Conference on Language Resources and Evaluation (LREC'16)*, pages 3291–3298.

Nasution, A. H., Murakami, Y., and Ishida, T. (2017a). A generalized constraint approach to bilingual dictionary induction for low-resource language families. *ACM Transactions on Asian and Low-Resource Language Information Processing (TALLIP)*, 17(2):1–29.

Nasution, A. H., Murakami, Y., and Ishida, T. (2017b). Plan optimization for creating bilingual dictionaries of low-resource languages. In *2017 International Conference on Culture and Computing (Culture and Computing)*, pages 35–41. IEEE.

Nasution, A. H., Murakami, Y., and Ishida, T. (2019). Generating similarity cluster of indonesian languages with semi-supervised clustering. *Interna-*

tional Journal of Electrical and Computer Engineering (IJECE), 9(1):531, feb.

Nasution, A. H., Murakami, Y., and Ishida, T. (2021). Plan optimization to bilingual dictionary induction for low-resource language families. *Transactions on Asian and Low-Resource Language Information Processing*, 20(2):1–28.

Paauw, S. (2009). One land, one nation, one language: An analysis of indonesia's national language policy. *University of Rochester working papers in the language sciences*, 5(1).

Schuster, M. and Paliwal, K. (1997). Bidirectional recurrent neural networks. *IEEE Transactions on Signal Processing*, 45(11):2673–2681.

Sennrich, R., Haddow, B., and Birch, A. (2016). Neural machine translation of rare words with subword units. In *Proceedings of the 54th Annual Meeting of the Association for Computational Linguistics (Volume 1: Long Papers)*. Association for Computational Linguistics.

Sutskever, I., Vinyals, O., and Le, Q. V. (2014). Sequence to sequence learning with neural networks. *Advances in neural information processing systems*, 27.

Yulita, I. N., Fanany, M. I., and Arymuthy, A. M. (2017). Bi-directional long short-term memory using quantized data of deep belief networks for sleep stage classification. *Procedia Computer Science*, 116:530–538.

Zhang, H., Li, J., Ji, Y., and Yue, H. (2016). A character-level sequence-to-sequence method for subtitle learning. In *2016 IEEE 14th International Conference on Industrial Informatics (INDIN)*. IEEE, jul.

Proceedings of SIGUL2022 @LREC2022, pages 129–136
Marseille, 24-25 June 2022

Machine Translation from Standard German to Alemannic Dialects

Louisa Lambrecht, Felix Schneider, Alexander Waibel
Interactive Systems Lab, Karlsruhe Institute of Technology (KIT)
Karlsruhe, Germany
louisa.lambrecht@student.kit.edu, felix.schneider@partner.kit.edu,
waibel@kit.edu

Abstract

Machine translation has been researched using deep neural networks in recent years. These networks require lots of data to learn abstract representations of the input stored in continuous vectors. Dialect translation has become more important since the advent of social media. In particular, when dialect speakers and standard language speakers no longer understand each other, machine translation is of rising concern. Usually, dialect translation is a typical low-resourced language setting facing data scarcity problems. Additionally, spelling inconsistencies due to varying pronunciations and the lack of spelling rules complicate translation. This paper presents the best-performing approaches to handle these problems for Alemannic dialects. The results show that back-translation and conditioning on dialectal manifestations achieve the most remarkable enhancement over the baseline. Using back-translation, a significant gain of +4.5 over the strong transformer baseline of 37.3 BLEU points is accomplished. Differentiating between several Alemannic dialects instead of treating Alemannic as one dialect leads to substantial improvements: Multi-dialectal translation surpasses the baseline on the dialectal test sets. However, training individual models outperforms the multi-dialectal approach. There, improvements range from 7.5 to 10.6 BLEU points over the baseline depending on the dialect.

Keywords: machine translation, low-resource languages, dialect

1. Introduction

For almost a decade, neural networks have become an integral part of machine translation (MT) (Kalchbrenner and Blunsom, 2013). However, neural machine translation (NMT) struggles when only limited amounts of data are available. A typical low-resourced language setting is the translation of dialects. Though usually spoken, written dialect translation has gained more importance since the advent of social media in everyday life (Sajjad et al., 2020).

There are two main problems concerning dialect translation: firstly, data acquisition. Since dialects (even in written form) are primarily used in conversational settings, data is usually not publically available. Even less often is there actual parallel data. The second problem regards the language itself: dialects do not have uniform spelling rules. Many words have multiple spellings reflecting the varying pronunciations from region to region. That impairs the BLEU score (Papineni et al., 2002) checking for exact word matches. BLEU is the standard used metric to evaluate MT models. It is based on the amount of overlapping words and phrases (n-grams) between hypothesis and reference translation.

The Alemannic dialect is mostly spoken in Central Europe, i.e., southwestern Germany, German-speaking Switzerland, France (Alsace), Liechtenstein, and Austria (Vorarlberg). There are around 10 million people who speak Alemannic. The Alemannic language area can be divided into different regions. Figure 1 shows a map of the Alemannic language area and the Alemannic dialects spoken there.

Different language characteristics mark each region.

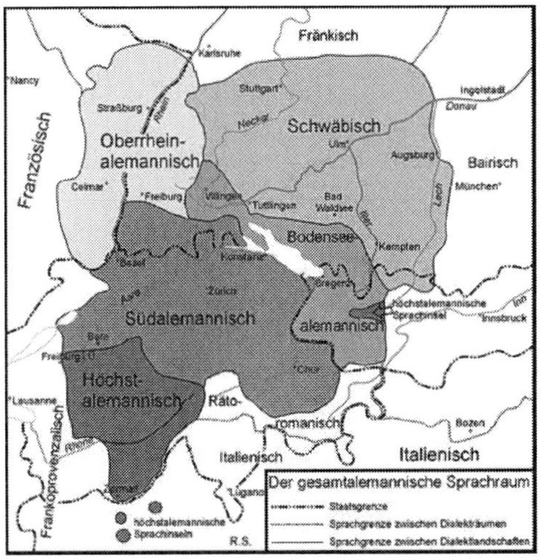

Figure 1: Alemannic language area in Central Europe (Schrambke, 2021)

Alemannic differs from Standard German in orthography, grammar and some vocabulary. For example, there are patterns in which orthography often changes (*st* → *scht* as in *Angst* → *Angscht* (fear) or prefix *ge* → *g* as in *gewöhnlich* → *gwöönlig* (usual, common)). Alemannic prefers perfect tense (more informal in Standard German) and passive voice over imperfect tense and active voice (Weinhold, 1863). Furthermore, the genitive is avoided in Alemannic and a small subset of the vocabulary is not derived from Standard German (e.g., *Grundbirne, Erdapfel, Häppere-Brägu,*

Häärpfel, Grompera, Gummel all denote the potato - Standard German: *Kartoffel*) (Christen et al., 2013; Bühler, 2019).

This paper describes the most promising approaches using back-translation and a more fine-grained differentiation of dialects to handle Alemannic dialect translation and the problem of inconsistent orthography. Section 2 gives a short overview over related work concerning low-resourced MT, dialect translation in general and Alemannic (mostly Swiss German) dialect translation. In Section 3, the corpora, a dialect classifier, and the experiments are described. Section 5 presents the evaluation results as well as some examples. A more fine-grained differentiation between Alemannic dialects using the dialect classifier proved highly efficient in combination with back-translation. The dialects Margravian, Basel German, and Swabian were examined in more detail. The first two achieved their best results in separate models while the lowest-resourced dialect, Swabian, profited from a multilingual setting. Due to the limited size of the Swabian test set, this effect should not be overestimated, though.

2. Related Work

Methods for improving (low-resourced) NMT in general are byte pair encoding (BPE) (Sennrich et al., 2016b; Gage, 1994), transfer learning (Zoph et al., 2016), back-translation (Sennrich et al., 2016a), and multilingual MT (Dong et al., 2015; Luong et al., 2015; Ha et al., 2016; Johnson et al., 2017). Translating dialects has been a topic for several languages, e.g., Arabic (Baniata et al., 2018; Tachicart and Bouzoubaa, 2014; Salloum and Habash, 2013), Chinese (Wan et al., 2020; Huang et al., 2016), and Indian languages (Chakraborty et al., 2018). Most of the dialect translation research focuses on the translation into the standard language or vice-versa.

Concerning the Alemannic dialect, there are mainly works focusing on Swiss German rather than the full range of the Alemannic dialects. Most of them translate (or normalize) from Swiss German into Standard German. Many works applied rule-based approaches or statistical machine translation (Samardzic et al., 2015; Garner et al., 2014; Scherrer and Ljubešić, 2016). Two more recent works, that employ (at least partially) NMT are (Honnet et al., 2018) and (Arabskyy et al., 2021). Honnet et al. combine character-based neural machine translation with phrase-based statistical machine translation to translate from written Swiss German to Standard German. Arabskyy et al. propose a hybrid system that combines automatic speech recognition (ASR), a lexicon, an acoustic model, and a neural language model to recognizes Swiss German speech data and translate it to Standard German text.

The only work translating into Alemannic or Swiss German is a rule-based system that generates sentences in multiple Swiss German dialects using hand-written transformation rules (Scherrer, 2012). Most of these rules are georeferenced as they utilize probability maps to determine the dialectal differences. Scherrer also describes the challenge of evaluation: due to minimal changes in the dialectal orthography the exact word matching implemented in the BLEU metric often fails. This problem has also been detected for morphologically rich languages like Hindi, Finnish, and German (Chauhan et al., 2021; Niehues et al., 2016). Therefore, Scherrer utilizes the longest common subsequence ratio (LCSR) (Melamed, 1995) that calculates the proportion of identical letters between candidate and reference translations. However the score comparing hypothesis to reference was hardly different from the one comparing hypothesis to source text (83.30% vs. 82.77%).

3. Methodology

This section first describes the existing parallel corpus and the collection of a monolingual corpus from the Alemannic Wikipedia[1]. Secondly, the training of a dialect classifier is presented using additional dialect information extracted from the Wikipedia dump. This classifier was used to split the corpora into smaller dialectal corpora. Then, general preprocessing steps applied to both corpora are listed. In the end, the baseline used for comparison is described.

3.1. Data

The Alemannic Wikipedia is, like any language Wikipedia, an encyclopedia that relies on a community of volunteers who collaborate to write and maintain articles in Alemannic. Some of the Alemannic articles are direct translations of the Standard German correspondence. In 2019 prior to this work, Ann-Kathrin Habig sentence-aligned these articles manually with their Standard German equivalent. Thus, the parallel corpus of 16 438 sentences emerged.

Additional monolingual data was gathered in this work. As of June 15, 2021, the Alemannic Wikipedia consisted of 25 032 articles (and 8 564 forwarding articles coming along). The monolingual corpus was created from the entire Alemannic Wikipedia dump. Forwarding articles and short articles containing less than 50 words were filtered from the Wikipedia dump. The sentences present in the parallel and this monolingual data were deleted from the monolingual corpus to keep both corpora independent. Due to changes between 2019 and 2021 in the Alemannic Wikipedia, 10% of the parallel sentences could not be identified in the monolingual corpus. This was considered a reasonable amount to keep as the sentences had to have considerably changed that they were not recognized anymore. The monolingual corpus held 522 018 sentences by then.

[1] https://als.wikipedia.org/

dialect	#articles	parallel	mono
Markgräflerisch (mg)	852	8 253	128 825
Basel German (bd)	1 002	5 613	88 169
Swabian (sw)	873	128	23 683
High Alemannic (ha)	499	1 722	104 205
Low Alemannic (na)	145	243	6 952
Highest Alemannic (hoe)	56	43	5 615
Alsatian (els)	1 896	107	29 358
others* (so)	139	32	3 754
not classified	n/a	297	131 457
sum	5 462	16 438	522 018

Table 1: Number of tagged articles in the Alemannic Wikipedia and sentences per dialect in the two corpora. *: others consists of "Liechtensteinerisch" and "Vorarlbergisch"

l* \ p*	mg	bd	sw	ha	na	hoe	els	so	sum
mg	370	1	0	3	0	2	1	0	377
bd	1	382	0	1	0	0	0	0	384
sw	2	0	454	0	0	0	1	1	458
ha	2	10	0	333	0	1	0	0	346
na	10	0	2	2	63	1	1	0	79
hoe	0	0	0	3	0	22	0	1	26
els	1	0	0	1	0	0	506	0	508
so	0	0	0	0	0	0	1	49	50
sum	386	393	456	343	63	26	510	51	2228

Table 2: Confusion matrix of the dialect classifier. *: l=label, p=prediction

3.2. Dialect Classifier

Authors submitting an article to the Alemannic Wikipedia have the option of tagging the article with their local dialect. 5 462 articles in the Wikipedia dump included dialect tags. 29 such dialect tags were extracted from the data. Some tags were present in only one or two articles, e.g., "Nidwaldnerdeutsch", "Issimedeutsch", others have several hundred associated articles, e.g., Swabian, Basel German, Alsatian. A rough linguistic analysis of the data based on frequently occurring words like *Einwohner* (inhabitant), *größte* (biggest, largest, greatest), *können* (can) and *haben* (have) conveyed similarities between the dialects. The dialect tags were grouped according to this linguistic analysis and the systematics of Alemannic dialects. The goal was to identify a rather rough clustering, i.e., few classes of dialects, but keeping the extent of inconsistencies within a dialect class minor. Furthermore, the classes should be balanced to prevent a bias to a certain dialect. Table 1 shows the identified classes (column 1), and the number of corresponding tagged articles (column 2).

Since most of the monolingual data did not have any dialect information, we trained a classifier with the extracted tagged data to identify the dialects of the remaining 19 570 articles in the monolingual corpus. The tagged articles were sliced into paragraphs of six sentences or at most 250 tokens to generate more data. These were added the corresponding label. This yielded 22 277 data points. The classifier was trained by fine-tuning the pre-trained RoBERTa (Liu et al., 2019) base model. Fine-tuning RoBERTa for a classification task was done according to the suggested design and hyperparameter choices[2] by Fairseq (Ott et al., 2019). After ten epochs of training, the classifier reached an accuracy of 97.80%. Table 2 shows the confusion matrix for the independent test set.

[2] `https://github.com/pytorch/fairseq/blob/main/examples/roberta/README.custom_classification.md`

The untagged data was classified by slicing the articles into paragraphs as well. These were classified, and only if there was a majority on the labels of the paragraphs, the article received this label. The other articles remained unclassified and were removed from the monolingual corpus. Table 1 also shows the statistics for the corpora after classification (column 3 and 4). In the end, the monolingual corpus held 390 561 classified sentences. The distribution of dialects in the corpora and of the original Wikipedia dialect tags differs greatly as Figure 2 illustrates.

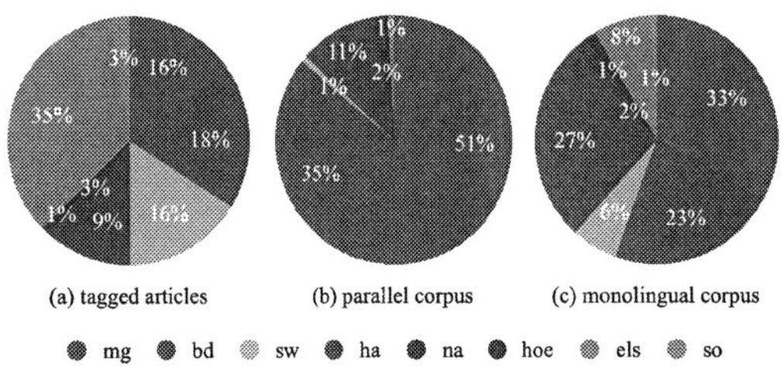

Figure 2: Distribution of dialects in (a) tagged articls, (b) the parallel corpus, and (c) the monolingual corpus

3.3. Preprocessing

Both corpora were split in training, validation and test data. Due to the limited size of the corpora only 10% was used as test data. The remaining 90% were also split 90:10 between training and validation data. All sets represent the dialectal classes in size according to their distribution over the entire corpus. That leads to small test sets (< 25 sentences) in the dialects that are underrepresented in the parallel corpus, i.e., Swabian, Low Alemannic, Highest Alemannic, and Alsatian

As preprocessing, the data was normalized (accent removal), tokenized (sacremoses), and byte pair encoding was applied (subword-nmt). The byte pair encoding was learned on the German and Alemannic parallel training sets limited to 8 000 BPE codes producing a joint dictionary of 8 340 subwords. These codes were applied to the train/validation/test sets and used in the baseline and the further experiments.

3.4. Baseline

As a baseline, a transformer model (Vaswani et al., 2017) was trained on the parallel corpus. Embedding dimensions for the baseline and in the other experiments were chosen as proposed by the authors. Merely the number of layers and attention heads was reduced to 4 and 2/4 in some experiments. All trained models were set higher dropout rates as suggested by Araabi and Monz (2020).

4. Experiments

This section presents three experiments to overcome the challenges of data scarcity and inconsistent orthography in the Alemannic dialects. The first experiment adds the monolingual corpus by using back-translation. Both other experiments are based on the classified split corpora training separate models for three chosen dialects first and secondly combining several dialects in a multilingual model.

4.1. Back-translation

The model that was used to translate the Alemannic monolingual corpus into Standard German was trained on the parallel training data and combined with a Standard German language model (LM). This LM was trained on the German Wikipedia and weighted at 0.52. Together the models reached a BLEU score of 55.3 producing acceptable translations.

The parallel corpus's test set is used to assess the model's performance despite the size discrepancy (351.5k training vs. 1 644 test sentences). That ensures correct measurement of translation quality despite the imperfect synthetic data and enables comparability with the baseline.

Since the amount of synthetic data is significantly higher than the number of sentences in the parallel corpus (16.4k vs. 390.6k sentences), the learning opportunities are increased. On the other hand, the quality of this data is certainly lower than that of the parallel corpus.

The back-translated monolingual corpus was split into 10% validation and 90% training data. A transformer model was trained on this data first. Afterwards, the model was fine-tuned on the parallel corpus. Note that the distribution of dialectal classes in the monolingual corpus differs from that of the parallel corpus.

4.2. Individual Models for the Dialects

In order to reduce the spelling possibilities based on the clustering of Alemannic dialects, three end-to-end transformer models were trained for the dialects Margravian ("Markgräflerisch"), Basel German ("Baseldeutsch"), and Swabian ("Schwäbisch"). Margravian was selected since it has the most extensive dialectal corpus. Basel German with its slightly smaller corpus is at the border between High and Low Alemannic and, therefore, interesting as it might still hold many ambiguities. Swabian was chosen due to its unique position among the dialectal variants. Its spelling differs more clearly from the other Alemannic variants. All three dialectal variants have in common that they have their own tag in the Alemannic Wikipedia, which might be an advantage considering the number of inconsistent spellings.

The end-to-end models for the three Alemannic dialects were trained with the same transformer architecture. Dropout rates were slightly increased compared to the baseline. The trainings were stopped early to prevent overfitting. Afterwards, the models were fine-tuned on their respective dialectal parallel training data.

4.3. Multi-dialectal Model

As mentioned in Section 2, many low-resourced language settings profit from integrating other (closely related) languages into a multilingual setting. In theory, shared embeddings and hidden representations soften the data sparsity problem and enable zero-shot translations (Zoph et al., 2016; Artetxe and Schwenk, 2019). Therefore, a multi-dialectal translation model was trained with five of the eight Alemannic dialects (mg, bd, sw, ha, els). The other dialects were not included due to their small corpus size and heterogeneous nature found in the linguistic analysis.

The multilingual transformer was trained to translate from German into the specified dialects. One encoder was used to encode Standard German input and one decoder each for decoding the Alemannic variants. The embeddings were not shared across the dialects. The multilingual transformer training was terminated after 103 epochs. Fine-tuning was performed for ten epochs. We also trained models with shared embeddings and shared decoders. However, these setups did not yield as good results as using one decoder for each output dialect.

5. Evaluation

The evaluation was done with sacrebleu[3] (Post, 2018) after generating translations with Fairseq's generation tool that also takes care of BPE removal and detokenization. All translations are generated with the parameters beam=5 (default) and no-repeat-ngram-size=3.

The results of the baseline and the experiments are listed in Table 3. The table shows the BLEU scores on the entire parallel test set (column *total*) and additionally the scores for the dialectal test sets. The dialectal test sets are subsets of the parallel test set and hold the test sentences of the respective dialect, i.e., column *mg* shows the BLEU scores for the Margravian test sentences that are part of the entire test set (*total*).

The baseline and the model incorporating back-translated monolingual data should be evaluated on the entire parallel test set (column *total*). In contrast, the

[3]sacrebleu configuration: `BLEU+case.mixed+numrefs.1+smooth.exp+tok.13a+version.1.4.14`

	mg	bd	sw	ha	na	hoe	els	so	total
baseline	**43.4**	**32.8**	**13.0**	<u>28.3</u>	25.1	5.0	27.1	3.8	**37.3**
with back-translation	48.6	38.0	12.9	26.5	23.5	4.6	<u>45.8</u>	5.4	**<u>41.8</u>**
separate dialect (mg)	**<u>50.9</u>**	18.8	10.7	20.9	<u>25.4</u>	4.6	29.2	3.1	35.5
separate dialect (bd)	19.9	**<u>43.0</u>**	13.2	25.2	16.2	4.8	22.1	6.0	29.3
separate dialect (sw)	12.7	11.0	**23.6**	12.1	10.1	6.1	17.0	<u>8.9</u>	12.1
multilingual (mg)	**44.8**	16.7	11.4	20.0	22.7	6.3	29.9	3.2	31.5
multilingual (bd)	18.1	**39.3**	10.4	22.4	13.2	<u>6.6</u>	19.1	6.0	26.6
multilingual (sw)	9.1	8.8	**<u>31.3</u>**	9.5	9.0	4.4	13.9	3.7	9.3

Table 3: BLEU scores of the different experiments: relevant test sets for comparison in bold, best results underlined.

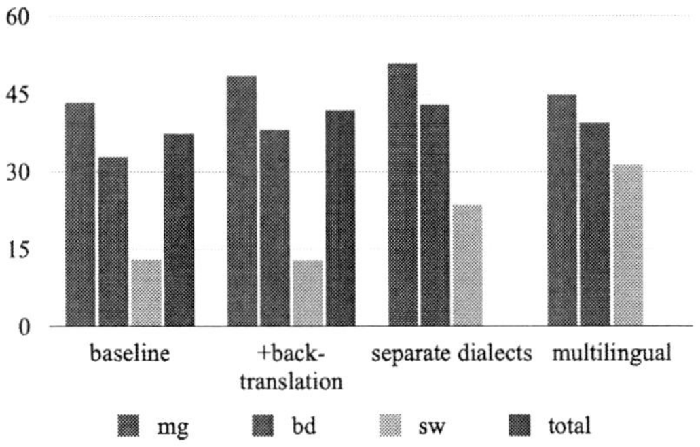

Figure 3: BLEU scores of the different experiments in total and on the relevant dialectal test sets

dialectal models and the multilingual model should not be evaluated on the whole test set as they are designed for a specific dialect. Therefore, the results of the corresponding relevant test sets are highlighted in bold font in Table 3. The scores on the other dialectal subsets were included for comparison. In addition, that might disclose some correlations among the dialects.

The baseline trained only on the parallel data achieves a BLEU score of 37.3 on the independent test set. Naturally, the dialectal variants with higher data proportions (mg, bd) perform better than the others.

5.1. Results

The model incorporating back-translated monolingual data reaches a BLEU score of 41.8 after fine-tuning. It shows an increase of performance in comparison to the baseline in the dominant dialects but decreases in most of the other dialects. Alsatian is a strong outlier. However, a large number of the Alsatian articles seem to focus on municipalities in Alsace. These articles are so similar to each other that they could be generated automatically. This would certainly create a strong bias within the Alsatian dialect.

Differentiating more fine-grained between Alemannic dialects showed improvements in both respective experiments in all three examined dialects. In the dialects Margravian and Basel German, the separate dialect models dominated. According to the corpus size, the model for Margravian achieved its best result after 300 epochs of training, the Basel German model trained 236 epochs, and the Swabian 162 epochs. For Margravian the BLEU score is improved by 7.5 points to 50.9 while the Basel German model surpasses the baseline by 10.2 BLEU points on the respective dialectal test set. The multilingual model also improves upon the baseline. The best model was reached after five epochs of fine-tuning. Its results show that mainly the lowest-resourced language, Swabian, benefits from the multilingual setting. Translating into Swabian the multilingual model surpasses the baseline by 18.3 BLEU points. Figure 3 summarizes the results of the experiments for the considered dialects.

5.2. Example

Table 4 lists the hypotheses of the different experiments for a sentence in Margravian. As the baseline's BLEU scores are very high from the beginning, translation quality is high in all hypotheses and differences between the experiments are minor. The hypotheses specific to Margravian agree in orthography for a great part. The baseline and the model using back-translated data are influenced by other dialectal orthography and their hypotheses show more differences. The translations of Standard German *Dokument* (*Dokumänt*; document) and *Jahr* (*Johr*; year) show how spelling is altered in Alemannic to match pronunciation. *aus* (out) is an example of one pronunciation having multiple spellings (*us, uss*) in the same Alemannic dialect (compare target and Margravian hypotheses) while *älteste* (oldest) has multiple spellings and pronunciations, e.g., *ältst* (in the target) and *eltscht* (in the dialectal hypotheses). Finally, there are some changes in the choice of words in Alemannic, e.g. *genannt* (*gnännt, gnennt*; call) instead of *erwähnt* (*erwäänt*; mention), *kommt* (*chunnt*; come) instead of *stammt* (date back). These lexical differences and paraphrasing proved most difficult for all models as most of the data contains only simpler reorderings due to changes in tense and case.

In contrast, Table 5 shows the hypotheses for the same sentence in the different dialects. The Margravian and Basel German hypotheses were produced with the individual dialectal models while the Swabian hypothesis was produced with the multilingual model. This table demonstrates the orthographic differences between the

Alemannic dialects. For example, *älteste* (oldest) had multiple spellings and pronunciations in Margravian alone. However, the baseline and the model with the back-translated monolingual corpus were trained with the full range of Alemannic and produce other valid translations and pronunciations of *älteste*. The dialects Basel German and Swabian add even more, e.g., the characteristic Swiss German *i* in the end of adjectives is preferred by the model with the back-translated monolingual corpus (Table 4) and the Swabian model (Table 5) produces "softer" pronunciations by choosing *d* over *t* as in *eldeschde* (and also *bekannde* (known)).

6. Discussion

Assessing translation quality using BLEU scores has become the predominant method. Compared to human evaluation it is less costly and less subjective. However, BLEU as an evaluation method has its drawbacks when it comes to morphologically rich languages. The high range of spelling possibilities can be viewed in the same way: there are several correct ways of expressing (or spelling) certain content. Usually, no more than one reference translation is available. That can diminish the BLEU scores for such languages. The examples shown in Table 4 demonstrate that translation quality is high concerning grammar, legibility, and correctness. However, concerning the separate dialect model's hypothesis and the target, five unigrams are incorrect - three of them differ in just one letter (*wu/wo, as/als, us/uss*). That can have tremendous effects on the BLEU score, and human evaluation might be an adequate alternative in this setting.

Nevertheless, some of the reported BLEU scores are relatively high. Note that the Alemannic dialects and Standard German are highly related. In contrast to spoken Alemannic, most written Alemannic texts (except Highest Alemannic) are intelligible for Standard German speakers without dialect background. BLEU scores reported in related work translating from Alemannic/Swiss German into Standard German are at a similar level. They range from 36 (Honnet et al., 2018) to 46 (Arabskyy et al., 2021), and 75 BLEU points (Garner et al., 2014).

The gain of 4.5 BLEU points by using back-translation is in the expected range. Splitting the data into smaller dialectal groups lead to respectable improvements. It was surprising that the multilingual model could not reach up to the individual dialect models (concerning Margravian and Basel German). Perhaps the multilingual model could benefit from other Germanic languages with larger corpora or transfer learning on the encoder side.

The BLEU scores found for the other dialects (apart from Margravian, Basel German, and Swabian) show some interesting correlations: All models perform considerably worse on the Highest Alemannic dialects and the data grouped in "others" than the other dialectal test sets. This supports the subjective impression that these dialects differ greatly from the other Alemannic data and endorses the decision of excluding this data from the multilingual setting. Similarly, the BLEU scores emphasize the differences to Swabian. Swabian does not only receive low scores in the baseline/with back-translation models but the Swabian models also perform very poor on the other dialectal test sets. However, the Swabian data was limited. That might inhibit Swabian models from performing well in general. Thus, the tremendous improvement by the multilingual model on the Swabian data (+18.3 BLEU points) also has to be interpreted with care as the Swabian test set contains less than 20 sentences.

Model/Language	Example
English	The oldest known document that mentions Aichen as a village dates back to 1275.
Standard German	Das älteste bekannte Dokument, das Aichen als Ort erwähnt, stammt aus dem Jahre 1275.
Alemannic Target (mg)	S ältst bekannt Dokumänt, wo Aiche als Ort gnännt wird, chunnt uss em Johr 1275.
Baseline	S älteschte Dokumänt, wo Aiche als Ort erwäänt, stammt us em Johr 1275.
with back-translation	S ältischti bekannti Dokument, wo Aiche als Ort erwähnt, stammt us em Johr 1275.
separate dialect (mg)	S eltscht bekannt Dokumänt, wu Aiche as Ort gnännt, stammt us em Johr 1275.
multilingual (mg)	S eltscht bekannt Dokumänt, s Aiche as Ort gnännt, stammt us em Johr 1275.

Table 4: Example of a Margravian (mg) sentence translated by the models of the different experiments

Model/Language	Example
English	The oldest known document that mentions Aichen as a village dates back to 1275.
Standard German	Das älteste bekannte Dokument, das Aichen als Ort erwähnt, stammt aus dem Jahre 1275.
Alemannic Target (mg)	S ältst bekannt Dokumänt, wo Aiche als Ort gnännt wird, chunnt uss em Johr 1275.
Margravian	S eltscht bekannt Dokumänt, wu Aiche as Ort gnännt, stammt us em Johr 1275.
Basel German	S eltiste bekannte Dokumänt, wo Aiche as Ort erwäänt, stammt us em Joor 1275.
Swabian	S eldeschde bekannde Dokument, wo Aiche als Ort zom erschte Mol gnennt, stammt us-em Johr 1275.

Table 5: Example of a Margravian (mg) sentence translated into different dialects

7. Conclusion

This work presents several experiments to improve machine translation of low-resourced languages on the example of the Alemannic dialects. Dialect translation has two primary problems: few parallel resources are available, and the colloquial nature of dialects often leads to inconsistent orthography. Using back-translation the parallel corpus of approximately 16k sentences could be expanded with a monolingual corpus holding 390k sentences. Tackling the problem of spelling inconsistencies does not have a definite course of action. Splitting the data into dialect groups and thus splitting the problem over several "languages" was rewarding. There are still spelling inconsistencies within these dialect groups, but the number certainly decreases. Individual models were trained for three Alemannic dialects on the corresponding subsets of the Alemannic monolingual data. Fine-tuning was performed with the analogous subset of the parallel corpus. BLEU scores on the dialectal test sets outperform the baseline by 7-10 BLEU points. A multi-dialectal model was trained on five Alemannic dialects. Its BLEU scores outperform the baseline on the dialectal test sets, but mainly the lowest-resourced dialect profited from the multilingual setting. The models trained for the separate Alemannic dialects achieved the best results. They produce high quality translations that account for the diversity of the Alemannic dialect by differentiating between Alemannic variants. Thus, the results propose a solid approach to deal with the problems of inconsistent orthography in dialects.

8. Acknowledgments

The compilation of the parallel corpus was carried out by research assistant Ann-Kathrin Habig in 2019.

9. References

Araabi, A. and Monz, C. (2020). Optimizing transformer for low-resource neural machine translation. In *Proceedings of the 28th International Conference on Computational Linguistics*, pages 3429–3435, Barcelona, Spain (Online). International Committee on Computational Linguistics.

Arabskyy, Y., Agarwal, A., Dey, S., and Koller, O. (2021). Dialectal speech recognition and translation of swiss german speech to standard german text: Microsoft's submission to swisstext 2021. Arxiv.

Artetxe, M. and Schwenk, H. (2019). Massively Multilingual Sentence Embeddings for Zero-Shot Cross-Lingual Transfer and Beyond. *Transactions of the Association for Computational Linguistics*, 7:597–610.

Baniata, L. H., Park, S., and Park, S.-B. (2018). A neural machine translation model for arabic dialects that utilizes multitask learning (mtl). *Computational intelligence and neuroscience*, 2018.

Bühler, R. (2019). Sprachalltag ii: Sprachatlas–digitalisierung–nachhaltigkeit und das arno-ruoff-archiv am ludwig-uhland-institut für empirische kulturwissenschaft der universität tübingen. *Linguistik online*, 98(5):411–423.

Chakraborty, S., Sinha, A., and Nath, S. (2018). A bengali-sylheti rule-based dialect translation system: Proposal and preliminary system. In *Proceedings of the International Conference on Computing and Communication Systems*, pages 451–460. Springer.

Chauhan, S., Daniel, P., Mishra, A., and Kumar, A. (2021). Adableu: A modified bleu score for morphologically rich languages. *IETE Journal of Research*, 0(0):1–12.

Christen, H., Glaser, E., and Friedli, M. (2013). *Kleiner Sprachatlas der deutschen Schweiz*. Huber.

Dong, D., Wu, H., He, W., Yu, D., and Wang, H. (2015). Multi-task learning for multiple language translation. In *Proceedings of the 53rd Annual Meeting of the Association for Computational Linguistics and the 7th International Joint Conference on Natural Language Processing (Volume 1: Long Papers)*, pages 1723–1732.

Gage, P. (1994). A new algorithm for data compression. *C Users Journal*, 12(2):23–38.

Garner, P. N., Imseng, D., and Meyer, T. (2014). Automatic speech recognition and translation of a Swiss German dialect: Walliserdeutsch. In *Proc. Interspeech 2014*, pages 2118–2122.

Ha, T.-L., Niehues, J., and Waibel, A. (2016). Toward multilingual neural machine translation with universal encoder and decoder. In *Proceedings of the 13th International Conference on Spoken Language Translation*, Seattle, Washington D.C. International Workshop on Spoken Language Translation.

Honnet, P.-E., Popescu-Belis, A., Musat, C., and Baeriswyl, M. (2018). Machine translation of low-resource spoken dialects: Strategies for normalizing Swiss German. In *Proceedings of the Eleventh International Conference on Language Resources and Evaluation (LREC 2018)*, Miyazaki, Japan, May. European Language Resources Association (ELRA).

Huang, G., Gorin, A., Gauvain, J.-L., and Lamel, L. (2016). Machine translation based data augmentation for cantonese keyword spotting. In *2016 IEEE International Conference on Acoustics, Speech and Signal Processing (ICASSP)*, pages 6020–6024. IEEE.

Johnson, M., Schuster, M., Le, Q. V., Krikun, M., Wu, Y., Chen, Z., Thorat, N., Viégas, F., Wattenberg, M., Corrado, G., et al. (2017). Google's multilingual neural machine translation system: Enabling zero-shot translation. *Transactions of the Association for Computational Linguistics*, 5:339–351.

Kalchbrenner, N. and Blunsom, P. (2013). Recurrent continuous translation models. In *Proceedings of the 2013 conference on empirical methods in natural language processing*, pages 1700–1709.

Liu, Y., Ott, M., Goyal, N., Du, J., Joshi, M., Chen, D., Levy, O., Lewis, M., Zettlemoyer, L., and Stoyanov, V. (2019). Roberta: A robustly optimized bert pretraining approach. *arXiv preprint arXiv:1907.11692*.

Luong, M.-T., Le, Q., Sutskever, I., Vinyals, O., and Kaiser, L. (2015). Multi-task sequence to sequence learning. *Proceedings of ICLR, San Juan, Puerto Rico*, 11.

Melamed, I. D. (1995). Automatic evaluation and uniform filter cascades for inducing n-best translation lexicons. *arXiv preprint cmp-lg/9505044*.

Niehues, J., Peter, J.-T., Guillou, L., Huck, M., Sennrich, R., Bojar, O., Kocmi, T., Burlot, F., Skadina, I., and Deksne, D. (2016). Intermediate report: Morphologically rich languages.

Ott, M., Edunov, S., Baevski, A., Fan, A., Gross, S., Ng, N., Grangier, D., and Auli, M. (2019). fairseq: A fast, extensible toolkit for sequence modeling. In *Proceedings of NAACL-HLT 2019: Demonstrations*.

Papineni, K., Roukos, S., Ward, T., and Zhu, W.-J. (2002). Bleu: a method for automatic evaluation of machine translation. In *Proceedings of the 40th annual meeting of the Association for Computational Linguistics*, pages 311–318.

Post, M. (2018). A call for clarity in reporting BLEU scores. In *Proceedings of the Third Conference on Machine Translation: Research Papers*, pages 186–191, Belgium, Brussels. Association for Computational Linguistics.

Sajjad, H., Abdelali, A., Durrani, N., and Dalvi, F. (2020). Arabench: Benchmarking dialectal arabic-english machine translation. In *Proceedings of the 28th International Conference on Computational Linguistics*, pages 5094–5107.

Salloum, W. and Habash, N. (2013). Dialectal arabic to english machine translation: Pivoting through modern standard arabic. In *Proceedings of the 2013 Conference of the North American Chapter of the Association for Computational Linguistics: Human Language Technologies*, pages 348–358.

Samardzic, T., Scherrer, Y., and Glaser, E. (2015). Normalising orthographic and dialectal variants for the automatic processing of swiss german. In *Proceedings of the 7th Language and Technology Conference*.

Scherrer, Y. and Ljubešić, N. (2016). Automatic normalisation of the swiss german archimob corpus using character-level machine translation. In *Proceedings of the 13th Conference on Natural Language Processing (KONVENS)*.

Scherrer, Y. (2012). *Generating Swiss German sentences from Standard German: a multi-dialectal approach*. Ph.D. thesis, University of Geneva.

Schrambke, R. (2021). Die gliederung des alemannischen sprachraums. [Online; accessed August 23, 2021].

Sennrich, R., Haddow, B., and Birch, A. (2016a). Improving neural machine translation models with monolingual data. In *Proceedings of the 54th Annual Meeting of the Association for Computational Linguistics (Volume 1: Long Papers)*, pages 86–96, Berlin, Germany. Association for Computational Linguistics.

Sennrich, R., Haddow, B., and Birch, A. (2016b). Neural machine translation of rare words with subword units. In *Proceedings of the 54th Annual Meeting of the Association for Computational Linguistics (Volume 1: Long Papers)*, pages 1715–1725, Berlin, Germany. Association for Computational Linguistics.

Tachicart, R. and Bouzoubaa, K. (2014). A hybrid approach to translate moroccan arabic dialect. In *2014 9th International Conference on Intelligent Systems: Theories and Applications (SITA-14)*, pages 1–5. IEEE.

Vaswani, A., Shazeer, N., Parmar, N., Uszkoreit, J., Jones, L., Gomez, A. N., Kaiser, L. u., and Polosukhin, I. (2017). Attention is all you need. In I. Guyon, et al., editors, *Advances in Neural Information Processing Systems*, volume 30. Curran Associates, Inc.

Wan, Y., Yang, B., Wong, D. F., Chao, L. S., Du, H., and Ao, B. C. (2020). Unsupervised neural dialect translation with commonality and diversity modeling. In *Proceedings of the AAAI Conference on Artificial Intelligence*, volume 34, pages 9130–9137.

Weinhold, K. (1863). *Alemannische Grammatik*. Ferd. Dümmler's Verlagsbuchhandlung Harrwitz und Gossmann.

Zoph, B., Yuret, D., May, J., and Knight, K. (2016). Transfer learning for low-resource neural machine translation. In *Proceedings of the 2016 Conference on Empirical Methods in Natural Language Processing*, pages 1568–1575, Austin, Texas. Association for Computational Linguistics.

Proceedings of SIGUL2022 @LREC2022, pages 137–145
Marseille, 24-25 June 2022

Question Answering Classification for Amharic Social Media Community Based Questions

Tadesse Destaw Belay[1], **Seid Muhie Yimam**[2],
Abinew Ali Ayele[2, 3], **Chris Biemann**[2]
Wollo University, Dessie, Ethiopia[1],
Universität Hamburg, Hamburg, Germany[2],
Bahir Dar University, Bahir Dar, Ethiopia[3]
tadesseit@gmail.com, {seid.muhie.yimam, abinew.ali.ayele, christian.biemann}@uni-hamburg.de

Abstract

In this work, we build a Question Answering (QA) classification dataset from a social media platform, namely the Telegram public channel called @AskAnythingEthiopia. The channel has more than 78k subscribers and has exists since May 31, 2019. The platform allows asking questions that belong to various domains, like politics, economics, health, education, and so on. Since the questions are posed in a mixed-code, we apply different strategies to pre-process the dataset. Questions are posted in Amharic, English, or Amharic in Latin script. As part of the pre-processing tools, we build a Latin-to-Ethiopic-Script transliteration tool. We collect 8k Amharic and 24K Amharic but written in Latin script questions and develop deep learning-based questions answering classifiers that attain an F-score of 57.79 in 20 different question categories. The datasets and pre-processing scripts are open-sourced to facilitate further research on the Amharic community-based question answering.

Keywords: question answering, Latin transliteration, question classification, Amharic question answering, social media questions

1. Introduction

Question classification (QC) is growing in popularity as it has an important role in Question Answering (QA) systems, and Information Retrieval (IR) and it can be used in a wide range of other domains (Sangodiah et al., 2015). The main aim of question classification is to accurately assign labels to questions based on the expected answer type (Metzler and Croft, 2005). It plays an important role in finding or constructing accurate answers and therefore helps to improve the quality of automated question answering systems (Van-Tu and Anh-Cuong, 2016). To correctly answer a question, one needs to understand what the question asks for.

Moreover, question classification, which focuses on putting the questions into several semantic categories, can minimize constraints on the possible answers and suggest different processing strategies. For example, if the system understands the question “Who will win the Presidential election?” asks for a person name from a "politics" category, the search space of possible answers will be significantly reduced. It aims to solve answer generating issues by extracting the relevant features from the questions and by assigning them to the correct class category. More specifically, knowing the possible classes of the question before answering narrows down the number of possibilities a question answering system has to consider (May and Steinberg, 2004).

While there are some attempts in building question answering systems for Amharic (Yimam and Libsie, 2009; Taffa and Libsie, 2019; Abedissa, 2013), as far as we know, there are no publicly available datasets for question classification tasks. To address this gap, we have collected question answer datasets from a social media platform community question and answer channel. The @AskAnythingEthiopia[1] Telegram channel has been established in 2019, where users are allowed to ask questions of various categories such as science, education, religion, art, and so on. Figure 2 shows the distributions of questions per different question classes or categories. The community give answers for each question, which is governed by administrators of the channel.

The main contributions of this work are:

1. Introduce the first public question answering classification dataset for Amharic.
2. Implement a transliteration algorithm that converts questions written in Latin script to Amharic Ethiopic or Fidäl representation.
3. Build deep learning models to classify questions into pre-defined categories.
4. Investigate the quality of the different question categories that have been collected from

[1]`https://t.me/askAnythingEthiopia`

the social media platform.

5. Publicly releases the QA dataset along with the Amharic semantic models and resource repository (Yimam et al., 2021).

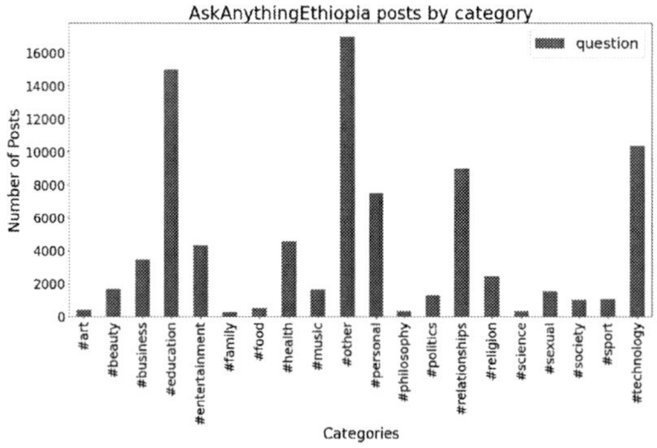

Figure 1: Distribution of questions per question categories.

In Section 2, basic information about the Amharicn language and the writing systems are discussed. In Section 3, we have presented the related works about question classification and some of the existing question answering systems for Amharic. While Section 4 and 5 discussed the data collection and pre-processing strategies, we have presented the Latin to Ethiopic/Fidäl transliteration processes in Section 6. In Section 7 and 8, deep learning question classification models and the results obtained are discussed. Finally, we have presented the main finding and future works in Section 9.

2. Amharic Language

Amharic (**አማርኛ**, amarəñña) is written from left to right in Ge'ez alphabets called Fidäl (**ፊደል**), also known as Ge'ez or Ethiopic script (Amha, 2009). Fidäl is a syllable-based writing system where the consonants and vowels co-exist within each graphic symbol. Amharic is the working language of the Federal Democratic Republic of Ethiopia and for many regional states in the country. It is the second old-most commonly spoken Semitic language after Arabic. Including the vowels, there are a total of 34 major letters each having up to seven major derivatives. Amharic uses a total of more than 300 characters.

3. Related Works

Many studies have addressed the question classification tasks, especially for high-resource languages like English. Among these, the work done by (Van-Tu and Anh-Cuong, 2016; May and Steinberg, 2004; Li and Roth, 2006; Li and Roth, 2002) proposed a method of using a feature selection algorithm to determine appropriate features corresponding to different question types. These proposed approaches are also used by the Text REtrieval Conference (TREC) shared task. The TREC dataset[2] is for question classification consisting of open-domain, fact-based questions divided into broad semantic categories. It has both a six-class called TREC-6, namely, Abbreviation, Description, Entities, Human Beings, Locations, or Numeric Values, and a fifty-class (TREC-50) version. Lei et al. (2018) proposed a novel CNN-based method for question classification in intelligent question answering using 5 different dataset types to test the performance of the proposed method. The work by Yang et al. (2018) built an attention-based LSTM to conduct Chinese questions classification. This work used Fudan University's question classification dataset, including 17,252 Chinese questions and classification results. Even though QC has been studied for various languages, it was barely studied for Amharic language and there is no benchmark dataset for question categorization. The work by Nega et al. (2016) presented Amharic question classification using machine learning (SVM) approaches. However, the dataset set used in this research consists of a very small dataset and is not publicly available, where a total of 180 questions are collected from the Agriculture domain.

Habtamu (2021) prepared an Amharic question dataset by labeling the sample questions into their respective classes and implemented an Amharic Question Classification (AQC) model using Convolutional Neural Network (CNN). The collected dataset was around 8,000 generic Amharic questions from different websites and labeled into 6 classes, similar to the question classes proposed by Li and Roth (2006). However, the dataset is still not available for further investigation. The work by Taffa and Libsie (2019) and Abedissa (2013) have developed Amharic non-factoid QA for biography, definition, and description questions. Yimam and Libsie (2009) developed an Amharic question answering system for factoid questions.

To the best of our knowledge, there are no publicly available question classification datasets that address the growing community-based question and answer platforms. We have collected the largest Amharic QC dataset to date.

4. Data Collection

One of the big challenges for low-resource languages such as Amharic is the unavailability of general-purpose datasets for various NLP tasks. For the question answering task, there is no publicly available benchmark dataset for Amharic. Some of the QA tasks, such as those by Yimam and Libsie (2009) and Nega et al. (2016) dealt

[2] http://l2r.cs.uiuc.edu/cogcomp/Data/QA/QC/

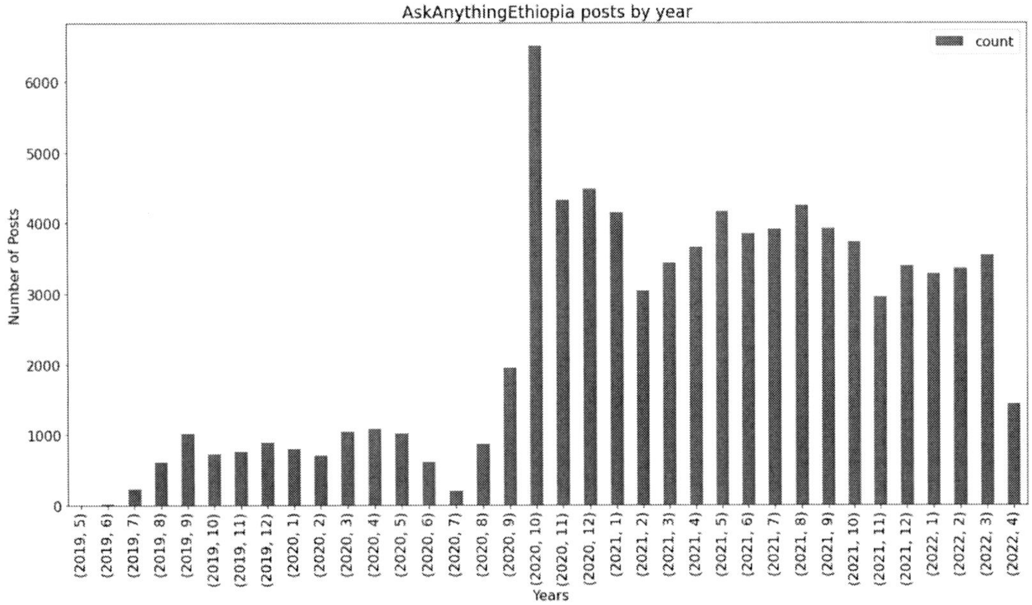

Figure 2: Distribution of questions over the last three years per each month (**year**, **month**).

with an end-to-end QA pipeline for factoid and domain-specific questions based on specific patterns. However, to build machine learning-based QA systems, manually annotated datasets are required. In this work, to build the QC datasets, we have exploited an existing social media platform community-based question and answer channel. Among several social media platforms, Telegram is one of the fastest-growing social networks platform in Ethiopia that has different features like bot services, personal chatting, and group calling/messaging. We have collected the Amharic question dataset from the public Telegram group channel called @AskAnythingEthiopia. The questions are freely available to the public who joined the group.

4.1. About @AskAnythingEthiopia

This Telegram group was created by @JvHaile and @da_king Telegram users. It was created for only questions that can not be answered with a simple Google search. Among the rules, 1) users are suggested to select the proper question category, 2) do not spread false information, 3) do not use it for announcements, and 4) don not ask questions that can be answered with a simple Google search. If users violate one of the rules, they will not be approved to ask further questions. Users that do not adhere to the rules will receive a warning, and if they continue breaking the rules, they will be banned from the channel permanently. It is the first of its kind in Ethiopia that serves only question answering in Amharic and/or English languages, which is a reward-based channel. Figure 3 shows the top 6 all-time leaders in reputation from the group.

Figure 3: Top 6 all-time reputation leaders of the bot (accessed on 18 April 2021).

Reputation is the number of points that each user has obtained weekly, monthly, and all time. It is an indicator of how helpful their answers were as well as how often the answers were seen. The more reputation they have, the more privileges they have on the bot. For example, asking an unlimited amount of questions per day depends on the reputation. In addition to this, they will also be eligible to be rewarded with 500 Ethiopian Birr at the end of each month.

4.2. Posing a Question

The question is asked to a bot under the group called @ask_anything_ethiopia_bot. At the time of writing, this bot has 287,557 subscribers. Figure 4 shows the user interface displayed by the bot to facilitate asking a question and selecting the appropriate question categories. Once the user entered the */start* command, the bot is initiated and displays the list of options including **Ask a question**. If the question type does not fall in one of the existing 20 categories, users are forced to select the category "other". Once the questions are posed to the group, they will be displayed under the @AskAnythingEthiopia channel where users respond to the questions. Using the Python Telethon[3] library, we have extracted 83,851 questions with their categories. Figure 1 shows the distribution of questions per question class or category while Figure 2 shows the number of questions over the past years. As we can see from Figure 2, the number of questions asked in the channel increases over time.

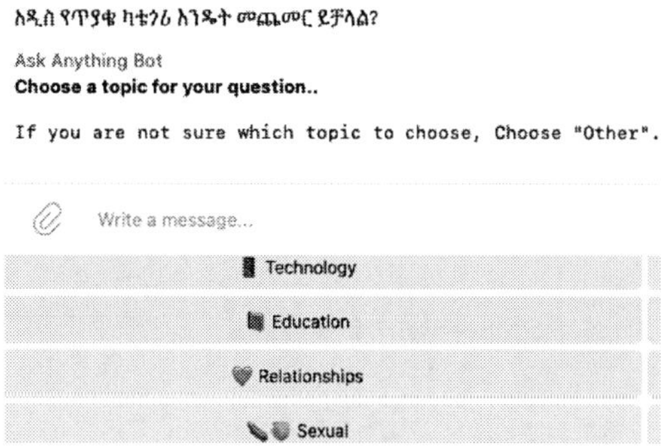

Figure 4: @ask_anything_ethiopia_bot Telegram bot user interface to ask questions.

5. Data Pre-processing

The platform allows asking questions both in English and Amharic. We have found that the questions are asked in different forms such as 1) all questions in Amharic, 2) all questions in English, 3) questions mixed in English and Amharic, or 4) Questions asked in Amharic language but written in Latin script.

The Python Compact Language Detection library (CLD2)[4] package is used to detect the script of the questions and we have found that 7,967, 51,424, and 24,446 questions are posed in Amharic, English, and Amharic with a Latin script respectively. In this study, we have considered questions written in Amharic Fidäl or Latin scripts to build the machine learning models. In the future, the questions posed in English will be used to build a multilingual question classification model. For questions written in the Latin script, we have implemented an algorithm that tries to convert the text to its nearest possible Amharic Fidäl representation, as discussed in Section 6 below.

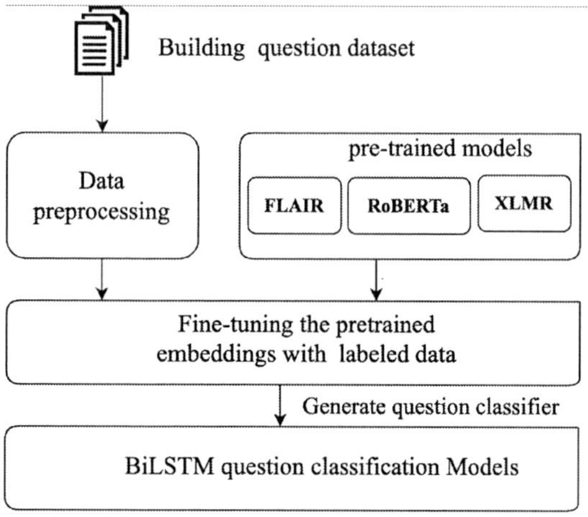

Figure 5: A general framework for the proposed Amharic question classification

6. Latin to Ethiopic Script Transliteration

Due to various reasons, users prefer to write Amharic text in Latin scripts. The following are some of the probable reasons to use the Latin script for Amharic text: 1) the mobile or computer keyboard does not support Ethiopic scripts, 2) writing in Latin script is faster than using the Ethiopic keyboard which usually requires multiple keystrokes for a single character representation, and 3) most of the emojis and special character representation are easier to type using the English keyboards. Our analysis shows users prefer to write using the Latin script as much as three-time (24,446 questions) compared to using the Ethiopic scripts (7,967 questions).

There is no word embedding or transformer-based language models for Amharic text written in Latin scripts. Hence, in this work, we have implemented the first Latin to Ethiopic transliteration algorithm and publicly release the script alongside the **amharicprocessor**[5] Amharic text segmentation, normalization, and romanization tool (Belay et al., 2021) which is one of the resources built along with the Amharic semantic models (Yimam et al., 2021)[6]. Transliteration is a process of converting ASCII represented Amharic texts back to the canonical Amharic letter representations (which

[3]https://github.com/LonamiWebs/Telethon

[4]https://pypi.org/project/pycld2/

[5]https://pypi.org/project/amseg/

[6]https://github.com/uhh-lt/amharicmodels/

Amharic Questions		RoBERTa			AmFLAIR		
Q. Categories	No. of Q.	P	R	F1	P	R	F1
Education	1118	63.71	68.70	66.11	59.26	69.57	64.00
Personal	763	27.71	28.40	28.05	24.49	14.81	18.46
Relationships	684	71.88	74.19	73.02	60.47	83.87	70.27
Technology	681	71.15	52.86	60.66	58.57	58.57	58.57
Religion	305	70.59	68.57	69.57	73.97	77.14	75.52
Health	519	54.55	67.92	60.50	50.00	62.26	55.46
Business	363	34.78	47.06	40.00	33.33	32.35	32.84
Entertainment	305	14.29	16.67	15.38	30.77	22.22	26.81
Politics	269	67.86	76.00	71.70	57.58	76.00	65.52
Music	218	47.62	66.67	55.56	43.75	46.67	45.16
Society	194	22.22	21.05	21.62	00.00	00.00	00.00
Beauty	125	40.00	23.53	29.63	100.0	11.76	21.05
Sexual	108	100.0	42.86	60.00	100.0	28.57	44.44
Philosophy	102	33.33	44.44	38.10	00.00	00.00	00.00
Sport	93	70.00	46.67	56.00	100.0	26.67	42.11
Art	56	66.67	50.00	57.14	00.00	00.00	00.00
Food	53	33.33	25.00	28.57	00.00	00.00	00.00
Family	39	14.29	33.33	20.00	00.00	00.00	00.00
Science	24	20.00	100.0	33.33	00.00	00.00	00.00
Other	1518	39.71	33.75	36.49	31.75	41.88	36.12
Av. f1 (micro)				50.82			48.93
Av. f1 (macro)				46.07			32.77

Table 1: Amharic question distributions and classification model results using AmRoBERTa and AmFLAIR embeddings.

are known as Ethiopic or Fidäl scripts). For example, the phrase "zare sint ken new?" written in classical Latin script can be transliterated to its Ethiopic representation as "**ዛሬ ስንት ቀን ነው?**" (Translation: what is the date of today?).

To transliterate Latin-based Amharic texts to their Fidäl/Ethiopic based Amharic representation, we have constructed rules, that try to reproduce the Ethiopic representation with minimal errors, as a perfect reproduction is difficult. The rule is compiled with a list containing the ASCII combinations and the corresponding Amharic letters where the largest possible chunk are first transliterated before transliterating smaller units. For example, we first look for sh (**ሽ**) before attempting to transliterate s (**ስ**).

It should be noted that the transliteration effort is different from the standard International Phonetic Alphabet (IPA) representation (Tedla, 2015), as users generally ignored the IPA pronunciation of words in different accents.

Example 1 shows an Amharic question from our dataset posed in a Latin script; the 'Original' line is the original question, and the 'Transliterated' line is the question transliterated to its Fidäl script equivalent, while the 'English' line is the translation of the given question to English. The red colored text indicated errors introduced by the transliteration algorithm. Here, the first error is introduced as the word is written in English (Hi) while the remaining errors are introduced because the Amharic characters **ቀ** and **ጠ** have similar representation in the non-IPA Latin script with **ከ** and **ተ**, which are **ke** and **te** respectively.

Example 1
Original: Hi menjafekad lemawtat ke sent amet jemro new?
Transliterated: **ሂ መንጃፈከድ ለማውታት ከ ሰንት አመት ጀምሮ ነው?**
English: Hi, what is the minimum age to obtain a driving licence?

7. Classification Models

A great deal of current research works on question classification are based on deep learning approaches with contextual embeddings rather than statistical approaches. In this experiment, we have employed three different contextual embedding approaches, where two of them are from the Amharic Semantic resource repository (Yimam et al., 2021) while the third one is from a publicly available embedding model from HuggingFace[7].

1. XLMR: Unsupervised Cross-lingual Representation Learning at Scale (XLMR) is a generic cross-lingual sentence encoder that is trained on 2.5 TB of newly-created clean CommonCrawl data in 100 languages including

[7]https://huggingface.co/xlm-roberta-base

Amharic (Conneau et al., 2019). Among this, 68m tokes are for Amharic.

2. AmRoBERTa: Is a RoBERTa model (Liu et al., 2019), that is trained for Amharic using a 6.5m sentences crawled from different sources (Yimam et al., 2021).

3. AmFLAIR: is based on FLAIR, a framework designed to facilitate experimentation with different embedding types, as well as training and distributing sequence labeling and text classification models (Akbik et al., 2018). This is a new FLAIR embedding model that was trained from scratch using a 6.5m Amharic corpus (Yimam et al., 2021).

AmRoBERTa and AmFLAIR embedding models are publicly available on GitHub[8] with the different benchmark datasets and NLP models.

A general framework using the deep learning method for our question classification is shown in Figure 5. As shown in the diagram, first, we need to build a question classification training dataset scraped from @AskAnythingEthiopia Telegram public channel. For all experiments, the data are further split into training, development, and test instances using an 80:10:10 split.

We have fine-tuned the pre-trained transformer/contextual pre-trained language models using the question classification datasets using a BiLSTM-based text classification model from FLAIR. The Text classification architecture is composed of respective embedding layers as an input layer with the sequence of 4 dense layers and an output layer. The training parameters for the architecture constitute a learning_rate of 0.5e5, mini_batch_size of 4, and max_epochs of 10. The models are trained on a 'Quadro RTX 6000' GPU server. While the Amharic dataset training took about 3 hours, the transliterated and merged (transliterated and Amharic) training took about half a day. We did not use the English dataset for model training.

The experimental results for the three different datasets (Amharic, Transliterated, and Merged) using the models fine-tuned on the two pre-trained embeddings (AmRoBERTa and AmFLAIR) are shown in Table 1, 2, and 3 respectively. Since the finetuned model based on XLMR could not produce meaningful results (it miss classify almost all of the cl assess, except the "others" class), we have excluded the results from the Tables. The cross-evaluation of the different models are shown in Table 4.

[8]`https://github.com/uhh-lt/amharicmodels`

Example 2
Amharic: ሰላም ስለ ኤርትራ እንደ ሀገር መመስረት በደንብ ሚገልፅ መፅሃፍ ጠቁሙኝ እባካችሁ?
Translation: Hi, Please tell me a book that clearly describes Eritrea as a nation
- Gold: education
- Pred: politics

Example 3
Amharic: አልወደኩም በፈራሁት ላይ የምለውን መዝሙር ላኩልኝ እባካችሁ?
Translation: Please send me a Mezmur (religious song) entitled as I did not fail on what I was scared of?
- Gold: music
- Pred: religion

Example 4
Amharic: ያፈቀሩትን ሠው መርሣት ይቻላል ይባላል እንዴት መርሳት ይቻላል?
Translation: It is said that the person you love can be forgotten. How to forget?
- Gold: relationships
- Pred: technology

Example 5
Amharic:አሁን በዚህ ሰአት ምን እየተሰማቹ ነው?
Translation:what are you feeling right now?
- Gold: other
- Pred: politics

8. Discussion

In this section, we will discuss the results of the Amharic question classification experiments we have presented in Section 7. We have used the F1-score (F1), Precision (P), and Recall (R) for the comparison of the models' performances for each question class. For the overall performances of the models, we have reported the average micro F1-scores as it shows us the overall performance. For completeness, we have reported the average macro F1-scores, but the scores will not be concrete as the classes are not balanced. The models fine-tuned on the AmRoBERTA pre-trained model have achieved an F1 score of 57.29 while those on AmFLAIR have achieved an F1 score of 54.20. Models fine-tuned from the multi-lingual XLMR embedding could not able to predict the question classes at all, except for the "Others" class with an F1 score of less than 20%. Hence, we have excluded the results from all tables.

When we see the results at the class label, questions under **Politics** and **Religion** classes are relatively accurately predicted. The class on **Entertainment** is the worst classified by the models. The class under **Other** has more questions than the other class but still, the model wrongly predicts most of the questions. One possible reason could be that the questions under **Other** are not seman-

Transliterated Questions		RoBERTa			AmFLAIR		
Q. Categories	No. of Q.	P	R	F1	P	R	F1
Education	4542	74.09	79.36	76.63	64.65	78.44	70.88
Personal	2127	23.78	22.00	22.86	30.97	17.50	22.36
Relationships	3007	76.70	81.72	79.13	66.37	77.59	71.54
Technology	2703	70.55	71.03	70.79	65.46	68.62	67.00
Religion	933	76.47	66.67	71.23	56.96	57.69	57.52
Health	1427	65.71	62.59	64.11	50.98	53.06	52.00
Business	861	42.03	31.52	36.02	28.95	11.96	16.92
Entertainment	880	36.59	32.61	34.48	33.33	14.13	19.85
Politics	296	47.62	41.67	44.44	72.73	33.33	45.71
Music	761	61.97	69.84	65.67	53.32	69.84	61.11
Society	254	06.67	05.26	05.88	00.00	00.00	00.00
Beauty	571	43.48	33.33	37.74	41.67	08.33	13.89
Sexual	325	50.00	41.38	45.28	00.00	00.00	00.00
Philosophy	50	11.11	100.0	20.00	00.00	00.00	00.00
Sport	300	34.78	23.53	28.07	42.86	08.82	14.63
Art	116	50.00	36.36	42.11	00.00	00.00	00.00
Food	144	14.29	20.00	16.67	00.00	00.00	00.00
Family	81	14.29	16.67	15.38	00.00	00.00	00.00
Science	41	33.33	16.67	22.22	00.00	00.00	00.00
Other	4542	41.57	44.71	43.08	38.72	53.78	45.03
Av. f1 (micro)				57.29			53.47
Av. f1 (macro)				42.09			27.91

Table 2: Transliterated classification model results using AmRoBERTa and AmFLAIR embeddings

Mixed Questions		RoBERTa			AmFLAIR		
Q. Categories	No. of Q.	P	R	F1	P	R	F1
Education	5660	70.16	78.95	74.30	63.88	80.58	71.27
Personal	2890	23.73	26.69	25.13	30.30	17.79	22.42
Relationships	3691	75.96	78.98	77.44	66.59	78.12	71.90
Technology	3384	69.49	68.33	68.91	66.04	68.61	67.30
Religion	1238	72.39	65.54	68.79	66.67	68.92	67.77
Health	1946	60.39	62.50	61.43	54.75	60.50	57.48
Business	1224	41.75	34.13	37.55	40.48	26.98	32.38
Entertainment	1185	44.29	28.18	34.44	32.73	16.36	21.82
Politics	565	56.00	57.14	56.57	59.57	57.14	58.33
Music	979	66.18	57.69	61.64	54.95	64.10	59.17
Society	448	07.14	07.89	07.50	00.00	00.00	00.00
Beauty	696	41.18	27.27	32.81	44.44	15.58	23.08
Sexual	433	43.48	27.78	33.90	50.00	11.11	18.18
Philosophy	152	18.75	30.00	23.08	00.00	00.00	00.00
Sport	393	53.85	28.57	37.33	53.33	16.33	25.00
Art	172	42.11	34.78	38.10	00.00	00.00	00.00
Food	197	44.44	28.57	34.78	00.00	00.00	00.00
Family	120	00.00	00.00	00.00	00.00	00.00	00.00
Science	65	16.67	14.29	15.38	00.00	00.00	00.00
Other	6060	39.47	40.93	40.19	39.12	49.92	43.86
Av. f1 (micro)				54.77			54.20
Av. f1 (macro)				41.46			32.00

Table 3: The mixed of Amharic and transliterated question and classification model results using AmRoBERTa and AmFLAIR embeddings.

tically similar enough to each other, and hence, we suggest that the platform should allow the creation of new question categories by the users.

We have made some error analyses to explore the strength and weaknesses of the model as well as to see if there are issues in the datasets. As it can be seen from Examples **2** and **3**, the model predicts the questions correctly while the samples were wrongly annotated. Some possible explanations for this wrong annotation of such samples could be either the users did not understand the question classification task (Example **2**) or the question itself is ambiguous (Example **3** has the word 'music' but it specifically refers to religious songs).

When we analyzed the model predictions, the most miss-classified classes are from the "Other" class. From Example **4**, we can see the model wrongly classified the question as "Technology", even though there are no contexts provided regarding technology. Similarly, Example **5** is predicted as "Politics" even though the question does not have a clear connection to politics.

Model	Test	P	R	F1
Merged	Amharic	47.61	39.65	42.11
Amharic	Trans.	25.71	20.37	21.44
Merged	Trans.	42.24	37.78	39.39
Trans.	Amharic	43.67	34.33	36.92

Table 4: The cross model evaluations results. "Trans." stands for Transliterated questions while 'Merged' stands for the merged questions (Amharic and transliterated). The hypothesis tested here is evaluating different models using different test sets.

Moreover, we have conducted a cross-model evaluation, mainly to verify the performance of the transliterated models. The results based on the pre-trained AmRoBERTa pre-trained embeddings are presented in Table 4. The results indicated that the Amharic model fails to properly classify transliterated texts while the transliterated model works better for Amharic test sets. Mixing the dataset increases the performance, but it is still very far from the performances of the models on the same dataset instances.

9. Conclusion and Future Works

In this paper, we presented the first work on the Amharic question classification task. Similar to the Reddit social news website, the @AskAnythingEthiopia Telegram public channel is established in 2019, which attracted as many as 78k subscribers to ask a question. The community asked any questions that could cover a wide range of question categories such as "Politics", "Music", "Technology", "Religion" and so on.

As the questions are manually tagged, and users are enforced to choose a category by the platform, it is a gold-standard dataset for question answering classification tasks. In this paper, we focused only on the question classification task. Since questions are asked both in English and Amharic, we apply language detection to consider questions only posed in Amharic. As most of the online community uses the Latin script to write Amharic questions, we also developed a Latin to Ethiopic transliteration algorithm. Using the cleaned dataset, we built deep learning-based question classification models using a pre-trained transformer and contextual embeddings. The question classification models performed at 57.79% F1 score on a total of 20 question categories, which is quite a promising result. The resources such as question classification datasets for Amharic, the models, transliteration and Pre-processing tools are released in our GitHub repository[9]. We anticipate that this dataset can be used and extended for several use-cases such as 1) extracting the answers and implementing an end-to-end QA system, 2) building multilingual question classification (Amharic + English) systems, 3) improving the transliteration system using a dictionary and contextual embeddings for word correction, 4) extracting the associated multi-modal data (images, sounds, and videos) to build a multi-modal QC and QA systems.

10. Bibliographical References

Abedissa, T. (2013). Amharic question answering for definitional, biographical and description questions. *Unpublished Master's Thesis, Computer Science Department, Addis Ababa University, Addis Ababa, Ethiopia.*

Akbik, A., Blythe, D., and Vollgraf, R. (2018). Contextual string embeddings for sequence labeling. In *Proceedings of the 27th international conference on computational linguistics*, pages 1638–1649, New Mexico, USA.

Amha, A. (2009). On loans and additions to the Fidäl (Ethiopic) writing system. In *The Idea of Writing*, pages 179–196. Brill.

Belay, T. D., Ayele, A. A., Gelaye, G., Yimam, S. M., and Biemann, C. (2021). Impacts of homophone normalization on semantic models for Amharic. In *2021 International Conference on Information and Communication Technology for Development for Africa (ICT4DA)*, pages 101–106, Bahir Dar, Ethiopia. IEEE.

Conneau, A., Khandelwal, K., Goyal, N., Chaudhary, V., Wenzek, G., Guzmán, F., Grave, E., Ott, M., Zettlemoyer, L., and Stoyanov, V. (2019). Unsupervised cross-lingual representation learning at scale. *arXiv 2019 preprint arXiv:1911.02116*, page 8440–8451.

Habtamu, S. (2021). *Amharic Question Classification System Using Deep Learning Approach.*

[9]`https://github.com/uhh-lt/amharicmodels`: The dataset are released under a permissive license

Unpublished master thesis, Addis Ababa University.

Lei, T., Shi, Z., Liu, D., Yang, L., and Zhu, F. (2018). A novel cnn-based method for question classification in intelligent question answering. In *Proceedings of the 2018 International Conference on Algorithms, Computing and Artificial Intelligence*, pages 1–6, Sanya China.

Li, X. and Roth, D. (2002). Learning question classifiers. In *COLING 2002: The 19th International Conference on Computational Linguistics*, page 1–7, Taipei, Taiwan.

Li, X. and Roth, D. (2006). Learning question classifiers: the role of semantic information. *Natural Language Engineering*, 12(3):229–249.

Liu, Y., Ott, M., Goyal, N., Du, J., Joshi, M., Chen, D., Levy, O., Lewis, M., Zettlemoyer, L., and Stoyanov, V. (2019). RoBERTa: A robustly optimized BERT pretraining approach. *arXiv preprint arXiv:1907.11692*.

May, R. and Steinberg, A. (2004). Al, building a question classifier for a TREC-style question answering system. *AL: The Stanford Natural Language Processing Group, Final Projects*.

Metzler, D. and Croft, W. B. (2005). Analysis of statistical question classification for fact-based questions. *Information Retrieval*, 8(3):481–504.

Nega, A., Chekol, W., and Kumlachew, A. (2016). Question classification in amharic question answering system: Machine learning approach. *International Journal of Advanced Studies in Computers, Science and Engineering*, 5(10):14–21.

Sangodiah, A., Muniandy, M., and Heng, L. E. (2015). Question classification using statistical approach: A complete review. *Journal of Theoretical & Applied Information Technology*, 71(3):386–395.

Taffa, T. A. and Libsie, M. (2019). Amharic question answering for biography, definition, and description questions. In *Proceedings of the 2019 Workshop on Widening NLP*, pages 110–113, Florence, Italy. Association for Computational Linguistics.

Tedla, T. (2015). amLite: Amharic Transliteration Using Key Map Dictionary. *arXiv preprint arXiv:1509.04811*.

Van-Tu, N. and Anh-Cuong, L. (2016). Improving question classification by feature extraction and selection. *Indian Journal of Science and Technology*, 9(17):1–8.

Yang, Y., Liu, J., and Liaozheng, Y. (2018). Chinese question classification based on deep learning. In *Advanced Multimedia and Ubiquitous Engineering*, pages 315–320. Springer.

Yimam, S. M. and Libsie, M. (2009). TETEYEQ: Amharic question answering for factoid questions. *IE-IR-LRL*, 3(4):17–25.

Yimam, S. M., Ayele, A. A., Venkatesh, G., Gashaw, I., and Biemann, C. (2021). Introducing various semantic models for Amharic: Experimentation and evaluation with multiple tasks and datasets. *Future Internet*, 13(11).

Proceedings of SIGUL2022 @LREC2022, pages 146–154
Marseille, 24-25 June 2022

Automatic Detection of Morphological Processes in the Yorùbá Language

Tunde Adegbola
African Languages Technology Initiative
11 Oluyole Way, New Bodija, Ibadan, Nigeria
taintransit@hotmail.com

Abstract

Automatic morphology induction is important for computational processing of natural language. In resource-scarce languages in particular, it offers the possibility of supplementing data-driven strategies of Natural Language Processing with morphological rules that may cater for out-of-vocabulary words. Unfortunately, popular approaches to unsupervised morphology induction do not work for some of the most productive morphological processes of the Yorùbá language. To the best of our knowledge, the automatic induction of such morphological processes as full and partial reduplication, infixation, interfixation, compounding and other morphological processes, particularly those based on the affixation of stem-derived morphemes have not been adequately addressed in the literature. This study proposes a method for the automatic detection of stem-derived morphemes in Yorùbá. Words in a Yorùbá lexicon of 14,670 word-tokens were clustered around "word-labels". A word-label is a textual proxy of the patterns imposed on words by the morphological processes through which they were formed. Results confirm a conjectured significant difference between the predicted and observed probabilities of word-labels motivated by stem-derived morphemes. This difference was used as basis for automatic identification of words formed by the affixation of stem-derived morphemes.

Keywords: Unsupervised Morphology Induction, Recurrent Partials, Recurrent Patterns, Stem-derived Morphemes, Word-labels.

1. Introduction

The automatic detection of morphological influences in words found on a simple list obtained from a reasonably sized corpus of unannotated written texts in natural language is an important problem in computational linguistics. There are widely varying morphological strategies for the formation of words from morphemes as sub-word elements in various natural languages. This presents a computational problem that needs to be addressed. There is a need to develop efficient algorithms that can be used to automatically identify morphemes as well as morphemic boundaries effectively in most, if not all of the languages spoken worldwide. As in all data-driven approaches to the processing of natural language, resource-scarcity poses a problem in the automatic induction of morphology.

Valuable work has been done in the unsupervised automatic induction of the morphology of some languages. Examples include Déjean (1998); Goldsmith (2000); Creutz and Lagus (2002); Creutz (2003); Creutz and Lagus (2004); Monson et al. (2007) as well as Hammarström (2009). Some of these studies have motivated the production of useful open-source application packages such as Linguistica, Morfessor and Paramor. However, it has been observed that the methods adopted in these efforts may not always scale-up to accommodate many more languages than the ones for which they were originally developed. In this regard, De Pauw and Wagacha (2007) noted the limitations of the popular methods that have been used effectively for some European languages when applied to Bantu languages of Africa. They observed in particular, that the established AutoMorphology method such as applied by Goldsmith (2000) is biased towards Indo-European languages and therefore puts it at a disadvantage when applied to a Bantu language such as Gĩkũyũ. Also, Adegbola (2016) highlighted the limitations of these methods in addressing the morphology of some other African languages. He made particular reference to the automatic induction of morphological processes such as full and partial reduplication, interfixation, compounding and others that are productively employed in Igbo, Yorùbá and some other Nigerian languages.

These methods, having been originally developed to address the morphology of a relatively few languages of Europe and Asia, essentially assume simple concatenative morphology which, even though employed in Igbo and Yorùbá, has been found to be less productively engaged in these languages than other morphological processes. Morphological processes that employ stem-derived morphemes in which affixes are dependent on and are therefore a reflection of stems cannot be automatically induced through computational methods that seek to identify recurrent partials as is used in applications such as Linguistica (Goldsmith, 2000); Morfessor (Creutz, Lagus and Virpioja, 2005) and Paramor (Monson et al,, 2007).

Hammarström and Borin (2011) prepared a comprehensive survey report on the unsupervised learning of Morphology. None of the studies in the survey addressed the unsupervised induction of partial or full reduplication, infixation, interfixation, compounding or any other morphological processes based on the affixation of stem-derived morphemes. Can and Manandhar (2014) also undertook a panoramic view of methods and algorithms used in unsupervised learning of morphology and yet strategies for addressing stem-derived morphemes did not reflect. Marelli (2021) engaged the general subject of quantitative morphology and still yet no methods that address stem-derived morphemes featured. This study therefore addresses this important but yet outstanding problem of the automatic detection of morphological processes that employ stem-derived morphemes.

2. Recurrent Partials and Recurrent Patterns

Adegbola (2016), demonstrated that the automatic induction of Yorùbá morphology depends to a large extent on the identification of recurrent patterns rather than the identification of recurrent partials, just as Iheanetu (2015) demonstrated for Igbo. For instance, inflection of, as well as the derivation of gerunds from English verbs may be achieved by the simple suffixation of the recurrent partial *'ing'*.

In Yorùbá, however, similar derivations of nouns from verbs are achieved by prefixation, not of recurrent partials, but through a process of partial reduplication in which a consonant-vowel (CV) template is prefixed to a stem. The C being a copy of the first consonant of the stem while the V is the high tone vowel *'í'* (Oyebade, 2007a), Yorùbá, being a tone language. This implies that the CV template that is prefixed to the stem is in itself derived from the stem. Hence the idea of a stem-derived morpheme.

Table 1 shows examples of the production of nouns from verbs through the process of partial reduplication by use of stem-derived affixes in Yorùbá:

Verb	Gloss	Derived Noun	Gloss
Ṣe	Do	Ṣíṣe	Doing (N)
Lọ	Go	Lílọ	Going (N)
Pè	Call	Pípè	Calling (N)
Gbà	Accept	Gbígbà	Acceptance

Table 1: Yorùbá examples of partial reduplication

Other common and highly productive processes of Yorùbá morphology such as full reduplication and interfixation also conform to this approach of affixation in which affixes are derived from the stems. Tables 2 and 3 show examples of these morphological processes and the resulting words, showing clearly identifiable word patterns:

Verb	Gloss	Derived Noun	Gloss
Pa iná	Put out fire	Panápaná	Fire fighter
Tú ilé	Undo household	Túlétúlé	Disruptive person
Gbé ọmọ	Steal child	Gbọ́mọgbọ́mọ	Kidnaper
Wo ìran	View scene	Wòranwòran	Spectator

Table 2: Yorùbá examples of full reduplication

Based on the assumption of morphemes as recurrent partials in English, for example, Goldsmith (2001), Creutz and Lagus (2004) as well as Hammarström (2009) have developed algorithms that use probability to differentiate between random sub-word elements and recurrent partials which are valid morphemic units.

Noun	Gloss	Derived Form	Gloss
Ọmọ	Child	Ọmọkọ́mọ	Any child/bad child
Iye	Value	Iyebíye	Invaluable
Àgbà	Adult	Àgbàlagbà	Old/matured person
Aṣe	Doer	Aṣemáṣe	Inappropriate behaviour

Table 3: Yorùbá examples of interfixation

However, the widely used affixation of stem-derived morphemes rather than recurrent partials in Yorùbá poses a problem in the fact of the dependence of an affix on its stem. This obviates the expected relatively high frequency of such affixes to enable their classification into one of two classes of "random sub-word segments" or "significant morphemic units" based on their probabilities of occurrence.

In a bid to cluster words produced through morphological processes based on stem-derived morphemes, Iheanetu (2015) used the idea of "word-labels" derived from the patterns of arrangements of consonants and vowels in the Igbo language to cluster words according to the morphological processes through which they were formed.

3. Word-labels

As proposed by Iheanetu (2015), a word-label can be described as a textual proxy of the pattern of arrangements of consonants and vowels in a word. It provides basis for clustering words of identical patterns, in a process of unsupervised learning, thereby identifying them as derived through identical morphological processes.

Word-labels are derived from words by assigning a sequence of symbols CX or VX representing consonants (C) or vowels (V) accompanied by a numerical index (X) indicating the occurrence or reoccurrences of specific consonants or vowels in the words, from left to right (Adegbola, 2016). Table 4 shows examples of a few English words and their derived word-labels.

Word	Word-label
Deal	C0V0V1C1
Said	C0V0V1C1
Deed	C0V0V0C0
Seek	C0V0V0C1

Table 4: Some English words and their word-labels

The word "deal", for example, takes the word-label C0V0V1C1 because the first character, 'd' is assigned the symbol C0 and the first vowel 'e' is assigned the symbol V0. Succeeding characters 'a' and 'l' are assigned the symbols V1 and C1 respectively because they are the second occurring vowel and consonant respectively. Using a zero-based indexing, the first occurrence of a consonant or vowel is assigned the index 0. Freshly used succeeding consonants or vowels are assigned succeeding numbers as indexes, while the reoccurrence of a consonant or vowel is reassigned the already assigned index. Based on this scheme, the word 'deed' takes the word-label C0V0V0C0 because the first and second occurring consonant as well as the first and second occurring vowel are the same. The facilitation of word-labels for the unsupervised induction of English morphology is yet to be investigated. In a Yorùbá lexicon, however, the patterns of morphological processes are clearly reflected in word-labels and it therefore becomes possible to cluster or classify words according to their morphological process, based on the manifest patterns in the words as reflected in their word-labels. The use of word-labels to cluster or classify words according to the morphological processes through which they are derived is justified by the fact that affixes derived from templates based on stems impose patterns on the produced words. These patterns are therefore reflected in the words so formed to the extent that commonality in morphological processes is reflected in a commonality in word patterns and therefore word-labels. The following examples of Yorùbá words of common morphological derivation clustered around the word-label C0V0C0V1 demonstrate this fact in Table 5. It should be noted that vowels with differing tone marks are regarded as different and that Yorùbá orthography uses the character *'n'* in three distinct ways. It is used in certain instances as a consonant, in some other instances as a syllabic nasal and in yet other instances as a nasalization indicator for a preceding vowel.

Stem	Gloss	Derived Word	Gloss	Common W. Label
Lọ	Go	Lílọ	Going (N)	C0V0C0V1
Wá	Come	Wíwá	Coming (N)	C0V0C0V1
Ṣe	Do	Ṣíṣe	Doing (N)	C0V0C0V1
Kọ	Write	Kíkọ	Writing (N)	C0V0C0V1
Ké	Cry	Kíké	Crying (N)	C0V0C0V1
Sè	Cook	Sísè	Cooking (N)	C0V0C0V1

Table 5: Some Yorùbá words (nouns) derived by partial reduplication to produce a common word-label

4. Identifying Morphologically Motivated Patterns

Every word has a word pattern. There is a need therefore to differentiate between random patterns and morphologically motivated patterns in order to be able to automatically identify words that are products of given morphological processes. The main objective of this study is to devise a means that can be used to automatically recognize pattern-inducing morphological processes in a language, using Yorùbá as an example, towards exploring the possibility of generalisation for other languages in future. Hence, we here present a scheme for automatically recognizing pattern-inducing morphological processes in Yorùbá.

To distinguish between word-labels that manifest by chance as against word-labels motivated by pattern-inducing morphological processes, it would be instructive to compute two probability measures for each word-label. The first is a predicted probability of a word-label based on an assumption of random choice of consonants and vowels in the words that produce the word-label and the second is the observed probability of the word-label in a sizable corpus of written texts in Yorùbá. These predicted and observed probabilities of word-labels may then be compared. A significant difference in the predicted and the observed probabilities of a word-label will be usable as basis for classifying word-labels as either resulting from random choice of consonants and vowels in the words that produce them or word-labels that result from significant patterns induced by morphological processes.

5. Predicted Probability of a Word-label

The predicted probability of the manifestation of a word-label is based on the assumption that all allowable consonants and vowels of the language in question occur equiprobably in words that produce such a word-label. In addition, it assumes independence between the individual consonants and vowels that make up the word. These assumptions would be valid only if there are no external influences on the choices of these consonants and vowels.

To compute this predicted probability, we consider a word-label as consisting of symbols A_iX_i where:

$$A_i \in \{C, V\}$$

$$X_i \in \{0, 1, 2, \ldots. n\}$$

In this light, the word-label C0V0C1V1 for the English word "make" for example, can be thought of as containing symbols $A_1X_1A_2X_2A_3X_3A_4X_4$, where $A_1 = C, X_1 = 0, A_2 = V, X_2 = 0, A_3 = C, X_3 = 1, A_4 = V \text{ and } X_4 = 1$.

Given a language of c consonants and v vowels, the probability of obtaining a symbol C0 for the first occurring consonant is $^{c}/_{c}$ as any of the c consonants can be chosen. This is equal to 1, implying certainty. The probability of obtaining another symbol C0 after the first consonant has taken the symbol C0 is $^{1}/_{c}$ because the only one consonant that caused the first consonant symbol to be C0 must have reoccurred. By the same token, the probability of any other consonant taking the symbol C1 is $^{(c-1)}/_{c}$, having excluded the consonant that produced C0. We can thus generalise the probability of any symbol CX as $^{(c-X)}/_{c}$. In the same vein, the probability of obtaining a symbol V0 for the first occurring vowel is $^{v}/_{v}$ and the probability of any symbol VX can be generalised as $^{(v-X)}/_{v}$ as argued above.

By virtue of the assumption of independence in the predicted probabilities of each of the symbols that make up a word-label, the likelihood $L(A_1X_1A_2X_2 \ldots A_nX_n)$ of a word-label can be computed as the naive product of the individual probabilities of each of the symbols thus:

$$L(A_1X_1A_2X_2 \dots A_nX_n) = \prod_{i=1}^{n} P(A_iX_i) \qquad (1)$$

The product of two or more probabilities may not necessarily yield a probability. Hence, to normalise the likelihood in formular (1) above into a probability, we shall multiply it by the reciprocal of the cumulative likelihoods of all conceivable word-labels in a group as shown in formular (2). This will guarantee that the probabilities of all conceivable word-labels in each group sums up to unity in accordance with probability theory.

$$P(A_1X_1A_2X_2 \dots A_nX_n) = {}^{1}/_{S} \prod_{i=1}^{n} P(A_iX_i) \qquad (2)$$

$$S = \sum_{j=1}^{m} L_j(A_1X_1A_2X_2 \dots A_nX_n) \qquad (3)$$

Where m is the total number of conceivable word-labels in each group and S is the cumulative likelihood of all the m conceivable word-labels in a group of equal lengths and common structure.

We define the structure of a word-label as the sequence of consonants and vowels without considering the indexes. For example, the word-labels C0V0V0 and C0V0V1 both have the same structure because they both consist of the same consonant and vowel sequence of CVV, differing only in their indexes.

6. Observed Probability of a Word-label

In considering the observed probability of a word-label, the manifestation of a given word-label is taken as a single event with a single outcome while the manifestations of all word-labels in a group is the total number of possible outcomes. Hence, the observed probability of a given word-label can be calculated as the frequency of occurrence of the word-label, based on the number of words that produced it and are thereby clustered around it, divided by the total number of occurrences of all word-labels in the same group, based on the total number of words that produced them.

To compute the observed probability of a word-label i that manifests in a given group of identical length and structure, having a cumulative total of n word-tokens, we observe the number of word-tokens n_i that produced the given word-label i. Each of the n word-tokens in the group will produce one word-label each. Hence, the probability $P(i)$ of the word-label i would be the number of word-tokens n_i that produced the word-label i divided by the total number of word-tokens n_i in the group, computed as:

$$P(i) = {}^{n_i}/_{n} \qquad (3)$$

7. Automatic Detection of Morphological Processes

As already explained, the predicted probability of a word-label as computed above assumes equiprobability in the occurrences of the individual consonants and vowels combined to form the word that produced the word-label. In addition, independence between the occurrences of the consonants and the vowels is assumed. However, if the formation of a word is motivated by a morphological process, these assumptions become invalidated. For example, as Oyebade (2007a) noted, in the morphological process of partial reduplication in Yorùbá, a consonant and vowel (CV) template is prefixed to a stem, the C being a copy of the first consonant of the stem while the V is the high tone vowel 'í'. The fact that the C is a copy of the first consonant of the stem violates the assumption of independence in the choice of that consonant. As for the assumption of equiprobability, the fact that the V in the prefix template is unconditionally the high tone vowel 'í' violates the assumption of equiprobability. Hence, we hypothesize that the contribution of a morphological process in the formation of a word will bring about a significant difference in the predicted and observed probabilities of its word label. Word-labels derived from such a word whose formation is motivated by a morphological process that employs a stem-derived morpheme will surely feature a sufficiently significant difference to signal the involvement of such a process.

To automatically detect the morphological processes used in word formation in a language, we may therefore compare the observed and predicted probabilities of word-labels encountered in a lexicon obtained from a sizable corpus of texts in the language. It is hypothesised that in the absence of any morphological influences, we expect no significant differences in the observed and predicted probabilities of a word-label. We can therefore conclude that any significant differences between the predicted and the observed probabilities of a word-label would have been brought about by morphological influences.

The predicted probability of a word-label as described in Section 5 is a normalised product over the set of probabilities of the individual symbols that make up the word-label. The product of two proper fractions will always produce a lower value than both. Hence, the predicted probability of a word-label will depend on its length. For this reason, we opted to group together word-labels of the same lengths and structures as defined in section 5 together for consistency in the comparison of word-labels.

8. Tests and Results

To explore the difference between the predicted and observed probabilities of a word-label produced by word-tokens whose formation is motivated by a morphological process based on the affixation of stem-derived morphemes, we extracted a lexicon of 14,670 word-tokens from a Yorùbá corpus. The 14,670 tokens produced 1,282 distinct word-labels. The word-labels were grouped according to their lengths and structures and both their predicted and observed probabilities were computed, all as described in sections 5 and 6. The computed predicted probability was based on 18 consonants and 12 vowels as specified in the literature for the number of consonants and vowels of the Yorùbá language (Oyebade, 2007b). Comparison of the predicted and observed probabilities were made and the following results were obtained.

The most productive word-label was C0V0C1V1, with a cluster of 2,716 word-tokens. This represents 18.51% of the 14,670 word-tokens in the lexicon. Examples of word-tokens that produced this word-label include *balẹ̀, dewé, fijó, gbaṣọ* and *jíṣẹ́*. The overwhelming majority of these are formed by the morphological process of compounding, suggesting that the word-label C0V0C1V1 clusters Yorùbá words formed mainly by compounding. A predicted probability of 0.8657 was computed for this word-label, while the computed observed probability was 0.7690.

W. Label	P. Prob.	O. Prob.	Cardinality
C0V0C0V0	0.0046	0.0416	147
C0V0C0V1	0.0509	0.0994	351
C0V0C1V1	0.8657	0.7690	2716
C0V0C1V0	0.0787	0.0900	318
Cumulative	1.0000	1.0000	3532

Table 6: Predicted and observed probabilities of word-labels of the CVCV group

Table 6 shows all conceivable word-labels in the group (CVCV) to which it belongs. Word-labels (W. Label) are shown in the first column, while the predicted and observed probabilities (P. Prob. and O. Prob.) are shown in columns two and three respectively. The fourth column shows the number of word-tokens (Cardinality) clustered around each word-label. The fact that the cumulative predicted probability adds up to unity indicates that word-tokens producing all conceivable word-labels in this group were encountered in the corpus.

The word-label C0V0C0V0, which is a member of the CVCV group suggests a cluster of words produced by the morphological process of full reduplication. The glaring difference in its predicted and observed probabilities bears eloquent testimony to its easily perceptible symmetry.

The second most productive word-label is V0C0V1, with a cluster of 1,446 word-tokens, representing 9.86% of the 14,670 word-tokens in the lexicon. Examples of words that produced this word-label include *abi, abẹ, egbé, idán, àgbo* and *ẹ̀rọ*, all derived through the nominalisation of single syllable Yorùbá verbs by the concatenative morphological process of vowel prefixation. While we acknowledge seeming exceptions such as *abẹ́*, which, though a noun is not easily associated with a one-syllable verb with related meaning, we can say generally that this word-label clusters words formed mainly through the morphological process of concatenation by vowel prefixation. As can be observed from the sample of words shown here from this cluster, various vowels featured as the prefixed morphemes. This is consistent with Awobuluyi's (2001) observation that all Yorùbá vowels apart from *'u'* and the nasal vowels are used freely as prefixes. It stands to reason however, that these prefixes may not occur sufficiently frequently to be easily detectable automatically as recurrent partials, based solely on frequency in a process of unsupervised induction of the morphological process. The proposed approach of clustering relevant words around word-labels, however, makes it easy to perceive the prefixes, generally as vowels rather than a particular individual vowel.

The only other word-label in the group VCV is V0C0V0. Table 7 shows the predicted and observed probabilities of these two word-labels of this group.

W. Label	P. Prob.	O. Prob.	Cardinality
V0C0V1	0.9167	0.9335	1446
V0C0V0	0.0833	0.0665	103
Cumulative	1.0000	1.0000	1549

Table 7: Predicted and observed probabilities of word-labels of the VCV group

The third most productive word-label is V0C0V1C1V2, with a cluster of 1,417 word-tokens, representing 9.66% of the 14,670 word-tokens in the lexicon. Examples of words that produced this word-label include *abetí, ìbínú, ojúgbó, àbùṣán, èlùbọ́, ìbùkún, òkúta, ẹlẹ́wù* and *ọmùtí*. Apart from *èlùbọ́* and *òkúta* in which the word formation processes may not be glaring to this investigator, the other words in this small sample and most of the others in the cluster feature mainly concatenation by vowel prefixation as well as compounding. For example, *ìbùkún* meaning "blessing" is a noun formed by the compounding of two words *bù* (take) and *kún* (fill) to form the verb "*increase*" followed by nominalisation of the verb *bùkún* by vowel prefixation to form the noun *ìbùkún*.

W. Label	P. Prob.	O. Prob.	Cardinality
V0C0V0C0V0	0.0004	0.0039	8
V0C0V0C1V1	0.0675	0.0640	132
V0C0V0C1V0	0.0061	0.0194	40
V0C0V1C1V1	0.0675	0.1024	211
V0C0V1C1V2	0.6745	0.6870	1417
V0C0V1C0V1	0.0040	0.0388	80
V0C0V1C1V0	0.0675	0.0344	71
V0C0V1C0V0	0.0040	0.0040	9
V0C0V1C0V2	0.0397	0.0432	89
V0C0V0C0V1	0.0040	0.0029	6
V0C0V0C0V2	0.0036	0.0000	0
V0C0V0C1V2	0.0612	0.0000	0
Cumulative	1.0000	1.0000	2063

Table 8: Predicted and observed probabilities of word-labels of the VCVCV group

The other word-labels of the VCVCV group to which V0C0V1C1V2 belongs are shown in Table 8. As would be noticed, no words that could have produced two valid word labels; V0C0V0C0V2 and V0C0V0C1V2 featured in the corpus used for this study. Particularly curious is V0C0V0C1V2 with a predicted probability of 0.0612, being the 5th highest probability in the group. A few other relatively productive word-labels are shown in Table 9.

W. Label	P. Prob	O. Prob	Cardinality
C0V0C1V1C2V2	0.6413	0.4711	620
V0C0V1C1V2C2V3	0.4810	0.5060	506
C0V0	1.0000	1.0000	430
C0V0C0V1	0.0509	0.0994	351
C0V0C1V0	0.0787	0.0900	318
C0V0V1C1V2	0.7215	0.5333	272
C0V0V1	0.9167	0.7220	226

Table 9: Predicted and observed probabilities as well as cardinality of the 4th to the 10th most productive word-labels

The core concern of this study is to automatically identify words that feature morphological processes based on stem-derived morphemes by comparing the predicted and observed probabilities of their word-labels.

Figure 1 and Figure 2 show that comparison of predicted and observed probabilities of word-labels is capable of making this important distinction. As can be observed in the charts, the observed probabilities of word-labels that incorporate stem-based morphemes are generally higher than their predicted probabilities, while the contrary holds in the case of word-labels without stem-based morphemes.

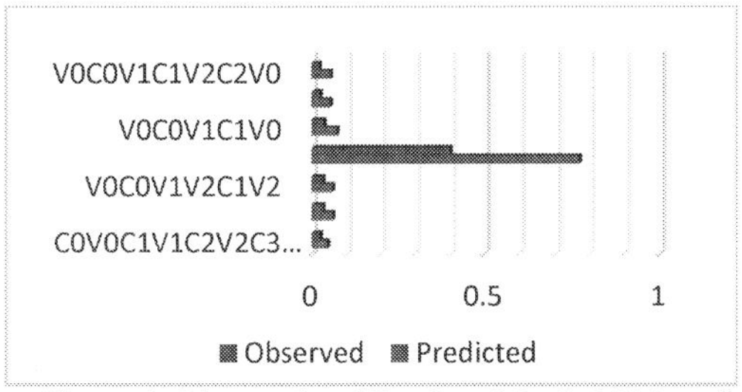

Figure 1: Observed and Predicted Probabilities of Word-labels with Stem-derived Words

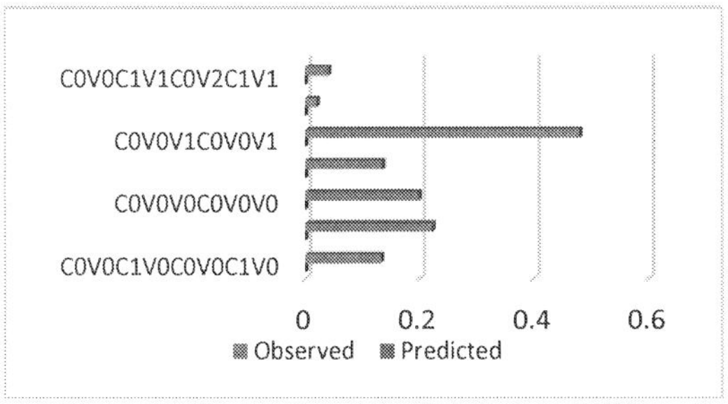

Figure 2: Observed and Predicted Probabilities of Word-labels without Stem-derived Words

We recognise the ratio of the observed and predicted probabilities of word-labels as a convenient indicator of the involvement of stem-derived morphemes.

$$ratio = {}^{O\ Prob}/_{P\ Prob}$$

Where $O\ Prob$ and $P\ Prob$ are the predicted and probabilities.

We also acknowledge two factors that would have effects on the predicted and observed probabilities of word-labels. On the one hand, as discussed in section 7, the longer a word-label, the lower its probability. Hence, the length of a word-label will affect its predicted probability to the extent that short word-labels may tend to have high probabilities while long word-labels may tend to have low probabilities. On the other hand, sampling error owing to resource-scarcity may affect the observed probability of word-labels in a group in which the word-labels cluster few words, causing them to have high observed probabilities.

The predicted probability of a word-label is computed as explained in section 5 by obtaining the normalised product of the probabilities of the individual symbols that make up the word-label, while the observed probability is computed as explained in section 6 by normalising the cardinality of a word-label with the overall cardinality of its group.

Table 10 shows a selection of word-labels, their ratios of observed and predicted probabilities and some sample word-tokens each. It can be observed from the table that the more the repetition of characters in a word-token as reflected in the word-label, the greater the ratio of the observed and predicted probabilities. Obviously, the word-labels, C0V0C1V0C0V0C1V0 and C0V0C1V1C0V0C1V1 are motivated by the morphological process of full reduplication as can be observed from the symmetry brought about by the duplication of C0V0C1V0 and C0V0C1V1 respectively. This is reflected in their relatively high ratios of 127145.48 and 19452.41 and the sample words; *biribiri* and *bọ̀lọ̀bọ̀lọ̀* as well as *bojúbojú* and *bàmùbàmù* respectively. The succeeding word-label, C0V0V0C1V0C0V0 must have been motivated by the morphological process of partial reduplication and this is reflected in the ratio of 6174.55 and the sample words: *fẹ́ẹ́rẹ́fẹ́* and *gbuurugbu*.

The word-label, C0V0C1V1C0V2 with a ratio of 0.85 and sample words of *jogójì* and *kàgbákò* as well as the word-label C0V0C1V1C2V1C3V2 with its ratio of 0.53 and sample words of *kòbọmọjẹ́* and *mójúkúrò* provide convincing evidence that the ratio of the observed and predicted probabilities is a faithful indicator of the involvement of stem-based morphemes in certain word-labels and their absence in some others.

Word-label	Ratio	Morphological Process	Sample words
C0V0C1V0C0V0C1V0	127145.48	Full Reduplication	biribiri, bọlọ̀bọ̀lọ̀, fírífírí, gbẹ̀jẹ̀gbẹ̀jẹ̀
C0V0C1V1C0V0C1V1	19452.41	Full Reduplication	bojúbojú, bàmùbàmù, fọ́rífọ́rí, jayéjayé
C0V0V0C1V0C0V0	6174.55	Partial Reduplication	fẹ́ẹ́rẹ́fẹ́, gbuurugbu, tààràtà, pẹẹrẹpẹ
C0V0C0V0C0V0	1074.26	Full Reduplication	dandandan, gangangan, jẹ́jẹ́jẹ́, tantantan
C0V0C1V1C0V2C1V1	352.40	Full Reduplication	fálafàla, jágbajàgba, kóbokòbo, pálapàla
V0C0V0C1V1C0V0	20.58	Interfixation	àgbàlágbà, ọmọkọ́mọ, ọ̀pọ̀lọpọ̀
V0C0V1C1V2C2V2	1.88	Prefixation	alágídí, alákàrà, ọlọ́gẹ̀dẹ̀, ónígbèsè
V0V1C0V2C1V3	1.30	Prefix+Compounding	àìdúpẹ́, àìlera, àìmọ̀kan, àìrójú, àìgbọràn
C0V0C0V1C1V2	1.30	Partial Reduplication	dídọ́gba, jíjóná, kíkorò, lílépa, pípadà
C0V0C1V1C0V2	0.85	Compounding	jogójì, kàgbákò, láyọ̀lé, pawọ́pọ̀, ṣojúṣe
C0V0C1V1C2V1C3V2	0.53	Desentencialisation	kòbọmọjẹ́, mójúkúrò, yírapadà, ṣàfarawé

Table 10: Word-label, Ratio, Morphological Process and Sample Words

It can be inferred from the fore-going that while the predicted probability of a word-label is affected by its length, the observed probability is totally insulated from this factor. Conversely, while the observed probability may be affected by sampling error occasioned by resource-scarcity, the predicted probability is totally insulated from this effect. The sampling error is reflected in the cardinality of each word-label, which in turn reflects on the cumulative cardinality of each group.

To address the problem of disparate lengths and their effects on probabilities, word-labels of identical lengths were considered together, regardless of their structures. However, it was noticed that the effect of disparity in lengths tended to reduce as the lengths of the word-labels increased. It was also noticed that the cardinality of word-labels correlates negatively with their lengths. By treating word-labels of disparate lengths separately, it was possible to localise the effects of sampling error to extremely long word-labels that featured very low cardinality. Hence, the effect of sampling error appears to be localised to each length-based cluster of word-labels.

The 1,282 word-labels generated from the lexicon of 14,670 word-tokens extracted from the Yorùbá corpus were grouped into 24 sets of word-labels based on their lengths. The word-labels in each set were sorted according to the values of their *O Prob* and *P Prob* ratios. It was observed that in each of the 24 sets of same-length word-labels as sorted based on their ratios, the first bunch of word-labels to be encountered are those that cluster words formed by full reduplication. Followed by this first bunch of word-labels, come word-labels that cluster words formed by either partial reduplication or interfixation. We then encounter word-labels that cluster words formed by simple affixation of recurrent partials as well as compounding and then word-labels that cluster all other types of words. This is observable in Table 10 in which C0V0C1V0C0V0C1V0 and C0V0C1V1C0V0C1V1 are examples of word-labels that conform to full reduplication, C0V0V0C1V0C0V0 conforms to partial reduplication while V0C0V0C1V1C0V0 conforms to interfixation. The word-labels C0V0C1V1C0V2 and C0V0C1V1C2V1C3V2 conform to compounding and desentencialisation respectively. The successive and consistent reduction in the values of the *O Prob*/*P Prob* ratios is instructive.

All morphological processes reported in the literature of Yorùbá morphology were observed and words formed by each process were found to cluster around specific word-labels. As noted in Adegbola (2016), some word-labels clustered word-tokens formed by more than one morphological process and in some cases, a single morphological process was found to produce word-tokens that clustered around more than one word-label. In the final analysis however, the word-labels showed themselves creditably as effective purveyors of the patterns imposed on words by stem-derived morphemes and therefore an effective and efficient means of identifying the morphological processes featured in a language.

9. Conclusion

It is apparent from the results obtained in this study that the ratio of the predicted and observed probabilities of word-labels is a valuable metric for the identification of word-labels that incorporate stem-derived morphemes. This is to be expected because the involvement of morphological processes in the formation of words that produce such word-labels contradict the assumptions of equiprobability and independence in the choice of characters for the affected word-tokens. This is a radically new approach to the unsupervised induction of morphology. It should become a valuable supplement to the approach proposed by Harris (1955), which has continued to guide the approaches used in more recent studies undertaken by investigators such as Déjean (1998); Goldsmith (2000); Creutz and Lagus (2002); Creutz (2003); Creutz and Lagus (2004) as well as Hammarström (2009) as was earlier discussed.

The resource-scarce status of the Yorùbá language played out significantly in this study. The lexicon used contained only 14,670 word-tokens, which certainly left many Yorùbá words unaccounted for. Many word-labels that obviously feature stem-derived morphemes had low cardinality, some of them as low as one. The incidence of a stem-derived morpheme in a word-label is indicative of a morphological process. A morphological process is not likely to produce only one word for a language and so, these word-labels with low cardinality are expected to have more than a few word-tokens each in their clusters. Towards addressing the resource-scarcity of Yorùbá, it should be possible to use such low cardinality word-labels to project and thereby validate or even generate out-of-vocabulary words in certain Natural Language Processing (NLP) circumstances. This is a worthy endeavour for a future study.

The cumulative values of the observed probabilities of each group of word-labels added up to unity in conformity with probability theory. This is ensured by the fact that these probabilities were computed, based solely on word-tokens that featured in the corpus that produced the study lexicon. However, the cumulative values of the predicted probabilities of some groups of word-labels did not add up to unity. This implies that certain word-labels in such groups did not feature in the modest corpus that produced the study lexicon.

As noted in Section 5, the predicted probability for each of all conceivable and valid word-labels in each group is guaranteed to sum up to unity. All word-labels that did not feature in their appropriate groups as a result of sampling error occasioned by the resource-scarcity are computationally derivable and their individual predicted probabilities can be computed with consistency. Hence, the cumulative predicted probability of all conceivable word-labels in a group is guaranteed to add up to unity. The corresponding observed probabilities of each of the unencountered word-labels due to sampling error will logically take a value of zero each, thereby ensuring that the predicted and observed probabilities for each group sums up to unity in conformity with probability theory. This was the case with the VCVCV group of word-labels as shown in Table 8, where the word-labels V0C0V0C0V2 and V0C0V0C1V2 had predicted probability values of 0.0036 and 0.0612 respectively but a cardinality of zero each and therefore observed probability values of zero each.

Unencountered word-labels, being validly computationally derivable may be useful in projecting and validating or even generating out-of-vocabulary words. The fact that the predicted probabilities of such unencountered word-labels can be calculated is of high value. Such probability values offers an important metric for assessing the coverage of available corpora in a language. The systematic use of such a metric to assess the level of coverage of available corpora of resource-scarce languages is yet another worthy issue for future study.

One interesting surprise encountered within the C0V0C1V1 cluster is the word *benson*, a foreign proper noun. Though a foreign word, it is understandable that it found its way into a Yorùbá corpus, being proper noun. It found its way into the C0V0C1V1 cluster in particular by virtue of the fact that the character *"n"* is used as the indicator for nasalisation of a preceding vowel in Yorùbá orthography as explained in Section 3. For this reason, the *"en"* and *"on"* in the word *benson* were erroneously construed as Yorùbá nasal vowels.

Many non-Yorùbá words in the corpus clustered around word-labels that admit consonant clustering which happens not to be a feature of Yorùbá syllable structure. An example of such a word-label is C0C1V0C2 under which the English words *show*, *this* and *what* were found. The words were traced to certain lines of a Yorùbá play in the corpus, in which one of the characters was showing off ability to speak the English language. In this light, it is interesting that word-labels may be usable as a means of identifying and extracting foreign words in a corpus.

Another interesting cluster is the cluster designated as "XXX", which was deliberately used to cluster words that incorporate consonants such as X, C, V and Q, which are not used in the Yorùbá language. Some of the words that found their ways into this cluster consisting of 40 words include *academic*, *achaempong*, *african* and *america*.

The problem of recognizing the presence of stem-derived morphemes in words is yet to be effectively addressed in the literature of computational morphology. Results obtained from this study show the potentials of word-labels as an effective and efficient tool for addressing this problem. A number of other important applications of word-labels have also been suggested. Locating the word-label as a proxy of words within the Chomsky hierarchy and the possible use of automata to parse and recognise valid word-labels of the Yorùbá language or any other languages for that matter are not only desirable but also pertinent. All these need to be actively engaged and further investigated in future studies.

10. Acknowledgments

We acknowledge the valuable suggestions in the excellent reviews offered by members of SIGUL2022 program committee. The Yorùbá lexicon used in this study was obtained from materials collected for the project; Development of a Yorùbá Speech Synthesizer funded by the Lagos State Research Development Council (LRDC).

11. Bibliographical References

Adegbola, T. (2016, April). Pattern-based unsupervised induction of Yorùbá Morphology. In Proceedings of the 25th International Conference Companion on World Wide Web (pp. 599-604).

Awobuluyi, O. (2001). Mọfọ́lọ́jì Èdè Yorùbá, in Ajayi B. (ed) Ẹ̀kọ́ Ìjìnlẹ̀ Yorùbá: Ẹdá Èdè, Lítíréṣọ̀, àti Aṣà. Ìjẹ̀bú-òde: Shebiotimo Publications. pp47-70

Can, B., & Manandhar, S. (2014, April). Methods and algorithms for unsupervised learning of morphology. In International Conference on Intelligent Text Processing and Computational Linguistics (pp. 177-205). Springer, Berlin, Heidelberg.

Creutz, M. & Lagus, K. (2002). Unsupervised discovery of morphemes. In Proceedings of the Workshop on Morphological and Phonological Learning of ACL. Philadelphia, PA. 21–30.

Creutz, M. (2003). Unsupervised segmentation of words using prior distributions of morph length and frequency. In *Proceedings of the 41st annual meeting of the Association for Computational Linguistics* (pp. 280-287).

Creutz, M., & Lagus, K. (2004). Induction of a simple morphology for highly-inflecting languages. In *Proceedings of the 7th meeting of the ACL special interest group in computational phonology: Current themes in computational phonology and morphology* (pp. 43-51).

Creutz, M., Lagus, K., & Virpioja, S. (2005, September). Unsupervised morphology induction using morfessor. In International Workshop on Finite-State Methods and Natural Language Processing (pp. 300-301). Springer, Berlin, Heidelberg.

De Pauw, G., & Wagacha, P. W. (2007). Bootstrapping morphological analysis of Gĩkũyũ using unsupervised maximum entropy learning. In In Proceedings of the eighth INTERSPEECH conference.

Déjean, H. (1998). Morphemes as necessary concept for structures discovery from untagged corpora. In *New Methods in Language Processing and Computational Natural Language Learning*.

Goldsmith, J. (2000) Linguistica: An automatic morphological analyzer. In Proceedings from the Main Session of the Chicago Linguistic Society's 36th Meeting, pages 125–139, Chicago, IL.

Goldsmith, J. (2001). Unsupervised learning of the morphology of a natural language. *Computational Linguistics*, *27*(2), 153-198.

Hammarström, H. (2009). Unsupervised learning of morphology and the languages of the world. Ph.D. thesis, Chalmers University of Technology and University of Gothenburg

Hammarström, H., & Borin, L. (2011). Unsupervised learning of morphology. *Computational Linguistics*, *37*(2), 309-350.

Harris, Z. (1955). From phoneme to morpheme. Language 31(2). 190–222.

Iheanetu, O. U. (2015). A data-driven model of Igbo morphology. *University of Ibadan, Nigeria (Unpublished Ph. D. Thesis)*.

Marelli, M. (2021). Quantitative Methods in Morphology: Corpora and Other "Big Data" Approaches. In Oxford Research Encyclopaedia of Morphology.

Monson, C. Carbonell, J., Lavie, A., & Levin, L. (2007). ParaMor: Finding paradigms across morphology. In Workshop of the Cross-Language Evaluation Forum for European Languages (pp. 900–907). Berlin, Germany: Springer.

Oyebade, F.O. (2007a) Yorùbá Morphology. In Orẹ Yusuf (ed.) Basic linguistics for Nigerian languages teachers. Port Harcourt: M & J Grand Orbit Communications Ltd. and Emhai Press. 241-255.

Oyebade, F.O. (2007b) Yorùbá Phonology. In Orẹ Yusuf (ed.) Basic linguistics for Nigerian languages teachers. Port Harcourt: M & J Grand Orbit Communications Ltd. and Emhai Press. 221-239.

Proceedings of SIGUL2022 @LREC2022, pages 155–160
Marseille, 24-25 June 2022

Evaluating Unsupervised Approaches to Morphological Segmentation for Wolastoqey

Diego Bear, Paul Cook
Faculty of Computer Science
University of New Brunswick
{diego.bear, paul.cook}@unb.ca

Abstract

Finite-state approaches to morphological analysis have been shown to improve the performance of natural language processing systems for polysynthetic languages, in-which words are generally composed of many morphemes, for tasks such as language modelling (Schwartz et al., 2020). However, finite-state morphological analyzers are expensive to construct and require expert knowledge of a language's structure. Currently, there is no broad-coverage finite-state model of morphology for Wolastoqey, also known as Passamaquoddy-Maliseet, an endangered low-resource Algonquian language. As this is the case, in this paper, we investigate using two unsupervised models, MorphAGram and Morfessor, to obtain morphological segmentations for Wolastoqey. We train MorphAGram and Morfessor models on a small corpus of Wolastoqey words and evaluate using two annotated datasets. Our results indicate that MorphAGram outperforms Morfessor for morphological segmentation of Wolastoqey.

Keywords: Morphological segmentation, unsupervised morphology, low-resource languages

1. Introduction

Wolastoqey is an Indigenous language spoken in parts of what are now the provinces of New Brunswick and Quebec, Canada, and the state of Maine, United States. This language is often referred to as Passamaquoddy-Maliseet, with Passamaquoddy and Maliseet being two dialects of this language. Many speakers of the Maliseet dialect in the communities where the authors of this paper live and work refer to their language as Wolastoqey. We therefore use the term *Wolastoqey* (as opposed to Passamaquoddy-Maliseet) in this paper.

Wolastoqey is a polysynthetic eastern Algonquian language. It is endangered, with only roughly 300 remaining first language speakers in Canada (Statistics Canada, 2017). It is a low-resource language with no large corpora or annotated datasets available. There is, however, the Passamaquoddy-Maliseet Dictionary (Francis and Leavitt, 2008). This Wolastoqey–English dictionary provides English definitions for roughly $19k$ Wolastoqey headwords. A version of this dictionary is available online.[1]

Relatively little prior computational work has considered Wolastoqey. Farber (2015) presents a preliminary finite-state model of Passamaquoddy-Maliseet noun morphology. Bear and Cook (2021) propose a cross-lingual Wolastoqey–English definition modelling system which generates English definitions for Wolastoqey words. They show that, for this definition modelling task, sub-word representations from byte-pair encoding (Sennrich et al., 2016) can be used to overcome the limitations of not having a large monolingual Wolastoqey corpus available for learning Wolastoqey word representations. Bear and Cook (2022) show that English definitions for Wolastoqey words can be used to form Wolastoqey word representations that encode syntactic and semantic information.

Morphological analysis is particularly important for building language technology and natural language processing systems for morphologically-rich languages. For example, Bowers et al. (2017) develop a morphological parser for the Odawa dialect of Ojibwe (also an Algonquian language) and discuss applications of this parser for building language technology such as morphologically-aware dictionary search to help a dictionary user to find a lemma from an inflected form and spelling correction. A Wolastoqey morphological analyzer could similarly enable such language technologies for this language. Finite-state morphology has also been shown to give improvements in language modelling for polysynthetic languages (Schwartz et al., 2020). Language models are a key component for many NLP systems. As such, a Wolastoqey morphological analyzer could support the development of future applications such as text prediction.

Finite state morphological analyzers have been developed for several Algonquian languages including Plains Cree (Snoek et al., 2014), Odawa (Bowers et al., 2017), and Arapaho (Kazeminejad et al., 2017). However, other than the preliminary work of Farber (2015) on noun morphology, there is currently no broad coverage finite state morphological analyzer for Wolastoqey.

In the absence of a finite state morphological analyzer for Wolastoqey, in this paper, we consider unsupervised approaches to morphological segmentation. MorphAGram (Eskander et al., 2020) is an unsupervised approach to morphological segmentation based on adaptor grammars, models that generalize probabilistic context-free grammars by introducing depen-

[1] Passamaquoddy-Maliseet Language Portal (http://www.pmportal.org); Language Keepers and Passamaquoddy-Maliseet Dictionary Project.

dencies between successive uses of rewrite rules. It has recently been shown to outperform other unsupervised approaches to morphological segmentation on a range of languages, including polysynthetic languages. In this paper, we evaluate MorphAGram on Wolastoqey, and compare it to Morfessor (Smit et al., 2014), an unsupervised morphological segmentation model that defines a segmentation vocabulary using minimum description length as a training objective. We find that MorphAGram also outperforms Morfessor for Wolastoqey.

The rest of the paper is organized as follows. In Section 2 we describe our experimental setup including the models considered, the training and evaluation datasets, and the evaluation metric. We present results for MorphAGram and Morfessor in Section 3. In Section 4 we summarize our findings and identify directions for future work.

2. Experimental Setup

In this section we describe the settings of MorphAGram and Morfessor used in our experiments, the training and evaluation data, and the evaluation metrics we use.

2.1. MorphAGram

To run our experiments with MorphAGram, we use the implementation of MorphAGram published by Eskander et al. (2020). This implementation requires an off the shelf adaptor-grammar sampler to train; we use the recommended adapter-grammar sampler.[2] To train our MorphAGram models, we use the same training parameters as the original paper as described in the source code of the implementation.[3]

As we wish to evaluate the performance of MorphAGram on Wolastoqey, we first must identify the best performing grammar for this language. For this, we consider running preliminary experiments in which we train multiple MorphAGram models using the grammars considered by Eskander et al. (2020). We evaluate the performance of each grammar on a small dataset of morphologically segmented words from the Passamaquoddy-Maliseet Dictionary (the PMLP dataset described in 2 4). In these preliminary experiments, we observed that a grammar consisting of prefixes, stems and suffixes, referred to PrStSu in the original paper, performed the best. We therefore choose to focus on this grammar, as well as the best performing grammar from the original paper, which, in-addition to prefixes, stems and suffixes, includes submorphs. This grammar is referred to as PrStSu + SM.

We choose to run our experiments both in a language-independent and scholar-seeded configuration. To train our models in a scholar-seeded setup, we seed our grammars using preverbs from the Passamaquoddy-Maliseet Dictionary. In total, we seed our scholar-seeded grammars with 813 preverbs.[4]

2.2. Morfessor

To establish a baseline for comparison, we train a Morfessor 2.0 (Smit et al., 2014) model on the same datasets used to train our MorphAGram models. For this we use the implementation of Morfessor 2.0 available in the python Morfessor library.[5] The Morfessor model used in our experiments is trained using the default training parameters on the types that occur in our training dataset.

2.3. Training Data

To construct the training dataset used in our experiments we use contents from the Passamaquoddy-Maliseet Dictionary. In addition to English definitions for Wolastoqey headwords, this dictionary includes parallel Wolastoqey–English example sentences. As we require a list of words to train our morphological segmentation models, we define our training dataset as the set of unique types that occur in the Wolastoqey example sentences of each dictionary entry. We choose to use the types that occur in the dictionary example sentences instead of the set of dictionary headwords, as all verb headwords are given in a third-person present-tense form, meaning many morphemes associated with particular inflected forms would not occur in the training data.

To obtain a list of types from our Wolastoqey sentences, we first tokenize each sentence using a regular expression tokenizer from NLTK (Bird and Loper, 2004). We define a token as a contiguous string of alphanumeric characters, underscores, hyphens and apostrophes. As many example sentences code-switch with English and thus contain English words, we remove all English words from our dataset using an English word list available in NLTK. Using this approach, we obtain a set of $30.1k$ unique types to train our models from $18.5k$ example sentences, containing a total of $147k$ tokens.

As both Morfessor and MorphAGram are unsupervised approaches to morphological segmentation, we choose to evaluate our models in a transductive setup in which words the model will be evaluated on (but not their gold-standard segmentations) are included in the training data. Given new unknown words to segment, the models could be simply retrained to obtain segmentations for them. Operating under this assumption, for each of our experiments, we add all words from the evaluation set (described below) to the training data.

[2] `https://web.science.mq.edu.au/~mjohnson/Software.htm`

[3] `https://github.com/rnd2110/MorphAGram`

[4] Many preverbs are listed in the Passamoquoddy-Maliseet Dictionary as headwords and as such can easily be identified to use in a scholar-seeded setting. In future work we intend to also consider including common suffixes in the scholar-seeded setting.

[5] `https://github.com/aalto-speech/morfessor`

2.4. Evaluation Datasets

For evaluation, we compare the output of MorphAGram and Morfessor to gold standard segmentations. We use two segmentation datasets for evaluation, one obtained from information available on the Passamaquoddy-Maliseet Language Portal, and the other from a morphologically-annotated sample text (Leavitt, 1996, 5.4).

The Passamaquoddy-Maliseet Language Portal includes word-building examples to help teach learners how words are formed.[6] These examples include information about morphological segmentation. We use all of the available examples to form a dataset for evaluation. The resulting dataset, which we refer to as PMLP, contains segmentations for 30 Wolastoqey words, composed of an average of 4.23 morphemes per word.

We build a second evaluation dataset from a morphologically-annotated sample text (Leavitt, 1996, 5.4). In this text, the morphological segmentation of each word is shown. We manually transcribe this sample text to create an additional evaluation dataset. This dataset, which we refer to as LEAVITT-1996, is composed of segmentations for 102 unique words (types), consisting of an average of 2.32 morphemes per word. LEAVITT-1996 is derived from running text. As such, it includes words corresponding to all parts-of-speech, including mono-morphemic particles and preverbs. This is in contrast to PMLP in which all instances in the dataset consist of multiple morphemes. Particles and preverbs can, however, be easily identified using a wordlist. As such, we are particularly interested in how a morphological segmenter performs on other parts-of-speech. We therefore construct a version of LEAVITT-1996 in which particles and preverbs are removed. We refer to this dataset as LEAVITT-1996-FILTERED. This results in a dataset consisting of segmentations for 71 words, being composed on average of 2.89 morphemes. For evaluations using LEAVITT-1996-FILTERED, we also remove particles and preverbs from the training data. This reduces the training data to 29.5k types as 624 particles and preverbs are removed from the training data.

2.5. Evaluation Metrics

A range of evaluation metrics have been considered for evaluating unsupervised morphological analyzers including boundary evaluations and morpheme assignment approaches such as EMMA-2 (Virpioja et al., 2011). In the case that both the predicted analysis and gold-standard are segmentations, Virpioja et al. (2011) find that boundary evaluations are appropriate. In our experimental setup both the predicted analyses and gold-standard annotations are segmentations, and so we use boundary precision-recall (BPR) for evaluation. BPR is a metric based on the precision, recall and F1 score of predicted segmentation splits.

[6] `https://pmportal.org/word-building`

3. Results

We report results for MorphAGram and Morfessor on each dataset in Table 1. For MorphAGram we consider a grammar with prefixes, stems, and suffixes (PrStSu) and the same grammar additionally with submorphs (PrStSu + SM). We consider each grammar in both a standard language-independent setting (Std.) and a scholar-seeded setting in which the model is seeded with knowledge of preverbs (Sch.). Results for MorphAGram approaches are averaged across ten runs with different random seeds.

We first consider results on PMLP (shown in the top panel of the Table 1). Focusing on F1, we observe that all MorphAGram approaches considered outperform the Morfessor baseline. This is inline with the findings of Eskander et al. (2020) that MorphAGram improves over Morfessor. Among the MorphAGram approaches considered we observe that the best approach is Std. PrStSU, i.e., a model without submorphs that does not use scholar seeding. We find that both approaches that do not use submorphs outperform those that do, and that using scholar seeding leads to a reduction in performance.

We now turn to consider results on LEAVITT-1996 (middle panel of Table 1). Focusing again on F1, we observe that for this dataset, not all MorphAGram models outperform the Morfessor baseline. In particular, only models that incorporate submorphs (indicated with +SM) outperform Morfessor. In contrast to experiments on PMLP, here we observe that both approaches that incorporate submorphs outperform those that do not.

We further see mixed results here for scholar seeding. In particular, scholar seeding gives a small improvement for models that do not use submorphs, but does not give improvements when submorphs are included. The best results on this dataset use submorphs and no scholar seeding (i.e., Std. PrStSu + SM). The inconsistent behaviour of scholar seeding could possibly be attributed to the fact that we only use prefixes as seeds in our experiments, and do not use stems or suffixes as seeds. Additionally providing stems and suffixes as part of the scholar seeding could potentially lead to improvements. However, the finding that scholar-seeding does not lead to uniform benefits is not inconsistent with Eskander et al. (2020) who find that scholar-seeding did not improve performance on some languages.

In the PMLP evaluation, all instances consist of multiple morphemes. In contrast, for LEAVITT-1996, the instances are drawn from running text and include many particles and preverbs (the latter of which are in certain cases written as separate words) which are mono-morphemic. In preliminary investigations we observed that MorphAGram over-segmented many of these monomorphemic forms, which seems to have contributed to the relatively low precision of MorphAGram approaches compared to Morfessor on LEAVITT-

Grammar	P		R		F1	
PMLP						
Morfessor	0.678		0.377		0.485	
Std. PrStSu	0.619	(0.026)	**0.623**	(0.021)	**0.621**	(0.021)
Std. PrStSu + SM	0.736	(0.021)	0.504	(0.027)	0.598	(0.024)
Sch. PrStSu	0.644	(0.022)	0.571	(0.030)	0.605	(0.025)
Sch. PrStSu + SM	**0.738**	(0.031)	0.466	(0.025)	0.571	(0.026)
LEAVITT-1996						
Morfessor	**0.710**		0.588		0.643	
Std. PrStSu	0.417	(0.022)	**0.800**	(0.022)	0.548	(0.023)
Std. PrStSu + SM	0.611	(0.021)	0.757	(0.017)	**0.676**	(0.018)
Sch. PrStSu	0.450	(0.025)	0.737	(0.019)	0.559	(0.022)
Sch. PrStSu + SM	0.605	(0.025)	0.747	(0.016)	0.668	(0.017)
LEAVITT-1996-FILTERED						
Morfessor	0.668		0.452		0.539	
Std. PrStSu	0.544	(0.025)	**0.668**	(0.021)	0.599	(0.022)
Std. PrStSm + SM	**0.772**	(0.032)	0.616	(0.022)	**0.685**	(0.022)
Sch. PrStSm	0.630	(0.022)	0.617	(0.019)	0.623	(0.018)
Sch. PrStSm + SM	0.763	(0.019)	0.599	(0.020)	0.671	(0.016)

Table 1: Boundary precision, recall and F1 scores on each dataset for MorphAGram and a Morfessor 2.0 baseline. The standard deviation for these evaluation metrics for MorphAGram is shown in parentheses. The best results for each method, on each dataset, are shown in boldface.

Word	Approach	Segmentation
	Gold standard	ali+tahas+uwin+uwok
alitahasuwinuwok	MorphAGram	ali+tahas+uwin+uwok
	Morfessor	al+itahasu+winuwok
	Gold standard	k+peci+pt+ul+on+ en
kpeciptulonen	MorphAGram	k+pecip+t+ul+on+en
	Morfessor	kpeci+ptul+onen
	Gold standard	wici+ht+aq+ik
wicihtaqik	MorphAGram	wi+ci+ht+a+qik
	Morfessor	wici+htaq+ik

Table 2: The segmentations for the gold standard, MorphAGram, and Morfessor for three words in LEAVITT-1996.

1996. For example, MorphAGram segments the mono-morphemic preverb *cuwi* as c+uwi while Morfessor does not segment this word. These findings led us to consider a further evaluation on LEAVITT-1996-FILTERED in which particles and preverbs are excluded from the evaluation.

Results for LEAVITT-1996-FILTERED are shown in the bottom panel of Table 1. In this evaluation, as for the evaluation on PMLP, all MorphAGram methods outperform the Morfessor baseline. For this evaluation the results follow a similar pattern to those on the full LEAVITT-1996 dataset. Including submorphs gives improvements, while the results for scholar seeding are mixed; the best results are again obtained using submorphs and no scholar seeding (i.e., Std. PrStSu + SM).

Further comparing the results between LEAVITT-1996 and LEAVITT-1996-FILTERED, we observe that Morfessor performs notably worse on the latter. This suggests that Morfessor performs well at (not) segmenting mono-morphemic words such as particles and preverbs. Such words can, however, be easily identified using a wordlist. We further observe that each MorphAGram approach achieves higher precision on LEAVITT-1996-FILTERED than on LEAVITT-1996. This finding is inline with the observation that MorphAGram over-segments monomorphemic items, which are included in LEAVITT-1996 but not LEAVITT-1996-FILTERED.

Table 2 shows some examples of the segmentations produced by MorphAGram and Morfessor. For *alitahasuwinuwok* ('the wise men') MorphAGram produces the same segmentation as the gold standard, while none of the boundaries predicted by Morfessor are correct. In the case of *kpeciptulonen* ('constant battles') MorphAGram produces an almost correct segmentation, but one boundary is incorrectly identified. For Morfessor, all predicted boundaries are correct, but recall is poor in that some boundaries are not predicted. For *wicihtaqik* ('make jointly') MorphAGram makes several errors, while Morfessor only fails to identify one boundary.

4. Conclusions

A morphological analyzer can be leveraged to give improvements for NLP tasks such as language modelling for polysynthetic languages. There is, however, currently no broad-coverage morphological analyzer for Wolastoqey. In this paper we therefore considered unsupervised approaches to morphological segmentation for Wolastoqey. MorphAGram has previously been shown to outperform Morfessor on polysynthetic languages. In this paper we evaluated MorphAGram and Morfessor and showed that this is also the case for Wolastoqey.

In future work, we intend to develop a finite-state morphological analyzer for Wolastoqey. Such a system could subsequently be leveraged to train a neural morphological analyzer with broader coverage (Micher, 2017; Lane and Bird, 2020). We are further interested in extrinsic evaluation of the segmentations produced by MorphAGram and leveraging them in applications. For example, we intend to consider whether cross-lingual Wolastoqey–English definition modelling could be improved by replacing BPE-based subword representations with segmentations from MorphAGram in the approach of Bear and Cook (2021). We are further interested in applications of morphological segmentations for semi-automated lexicography. For example, dictionaries of other Algonquian languages include entries for stems, roots, and affixes (Frantz and Russell, 2017). We are interested in whether MorphAGram segmentations could be leveraged to help lexicographers to add similar entries to a Wolastoqey dictionary.

5. Bibliographical References

Bear, D. and Cook, P. (2021). Cross-lingual wolastoqey-English definition modelling. In *Proceedings of the International Conference on Recent Advances in Natural Language Processing (RANLP 2021)*, pages 138–146, Held Online, September. INCOMA Ltd.

Bear, D. and Cook, P. (2022). Leveraging a bilingual dictionary to learn wolastoqey word representations. To appear in *Proceedinsg of LREC 2022*.

Bird, S. and Loper, E. (2004). NLTK: The natural language toolkit. In *Proceedings of the ACL Interactive Poster and Demonstration Sessions*, pages 214–217, Barcelona, Spain, July. Association for Computational Linguistics.

Bowers, D., Arppe, A., Lachler, J., Moshagen, S., and Trosterud, T. (2017). A morphological parser for odawa. In *Proceedings of the 2nd Workshop on the Use of Computational Methods in the Study of Endangered Languages*, pages 1–9, Honolulu, March. Association for Computational Linguistics.

Eskander, R., Callejas, F., Nichols, E., Klavans, J., and Muresan, S. (2020). MorphAGram, evaluation and framework for unsupervised morphological segmentation. In *Proceedings of the 12th Language Resources and Evaluation Conference*, pages 7112–7122, Marseille, France, May. European Language Resources Association.

Farber, A. (2015). A finite-state grammar of passamaquoddy-maliseet nouns. `http://dx.doi.org/10.13140/RG.2.1.2836.6967`.

Kazeminejad, G., Cowell, A., and Hulden, M. (2017). Creating lexical resources for polysynthetic languages—the case of Arapaho. In *Proceedings of the 2nd Workshop on the Use of Computational Methods in the Study of Endangered Languages*, pages 10–18, Honolulu, March. Association for Computational Linguistics.

Lane, W. and Bird, S. (2020). Bootstrapping techniques for polysynthetic morphological analysis. In *Proceedings of the 58th Annual Meeting of the Association for Computational Linguistics*, pages 6652–6661, Online, July. Association for Computational Linguistics.

Micher, J. (2017). Improving coverage of an Inuktitut morphological analyzer using a segmental recurrent neural network. In *Proceedings of the 2nd Workshop on the Use of Computational Methods in the Study of Endangered Languages*, pages 101–106, Honolulu, March. Association for Computational Linguistics.

Schwartz, L., Tyers, F., Levin, L., Kirov, C., Littell, P., Lo, C.-k., Prud'hommeaux, E., Park, H. H., Steimel, K., Knowles, R., Micher, J., Strunk, L., Liu, H., Haley, C., Zhang, K. J., Jimmerson, R., Andriyanets, V., Muis, A. O., Otani, N., Park, J. H., and Zhang, Z. (2020). Neural polysynthetic language modelling.

Sennrich, R., Haddow, B., and Birch, A. (2016). Neural machine translation of rare words with subword units. In *Proceedings of the 54th Annual Meeting of the Association for Computational Linguistics (Volume 1: Long Papers)*, pages 1715–1725, Berlin, Germany, August. Association for Computational Linguistics.

Smit, P., Virpioja, S., Grönroos, S.-A., and Kurimo, M. (2014). Morfessor 2.0: Toolkit for statistical morphological segmentation. In *Proceedings of the Demonstrations at the 14th Conference of the European Chapter of the Association for Computational Linguistics*, pages 21–24, Gothenburg, Sweden, April. Association for Computational Linguistics.

Snoek, C., Thunder, D., Lõo, K., Arppe, A., Lachler, J., Moshagen, S., and Trosterud, T. (2014). Modeling the noun morphology of Plains Cree. In *Proceedings of the 2014 Workshop on the Use of Computational Methods in the Study of Endangered Lan-*

guages, pages 34–42, Baltimore, Maryland, USA, June. Association for Computational Linguistics.

Statistics Canada. (2017). *Canada [Country] and Canada [Country] (table). Census Profile.* 2016 Census. Statistics Canada Catalogue no. 98-316-X2016001. Ottawa. Released November 29, 2017. `https://www12.statcan.gc.ca/census-recensement/2016/dp-pd/prof/index.cfm?Lang=E` (accessed August 13, 2021).

Virpioja, S., Turunen, V. T., Spiegler, S., Kohonen, O., and Kurimo, M. (2011). Empirical comparison of evaluation methods for unsupervised learning of morphology. *Traitement Automatique des Langues*, 52(2):45–90.

6. Language Resource References

David A. Francis and Robert M. Leavitt. (2008). *A Passamaquoddy-Maliseet Dictionary*. The University of Maine Press and Goose Lane Editions.

Frantz, D. G. and Russell, N. J. (2017). *Blackfoot Dictionary of Stems, Roots, and Affixes*. University of Toronto Press, third edition.

Leavitt, R. (1996). *Passamaquoddy-Maliseet*. Languages of the world / Materials: Materials. Linde.

Proceedings of SIGUL2022 @LREC2022, pages 161–168
Marseille, 24-25 June 2022

Baseline English and Maltese-English Classification Models for Subjectivity Detection, Sentiment Analysis, Emotion Analysis, Sarcasm Detection, and Irony Detection

Keith Cortis, Brian Davis
ADAPT Centre
Dublin City University
Glasnevin, Dublin 9, Ireland
{keith.cortis, brian.davis}@adaptcentrie.ie

Abstract

This paper presents baseline classification models for subjectivity detection, sentiment analysis, emotion analysis, sarcasm detection, and irony detection. All models are trained on user-generated content gathered from newswires and social networking services, in three different languages: English —a high-resourced language, Maltese —a low-resourced language, and Maltese-English —a code-switched language. Traditional supervised algorithms namely, Support Vector Machines, Naïve Bayes, Logistic Regression, Decision Trees, and Random Forest, are used to build a baseline for each classification task, namely subjectivity, sentiment polarity, emotion, sarcasm, and irony. Baseline models are established at a monolingual (English) level and at a code-switched level (Maltese-English). Results obtained from all the classification models are presented.

Keywords: opinion mining, social media, subjectivity analysis, sentiment analysis, emotion analysis, irony detection, sarcasm detection, social data, code-switching

1. Introduction

Finding out what other people think about a product or service has always been a very important part of an individual's and/or organisation's information gathering behaviour especially during a decision making process. Before the World Wide Web awareness, people asked their friends and colleagues about recommendations for an automobile mechanic, or about whom they plan to vote for in the upcoming elections, and checked with the consumer reports before buying a house appliance. Organisations usually conducted market analysis in the form of opinion polls, surveys, and focus groups in order to capture public opinion concerning their products and services (Liu, 2010). The advent of the Social Web and the massive increase of user-generated content posted on social media platforms and newswires commenting sections, allows users to create and share content and their opinions directly to the public, thus circumventing possible forms of bias (by acquaintance of experts only). Such user-generated content is invaluable for certain needs, such as improving an entity's service or perception and tracking citizen opinion to aid policy makers and decision takers (Hilts and Yu, 2010). Opinion-rich resources have been growing both in terms of availability and popularity.

The year of 2001 marked the beginning of widespread awareness of the research problems and opportunities for Opinion Mining and Sentiment Analysis (Pang and Lee, 2008). Online review sites and personal blogs were early examples of such opinionated resources, whereas social networking (e.g., Facebook[1]), microblogging (e.g., Twitter[2]), travel (e.g., TripAdvisor[3]), and newswire (e.g., Reuters[4]) services are nowadays the most popular. This created new opportunities and challenges for Opinion Mining, especially on user-generated content spread across heterogeneous sources, such as newswires and social networking services.

This paper presents baseline classification models for **five** opinion classification tasks: *subjectivity detection*, *sentiment analysis*, *emotion analysis*, *sarcasm detection*, and *irony detection*. These are based on a novel multidimensional and multilingual social opinion dataset in the Socio-Economic domain, specifically Malta's annual Government Budget, which comprises social data from the 2018, 2019, and 2020 budgets.

In terms of language, this social data is in one of the following languages: English —a high-resourced language, Maltese —a low-resourced language, and Maltese-English —a code-switched language. Baseline models are established at a monolingual level using user-generated content in English, and at a code-switched level using user-generated content in Maltese-English and Maltese. Section 2 presents a review of social datasets available for Opinion Mining, the algorithms generally used for evaluating them, and other relevant studies within this research area. The experiments carried out to establish the baseline models are discussed in Section 3, with some conclusions and future work presented in Section 4.

[1]`https://www.facebook.com`

[2]`https://www.twitter.com`

[3]`http://www.tripadvisor.com`

[4]`https://www.reuters.com`

2. Related Work

Studies focusing on text classification tasks, such as sentiment analysis, at a binary (two classes) and/or multi-class (more than two classes) level generally use machine learning (ML) and deep learning (DL) supervised algorithms for building their baseline models. A Social Opinion Mining systematic review (Cortis and Davis, 2021b) analysed a large number of studies that make use of social data, such as user-generated content from social media platforms, and identified techniques used for carrying out classification tasks in this research area. In terms of traditional supervised learning algorithms, the most common ones used for baseline, experimentation, evaluation and/or comparison purposes are Naïve Bayes (NB) (Lewis, 1998), Support Vector Machine (SVM) (Cortes and Vapnik, 1995), Logistic Regression (LR) (McCullagh, 1984) / Maximum Entropy (MaxEnt)–generalisation of LR for multi-class scenarios (Yu et al., 2011), Decision Tree (DT) (Quinlan, 1986), and Random Forest (RF) (Breiman, 2001). The choice of traditional supervised learning algorithms selected is supported by other Opinion Mining reviews, such as (Ravi and Ravi, 2015), (Hemmatian and Sohrabi, 2019), (Carvalho and Plastino, 2021), (Ligthart et al., 2021). Even though recent advances in Opinion Mining has seen an increase in the use of DL approaches, such as the Transformer model architecture (Vaswani et al., 2017), traditional ML algorithms are still very much used to carry out Opinion Mining classification tasks, with good results obtained especially on small datasets (Ligthart et al., 2021).

Several high-quality Opinion Mining social datasets are available for research purposes as part of shared evaluation tasks, such as the International Workshop on Semantic Evaluation (SemEval)[5] and/or through open access repositories, such as Zenodo[6]. Teams submitting their systems in the SemEval sentiment analysis task on code-mixed tweets (Patwa et al., 2020) used the following techniques, traditional ML algorithms such as NB, LR, RF, and SVM; word embeddings such as word2vec (Mikolov et al., 2013), GloVe (Pennington et al., 2014), and fastText (Joulin et al., 2016); and DL algorithms such as Convolutional Neural Network (CNN) (LeCun et al., 1990), and Bidirectional Enconder Representations from Transformers (BERT) (Devlin et al., 2018). In (Gupta et al., 2017), several ML (SVM best performer) and DL algorithms are used as baselines for contextual emotion detection on tweets.

A baseline SVM system was trained in numerous SemEval tasks, such as (Mohammad et al., 2018) for affect in tweets and (Pontiki et al., 2016) for aspect-based sentiment analysis. Similarly, SVM performed well on irony detection (Van Hee et al., 2018) and sentiment analysis (Rosenthal et al., 2017) in tweets. Participants in the SemEval task focusing on fine-grained sentiment analysis on financial microblogs and news (Cortis et al., 2017) made use of lexicon-based, ML, DL, and hybrid techniques, similar to (Patwa et al., 2020). An approach based on SVM was used in (Kothari et al., 2013) for subjectivity classification of news articles' comments and tweets. In (Appidi et al., 2020), ML algorithms such as SVM were used for emotion classification experiments on an annotated corpus of code-switched Kannada-English tweets. Bansal et al. used SVM and RF for training baseline models to show how code-switching patterns can be used to improve several downstream Natural Language Processing (NLP) applications (Bansal et al., 2020). In (Mamta et al., 2020), the authors also implemented baseline models for sentiment analysis using ML and DL algorithms, such as SVM and CNN. Similarly, the authors in (Yimam et al., 2020) built several baseline models for Amharic sentiment analysis from social media text using ML algorithms, such as SVM and LR.

[5]`https://semeval.github.io/`

[6]`https://zenodo.org/`

3. Experiments

In this paper, we experimented with multiple classification models catering for the English, Maltese, and Maltese-English languages across **five** different social opinion dimensions, namely *subjectivity*, *sentiment polarity*, *emotion*, *irony*, and *sarcasm*. All experiments have been carried out in the Python using Jupyter Notebook[7] on a machine with an Intel(R) Core(TM) i7-8550U CPU @ 1.80GHz 1.99 GHz processor and 8.00 GB (7.88 GB usable) installed memory (RAM).

3.1. Baseline Models

Baseline models for each social opinion dimension were built using the following eight supervised learning algorithms:

- **NB**: Multivariate Bernoulli NB (MBNB)–classifier suitable for discrete data and is designed for binary/boolean features (scikit learn, a), and Complement NB (CNB)–designed to correct "severe assumptions" made by the standard Multinomial NB classifier and suited for imbalanced datasets (scikit learn, b);
- **SVM**: Support Vector Classification (SVC)–C-SVC implementation based on libsvm (a library for SVM) (scikit learn, h), Nu-Support SVC (NuSVC)–similar to SVC however can control the number of support vectors (scikit learn, f), and Linear SVC–similar to SVC however has more flexibility and supports both dense and sparse input (scikit learn, d);
- **LR**: a probabilistic classifier also known as logit or Maximum Entropy (scikit learn, e);
- **DT**: an optimised version of the Classification and Regression Trees (CART) algorithm (scikit learn, c); and
- **RF**: an ensemble of decision tree algorithms (scikit learn, g).

[7]`https://jupyter.org/`

The scikit-learn[8] ML library was used for building the baseline models. This consists of a set of tools for data mining and analysis, such as pre-processing, model selection, classification, regression, clustering, and dimensionality reduction.

3.2. Approach

The Opinion Mining approach for building baseline models consists of the following steps, namely data acquisition, pre-processing, model generation, and model evaluation.

3.2.1. Dataset

The dataset of multidimensional and multilingual social opinions for Malta's Annual Government Budget[9] (Cortis and Davis, 2021a) has been used for the work carried out in this paper. This dataset contains 6,387 online posts for the 2018, 2019, and 2020 budgets, which user-generated content was collected from three newswires, namely Times of Malta[10], MaltaToday[11], and The Malta Independent[12], and one social networking service, namely Twitter. In terms of languages, the majority of the online posts were in English (74.09%) with most of the rest being in Maltese-English or Maltese (24.99%). It is important to note that the online posts in Maltese-English and Maltese have been merged together due to the low amount of online posts in Maltese only. Each online post is annotated for the following five social opinion dimensions: subjectivity, sentiment polarity, emotion, sarcasm, and irony. Table 1 presents the overall class distribution of online posts for each social opinion dimension and the language annotation. Statistics are provided for the entire dataset (columns 2 and 3), the subset of online posts in English (columns 4 and 5), and subset of online posts in Maltese-English and Maltese (columns 6 and 7).

3.2.2. Pre-processing

Pre-processing on the online posts used for building the baseline models was carried out, using the following NLP tasks of a syntactic nature:

- **Data cleaning**: Removal of any numbers, HTML/XML tags, special characters and whitespaces;
- **Tokenisation**: text composed of string of words or sentences split into tokens, in terms of alphabetic and non-alphabetic characters, using the NLTK (Bird et al., 2009) word punctuation tokeniser;
- **Stemming**: removes suffices or prefixes used with a word to reduce inflectional forms to a common base form, using NLTK's implementation of the Porter stemming algorithm[13]; and
- **Conversion of textual data into numerical representations**: term frequency and inverse document frequency (TF-IDF) (Salton and McGill, 1986) statistical measure (using the scikit-learn TfidfVectorizer function) used to evaluate the word relevance in online posts and hence represent the online posts into a feature vector for training a classifier using any algorithm discussed in Section 3.1.

3.2.3. Model Generation

Given that the dataset used is relatively small in terms of data volume, we are not in a position to omit a chunk of data for model generation. Therefore, cross-validation provides us with a better modelling approach for small datasets, as opposed to the traditional training-validation-test set split. Stratified 10-fold cross-validation is applied on the entire dataset being used for model generation and evaluation. This cross-validation technique is used since the ratio between the target classes is preserved as is in the full dataset. It is also adequate for imbalanced datasets such as the one being used, as reflected in Table 1. Moreover, this technique just shuffles and splits the dataset once into 10 folds. Therefore, the test sets used for validating the trained model (on k - 1 of the folds used as training data) do not overlap between any of the 10 splits. Lastly, the model itself is trained 10 times, with the weights and any biases being reset with each new model. This cross-validation procedure was applied for each baseline model built using the supervised learning algorithms discussed in Section 3.1. Baseline classification models for *subjectivity*, *sentiment polarity*, *emotion*, *sarcasm*, and *irony*, were built on i) the subset of English online posts and ii) the subset of Maltese-English and Maltese online posts.

3.3. Results and Discussion

Results of the baseline classification models mentioned in Section 3.2.3 are presented and discussed in this section. Table 2 displays results obtained on the subset of English online posts, whereas Table 3 displays results obtained on the subset of Maltese-English and Maltese online posts (merged together due to the low amount of online posts in Maltese only).

The following evaluation metrics were used to measure the classification performance of the models generated for each social opinion dimension:

- **F1 score weighted** (Chinchor, 1992): F1 score is the weighted average of precision and recall. The weighted score calculates the F1 score for each label with their average being weighted by support,

[8]https://scikit-learn.org/

[9]https://doi.org/10.5281/zenodo.4650232

[10]https://www.timesofmalta.com/

[11]https://www.maltatoday.com.mt/

[12]https://www.independent.com.mt/

[13]https://tartarus.org/martin/PorterStemmer/

Dataset	All		English		Maltese-English and Maltese	
	Count	**Percentage**	**Count**	**Percentage**	**Count**	**Percentage**
Subjectivity						
Subjective	2591	40.57%	1713	36.20%	852	53.38%
Objective	3796	59.43%	3019	63.80%	744	46.62%
Sentiment Polarity						
Negative	1232	19.29%	775	16.38%	441	27.63%
Neutral	1605	25.13%	1355	28.63%	219	13.72%
Positive	3550	55.58%	2602	54.99%	936	58.65%
Emotion						
Joy	2636	41.27%	1976	41.76%	648	40.60%
Trust	363	5.68%	219	4.63%	144	9.02%
Fear	72	1.13%	61	1.29%	11	0.69%
Surprise	177	2.77%	116	2.45%	60	3.76%
Sadness	245	3.84%	176	3.72%	67	4.20%
Disgust	498	7.80%	275	5.81%	216	13.53%
Anger	369	5.78%	238	5.03%	127	7.96%
Anticipation	2027	31.74%	1671	35.31%	323	20.24%
Sarcasm						
Sarcastic	177	2.77%	101	2.13%	74	4.64%
Not Sarcastic	6210	97.23%	4631	97.87%	1522	95.36%
Irony						
Ironic	329	5.15%	189	3.99%	136	8.52%
Not Ironic	6058	94.85%	4543	96.01%	1460	91.48%
Language						
English	4732	74.09%	4732	100%		
Maltese	299	4.68%			299	18.73%
Maltese-English	1297	20.31%			1297	81.27%
Other	59	0.92%				

Table 1: Class distribution for each annotation per dataset

that is, the number of true instances for each label. This metric caters for label imbalance.

- **Balanced accuracy** (Brodersen et al., 2010): defined as the average of recall scores obtained per class. This metric is used for imbalanced binary and multi-class classification.

Both tables present the mean and standard deviation F1 score (weighted) and balanced accuracy results obtained for all eight supervised learning algorithms using the stratified 10-fold cross-validation technique.

With respect to the English data, the LR algorithm obtained the best F1 score (weighted) results for the subjectivity and irony classification models. The SVC and RF obtained the same results for the latter model. The CNB algorithm produced the best F1 score (weighted) for the sentiment polarity and emotion classification models, whereas NuSVC fared best for the sarcasm classifier. When considering the balanced accuracy, the CNB algorithm produced the best results for all the social opinion dimensions.

As for the results on the Maltese-English and Maltese data, the CNB algorithm fared best in terms of F1 score (weighted) for the subjectivity, emotion (same as for English data), and irony classification models. The LinearSVC algorithm produced the best F1 score (weighted) for the sentiment polarity classifier, whereas the LR, SVC, and RF algorithms obtained the best and same results for sarcasm. Similar to the results obtained on the English data, the CNB algorithm produced the best balanced accuracy results for subjectivity, sarcasm, and irony. On the other hand, LinearSVC obtained the best balanced accuracy results for sentiment polarity, whereas RF fared best for emotion.

The following are some observations on the results obtained:

- The CNB algorithm obtained good performance for all languages and handled the imbalanced classes better than the other algorithms.

- Results obtained for the subjectivity and sentiment polarity classifiers are very promising for the English subset and Maltese-English and Maltese subset, even though the latter subset only amounts to 1596 online posts and the classes are not evenly balanced (for both subsets).

- Further evaluation using online posts unseen by the trained models is needed on the emotion, sarcasm, and irony classifiers to ensure that they are not biased towards the majority classes (Padurariu and Breaban, 2019), due to small amount of online posts available for the minority classes. Resampling techniques (Cateni et al., 2014; More, 2016) such as over-sampling and under-sampling can be used for handling such imbalances.

Opinion Dimension	LR	LinearSVC	NuSVC	SVC	BNB	CNB	DT	RF
Subjectivity								
F1 score (weighted)								
Mean	**0.883841**	0.879541	0.876273	0.496998	0.840135	0.883805	0.836563	0.8721
Standard Deviation	0.090688	0.076603	0.099753	0.000954	0.100051	0.077748	0.080797	0.09332
Execution time (sec)	0.366402	0.152594	133.560791	138.974958	0.056846	0.049864	3.255599	38.103134
Balanced accuracy								
Mean	0.866635	0.86671	0.855156	0.5	0.811524	**0.873531**	0.827453	0.85808
Standard Deviation	0.109981	0.095431	0.118991	0	0.11106	0.09623	0.099956	0.108103
Execution time (sec)	0.325131	0.147605	128.942503	138.723404	0.051897	0.038896	3.552703	32.025443
Sentiment Polarity								
F1 score (weighted)								
Mean	0.773488	0.766855	0.777319	0.390174	0.776828	**0.783019**	0.722608	0.763451
Standard Deviation	0.070612	0.054157	0.053882	0.000444	0.053359	0.073829	0.049837	0.065426
Execution time (sec)	4.067413	0.409448	173.671773	146.321687	0.063825	0.044364	4.606840	35.520771
Balanced accuracy								
Mean	0.722771	0.717044	0.739063	0.333333	0.727495	**0.766624**	0.685624	0.714724
Standard Deviation	0.077534	0.058836	0.059551	0	0.056173	0.075009	0.063942	0.070536
Execution time (sec)	3.950933	0.397628	173.383033	144.026906	0.041853	0.037899	4.462762	41.809123
Emotion								
F1 score (weighted)								
Mean	0.558523	0.573032	0.565908	0.246018	0.559174	**0.597985**	0.53082	0.538238
Standard Deviation	0.028066	0.04086	0.032799	0.000952	0.050814	0.059299	0.047546	0.048382
Execution time (sec)	12.094085	1.239142	249.117511	153.079795	0.119210	0.055034	5.528538	42.201759
Balanced accuracy								
Mean	0.247898	0.282854	0.268255	0.125	0.248973	**0.319283**	0.265121	0.237785
Standard Deviation	0.023119	0.025369	0.025894	0	0.034061	0.035876	0.032245	0.028137
Execution time (sec)	11.447332	0.969887	237.525686	134.157565	0.097378	0.045877	5.374176	42.332807
Sarcasm								
F1 score (weighted)								
Mean	0.9681	0.967914	**0.968939**	0.9681	0.956555	0.954114	0.961048	0.9681
Standard Deviation	0.000925	0.001536	0.001145	0.000925	0.023294	0.050832	0.007896	0.000925
Execution time (sec)	0.190490	0.132643	58.925297	8.298284	0.066821	0.050832	2.718095	19.604499
Balanced accuracy								
Mean	0.5	0.508466	0.509438	0.5	0.558462	**0.566324**	0.555348	0.5
Standard Deviation	0	0.018602	0.018891	0	0.055718	0.072913	0.042625	0
Execution time (sec)	0.186504	0.116689	63.924314	8.433631	0.054854	0.040890	2.684616	20.277674
Irony								
F1 score (weighted)								
Mean	**0.940496**	0.940348	0.940073	**0.940496**	0.917422	0.92766	0.934038	**0.940496**
Standard Deviation	0.000932	0.003619	0.000979	0.000932	0.046925	0.023662	0.018002	0.000932
Execution time (sec)	0.208476	0.151596	87.929416	17.331174	0.080325	0.050864	2.785665	27.825442
Balanced accuracy								
Mean	0.5	0.510847	0.49956	0.5	0.535921	**0.561683**	0.558459	0.502632
Standard Deviation	0	0.019195	0.00073	0	0.073153	0.038838	0.051882	0.007895
Execution time (sec)	0.209446	0.134637	88.003576	16.294276	0.053856	0.041888	2.464509	30.312636

Table 2: Classification model results - English dataset

4. Conclusions and Future Work

The paper discusses preliminary results of baseline classification models for subjectivity detection, sentiment analysis, emotion analysis, sarcasm detection, and irony detection. In this respect, language specific models for English (monolingual) and Maltese-English (code-switched Maltese-English and monolingual Maltese) have been built. Deep neural network language models like BERT shall be fine-tuned to adapt to new domains, transfer knowledge from one language to another, and build new classification models. In this regard, multiple neural-based classification models for subjectivity, sentiment polarity, emotion, sarcasm, and irony, at a multilingual level using user-generated content in English, Maltese, and Maltese-English have already been published in (Cortis et al., 2021). Models capable of understanding English and Maltese data, both being Malta's official languages, can be used by governments for policy formulation, policy making, decision making, and decision taking. Multidimensional Social Opinion Mining provides a nuanced voice to the citizens and residents of Malta and hence leaves a positive impact on society at large.

Opinion Dimension	LR	LinearSVC	NuSVC	SVC	BNB	CNB	DT	RF
Subjectivity								
F1 score (weighted)								
Mean	0.839627	0.841091	0.845513	0.371596	0.772777	**0.854936**	0.817842	0.842926
Standard Deviation	0.103584	0.092145	0.096013	0.002719	0.15322	0.105658	0.112311	0.141601
Execution time (sec)	0.140372	0.126745	19.511326	18.196656	0.075907	0.024654	0.911396	11.830028
Balanced accuracy								
Mean	0.843608	0.842783	0.847955	0.5	0.802879	**0.864388**	0.83255	0.847062
Standard Deviation	0.088045	0.08498	0.084147	0	0.114555	0.09073	0.105097	0.119309
Execution time (sec)	0.088763	0.091463	19.070196	18.066252	0.055128	0.040290	0.844383	11.074797
Sentiment Polarity								
F1 score (weighted)								
Mean	0.689206	**0.739622**	0.725397	0.433592	0.593306	0.724719	0.711952	0.720501
Standard Deviation	0.081683	0.096397	0.106766	0.001532	0.060966	0.102363	0.089007	0.10021
Execution time (sec)	3.230092	0.266272	23.310936	16.025399	0.043515	0.036038	1.418103	12.771962
Balanced accuracy								
Mean	0.562462	**0.638019**	0.618941	0.333333	0.449516	0.612975	0.601	0.619531
Standard Deviation	0.063686	0.091922	0.101573	0	0.049415	0.08929	0.087626	0.101987
Execution time (sec)	2.763433	0.185026	22.411216	16.399088	0.030229	0.027661	1.324603	15.214964
Emotion								
F1 score (weighted)								
Mean	0.376882	0.427224	0.375519	0.234498	0.314026	**0.432851**	0.403896	0.418661
Standard Deviation	0.034389	0.054136	0.049605	0.002648	0.035831	0.047303	0.070764	0.06
Execution time (sec)	8.288645	0.411707	32.969826	21.907470	0.056324	0.036504	1.851777	17.749398
Balanced accuracy								
Mean	0.205188	0.275239	0.241458	0.125	0.162991	0.254581	0.246939	**0.276573**
Standard Deviation	0.022074	0.062415	0.05161	0	0.02325	0.031079	0.061356	0.054324
Execution time (sec)	7.956497	0.351134	32.464855	22.532657	0.044598	0.040448	2.101381	19.586962
Sarcasm								
F1 score (weighted)								
Mean	**0.931012**	0.929747	0.930699	**0.931012**	0.921376	0.9097	0.915169	**0.931012**
Standard Deviation	0.004388	0.006875	0.004848	0.004388	0.016343	0.036802	0.023135	0.004388
Execution time (sec)	0.107805	0.094377	14.096916	2.055357	0.058842	0.040891	1.042049	8.552041
Balanced accuracy								
Mean	0.5	0.498684	0.499671	0.5	0.507068	**0.530167**	0.491371	0.499671
Standard Deviation	0	0.003947	0.000987	0	0.035031	0.087631	0.027111	0.000987
Execution time (sec)	0.090132	0.085380	15.818028	1.977244	0.043882	0.035901	0.930696	8.509591
Irony								
F1 score (weighted)								
Mean	0.874091	0.87929	0.872834	0.874091	0.855613	**0.884021**	0.880597	0.873464
Standard Deviation	0.00409	0.009558	0.005784	0.00409	0.031979	0.042444	0.031066	0.004947
Execution time (sec)	0.092754	0.089761	12.690590	3.377020	0.040492	0.044879	1.090016	10.739472
Balanced accuracy								
Mean	0.5	0.518964	0.49863	0.5	0.507704	**0.611068**	0.584066	0.506458
Standard Deviation	0	0.030468	0.003139	0	0.034832	0.057851	0.049402	0.013006
Execution time (sec)	0.076793	0.091754	14.075315	3.323173	0.038205	0.032164	1.082346	10.587719

Table 3: Classification model results - Maltese-English and Maltese dataset

5. Acknowledgments

This research was conducted with the financial support of Science Foundation Ireland under Grant Agreement No. 13/RC/2106_P2 at the ADAPT SFI Research Centre at Dublin City University. ADAPT, the SFI Research Centre for AI-Driven Digital Content Technology, is funded by Science Foundation Ireland through the SFI Research Centres Programme.

6. Bibliographical References

Appidi, A. R., Srirangam, V. K., Suhas, D., and Shrivastava, M. (2020). Creation of corpus and analysis in code-mixed kannada-english twitter data for emotion prediction. In *Proceedings of the 28th International Conference on Computational Linguistics*, pages 6703–6709.

Bansal, S., Garimella, V., Suhane, A., Patro, J., and Mukherjee, A. (2020). Code-switching patterns can be an effective route to improve performance of downstream NLP applications: A case study of humour, sarcasm and hate speech detection. In *Proceedings of the 58th Annual Meeting of the Association for Computational Linguistics*, pages 1018–1023, Online, July. Association for Computational

Linguistics.

Bird, S., Klein, E., and Loper, E. (2009). *Natural language processing with Python: analyzing text with the natural language toolkit.* " O'Reilly Media, Inc.".

Breiman, L. (2001). Random forests. *Machine learning*, 45(1):5–32.

Brodersen, K. H., Ong, C. S., Stephan, K. E., and Buhmann, J. M. (2010). The balanced accuracy and its posterior distribution. In *2010 20th international conference on pattern recognition*, pages 3121–3124. IEEE.

Carvalho, J. and Plastino, A. (2021). On the evaluation and combination of state-of-the-art features in twitter sentiment analysis. *Artificial Intelligence Review*, 54(3):1887–1936.

Cateni, S., Colla, V., and Vannucci, M. (2014). A method for resampling imbalanced datasets in binary classification tasks for real-world problems. *Neurocomputing*, 135:32–41.

Chinchor, N. (1992). Muc-4 evaluation metrics. In *Proceedings of the 4th Conference on Message Understanding*, MUC4 '92, page 22–29, USA. Association for Computational Linguistics.

Cortes, C. and Vapnik, V. (1995). Support-vector networks. *Machine learning*, 20(3):273–297.

Cortis, K. and Davis, B. (2021a). A dataset of multidimensional and multilingual social opinions for malta's annual government budget. In *Proceedings of the International AAAI Conference on Web and Social Media*, volume 15, pages 971–981.

Cortis, K. and Davis, B. (2021b). Over a decade of social opinion mining: a systematic review. *Artificial intelligence review*, pages 1–93.

Cortis, K., Freitas, A., Daudert, T., Huerlimann, M., Zarrouk, M., Handschuh, S., and Davis, B. (2017). SemEval-2017 task 5: Fine-grained sentiment analysis on financial microblogs and news. In *Proceedings of the 11th International Workshop on Semantic Evaluation (SemEval-2017)*, pages 519–535, Vancouver, Canada, August. Association for Computational Linguistics.

Cortis, K., Verma, K., and Davis, B. (2021). Fine-tuning neural language models for multidimensional opinion mining of english-maltese social data. In *Proceedings of the International Conference on Recent Advances in Natural Language Processing (RANLP 2021)*, pages 309–314.

Devlin, J., Chang, M.-W., Lee, K., and Toutanova, K. (2018). Bert: Pre-training of deep bidirectional transformers for language understanding. *arXiv preprint arXiv:1810.04805*.

Gupta, U., Chatterjee, A., Srikanth, R., and Agrawal, P. (2017). A sentiment-and-semantics-based approach for emotion detection in textual conversations. *arXiv preprint arXiv:1707.06996*.

Hemmatian, F. and Sohrabi, M. K. (2019). A survey on classification techniques for opinion mining and sentiment analysis. *Artificial Intelligence Review*, 52(3):1495–1545.

Hilts, A. and Yu, E. (2010). Modeling social media support for the elicitation of citizen opinion. In *Proceedings of the International Workshop on Modeling Social Media*, pages 1–4.

Joulin, A., Grave, E., Bojanowski, P., and Mikolov, T. (2016). Bag of tricks for efficient text classification. *arXiv preprint arXiv:1607.01759*.

Kothari, A., Magdy, W., Darwish, K., Mourad, A., and Taei, A. (2013). Detecting comments on news articles in microblogs. In *Proceedings of the International AAAI Conference on Web and Social Media*, volume 7.

LeCun, Y., Boser, B. E., Denker, J. S., Henderson, D., Howard, R. E., Hubbard, W. E., and Jackel, L. D. (1990). Handwritten digit recognition with a back-propagation network. In *Advances in neural information processing systems*, pages 396–404.

Lewis, D. D. (1998). Naive (bayes) at forty: The independence assumption in information retrieval. In *European conference on machine learning*, pages 4–15. Springer.

Ligthart, A., Catal, C., and Tekinerdogan, B. (2021). Systematic reviews in sentiment analysis: a tertiary study. *Artificial Intelligence Review*, pages 1–57.

Liu, B. (2010). Sentiment analysis and subjectivity. In *Handbook of Natural Language Processing, Second Edition. Taylor and Francis Group, Boca*.

Mamta, Ekbal, A., Bhattacharyya, P., Srivastava, S., Kumar, A., and Saha, T. (2020). Multi-domain tweet corpora for sentiment analysis: Resource creation and evaluation. In *Proceedings of the 12th Language Resources and Evaluation Conference*, pages 5046–5054, Marseille, France, May. European Language Resources Association.

McCullagh, P. (1984). Generalized linear models. *European Journal of Operational Research*, 16(3):285–292.

Mikolov, T., Chen, K., Corrado, G., and Dean, J. (2013). Efficient estimation of word representations in vector space. *arXiv preprint arXiv:1301.3781*.

Mohammad, S., Bravo-Marquez, F., Salameh, M., and Kiritchenko, S. (2018). Semeval-2018 task 1: Affect in tweets. In *Proceedings of the 12th international workshop on semantic evaluation*, pages 1–17.

More, A. (2016). Survey of resampling techniques for improving classification performance in unbalanced datasets. *arXiv preprint arXiv:1608.06048*.

Padurariu, C. and Breaban, M. E. (2019). Dealing with data imbalance in text classification. *Procedia Computer Science*, 159:736–745.

Pang, B. and Lee, L. (2008). Opinion mining and sentiment analysis. *Foundations and Trends® in Information Retrieval*, 2(1-2):1–135, January.

Patwa, P., Aguilar, G., Kar, S., Pandey, S., PYKL, S., Gambäck, B., Chakraborty, T., Solorio, T., and Das,

A. (2020). Semeval-2020 task 9: Overview of sentiment analysis of code-mixed tweets. In *Proceedings of the 14th International Workshop on Semantic Evaluation (SemEval-2020)*, Barcelona, Spain, December. Association for Computational Linguistics.

Pennington, J., Socher, R., and Manning, C. D. (2014). Glove: Global vectors for word representation. In *Empirical Methods in Natural Language Processing (EMNLP)*, pages 1532–1543.

Pontiki, M., Galanis, D., Papageorgiou, H., Androutsopoulos, I., Manandhar, S., Al-Smadi, M., Al-Ayyoub, M., Zhao, Y., Qin, B., De Clercq, O., et al. (2016). Semeval-2016 task 5: Aspect based sentiment analysis. In *International workshop on semantic evaluation*, pages 19–30.

Quinlan, J. R. (1986). Induction of decision trees. *Machine learning*, 1(1):81–106.

Ravi, K. and Ravi, V. (2015). A survey on opinion mining and sentiment analysis: tasks, approaches and applications. *Knowledge-based systems*, 89:14–46.

Rosenthal, S., Farra, N., and Nakov, P. (2017). Semeval-2017 task 4: Sentiment analysis in twitter. In *Proceedings of the 11th international workshop on semantic evaluation (SemEval-2017)*, pages 502–518.

Salton, G. and McGill, M. J. (1986). Introduction to modern information retrieval.

scikit learn. a). Bernoulli naïve bayes. `https://scikit-learn.org/stable/modules/generated/sklearn.naive_bayes.BernoulliNB.html`.

scikit learn. b). Complement naïve bayes. `https://scikit-learn.org/stable/modules/generated/sklearn.naive_bayes.ComplementNB.html`.

scikit learn. c). Decision tree. `https://scikit-learn.org/stable/modules/tree.html`.

scikit learn. d). Linear support vector classification. `https://scikit-learn.org/stable/modules/generated/sklearn.svm.LinearSVC.html`.

scikit learn. e). Logistic regression. `https://scikit-learn.org/stable/modules/generated/sklearn.linear_model.LogisticRegression.html`.

scikit learn. f). Nu-support support vector classification. `https://scikit-learn.org/stable/modules/generated/sklearn.svm.NuSVC.html`.

scikit learn. g). Random forest. `https://scikit-learn.org/stable/modules/generated/sklearn.ensemble.RandomForestClassifier.html`.

scikit learn. h). Support vector classification. `https://scikit-learn.org/stable/modules/generated/sklearn.svm.SVC.html`.

Van Hee, C., Lefever, E., and Hoste, V. (2018). Semeval-2018 task 3: Irony detection in english tweets. In *Proceedings of The 12th International Workshop on Semantic Evaluation*, pages 39–50.

Vaswani, A., Shazeer, N., Parmar, N., Uszkoreit, J., Jones, L., Gomez, A. N., Kaiser, L., and Polosukhin, I. (2017). Attention is all you need. *arXiv preprint arXiv:1706.03762*.

Yimam, S. M., Alemayehu, H. M., Ayele, A., and Biemann, C. (2020). Exploring amharic sentiment analysis from social media texts: Building annotation tools and classification models. In *Proceedings of the 28th International Conference on Computational Linguistics*, pages 1048–1060.

Yu, H.-F., Huang, F.-L., and Lin, C.-J. (2011). Dual coordinate descent methods for logistic regression and maximum entropy models. *Machine Learning*, 85(1-2):41–75.

Proceedings of SIGUL2022 @LREC2022, pages 169–175
Marseille, 24-25 June 2022

Building Open-Source Speech Technology for Low-Resource Minority Languages with Sámi as an Example – Tools, Methods and Experiments

Katri Hiovain-Asikainen, Sjur Nørstebø Moshagen
Department of Language and Culture
UiT the Arctic University of Norway
firstname.lastname@uit.no

Abstract

This paper presents a work-in-progress report of an open-source speech technology project for indigenous Sámi languages. A less detailed description of this work has been presented in a more general paper about the whole *GiellaLT* language infrastructure, submitted to the LREC 2022 main conference. At this stage, we have designed and collected a text corpus specifically for developing speech technology applications, namely Text-to-speech (TTS) and Automatic speech recognition (ASR) for the Lule and North Sámi languages. We have also piloted and experimented with different speech synthesis technologies using a miniature speech corpus as well as developed tools for effective processing of large spoken corpora. Additionally, we discuss effective and mindful use of the speech corpus and also possibilities to use found/archive materials for training an ASR model for these languages.

Keywords: speech corpus, speech processing, minority languages, indigenous languages, TTS, ASR, speech technology

1. Introduction

The current paper will describe ongoing work for developing open-source speech technology applications for two Sámi languages, Lule and North Sámi. The Sámi languages, belonging to the Uralic language family, are related to, e.g. Finnish and Estonian and thus share some structural and lexical features. Lule and North Sámi are neighboring languages, spoken in the northernmost parts of Scandinavia. While Lule Sámi is spoken in Norway and Sweden, North Sámi is spoken in three countries: Norway, Sweden and Finland. For both languages, generally all speakers are bilingual in Sámi and at least one of the majority languages: Norwegian, Swedish and Finnish. The two languages are structurally similar, and after some training, they are mutually intelligible to some extent. However, as part of language revitalization and preservation as well as accelerating digitalization, separate languages need separate language and speech technology tools to meet the needs of modern language users.

Lule and North Sámi differ remarkably in terms of the amount of speakers or language users. According to Ethnologue (Lewis, 2009), North Sámi has by far the largest number of language users among the Sámi languages: 25 000 in all three countries. Lule Sámi, on the other hand, has considerably fewer speakers: total of 2000 in both countries it is spoken in. All Sámi languages are classified as endangered by UNESCO (Moseley, 2010) and Lule Sámi as severely endangered. Perhaps consequently, as North Sámi has most language users among the Sámi languages, it has also most language resources and tools available. An infrastructure of dictionaries, morphological analyzers, spell checkers and language learning tools etc. have been maintained and developed since 2001 by the Divvun and Giellatekno groups[1].

A Text-to-speech tool is made to be able to synthesize intelligible speech output from any unseen text input in a particular language. A key objective for developing speech technology tools for indigenous languages generally is to meet the needs of modern language users in all language communities equally. For the Sámi languages, this would mean equal possibilities to use Sámi in the same contexts as the majority languages are being used. In this way, developing speech and language technology tools for the Sámi languages also contribute to the revitalisation of these languages. Additionally, speech technology tools are important for many language users, also those with special needs. These include language learners (see, e.g., (Yaneva, 2021)), people with dyslexia, vision impaired individuals, (native) users of the language that are not used to read Sámi etc. Additionally, speech technology is bringing more accessibility to many kinds of contents and utilities: a user can for example choose to listen to the news instead of reading the text, or a speech synthesis tool could be integrated into an online dictionary to allow listening to the correct pronunciations of the words.

The first Text-to-speech (TTS) tool for the Sámi languages was developed in 2015 for North Sámi by Divvun and Acapela[2]. This tool was produced as closed-source and thus neither the framework used to develop the tool nor the speech corpus used for it are publicly available[3]. Also, the company has ended support for certain operating systems, blocking access to

[1] https://giellatekno.uit.no/, https://divvun.no/fi/

[2] `https://divvun.no/fi/tale/tale.html`

[3] We hope to be able to make the speech corpus publicly available in the future.

the voices for new users on these operating systems. For this reason, we are now working on a modern, open-source TTS system that could be openly available for anyone who wants to develop speech technology for minority languages. The system will make all language-independent parts integrated into the larger GiellaLT infrastructure[4], ensuring that maintenance and updates are done regularly. When finished, it will also ensure that all voices will be available on all supported platforms, and that new platforms will be available to all existing voices. The research and development groups behind the GiellaLT infrastructure have existed for about twenty years, and given the governmental support for the Sami languages, the sustainability prospects are good.

2. Requirements and Related Works

Developing TTS for an indigenous language with few resources (such as grammars, language learning books or phonetic descriptions) available can be challenging. Such resources are important in designing the project, building and checking the corpora and evaluating the TTS output phonetically. If a phonetic description of the language is scarce or it is made within a different framework, one might need to make a description from scratch. Any linguistic description is useful for this, but for speech technology purposes, what is important is to have at least some amount of speech material and corresponding text, provided by a native speaker of the language. In this way, it is possible to study the relationship between text and speech in a particular language and to produce a phonetic description in a form of a grapheme-to-phoneme mapping. This mapping (or *text-to-IPA* rule set) can already be used to build a very simple and "old-fashioned" but still usable TTS application, such as the Espeak formant synthesis (Kastrati et al., 2014; Pronk et al., 2013). As this framework does not require a speech corpus but only a set of phonetic and phonological rules, any language can be added to the list of the languages covered by Espeak, only utilising the knowledge of native speakers. The downside of this is that while it might be a working synthesizer, the users' expectations for the quality of a TTS system are very high due to the examples from well-resourced languages such as English.
The development of a TTS system as a whole requires multidisciplinary input from fields like natural language processing (NLP), phonetics and phonology, machine learning (ML) and digital signal processing (DSP). Tasks connected to NLP are important in developing the text front-end for the TTS – these are, for example, automatically converting numbers and abbreviations to full words in a correct way. Phonetics and phonology are essential in corpus design, making text-to-IPA rules and evaluating the TTS output. Also, by using phonetic annotations of the texts, it is possible to address phenomena that are not visible in the orthographic texts. The importance of ML is growing in the field of speech technology, as neural networks are used to model the acoustics of human speech, allowing for realistic and natural-sounding TTS. Procedures related to DSP are important in (pre)processing the audio data: these include filtering, resampling and normalizing the corpus for suitable audio quality. Furthermore, the resulting TTS system can be used in developing more advanced speech technology frameworks, such as dialogue systems (see, e.g. Jokinen et al. (2017; Wilcock et al. (2017; Trong et al. (2019)) and various kinds of mobile applications.
Some of the typological and phonetic features of for example North and Lule Sámi are setting challenges in building a high quality TTS. One of these is the ternary quantity system in both of these languages. In both North and Lule Sámi, there are triplets of word forms that differ only by the quantity, the length of the intervocalic consonant in a disyllabic foot. The orthography does not differentiate between the Quantity 3 (Q3) and Quantity 2 (Q2) forms in all contexts, and the long (Q2) and overlong (Q3) geminates are written identically in those cases (see Tables 1 and 2 for examples). Our first experiments on building an open-sourced TTS have shown that a simple rule-based formant synthesis (such as Espeak) is not able to fully cover for this phonetic phenomenon without a separate syntactically disambiguated text-processing pipeline.

At present, several minority language communities with a weak literary tradition try to strengthen the position of the language in society. In doing so, they find themselves in a situation lacking the infrastructure needed to do so, infrastructure that majority language speakers take for granted. Minority language communities do not equally benefit from the technological advances, compared to languages like English or Mandarin. By adapting existing state-of-the-art speech technology to a form suitable for low-resource languages, we contribute to the strengthening the language infrastructure for the Sámi languages and widening the modalities where the languages can be used.
In what follows, we present our plans for our Sámi TTS project and discuss some directions for our future work.

3. Methodology

3.1. Building the Corpora

3.1.1. Text Corpus

Building a corpus with good quality requires selecting native language texts from different domains to build a special-purpose corpus (i.e. for speech technology) from scratch.
Texts in Sámi languages are published daily in both media and by public bodies required to communicate in writing in Sámi. Since most of the publishers (typically online) have to provide their site in both Sámi and the majority languages. Having gathered text since 2005,

[4] giellalt.github.io, github.com/divvun

the largest Sámi corpus is the one for North Sámi, with 38.94 million tokens. The North Sámi corpus is a quite big corpus for an indigenous language, but on the other hand small compared to majority languages.
Our aim is to have a balanced corpus for the other Sámi languages as well, with regard to regional dialects of the same language. As the majority of North Sámi speakers are in Norway, and the legal protection for the Sámi languages is stronger in Norway than in Sweden, both our North Sámi and our Lule Sámi corpus therefore mostly consist of text written in Norway. This has consequences for some of the tools we are developing, including TTS: the synthesis will reflect the characteristics of the Norwegian variety better.

3.1.2. Speech Corpus

The modern approaches to TTS involve machine learning and complex modelling of speech, which brings in the requirement for relatively big amounts of speech data to build the models from. This is because in a data-driven or *corpus-based* speech synthesis, that utilize deep neural networks, the association between textual features and acoustic parameters is learned directly from paired data – the sentence-long sound files and the corresponding texts. The sum of the learned knowledge from the paired data construct the acoustic model (see, e.g., Watts et al. (2016)). This is especially the case in the modern end-to-end or sequence-to-sequence approaches that merge the front-end to the neural model, such as in the Tacotron 2 framework (Shen et al., 2018).
The building of the speech corpus starts from collecting a suitable multi-domain text corpus which corresponds to at least 10 hours of recorded read speech, that has been shown to be enough to achieve an end-user suitable TTS system for North Sámi (Makashova, 2021). This amount is also going to be recorded to build our Lule Sámi voice. Our plan is to build both male and female voices and thus altogether 20 hours of speech is going to be recorded.
A question of *data efficiency* has been discussed in a new study by Săracu and Stan (2021). This study evaluated the amount of data required by the Tacotron 2 speech synthesis model to produce good quality output, and showed that if the training data is carefully constructed to present all common graphemes in a language, the data requirement can be significantly lowered. In the present project, we have checked that our corpus covers all important phonological contrasts and sound combinations by calculating frequencies of all trigrams in our corpus. Additionally, we calculated frequencies of all consonant gradation patterns from the Lule Sámi TTS corpus, using a grammatical description of the language (Spiik, 1989). In the case of missing gradation patterns, we added additional sentences to cover for these as well.
In the present project, we focus on open-source methodologies, in which case it is important to build a collection of open source texts as well, with a CC-BY (Creative Commons) licence.

To build our new TTS text corpus, we reused a part of the Lule Sámi gold corpus[5] developed in 2013 within the GiellaLT community, and collected additional texts of various text styles we knew to be well written. The resulting Lule Sámi text corpus for TTS consists of text styles such as news, educational, parliament etc. with altogether over 74,000 words (see Figure 4 for word counts per domain).

3.2. Corpus Processing and Modeling

When using machine-learning methods to build up a speech model for TTS, the quality of the recordings has to be excellent, i.e., room reverberation or background noise has to be avoided in the recordings, because the noise would be modelled as well. Thus, the recordings have to be done in a sound-treated room with professional microphones and recording set-up. The minimal requirement for the audio recording is so-called *CD quality* (44.1 kHz sample, 16-bit).

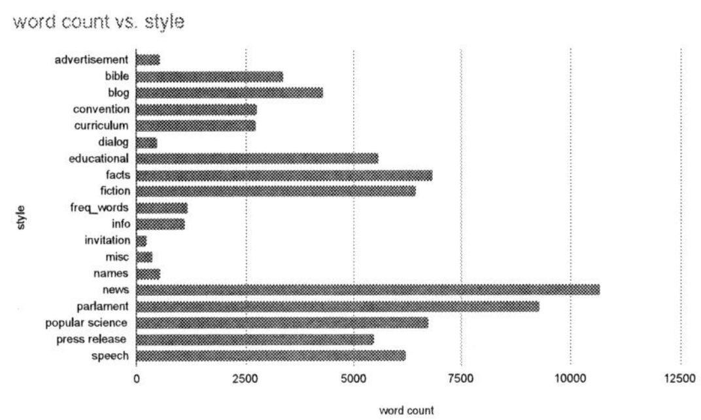

Figure 1: The word counts per style of the Lule Sámi text corpus for TTS. Altogether, 74,737 words that correspond roughly to 12.46 hrs of speech recordings.

3.2.1. Text Processing

Most orthographies are underspecified with respect to the pronunciation of the text. This creates interesting questions when converting a standard orthographic text to audio waves. In the cases of Lule and North Sámi there is a class of nouns where consonant gradation (i.e. length alternation) is not expressed in the orthography, while still being grammatically crucial, as it is the sole marker of the difference between different syntactic functions, especially *singular nominative* vs *singular genitive*, and for North Sámi also *singular accusative*. That is, for this class of nouns the only difference between the subject and the possessor or (for North Sámi) between the subject and the object, is expressed through a length distinction that is *not* present in the standard orthography, as seen in Tables 1 and 2. This distinction is phonetically significant, as shown in a number of acoustic phonetic studies, such as in Magga

[5] gtsvn.uit.no/freecorpus/goldstandard/converted/smj/

(1984) and Hiovain et al. (2020) for North Sámi and Fangel-Gustavson et al. (2014) for Lule Sámi.
The distinction has to be recreated when converting the orthographic text to a phonemic representation. There are also other underspecifications in the orthography, but these are the most crucial.

	Orth.	IPA	Transl.
Q3	*oarre*	[ʔo͡ɑrːrɪɛ]	'a squirrel' Nom.Sg
Q2	*oarre*	[ʔoɑrːɪɛ]	'a squirrel's' Gen.Sg
			'a reason' Nom.Sg
Q1	*oare*	[ʔoɑrɪɛ]	'a reason's' Gen.Sg

Table 1: Ternary length contrast of consonants in Lule Sámi, underspecified in the orthography. Abbreviations: Q3 – overlong, Q2 – long, Q1 – short. Examples originally presented in Fangel-Gustavson et al. (2014).

	Orth.	IPA	Transl.
Q3	*beassi*	[pe͡æsːsɪ]	'birchbark' Nom.Sg
Q2	*beassi*	[peæsːɪ]	'birchbark' Acc.Sg
			'(bird's) nest' Nom.Sg
Q1	*beasi*	[peæsɪ]	'(bird's) nest' Acc.Sg

Table 2: Ternary length contrast of consonants in North Sámi, underspecified in the orthography. Abbreviations as in Table 1.

The foundation for all linguistic processing and thus also for the text processing for speech technology in the *GiellaLT* infrastructure is the morphological analyser, built using formalisms from Xerox. From these source files, the *GiellaLT* infrastructure creates *finite state transducers* (FST's) using one of three supported FST compilers: Xerox tools (Beesley and Karttunen, 2003), *HFST* (Lindén et al., 2013), or Foma (Hulden, 2009). All language models are written as rule-based, full form lexicons with explicit morphological descriptions and morphophonological alternations. This makes it possible to create language models for any language, including minority and indigenous languages with few or non-existing digital resources.
FST's are useful in speech technology especially in the task of converting orthographic texts to IPA characters, by using an FST model of the language to analyze the corpus texts. The length contrast is encoded in the FST model at an intermediate level, but during compilation, this information is lost. We have enhanced the code for the *HFST* utility `hfst-pmatch` to allow the analyser/-tokeniser FST to be an on-the-fly composition of two separate FST's, and outputting that intermediate string representation, in effect creating a fake three-tape FST. With the morphological analysis of all tokens available, we can proceed by disambiguating the sentence, and leaving only the analyses that fit the morphosyntactic context. The end result is that we will be left with the proper analysis (subject or object) *and* with information of the proper length of the word form, to be fed to the module for conversion to IPA. As always, this is done using rule-based components, to have full control of every step and be able to correct errors in the IPA transcription. There is still a fallback module for cases of unknown words and names.
The IPA transcription provided by the FST technology described above can further improve the accuracy of the TTS, especially for the alignment between sounds and characters. When training a speech model with the IPA transcriptions as text input instead of standard orthography, in a deep neural network structure, the letter-to-sound correspondence will likely be more transparent, especially with ternary quantity cases described above. This rule-based approach, reusing many components from other parts of the *GiellaLT* infrastructure, also means that high quality speech synthesis is within reach for not only Sámi languages, but for other low-resource languages as well.

3.2.2. Experiments with Different TTS Frameworks

We have experimented with two different open source ML based TTS methodologies: Ossian (Suni et al., 2014) and a *Tacotron implementation* (largely based on Shen et al. (2018)), specially adapted for low-resource languages, like the Sámi languages (Makashova, 2021). Both of these methodologies require standard preprocessing procedures such as splitting the training data into sentence-long files as well as some sound filtering and normalisation techniques to ensure good quality and accuracy of the speech modeling.
The texts have to accurately match the corresponding audio files for the modelling to be successful, thus, a text normalisation procedure (part of the front-end) has to be conducted for the whole data. This covers, e.g., converting numbers, acronyms and abbreviations to orthographic text. Also, as explained in Section 3.2.1., it is useful to make a letter to sound (or text-to-IPA) rule mapping of a given language as this makes the relationship between speech and the corresponding text (when used as training data for speech modeling) more transparent.
In our first experiment, we used a data set consisting of approximately one hour of speech from a native speaker of Lule Sámi, using the Ossian TTS. Ossian consists of a rule-based, statistical front-end and a deep neural network-based acoustic modelling. We used Ossian with the HTS (HMM/DNN-based Speech Synthesis System, see also Zen et al. (2007)) recipe to train an experimental Lule Sámi voice, generating relatively intelligible speech (see Figure 2 for a spectrogram image of a sample sentence).
With one hour of training data and an HP ZBook 15 G6 (Intel i7 CPU), it took approximately 3 hours to train an experimental Lule Sámi voice. Although Ossian TTS or similar would technically be more suitable for a low-resource setup, its machine-like voice quality does not meet the requirements of a modern speech technology user. However, from this experiment, it was clear that

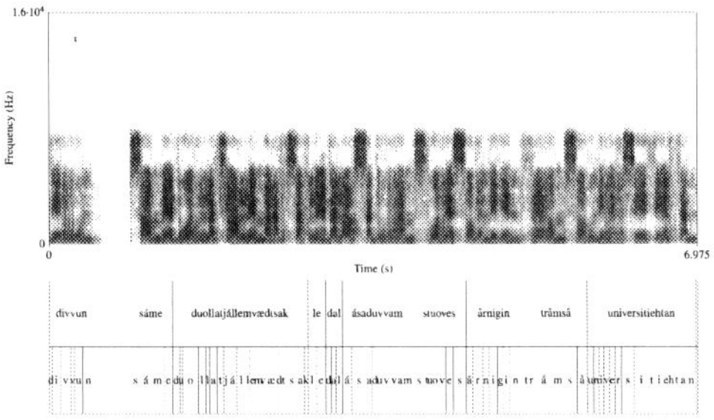

Figure 2: A spectrogram of a sample sentence from the Ossian TTS model trained on 1 hour of Lule Sámi speech. Sentence text: *"Divvun, sáme duollatjállemvædtsak, le dal ásaduvvam stuoves årnigin Tråmså universitiehtan."*

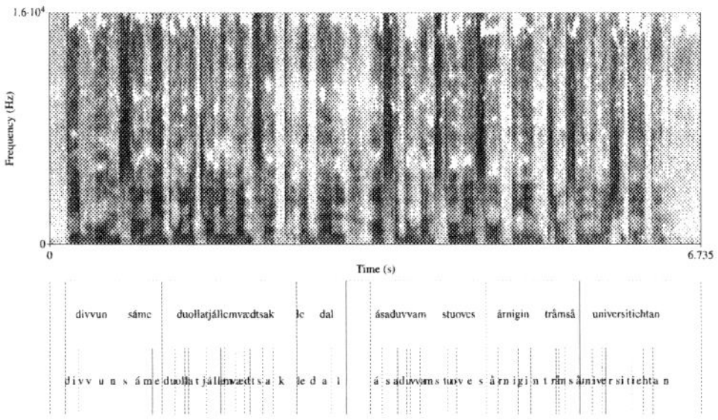

Figure 3: A spectrogram of a sample sentence from a human native speaker of Lule Sámi, reading the exact same sentence as in the Ossian sample.

for getting better results, more training data would be needed, but piloting the methods using small experimental data gives us better insight on the requirements for the speech corpus, i.e. the size and audio quality of the data.

As the expectations for the quality of TTS are very high due to the examples from well-resourced languages such as English, using a neural vocoder (such as *WaveNet*, Oord et al. (2016) or *WaveGlow*) that produces realistic, human-like speech is necessary for good usability and user experience.

As described in Makashova (2021), the North Sámi TTS voice was trained with a female voice, data set consisting of 3500 training sentences. The TTS model consisted of four components: Tacotron, ForwardTacotron, Tacotron2 and WaveGlow, the two latter ones from the official Nvidia repository. The training of this successful and good quality Tacotron model and the WaveGlow model took one month, and for the ForwardTacotron for three days, on a single GPU. In Divvun, we have access to the Norwegian academic high-performance computing and storage service (Sigma2) and thus the training time could be significantly shorter.

As can be seen from comparing the spectrograms in

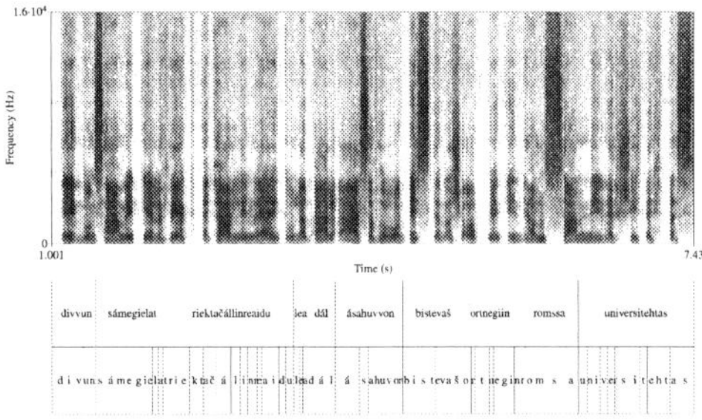

Figure 4: A spectrogram of a sample sentence generated using a Tacotron model of North Sámi. The text is the North Sámi equivalent of the Lule Sámi sentence in the previous figures: *"Divvun, sámegielat riektačállinreaidu, lea dál ásahuvvon bistevaš ortnegiin Romssa Universitehtas."*

Figures 2, 3 and 4, the Tacotron sample is also visually similar to the human speech in Figure 3. The Ossian sample has a lot lower frequency range compared to the Tacotron and human samples, and the formant transitions are not smooth. Figure 4 also shows the promising quality of the Tacotron sample: with few hours of training data, realistic and good quality TTS is achievable. Thus, a similar workflow, following the North Sámi one for training the Lule Sámi TTS voice has been planned and started in our project.

It has to be taken into account that the environmental cost for the complex modelling of speech is high in terms of electricity and technical components such as graphical processing units (GPUs). For reducing these costs, there are possibilities to adapt existing speech models by training the models further with additional data and pre-trained models from a "neighbouring" language. This so-called *transfer learning* (Tu et al., 2019; Debnath et al., 2020) allows for utilising smaller data sets for training, making it possible, for example, to use the North Sámi TTS model as the starting point for the Lule Sámi TTS.

At this point, we have made some experiments on a TTS model using transfer learning between North and Lule Sámi. With a miniature data set (approx. one hour of speech data recorded with a cell phone), we were able to train a Lule Sámi voice, but the quality of the output showed that this corpus did not cover all necessary phonemes of the language and thus there were some phonological inaccuracies. Moreover, as the North and Lule Sámi orthographies are somewhat different (for example, the alveolar fricative sound written in English as *sh*, is written as *š* in North Sámi, and as *sj* in Lule Sámi), there were errors in this kind of cases. By converting both North and Lule Sámi texts to IPA characters these differences could be "eliminated" and thus the transfer learning would presumably be more successful.

A good quality speech corpus of Lule Sámi is going to be produced by autumn 2022. Having experimented with different frameworks and experimental data sets, we have now the required tools and technologies to proceed quickly to producing the end-user suitable TTS for Sámi.

3.3. Future Work: Approaches to Automatic Speech Recognition

In addition to TTS, we are working towards developing a tool for *automatic speech recognition* (ASR) for Sámi. This section describes materials and experiments only for North Sámi, but in the future, we hope to expand our work to Lule Sámi ASR as well.

In Makashova (2021), TTS and ASR models were trained simultaneously in a dual transformation loop, using the same *read speech* data set, corresponding to only six hours of speech from two speakers, three hours each. The ASR model in this work was based on the Wav2Vec model which is a part of the HuggingFace library. The model was trained for 30 000 steps and it reached a WER (Word-Error-Rate) of 41% and 0.5 loss. The most common error types in the ASR predictions seem to be in word boundaries (**earáláhkai – eará láhkái* and in lengths of some sounds (**rinškit – rinškkit*). However, these kinds of errors would be easy to correct using Divvun's spell checking software.

One of the most important differences between training the TTS and ASR models would be that for TTS, the training material needs to be very clean in terms of sound quality and there needs to be as many recordings from a single speaker as possible. For ASR, on the other hand, the recorded materials can be of poorer sound quality and preferably from multiple speakers and from different areal varieties of a language as long as there are good transcriptions of the speech.

State-of-the-art ASR frameworks normally require up to 10,000 hours of multi-speaker data for training reliable and universal models that are able to generalise to any unseen speaker (Hannun et al., 2014). As collecting these amounts of data from small minority languages is not a realistic goal, alternatives such as utilising existing archive materials can be considered for developing speech technology for Sámi. These are provided by, e.g., *The language bank of Finland* and *The language bank of Norway*. These archive materials contain spontaneous, transcribed spoken materials from various dialects and dozens of North Sámi speakers.

The huge amounts of speech data normally used for ASR thus might require *massive* online data sourcing campaigns, such as the ongoing *Lahjoita puhetta – "Donate your speech"*[6] project for developing Finnish ASR. A similar campaign but in a smaller scale could be considered for the Sámi languages.

The first experiments on using the ASR model from (Makashova, 2021) to predict unseen *spontaneous* North Sámi speech have been promising and there is ongoing work on further development of an ASR tool.

We believe such a tool will contribute to the documentation and to better usability of any untranscribed Sámi archive speech corpora. By providing automatic text transcriptions of the materials, they could be easily searchable and thus utilized for, e.g. linguistic research. Additionally, ASR has an important role in modern language-learning applications that have spoken language exercises, such as in Duolingo (Teske, 2017).

4. Conclusion

In summary, the procedures and pipelines described above could be applied to any (minority) language with a low-resource setting, in the task of developing speech technology applications. Most of the applications discussed here can be piloted with or further developed with relatively small data sets (even with < 10 hrs of paired data), compared to the amounts of data used for respective tools for majority languages. This is largely possible thanks to the available open source materials and technologies, especially those relying on, e.g., *transfer learning* methodologies that allow for adapting speech models between related/similar languages.

Additionally, Cooper (2019) suggests that for low-resource languages, certain types of *found data* could be used to build TTS, instead of collecting a synthesis corpus from scratch. In this research, non-traditional sources of data such as (read) ASR data, radio broadcast news and audio books were used to develop usable and natural sounding TTS.

Finally, for tasks like TTS, if a speech corpus must be built from scratch, it has to be designed to prioritise quality over quantity of the corpus. We ensure a good quality and multi-purpose speech corpus by working with professional voice talents and language experts that are native speakers of the language. Additionally, by making the speech corpus used for developing TTS openly available, future needs to collect similar corpora are reduced.

Bibliographical References

Beesley, K. R. and Karttunen, L. (2003). Finite-state morphology: Xerox tools and techniques. *CSLI, Stanford*.

Cooper, E. (2019). *Text-to-speech synthesis using found data for low-resource languages*. Columbia University.

Debnath, A., Patil, S. S., Nadiger, G., and Ganesan, R. A. (2020). Low-resource end-to-end sanskrit tts using tacotron2, waveglow and transfer learning. In *2020 IEEE 17th India Council International Conference (INDICON)*, pages 1–5. IEEE.

Fangel-Gustavson, N., Ridouane, R., and Morén-Duolljá, B. (2014). Quantity contrast in Lule Saami: A three-way system. In *Proceedings of the 10th International Seminar on Speech production*, pages 106–109.

[6] yle.fi/aihe/lahjoita-puhetta

Hannun, A., Case, C., Casper, J., Catanzaro, B., Diamos, G., Elsen, E., Prenger, R., Satheesh, S., Sengupta, S., Coates, A., et al. (2014). Deep speech: Scaling up end-to-end speech recognition. *arXiv preprint arXiv:1412.5567*.

Hiovain, K., Vainio, M. T., and Šimko, J. (2020). Dialectal variation of duration patterns in Finnmark North Sámi quantity. *The Journal of the Acoustical Society of America*, 147(4):2817–2828.

Hulden, M. (2009). Foma: a finite-state compiler and library. In *Proceedings of the Demonstrations Session at EACL 2009*, pages 29–32.

Jokinen, K., Hiovain, K., Laxström, N., Rauhala, I., and Wilcock, G. (2017). Digisami and digital natives: Interaction technology for the North Sami language. In *Dialogues with social robots*, pages 3–19. Springer.

Kastrati, R., Hamiti, M., and Abazi, L. (2014). The opportunity of using espeak as text-to-speech synthesizer for Albanian language. In *Proceedings of the 15th International Conference on Computer Systems and Technologies*, pages 179–186.

M. Paul Lewis, editor. (2009). *Ethnologue: Languages of the World*. SIL International, Dallas, TX, USA, sixteenth edition.

Lindén, K., Axelson, E., Drobac, S., Hardwick, S., Kuokkala, J., Niemi, J., Pirinen, T. A., and Silfverberg, M. (2013). Hfst—a system for creating nlp tools. In *International workshop on systems and frameworks for computational morphology*, pages 53–71. Springer.

Magga, T. (1984). *Duration in the quantity of bisyllabics in the Guovdageaidnu dialect of North Lappish*, volume 11. University of Oulu.

Makashova, L. (2021). Speech synthesis and recognition for a low-resource language: Connecting TTS and ASR for mutual benefit. Master's thesis, University of Gothenburg.

Moseley, C. (2010). *Atlas of the World's Languages in Danger*. Unesco.

Oord, A. v. d., Dieleman, S., Zen, H., Simonyan, K., Vinyals, O., Graves, A., Kalchbrenner, N., Senior, A., and Kavukcuoglu, K. (2016). Wavenet: A generative model for raw audio. *arXiv preprint arXiv:1609.03499*.

Pronk, R., Intelligentie, B. O. K., and Weenink, D. D. (2013). Adding Japanese language synthesis support to the espeak system. *University of Amsterdam*.

Săracu, G. and Stan, A. (2021). An analysis of the data efficiency in Tacotron2 speech synthesis system. In *2021 International Conference on Speech Technology and Human-Computer Dialogue (SpeD)*, pages 172–176. IEEE.

Shen, J., Pang, R., Weiss, R. J., Schuster, M., Jaitly, N., Yang, Z., Chen, Z., Zhang, Y., Wang, Y., Skerrv-Ryan, R., et al. (2018). Natural tts synthesis by conditioning WaveNet on mel spectrogram predictions. In *2018 IEEE international conference on acoustics, speech and signal processing (ICASSP)*, pages 4779–4783. IEEE.

Spiik, N. E. (1989). *Lulesamisk grammatik*. Sameskolstyrelsen.

Suni, A., Raitio, T., Gowda, D., Karhila, R., Gibson, M., and Watts, O. (2014). The simple4all entry to the Blizzard Challenge 2014. In *Proc. Blizzard Challenge*. Citeseer.

Teske, K. (2017). Duolingo. *calico journal*, 34(3):393–401.

Trong, T. N., Jokinen, K., and Hautamäki, V. (2019). Enabling spoken dialogue systems for low-resourced languages—end-to-end dialect recognition for North Sami. In *9th International Workshop on Spoken Dialogue System Technology*, pages 221–235. Springer.

Tu, T., Chen, Y.-J., Yeh, C.-c., and Lee, H.-Y. (2019). End-to-end text-to-speech for low-resource languages by cross-lingual transfer learning. *arXiv preprint arXiv:1904.06508*.

Watts, O., Henter, G. E., Merritt, T., Wu, Z., and King, S. (2016). From HMMs to DNNs: where do the improvements come from? In *2016 IEEE International Conference on Acoustics, Speech and Signal Processing (ICASSP)*, pages 5505–5509. IEEE.

Wilcock, G., Laxström, N., Leinonen, J., Smit, P., Kurimo, M., and Jokinen, K. (2017). Towards samitalk: a Sami-speaking robot linked to Sami wikipedia. In *Dialogues with Social Robots*, pages 343–351. Springer.

Yaneva, A. (2021). Speech technologies applied to second language learning. A use case on Bulgarian. Bachelor's thesis.

Zen, H., Nose, T., Yamagishi, J., Sako, S., Masuko, T., Black, A. W., and Tokuda, K. (2007). The HMM-based speech synthesis system (hts) version 2.0. In *SSW*, pages 294–299. Citeseer.

Proceedings of SIGUL2022 @LREC2022, pages 176–184
Marseille, 24-25 June 2022

Investigating the Quality of Static Anchor Embeddings from Transformers for Under-Resourced Languages

Pranaydeep Singh, Orphée De Clercq, Els Lefever
LT3, Language and Translation Technology Team
Department of Translation, Interpreting and Communication – Ghent University
Groot-Brittanniëlaan 45, 9000 Ghent, Belgium
{firstname.lastname}@ugent.be

Abstract

This paper reports on experiments for cross-lingual transfer using the anchor-based approach of Schuster et al. (2019) for English and a low-resourced language, namely Hindi. For the sake of comparison, we also evaluate the approach on three very different higher-resourced languages, viz. Dutch, Russian and Chinese. Initially designed for ELMo embeddings, we analyze the approach for the more recent BERT family of transformers for a variety of tasks, both mono and cross-lingual. The results largely prove that like most other cross-lingual transfer approaches, the static anchor approach is underwhelming for the low-resource language, while performing adequately for the higher resourced ones. We attempt to provide insights into both the quality of the anchors, and the performance for low-shot cross-lingual transfer to better understand this performance gap. We make the extracted anchors and the modified train and test sets available for future research at https://github.com/pranaydeeps/Vyaapak

Keywords: cross-lingual transfer, bilingual lexicon induction, natural language inference

1. Introduction

Despite the great progress witnessed in recent years for various NLP tasks, low(er)-resourced languages are often lagging behind because of data scarcity. To overcome this lack of resources, researchers have started to investigate the use of cross-lingual information, where knowledge or data from a rich-resourced language, like English, is used to improve the modeling in a low(er)-resourced target language. With the new dawn of extremely data hungry (pre-trained) transformers, the field of cross-lingual knowledge transfer has become even more effective, since large pre-trained models are not always available for a certain language or task.

The idea of cross-lingual embeddings originally stems from the idea of Mikolov et al. (2013) that vector spaces in different languages share a certain similarity, and that a projection can be learned from one language to another. A lot of research has been proposed to perform cross-lingual alignment (see Section 2 for an overview). The most recent approaches incorporating contextual embeddings, such as multilingual BERT (mBERT, Devlin et al. (2019)) and XLM (Conneau and Lample, 2019) apply joint training on multiple languages, obtaining very promissing results for a wide range of cross-lingual tasks. Main drawback of these approaches is that they require a huge amount of processing time and power, which makes them almost impossible to retrain for additional languages. In addition, research has shown that low-resourced languages are under-represented in joint models like mBERT and perform poorly on downstream tasks compared to high-resourced languages (Wu and Dredze, 2020).

The approach under investigation here has initially been proposed by Schuster et al. (2019). They demonstrate that contextual embeddings can be treated as having a static anchor component, and a dynamic context component for every token. In this paper, we revisit and investigate the potential of this static anchor component for the cross-lingual transfer of transformer representations for under-represented languages, Hindi in this case. We compare all results with a set of control target languages having more resources and which are either closely (Dutch) or more distantly related (Russian, Chinese) to the source language English. Although a language like Hindi has a large number of native speakers (around 370 million worldwide), NLP researchers consider a language to be low-resourced when it is difficult to gather corpora or tools for that specific language (e.g. the size of the Wikipedia available for training language models (Wu and Dredze, 2020)).

We extend the original anchor-based approach in several ways. First, up to date the original approach has not been evaluated for BERT or other language models from the transformer family since it was proposed in a pre-transformers era. Second, it has only been evaluated on a set of higher-resourced Western European languages, and not on under-resourced languages, such as Hindi. Third, the original work demonstrated its use case solely for dependency parsing, while we evaluate the quality of the anchors for two sets of tasks: (1) monolingual tasks: Word Polarity Prediction, and (2) cross-lingual tasks: Bilingual Lexicon Induction (a lexical task) and zero-shot Natural Language Inference (a sentence-based task). For each task, we compare our approach to the state-of-the-art methodologies. We provide a detailed overview of all experimental results

and also attempt to analyze in detail the inherent drawbacks and failures of the approach.
The remainder of this paper is organized as follows. Section 2 describes the related research on cross-lingual approaches, whereas Section 3 further elaborates the anchor-based approach we extended to obtain cross-lingual representations from pre-trained transformers. Section 4 gives an overview of the experimental setup and results, both for the mono and cross-lingual downstream tasks. Section 5 provides a qualitative analysis and discussion, while Section 6 ends this paper with concluding remarks and indications for future research.

2. Related Research

There are various research strands using cross-lingual information to circumvent the lack of resources in a given target language.
A first line of research uses machine translation (MT) systems to map lexicons or labeled data to other languages (e.g., (Mihalcea et al., 2007) for the task of Sentiment Analysis). Balahur and Turchi (2014), however, showed that working with translated data implies an incremented number of features, sparseness and noise in the data for classification. They also revealed that the quality of these methods largely depends on the availability of large parallel corpora for training the MT system, which are often lacking for low-resourced languages. Related approaches only use parallel data without building machine translation systems. Rasooli et al. (2018) used annotation projection to project supervised labels from the source languages to the target language and a direct transfer approach to develop sentiment analysis systems.
Other approaches extract paired sentences from large parallel corpora to learn bilingual embeddings. Chandar et al. (2014), for instance, explored the use of autoencoder-based methods for learning vectorial word representations that are aligned between the two languages without relying on word-level alignments. They reported state-of-the-art performance for the task of cross-language text classification. In sum, all these approaches require large amounts of high-quality parallel data, which are often lacking for low-resourced languages.
Another promising line of research, one that does not require large parallel corpora, are cross-lingual embeddings. These cross-lingual embeddings, which are obtained by mapping monolingual word embeddings into a common space, have already been successfully applied for low-resourced languages (Duong et al., 2016). The concept entails the possibility of learning a perfect mapping by traversing between vector spaces in different languages. In other words, by creating monolingual spaces and then learning a projection from one language to another the need for large parallel corpora for cross-lingual supervision can be eliminated. Mikolov et al. (2013) attempted to learn a linear mapping from one space to another and optimized the performance by using the most common words from both languages and by using a bilingual lexicon to guide the learning of the mapping in the right direction. As large bilingual lexicons are often not available for low-resourced languages or specific domains, there was a need to either completely eliminate or drastically reduce the size of the required bilingual lexicon. Artetxe et al. (2017) further explored these ideas by using a combination of back translation and denoising. This approach was, however, severely lacking in terms of performance as compared to a method with cross-lingual signals. The advent of adversarial networks brought on some unique ideas which opened up a lot of new research directions: a discriminator is trained to identify whether an embedding originates from a source language or a target language and a mapping is trained to fool the discriminator. The underlying principle is that there is an orthogonal matrix W, which can transform embeddings in one language to embeddings in another language.

With the arrival of the new generation of language models, contextual embeddings came into the picture. Contextual embeddings significantly enhanced word and sentence representations, and improved upon previous methods of cross-lingual alignment like MUSE (Lample and Conneau, 2019) and VecMap (Artetxe et al., 2018) due to their dynamic nature. Multilingual BERT (mBERT, Devlin et al. (2019)) and XLM (Conneau and Lample, 2019) were jointly trained for Masked Language Modelling on 104 languages and significantly outperformed previous approaches for a variety of zero-shot cross-lingual tasks. While joint training is an excellent solution, it is computationally expensive to train and not receptive to new languages after the initial training. A number of recent works (Wu and Dredze, 2020; Wang et al., 2020) investigating mBERT have also uncovered that under-resourced languages have much poorer representations compared to the higher-resourced languages, making these models not the optimal choice when working with a low-resource language.

Artexte et al. (2020) introduce another clever alternative to joint training (mBERT, XLM), by freezing the encoder layers of a transformer after the initial pre-training, and re-learning only the embeddings on a target language. This results in a very similar performance to mBERT while keeping the training time significantly lower. Schuster et al. (2019), for their part, treat contextual embeddings as having a static anchor component, and a dynamic context component for every token. This once again enabled the static components to be aligned with methods like MUSE. Tran et al. (2020) proposed a further improvement on the joint training direction of research, by forcing foreign language embeddings to be initialized in the same space as the source language, thus increasing the performance of mBERT and XLM.

In this paper, we seek to investigate viable approaches to zero-shot cross-lingual transfer of transformer representations for a lower-resourced and often under-performing language, namely Hindi. At the same time we wish to compare the performance of these approaches on higher-resourced languages from different families. To this end, we revisit the anchor-based approach of Schuster et al. (2019) which decomposes contextual embeddings into anchors and contexts. Given that this original approach has only been validated on ELMo (Peters et al., 2018), we investigate the scalability of this method on modern transformers such as BERT and RoBERTa (Liu et al., 2019). In order to assess the viability of this approach on Hindi in different settings, we perform detailed experiments for three different downstream tasks.

3. Static Anchors from Transformers

Even though approaches like RAMEN (Tran, 2020) and MonoTrans (Artetxe et al., 2020) have replaced the older, orthogonal alignment with Procrustes refinement strategies, these newer approaches are solely designed for certain architectures requiring additional training steps. In this paper we choose to investigate an approach which is intuitively sound and model-agnostic. The approach in question, henceforth referred to as Cross-lingual ELMo (Schuster et al., 2019), theorizes that the average for all contextual embeddings of a word over a large corpus adequately represents a static anchor for the token in question. Given a source language s and a target language t, the objective of the classical alignment methods is to learn a transformation

$$E_{s,t} \approx W^{s \to t} E_{s,s} \quad (1)$$

where $E_{s,s}$ represents the embeddings of the source language in their original space, while $E_{s,t}$ represents the embeddings of the source language in the target language's multi-dimensional space. For classical word embeddings like word2vec (Mikolov et al., 2013) and FastText (Bojanowski et al., 2016), this becomes a simple optimisation problem for an orthogonal matrix W. VecMap achieves this by maximizing for similarity over a sparse seed dictionary (which can be initialized with zero supervision or using identical words if a seed dictionary is not available), and iteratively improving the dictionary and relearning the alignment after each optimisation step. MUSE achieves the same objective by initializing W using an adversarial objective, where W is optimized such that a discriminator model is unable to differentiate between the embeddings originating from $E_{t,t}$ and $WE_{s,s}$.

However, the dynamic nature of the embedding spaces E in the case of transformers makes the solutions slightly more complicated and requires some assumptions to simplify the problem. To obtain an approximation of the embedding spaces $E_{s,s}$ and $E_{t,t}$, for a token i in the context c,

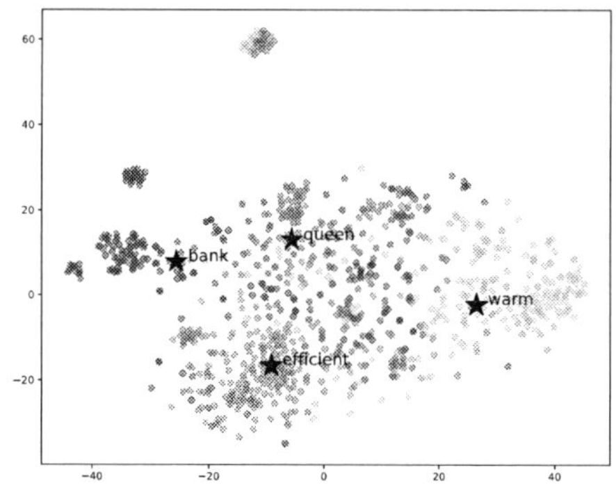

Figure 1: Distribution of token embeddings from all Wikipedia contexts for the words *bank, efficient, queen* and *warm*, and their respective static anchors ($\star$).

$$e_{i,c} = A_i + \hat{e_{i,c}} \quad (2)$$

where A_i is the fixed Anchor for the token i obtained by averaging embeddings over all available contexts c, while $\hat{e_{i,c}}$ is the additional context component of the embedding. This decomposition means that the complete embedding space $E_{s,s}$ once again can be simplified as a static space $A_{s,s}$, the space of all anchors for a source language s. The outcome of the anchor extraction approach is shown in Figure 1 for four example words (*bank, efficient, queen* and *warm*). The individual dots represent the embeddings of the tokens in various contexts from the Wikipedia corpus, while the $\star$ represents their obtained anchors. In their paper Schuster et al. (2019) demonstrated that for the ELMo embeddings the point clouds for individual tokens can be seperated much more distinctly and thus may result in better anchors. However, if we look at Figure 1, more intersecting clouds can be observed for our BERT embeddings.

After the static anchor space is obtained, a transformation

$$A_{s,t} \approx U^{s \to t} A_{s,s} \quad (3)$$

can then be learned with methods like MUSE and VecMap, to align monolingual anchors with their counterparts in other languages. Figure 2 illustrates the outcome of this alignment for the same four words in English and Dutch: we indeed observe that the anchor in English ($\star$) is well-aligned with the anchor in Dutch ($\triangle$). However, 'bank' being a homonym in English interferes with the alignment of its different meanings in Dutch. This again in contrast to the ELMo anchors where homonyms were often found to be resolved succesfully.

While this alignment method for dynamic contextual embeddings has been shown to perform well

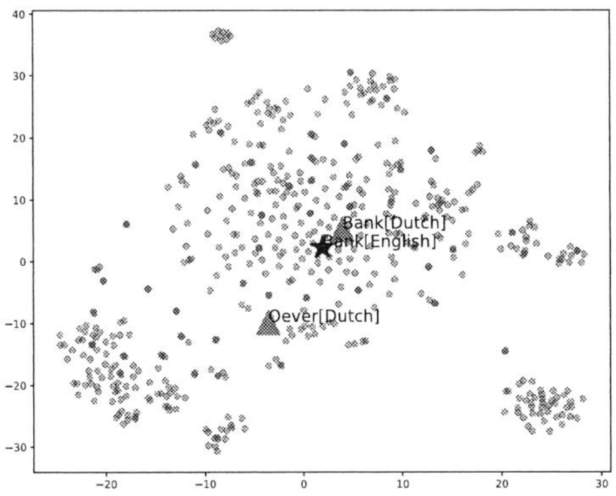

Figure 2: Homonyms: different meanings of the word 'bank' in Dutch (financial: *bank* /vs/ river bank: *oever*) are anchored similarly to 'bank' in English.

using ELMo anchors for dependency parsing, we further probe the potential of this methodology for transformer-based architectures to under-resourced languages. Below, we perform detailed experiments to probe the quality of the anchors, first in a monolingual setting to judge the quality of their pre-alignement, then in a cross-lingual setting by aligning anchors with VecMap and testing them for the tasks of Bilingual Lexicon Induction and and Zero-shot Natural Language Inference.

4. Experimental Setup and Results

The initial step for both sets of experiments is identical, i.e. the extraction of anchors from a BERT-based model. We aim to study the anchors for a wide variety of BERT-based transformers. While for English[1], Hindi[2] and Chinese[3], anchors extracted from more standard BERT models, we relied on RuBERT (Kuratov and Arkhipov, 2019) for Russian, which is a cased BERT model initialized with mBERT, and on Robbert (Delobelle et al., 2020) for Dutch, which is a RoBERTa-based architecture. We use these pre-trained LMs, along with a random subset (1 million sentences) of Wikipedia in the respective languages, to extract embeddings for the 50,000 most common words in the corpus. All the different contexts are then averaged to obtain the anchors as described in Section 2. We perform all described experiments on a singular Tesla V100 (16GB) which takes about 30 hrs per language. Since this is the only major bottleneck in the experiments, we make the obtained anchors available for use.

[1]https://huggingface.co/bert-base-uncased

[2]https://huggingface.co/monsoon-nlp/hindi-bert

[3]https://huggingface.co/bert-base-chinese

4.1. Monolingual Evaluation

To judge the quality of the anchors' pre-alignment, we perform baseline experiments to compare them with FastText embeddings trained on an identical Wikipedia corpus. We train both sets of embeddings with an additional linear layer for classificitation, viz. to predict the polarity of words contained by the Multilingual Sentiment Lexicon (Chen and Skiena, 2014). We use 2,000 random words from the lexicon for training and 400 for testing for each language (except for Chinese (*) where we only had 1000 words for training). The experiments are performed for all 5 languages used in the cross-lingual setup, English (EN), Hindi (HI), Dutch (NL), Russian (RU) and Chinese (ZH). Working with a token-based polarity prediction instead of sentence-based sentiment analysis made more sense for this evaluation since we aim to study the lexical strength of the embeddings before proceeding to more complicated tasks.
The scores for the monolingual setup are shown in Table 1. There is a significant performance gap between FastText and the obtained anchors for most languages except for Russian and Chinese, with Chinese being the only language where the static anchor approach outperforms FastText. The performance for the anchors was found to be especially poor for Hindi and Dutch, while the FastText counterparts remain more or less consistent for all languages. The results clearly demonstrate that on a purely lexical basis, FastText embeddings are still quite superior, even for an under-resourced language like Hindi.

Language	FastText	Static Anchors
EN	**0.8425**	0.7575
HI	**0.8125**	0.5625
NL	**0.7300**	0.5750
RU	**0.7575**	0.7175
ZH*	0.5200	**0.5780**

Table 1: Results for the Monolingual Setup (word polarity predictions) for the five considered languages: English (EN), Hindi (HI), Dutch (NL), Russian (RU) and Chinese (ZH)

4.2. Cross-lingual Evaluation

4.2.1. Bilingual Lexicon Induction

For the first part of the cross-lingual evaluation, we perform Bilingual Lexicon Induction (BLI) experiments for four language pairs, for each pair using English as both a source (EN-XX) and target language (XX-EN). All datasets have been derived from the MUSE bilingual dictionaries[4]. Since our intention is to evaluate contextual models, the respective MUSE train and test sets had to be reduced to accommodate for the smaller BERT sub-word based vocabularies as compared to the

[4]https://github.com/facebookresearch/MUSE

	EN-HI	HI-EN	EN-NL	NL-EN	EN-RU	RU-EN	EN-ZH	ZH-EN
FASTTEXT EMBEDDINGS WITH VECMAP								
Full Train Set	0.5679	0.7098	0.8604	0.8467	0.6465	0.8137	0.8325	0.549
1k Supervision	0.4864	0.5268	0.8234	0.7660	0.5525	0.7561	-	-
ALIGNED ANCHORS WITH VECMAP								
Full Train Set	0.4955	0.5994	0.6382	0.7350	0.6210	0.8043	0.8010	0.4510
1k Supervision	0.3620	0.2997	0.2300	0.3860	0.3276	0.5940	-	-

Table 2: BLI Results for the four language pairs, including English both as source and target language.

Model	**HI**	**RU**	**ZH**
XNLI Transfer Learning Baseline	0.563	0.578	0.588
mBERT (Devlin et al., 2019)	0.600	0.638	-
XLM (MLM) (Lample and Conneau, 2019)	0.657	0.731	0.719
MonoTrans (Artetxe et al., 2020)	**0.660**	0.704	0.703
RAMEN (Tran, 2020)	0.656	**0.736**	**0.737**
CL ELMo (Schuster et al., 2019)	0.548	-	-
CL-anchor-BERT	0.583	0.644	0.662

Table 3: Results on the Zero-Shot XNLI Test Set

FastText or word2vec variants. Using the full dictionaries would be misleading, since, for example, for Russian, our model was only able to use around 3500 samples for training, as compared to the 5000 available in the full train set. To keep the comparisons consistent, we evaluated the two methods incorporating static FastText embeddings (VecMap and MUSE) on the reduced train/test sets as well, and make the reduced dictionaries available[5] for reproducibility. Two sets of experiments have been performed for each language pair: one with the full train set, and a second one where only 1000 samples are available for supervision, (except for Chinese where the full train set consisted of less than 1000 entries, so a run with 1000 samples was not possible). We use FastText vectors aligned with the same hyperparameters as the anchors, using VecMap for comparison.

Table 2 lists the accuracy scores for the BLI experiments. The anchor alignment methods again fail to compete in lexical strength with the SOTA VecMap alignments using FastText, except for Russian where the two methods perform quite similarly. A reason why FastText embeddings align significantly better could be attributed to the isomorphism assumption. Vulić et al. (2020) pointed out that two sets of embeddings are more likely to be isomorphic given similar environmental factors, like similar amounts of training data, time and parameters. This makes FastText very robust since embeddings for all the languages are trained in a near identical fashion.

4.2.2. Zero-Shot Natural Language Inference

In our final evaluation, we use the aligned anchors in a basic setup for zero-shot cross-lingual NLI using the XNLI (Conneau et al., 2018) dataset. As this dataset does not include Dutch, we perform the experiments for Hindi, Russian and Chinese. We first fine-tune a classifier using the English train set, with the language model fully frozen to prevent the embeddings from being altered, since the alignment matrix $W^{EN \to TRG}$ was obtained for the embedding space prior to the training step. In a second step, we use the embeddings for a transformer from the target language, using the alignment matrix to transfer the embeddings to the shared space, and use the pre-trained classifier to perform zero-shot NLI in the target language. We use a learning rate of $1e-5$, gradient accumulation for every 2 steps for a batch size of 8, and train for a total of 5 epochs for the English training phase.

We report results for the anchor-based systems, CL-anchor-BERT, for all languages, as well as results for other state-of-the-art cross-lingual methods in Table 3. We were unable to find ELMo models for Russian and Chinese, which is why these scores are only reported for Hindi. The results reported for MonoTrans, XLM and RAMEN are of the variants of the models that use no parallel corpus since the approach investigated in this paper also does not require a parallel corpus.

As can be seen in the results, CL-anchor-BERT outperforms the XNLI transfer learning baseline for all languages in question, but fails to close the gap on the state-of-the-art approaches XLM (Joint training SOTA approach), and MonoTrans/RAMEN (cross-lingual transfer SOTA approach). It is a key detail that all of the listed SOTA approaches do fine-tune the language model for the English pre-training step, while the anchors approach works with a frozen encoder, which potentially explains the gap in performance. Another potential cause for this can be the dynamic context of the embeddings being impactful for methods like RAMEN and MonoTrans, whereas CL ELMo, and by extension CL-anchor-BERT, only

[5]https://github.com/pranaydeeps/Vyaapak

use the static anchors to learn the alignment matrices, which could be a hindrance when used with context-rich BERT embeddings. It is also worth noting that CL-anchor-BERT significantly outperforms the previously used CL ELMo variant, hence also proving that the static anchor hypothesis does indeed extend to BERT and outperforms results on ELMo for Hindi.

5. Discussion

Based on the results a few observations can be made. Firstly, for the BLI evaluation, we note that with the anchor-based approach, the transfer from English is significantly harder than just relying on English as the target language, especially for Hindi and Russian. Another outcome is that the drop in performance for the 1,000 training samples experiments seems to be consistently higher for the anchor alignments compared to FastText. This could be attributed to the larger vocabulary of FastText allowing the alignment refinement steps to have a better understanding of the embedding space, thus making the anchor-based approach only viable with slightly larger seed dictionaries. This can obviously be mitigated by expanding the vocabulary of the anchors, but will exponentially increase the compute bottleneck for anchor extraction.

In order to gain more insights into the ouput of our approach, native linguists performed a qualitative error analysis on the BLI output of the first 100 instances of the test sets of Hindi, Dutch and Russian. Interestingly, we found that even though these three languages are far apart, they exhibit similar errors. Figure 4 represents the distribution of the error categories per language. As can be observed, the largest error category in Hindi constitutes nonsensical words, a problem likely caused again due to the BERT sub-word tokenization not being perfectly suited for under-represented languages. For Russian, especially morphological and syntax-related errors prevail (the latter has mostly to do with different cases or inflections of nouns, a typical difficulty of the Russian language). The other error types are related to semantics (antonyms, synonyms, polysemous words). An important category (especially in Hindi and Russian) are words that are no real translations, but are semantically related (example EN-HI: 'chicken' was translated to *elephant*, example EN-RU: 'promise' was translated to *hope*, example EN-NL: 'inches' was translated by *meters*, which is actually the Dutch standard distance metric).

In Figure 3 we, also attempt to visualize some selected embeddings that have been correctly (green) and incorrectly (red) aligned for Hindi, Dutch and Russian using PCA dimensionality reduction. The embeddings in blue are the source words. The visualizations demonstrate (again) that a lot of the mistakes can be attributed to semantics, as well as ambiguity in the test set (e.g. 'bladen' in Dutch can be interpreted as both 'sheets' (*of paper*) and 'leaves' (*of a tree*), but only 'sheets' is accepted by the gold standard test set). During the qualitative error analysis lots of such translations were indicated as missing from the gold standard.

Secondly, for the XNLI evaluation, we performed an analysis of the mistakes made by the CL-anchor-BERT model where MonoTrans and RAMEN were often found to be correct. We observed that most of these errors occurred for sentences containing words with less than 10 samples in the validation set of Hindi Wikipedia that was use for the anchor extraction phase. This means these instances resulted in unrefined anchors and therefore, by extension, poor alignments. This issue also potentially correlates with the frequent semantically rooted mistakes found in the BLI evaluation (such as *Persia* was was translated as Iran in Hindi). This problem could be solved by adding more monolingual data (from Common Crawl, for example) for the anchor extraction step. We also noticed that for cases where the anchors are sufficiently refined – with more than 50 occurrences of the token – CL-anchor-BERT is more consistent than MonoTrans and RAMEN. Figure 5 shows example sentences from the test set, with words occurring less than 10 times marked in red. As can be expected, the marked words have poor anchors, thus compromising the sentence representations. A manual analysis of a random sample of 20 test sentences containing no tokens with less than 50 occurrences showed that CL-anchor-BERT correctly predicts 16 instances, while MonoTrans and RAMEN correctly predict 13 and 12 instances, respectively. This demonstrates that the anchor extraction and alignment methodology has the same potential as any other proposed approach to convert a transformer from one language to another, provided that enough data is available to extract high-quality anchors.

Our final point of discussion attempts to justify the lower performance for Hindi (and by extension other under-resourced languages). In the past a possible explanation for this has been that the sub-word tokenization scheme does not benefit languages like Hindi and Urdu, which has already been studied extensively by Wu and Dredze (2020) and Wang et al. (2020). Moreover, reference can also be made to the limits of relying on unlabelled monolingual data. Since most methodologies use the Wikipedia and/or the Common Crawl corpus as initial pre-training data, the performance of under-resourced languages can be justified by directly comparing their performance as a function of the amount of available monolingual data. To this end, we compared the test accuracy of a language for the XNLI dataset using the MonoTrans methodology, with the number of pages available in the language's Wikipedia. Figure 6 shows a significant correlation (R^2 value of 0.882 for the trendline) between the availability of monolingual data and the XNLI test accuracy for the MonoTrans SOTA methodology (in %). It is interesting to note that two languages as varied

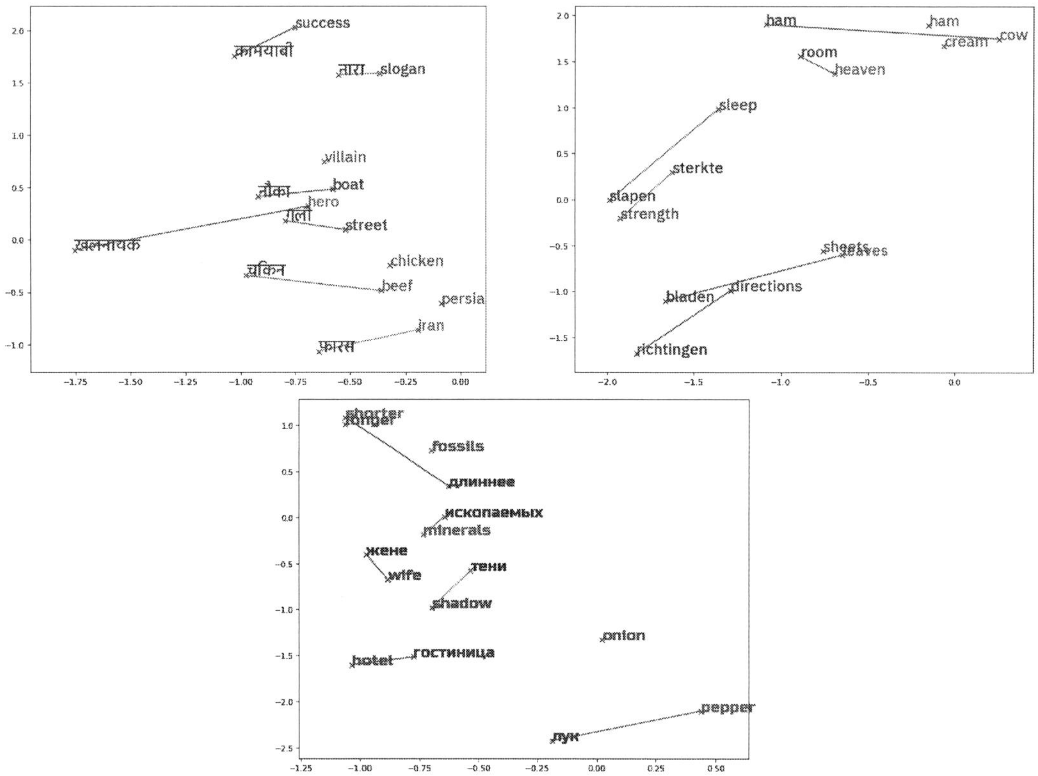

Figure 3: Illustration of the Hindi, Dutch and Russian example words (blue), respectively, that have been correctly (green) and incorrectly (red) aligned according to the gold standard.

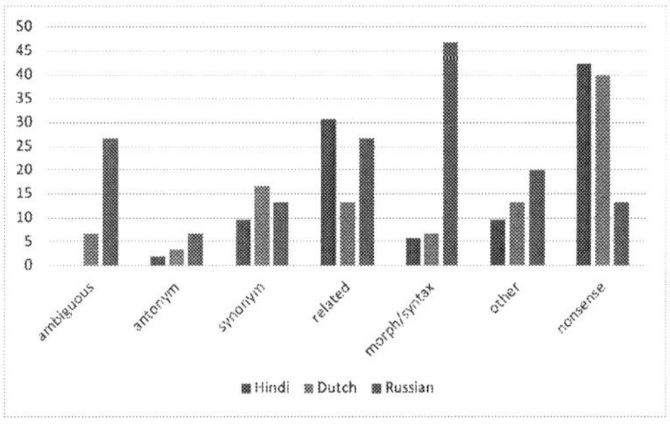

Figure 4: Distribution of error types per language (%)

as Chinese/Russian, and Thai/Hindi have near identicaly performance since they have more or less the same amounts of Wikipedia data. This really stresses the notion that the availability of monolingual resources is the primary bottleneck, while other reasons like language typology and sub-word tokenization might be secondary.

6. Conclusion

In this paper, we report cross-lingual transfer results for the extended anchor-based approach of Schuster et al (2019). Initially designed for ELMo embeddings, we evaluate the approach for the more recent BERT family of transformers for various monolingual and cross-lingual downstream tasks. We evaluate on one lower-resourced language, Hindi, while also presenting control results for three higher-resourced languages from a variety of language families, being Dutch, Russian and Chinese. It is clear from the experimental results that the language models and alignment methods perform worse for a lower-resourced language such as Hindi. Even though the method lags behind in lexical strength when compared to static word vectors, it beats a few baselines on the zero-shot XNLI task, but is unable to compete with the best approaches. We also attempted to analyze why the anchor approach, and most related cross-lingual approaches fail to perform for under-resourced languages. These results are in sync with works such as Wu et al. (2020), which demonstrate the under-representation of these languages even in a joint model like mBERT.

In future work, we would like to focus on developing high-quality evaluation sets for low-resourced languages so the state-of-the-art can be better assessed on tasks with a wider scope than NLI. Another interesting research direction is finding better transfer languages than English, since English is not an optimal pivot for most non-European languages (de Vries et

Sentence 1: एकीकरणवाद में विश्वास रखने वाले काला उदारवादी है जैसे प्रोफेसर हेनरी लुई गेट्स और कर्नेल वेष्ट।
(There are black liberals who believe in integrationism such as Professor Henry Louis Gates and Cornel West.)

Sentence 2: क्या कोई अगला पचास साल के बाद विश्व व्यापार संगठन को याद करेंगे ?
(Will anyone remember the World Trade Organization after the next fifty years?)

Sentence 3: कभी-कभी परिपक्वता या खराबी कि इस व्यक्तिगत प्रक्रिया को संस्कृति में आने वाले बदलाव से कोई प्रभाव नहीं पड़ता।
(Sometimes this individual process of maturation or malfunction is unaffected by the pressures that come into the culture.)

Figure 5: Examples from the XNLI Hindi test set for problematic sentences containing words (marked in red) with less than 10 occurrences in the Wikipedia validation set.

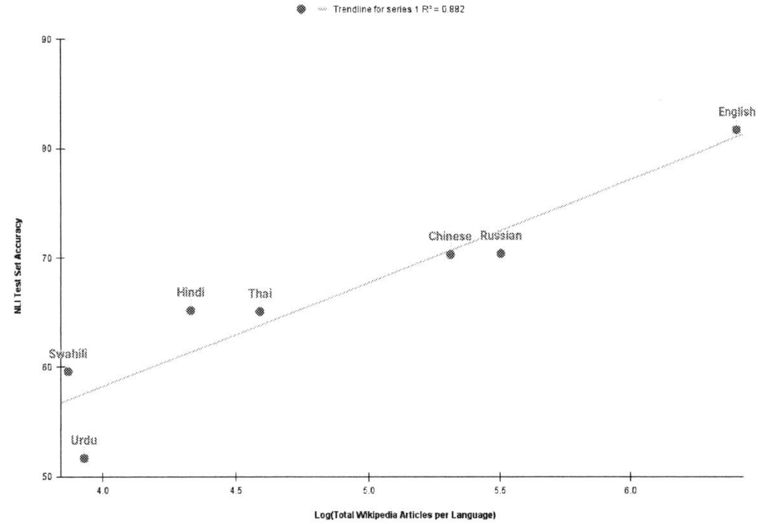

Figure 6: Plotting of different languages when taking the XNLI test accuracy (Y-axis) and number of Wikipedia pages (on a log scale) available for training (X-axis) into account.

al., 2022). Therefore, focusing on creating language-specific transformers jointly trained for a selection of closely related languages from the same language family could be a viable approach as well.
The extracted anchors for all 5 languages, modified MUSE dictionaries and other resources are made available at https://github.com/pranaydeeps/Vyaapak.

7. Bibliographical References

Artetxe, M., Labaka, G., and Agirre, E. (2017). Learning bilingual word embeddings with (almost) no bilingual data. In *Proceedings of the 55th Annual Meeting of the Association for Computational Linguistics (Volume 1: Long Papers)*, pages 451–462, Vancouver, Canada. ACL.

Artetxe, M., Labaka, G., and Agirre, E. (2018). A robust self-learning method for fully unsupervised cross-lingual mappings of word embeddings. In *Proceedings of the 56th Annual Meeting of the Association for Computational Linguistics (Volume 1: Long Papers)*, pages 789–798.

Artetxe, M., Ruder, S., and Yogatama, D. (2020). On the cross-lingual transferability of monolingual representations. In *Proceedings of the 58th Annual Meeting of the Association for Computational Linguistics*, pages 4623–4637, Online, July. Association for Computational Linguistics.

Balahur, A. and Turchi, M. (2014). Comparative experiments using supervised learning and machine translation for multilingual sentiment analysis.

Computer Speech Language, 28(1):56–75.

Bojanowski, P., Grave, E., Joulin, A., and Mikolov, T. (2016). Enriching word vectors with subword information. *arXiv preprint arXiv:1607.04606*.

Chandar, S., Lauly, S., Larochelle, H., Khapra, M., Ravindran, B., Raykar, V., and Saha, A. (2014). An autoencoder approach to learning bilingual word representations. *Advances in Neural Information Processing Systems*, pages 1853–1861.

Chen, Y. and Skiena, S. (2014). Building sentiment lexicons for all major languages. In *Proceedings of the 52nd Annual Meeting of the Association for Computational Linguistics (Volume 2: Short Papers)*, pages 383–389, Baltimore, Maryland, June. Association for Computational Linguistics.

Conneau, A. and Lample, G. (2019). Cross-lingual language model pretraining. In H. Wallach, et al., editors, *Advances in Neural Information Processing Systems*, volume 32. Curran Associates, Inc.

Conneau, A., Rinott, R., Lample, G., Williams, A., Bowman, S., Schwenk, H., and Stoyanov, V. (2018). XNLI: Evaluating cross-lingual sentence representations. In *Proceedings of the 2018 Conference on Empirical Methods in Natural Language Processing*, pages 2475–2485, Brussels, Belgium, October-November. Association for Computational Linguistics.

de Vries, W., Nissim, M., and Wieling, M. (2022). Make the best of cross-lingual transfer: Evidence from pos tagging with over 100 languages. In *Proceedings of the 60th Annual Meeting of the Association for Computational Linguistics*, Online, May. Association for Computational Linguistics.

Delobelle, P., Winters, T., and Berendt, B. (2020). Robbert: a dutch roberta-based language model.

Devlin, J., Chang, M.-W., Lee, K., and Toutanova, K. (2019). BERT: Pre-training of deep bidirectional transformers for language understanding. In *Proceedings of the 2019 Conference of the North American Chapter of the Association for Computational Linguistics: Human Language Technologies, Volume 1 (Long and Short Papers)*, pages 4171–4186, Minneapolis, Minnesota. Association for Computational Linguistics.

Duong, L., Kanayama, H., Ma, T., Bird, S., and Cohn, T. (2016). Learning crosslingual word embeddings without bilingual corpora. In *Proceedings of EMNLP 2016*, pages 1285–1295. Association for Computational Linguistics.

Kuratov, Y. and Arkhipov, M. (2019). Adaptation of deep bidirectional multilingual transformers for russian language.

Lample, G. and Conneau, A. (2019). Cross-lingual language model pretraining. *CoRR*, abs/1901.07291.

Liu, Y., Ott, M., Goyal, N., Du, J., Joshi, M., Chen, D., Levy, O., Lewis, M., Zettlemoyer, L., and Stoyanov, V. (2019). Roberta: A robustly optimized BERT pretraining approach. *CoRR*, abs/1907.11692.

Mihalcea, R., Banea, C., and Wiebe, J. (2007). Learning multilingual subjective language via cross-lingual projections. In *Proceedings of the 45th Annual Meeting of the Association for Computational Linguistics*, pages 976–983.

Mikolov, T., Chen, K., Corrado, G., and Dean, J. (2013). Efficient estimation of word representations in vector space. In *Proceedings of the ICLR Workshop Papers*.

Peters, M., Neumann, M., Iyyer, M., Gardner, M., Clark, C., Lee, K., and Zettlemoyer, L. (2018). Deep contextualized word representations. In *Proceedings of the 2018 Conference of the North American Chapter of the Association for Computational Linguistics: Human Language Technologies, Volume 1 (Long Papers)*, pages 2227–2237, New Orleans, Louisiana, June. Association for Computational Linguistics.

Rasooli, M., Farra, N., Radeva, A., Yu, F., and McKeown, K. (2018). Cross-lingual sentiment transfer with limited resources. *Machine Translation*, 32(1–2):143–165.

Schuster, T., Ram, O., Barzilay, R., and Globerson, A. (2019). Cross-lingual alignment of contextual word embeddings, with applications to zero-shot dependency parsing. In *Proceedings of the 2019 Conference of the North American Chapter of the Association for Computational Linguistics: Human Language Technologies, Volume 1 (Long and Short Papers)*, pages 1599–1613, Minneapolis, Minnesota, June. Association for Computational Linguistics.

Tran, K. M. (2020). From english to foreign languages: Transferring pre-trained language models. *CoRR*, abs/2002.07306.

Vulić, I., Ruder, S., and Søgaard, A. (2020). Are all good word vector spaces isomorphic?

Wang, Z., K, K., Mayhew, S., and Roth, D. (2020). Extending multilingual BERT to low-resource languages. *CoRR*, abs/2004.13640.

Wu, S. and Dredze, M. (2020). Are all languages created equal in multilingual bert? *CoRR*, abs/2005.09093.

Proceedings of SIGUL2022 @LREC2022, pages 185–188
Marseille, 24-25 June 2022

Introducing YakuToolkit

Yakut Treebank and Morphological Analyzer

Tatiana Merzhevich, Fabrício Ferraz Gerardi
Universität Tübingen
Seminar für Sprachwissenschaft
{tatiana.merzhevich, fabricio.gerardi}@uni-tuebingen.de

Abstract

This poster presents the first publicly available treebank of Yakut, a Turkic language spoken in Russia, and a morphological analyzer for this language. The treebank was annotated following the Universal Dependencies (UD) framework and the morphological analyzer can directly access and use its data. Yakut is an under-represented language whose prominence can be raised by making reliably annotated data and NLP tools that could process it freely accessible. The publication of both the treebank and the analyzer serves this purpose with the prospect of evolving into a benchmark for the development of NLP online tools for other languages of the Turkic family in the future.

Keywords: Yakut, Sakha, Turkic languages, Universal Dependencies, Morphology, NLP, Finite State Morphology

1. Introduction

Yakut or Sakha (ISO sah, Glottocode yaku1245) is the easternmost member of the Turkic language family, spoken in the Republic of Sakha (Yakutia) in the Far Eastern Federal District of Russia. The distribution of Turkic languages, taken from Glottolog 4.5 (Nordhoff and Hammarström, 2011) is shown in Figure 1 with Republic of Sakha colored in green. In spite of their broad geographical distribution, all Turkic languages including Yakut are head final languages sharing features like SOV word order, agglutinative morphology, synthetic structure, and syllabic harmony. Although Yakut is not intelligible to speakers of other Turkic languages. Nonetheless, all Turkic languages still share many structural features that clearly allow then to be identified as Turkic (Johanson, 2021; Menz and Monastyrev, 2022).

The Federal State Statistics Service[1] estimated the population of the Republic of Sakha to be about 1 million people in 2021. Of these, the half is considered to be native Yakuts. Based on the 2002 census (Eberhard et al., 2021), 93% of the ethnic population speak Yakut and the language enjoys the official status of a provincial language and is thus used in education, work, mass media, and administration (Eberhard et al., 2021). Nonetheless, at the same time it is also categorized as an endangered language (ELP, 2020; Moseley, 2010), partly due to the increasing use of Russian among younger generations. The gradual loss of Yakut speakers can be indirectly seen in the higher density of monolingual speakers in rural areas.

[1] https://rosstat.gov.ru. Accessed on 16/04/2022.

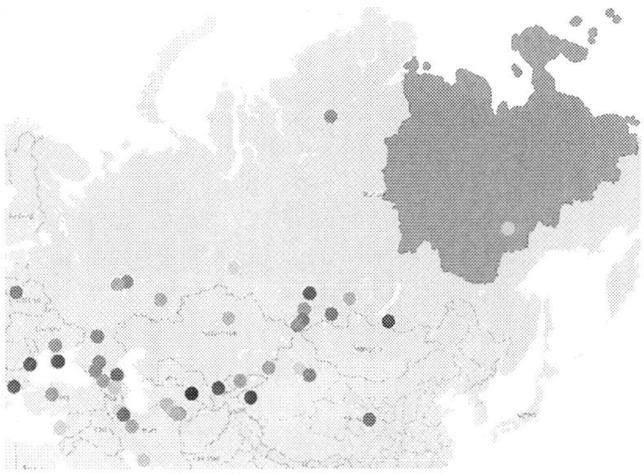

Figure 1: Distribution of Turkic languages according to Glottolog 4.5. Each language is represented by a single dot and a unique color. Yakut is spoken in the green shaded area.

Within the Turkic family, the importance of Yakut is evident due to its being the only language, besides Turkmen and Khalaj, to have maintained traces of primary vowel-length distinction (Johanson, 2021); and the presence of borrowings from Mongolic and Russian, with a Tungusic and Yeniseic substratum (Menz and Monastyrev, 2022). Still, although Yakut is used in education and public life, it can be considered to be an under-represented language. The major linguistic descriptions of the language are mainly available in Russian and, to our knowledge, little to no online NLP tools are able to process Yakut.

The lack of open access tools was the primary motivation behind the work on the Universal De-

pendencies Yakut treebank. By making syntactically and morphologically annotated texts of different genres and complexity available, the treebank will allow for more comprehensive understanding of both Turkic languages and languages in general. At the same time it serves as a departing point for the creation of NLP tools, which are practically non-existent. Parallel to the Yakut treebank we are also working a finite-state morphological analyzer which extends the potential of NLP tasks that can be carried out for Yakut.
Among available tools for Yakut we are aware of the following: 1) the morphological analyzer and generator for Sakha (WiN, 2021), 2) annotated morphological data, which is a part of the Universal Morphology project (Kirov et al., 2018), 3) an online Sakha-Russian-Sakha dictionary, which is apparently being expanded with English translation (Anonymous, 2012).
The rest of this paper is organized as follows: Section 2 introduces the UD-Yakut treebank, and Section 3 introduces the morphological analyzer. Section 4 concludes the papers with some brief remarks.

2. The UD-Yakut Treebank

Universal Dependencies (De Marneffe et al., 2021) is a multilingual formalism which offers annotation guidelines[2] for dependency relations, morphological analysis, part-of-speech tagging, among others. Despite some drawbacks of UD (Osborne and Gerdes, 2019), it is arguably the best open-access framework available nowadays. Alternatives such as SUD (Gerdes et al., 2018) are also worth considering and a conversion and parallel maintenance is planned.
Besides Yakut, five other Turkic languages are represented in UD: Kazakh, Old Turkish, Tatar, Turkish (with nine treebanks), and Uyghur. A Kyrgyz treebank has been announced but has not yet been released. A comparison of Turkic treebanks in UD is given in Table 1. The presence of Old Turkish is important because it can shed light on diachronic processes within the Turkic family. Yet the disparity in the amount of sentences and tokens from one language to another is significant and calls for additional work before large scale analyses can be run on the set of several or all of the Turkic languages.
The annotation of the treebank is carried out based on the UD standards (Nivre et al., 2020), which use the CoNLL-U format[3]. The CoNLL-U file format requires the presence of ten columns: index, form, lemma, universal part-of-speech, language specific part-of-speech, morphological features, head, dependency relation, enhanced dependency graph, and allows for an optional additional annotation

Language	Sentences	Tokens
Kazakh	1.078	10.383
Old Turkish	18	221
Tatar	66	1.119
Turkish	> 50.000	> 500.000
Uyghur	3.456	40.236
Yakut	96	495

Table 1: Turkic languages in UD and the current state of their treebanks. The counts for Turkish are from all nine treebanks taken together.

column. Although some columns only accept values from a pre-defined tagset, other columns can contain language specific features and values. For the Yakut treebank we carefully considered the terminology based not only on descriptions of Yakut, but also on more recent typological works and descriptions of other Turkic languages, especially the comparative ones (Deny et al., 1959; Johanson, 2021; Vinokurova, 2005). This decision allows researchers to grasp similar features of the Turkic languages more readily when working with the treebank.
The standardized documentation for features and their respective values as well as for dependency relations which are able to account for language specific constructions is a not only a useful reference but an essential step in developing NLP resources. An example of documented features in the current version of the Yakut treebank[4] is given in Figure 2 below. The full documentation can be accessed on the treebank hub page[5].

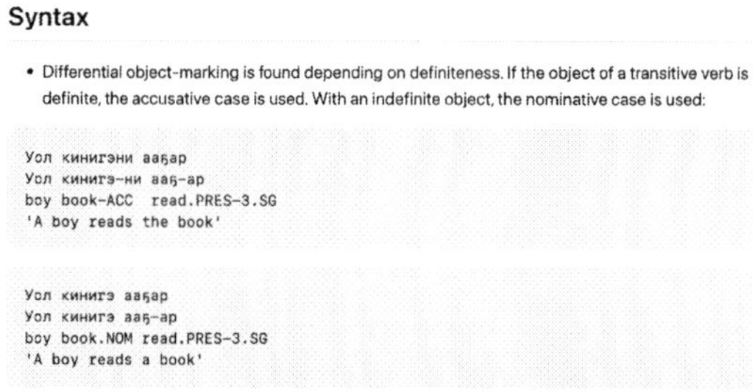
Syntax

- Differential object-marking is found depending on definiteness. If the object of a transitive verb is definite, the accusative case is used. With an indefinite object, the nominative case is used:

```
Уол кинигэни ааҕар
Уол кинигэ-ни ааҕ-ар
boy book-ACC  read.PRES-3.SG
'A boy reads the book'
```

```
Уол кинигэ ааҕар
Уол кинигэ ааҕ-ар
boy book.NOM read.PRES-3.SG
'A boy reads a book'
```

Figure 2: Documentation of a syntactic feature from the Yakut UD-treebank.

The competitive scores reached in the ConLL 2017 and 2018 Shared Tasks, illustrate the suitability of the UD framework for the development of high-accuracy parsers and other downstream NLP tasks (Zeman et al., 2018). It is based on the documentation of the features that the morphological analyzer is being built.

[2]https://universaldependencies.org/guidelines.html.
[3]https://universaldependencies.org/format.html.
[4]https://github.com/UniversalDependencies/docs/blob/pages-source/_sah/index.md.
[5]https://universaldependencies.org/treebanks/sah_yktdt/index.htm

2.1. The Annotation Process

Since Yakut has, since 1939, an official orthography, all texts available are written in it, which consists of the Cyrillic alphabet with five additional letters (Menz and Monastyrev, 2022). Some of the letters in the Russian alphabet are used exclusively in foreign words. As a consequence of this orthography, texts do not require pre-processing of transcription.

At present, only manual annotation is being carried out by these authors (TM and FFG)[6]. Supervised computational methods for the annotation are not yet possible due to the low amount of annotated sentences to be used as a training set. Once a few hundred sentences will have been manually annotated it will be possible to employ the UD-Pipe (Straka, 2018) to speed up the annotation process. This tool represents a trainable pipeline for processing CoNLL-U format, POS tagging, lemmatization, tokenization, and parcing. With ever growing training set, the growth of the treebank will thus also accelerate since expert judgment will be needed mostly for checking and correcting any erroneous tags made by the algorithm. So far transfer approaches have not been considered due to the small amount of annotated sentences.

3. Morphological analyzer

Morphological analysis is a basic component for a large number of automatic text processing systems, including machine translation, POS tagging, information retrieval, and information extraction. The effectiveness of the morphological analyzer largely depends on the effectiveness of all its subsequent stages.

The Yakut analyzer is being built based on data from (Kirov et al., 2018) with POS being extended manually. We are using a finite-state compiler Foma (Hulden, 2009), which is based on lexicon and rules. The lexicon stores a list of words to which morphological analysis is applied. The rule transducers are established from regular expressions and applied to the list of identified word forms. The rules are manually defined based on specialized literature and on native speakers judgement. Currently, approximately twenty rules have been implemented only regarding nouns and verbs. We suspect that with a couple hundred rules some meaningful results could be obtained.

For the system to perform better we need to have a large lexical database since the greater the number of unique word forms, the higher the accuracy of the morphological analysis. Therefore, we use the wordset for Yakut provided by the Universal Morphology project (UniMorph) (Kirov et al., 2018). UniMorph offers lists with lemmas and universal feature schemas with morphological categories. In the Yakut data nearly 600.000 different word forms were identified pertaining to almost 6.000 lemmata.

The morphological analyzer we are building for Yakut interacts with the morphological features and values on the Yakut treebanks, as exemplified in Figures 3, 4, and 5.

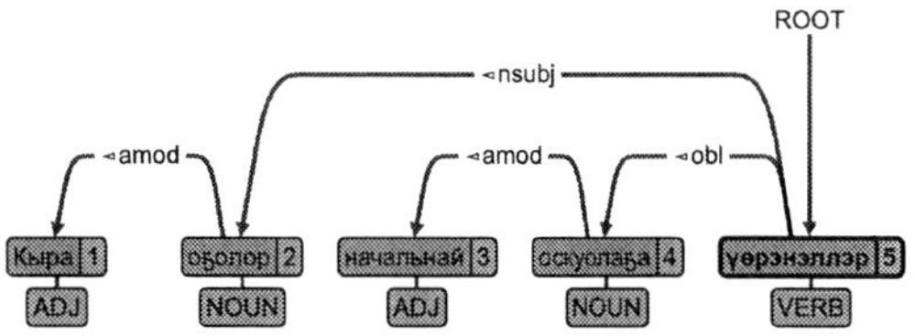

Figure 3: Example of dependency annotation from the Yakut UD-treebank.

```
# sent_id = 12
# text = Кыра оҕолор начальнай оскуолаҕа үөрэнэллэр
# text_rus = Маленькие дети учатся в начальной школе
# text_eng = Small children study at primary school
1   Кыра        кыра      ADJ  adj  _                          2  amod   _  _
2   оҕолор      оҕо       NOUN n    Case=Nom|Number=Plur       5  nsubj  _  _
3   начальнай   начальнай ADJ  adj  _                          4  amod   _  _
4   оскуолаҕа   оскуола   NOUN n    Case=Dat|Number=Sing       5  obl    _  _
5   үөрэнэллэр  үөрэн     VERB vi   Number=Plur|Tense=Pres     0  root   _  _
```

Figure 4: Example of dependency annotation in CoNLL-U format from the Yakut UD-treebank.

```
foma[1]: apply down оҕо+N+PL+NOM
оҕолор
foma[1]: apply down оскуола+N+SG+DAT
оскуолаҕа
```

Figure 5: Example of network generation using Finite-State transducer.

Unfortunately, at this point, initial stage, we cannot evaluate the analyzer. A test-set is being prepared along the increment of rules.

4. Conclusion

We have briefly introduced the Yakut UD-treebank and the Yakut morphological analyzer that we intend to complete by the end of the year. Although we are still at an initial phase of the project, its presentation intends to spread information on the Yakut language an motivate the development of other treebanks, morphological analyzers, and lend support to the UD framwork so that more under-represented languages might profit from it and build on the existing set of data and tools.

Future work will focus on improving the precision and coverage of the morphological analyzer. A sequence-to-sequence recurrent neural network model (Sutskever et al., 2014) which produces morphological analysis for given text as output is also

[6]Both authors are computational linguists. Tatiana Merzhevich has some command of Sakha.

planned. Future work should also seek a closer interaction with tools for other Turkic languages, which as a consequence could enable profit from Yakut tools. While aware that there is a long path ahead, we look forward to receiving suggestions and engaging with the NLP community through this work since we believe that such interaction is essential and results in more robust and user-friendly resources.

5. Acknowledgements

The research presented in this paper is supported by the by European Research Council (ERC) under the European Union's Horizon 2020 research and innovation programme (Grant agreement No. 834050).

6. Bibliographical References

Anonymous. (2012). Sakhatyla (online sakha-russian / sakha-english dictionary. https://sakhatyla.ru.

De Marneffe, M.-C., Manning, C. D., Nivre, J., and Zeman, D. (2021). Universal dependencies. *Computational linguistics*, 47(2):255–308.

Deny, J., Grønbech, K., Scheel, H., and Velidi, T. Z. (1959). *Philologiae turcicae fundamenta.* Aquis Mattiacis apud Franciscum Steiner.

Eberhard, D. M., Simons, G. F., and Fennig, C. D. (2021). *Ethnologue: Languages of the World. Twenty-fourth edition*, volume 16. SIL international, Dallas, TX.

ELP. (2020). Endangered Languages Project: Catalogue of endangered languages. http://www.endangeredlanguages.com.

Gerdes, K., Guillaume, B., Kahane, S., and Perrier, G. (2018). SUD or surface-syntactic Universal Dependencies: An annotation scheme near-isomorphic to UD. In *Proceedings of the Second Workshop on Universal Dependencies (UDW 2018)*, pages 66–74, Brussels, Belgium, November. Association for Computational Linguistics.

Hulden, M. (2009). Foma: a finite-state compiler and library. In *EACL*.

Johanson, L. (2021). *Turkic.* Cambridge Language Surveys. Cambridge University Press.

Kirov, C., Cotterell, R., Sylak-Glassman, J., Walther, G., Vylomova, E., Xia, P., Faruqui, M., Mielke, S. J., McCarthy, A., Kübler, S., Yarowsky, D., Eisner, J., and Hulden, M. (2018). UniMorph 2.0: Universal Morphology. In *Proceedings of the Eleventh International Conference on Language Resources and Evaluation (LREC 2018)*, Miyazaki, Japan, May. European Language Resources Association (ELRA).

Menz, A. and Monastyrev, V. (2022). Yakut. In Lars Johanson et al., editors, *The Turkic languages*, chapter 29, pages 444–460. Routledge, 2 edition.

Moseley, C. (2010). *Atlas of the World's Languages in Danger.* UNESCO, 3 edition.

Nivre, J., de Marneffe, M.-C., Ginter, F., Hajič, J., Manning, C. D., Pyysalo, S., Schuster, S., Tyers, F., and Zeman, D. (2020). Universal Dependencies v2: An Evergrowing Multilingual Treebank Collection.

Nordhoff, S. and Hammarström, H. (2011). Glottolog/langdoc: Defining dialects, languages, and language families as collections of resources. In *Proceedings of ISWC 2011.*

Osborne, T. and Gerdes, K. (2019). The status of function words in dependency grammar: A critique of universal dependencies (ud). *Glossa: a journal of general linguistics*, 4(1):1–28.

Straka, M. (2018). UDPipe 2.0 prototype at CoNLL 2018 UD shared task. In *Proceedings of the CoNLL 2018 Shared Task: Multilingual Parsing from Raw Text to Universal Dependencies*, pages 197–207, Brussels, Belgium, October. Association for Computational Linguistics.

Sutskever, I., Vinyals, O., and Le, Q. V. (2014). Sequence to sequence learning with neural networks. *CoRR*, abs/1409.3215.

Vinokurova, N. (2005). *Lexical categories and argument structure: A study with reference to Sakha.* Ph.D. thesis, Utrecht University. Unpublished PhD thesis.

WiNLP 2021 Workshop. (2021). *A Prototype Free/Open-Source Morphological Analyser and Generator for Sakha.* EMNLP. https://github.com/apertium/apertiumsah.

Zeman, D., Hajič, J., Popel, M., Potthast, M., Straka, M., Ginter, F., Nivre, J., and Petrov, S. (2018). CoNLL 2018 shared task: Multilingual parsing from raw text to universal dependencies. In *Proceedings of the CoNLL 2018 Shared Task: Multilingual Parsing from Raw Text to Universal Dependencies*, pages 1–21, Brussels, Belgium, October. Association for Computational Linguistics.

Proceedings of SIGUL2022 @LREC2022, pages 189–198
Marseille, 24-25 June 2022

A Language Model for Spell Checking of Educational Texts in Kurdish (Sorani)

Roshna Omer Abdulrahman and Hossein Hassani
University of Kurdistan Hewlêr
Kurdistan Region - Iraq
roshna.abdulrahman@ukh.edu.krd, hosseinh@ukh.edu.krd

Abstract

Spell checkers have become regular features of most word processing applications. They assist us in writing more correctly in various digital environments. However, this assistance does not exist for all languages equally. The Kurdish language, which still is considered a less-resourced language, currently, lacks well-known and well-tested spell checkers. We present a language model for the Kurdish (Sorani) based on educational texts written in the Persian/Arabic script. We also showcase a spell checker as a testing environment for the language model. Primarily, we use a probabilistic method and our language model with Stupid Backoff smoothing for the spell-checking algorithm. We test for spelling errors on a word and context basis. The spell checker suggests a list of corrections for misspelled words. The results show 88.54% accuracy on the texts in the related context, an *F1* score of 43.33%, and correct suggestions of an 85% chance of being in the top three positions of the corrections.

Keywords: Spell checker, Kurdish Language, Ngram Language Model, Low-Resourced, Error Detection.

1. Introduction

A spell checker is an application that detects grammatical and contextual spelling errors from a given text and tries to correct them according to an algorithm or a set of rules. Some spell checkers suggest a list of correct candidate words for a misspelled word or suggestions for a sequence of words. Automatic spell checking is a popular feature in word processors for most languages. Also, almost all web browsers provide built-in spell checkers.

Research on spell checkers dates back to the late 1950s, and they are now well established for many languages such as English, German, and Chinese. However, the Kurdish language is low-resourced, and the related research, data, and tools are still in their infancy.

About 19 to 28 million people speak the Kurdish language (Hassani and Medjedovic, 2016). Kurdish is written in different scripts, mostly in Persian/Arabic and Latin, and it includes several dialects (Hassani, 2018). The Kurdish language is less-resourced, and the Kurmanji dialect has had more research regarding spell checkers, for example, the Rastnivîs – Add-ons for Firefox while the Sorani dialect has recently had research regarding tools and corpora to be used for spell checkers. We discuss them in the following paragraphs.

We develop a spell checking application for the Sorani dialect focusing on scientific texts. Our application is based on a language model that is created over the segmented KTC corpus (Abdulrahman and Hassani, 2020) and uses the Stupid Backoff smoothing score (Brants et al., 2007) to find non-words and errors within the context of a sentence. We also use Edit Distance (Damerau, 1964) paired with the score for correction and then ranking the list of suggestions. The language model is publicly available at GNU V3.0 license at `https://github.com/KurdishBLARK/KTC-Language-Model`.

The rest of this paper is organized as follows. Section 2 reviews related work on Kurdish language models and spell checkers. Section 3 provides the methodology of the research. Section 4 presents the experiment environment and RastNus application that we created to use the language model. Section 5 presents the findings and results of the paper. Finally, in Section 6, we provide the conclusion.

2. Related Work

Even though the amount of research on the Kurdish language - for all of the dialects - was few and far between, we can say that recent research on the Kurdish language processing has gained popularity in the past decade.

A Spell checking system that already exists for Sorani is Renus, an error correction system that works on a word-level basis and uses lemmatization (Salavati and Ahmadi, 2018). Renus detects an error using lookup methods in a language model. Also, it corrects the erroneous word using Edit Distance. The system suggests a list of candidates' grams of the same position with an Edit Distance of less than three and ranks the suggested corrections based on the candidate's frequency and Edit Distance. Renus spell checker is evaluated by comparing the golden-standard word with first-ranked suggestions of the algorithm. The authors report that the lemmatizer has an accuracy of 86.7% while the spell checker's accuracy with a lexicon is 96.4% and without one is 87%. While most of their work revolves around the Peyv, the spell checker application in this paper is a step in the right direction.

Hawezi et al. (2019) create a spell checking algorithm for the Sorani dialect (Central Kurdish) with a focus on its morphological complexness - agglutinative. They store a list of base words in memory and use variants of a word in which the base stays the same but prefixes, suffixes, and infixes are changed according to a pattern. This method is similar to what spell checking libraries like Hunspell use. They report that 79.93% of the time, the first word is the correct word, 93.30% the correct word is in the top 3, and 97.01% the correct word is in the top 5 suggested words. They have also created a sample application to test the library, but the application is not open-source.

Ahmadi (2020) presents an open-source language processing toolkit for Kurdish (KLPT) that includes a spell checker based on Hunspell. The performance is not discussed since it was under review as of the writing of this article.

Hamarashid et al. (2021) present a word prediction system for Sorani and Kurmanji dialects of the Kurdish language. They use the ngram model where n=5. In other words, the system predicts the next five words after the input text. The authors suggest that the system is effective in correcting spelling errors. The authors develop an application that is not public nor is it open source.

AsoSoft text corpus is a Kurdish Sorani corpus that contains 188 million tokens. The corpus is mostly collected from websites, books, and magazines. The authors share a detailed look at the creation and cleaning process of the AsoSoft corpus. Veisi et al. (2020) create an ngram language model of the corpus to calculate perplexity. The corpus is available for usage on GitHub, while the language model was not shared publicly.

A spell checking web application that was published recently is by the AsoSoft Research Group is the Aso spell checker هەڵەچنی ئاسۆ that can be accessed through this website spell.kurdinus.com (Aso Mahmudi, 2022)

Our focus is on the Sorani dialect written using the Persian/Arabic script presented in table 1. In order to present a use case of the language model, we use the Python programming language for data processing and the spell checking algorithms, and finally developing a word processing environment that performs contextual spell checking on a word level.

ئ	ا	ب	پ	ت	ج	چ	ح
خ	د	ر	ڕ	ز	ژ	س	ش
ع	غ	ف	ڤ	ق	ک	گ	ل
ڵ	م	ن	هـ	و	ۆ	ی	ێ

Table 1: Kurdish Alphabet (from left to right)

As mentioned before, many languages have achieved acceptable accuracy in the spell checking task. We cannot use most of the spell checking algorithms for languages like Kurdish. Not only for script differences but also for inflection (Walther and Sagot, 2010) and grammatical rules. That makes the existing methods limiting and leads to needing different ones or modifying the existing methods to better suit the Kurdish language.

Compared with the Kurdish spell checkers mentioned previously, our work suggests a more robust language model for educational/scientific writing because it is built based on the textbooks edited by academic and professional editors for educational purposes. That allows the model to find errors and suggest corrections that are close to *de facto* writing standard that is currently formally followed in the Kurdistan Region of Iraq.

3. Methodology

In this section, we explain the steps we took for creating an ngram language model. The language model consists of lists of trigrams, bigrams, and unigrams with each ngram's frequency distribution. We look into the smoothing method that we used to make the language model more accurate when used in different scenarios. We also

Unigrams	1	<s>
	2	ئێوە
	3	هیوای
	4	دواڕۆژن
	5	.
	6	</s>
Bigrams	1	<s>, ئێوە
	2	ئێوە, هیوای
	3	هیوای, دواڕۆژن
	4	دواڕۆژن, .
	5	., </s>
Trigram	1	<s>, ئێوە, هیوای
	2	ئێوە, هیوای, دواڕۆژن
	3	هیوای, دواڕۆژن, .
	4	دواڕۆژن, ., </s>

Table 2: Unigrams, Bigrams, and Trigrams created from “<s> ئێوە هیوای دواڕۆژن.</s>”.

present the methodology of creating and testing our spell checking algorithm with a simple environment that we develop to test the usage of our language model.

3.1. Developing the Language Model

Chen and Goodman (1999) explain a language model as “a probability distribution over strings P(s) that attempts to reflect the frequency with which each string s occurs as a sentence in natural text.”

3.1.1. Ngram

When creating the ngram language model, we started by choosing the ready-made segmented Kurdish Textbook Corpus - KTC (Abdulrahman and Hassani, 2020). A Kurdish Sorani school textbook corpus with 31 books on twelve different subjects at the K-12 level including (Economics, Genocide, Geography, History, Human Rights, Kurdish, Kurdology, Philosophy, Physics, Theology, Sociology, Social Study). The (n) in ngram indicates a number that means it has n consecutive words. In our case, n=3, which is called a trigram. As an example, we take a word from the KTC corpus with two other words in a row in the context of a sentence “<s> ئێوە هیوای دواڕۆژن.</s>”. We can create 4 trigrams, 5 bigrams, and 6 unigrams from the above sentence, as shown in table 3.1.1.

We use an ngram language model so that our spell checker can correct not only wrong words but also specify the errors made in the context of a sentence.

3.1.2. Smoothing

Smoothing techniques are used to improve performance in many cases, but when data is sparse, which is the case for Kurdish Sorani, smoothing is more necessary. “The term smoothing describes techniques for adjusting the maximum likelihood estimate to hopefully produce more accurate probabilities.” (Chen and Goodman, 1999). There are many smoothing techniques, some are expensive and require a lot of training, such as Kneser-Ney Smoothing (Brants et al., 2007). We chose the funnily named Stupid Backoff Smoothing method by Brants et al. (2007) that most simply put multiplies the probability of a constant 0.4. We explain the smoothing method in more detail in the later sections. The point of using a smoothing method for our language model is to not get zeros too often when checking for a word or an ngram in our language model.

3.2. Testing Environment - A Spell Checking Application

In order to test the language model and have use cases for it, we develop a spell checking environment that uses the language model as its back-end. The spell checker consists of three main tasks that occur one after the other: error detection, error correction - which can be a list of candidate corrections, and ranking the correction list (Verberne, 2002). We look at the performance of of the mentioned tasks separately.

A significant component of our application is spell checking in context and not only a single word.

3.2.1. Algorithm

We build an algorithm that detects erroneous words and corrects them. The algorithm behind the application consists of many parts. We discuss them in the following subsections:

- Error detection: Given a body of text our algorithm uses a Trigram Language Model with Stupid Backoff smoothing (Brants et al., 2007) by checking the user's input text - which we refer to as (s) - for having more than three tokens, if (s) in less than three tokens we check the dictionary (lexicon or unigram list) lookup method, the method is more accurate when the RAM - random access memory - is not a problem (Kukich, 1992). In the case when (s) has more than three tokens, we check the Stupid Backoff score as shown in equation 1, where S is for Stupid Backoff score, w for word, and $\alpha = 0.4$. In equation 2, N is the total number of words in the unigram list (lexicon), and $f(w_i)$ is the frequency distribution of w_i, the current unigram. The researchers (Brants et al., 2007) chose 0.4 for the value of α based on good results in their experiments.

$$S(w_i|w_{i-k+1}^{i-1}) = \begin{cases} \frac{f(w_{i-k+i}^{i})}{f(w_{i-k+i}^{i-1})} & \text{if } f(w_{i-k+i}^{i}) > 0 \\ \alpha S(w_i|w_{i-k+1}^{i-1}) & \text{otherwise} \end{cases} \tag{1}$$

$$S(w_i) = \frac{f(w_i)}{N} \tag{2}$$

In our case of using trigrams, the score result is a relative frequency. As shown in equation 1 above, when the trigram has a frequency that is more than 0, the score is the trigram's frequency divided by the bigram frequency. This pattern continues until we reach the unigram level. When the unigram has a frequency more than 0, the score is the unigram's frequency divided by the total unigram frequency. Otherwise, the score is zero.

- List of candidate corrections: The erroneous word is modified by two Edit Distance (insertions, deletions, substitutions, and transpositions) by Damerau (1964) and Levenshtein and others (1966).
- Correction list ranking: We rank the suggestions based on the Stupid Backoff score using equation 1.
- Context correction: We use the Trigram Language Model within a sentence boundary.

To correct the errors the system found, it needs to find the types of errors starting from the smallest unit, letters, and more feasibly letters within a word boundary. We train our algorithm on what we consider the wrong word. We do not find "if" as a mistake unless it is used in the wrong context, such as "if course". Likewise, in Kurdish saying (بە) is all well and good unless used in the wrong context, such as (بە زانکۆ دەخوێنم).An incorrect letter substitute could have caused this type of spelling error. How many other types of errors can we find? Let us continue on the word level. Here is a list of error types our algorithm seeks to correct within a word boundary. We use the term *character* instead of using letters in the upcoming paragraphs:

1. Character substitution: زانکێ, the character □ is substituted with ێ.
2. Adding an extra character (insertion): زاینکۆ the character ی in the third position starting from the right.
3. A character missing or deleted: زاکۆ the character ن is missing
4. Neighboring character order transposition: زاکنۆ the characters ن and ك have changed positions.

Damerau–Levenshtein's (Bard, 2006) Edit Distance covers all of the word boundary errors we mentioned. Where Levenshtein's Distance (Levenshtein and others, 1966) measures the difference between two words by how many operations it is needed to turn one into the other, or in other words, correct the erroneous word. These operations include insertion, deletion, and substitution of a character.

Damerau (1964) adds a new operation, which is the transposition of neighboring characters within a word. The probability of the next word given the previous word is known as the chain rule (Samanta and Chaudhuri, 2013), and we are using Markov's assumption, the last n in the chain. We check for context within the sentence boundary. We take the start of the sentence token <s> and end of sentence token </s> into account to achieve a correctly normalized probability of the complete sentence.

Following equation 1, we take the user input of a set of serialized strings - a word, a sentence, or a paragraph. The algorithm segments the user input into sentences with the beginning of sentence tags <s> twice so that a trigram of (u, v, w) where w is the first word in a sentence u and v are the start of sentence indicators as well as the end of sentence tags </s>. Then the algorithm loops through each sentence and creates trigrams within its bounds, and then the index cursor starts at the beginning tag and gets the first trigram of (u, v, w) the tag included and continues until it reaches the end of the sentence tag. Within a sentence boundary, we check each ngram's - trigram, bigram, and unigram - Stupid Backoff score. If the score is bigger than zero S(wi) > 0, we create a confusion set by using an Edit Distance of two and putting each correct candidate word back into the trigram, then recheck the trigram's score, and then put the trigram in the suggestion list with its score.

The Stupid Backoff technique, as shown in equation 1 checks the given trigram of (u, v, w) in the list of trigram frequencies. If the trigram has a frequency of zero, it checks the bigram of the given words of (v, w) multiplied by α - as previously mentioned, we chose 0.4 because it was suggested by the (Brants et al., 2007) to be the optimal value. If the bigram score is zero, it checks the unigram of (w) by calculating equation 2 - where N is the total number of unigrams (length of the lexicon) again multiplied by α and returns the score, or it returns zero where all the iteration resulted in zero. The suggestion list contains the top five suggestions of each trigram that are sorted by the score. We highlight the erroneous tokens from the suggestion list, and when the user selects a suggested item, we check the text one more time.

3.3. Testing Methods

We test and evaluate our algorithm's error detection and error correction with suggestion ranking with written tests by students that study the textbooks. The test data is educational and in the same style of writing as our corpus. The test data has not been used in developing the language model.

We collect testing data by having students who have studied the textbooks from the KTC corpus. The students take dictation from the remaining 10% of the selected corpus's test data. We chose the student randomly. A teacher with a supervisor reads the dictation material to them, and they type it in a basic text processor with all hints and help turned off.

We prepare the dictation material by looking at research on the typing speed of students in the same age range as our participants. (Horne et al., 2011) report that 11-year-olds have a typing speed of over 13 words per minute (wpm). 12-year-olds over 16 and 13-year-olds over 20 wpm. 14-year-olds over 24 wpm, and another research on elementary schools in Georgia, (Gillespie and Leader, 2005) report that an average kindergarten through fifth-grade students have a speed of 5.1 wpm with no prior practice and 5.91 wpm after 7 lessons taking the speed of typing by age into account and the time limit we categorized the dictation material for each grade.

We manually evaluate the performance of error detection the chosen method by computing precision, recall, and accuracy from calculating each test's true positive, false positive, true negative, and false negative. The equations are listed in equations (3, 4, 5, 6) respectively. Then we manually evaluate our test set and the collected dictation of the test set via the human evaluation of the tests.

$$Precision = \frac{TP}{TP + FP} \tag{3}$$

$$Recall = \frac{TP}{TP + FN} \tag{4}$$

$$Accuracy = \frac{TP + TN}{TP + TN + FP + FN} \tag{5}$$

$$F1 = \frac{2 * TP}{2 * TP + FP + FN} \tag{6}$$

Moreover, similar to Samanta and Chaudhuri (2013), we rate the probability of the list of suggestions and flag where is suggestion is the correct candidate or a better wording in the context. We look into the top five positions in the suggestions that are retrieved from the algorithm.

4. The Test Environment - RastNus Application

In this section, we present the spell checking application created from the methodology of this paper. We show the application's user interface as well as the back-end of how the concept was implemented. We report the testing process, and we present the application's performance as well as other results in the results and discussion section.

4.1. User Interface

We named the spell checking application RastNus (RastNus ڕاستنوس - is a Kurdish noun that is composed of two other nouns; Rast means truthful and Nus means writing). When viewing the application as a user, RastNus has a simple interface of two components, the text editing area, and the "Spell Check" button. When the user inputs text in the text editing box and presses the spell check button, a table of erroneous words alongside its corrections is shown to the user with a select link next to each correct candidate word. The table of erroneous words and candidate selection is shown in figures 2 and 3, respectively.

After the user inputs text in the text area and selects the "Spell Check" button, the application follows a series of steps. A flow chart of the steps is shown in figure 1 - RastNus application process.

4.1.1. Algorithm

The algorithm behind the RastNus application first checks for non-words. If the given word is incorrect - using Edit Distance - the application shows the user a list of candidate words. RastNus's algorithm contains the following components:

- A Language Model consists of lists of trigrams, bigrams, and unigrams with each ngram's frequency distribution.
- A custom tokenizer trained on KTC's test set using Punkt (Kiss and Strunk, 2006).

The first step in the main method of the RastNus application is loading the prepared data by starting with calling the LoadTokenizer method. When the method is called, the program loads KTC's custom tokenizer. We manually added a list of abbreviations to the pickle file, and the abbreviations are: ['د', 'م', 'د.خ', 'پ', 'پ.ز']. Then the LoadNgramsInToDic method is called to load the ngram language model of trigrams, bigrams, and unigrams paired with frequency distribution created from our corpus. The SpellCheck method is triggered when the user clicks the "Spell Check" button. It starts by cleaning the user's input text (T). It removes extra space and replaces the character ک with ك because the first form of the sound /k/ does not appear in the KTC we take this step to avoid unnecessary flagging.
The cleaned text (T) is sent to KTC's custom tokenizer (trained using Punkt) so that (T) is made into trigrams. The resulting trigram is sent to get a Stupid Backoff smoothing score. If the score is zero, that ngram is appended to a list. Each word in that list is sent to the notKnown method to check whether that word exists in our dictionary list. If the word is unknown, it is sent to the candidatesSet2Prob method to get a list of words with an Edit Distance of two from the original unknown word. Each candidate word is put back into the ngram. We check for the Stupid Backoff score of each reconstructed ngram to check for the correction within the ngram context. If the score is more than zero, the ngram is considered as a candidate correction, and it is shown to the user in the form of a table shown in figure 2.

Once the user selects a suggested candidate, the updated text is once again checked, as presented in figure 3.

4.1.2. RastNus Testing Procedure

We manually tested the RastNus application by taking random paragraphs from the test set and running it through the application. We also checked the student dictation data and collected error types (tp, tn, fp, fn) while comparing RastNus's spell checking manually with a human checker. We tested and evaluated the algorithm that our spell checker - RastNus, uses. The results are displayed and discussed in the following paragraphs. We collected the test corpus of dictation to evaluate RastNus alongside the test set. Twenty-three students from 1st grade to 9th grade in total participated in the computer-based dictation. The first session with eight available computers, and in the second session of six participants, three laptops were available.
According to research, 4, 5, and 6-year-olds have a 5 to 13 word per minute speed, nine on average. In that case, a 250-word paragraph is sufficient for that age group and the time we have. However, 7th to 9th graders have a speed of 16 to 24 words per minute 20 on average, 1000 Word page dictation could be achieved in 30 minutes. In the first session, we selected the first n words (number of words needed per age group) for dictation from our test set, but for the second session, we selected a random set of sentences that made up n words or more.
We tested RastNus using the test set and the dictation data, by manually checking each word and flagging it as the corresponding error type (true positive, true negative, false positive, false negative). See an example in figure 4. Then we counted the error types and then calculated precision, recall, F1, and accuracy. We manually checked each suggestion of the test set and the dictation data by tagging the correct candidate in the top five suggestions the percentage of correct candidates suggested in the test set.

5. Results

In the following sections, we showcase the language model we created as well as present the results of our spell checking algorithm alongside it.
The trigram ngram language model of the KTC corpus consists of 94,188 unigrams, 372,903 bigrams, and 521,797 trigrams.

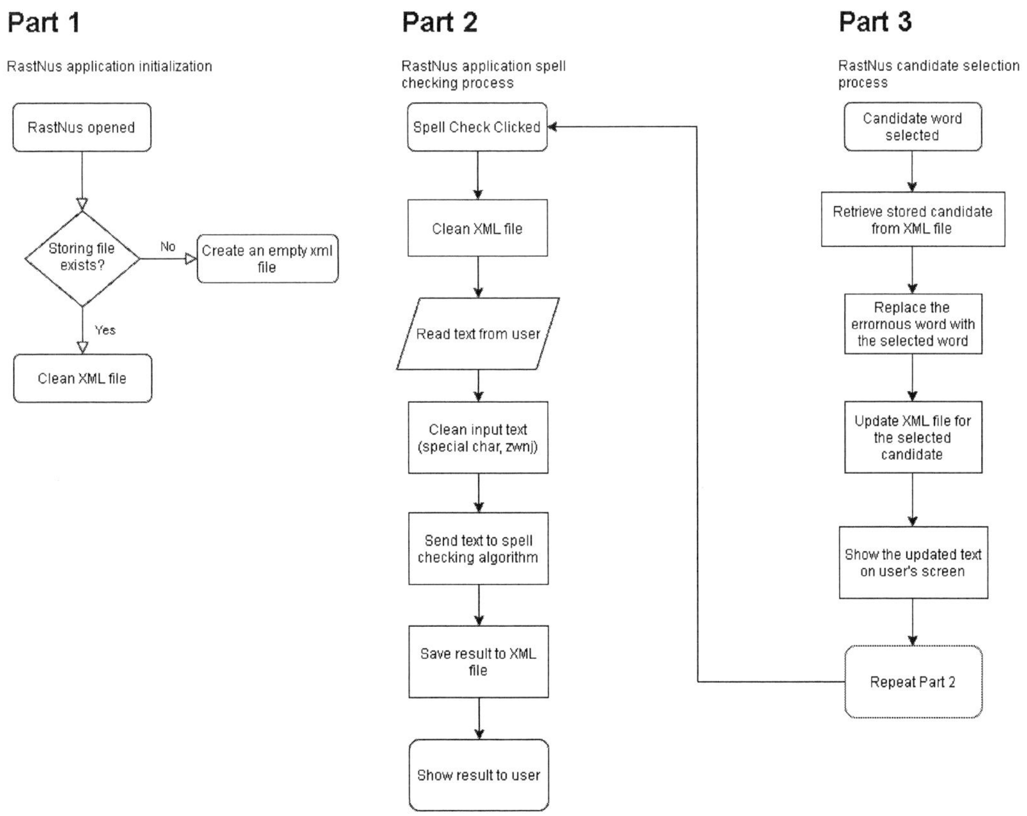

Figure 1: RastNus application process.

#	Unigram	Bigram	Trigram
1	و	. </s>	) . </s>
2	<s>	) .	... ...
3	</s>	... ...	: ((
4	.	: (	) و(
5	لە	) و	(د.خ)
6	)	) ی	2 . </s>
7	(	کە لە	1 . </s>
8	:	) ،	3 . </s>
9	بە	<s>لە	<s>2 .
10	کە	<s>2-	پێغەمبەر (د.خ

Table 3: Top 10 ngrams.

We present top the 10 ngrams of our language model that contains trigrams, bigrams, and unigrams in table 5.

The result of our spell checking algorithm is shown in table 5 it contains the error types (true positive, false positive, true negative, and false negative), and precision, recall, F1, and accuracy are calculated. From the first test using the dictation data, we can see that the F1 score is 65.94%, and the F1 score of testing the algorithm with our test set is 21.90%. The total F1 score of our method is 43.33%, while the accuracy is significantly higher. The dictation data has an accuracy of 82.27%, and the accuracy of testing the algorithm using our test set is 90%. Overall the accuracy of our method is 88.54%. The F1 score is a harmonic mean between precision and recall, while the accuracy measures all correctly flagged cases with equal importance.

The reason behind the notable difference in accuracy and F1 score is that unlike the F1 score, the accuracy takes true negatives into account.

Type	T.P	F.P	T.N	F.N	Precision	Recall	F1	Accuracy
Dictation	154	16	584	143	90.58%	51.85%	65.94%	82.27%
Test set	54	177	3,411	208	23.37%	20.61%	21.90%	90%
Total	208	193	3995	351	51.87%	37.20%	43.33%	88.54%

Table 4: RastNus spell checker performance.

Figure 2: RastNus Spell Checker testing.

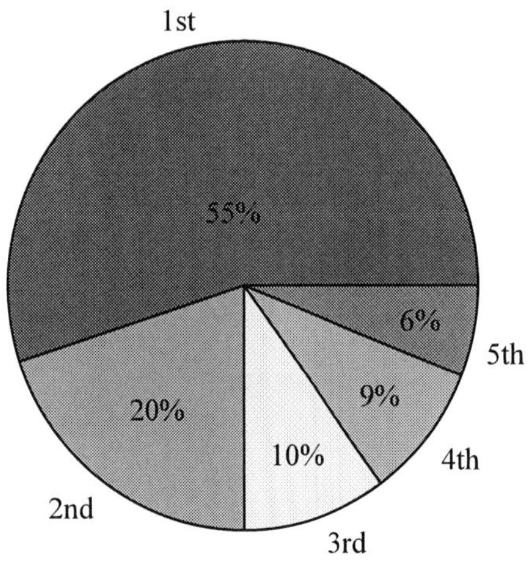

Figure 5: Total percentage of correct suggestion candidates in the top five positions.

Figure 3: RastNus Spell Checker: candidate word selected.

We manually checked each suggestion of the test set and the dictation data by tagging the correct candidate in the top five suggestions. The percentage of correct candidates suggested in the test set is presented in figure 5. The suggestion in the top three positions of the correct suggestion makes up over 85% of the correct suggestions.

6. Conclusion

We created an ngram language model made of lists of trigrams, bigrams, and unigrams with each ngram's frequency distribution, and we used the Stupid Backoff smoothing method.

We built a spell checking Web application RastNus to use the language that we aim at making it publicly available.

We used a desktop-based version of this application to test the error detection and correction of the language model using the developed spell checking algorithm. The spell checking algorithm uses a probabilistic method. Error detection uses a

کردار	ڕاستکردنەوە	هەڵە	ڕستە لە هەڵە	#
rank#1	خودای گەورە المهيـمن	الموهيمن	خودای گەورە الموهيمن	1
rank#0	الموهيمن : بەتواناو	بەتوانایەو	الموهيمن : بەتوانایەو	1
هەڵبژێرە	الموهيمن : بەتوانای	بەتوانایەو	الموهيمن : بەتوانایەو	2
هەڵبژێرە	الموهيمن : توانایەو	بەتوانایەو	الموهيمن : بەتوانایەو	3
هەڵبژێرە	الموهيمن : بەتوانایی	بەتوانایەو	الموهيمن : بەتوانایەو	4
rank#1	بەسەر گشت درووستکراوەکانیدا	دروسکراوەکانیدا	بەسەر گشت دروسکراوەکانیدا	1
هەڵبژێرە	وانەی یەکەم ناو	لاناو	وانەی یەکەم لاناو	1
rank#2	وانەی یەکەم لەناو	لاناو	وانەی یەکەم لاناو	2
هەڵبژێرە	وانەی یەکەم مانای	لاناو	وانەی یەکەم لاناو	3
هەڵبژێرە	وانەی یەکەم بەناو	لاناو	وانەی یەکەم لاناو	4
هەڵبژێرە	وانەی یەکەم پێناو	لاناو	وانەی یەکەم لاناو	5

وانەی یەکەم لاناو پیرۆزەکانی خودای گەورە
الموهيمن :بەتوانایەو تەواوی دەسەڵاتی بەسەر
گشت دروسکراوەکانیدا هەیە

Tagged

وانەیtn یەکەمtn لاناوtp پیرۆزەکانیtn
خودایtn گەورەtn الموهيمنtp :tnبەتوانایەوtp
تەواویtn دەسەڵاتیtn بەسەرtn گشتtn
دروسکراوەکانیداtp هەیەtn

Figure 4: RastNus output manual tagging.

dictionary lookup to find non-word mistakes, and for real-word errors, we use the Stupid Backoff method for each trigram within a sentence boundary. For error correction, the algorithm uses the Edit Distance of two to create a confusion set. Where the word of the set has a Stupid Backoff score of over zero, it adds the word to the candidate list. The algorithm ranks the list of candidates using the score of relative frequency, which is the output of the Stupid Backoff smoothing method. The error detection has an F1 score of 43.33% and an 88.54% accuracy, and the correct suggestion is in the top three positions in 85% of cases.

The aim of the language model creation is that it can be used in official settings.

For future work, we are interested in expanding the language model and with it, the spell-checking environment to cover other Kurdish dialects and include different scripts.

The spell checker could be improved further as usually these kinds of applications could, and we would like to work on expanding the language model further by adding more (official and educational) documents.

We hope the researchers in the field to use the language model to enrich the data and tools for the Kurdish language.

7. Acknowledgements

We would like to apprecia the assistance of Hakary Basic School's staff in allowing us to use their materials and test their students.

8. Bibliographical References

Abdulrahman, R. O. and Hassani, H. (2020). Using Punkt for Sentence Segmentation in non-

Latin Scripts: Experiments on Kurdish (Sorani) Texts . *arXiv preprint arXiv:2004.14134*.

Ahmadi, S. (2020). KLPT – Kurdish Language Processing Toolkit. In *Proceedings of Second Workshop for NLP Open Source Software (NLP-OSS)*, pages 72–84.

Aso Mahmudi, A. R. G. (2022). Aso Spell Checker.

Bard, G. V. (2006). Spelling-Error Tolerant, Order-Independent Pass-Phrases via the Damerau-Levenshtein String-Edit Distance Metric. *Cryptology ePrint Archive*.

Brants, T., Popat, A. C., Xu, P., Och, F. J., and Dean, J. (2007). Large Language Models in Machine Translation.

Chen, S. F. and Goodman, J. (1999). An Empirical Study of Smoothing Techniques for Language Modeling. *Computer Speech & Language*, 13(4):359–394.

Damerau, F. J. (1964). A Technique for Computer Detection and Correction of Spelling Errors. *Communications of the ACM*, 7(3):171–176.

Gillespie, C. and Leader, L. (2005). *We can...can they? Touch Typing for First Graders*. Ph.D. thesis, Citeseer.

Hamarashid, H. K., Saeed, S. A., and Rashid, T. A. (2021). Next word prediction based on the N-gram model for Kurdish Sorani and Kurmanji. *Neural Computing and Applications*, 33(9):4547–4566.

Hassani, H. and Medjedovic, D. (2016). Automatic Kurdish Dialects Identification. *Computer Science & Information Technology*, 6(2):61–78.

Hassani, H. (2018). BLARK for multi-dialect languages: towards the Kurdish BLARK. *Language Resources and Evaluation*, 52(2):625–644.

Hawezi, R. S., Azeez, M. Y., and Qadir, A. A. (2019). Spell checking algorithm for agglutinative languages "Central Kurdish as an example". In *2019 International Engineering Conference (IEC)*, pages 142–146. IEEE.

Horne, J., Ferrier, J., Singleton, C., and Read, C. (2011). Computerised assessment of handwriting and typing speed. *Educational and Child Psychology*, 28(2):52.

Kiss, T. and Strunk, J. (2006). Unsupervised Multilingual Sentence Boundary Detection. *Computational linguistics*, 32(4):485–525.

Kukich, K. (1992). Techniques for Automatically Correcting Words in Text. *Acm Computing Surveys (CSUR)*, 24(4):377–439.

Levenshtein, V. I. et al. (1966). Binary codes capable of correcting deletions, insertions, and reversals. In *Soviet physics doklady*, volume 10, pages 707–710. Soviet Union.

Salavati, S. and Ahmadi, S. (2018). Building a lemmatizer and a spell-checker for sorani kurdish. *arXiv preprint arXiv:1809.10763*.

Samanta, P. and Chaudhuri, B. B. (2013). A simple real-word error detection and correction using local word bigram and trigram. In *Proceedings of the 25th conference on computational linguistics and speech processing (ROCLING 2013)*, pages 211–220.

Veisi, H., MohammadAmini, M., and Hosseini, H. (2020). Toward Kurdish language processing: Experiments in collecting and processing the AsoSoft text corpus. *Digital Scholarship in the Humanities*, 35(1):176–193.

Verberne, S. (2002). Context-sensitive spellchecking based on word trigram probabilities. *Unpublished master's thesis, University of Nijmegen*.

Walther, G. and Sagot, B. (2010). Developing a Large-Scale Lexicon for a Less-Resourced Language: General Methodology and Preliminary Experiments on Sorani Kurdish. In *Proceedings of the 7th SaLTMiL Workshop on Creation and use of basic lexical resources for less-resourced languages (LREC 2010 Workshop)*.

Proceedings of SIGUL2022 @LREC2022, pages 199–206
Marseille, 24-25 June 2022

SimRelUz: Similarity and Relatedness scores as a Semantic Evaluation Dataset for Uzbek Language

Ulugbek Salaev*, Elmurod Kuriyozov†, Carlos Gómez-Rodríguez†
*Urgench State University, Department of Information Technologies
14, Kh.Alimdjan str, Urgench city, 220100, Uzbekistan
ulugbek0302@gmail.com

†Universidade da Coruña, CITIC
Grupo LYS, Depto. de Computación y Tecnologías de la Información
Facultade de Informática, Campus de Elviña, A Coruña 15071, Spain
{e.kuriyozov, carlos.gomez}@udc.es

Abstract

Semantic relatedness between words is one of the core concepts in natural language processing, thus making semantic evaluation an important task. In this paper, we present a semantic model evaluation dataset: SimRelUz - a collection of similarity and relatedness scores of word pairs for the low-resource Uzbek language. The dataset consists of more than a thousand pairs of words carefully selected based on their morphological features, occurrence frequency, semantic relation, as well as annotated by eleven native Uzbek speakers from different age groups and gender. We also paid attention to the problem of dealing with rare words and out-of-vocabulary words to thoroughly evaluate the robustness of semantic models.

Keywords: natural language processing, uzbek language, semantic evaluation, dataset, similarity, relatedness

1. Introduction

Having computational models that can measure the semantic relatedness and semantic similarity between concepts or words is an important fundamental task for many Natural Language Processing (NLP) applications, such as word sense disambiguation (Navigli, 2009; Agirre and Edmonds, 2007), thesauri, automatic dictionary generation (Mihalcea and Moldovan, 2001; Solovyev et al., 2020), as well as machine translation (Bahdanau et al., 2014; Brown et al., 1990). There are many language models that have been created that yield good quality semantic knowledge, yet their evaluation depends on gold standard datasets that have word/concept pairs scored by their semantic relations (such as synonymy, antonymy, meronymy, hypernymy, etc.), that come with cost due to their time-consuming context-generation process and high dependence on human annotators.

Many such datasets have been created so far for resource-rich languages (Hill et al., 2015; Finkelstein et al., 2001; Rubenstein and Goodenough, 1965). However, there is still a big gap of such datasets available for low-resource languages. Current work aims to fill that gap by providing, to our knowledge, the first semantic similarity and relatedness dataset for Uzbek language. In this paper, we describe all the steps we followed as a set of data collection and annotation guidelines, with the full statistics and results obtained. The main contributions of this paper are two-fold:

- Publicly available word pair semantic similarity and relatedness scoring web-based questionnaire software[1];
- Publicly available semantic evaluation dataset including both similarity and relatedness scores for the low-resource Uzbek language [2];

Furthermore, this paper also describes some important construction considerations about the dataset considering morphological and semantic attributes for a morphologically rich language, with their visualisations.

Uzbek language (native: *O'zbek tili*) is a member of the Eastern Turkic or Karluk branch of the Turkic language family, an official language of Uzbekistan, and also a second language in neighbouring Central-Asian countries. It has more than 30 million speakers inside Uzbekistan alone, and more than ten million elsewhere in Central Asian countries, Southern Russian Federation, as well as the North-Eastern part of China, making it the second most widely spoken language among Turkic languages (right after Turkish language)[3].

This paper has been organised as follows: It starts with a terminology section, explaining the basic definitions of terms used in the paper, then comes a related work section followed by a description of dataset creation and annotation process, moving onto some insights of the dataset, and in the end, authors describe their discussions, conclusions, as well as future work.

[1] Demo website: `https://simrel.urdu.uz`

[2] Both publicly available dataset and the source code of the web-application can be found here: `https://github.com/UlugbekSalaev/SimRelUz`.

[3] More information about Uzbek language: `https://en.wikipedia.org/wiki/Uzbek_language`

2. Terminology

In order to eliminate repetition, and to avoid confusion understanding the terms used in this paper, the terms similarity, relatedness, association, and distance may come with or without the prefix "semantic" interchangeably, but they are meant to mean the same respectively.

The term ***semantic similarity*** in general, stands for a sense of relatedness that is dependent on the amount of shared properties, thus the 'degree of synonymy'. Whereas the term ***semantic relatedness*** means a general sense of semantic proximity or semantic association, regardless of the causes of the connection humans can perceive. For instance *bus/train* are good examples of semantic similarity, where they share many properties, i.e. they are both means of transport, both consume similar sorts of energy, have engines to operate, etc. On the other hand, *teapot/cup* can be a good example of semantic relatedness, where they don't necessarily share common properties, but they are used in a similar context, since they both store tea, but teapot is for steeping tea in larger amounts, while a cup is for serving and drinking tea in smaller portions. Both above-mentioned examples can be used for semantic relatedness though, which means that semantic similarity is included inside semantic relatedness. Therefore, semantically similar things are, at the same time, semantically related, but the converse cannot be said to be the case in general.

3. Related Work

The first creation of a stand-alone semantic relation evaluation dataset dates back to the RG dataset (Rubenstein and Goodenough, 1965) , which was created for semantic similarity more than relatedness[4]. Although it was very small in size (limited to only 65 noun pairs), it clearly showed the scientific importance, so the research interest continued later with more datasets coming along. The FrameNet (Baker et al., 1998) dataset is a rich linguistic resource with morphological, as well as expert-annotated semantic information as well. Among the most important gold-standard semantic evaluation datasets, we can find the WordSim-353 (Finkelstein et al., 2001), MEN (Bruni et al., 2012), and SimLex-999 (Hill et al., 2015) datasets for English. WordSim-353[5] contains 353 noun pairs scored by multiple human annotators. Similar to SimLex-353, the MEN[6] dataset also is described as having similarity and relatedness distinctly, but the annotators only were asked to rate based on semantic relatedness. Later, introduction of the SimLex-999[7] dataset made it the state-of-the-art gold standard semantic relatedness evaluation source. Some popular datasets for other languages include the RG dataset's German translation (Gurevych, 2005), the database of paradigmatic semantic relation pairs for German (Scheible and Im Walde, 2014), and the Simlex-999's translation into three languages: Italian, German and Russian (Leviant and Reichart, 2015). The Multi-SimLex (Vulić et al., 2020) project includes datasets for 12 diverse languages, including both major languages (English, Russian, Chinese, etc.) and less-resourced ones (Welsh, Kiswahili). Multi-SimLex[8] was a project originated from Simlex-999, and was taken to another step by creating a larger and more comprehensive dataset. Linguistic databases such as VerbNet (Schuler, 2005) and WordNet (Miller, 1995; Fellbaum, 2010) together with their implementations for other languages also contain semantically rich information created by experts.

Since this is the first work of this kind for Uzbek language, the closest related work would be the related resources created for other Turkic languages, such as Turkish WordNets (Tufis et al., 2004; Bakay et al., 2021), and especially AnlamVer dataset (Ercan and Yıldız, 2018), where it contains both semantic similarity and relatedness scores annotated by many native speakers. Furthermore, the AnlamVer also shares useful knowledge of dataset design consideration when dealing with morphologially-rich and agglutinative languages.

Work on Uzbek language. Although there have been many papers published claiming that they have created NLP resources or developed some useful tools for Uzbek language, most of them, according to humble search results gathered by the authors, turned out to be "zigglebottom" papers (Pedersen, 2008). However, there are also many useful papers with publicly available resources, some of them are the first Uzbek morphological analyzer (Matlatipov and Vetulani, 2009), transliteration (Mansurov and Mansurov, 2021a), WordNet type synsets (Agostini et al., 2021), Uzbek stopwords dataset (Madatov et al., 2021), sentiment analysis (Rabbimov et al., 2020; Kuriyozov and Matlatipov, 2019), text classification (Rabbimov and Kobilov, 2020), and even a recent pretrained Uzbek language model based on the BERT architecture (Mansurov and Mansurov, 2021b). There is also a well established Finite State Transducer(FST) based morphological analyzer for Uzbek language with more than 60K lexemes in Apertium monolingual package[9].

[4]RG dataset: https://aclweb.org/aclwiki/RG-65_Test_Collection_(State_of_the_art)

[5]WordSim-353 datset: http://alfonseca.org/eng/research/wordsim353.html

[6]MEN dataset: https://staff.fnwi.uva.nl/e.bruni/MEN

[7]SimLex-999 dataset: https://fh295.github.io//simlex.html

[8]Multi-SimLex project and dataset: https://multisimlex.com

[9]https://github.com/apertium/apertium-uzb

4. Dataset Design and Methodology

The criterion for the construction of the dataset had to satisfy all the requirements available to make a high-quality semantic evaluation resource. So we followed the design choice and recommendations brought by authors of previous work (Finkelstein et al., 2001; Bruni et al., 2012; Hill et al., 2015; Ercan and Yıldız, 2018; Vulić et al., 2020), such as follows:

- `Clear definition`: The dataset must provide a clear definition of what semantic relation is supposed to be scored. So we decided to collect scores of both similarity and relatedness separately;
- `Language representativity`: The dataset should should be built considering diverse concepts of the language, such as parts of speech (i.e. verb, noun, adjective, ...), word formations (root, inflectional, or derivative), possible semantic relations (i.e. synonymy, antonymy, meronymy, ...), as well as the frequency range (i.e. frequent words, rare words, even out-of-vocabulary words);
- `Consistency and reliability`: Clear and precise scoring guidelines were provided to get consistent annotations from native speakers with different level of linguistic expertise.

More detailed information regarding each criteria are given below.

4.1. Design Choice

For the design of the dataset we followed the AnlamVer project (Ercan and Yıldız, 2018), where instead of building two separate datasets for semantic similarity and relatedness, we decided to rate each word pair with two separate scores: one for similarity, and another for relatedness. This way, the resulting dataset was smaller in size, but richer in information. Moreover, this approach gave us an opportunity to visualize the dataset as a semantic relation space, using two scores as two dimensions, and creating a scatter plot. According to the methodology proposed by AnlamVer (Ercan and Yıldız, 2018) project, it is possible to predict the semantic relation of word pairs, by their location in the "Sim-Rel vector space", which is given in Figure 1.

4.2. Word Candidates Selection

Probably a relatively easy way to obtain candidate words with minimum work would be translating words from gold-standard resources available for rich-resource languages (i.e. Multi-Simlex (Vulić et al., 2020)). However, there have been various relevant problems that have been reported to be caused by the use of such translations, such as:

- Two synonym pairs from a source language being mapped to one word in target language (Both words in *car - automobile* pair in English would be mapped to a single *avtomobil* in Uzbek);
- A translation of a single word in a source language that makes it multiple words in a target one (the word *asylum* in English would be translated as *ruhiy kasalliklar shifoxonasi* in Uzbek);
- Loss in the similarity/relatedness scores due to other cross-lingual aspects of pairs, such as translation accuracy or semantic/grammatical/cultural differences, require human annotators to re-score, leaving the costly part to be done again.

Therefore, we decided to choose the candidate wordlist ourselves for better quality. The first thing to make was a comprehensive list of words in the language using a big language corpus. For the language corpus mentioned in this work, we used the Uzbek corpus from the CUNI corpora for Turkic languages (Baisa et al., 2012), which is, to our knowledge, the biggest Uzbek corpus collected with 18M tokens. To obtain their part-of-speech (POS) tags, we used the UzWordNET dataset (Agostini et al., 2021) (which contains very limited information of root words with their POS classes), and Apertium-Uzb monolingual data[10] (contains more than 60K of Uzbek root words with their POS tags). Then we extracted nouns, adjectives and verbs only (with descending order relatively, according to their frequencies in the corpus), following the custom of similar gold-standard semantic evaluation resources. Apart from only root forms of words, we also did manual selection of words with inflectional and derivational forms of words.

4.3. Frequency-based Considerations

Considering the agglutinative nature of Uzbek language, creating the list of word frequencies in this language is not an easy task, since a single word can occur together with many different morphemes (either a single morpheme or a combination of many), making it difficult to obtain the actual count of occurrences of a single root-word. In this paper, we created a list of stems with their frequencies in Uzbek language using the biggest available Uzbek corpora (Baisa et al., 2012). Firstly, the CUNI corpus was tokenized into sentences, then all the sentences were fed to the Apertium morphological analyser tool for Uzbek language[11]. Then, all the parts except for the lemmas of the resulting output were removed, which allowed us to obtain a stem/root-word frequency list. Our priority was to include as many words with different frequencies as possible, so we used a technique similar

[10] `https://github.com/apertium/apertium-uzb`

[11] Although we have used the CLI version of the Apertium morphoological analyzer, it also can be accessed on the web to check its features: `https://turkic.apertium.org/index.eng.html?choice=uzb#analyzation`

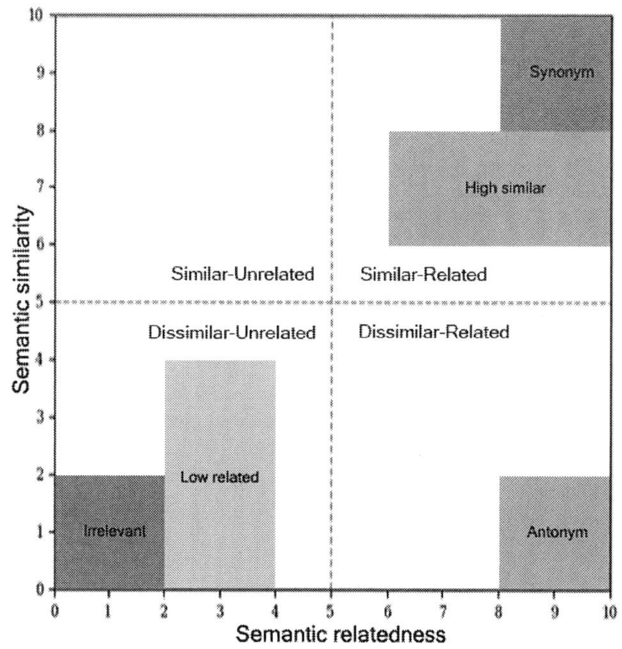

Figure 1: Semantic relation vector-space (proposed by AnlamVer project).

to the one issued by the RareWords dataset (Luong et al., 2013) - grouping words by their frequencies, dividing into three groups labeled as *low*, *medium*, *high* with [2,5],[6,49],[50+] count ranges respectively.

4.4. Rare and OOV Words

Furthermore, to make the dataset useful for checking the robustness of the semantic models, considering less-frequent words, even words that do not exist in the language dictionary but might appear in the context due to some morphological (surface words), syntactical (typo), or phonetical (homophones) reasons is also an important aspect. Thus, the words where their root form does not appear more than 3 times in the corpus were grouped as rare words, and their representatives were manually selected for the word list.

Considering the rich morphological aspect of Uzbek language, like other Turkic languages, there is a high inflection and derivation rate, where words are made in an agglutinative way: by combining stem and one or more morphemes (as prefix or suffixes). Hence, there is a high chance that a word may be grammatically wrong, but was created following surface-word creation rules (of which almost an unlimited number can be created). So we chose the following two most common out-of-vocabulary word cases, which are formally incorrect, but considered as acceptable forms for native speakers, and added some examples to the dataset:

- `Stem-morpheme ambiguation`: It is a frequent case in Uzbek where stem and morpheme are combined directly, skipping the slight changes to fit them. E.g. *yaxshiliq* instead of *yaxshilik* (goodness), *qamoqga* instead of *qamoqqa* (to jail);
- `Phonetic ambiguation`: Two letters in Uzbek alphabet: "x" and "h" are phonetically so close to each-other, it is hard to identify them when used in a context, so people frequently mistake one for another when writing. E.g. *pahta* instead of *paxta* (cotton), *shaxzoda* instead of *shahzoda* (prince).

In total, 128 examples from both rare and OOV words with diverse POS types and word forms were added to the dataset.

After going through all the above mentioned steps and considerations, we gathered 1963 unique words to construct pairs. All their distribution among ford types, word forms, as well as word frequencies are given in Table 1.

4.5. Word Pairs Selection

Choosing word pairs randomly and scoring them would require the dataset to be huge in size, taking a very long time to annotate, so we tried to provide best quality semantic evaluation dataset with a limited number of word pairs by pre-establishing common semantic relations, such as synonymity, antonymity, hypernymity, and meronymity. This way the dataset would achieve a diverse distribution of scores, rather than filled up with very low scores due to most words not being related. Thus, we selected common semantic relation categories, namely synonyms, antonyms, meronyms and

Word classes		Word forms		Word frequencies	
Nouns	1154	Root form	995	High frequency	1136
Verbs	351	Infelctional	423	Medium frequency	448
Adjectives	457	Derivational	544	Low frequency & OOV	378
Total number of unique words: 1962					

Table 1: Distribution of words by different word types, word forms, and word frequencies.

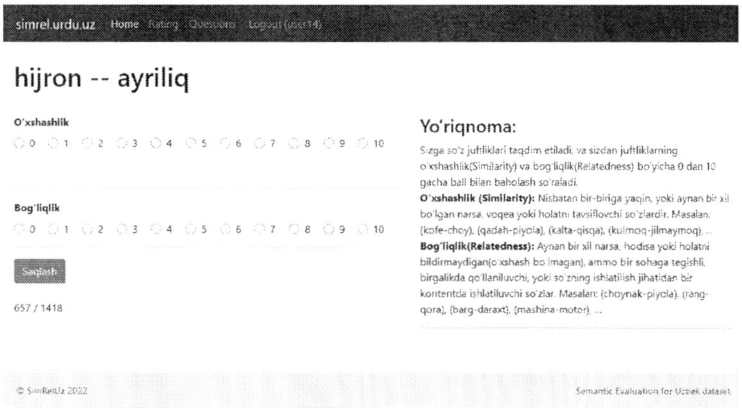

Figure 2: User interface of web-based annotation app.

hypernyms, and manually combined words from the word candidates list, tagging the pairs by a category where they most likely fit. Furthermore, we added word pairs by random allocation, which we named this category of pairs "irrelevant" (not in the sense of irrelevant pairs but in the sense of the magnitude of their semantic similarity and relatedness, as they are more likely to have very low scores on both sides).

Overall, 1418 word pairs were selected for the annotation, Table 2 shows the number of word pairs for each individual category.

Category	# of word pairs
Synonyms	639
Antonyms	239
Hypernyms	220
Meronyms	193
Irrelevant/Random	127
Total	**1418**

Table 2: Distribution of word pairs by their pre-established semantic relations.

5. Annotation Process

For the annotation process, we have created a web-based survey application where each annotator is given a unique username and password, where they can access the website and rate given word pairs with two separate scores at once. General user interface of the annotation page can be seen in Figure 2.

In total, eleven annotators (including two authors), who are native Uzbek speakers with different linguistic background, from different age groups and genders, have participated at the annotation, rating each pair once, with two scores (one for similarity, and the other for relatedness) from 0 to 10. Based on a statistical analysis from (Snow et al., 2008), more than ten annotators for a semantic evaluation are reliable enough. In the end, there were eleven scores of similarity and the same amount for relatedness for each word pair, and we took their averages as the final scores. Figure 3 shows the distribution of age and gender between annotators.

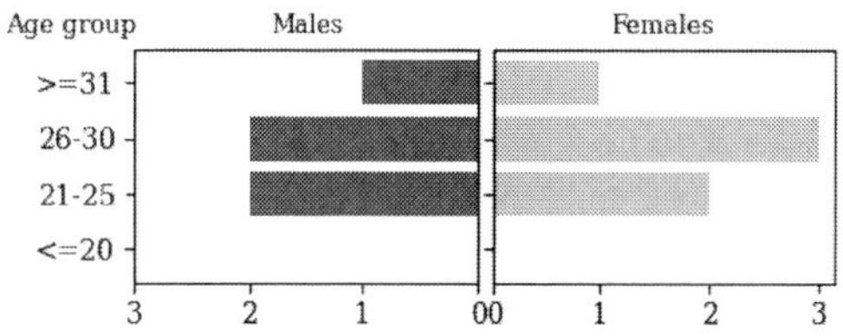

Figure 3: Distribution of annotators based on gender and age-groups.

6. Results

The resulting dataset is composed of 1418 word pairs from different word types (nouns, adjectives and verbs), different word forms (root, inflectional, derivational), with different frequencies (high, mid, low frequencies, rare and OOV words), and with diverse pre-established semantic relations (synonym, antonym, meronym, hypernym, not related). All the pairs have two scores, one for semantic similarity, while the other

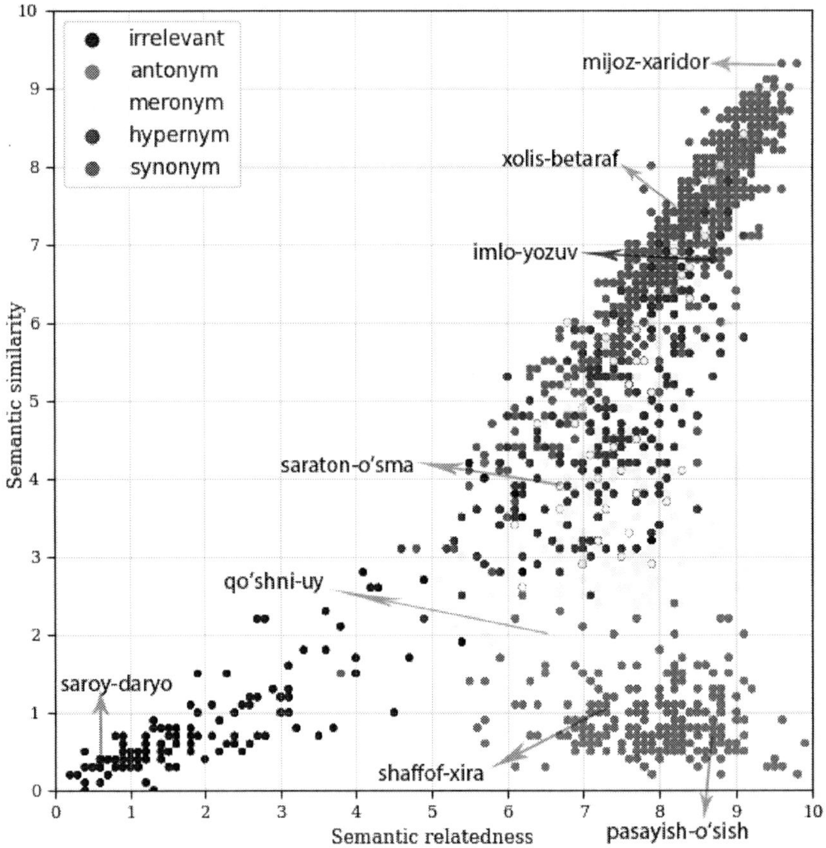

Figure 4: Visualisation of the created dataset in a Sim-Rel vector space.

is for semantic relatedness. No field in the dataset was left empty (as was requested from annotators in the guidelines, even for the OOV cases), and the average pairwise inter-annotator agreement scores (apia) were computed for both semantic similarity and relatedness separately, where we achieved 0.71 and 0.69 apia scores for semantic similarity and relatedness respectively, meaning that although we have scored less than AnlamVer dataset (0.75), it still performed better than most semantic evaluation datasets (SimLex=0.67, MEN=0.68). The resulting dataset can be plotted into the Sim-Rel vector space as shown in Figure 4.

Discussions. As can be seen from the scatter plot of the dataset in a vector space (Figure 4), it can be concluded that average scores of word pairs visually correlate to our pre-established relation types, since they are scattered mostly inside and around the determined areas in the vector-space. Irrelevant and random pairs can be easily detected from the plot, that it has no much overlap with other types. It is also worth mentioning that none of the word pair is in the Similar-Unrelated (top-left quarter of the vector-space) part of the plot, confirming its reliability, since a word cannot be similar, but not related at once. There is a big overlap between hypernym, meronym, and partially synonym pairs, as expected, as they share similar score ranges. Handling OOV words by annotators has also met our expectations, where they treated them as regular words and scored accordingly.

7. Conclusion

In this paper, we presented SimRelUz, a novel semantic evaluation dataset for the low-resource Uzbek language, with semantic similarity and relatedness scores for 1418 word pairs, which were selected based on their morphological classes, word-forms, frequencies, also including rare and out-of-vocabulary words for better evaluation of semantic language models. This kind of dataset is a useful resource to be used for evaluation of computational semantic analysis systems that will be created in the future for Uzbek, in simpler words, for formal analysis of meaning in language models. Moreover, we have also presented an open-source web-based semantic evaluation tool designed for multiple-user annotation. Our future work includes intrinsic and extrinsic analysis of created dataset, also creating big WordNet-type knowledge-base for Uzbek language.

8. Acknowledgements

This work has received funding from ERDF/MICINN-AEI (SCANNER-UDC, PID2020-113230RB-C21), from Xunta de Galicia (ED431C 2020/11), and from Centro de Investigación de Galicia "CITIC", funded by Xunta de Galicia and the European Union (ERDF - Galicia 2014-2020 Program), by grant ED431G 2019/01. Elmurod Kuriyozov was funded for his PhD by El-Yurt-Umidi Foundation under the Cabinet of Ministers of the Republic of Uzbekistan. The authors would also like to thank the NLP team of Urgench State University for their tremendous help with the web hosting, and annotation.

9. Bibliographical References

Agirre, E. and Edmonds, P. (2007). *Word sense disambiguation: Algorithms and applications*, volume 33. Springer Science & Business Media.

Agostini, A., Usmanov, T., Khamdamov, U., Abdurakhmonova, N., and Mamasaidov, M. (2021). Uzwordnet: A lexical-semantic database for the uzbek language. In *Proceedings of the 11th Global Wordnet conference*, pages 8–19.

Bahdanau, D., Cho, K., and Bengio, Y. (2014). Neural machine translation by jointly learning to align and translate. *arXiv preprint arXiv:1409.0473*.

Baisa, V., Suchomel, V., et al. (2012). Large corpora for turkic languages and unsupervised morphological analysis. In *Proceedings of the Eighth conference on International Language Resources and Evaluation (LREC'12), Istanbul, Turkey. European Language Resources Association (ELRA)*.

Bakay, Ö., Ergelen, Ö., Sarmış, E., Yıldırım, S., Arıcan, B. N., Kocabalcıoğlu, A., Özçelik, M., Sanıyar, E., Kuyrukçu, O., Avar, B., et al. (2021). Turkish wordnet kenet. In *Proceedings of the 11th global wordnet conference*, pages 166–174.

Baker, C. F., Fillmore, C. J., and Lowe, J. B. (1998). The berkeley framenet project. In *COLING 1998 Volume 1: The 17th International Conference on Computational Linguistics*.

Brown, P. F., Cocke, J., Della Pietra, S. A., Della Pietra, V. J., Jelinek, F., Lafferty, J., Mercer, R. L., and Roossin, P. S. (1990). A statistical approach to machine translation. *Computational linguistics*, 16(2):79–85.

Bruni, E., Boleda, G., Baroni, M., and Tran, N.-K. (2012). Distributional semantics in technicolor. In *Proceedings of the 50th Annual Meeting of the Association for Computational Linguistics (Volume 1: Long Papers)*, pages 136–145.

Ercan, G. and Yıldız, O. T. (2018). Anlamver: Semantic model evaluation dataset for turkish-word similarity and relatedness. In *Proceedings of the 27th International Conference on Computational Linguistics*, pages 3819–3836.

Fellbaum, C. (2010). Wordnet. In *Theory and applications of ontology: computer applications*, pages 231–243. Springer.

Finkelstein, L., Gabrilovich, E., Matias, Y., Rivlin, E., Solan, Z., Wolfman, G., and Ruppin, E. (2001). Placing search in context: The concept revisited. In *Proceedings of the 10th international conference on World Wide Web*, pages 406–414.

Gurevych, I. (2005). Using the structure of a conceptual network in computing semantic relatedness. In *International conference on natural language processing*, pages 767–778. Springer.

Hill, F., Reichart, R., and Korhonen, A. (2015). Simlex-999: Evaluating semantic models with (genuine) similarity estimation. *Computational Linguistics*, 41(4):665–695.

Kuriyozov, E. and Matlatipov, S. (2019). Building a new sentiment analysis dataset for uzbek language and creating baseline models. In *Multidisciplinary Digital Publishing Institute Proceedings*, volume 21, page 37.

Leviant, I. and Reichart, R. (2015). Judgment language matters: Multilingual vector space models for judgment language aware lexical semantics. *CoRR, abs/1508.00106*.

Luong, M.-T., Socher, R., and Manning, C. D. (2013). Better word representations with recursive neural networks for morphology. In *Proceedings of the seventeenth conference on computational natural language learning*, pages 104–113.

Madatov, K., Bekchanov, S., and Vičič, J. (2021). Lists of uzbek stopwords.

Mansurov, B. and Mansurov, A. (2021a). Uzbek cyrillic-latin-cyrillic machine transliteration. *arXiv preprint arXiv:2101.05162*.

Mansurov, B. and Mansurov, A. (2021b). Uzbert: pretraining a bert model for uzbek. *arXiv preprint arXiv:2108.09814*.

Matlatipov, G. and Vetulani, Z. (2009). Representation of uzbek morphology in prolog. In *Aspects of Natural Language Processing*, pages 83–110. Springer.

Mihalcea, R. and Moldovan, D. I. (2001). Automatic generation of a coarse grained wordnet.

Miller, G. A. (1995). Wordnet: a lexical database for english. *Communications of the ACM*, 38(11):39–41.

Navigli, R. (2009). Word sense disambiguation: A survey. *ACM computing surveys (CSUR)*, 41(2):1–69.

Pedersen, T. (2008). Last words: Empiricism is not a matter of faith. *Computational Linguistics*, 34(3):465–470.

Rabbimov, I. and Kobilov, S. (2020). Multi-class text classification of uzbek news articles using machine learning. In *Journal of Physics: Conference Series*, volume 1546, page 012097. IOP Publishing.

Rabbimov, I., Mporas, I., Simaki, V., and Kobilov, S. (2020). Investigating the effect of emoji in opinion classification of uzbek movie review comments. In

International Conference on Speech and Computer, pages 435–445. Springer.

Rubenstein, H. and Goodenough, J. B. (1965). Contextual correlates of synonymy. *Communications of the ACM*, 8(10):627–633.

Scheible, S. and Im Walde, S. S. (2014). A database of paradigmatic semantic relation pairs for german nouns, verbs, and adjectives. In *Proceedings of Workshop on Lexical and Grammatical Resources for Language Processing*, pages 111–119.

Schuler, K. K. (2005). *VerbNet: A broad-coverage, comprehensive verb lexicon*. University of Pennsylvania.

Snow, R., O'connor, B., Jurafsky, D., and Ng, A. Y. (2008). Cheap and fast–but is it good? evaluating non-expert annotations for natural language tasks. In *Proceedings of the 2008 conference on empirical methods in natural language processing*, pages 254–263.

Solovyev, V., Bochkarev, V., and Khristoforov, S. (2020). Generation of a dictionary of abstract/concrete words by a multilayer neural network. In *Journal of Physics: Conference Series*, volume 1680, page 012046. IOP Publishing.

Tufis, D., Cristea, D., and Stamou, S. (2004). Balkanet: Aims, methods, results and perspectives. a general overview. *Romanian Journal of Information science and technology*, 7(1-2):9–43.

Vulić, I., Baker, S., Ponti, E. M., Petti, U., Leviant, I., Wing, K., Majewska, O., Bar, E., Malone, M., Poibeau, T., et al. (2020). Multi-simlex: A large-scale evaluation of multilingual and crosslingual lexical semantic similarity. *Computational Linguistics*, 46(4):847–897.

Proceedings of SIGUL2022 @LREC2022, pages 207–212
Marseille, 24-25 June 2022

ENRICH4ALL: A first Luxembourgish BERT Model for a Multilingual Chatbot

Dimitra Anastasiou[+], Radu Ion[*], Valentin Badea[*], Olivier Pedretti[+], Patrick Gratz[+], Hoorieh Afkari[+], Valerie Maquil[+], Anders Ruge[&]
[+]Luxembourg Institute of Science and Technology,
[*]Romanian Academy Institute for AI, [&]SupWiz
[+]5 avenue des Hauts-Fourneaux, L-4362 Esch-sur-Alzette, *13 Calea 13 Septembrie, Bucharest 050711,
[&]Vesterbrogade 35, 1620 Copenhagen
{dimitra.anastasiou, olivier.pedretti, patrick.gratz, hoorieh.afkari, valerie.maquil}@list.lu,
{radu, valentin.badea}@racai.ro, a.ruge@supwiz.com

Abstract

Machine Translation (MT)-powered chatbots are not established yet, however, we see an amazing future breaking language barriers and enabling conversation in multiple languages without time-consuming language model building and training, particularly for under-resourced languages. In this paper we focus on the under-resourced Luxembourgish language. This article describes an experiment we have done with a dataset containing administrative questions that we have manually created to offer BERT QA capabilities to a multilingual chatbot. The chatbot supports visual dialog flow diagram creation (through an interface called *BotStudio*) in which a dialog node manages the user question at a specific step. Dialog nodes can be matched to the user's question by using a BERT classification model which labels the question with a dialog node label.

Keywords: administrative questions, BERT, chatbot, eTranslation, CEF, QA dataset, Luxembourgish

1. Introduction

This paper discusses our own solution of an AI chatbot powered with *eTranslation*[1], the Machine Translation (MT) system of the European Commission. Since we are developing a conversational chatbot answering user open-ended questions, Natural Language Understanding (NLU) plays an indispensable role in chatbot dialogue management (see Namazifar et al., 2020). In this paper, we describe our work-in-progress in creating a new BERT model for Luxembourgish to drive question classification and answering.

This work has been done within ENRICH4ALL, a CEF-funded project aiming at a Digital Single Market strategy, which is linked with lowering language barriers for online services and public administration procedures. Our chatbot is an AI-based, MT-powered, fully digital and secure service, which automatically simplifies procedures by providing readily available information to citizens 24/7 and reduces the administrative burden from public authorities. One of the goals of ENRICH4ALL is to deploy the chatbot in public services in the Consortium member countries, Luxembourg, Romania, and Denmark.

The goal of this paper is twofold: fine-tune a BERT model for Luxembourgish for i) question labeling and ii) question similarity. The paper is laid out as follows: In Section 2 we provide a short literature review with subsections on the evolution of chatbots, e-government chatbots as well as on multilingual aspects of chatbots. Section 3 describes BotStudio, our AI-based chatbot and its integration with *eTranslation* as well as one of the challenges of MT-enabled chatbots, which is language detection. Section 4 describes briefly the Luxembourgish language and the multilingual setting in Luxembourg. In section 5 we present our Luxembourgish dataset on administrative questions. The dataset is submitted as resource in LREC repository and is also freely available at the project's website[2]. In Section 6 we describe our training process of BERT models and in Section 7 we present our results on the aforementioned dataset. We conclude this paper in Section 8 with a few future prospects.

2. Literature Review

We begin this literature review on the history and evolution of chatbots (2.1) from simply answering questions to enabling human-like conversations, narrowing down the available infrastructure of chatbots in general to e-government chatbots (2.2) and multilingual chatbots (2.3).

2.1 Evolution of Chatbots

A chatterbot, chatbot, or simply bot is a software application that conducts an online chat conversation with human beings via text or voice through a messaging interface. The term "Chatterbot" was originally coined to describe conversational programs (Mauldin, 1994). However, the first known chatbot dates back to 1966 and its name was Eliza, whose purpose was to act as a psychotherapist returning the user utterances in a question form (Weizenbaum, 1966).
Today chatbots have evolved into "virtual personal assistants" and are mainly developed by Google, Amazon, Facebook, Apple, and Microsoft (GAFAM). Conversational agents are gaining attention and are applied today in many fields, such as e-commerce, education, health, entertainment, and public services to name just a few. According to Gao et al. (2018), conversational systems can be grouped into three categories: (1) question answering agents, (2) task-oriented dialogue agents, and (3) chatbots. The history, essential concepts, and classification of chatbots can be found at Adamopoulou & Moussiades (2020).

[1] Links of services or products are included in Section 10.

[2] https://www.enrich4all.eu/language-resources

The advancement of Machine Learning (ML), and particularly transfer learning has shown huge improvements in Natural Language Processing (NLP). Low code-free or open-source development platforms in combination with limited design efforts for a chatbot interface make chatbot development an easy task for developers. *Chatbot.org* is a comparison resource for chatbot buyers by providing user reviews, and research on thousands of chatbot platforms and solutions.

2.2 E-government Chatbots

The European Commission has a strategy on e-government in the digital single market concerning the electronic exchange of social security information, electronic payments & invoicing, etc. E-government chatbots are an essential AI application in advancing e-government and facilitating communication between citizens and public services. However, there are certain challenges, such as the large number of relevant services, the complexity of administrative services, the context-dependent relevance of user questions, the differences in expert-language and user-language as well as the necessity of providing highly reliable answers for all questions (Lommatzsch, 2018). While in the USA and India, government agencies use chatbots, in the EU and CEF (Connecting Europe Facility) Associated Countries, it is in its infancy. Currently, there are a few EU countries, where many e-government chatbots are deployed, whereas in other countries, such as Romania or Luxembourg, there are not. However, in 2019 the Directorate-General for Informatics (DIGIS) has published a document containing the components of a high-level architecture for public service chatbots.[3].

2.3 Multilingual Chatbots

By multilingual chatbot, we mean that a user can choose to ask their question in their preferred language and the chatbot answers respectively in this language. Multilingual communication between citizens and public administration is a major priority of the EU, as it provides customized services for citizens to facilitate their right to speak and write in their native language. Particularly for administrative procedures, there are many requests from citizens who enter a new country. Application for residence, importing a car, start-up a new business, family allowances, etc. are some of such requests. Multilingual bots and guides on how to create them are coming up increasingly in the last few years (Janarthanam, 2017; Boonstra, 2021), but also mainly by the industry and their business solutions.

Many multilingual bots are used for foreign language learning, such as Mondly (supporting 41 languages). Lothritz et al. (2021) tested two strategies for implementing a multilingual chatbot: (S1) For *n* languages, employ *n* chatbots, each of which is trained to handle requests in a single language. (S2) For *n* languages, employ one chatbot which is trained using data written in *n* languages. They compared these two strategies for chatbots in a multilingual environment on two tasks that represent Intent Classification and Slot Filling. They found that in the case of two languages, the combination of a language selector and two monolingual chatbots (S1) usually outperforms chatbots that are directly trained on bilingual datasets (S2).

In the ENRICH4ALL project, we develop a multilingual chatbot using MT, which to our knowledge, is the first multilingual bot in the domain of public administration. This chatbot is called *BotStudio* and is described in Section 3 below.

3. BotStudio

In ENRICH4ALL, we are using the AI-powered chatbot named *BotStudio*, developed by the Danish company SupWiz, which now integrates the eTranslation API. The BotStudio chatbot has the ability for a node to "match on" what the user writes. This matching can be done either by providing examples of possible user queries or through the usage of an NLU model which is trained on real sample-data from users' queries. BotStudio can use fine-tuned, BERT-like models to appropriately map user intents to developed chat nodes in specific domains.

eTranslation is the neural Machine Translation (MT) tool provided by the European Commission to all EU bodies, public services, and public administrations across EU, Iceland and Norway, as well as European SMEs and startups. It currently covers not only the 24 official languages of the EU, but also Russian, simplified Chinese, Turkish, and Arabic. eTranslation is a CEF building block that can be integrated into digital services to add translation capabilities.

eTranslation is available both as a stand-alone web service and as an API that can be integrated into other online services. One significant benefit of eTranslation over other MT solutions, for a government chatbot, is data privacy preservation. Personal data security is an essential requirement for the deployment and viability of e-government chatbots.

In ENRICH4ALL, BotStudio and the live chat solution *SupChat* have been integrated with eTranslation via the available API with a particular focus on ensuring real time communication with real time translation. The multilingual BotStudio chatbot uses eTranslation to automatically translate incoming questions into the language of the QA model and outgoing answers into the language of the user. However, the eTranslation API has not been used for the experiment described in this paper, so it is outside of its scope.

In order to automatically select the translation engine, a language identifier algorithm is needed and we adapted[4] Python's `langdetect`[5] package to the needs of our project. We built a custom Docker container[6] that serves language identification services to the caller, for the languages of the project. Luxembourgish was not supported by the latest distribution of `langdetect` (1.0.9) and thus, we have added it by training `langdetect` on a Luxembourgish Web-based corpus (Leipzig Corpora Collection) containing 1M sentences and more than 16M

[3] https://joinup.ec.europa.eu/sites/default/files/news/2019-09/ISA2_Architecture%20for%20public%20service%20chatbots.pdf

[4] https://github.com/racai-ai/e4a-langdetect

[5] https://pypi.org/project/langdetect/

[6] https://hub.docker.com/r/raduion/e4alangdetect

words; the used text material was taken from randomly chosen Web sites.

4. Luxembourgish Language

Luxembourg is a highly multilingual country with Luxembourgish as the national language, French as the legislative language, and French, German and Luxembourgish as the three administrative and judicial languages. Luxembourgish has received an official status only since 1984, and moreover, is still not an official language of the EU. The vocabulary of Luxembourgish has many loan words from French and German, the morpho-syntax follows Germanic patterns. According to the STATEC (as of May 2019), French is the most spoken language at work (78%), followed by English (51%) and Luxembourgish (48%). Luxembourgish is the most widely spoken language at home (53%), followed by French (32%) and Portuguese (19%). Luxembourgish is a low-resourced language when it comes to the availability of language resources or tools.

The latest version of the official Luxembourgish orthography can be found at the Zenter fir d'Lëtzebuerger Sprooch (ZLS)/Centre for the Luxembourgish Language and also downloaded as a PDF file[7]. The Luxembourgish orthography officially regulates the spelling of the Luxembourgish language for the areas for which the Luxembourg State is responsible (administrations, schools). The codification and subsequent implementation of orthography in Luxembourgish can be found at Gilles (2015). More information on the languages spoken in Luxembourg can be found at Lulling et al. (2010).

However, the focus on the Luxembourgish language has increased during the last few years both from the governmental side with its long-term strategy and the research side, as a consequence. On the one hand, the government aims at increasing the importance of Luxembourgish by advancing the standardization, use and study of Luxembourgish, promoting learning Luxembourgish and the Luxembourg culture, and promoting culture in the Luxembourgish language. The ZLS contributes to the realization of the government policy on the Luxembourgish language. On the other hand, we see that in the last few years, many research projects focus on Luxembourgish (Lingscape[8], Schnëssen[9]); both of these projects are based on crowdsourcing. This is an excellent example about creating large spoken, image, or written corpora quickly and by diverse users, which can contribute to developing language technology applications.

5. Luxembourgish Dataset on Administrative Questions

As in many countries in the EU, e-government and digitalization are managed by dedicated institutions. In Luxembourg, the Ministry for Digitalization was created on December 11th, 2018 and in Romania, this is the newly established Authority for the Digitalization of Romania. These authorities have helped the ENRICH4ALL project to become a reality and the language resources output of ENRICH4ALL will be fed into the European Language Grid project (Rehm et al., 2020), in which the Luxembourg Institute of Science and Technology and Romanian Academy Research Institute for Artificial Intelligence "Mihai Drăgănescu" are also partners.

In ENRICH4ALL we need targeted datasets, so that we can fine-tune BERT(-like) models for the project's languages and domains of interest. We chose three domains of interest to develop and test our multilingual chatbot: COVID-19 (in Romanian), construction permits (in Romanian) and administrative questions (in Luxembourgish). In this paper, we focus only on Luxembourgish.

Concerning the citizen´s online services with the State, Guichet.lu is the information portal in Luxembourg that simplifies citizen's exchanges with the State and offers them quick and user-friendly access to all the information, procedures and services offered by Luxembourg public bodies. The website of Guichet.lu is available in German, English, and French, but not in Luxembourgish.

We have manually created a set of 135 questions with their corresponding answers in Luxembourgish based on Guichet.lu. The questions cover questions about passport, asylum, or certificate requests (see Q1 example in Table 1, below), but also questions that a newly arrived person in Luxembourg might ask, e.g., about the minimum wage (Q2), unemployment rates, school enrollment, etc. Since there are many commuters working in Luxembourg, but living in neighboring countries, we also collected questions relevant to paying taxes in Luxembourg, while living in France or Germany.
Most questions (83%) are *wh*-questions, i.e. starting with Where/When/Whom/How, while 6% are in statement form (see Q3, Table 1). 11% of the questions include both a statement and a *wh*-question. The size of the questions varies from 4 to 15 words.

Q1	Wou muss ech d'Gebuert vu méngem Bebé umellen?	Where should I declare the birth of my baby?
Q2	Wat ass de soziale Mindestloun zu Lëtzebuerg?	Which is the minimum wage in Luxembourg?
Q3	Ech wëll fir e Pass rembourséiert ze kréien.	I want to be reimbursed for a passport.

Table 1: Examples of questions in Luxembourgish and their English translation[10]

This corpus is multilingual (LTZ-EN-DE-FR); we plan further experimentation in future months (see Section 8).

[7] https://portal.education.lu/zls/ORTHOGRAFIE

[8] https://lingscape.uni.lu/

[9] https://infolux.uni.lu/schnessen/

[10] The English text is provided only for reading comprehension in this paper, it is not used as a test set in the experiment.

6. Training/Fine-tuning of BERT Models

In BotStudio, one can upload a fine-tuned BERT language model and use it to label input questions so that the label maps onto the desired dialog node. Users can add labels and training questions for each label and BotStudio uses the fine-tuned BERT model to learn a sequence classifier for the label set.

To enable such functionality in BotStudio, we must train and/or fine-tune BERT models for the datasets of interest. An additional reason for using BERT models for such a task is to save many hours of manual work creating alternative/synonym sentences and manual labeling of these sentences. Luxembourgish did not have any BERT models and thus, we have created one from scratch. In the next subsection, we detail the training and fine-tuning of Luxembourgish models. In our experiment, we made a comparison between the fine-tuned version of the `bert-base-multilingual-cased` BERT model (Devlin, 2018) as the baseline model and a language-specific, fine-tuned BERT model called `luxmed`.

6.1 The Luxembourgish BERT model for administrative questions

Luxembourgish is a low-resourced language and it is a big challenge to train a standard BERT model for it. According to Wu & Dredze (2020), the multilingual BERT model covers 104 languages and the 30% of languages with the least pretraining resources perform worse than those using no pretrained language model at all.

To bring Luxembourgish among the languages with at least a BERT model and to benefit from language-specific fine-tuning for our evaluated tasks, we proceeded to train a Luxembourgish BERT medium model from scratch, using the 16M Luxembourgish Web-based corpus (Leipzig Corpora Collection) containing 1M sentences and more than 16M words; the used text material was taken from randomly chosen Web sites. This model is available on HuggingFace[11] and can be readily used with the transformers Python API. It was trained for 3 epochs and it reached a final perplexity of 58.76 on the validation set. It has 8 encoder blocks, the size of the hidden layer is 512 and it uses 16 attention heads. The vocabulary has 70K word pieces.

The fine-tuning for administrative questions labeling (see Table 3 below) was done by varying the epochs number (10, 50, 100, 200, 400), the batch size (8, 16, 32), learning rate (5 to 1e-5), and learning rate decay rate (polynomial decay with a learning rate decreasing with `step = size(trainset) * epochs`). The data used for training was 80% of the dataset and the rest for validation. The best results were obtained with 200 epochs, a batch size of 16, and starting learning rate of 1e-5. The whole training process was done using the Tensorflow version of HuggingFace. In what follows, we will refer to the Luxembourgish BERT medium model as `luxmed`.

7. Results

In this section we will evaluate the Luxembourgish fine-tuned BERT models' ability to label input questions with the appropriate label and the ability to find the most similar question to the input question from the train set.

7.1 QA datasets statistics

The dataset has been transformed into JSON objects which are available on GitHub[12]. Each QA dataset is organized into question groups, each group having a unique ID and containing multiple formulations of the same question. Each question group contains a single answer that is valid for any question formulation in the group.

Table 2 lists the average number of formulations per question group, the number of groups in the QA dataset, and the number of all questions in the QA dataset.

	Average alternatives	**QA groups**	**Total questions**
Administrative questions	1.5	93	135

Table 2: QA datasets statistics

7.2 Task evaluation

For our QA dataset, we will provide the following accuracy figures:

a. The accuracy of labeling a question with the correct label from the QA dataset label set;
b. The accuracy of correctly retrieving the ID of the question group (with at least two formulations), out of which one formulation is taken as the test input question, as explained next.

Figure 1 shows the label frequency and distribution in our dataset. To evaluate question similarity, given an input question from a question group that has at least two formulations, we aimed at recovering the ID of the parent question group. To achieve this, we fed the BERT model the input question and used the last hidden state tensor output to calculate a cosine similarity between the input question and *all* other questions in the QA dataset. The ID of the group in which the most similar QA dataset question is found is the ID we are looking for. If this ID matches the question group ID from which the input question was extracted, we get one accuracy point.

[11] https://huggingface.co/raduion/bert-medium-luxembourgish

[12] https://github.com/racai-ai/e4all-models

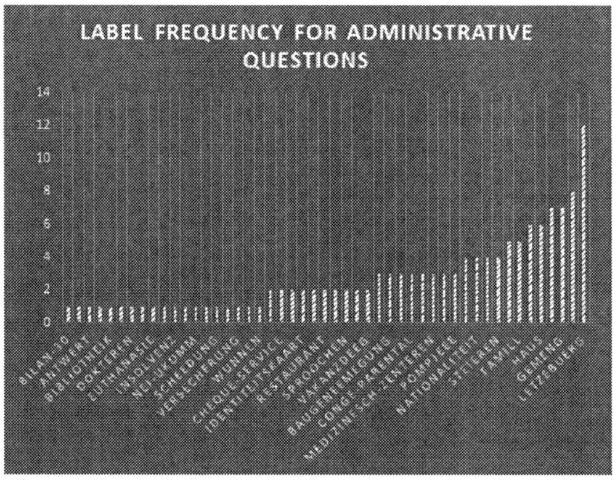

Figure 1: Label distribution for the Administrative questions dataset. The most frequent appears 12 times while there are 19 labels with a count of 1. There are 49 distinct labels in total.

To compute the performance of question similarity, we had to trim the QA datasets and remove all question groups in which a single formulation existed. We ended up with 22.2% of the administrative questions QA dataset.

To optimize the computation time, we introduced an early stop condition: if cosine similarity is over 95%, we assume a very similar question and stop the search for a better one. With this optimization, the whole accuracy calculation time was reduced from 12h to 6h, using an i5-10400 CPU.

We then took the fine-tuned version of the `bert-base-multilingual-cased` BERT model (Devlin, 2018) as the baseline model and we compared accuracy figures against `luxmed` which is a language-specific, fine-tuned BERT model.

Table 3 shows that the multilingual BERT model (`mling`) and the Luxembourgish BERT model (`luxmed`) gave the same accuracy when it came to question labeling. This can be justified by the small size of the administrative questions dataset (135 questions), coupled with the high number of labels (49). In Figure 1 we can see that 19 labels appear only once in our Administrative questions dataset.

When it comes to question similarity accuracy, using the language-specific `luxmed` BERT model is a better choice than using the generic multilingual BERT model (`mling`).

	mling	luxmed
Question labeling accuracy	40.7%	40.7%
Question similarity accuracy	23.3%	26.6%

Table 3: Question labeling and question similarity accuracy with `mling` vs. `luxmed` BERT models

8. Conclusion and Future Prospects

Multilingual communication between citizens and public services should be a requirement for a digital single market. Chatbots are completely missing in the public administration in Luxembourg, a highly multilingual country. A multilingual chatbot, enabling citizens to ask their questions in their preferred language, is a much-needed AI application in the e-government infrastructure.

The project ENRICH4ALL aims at deploying an MT and AI-enabled chatbot in public services in Luxembourg. Luxembourgish is an under-resourced language, and in addition, is not supported in eTranslation. Within the project ENRICH4ALL, we can overcome these limitations by using the new BERT models we trained for it.

We tested pre-trained and fine-tuned BERT models for question labeling and question similarity. The main limitation of this work was the small size and label imbalance of the QA dataset. In the meantime, we have been adding additional alternative questions under each label.

In the last weeks, we have been extending our Luxembourgish corpus with additional 1,700,000 sentences. We plan to train and validate another medium BERT size model from scratch using this extended corpus data in the coming weeks. Testing with data of similar languages is also among our future prospects. We expect that a subsequent fine-tuning with the improved QA dataset will mitigate the current limitations and yield improved results.

In the coming months we plan to deploy our chatbot in public administration in Luxembourg. Having user interaction logged will result in real user questions that will be added to our existing QA datasets. This will improve the performance of the chatbot, and we will have more data to fine-tune our BERT models. After chatbot deployment, we will analyze user feedback, which will be collected at the end of each conversation. We will calculate the amount of user questions, most used questions as well as the success rate per question.

9. Acknowledgements

The Action 2020-EU-IA-0088 has received funding from the European Union's Connecting Europe Facility 2014-2020 - CEF Telecom, under Grant Agreement No. INEA/CEF/ICT/A2020/2278547.

10. Bibliographical References

Adamopoulou, E. and Moussiades, L. (2020). An overview of chatbot technology. In *IFIP International Conference on Artificial Intelligence Applications and Innovations*, Springer, Cham, pp. 373-383.

Boonstra, L. (2021). Creating a multilingual chatbot. In *The Definitive Guide to Conversational AI with Dialogflow and Google Cloud,* pp. 187-194.

Devlin, J. (2018). Multilingual bert readme document.

Devlin et al. (2018). Devlin, J., Chang, M.-W., Lee, K., and Toutanova, K. (2018). Bert: Pre-training of deep bidirectional transformers for language understanding. arXiv preprint. arXiv:1810.04805.

European Language Grid: https://www.european-language-grid.eu/, 14.01.22

ENRICH4ALL: https://www.enrich4all.eu/, 13.01.22

eTranslation: https://ec.europa.eu/cefdigital/wiki/display/CEFDIGITAL/eTranslation, 13.01.22

eTranslation Web Service: https://ec.europa.eu/cefdigital/wiki/display/CEFDIGITAL/How+to+submit+a+translation+request+via+the+CEF+eTranslation+webservice, 13.01.22

Janarthanam, S. (2017). Hands-on chatbots and conversational UI development: build chatbots and voice user interfaces with Chatfuel, Dialogflow, Microsoft Bot Framework, Twilio, and Alexa Skills. Packt Publishing Ltd.

Gao, J., Galley, M., and Li, L. (2018). Neural approaches to conversational AI. In *The 41st International ACM SIGIR Conference on Research & Development in Information Retrieval,* pp. 1371-1374.

Gilles, P. (2015). From status to corpus: Codification and implementation of spelling norms in Luxembourgish. In *Language planning and microlinguistics*, pp. 128-149.

Guichet.lu: www.guichet.lu, 13.01.22

Leipzig Corpora Collection: Luxembourgish Wikipedia corpus based on material from 2021.

Leipzig Corpora Collection. Dataset. https://corpora.uni-leipzig.de?corpusId=ltz_wikipedia_2021.

Lommatzsch, A. (2018). A next generation chatbot-framework for the public administration. In *International Conference on Innovations for Community Services,* Springer, Cham, pp. 127-141.

Lothritz, C., Allix, K., Lebichot, B., Veiber, L., Bissyandé, T. F., & Klein, J. (2021). Comparing multilingual and multiple monolingual models for intent classification and slot filling. In *International Conference on Applications of Natural Language to Information Systems,* Springer, Cham, pp. 367-375.

Lulling, F. S. (2010). Lëtzebuergesch: la langue nationale du Grand-Duché de Luxembourg. *Lengas. Revue de sociolinguistique*, (60).

Mauldin, M. (1994), ChatterBots, TinyMuds, and the Turing Test: Entering the Loebner Prize Competition. In *Proceedings of the 11th National Conference on Artificial Intelligence*. https://www.reginamaria.ro

Mondly: https://www.mondly.com/

Namazifar, M., Papangelis, A., Tur, G., & Hakkani-Tür, D. (2021). Language model is all you need: Natural language understanding as question answering. In *ICASSP 2021-2021 IEEE International Conference on Acoustics, Speech and Signal Processing (ICASSP),* pp. 7803-7807.

SupWiz: https://www.supwiz.com/, 14.01.22

Tutor Mike: https://www.rong-chang.com/tutor_mike.htm, 14.01.22

Weizenbaum, J. (1966). ELIZA–a computer program for the study of natural language communication between man and machine. *Commun. ACM* 9, pp. 36-45.

Wu, S. and Dredze, M. (2020). Are all languages created equal in multilingual BERT? arXiv preprint arXiv:2005.09093Language Resource References.

Author Index

Abdulrahman, Roshna, 189
Adegbola, Tunde, 146
Allassonnière-Tang, Marc, 41
Anastasiou, Dimitra, 207
Anusha, Mudoor Devadas, 33
Aragon, Carolina, 48
Armengol-Estapé, Jordi, 59
Ayele, Abinew, 137

Bal, Bal Krishna, 106
Bear, Diego, 155
Besacier, Laurent, 1
Bhatt, Shiva, 106
Bhatta, Manish, 106
Biemann, Chris, 137
Bojar, Ondrej, 78

Calvo Figueras, Blanca, 59
Chakravarthi, Bharathi Raja, 33
Coelho, Sharal, 33
Coler, Matt, 16
Cook, Paul, 155
Cortis, Keith, 161

Davis, Brian, 161
De Clercq, Orphee, 176
de Gibert Bonet, Ona, 59
Destaw, Tadesse, 137
Dhungel, Sanket, 106
Dijkstra, Jelske, 16
Do, Phat, 16
Doğruöz, A. Seza, 92

Ferraz Gerardi, Fabrício, 185
Fong, Judy, 10

Gerardi, Fabrício F., 48
Gómez-Rodríguez, Carlos, 199
Gudnason, Jon, 10
Gunnarsson, Þorsteinn Daði, 10

Hassani, Hossein, 189
Hegde, Asha, 33
Hiovain-Asikainen, Katri, 169
Huggins Daines, David, 23
Hutin, Mathilde, 41

Joanis, Eric, 23

Kevers, Laurent, 112
Kharitonova, Ksenia, 59
Klabbers, Esther, 16
Kuriyozov, Elmurod, 199
Kvapilíková, Ivana, 78

Lambrecht, Louisa, 129
Lefever, Els, 176
Littell, Patrick, 23

Mabokela, Ronny, 70
Martín Rodríguez, Lorena, 48
Maskey, Utsav, 106
Melero, Maite, 59
Merzhevich, Tatiana, 48, 185
Moshagen, Sjur, 169
Murakami, Yohei, 122

Nasution, Arbi Haza, 122

Ondel, Lucas, 1
Örnólfsson, Gunnar Thor, 10

Pimienta, Daniel, 83
Pine, Aidan, 23

Rakhmanov, Ochilbek, 98
Resiandi, Kartika, 122

Salaev, Ulugbek, 199
Schlippe, Tim, 70, 98
Schneider, Felix, 129
Shashirekha, Hosahalli Lakshmaiah, 33
Silva, Wellington, 48
Singh, Pranaydeep, 176
Sitaram, Sunayana, 92

Tessier, Marc, 23
Þorsteinsdóttir, Sunneva, 10
Torkornoo, Delasie, 23
Tresoldi, Tiago, 48

Villavicencio, Aline, 1

Waibel, Alexander, 129

Yimam, Seid Muhie, 137
Yusuf, Bolaji, 1

Zanon Boito, Marcely, 1

Association for Computational Linguistics
209 N. Eighth Street
Stroudsburg, Pennsylvania 18360

ISBN 978-1-7138-6138-6

CURRAN ASSOCIATES INC.
proceedings.com